ONE WORLD DIVIDED

A Blaisdell Book in the Social Sciences

ONE WORLD
DIVIDED

A Geographer Looks at the Modern World

BY PRESTON E. JAMES
SYRACUSE UNIVERSITY

MAP DESIGN BY *Eileen W. James*

BLAISDELL PUBLISHING COMPANY
A DIVISION OF GINN AND COMPANY
Waltham, Massachusetts · Toronto · London

To the memory of

GEORGE BABCOCK CRESSEY

founder of geography at Syracuse University, enthusiastic traveler and observer of man and nature throughout the world, master of clarity and structure in professional writing, dedicated teacher of the highest principles of scholarship to many generations of students, a man of great courage

*this book is respectfully
dedicated*

PREFACE

A geographer's view of the state of affairs in the contemporary world provides a somewhat different perspective from that of other scholars. The difference is inherent in the structure of his field of learning. Geographic concepts are generalizations about the development of contrasts and similarities between places on the face of the earth. The purpose of geographic study is to throw light on the complex interaction of the processes of change that produce these contrasts and similarities. Why does one country differ from another? The geographer's approach to such a question makes use of the same basic information that is used by other students of contemporary conditions. But the geographer arranges this information in terms of areal association or areal interchange on the face of the earth. He is concerned with such questions as the significance of position with reference to other places. He is concerned with the pattern of movement into and out of areas. He is concerned with the processes that are interconnected in particular places, and with the resulting features that are areally associated.

All approaches to learning are essentially descriptive. Explanation in any ultimate sense is beyond the reach of human scholarship. "Explanatory description," the term used by William Morris Davis many decades ago, consists in adding the time dimension to mere description. To explain an existing situation, one reconstructs the geography of a past period and traces the developments or changes leading to present conditions. Projections into the future based on past trends permit the making of forecasts. But these are only more sophisticated approaches to description.

Description, however, goes beyond the formula, "how much of what is where?" Historical geography, which focuses attention on the recreation of past geographies, and on tracing geographic changes through time, reveals the nature of the processes at work on the face of the earth. Although the specific phenomena observed in any particular place are unique there are, at the same time, certain uniformities or recurring patterns among the sequences of change. These can be identified and used as the basis for the formulation of general concepts. Where concepts can be formulated in mathematical terms they become models or ideal constructs. But where they can be formulated only in word symbols they still contribute to the theoretical structure of geography.

The purpose of this book is to apply geographic methods and use geographic concepts in the search for meaning in the modern world. Many scholars have described the two sets of revolutionary changes now going on in the world—the technological changes and the many resulting readjustments which we call the Industrial Revolution, and the changes in the status and dignity of the individual which we call the Democratic Revolution. Social scientists have described the background and antecedents of these revolutions. The special purpose of this book, however, is to note the particular place or places on the earth where these movements originated, to discover the pattern and speed with which they spread, and to observe the results of the impact of change on pre-existing societies in particular places.

These two sets of fundamental change are in process of spreading over the earth.

Both have given rise to strong reactions. As a result the world is becoming more and more sharply divided. The contrast between developed and developing nations, between rich and poor nations, between those that have and those that have not, has become greater than ever before. At the same time the world is also sharply divided between those who favor one or the other of two basic political and social principles: democracy and autocracy. But these contrasts—between the economically developed and the economically underdeveloped, between the democratically organized and the autocratically organized—are more than abstract ideas. They are found in particular places, associated with particular kinds of habitats and resources, making impact with particular kinds of pre-industrial and pre-democratic institutions.

Let us follow the sequence of ideas:

1. The world is divided by differences in the physical and biotic character of the habitats, and by differences in the resource base of states.
2. It is divided, also, by differences in population, economy, and political condition.
3. For some two centuries two great processes of revolutionary change have been occurring, each spreading in a somewhat different pattern from the source region around the North Sea in Europe.
4. As they spread, the two processes of revolutionary change also continue to develop, so that they do not make the same impact today along their advancing fronts as they did a century ago.
5. Distinctive social, economic, and political reactions have been produced by the impact of these revolutionary changes on pre-existing societies.
6. The world can be divided into regions, each characterized by a distinctive set of reactions to the impact of revolutionary change.
7. In each distinctive culture region, so defined, the significance to man of the features of the habitat changes with changes in the attitudes, objectives, and technical skills of the inhabitants, requiring, therefore, repeated re-evaluations of the resource base of states.

The eleven culture regions presented in this book are, in a sense, a geographic hypothesis. It is assumed that the general picture of the contemporary world offered by this division into culture regions will serve to illuminate rather than obscure the nature of the processes of change that are at work. The regions are defined as contiguous areas because an important part of our analysis deals with the significance of position on the globe. They are defined in terms of political units because a major part of the analysis deals with the viability of states. It is recognized that the characteristics of each region are most clearly developed at the regional core, and that around the margins there are wide zones of transition where the characteristics of neighboring regions are mingled. Regional boundaries, therefore, are less important than regional cores. Regional boundaries are subject to change with increasing knowledge, and with the progress of the processes of revolutionary change over the world. The eleven culture regions are shown on the map inside the front cover.

The measurement of economic development has been the subject of careful statistical study by Brian J. L. Berry.[1] For 95 of

---

[1] Brian J. L. Berry, "An Inductive Approach to the Regionalization of Economic Development," in Norton Ginsburg (ed.), *Geography and Economic Development*, University of Chicago, Department of Geography, Research Paper No. 62, 1960; pp. 78-107; and Brian J. L. Berry, "Basic Patterns of Economic Development," in Norton Ginsburg *Atlas of Economic Development*, University of Chicago Press, 1961. For the grouping of countries on technological and demographic scales by culture regions the author is indebted to Berry and Perle.

the states of the world Berry applied 43 indices of economic development. For each index he ranked the countries from 1 to 95. A 95 × 43 table of ranks was thus prepared. The 95 countries are represented by dots in the diagrams on page x. The dots are arranged with reference to two scales, the median lines of which are indicated in the diagrams. The vertical scale measures technological development: the nearer to the top a point is the poorer is the country in terms of gross national product, amount of large-scale industry, efficiency of transportation, amount of economic specialization within the country and volume of internal interchange, ratio of urban to rural, and other similar measures of technological development. The horizontal scale measures demographic conditions: the farther to the left a point is the poorer is the country it represents in demographic terms—which include such conditions as high birth rates, high death rates, and high infant mortality rates. Since the dots form a continuum, sweeping from the top left to the bottom right, it is clear that there is a close correlation between technological and demographic underdevelopment.

In each of the ten diagrams the dots for the countries included in the specific culture region are covered with stars. The eleventh region—the Pacific—is omitted. A study of these diagrams shows that whereas in some culture regions the dots with the stars are clustered, in others there is a considerable variation in the position of the starred dots on the technological and demographic scales. The European region would be fairly homogeneous were it not for the inclusion of Cyprus and other countries of the Mediterranean. It might be argued from this analysis alone that Cyprus should be included in the North African-Southwest Asian region. The Afri-

can region would be more nearly homogeneous were it not for the inclusion of South Africa and Rhodesia. The regions with the largest spread between countries are Latin America and East Asia. The spread in these cases is, in fact, one of the regional characteristics. Both these regions are feeling the full impact of the two revolutions and have reacted violently: when the impact of revolutionary change is felt the first result is an increase in the contrasts between rich and poor, developed and developing.

It is also possible to apply measurements to the revolutionary changes produced by the struggle between democracy and autocracy. However, scholars are by no means in agreement regarding the criteria that are useful in measuring democracy—not nearly so much in agreement as are the students of economic development. The political scientist, Russell H. Fitzgibbon of the University of California at Los Angeles, has devised a scale for measuring democracy and has applied it to a study of the countries of Latin America.[2] The elements in the formula include a variety of attributes of the democratic state, for instance, whether elections are free and the ballots honestly counted; whether the minority accepts the decision of the majority; whether political parties are free, especially the opposition parties; whether the judiciary is independent; to what extent there are controls by the military or the clergy; whether the general public is aware of how public money is spent; whether there is open discussion of policy problems; how effective local governments are in responding to popular opinion; what proportion of the population can read and write, and what

[2] Russell H. Fitzgibbon, "How Democratic is Latin America?" *Inter-American Economic Affairs*, Vol. 9 (Spring, 1956); pp. 65-77.

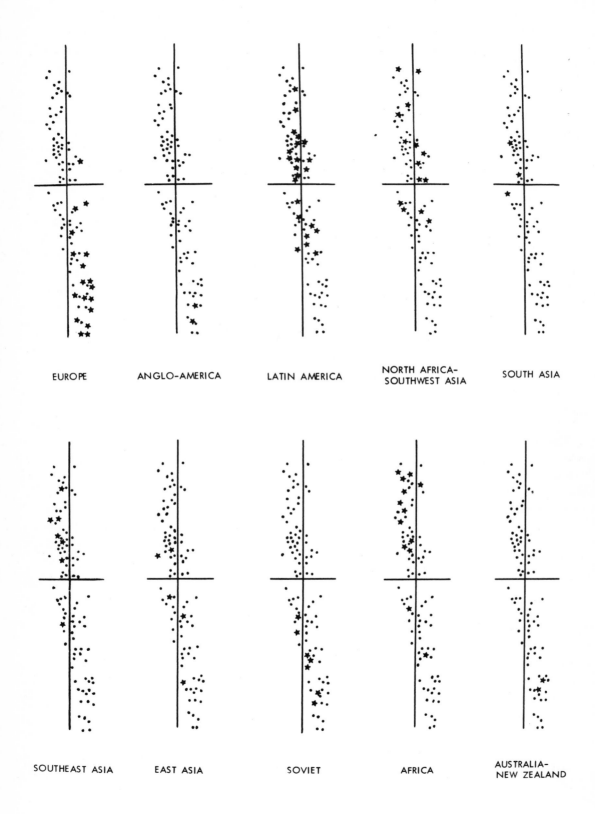

EUROPE   ANGLO-AMERICA   LATIN AMERICA   NORTH AFRICA-   SOUTH ASIA
                                                              SOUTHWEST ASIA

SOUTHEAST ASIA   EAST ASIA   SOVIET   AFRICA   AUSTRALIA-
                                                                           NEW ZEALAND

the facilities are for education; and whether there is free access to knowledge? These and other elements were used to rate the countries of Latin America by a number of scholars who are specialists in the study of this region. Top rating went to Uruguay and Costa Rica; but the ratings included a wide variety of conditions from the most thoroughly democratic to the completely autocratic, as in the case of Paraguay (and now Cuba). The wide spread from democracy to autocracy among the countries reveals again the results of the full impact of revolutionary change now occurring.

These two efforts at measurement point the way toward further research. The culture regions, as presented in this book, were outlined by intuitive judgment based on a wide variety of sources and some direct field observation. Clearly, this is an initial step in the work of providing a more precise description of the processes of change in the modern world.

The author is indebted to many of his professional colleagues for assistance and critical comments. Donald W. Meinig read the whole of the manuscript and offered many valuable suggestions. George B. Cressey read the chapters concerned with parts of Asia and the Soviet Union. The Soviet chapters were also read by the historian, Warren B. Walsh, and by several geographers who, with the author, visited the Soviet Union in 1961: Chauncy D. Harris, Edward Espenshade, Joseph A. Russell, and H. H. McCarthy. The chapter on Southeast Asia was read by the anthropologist Donn V. Hart. Peter Gould read the chapter on Africa. Eric Faigle and John H. Thompson read Anglo-America. The appendix on vegetation, and the map of world vegetation, were prepared by David J. deLaubenfels. Many other persons with special knowledge of certain places have been over smaller parts of the manuscript. For all this work the author is very grateful.

For the compilation of the maps and the map design the author is indebted to his wife, Eileen W. James.

The author also expresses his thanks for painstaking editorial work to Miss Karla Weatherall, and for the collection of statistical data to Miss Virginia Edwards.

Preston E. James

Syracuse, 1963

CONTENTS

1 INTRODUCTION:

THE WORLD'S CULTURE REGIONS

All men are brothers. This idea is the theme given passionate affirmation in the Ninth Symphony, and in the words of the poets since poetry was first written. It is basic to the teachings of Confucius, and Jesus, and Gandhi, and many other religious leaders. No generation since the dawn of history has been without those who have tried to model their lives on this ideal. And with the aid of the newest technology of instant communications all men are brought so closely into contact with each other that distance seems to have been annihilated, and we find ourselves living in one world together. Yet never has our one world seemed so divided. How does it happen that the realities differ so much from the vision of what might be?

The fact is that the one world has always been divided. In simplest terms it is divided into "home" and "away from home." Just as the child begins timidly to explore the tangle of bushes at the end of the yard, so man in all the million or so years of his presence on the earth has sought to discover what lies beyond the horizon. On the curved surface of the earth there is always a horizon, and beyond the range of the familiar lurks danger. The geographers have found ways to tell what it is like away from home, and to put the unfamiliar into the context of the familiar. The philosophers and religious teachers have done more: their minds have soared beyond the limitations of home and have created a vision of a world of many homes, each occupied by members of the same human species, preoccupied with the same kinds of problems, inhibited by the same kinds of fear about what might be found beyond the horizon.

Our one world is divided by many things. It is divided by mountains, by rivers and oceans, and by differences of climate. It is divided by the use of thousands of different languages. It is divided by the practice of many different religions, by contrasts in economic institutions and forms of government. It is divided by the existence of very different levels of technical skill and of material well-being. It is divided by great contrasts between wealth and poverty, abundance and hunger. As a result of all these differences man himself has created divisions and barriers far more difficult to cross than those created by nature. Man has brought into being mountains of hate, rivers of inflexible tradition, oceans of ignorance. And as technology brings men closer together the man-made barriers loom larger and more forbidding.

This book attempts to put the divisions of our one world into perspective. It identifies and defines the divisions of the world that are important to an understanding of the problems of public policy. It shows how these divisions have been created, and seeks to throw light on the significance of the pattern of arrangement of these divisions. It presents a picture of the contemporary world as a background for the formulation of policy.

The Earth as the Home of Man. The face of the earth is the habitat of man. Here, in the narrow zone of contact between land, air, and water, on the surface of a medium-sized planet in a medium-sized solar system, the human genus appeared. During the two million years of his presence on the earth man has groped toward a better and better understanding of his habitat, and of ways to modify it to his advantage. Yet, in spite of the fact that no major part of the earth's surface remains unexplored, and in spite of the rapidly increasing capacity to transform the natural features of the habitat into man-made landscapes, the human population is still very unevenly spread over

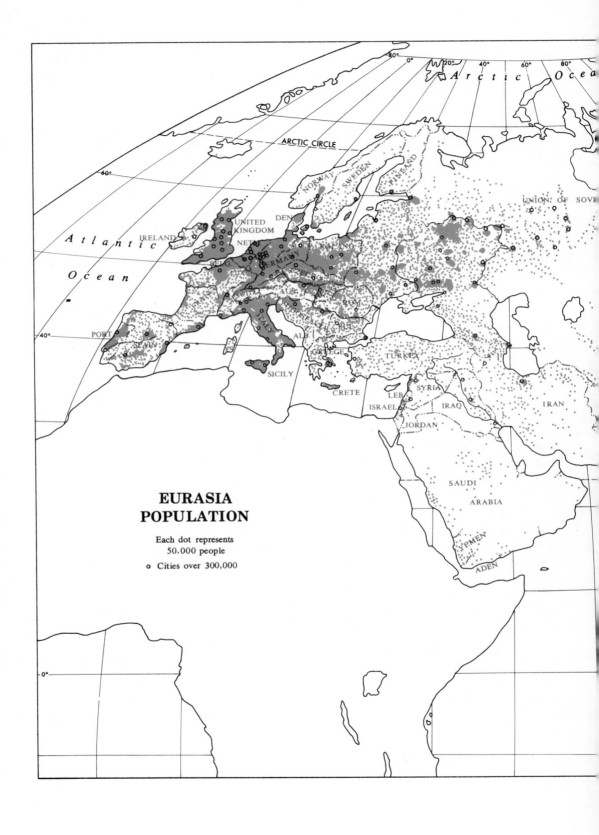

EURASIA POPULATION

Each dot represents
50,000 people

o Cities over 300,000

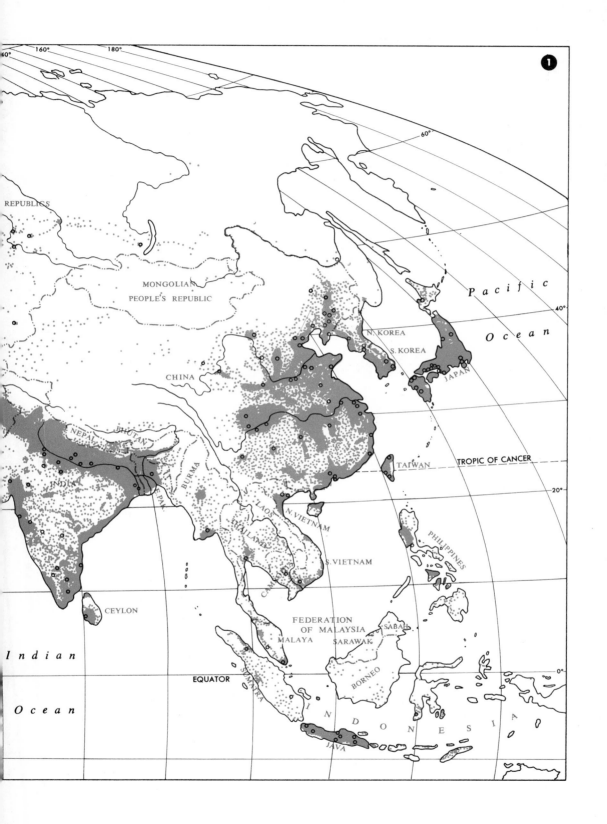

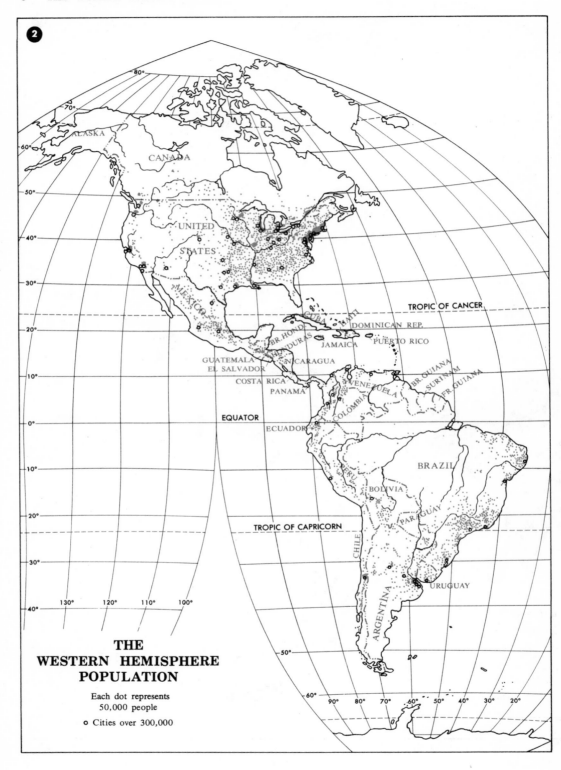

2

ALASKA

CANADA

UNITED
STATES

MEXICO

TROPIC OF CANCER

CUBA   HAITI
DOMINICAN REP.
BR.HOND
HONDURAS
JAMAICA   PUERTO RICO
GUATEMALA   NICARAGUA
EL SALVADOR
COSTA RICA
PANAMA

VENEZUELA
BR.GUIANA
SURINAM
FR.GUIANA
COLOMBIA

EQUATOR

ECUADOR

BRAZIL
PERU
BOLIVIA

TROPIC OF CAPRICORN

PARAGUAY

CHILE

URUGUAY

ARGENTINA

**THE
WESTERN HEMISPHERE
POPULATION**

Each dot represents
50,000 people

o Cities over 300,000

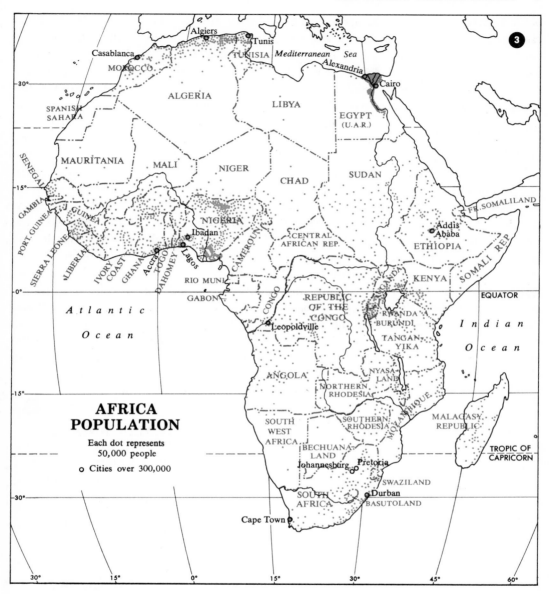

**AFRICA
POPULATION**

Each dot represents
50,000 people

o Cities over 300,000

the earth. Vast areas remain essentially empty of human inhabitants, while the major part of mankind is densely crowded into relatively small areas (Maps 1, 2, 3, and 4). Furthermore, the trend is for the thinly peopled areas to lose population while the more densely peopled areas gain.

How is this uneven distribution of population related to the varying physical conditions of the earth's habitats? This is a ques-

tion we must repeatedly try to answer, not only while we are looking at the world as a whole, but also when we examine the parts of the earth more closely. Are some places more favorable for human settlement than others? Does human settlement tend to concentrate in certain kinds of habitats, and to avoid other kinds?

The word *habitat* refers to the features of the human abode that are the result of natural processes. Some of the natural processes of change operating on the face of the earth go on slowly, some rapidly. The geological processes, by which lands are raised or lowered in relation to sea level, by which rocks are formed and distorted by movements of the earth's crust, by which the uplifted lands are worn down by rivers and other agents of erosion—most of these processes go on so slowly in relation to individual human lives that the hills seem to be everlasting. On the other hand some natural processes, even some geologic ones, go on very rapidly. The processes of physical change that we call weather go on so rapidly that not until the age of the electronic computer could men record observations and perform calculations fast enough to make meaningful forecasts. Some of the natural processes are described by the laws of physics and chemistry, some by the laws of

biology. It is the interaction of these various processes that results in the differentiation of the face of the earth into natural regions.

The face of the earth is made up of four spheres, closely fitted together to form the human habitat. One is the *atmosphere,* the thin film of gases clinging to the earth's surface. The state of the atmosphere at any one moment is known as *weather,* and the average of weather which characterizes a particular part of the earth is known as *climate* (Maps 5, 6, and 7, and Appendix A, p. 434). The second of the spheres is the *lithosphere,* the rock crust of the earth. The surface features of the lithosphere include mountains, plains, valleys, and so on (defined in Appendix B, p. 438). This sphere also includes the mantle of loose material over the rock surface in which soils are formed, and the minerals contained in the rocks which from time to time are found to

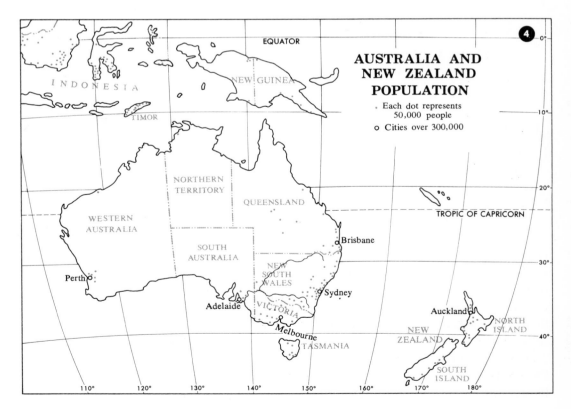

AUSTRALIA AND
NEW ZEALAND
POPULATION

. Each dot represents
50,000 people

o Cities over 300,000

be useful for man. Third is the *hydrosphere,* the water in liquid form which fills the ocean basins and overflows the margins of the continents (Map 8). Only 29.4 per cent of the whole surface of the earth stands high enough to rise above the water. From the warm oceans, moreover, the air picks up water through evaporation and carries it over the land where it drops as rain or snow (Map 6), supporting rivers, lakes, ground water, or glaciers and ice caps. And fourth is the *biosphere,* the cover of plants and animals living in intimate connection with the climate, the soil, and the water (Map 8, and Appendix C).

The study of these natural features brings an understanding of how very great are the differences that distinguish one place on the earth from another. There are enormous differences in climate, in surface features and soils, in minerals, and vegetation cover—for the earth's resources are notably uneven in their distribution. Does this diversity of natural features, this uneven distribution of resources, in any way account for the divisions among men?

Race and Culture. To answer this question we must examine man himself. We must make a clear distinction between *race* and *culture.* An individual is born the member of a race, and the racial traits that he inherits from his parents can be described by the laws of biology. But the individual learns to accept the attitudes and objectives, and to practice the technical skills of his culture. The child learns from his parents, his teachers, and from other children; and those who cannot learn to conform to the pattern of behavior accepted by the culture group become outcasts. Culture is not inherited: it is "learned behavior."

To define a race is not a simple matter. The popular distinction between races on the basis of skin color is not accepted by the anthropologists. Skin color, they point out, is only one of a number of hereditary traits. There are also such traits as stature, head form, hair color and texture, eye color and shape, and nose shape. These traits are not necessarily associated with skin color. Races develop as geographically separate divisions of a species; but the races of man have been so thoroughly intermingled that no "pure" types exist. The anthropologist, Carleton S. Coon, defines five chief races as follows: 1) the *Australoids,* including the Australian aborigines, the Melanesians, and the Negritos, who are scattered from the Philippines to the Andaman Islands and mainland India; 2) the *Mongoloids,* found today in eastern Asia, Polynesia, and throughout the Americas; 3) the *Caucasoids,* including the Europeans and people of European ancestry, the people of North Africa and Southwest Asia, the people of India, and the Ainus of Japan; 4) the *Capoids,* the Bushmen and Hottentots who lived in the southern part of Africa when the Europeans first came upon them; and 5) the *Congoids,* the people of the Congo Basin, including the modern Negroes and Pygmies of African origin.[1]

Culture is, by definition, distinct from race. Modern anthropological studies, however, recognize that race and culture are in fact intimately related, for the process of biological selection is to a certain extent the result of the way of life of a people. In this book the term culture is used to refer to the attitudes, objectives, and technical skills of a people. The outline formulated by the anthropologist Melville J. Herskovits suggests the range of traits that are included in this concept:[2]

[1] Carleton S. Coon, *The Origin of Races,* Alfred A. Knopf, Inc., New York, 1962. See also William W. Howells, 1960. For full references see the bibliography at the end of the book.
[2] Melville J. Herskovits, *Man and His Works,* Alfred A. Knopf, Inc., New York, 1948; p. 239.

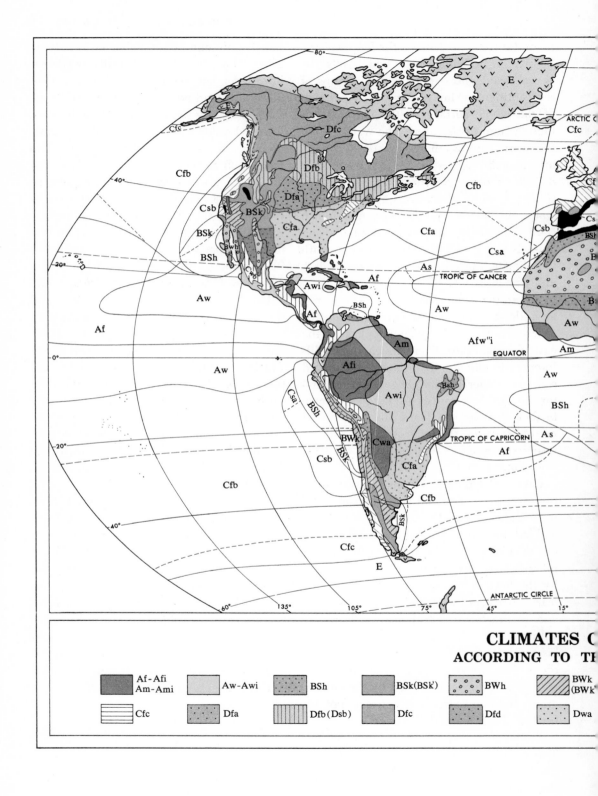

CLIMATES C
ACCORDING TO TH

Af-Afi Am-Ami	Aw-Awi	BSh	BSk(BSk̓)	BWh	BWk (BWk̓)
Cfc	Dfa	Dfb(Dsb)	Dfc	Dfd	Dwa

Map labels:

Cfc, E, ARCTIC C, Cfc, Dfc, Cfb, Cfb, Dfb, Cfb, Csb, BSk, Dfa, Csb, Cs, BSk, Cfa, Csa, Csb, BSk, BSh, As, TROPIC OF CANCER, Af, Aw, Awi, Af, BSh, Aw, Aw, Afw"i, Am, BWh, Af, Am, Afi, EQUATOR, Aw, Aw, Awi, BSh, BSh, Csa, As, BWk, Cwa, TROPIC OF CAPRICORN, Af, BSh, Csb, BSk, Cfa, Cfb, Cfb, BSk, Cfc, E, ANTARCTIC CIRCLE

80°, 40°, 20°, 0°, 20°, 40°, 60°, 135°, 105°, 75°, 45°, 15°

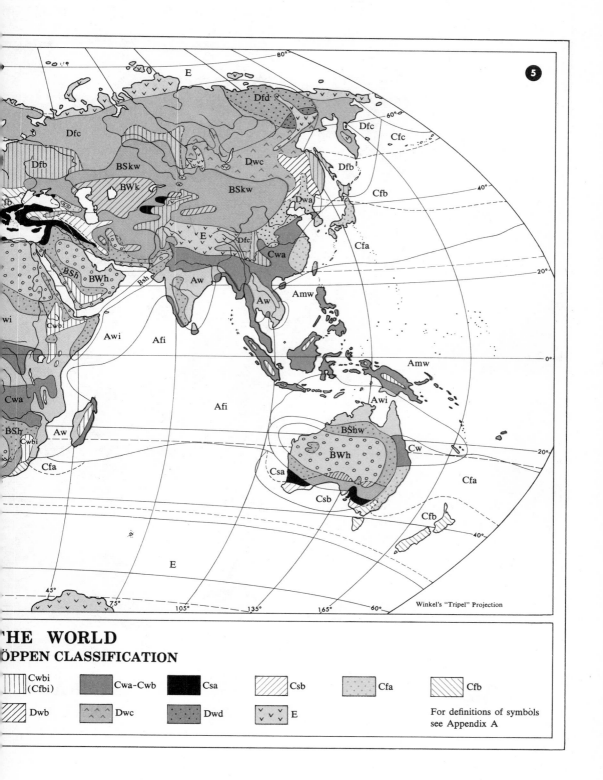

THE WORLD
KÖPPEN CLASSIFICATION

Cwbi (Cfbi)		Cwa-Cwb		Csa		Csb	
Dwb		Dwc		Dwd		E	

Cfa   Cfb

For definitions of symbols see Appendix A

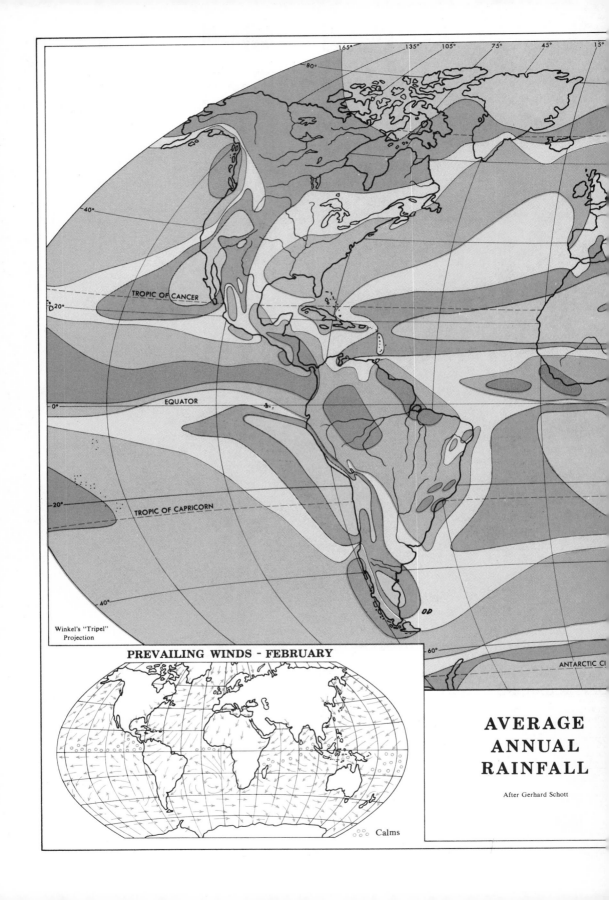

PREVAILING WINDS - FEBRUARY

Calms

AVERAGE
ANNUAL
RAINFALL

After Gerhard Schott

Winkel's "Tripel"
Projection

TROPIC OF CANCER

EQUATOR

TROPIC OF CAPRICORN

ANTARCTIC CI

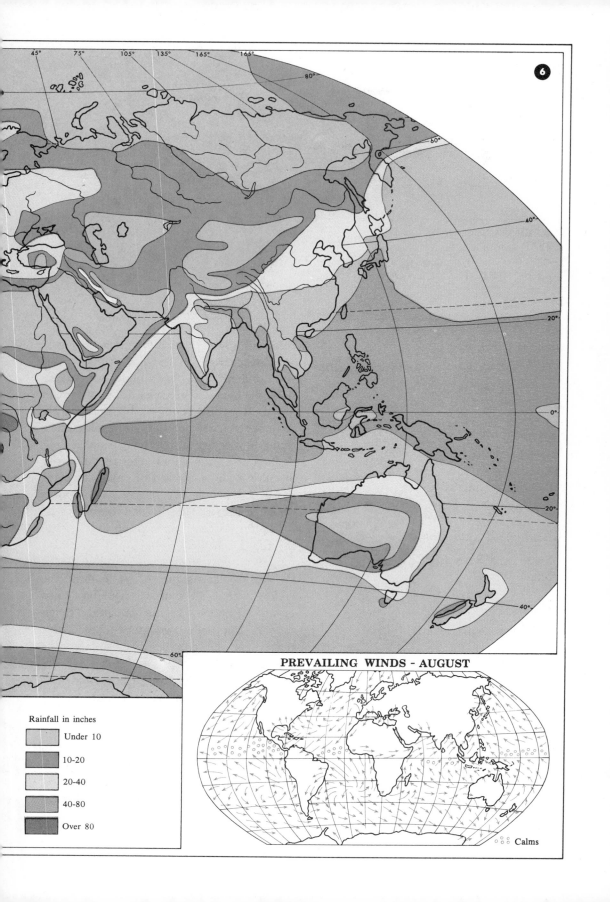

6

	Rainfall in inches
	Under 10
	10-20
	20-40
	40-80
	Over 80

PREVAILING WINDS - AUGUST

Calms

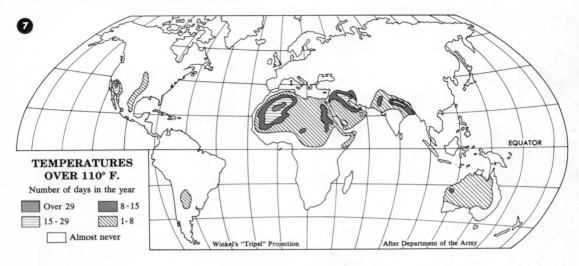

7

TEMPERATURES
OVER 110° F.

Number of days in the year

Over 29   8 - 15
15 - 29   1 - 8
Almost never

Winkel's "Tripel" Projection   After Department of the Army

EQUATOR

Material Culture

Tools and technical skills, including crops
and animals
Economic systems

Social Institutions

Social organization
Education
Political groups
Government

Attitude toward the Unknown

Religious beliefs
Magic

Art

Graphic and plastic arts
Folklore
Music, drama, and the dance

Language

These are the elements that combine to
make up a culture, or the way of life of a
people. We, in the twentieth century, live
in a period of rapid cultural change, when
long-cherished values are challenged. But,
throughout the long course of human history, the way people live has been characterized more by stability and permanence
than by change. In the days when travel
was difficult and communications were
slow, the contacts between different human
groups were few: cultures became sharply
distinct from one another, and each culture
came to occupy a relatively small, well-
defined area. Can we say that this diversity
of culture, the contrast from place to place
in the way people live, in any way accounts
for the contemporary divisions among men?

The fact is that both habitat and culture
must be examined in relation to each other
to gain a full perspective of the divisions of
the world. The nature of the habitat, the
endowment of resources available to a
group of people, is the essential "stage-
setting." But modern geographers recognize
that it is the culture that explains the
significance to man of the physical features
of his habitat. No land can be properly
described as rich or poor, friendly or unfriendly, except in relation to a particular
culture. For the same land may be considered richly endowed by the members of
one culture, and poorly endowed by another. Even so-called "natural resources"
only become resources as a result of human
technology. Consider, for example, the case
of coal: for the Indians of Pennsylvania

coal was not a natural resource; it only became a resource as a result of the development of the skills and the machines to use it. Soils can be described as fertile or infertile in terms of a specific crop, cared for by specific kinds of farm practices. Slopes that can be cultivated with the hoe are too steep to cultivate when the hoe is replaced by the plow and tractor. This means that with each change in any element of a culture, the meaning of the habitat must be reappraised. The geographic principle may be stated as follows: *the significance to man of the physical features of the habitat is a function of the attitudes, objectives, and technical skills of man himself.*

MAN ON THE EARTH

The anthropologists tell us that the story of man on the earth has been made up of long periods when there have been no fundamental changes in culture, separated by revolutionary periods when man's relation to the earth has been radically altered. We know little of the early period of the presence of the genus *homo* on the earth. Nearly two million years ago the earliest representatives of this genus appeared in the tropical zone extending from central Africa to southeastern Asia. At some stage he learned how to communicate by language, how to make tools and weapons, and how to use fire, and to cook food; and at some stage, it seems, he was joined by the dog. But he still knew nothing of agriculture, and he had no domestic animals other than the dog. Aided by weapons he could hunt and fish, and he could collect the seeds and fruits of wild plants. He used fire to aid in the hunt, and his fires, raging out of control, had the effect of greatly changing the original vegetation cover by favoring plants that could survive burning.

The only surviving species of the genus *homo* is known as *homo sapiens*. It is believed that the human species originated perhaps 50,000 years ago, probably also in the tropical zone of Africa and Asia. During the 50,000 years of the presence of *homo sapiens* on the earth there have been three periods of fundamental, revolutionary change in culture. The first, starting about 8000 B.C., was the *Agricultural Revolution,* when man first learned how to cultivate crops and domesticate animals. The second, starting about 4000 B.C., was marked by the rise of the *Early Civilizations.* The third, which started during the last two centuries, is made up of two kinds of culture change—the *Industrial Revolution* and the *Democratic Revolution.*

The Agricultural Revolution.[3] The Agricultural Revolution marked the first fundamental change, in man's relation to the resources of the land, that can be reconstructed from observable evidence. It is thought that this revolution took place in the highlands bordering the dry lands of Southwest Asia. These highlands extend in an arc from the eastern side of the Persian Gulf and of the Tigris-Euphrates Valley, through what is now southern Turkey to the eastern side of the Mediterranean. The world's first farmers began to cultivate several plants that were native to the area: wheat, barley, peas, lentils, and vetch. They also domesticated two native animals: goats and sheep. For the first time in man's experience it was unnecessary to spend almost every waking moment in the search for the next meal. As these people spread down valley to the bordering lowlands they added the date palm to their cultivated crops; and they made three important inventions: the wheel, the plow, and the spinning frame.

The Agricultural Revolution came at more or less the same time to the area farther east. In India cattle were domesti-

---

[3] R. J. Braidwood, 1960.

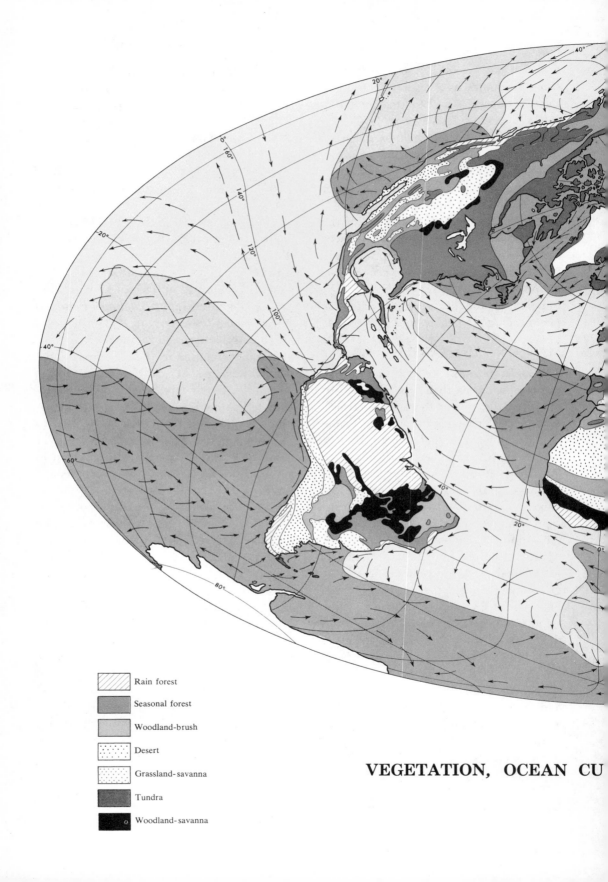

Rain forest

Seasonal forest

Woodland-brush

Desert

Grassland-savanna

Tundra

o Woodland-savanna

VEGETATION, OCEAN CU

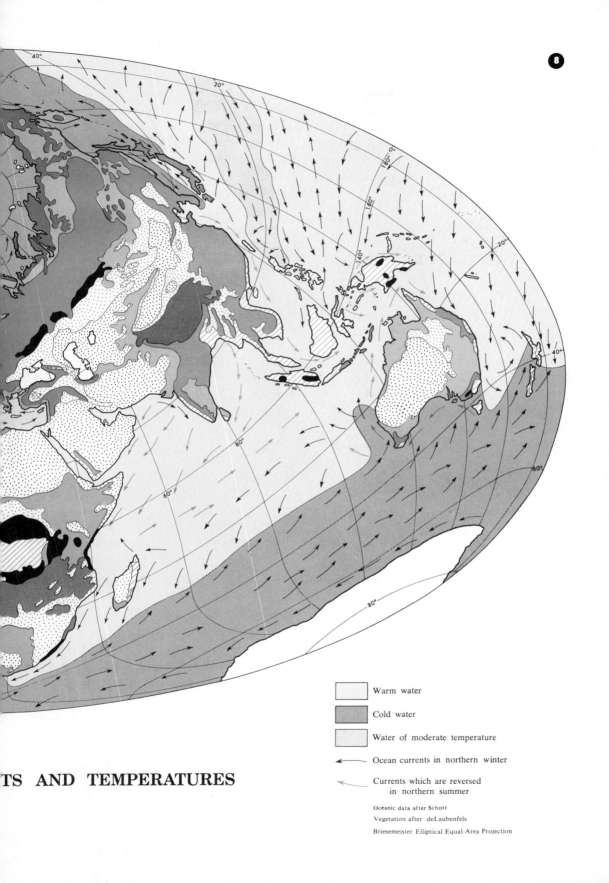

8

TS AND TEMPERATURES

Warm water

Cold water

Water of moderate temperature

Ocean currents in northern winter

Currents which are reversed
in northern summer

Oceanic data after Schott

Vegetation after deLaubenfels

Briesemeister Elliptical Equal-Area Projection

cated; in Southeast Asia pigs, poultry, rice, taro, and bananas; in the bordering grasslands of Southwest and Central Asia, horses, camels, and other animals. This kind of revolution also took place, apparently quite independently, when maize[4] was cultivated in Central America, and the potato in the Andes of South America.

From these centers the new way of life—which the anthropologists describe as *Neolithic* (in contrast to the earlier *Paleolithic*) —spread outward along the lines of human migration. Crops and animals were brought to the eastern side of the Mediterranean, and on through Egypt to Africa south of the Sahara. Along with the wheat and barley that were brought into Europe came two weeds—rye and oats: and in the cool climate of maritime Europe the weeds became more important. Wheat, rice, and domestic animals were brought to China. As the new way of life was adopted, the more primitive peoples were pushed out of the lands that were better suited to the new technology, and the density of population was greatly increased.

The Early Civilizations. The second of the great revolutions in human living began at the dawn of written history, and close to the area where the Agricultural Revolution had taken place some 4,000 years earlier. There were three of these Early Civilizations in, and close to, Southwest Asia; but there were also three others in more distant parts of the earth that developed somewhat later. The first three (about 4000 B.C.) were in Mesopotamia, in the Nile Valley of Egypt, and in the Indus Valley of what is now Pakistan.[5] The other three included the Chinese Civilization of East Asia, which began a little before 2000 B.C.; the Andean Civilization of South America, which started about 1000 B.C.; and the Mayan Civilization of Central America, about the seventh century A.D. The origins of the last two are not so well known as the others because of the absence of any kind of writing among the Indians of the Americas.

Each of the Early Civilizations was marked by the development of a central government backed by military force. But government and armed forces require the services of many individuals who are freed from the necessity of producing their own supplies of food and other necessities. There had to be an agricultural surplus in order to support those people who were not engaged in farming. First there were priests, and the earliest signs of this development can be seen in the construction of temples. The priests not only performed the religious rites but also acted as administrators of the economy. As larger numbers of people came together in cities, it was necessary to build walls and to organize armies to defend against the raids of the less civilized outsiders. The first kings, it seems, were selected to act as military leaders in time of danger; but soon they were accepted as peace-time rulers. With the kings came landowners, and army officers who maintained order. And along with the institution of kingship came the idea of conquest, and the desire of the ruling group not only to perpetuate its power, but also to control the territory from which the whole state derived its food and raw materials. The Early Civilizations had the effect of intensifying

---

[4] Maize is the word which refers specifically to the grain which we in the United States commonly call Indian corn, or just corn. According to general English usage, however, corn refers to any common grain. In England corn is the word used to refer to wheat, in Scotland to oats. In this book, therefore, we use the Indian word *maize* to designate Indian corn.

[5] R. M. Adams, 1960.

warfare and empire-building—all except the Inca Empire of the Andes, which occupied a position almost free from threatening neighbors, and where the world's only example of a true communist state was built.

For thousands of years after the rise of these Early Civilizations there were no revolutionary changes in man's relation to the land. Crops were cultivated and work done with human and animal muscles. In the course of time wind power and the power of falling water were added to muscle power. In such a society land was wealth, and the owners of land became the aristocracy. Associated with the aristocracy were the priests and army officers, the latter administering the political authority in the name of the aristocracy. The wealthy minority supported the priests of the church, and patronized the artists, musicians, and writers—except in the two American civilizations where there was no written language. In each case the economic burden rested on the farmers, who worked end-lessly and monotonously to raise food, and who lived in poverty, illiteracy, and often in hunger.

At first the separate centers, and the territory into which the idea of an ordered society under a supreme authority spread, remained distinctive. The crops and animals, and even the people of each area, differed from those of other civilized areas. But it was not long before interconnections were established overland among the four Old World centers, with a resulting spread of crops, animals, and techniques. It was not until the age of exploration, which began in the fifteenth century, that Old-World crops and New-World crops were interchanged, and for the first time the Old-World domestic animals were brought to the Americas. Furthermore, starting in the sixteenth century, large numbers of Negroes from Africa were brought to the Americas.

During all this time there were no fundamental changes in the basic technology, the kinds of social and political institutions,

The ruins of Persepolis, once the center of the Persian culture hearth. The city was destroyed by Alexander in 330 B.C.

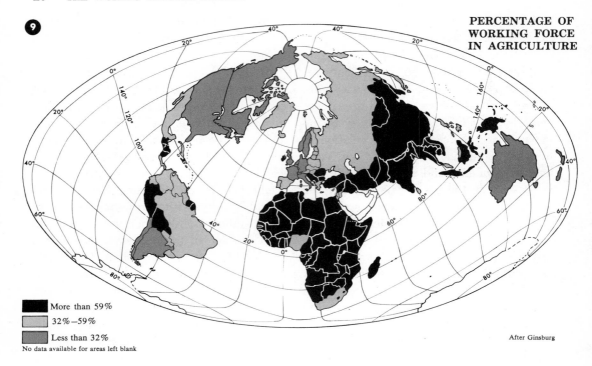

9

PERCENTAGE OF
WORKING FORCE
IN AGRICULTURE

■ More than 59%
▨ 32%–59%
▨ Less than 32%
No data available for areas left blank

After Ginsburg

·and the common attitudes and objectives. In all these areas, organized political authority felt the impelling need to extend its range by force through the conquest of other competing authorities. The idea, that one state should use its military force to impose its will on another state, first appeared in Southwest Asia—a region which has the longest and bitterest record of conquest and reconquest of any part of the world. But the idea of conquest was not lacking among the other Early Civilizations. The spread of civilization from the early centers, until it covered almost the whole inhabited world, was accompanied by conflict among states, by repeated invasions, by repeated changes of territory and boundaries. The only state that could be described as strong was one that was self-sufficient because it controlled within its own territory the essential resources needed to maintain its economy. In the modern world all these objectives, as we shall see, are out-

moded, because an industrialized state that is self-sufficient cannot be strong, and the conquest of other states is no longer practical in an era of total warfare. Yet the ideas generated in the Early Civilizations still persist to trouble the contemporary world.

During this long period when no fundamental culture changes were taking place, population increased slowly. When weather was good for crops, and when there was no warfare, the death rate would fall and the population would increase. Then there would be natural disasters of flood or drought or violent storm, or man-made disasters of war and destruction, or resulting famines and epidemics of disease. The death rates would rise; there would follow a net decrease in the total number of people. It is estimated that, at the time of Christ, the total population of the world was between 200,000,000 and 300,000,000. Of these some 9,000,000 lived in Egypt, and 54,000,000 were in territory ruled by Rome.

In the year A.D. 2 the world's first attempt at a census was made in China, at which time between 60,000,000 and 70,000,000 people were reported in that region. Vast areas of the world were very thinly populated or remained entirely empty. Thereafter the population of the world increased slowly, and irregularly, to an estimated 545,000,000 in 1650, and 728,000,000 in 1750.[6]

The Contemporary Revolutions. The third great period of revolutionary change in human living is now going on. We are living in the early period of change, when ancient concepts still claim the adherence of many people; but these concepts are now challenged by a new order, the shape of which it is not easy to discern. This is a period of conflict and chaos. The nature of our revolutionary period can best be understood if we recognize the existence of two revolutions going on together, but each in a somewhat different area: the Industrial Revolution and the Democratic Revolution.

The one world is now divided, as never before, by the impact of these two contemporary revolutions. Both originated around the shores of the North Sea in Europe, and both have been spreading from that core area, each at a somewhat different tempo and in a somewhat different pattern. It is possible to map the areas of the world's inhabited lands over which the new ways of life have spread, decade by decade during the past two centuries, and to identify the border zones where the old order is in process of violent conflict with the new. It is the main theme of this book that the world is now divided into regions within each of which the changes and conflicts, resulting from the spread of these two contemporary revolutions, are producing a

series of interrelated problems and developments; and that the modern world can best be seen in perspective when these changes are viewed through the eyes of both history and geography.

THE INDUSTRIAL REVOLUTION

The Industrial Revolution began in the late eighteenth and early nineteenth centuries. It started, we may say, when James Watt patented his first successful steam engine (in Glasgow in 1769), and when the firm of Boulton and Watt of Birmingham built the first working steam engine and placed it in operation (to pump water out of a coal mine in 1775). Among the famous dates that mark the beginnings of the new technology are: 1785, the first use of steam to move the machinery of a textile factory (at Popplewick, near Nottingham in England); 1788, the first use of steam to propel a boat (on a Scottish lake), although the first practical steamboat was a tug used in 1802 on the canal between the Clyde and the Forth rivers in Scotland; 1807, the first use of a Boulton and Watt engine to operate a regular passenger boat (on the Hudson River); 1813, the first locomotive (to haul coal between the mines and docks on the River Tyne in England); 1819, the first steamship to cross the Atlantic (the Savannah, from Savannah to Liverpool in twenty-nine days); and 1825, the first steam passenger railroad (Stockton to Darlington in England).

Changes in Technology. These dates mark the beginning of a revolution in technology. For the first time in the million years of man's existence on the earth he made use of controlled inanimate power instead of the muscle power of man or beast, or the uncontrolled power of wind or falling water. For the first time man could cease to be a lifter, a digger, and a mover:

[6] A. M. Carr-Saunders, 1935.

he had to learn how to be a puller of levers, a pusher of buttons, a skilled builder and repairer of complex machinery, an industrial engineer, a planner and manager of intricate operations. With less expenditure of his own physical energy man could now produce a vastly expanded volume and variety of goods. At first controlled, inanimate power was supplied by the steam engine, but later other kinds of power were added—the electric motor, the internal combustion motor, and most recently the nuclear reactor. With these new machines man has suddenly increased his capacity to produce food, clothing, housing, and many other things that were once listed as luxuries; and he has vastly increased his capacity to transport large volumes of things at high speed from one place to another on the earth. This enlarged capacity to produce and to transport has resulted in an unprecedented increase in the volume and variety of raw materials required to maintain the new economy. And this new capacity to produce and to transport things over the earth has resulted in an appalling new destructive potential in warfare, so that war is now "total war," involving all the people of a state and not just a body of professional soldiers. Yet, those peoples who have gone through the Industrial Revolution can now live at a standard of material comfort, and with a freedom from the threat of natural disasters, that even the well-to-do could not have attained in the pre-industrial world.

Geographic Changes. The Industrial Revolution, however, is much more than just a change in technology. The new capacity to produce and to transport requires a reappraisal of the significance of the physical features of the habitat. Of special importance are the changes in the patterns of circulation, changes in the significance of

barriers to circulation, changes in the size and complexity of cities, and changes in the use of raw materials.

The Patterns of Circulation. One of the distinguishing features of countries that have felt the impact of the Industrial Revolution is the increased volume of movement of goods and people from place to place. This may be described by the general term *circulation.* Map 10 shows the extent to which both railroads and highways are concentrated in the economically most highly developed regions—notably Europe and the United States. Furthermore the arrangement of ships at sea on any one day shows a concentration on certain busy routes, especially the route connecting Europe with North America. A map of airplanes in flight would show a similar pattern of arrangement.

The kinds of routes selected have changed with changes in the technology of transport. The easiest routes for men on foot or horseback had been discovered and developed by the earliest inhabitants, and had been used as lines of movement for thousands of years. But with the coming of the railroad, and with the increased size of ocean vessels, some routes and ports had to be abandoned. Railroads, and modern motor highways, are less restricted by such features as river crossings and swamps than were the older roads; but on the other hand railroads, and to a certain extent motor highways, are more restricted to the easier grades through mountains and hilly uplands.

The Significance of Barriers. What constitutes a barrier to circulation? What features of the terrain are important because they impede the movement of goods and people, or provide protection against invading armies? The answer depends on the technology of transport. Is a river to be considered as a boundary line because it constitutes a barrier, or is it to be recognized as a major line of circulation, an axis rather than a boundary? These questions must always be asked with reference to a particular kind of culture, for the features that would be barriers to some people offer easy lines of circulation to others.

This principle can be illustrated with reference to warfare. For the first time in World War II the pattern of paved roads for a mechanized army was of greater importance than the arrangement of hills and slopes. No longer were ridges and scarps important as strong points in defense: the new strong points were offered by the stone houses and narrow streets of towns where the roads came together, and around which it was impossible to pass without leaving the roads. Now with air-borne armies and rocket projectiles the significance of the terrain must be interpreted anew.

The Size and Complexity of Cities. Another change associated with the Industrial Revolution is in the size and complexity of cities. Early in the nineteenth century old cities began to grow rapidly, and new cities appeared in the midst of formerly rural country. The number of cities with more than a million population, and the number of *conurbations,* or clusters of great cities, increased at a more and more rapid rate. The first city to reach a million in population was London in 1802. Paris reached this size about 1850, New York about 1870, Vienna in 1878, Berlin in 1880, Tokyo, Chicago, and Philadelphia about 1890, Calcutta in 1900, Buenos Aires about 1906. In 1930 there were thirty-nine such great cities; but by 1963 the number of great cities and conurbations in the world had passed 100 (see Appendix D). As the Industrial Revolution sweeps over a country the proportion of the population living in cities rises from perhaps less than 10 per cent to more than 50

per cent—in some places to as high as 90 per cent.

All this urban growth took place basically because there were more jobs available in cities than in rural areas. The city people were called on to perform a wider and wider range of services for their service areas. Since the rise of the Early Civilizations, the traditional urban functions have included worship, commerce, and administration. There have been religious centers, trading centers, and places where the activities of government were carried on. Usually all three functions have been combined in one central place. In the typical pre-industrial cities manufacturing was carried on in workshops located under the same roofs as the salesrooms and living quarters. But the Industrial Revolution greatly enlarged the need for urban services, and caused an increase in the complexity of urban areas. The commercial function is now usually concentrated in the central business district. Parts of the urban area are devoted to banking and finance, to business and professional services, and to recreation. Distinctive industrial districts have appeared, and industries of any one kind have tended to group together in compact areas. For the first time in history manufacturing cities have begun to grow at, or near, coal fields because of the new need for a source of power.

The change in the technology of transport made all this urban growth possible and guided its form and structure. Without railroads and steamships enough food could not have been brought to the small area of a city to feed so many non-farming people. Furthermore, within the pre-industrial cities people moved about on foot or horseback, and they built their streets for this purpose. Residences had to be as close as possible to the places of work. It was the electric street railroads that first permitted the spread of

Winkel's "Tripel"
Projection

TROPIC OF CANCER

Atlantic

EQUATOR

Ocean

TROPIC OF CAPRICORN

Pacific

Ocean

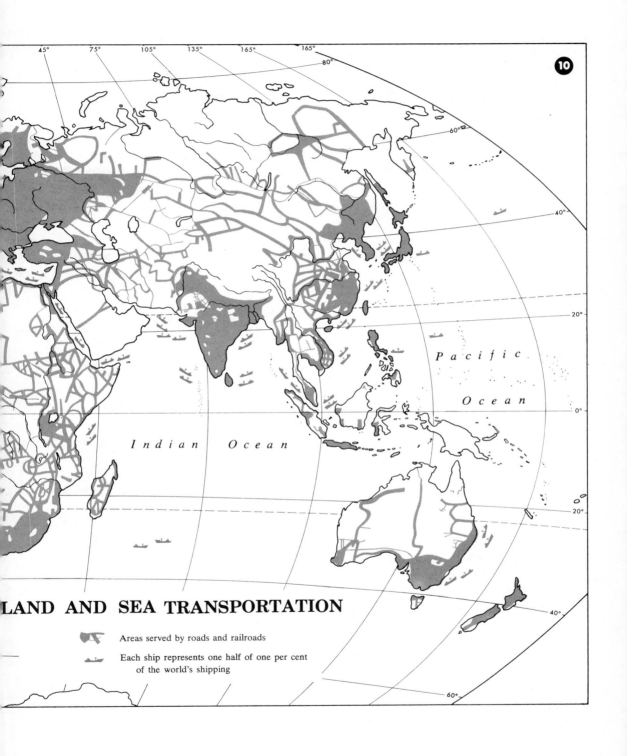

80°

60°

40°

20°

Pacific

Ocean

0°

Indian   Ocean

20°

LAND AND SEA TRANSPORTATION

Areas served by roads and railroads

Each ship represents one half of one per cent
of the world's shipping

40°

60°

residences to the suburbs—along lines of fast travel. Now motor buses and automobiles make the urban sprawl possible in many directions, not just along certain main lines. Around the cities are large areas of suburban countryside occupied by people who commute daily to work-places in the cities.

The Use of Raw Materials. Another geographic change of major importance associated with the Industrial Revolution is in the use of raw materials. The volume of earth resources that must be supplied daily to modern large-scale manufacturing centers is almost incredible. Water is the resource that is consumed in the greatest volume. For industrial purposes it is used on such a scale that even in rainy climates water shortages may develop. More than 250 tons of water are needed to make one ton of steel, and the water demands for some other industrial processes are even greater. In addition to water, there are the old familiar raw materials provided by the earth, such as copper, tin, iron, lead, and zinc, on which man's economic life has long been based. But in the past century a great variety of new materials have been added to the list of basic resources, such as coal and oil, and the hardeners of steel—manganese, tungsten, nickel, chromium, vanadium, molybdenum. Among other new resources are bauxite, the ore of aluminum, and uranium, the source of nuclear power.

None of these resources is evenly distributed over the earth. Even water is abundant in some places, lacking in others. Iron minerals are widespread among the rocks of the earth's crust, and iron ore has been mined in many parts of the world. But the demands of modern industry are so enormous that it is no longer possible to undertake mining operations on small ore bodies.

Only where there is an exceptionally large volume of ore does it pay to invest in the development of large-scale operations, yet only by the use of such operations can the ore be supplied at low cost. This has had the effect of bringing fundamental changes in the patterns of economic geography: in the modern world the greater part of the world's supply of raw materials comes from only a few places. For example, in 1954-1956 more than 60 per cent of the iron ore came from localities in three countries—the United States, the Soviet Union, and France. Nearly 60 per cent of the coal was mined in the United States, the Soviet Union, and Germany. Over 50 per cent of the tin came from Malaya and Indonesia. Nearly 40 per cent of the bauxite came from the Guianas. More than 86 per cent of the world's sulfur came from the Gulf Coast of the United States.

Meanwhile industrial society has been using up its best ore bodies at a rapid rate. As lower-grade ores come into use, costs of production increase, not rapidly, but in slow almost imperceptible steps. There are some economists who point to the possibility that gradually increasing costs could wipe out the advantages of large-scale production, and could bring the whole industrial world face to face with disaster—without dropping any bombs at all. It seems that the Industrial Revolution creates a situation in which there is a race between continued technological progress and resource exhaustion. The country that hopes to survive must devote the greatest possible effort to scientific research and engineering development. But this is not all.

The Population Explosion. As a result of all these interrelated changes that constitute the various aspects of the Industrial Revolution, there has been a sudden upsurge in the rate of population growth. Not only are more and more people concentrated now in cities, as we have said, but the thinly peopled areas are decreasing in density, while the densely peopled areas are increasing. Also, because of the unprecedented success of efforts to control disease and the causes of death, death rates, especially in the economically more developed areas, have taken a sudden drop. Death rates, which before World War II were as high as 30 per thousand in some countries, have been lowered in a few decades to less than 20 per thousand. With birth rates still high— as much as 40 to 50 per thousand in economically less developed countries—this decrease in the death rate has produced a sudden net increase in the rate of population growth, which in some places amounts to a "population explosion." From the 728,-000,000 people who were alive about 1750, the population of the world had increased to 2,995,000,000 in 1960. By the year 2000, the world's population could easily pass 5,000,000,000.

There is some evidence that as people are grouped together in cities there is a drop in the birth rate. There is a general correlation between the birth rate and the proportion of the population living in cities. But even in the United States, where more than half of the population is urban, the net rate of growth between 1953 and 1957 was 18 per thousand, at a time when the world mean was 16 per thousand.

If population growth is faster than the growth in the value of goods and services— in other words, if the number of people increases faster than the number of jobs— economic development may become impossible. The result of such a situation is only to increase the amount of poverty, hunger, and misery in the world. The fastest

possible rate of population growth, as determined by the biological process of reproduction, is about 3 per cent per year. If economic growth is to be started in a country with such a high net rate of population increase, it must be at a level of at least 4 per cent.

Conditions and Stages of Economic Growth. Under what conditions and by what means can the production of goods and services in an economy be increased at a rate fast enough to produce economic development? Essentially this question concerns the nature of the Industrial Revolution and the conditions of its spread across the world.

To increase the production of goods and services at a rate faster than that of the increase in population requires a massive investment of new capital. Economists estimate that it takes something like a 3 per cent increase in capital per year to produce a 1 per cent increase in the gross national product. In countries that are relatively productive and are occupied by well-to-do people who want to use some of their incomes for investment rather than for the building of country homes and other forms of luxury living, the capital may be supplied from domestic sources. Where the well-to-do people are reluctant to turn income into savings and investments, the capital may have to be provided by the government. And if the gross national product of a country is too small, large injections of foreign capital may be necessary to start the process of development going. In any case, investment means that there has been a postponement of consumption for the sake of larger consumption later.

The Initial Phase. The initial phase of the Industrial Revolution, according to the economist W. W. Rostow, requires that about 5 to 10 per cent of the gross national product should be used for new capital formation each year, over a period of two or three decades.[7] This is what happened in Great Britain during the late eighteenth century. James Watt could not have placed his steam engine in production without financial help. A large landowner by the name of Matthew Boulton sold his estates in Packington, England, and invested in the necessary equipment to start the manufacture of steam engines. An industrialist named John Wilkinson, who was engaged in the manufacture of cannons, invested money in the necessary research and development to make the boring of cannons cheaper and more accurate. His invention, applied to the manufacture of the cylinders of Watt's engine, made these engines far more efficient. Such investment in future profits would not have been possible in an unstable society where an uncertain future made the immediate use of income desirable, or in a society that frowned upon innovation and experiment. But Britain in the eighteenth century had both stability and social freedom. A member of the landed aristocracy did not lose his status before the law by selling his land and investing in an industry. People were free to seek individual profit from business enterprise. The initial phase of the Industrial Revolution, which was based on the new use of controlled inanimate power to increase the productivity of the textile industries, was started by an increase in investment from domestic sources. The low wages paid to labor, which were barely above subsistence levels, also had the effect of postponing consumption, and leaving a larger proportion of the gross national product to invest in new capital.

The new capital developed during this

[7] W. W. Rostow, 1960.

period had to include what Rostow calls "social overhead." The facilities for transportation, the supply of power, housing for urban workers, and many other facilities had to be provided, whether from private or public sources. The Industrial Revolution was made possible in Britain by the construction of docks, by the building of railroads, and by the expansion of urban residences.

The Mature Economy. Rostow describes a sequence of stages of economic development, based largely on European and American experience. The initial phase he describes as the "take-off." If from 5 to 10 per cent of the gross national product is invested in new capital formation over a period of two or three decades, and if other conditions of growth are present, economic development thereafter becomes self-sustaining, and the continued growth of the economy becomes the way of life of the people. The drive to maturity takes about forty to sixty years, during which time from 10 to 20 per cent of the gross national product is used in new capital formation each year.[8]

The mature economy is one in which the industries are highly diversified and produce a wide variety of consumer goods. The proportion of agricultural workers has dropped far below the ratios in manufactur-

[8] W. W. Rostow, *op. cit.*, pp. 38 and 59, offers the following tentative dates when certain countries passed through the take-off stage and reached maturity. Not all economists are in agreement that these stages do, in fact, illuminate the process of economic growth.

Country	Take-off	Maturity
Great Britain	1783-1802	1850
France	1830-1860	1910
United States	1843-1860	1900
Germany	1850-1873	1910
Sweden	1868-1890	1930
Japan	1878-1900	1940
Canada	1896-1914	1950

A product of the Industrial Revolution: nineteenth century working-class housing in the East End of London.

ing, commerce, and service occupations. Business promoters have been replaced by industrial engineers and managers. The old pre-industrial principle of "few sales, large profit per sale," has been replaced by "large volume of sales, small profit per sale." Self-sufficiency has given way to interdependence.

According to Rostow's analysis, countries that achieve maturity are able to make a choice between alternative policies. Some have continued to adhere to the old pre-industrial principle that the actual possession of resources and markets is both desirable and possible, and these countries have made use of their mature powers to extend their control over other countries by force. But it is also possible to move into a stage of "high mass consumption," in which a great variety of consumer goods is made widely available among the people. Another alternative is to establish a "welfare state," in which the people choose to sacrifice some of the potential material standards of living in favor of a guarantee of security.

THE DEMOCRATIC REVOLUTION

The Democratic Revolution is the second of the two great revolutions that are producing ever sharper divisions in our one world. It also started around the shores of the North Sea as did the Industrial Revolution, and more or less at the same time. But its pattern of spread has been quite different. The Democratic Revolution involves a fundamental change in the status of all the individuals of a state. Basically it means that the old religious ideas concerning the brotherhood of man are to be given wide application: that henceforth it is not "right" that men should be free to inflict harm on other men through the use of force. It means that government is to be with the consent of the governed. It means that conflicts of interest among men are to be resolved by mutual discussion and agreement, not by the dictation of those who command the greatest force. This means that the "law of contract" replaces the "law of status." The spread of the Democratic Revolution clothes the individual with a new dignity never before enjoyed by all the citizens of a state. Even in ancient Athens, where many

democratic ideas were generated, half the population was not included among the free citizens.

The political scientist, J. L. Busey, defines democracy as a political condition where the maximum possible number of people enjoy the maximum possible degree of freedom of choice, political and social participation, and of security under a rule of law. There are five chief elements in this new, revolutionary definition of the status of the individual: (1) the acceptance of the principle of equal treatment before the law; (2) the guarantee of protection from the arbitrary acts of those in authority; (3) the right of the individual to be represented where taxes are levied or laws formulated; (4) the acceptance of the principle of majority rule, and of the secret ballot; and (5) the right of freedom of access to knowledge, and the open discussion of issues of public policy. Even the idea that such objectives might be possible for all the citizens of a country represents one of the most revolu-

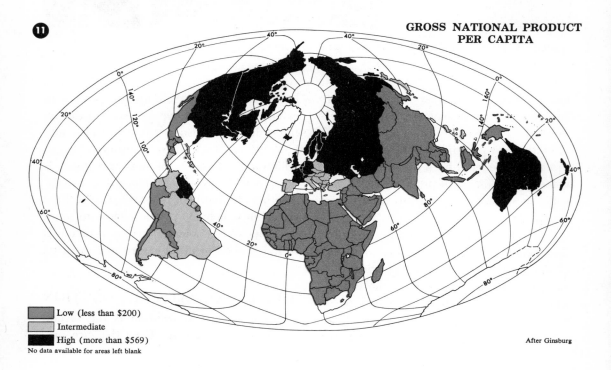

11

GROSS NATIONAL PRODUCT
PER CAPITA

Low (less than $200)
Intermediate
High (more than $569)
No data available for areas left blank

After Ginsburg

tionary changes in man's relation to man that has appeared in thousands of years.

The ideas of the Democratic Revolution, like those of the Industrial Revolution, first appeared in practice around the shores of the North Sea. The concepts of the legal status of the individual were a part of English common law, drawn from the experience of some five centuries. British, also, was the tradition of free speech, and free access to knowledge. The idea that government should be by consent of the governed was first written down as a basis for political unity in the Mayflower Compact of 1620, by men of English origin who had been living in the Netherlands. The demand for popular sovereignty originated in France—in fact adult male suffrage was only adopted in Britain in the 1880's. But, settlers from Europe who had moved to America were among the first to use these ideas as a basis for government. And many of the basic ideas of democracy were presented with great eloquence in the Declaration of Independence of the United States, and in its Constitution.

The ideas of the Democratic Revolution spread rapidly in eighteenth century Europe. The period from 1760 to 1800 was notable for a whole series of revolts against traditional authorities; and by the beginning of the nineteenth century the word "democracy" had, for the first time, come into wide use from the North Sea to Switzerland.[9] The ideas of democracy continued to spread rapidly to Anglo-America, and to Australia and New Zealand. But the spread of the Democratic Revolution has not ended yet. It is sweeping today into other pre-democratic parts of the world. To be sure, the content of the revolution has been changed—so much so that, in some areas where individual inequality has yet to be

[9] R. R. Palmer, 1959.

challenged, there is a mounting demand for an end to inequalities of status based on race or on the ownership of property. If men cannot expect to be equal, they can expect their countries to be treated on terms of equality with other countries.

Such radical new ideas could not fail to arouse opposition. In Europe, where pre-democratic society was strongly developed, the reaction against democratic ideas has been strong, especially among the fascist countries. But the strongest reaction against the Democratic Revolution, as defined above, has appeared in the Soviet Union, where all five basic elements are specifically denied. In communist terminology a "People's Democracy" is a dictatorship operated in the name of the proletariat. The use of this word in such opposite meanings has the effect of confusing the unwary.

THE CONCEPT OF THE CULTURE REGION

These twin revolutions of the contemporary world are creating unprecedented changes in man's way of life. Inevitably there is conflict and disorder. The shape of the new world which will eventually emerge is not yet predictable, but it is clear that the traditional ways of life are in process of modification, as the pre-industrial and pre-democratic ideas are challenged. The communists believe in the Marxist-Leninist concept that the ultimate victory of communism is inevitable, due to fundamental contradictions within the capitalist system. Those who have faith in the ideas of democracy are equally certain that these ideas constitute the "wave of the future."

The purpose of this book is to look at the modern world in the perspective of historical process and areal differentiation. The two revolutions and the reactions they set up have created a pattern of regional divisions, each characterized by a particular set of economic, social, and political conditions and problems. Each region is a unique segment of the earth's surface, within which there is a unique assortment of resources and habitat conditions, a unique pattern of political organizations, and an arrangement of people and production that is peculiar to the area. Each individual country or state exists in the context of the culture region of which it is a part, and the interactions among countries reveal the nature of international tensions and conflicts. The significance of these tensions and conflicts is related in part to the position of the culture region in its areal relation to other regions.

It is important to understand that no region can be completely uniform, for no two pin-points on the face of the earth are identical. The "region" is a geographic generalization—analagous to the "period" in history. The characteristics described in each region are most fully developed in the regional cores, and they become less clearly exhibited toward the peripheries. There are areas which are transitional between neighboring culture regions, and share the characteristics of both. Clearly the cores of regions are more important than the peripheral zones. But, because of the convenience of using statistical data and other information, the regions are defined in terms of whole states. Eleven major culture regions are defined, as follows:[10]

European
Soviet
Anglo-American
Latin American
North African-Southwest Asian
South Asian
Southeast Asian
East Asian
African
Australia-New Zealand
Pacific

[10] Shown on the map inside the front cover.

The Analysis of States. Within the culture regions the basic units of action and reaction are the politically organized areas, the states. Each state has within its national territory a particular arrangement of natural features and resources, and this resource base must be appraised in relation to the attitudes, objectives, and technical skills of the people. The pattern of population—of areas of concentrated settlement with central cities, of areas thinly populated, and even of areas outside the effective national territory (that is, areas from which the citizens of the state do not derive a living)—is in relation to the habitat. Also in relation to habitat and population is the pattern of the economy: agriculture, mining, the manufacturing industries, and transportation facilities. And finally, all these elements are included in an analysis of the viability of a state.

The viability of a state refers to the effectiveness with which it can be operated to fulfill its purposes. A state exists for the purpose of preserving the traditions and carrying out the objectives of its people. The particular body of traditions and objectives that the people have in mind is known as the *state-idea*. This is the *raison d'être* of a state, the reason why people give their support to the state, the reason why the state continues to exist.

There is a difference between a nation and a state. A nation is a body of people with common traditions, conscious of belonging together. Often a nation is tied together by the use of a common language, and by the literary traditions inscribed in that language, although there are nations that have overcome the handicap of using different languages, and have nevertheless achieved unity and coherence. A state, on the other hand, is any politically organized territory. A nation-state exists when the people of one nation are organized in one state, but there are many examples of nations that are divided among several states, and of states that include more than one nation. The interplay of state and nation is an important element in world tensions, and in the analysis of viability.

In any state there are integrating and disintegrating forces. Those that tend to hold a state together are integrating forces, but these are always competing with the forces of disintegration which tend to break a state into separate parts. A strongly held state-idea is an integrating force. But where a national territory is divided into two parts, in each of which people adhere to a somewhat different state-idea, there is a great danger that the state will break apart. However a state divided into three parts is in less danger, and if strongly held differences of opinion are intermingled throughout the state, there is still less danger of disintegration. A state that lacks a strong state-idea may have to be held together by the power of a central authority, forming a police state in which differences of opinion are not permitted expression. All these and many other alternatives must be considered in any analysis of the viability of a state.

The Method. This method of studying a culture region, and of analyzing the viability of the more important states, uses the approach of historical geography. If the sequence of cause and effect is to be followed it is impossible to limit discussion to strictly contemporary conditions. It is necessary to go back to origins, and to follow the geographic changes through time. The processes of economic, social, and political change are still going on, so that the contemporary regional divisions of the earth will be subject to change in the future. Approached from the point of view of history alone, there would be more attention to the sequence of events, and to the chain of cause and effect that ties events together in a coherent series. Historical geography reconstructs past geographies, and notes the changes in geography through time. The emphasis is less on sequences of events than on the reflection of these events in the arrangement of things on the face of the earth, and in the significance attached to features of the habitat that are related to changes in culture.

The purpose is to put the divisions of our one world into perspective. This is done by tracing the geographic changes through time, recognizing that the present geographic division of the world into culture regions is only the most recent such division, and that it is in no sense the end of the series. By understanding the causes and consequences of the regional divisions of the earth a background is created for the study of specific problems, or for the formulation of policies for action.

2

THE
EUROPEAN
CULTURE REGION

Country	Political Status	Latest Estimate Population	Capital City
Andorra	Republic	8,000 ('60)	Andorra
Austria	Federal Republic	7,100,000 ('62)	Vienna
Belgium	Constitutional Monarchy	9,300,000 ('62)	Brussels
Cyprus	Republic	600,000 ('62)	Nicosia
Denmark	Constitutional Monarchy	4,600,000 ('62)	Copenhagen
Faeroe Is.	Autonomous part of Denmark	34,000 ('60)	
Greenland	Integral part of Denmark	31,000 ('60)	
Finland	Republic	4,500,000 ('62)	Helsinki
France	Republic	46,400,000 ('62)	Paris
Incl. Corsica			
Germany, West	Federal Republic	56,900,000 ('62)	Bonn
Incl. W. Berlin			
Greece	Constitutional Monarchy	8,500,000 ('62)	Athens
Iceland	Republic	200,000 ('62)	Reykjavík
Ireland, Rep. of	Republic	2,800,000 ('62)	Dublin
Italy	Republic	50,463,762 ('61)	Rome
Liechtenstein	Constitutional Monarchy	16,628 ('60)	Vaduz
Luxembourg	Constitutional Monarchy	314,889 ('60)	Luxembourg
Malta	Constitutional Monarchy	328,461 ('60)	Valleta
Monaco	Monarchy	22,297 ('61)	
Netherlands	Constitutional Monarchy	11,800,000 ('62)	Amsterdam
Norway	Constitutional Monarchy	3,600,000 ('62)	Oslo
Excl.			
Svalbard Arch. ⎱			
Jan Mayen ⎰		4,276 ('57)	
Portugal	Republic	9,300,000 ('62)	Lisbon
Incl. Azores		318,558 ('56)	
Madeira		280,000 ('56)	
San Marino	Republic	17,000 ('60)	San Marino
Spain	Monarchy	30,600,000 ('62)	Madrid
Incl. Balearic Is.		441,842 ('59)	
Canary Is.		908,718 ('59)	
Sweden	Constitutional Monarchy	7,600,000 ('62)	Stockholm
Switzerland	Federal Republic	5,600,000 ('62)	Bern
United Kingdom of Great Britain & Northern Ireland	Constitutional Monarchy	53,200,000 ('62)	London
Incl. England ⎱ Wales ⎰		46,071,604 ('61)	
Scotland		5,178,490 ('61)	Edinburgh
Northern Ireland		1,425,462 ('61)	Belfast
Excl. Gibraltar	British Colony	26,000 ('60)	
Isle of Man		48,150 ('61)	
Channel Is.		108,471 ('61)	
Vatican City State	Ecclesiastical State	1,000	

There are several reasons why Europe is the key to an understanding of the modern world. This is the source region for the two great contemporary revolutions, and also the region in which some of the strongest reactions against these revolutions have originated. The modern concept of the nation-state first developed in Europe, and along with it the pre-industrial idea that to be strong a state must be self-sufficient. Since the age of exploration, which started in the fifteenth century, the western part of Europe has occupied a focal position in world communications, which was given additional emphasis by Great Britain's early start in modern economic development.

◄ *Holland, the Zuyder Zee Works: A gap being closed.*

THE LAND HEMISPHERE

THE WATER HEMISPHERE

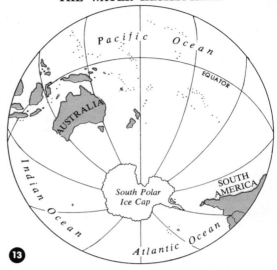

Now the technology of the air and space age requires that we take a new view of the globe: it has become significant that Europe is at the center of the world's Land Hemisphere, the half of the globe within which most of the world's people live. What happens in Europe is of vital concern to everyone.

Revolution and Reaction. The Industrial Revolution had its beginnings in England and Scotland. Here were the earliest applications of controlled inanimate power to manufacturing industry and transportation. Here was the first large-scale steel industry based on coal. Great Britain was the first country in the world to achieve industrial maturity, and for more than half a century Britain held a position of economic and military superiority. On this little island arose the world's first concentration of more than a million urban people. Most of the problems involved in transforming a pre-industrial, agricultural country into an industrial and predominantly urban country were faced first in Britain and then around the continental shores of the North Sea.

Similarly the Democratic Revolution had its beginnings in England, Scotland, the Netherlands, and France. To be sure, the world's oldest parliament was established in Iceland in A.D. 930; but the idea of representative government did not spread from there. In the late eighteenth century revolutionary new concepts regarding the rights of individual citizens burst into the open in Europe and Anglo-America.

One of the distinctive characteristics of the European Culture Region, however, is the strength and persistence of the reaction against these new concepts. The reason for the resistance is clear. Europe is the part of the world in which pre-industrial and pre-democratic institutions were strongest. The landowning aristocracy, and the army officers and churchmen who controlled the political life, were not eager to change the system. The great majority of the people were peasant farmers on whose incessant toil for meager returns the whole system rested. Most of the people were illiterate, and had little idea of the state of affairs in the world outside their small communities. Even today in Great Britain, the Scandinavian countries, the Netherlands, Belgium, Luxembourg, and Greece, the pre-democratic forms—royalty and titled nobility—

have been preserved and are greatly admired by the people. Monarchs have no political power, but they continue to constitute a symbol which has the effect of bringing unity to the states over which they preside.

Until recently there has been strong resistance to the idea of economic interdependence among states. The Industrial Revolution, with its resulting increase in productivity, its ever-mounting need for larger and larger volumes of raw materials, its need for large markets, and its new-found capacity to transport bulky goods at low cost, makes interdependence both possible and necessary. In the pre-industrial world a state had to be self-sufficient in order to be strong: the possession of territory richly endowed with resources and separated from enemies by easily defended barriers helped in the formation of a powerful state. But no modern state can be both strong and self-sufficient. Even the persistence of the idea that self-sufficiency is desirable has the effect of thwarting economic development and of withholding from the people the full beneficial effects of more abundant living which is made possible by the revolution in technology.

In the European Culture Region the need to accept the principle of economic interdependence has been emphasized by the geographic arrangement of the basic resources. Europe has an ample supply of the world's anthracite and bituminous coal; but more than 50 per cent of it is located in the Ruhr of Germany, and nearly 40 per cent is in Great Britain. For many years after coal became a major natural resource the European world was disturbed by the inescapable geographic fact that Germany had most of the coal and France most of the iron ore, yet France and Germany had become bitter rivals. With this culture region partitioned among nineteen sovereign

states, many of them strongly moved to seek self-sufficiency at whatever cost, the low-cost products promised by the new technology could not be supplied. Frustrated in the attempt to raise living standards and increase per capita production, some countries turned to fascist dictatorships, hoping to provide for economic development by decree, while at the same time denying all the ideas of democracy.

The Rise of the Nation-States. Another feature of the modern world which had its origin in the European Culture Region is the nation-state. Portugal and France were the first countries in the world where people, strongly conscious of their distinctive national character, were brought together under one political organization. This was accomplished through the success of a central authority in asserting political control over lesser authorities, and through the development of strong state-ideas powerful enough to overcome the forces of disintegration. But not all the states of Europe are nation-states—within the politically organized territory of many there is more than one nationality, and sometimes nations are split between two states. In the case of Switzerland people who talk four different languages, who profess different religions and practice different kinds of economy, are united by a powerful state-idea into a coherent and integrated state. Throughout this culture region state-ideas are strongly developed; yet not strongly enough to save Spain from civil war, nor to hold Ireland to the United Kingdom.

The European Culture Region has been handicapped by the existence of too many separate states. When each state is motivated by the pre-industrial concept of self-sufficiency, and feels impelled to expand the national territory at the expense of neighbors, and when international boundaries are reinforced by high tariff walls to

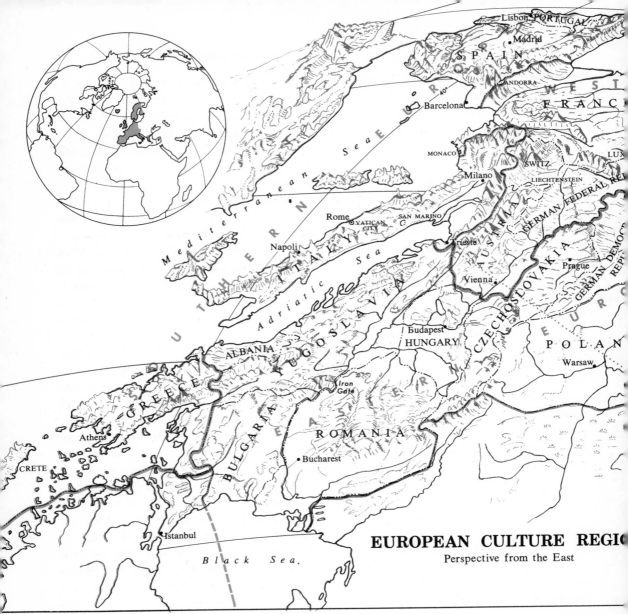

EUROPEAN CULTURE REGION

Perspective from the East

Map labels: Lisbon, PORTUGAL, Madrid, SPAIN, ANDORRA, Barcelona, MONACO, Milano, SWITZ., LIECHTENSTEIN, GERMAN FEDERAL REP., LUX., WEST FRANCE, Rome, VATICAN CITY, SAN MARINO, AUSTRIA, CZECHOSLOVAKIA, Prague, Napoli, ITALY, Trieste, Vienna, GERMAN DEMOC. REP., POLAND, Budapest, HUNGARY, Warsaw, ALBANIA, YUGOSLAVIA, Iron Gate, ROMANIA, GREECE, Athens, BULGARIA, Bucharest, CRETE, Istanbul, Black Sea, Adriatic Sea, Mediterranean Sea, SOUTHERN EUROPE, EASTERN EUROPE

obstruct the movement of goods from place to place, the result can only be frustration and intensified conflict. Ironically, the very strength of the state-ideas has hindered the acceptance of the changes made necessary by the Industrial Revolution, and has kept that revolution from raising the standards of living—until after World War II. Now, under threat of communist expansion, the first steps have been taken to eliminate the barriers to the free flow of goods and people, and to develop a European Economic Community. Within a few years the effect of this effort on living standards has been spectacular. Europe, united by the acceptance of interdependence among states, can become an economic and military power capable of standing side by side with the United States and the Soviet Union.

The Land Hemisphere. These developments are of special importance in the world picture because of the global position of the European Culture Region. If we turn the globe about until we discover the

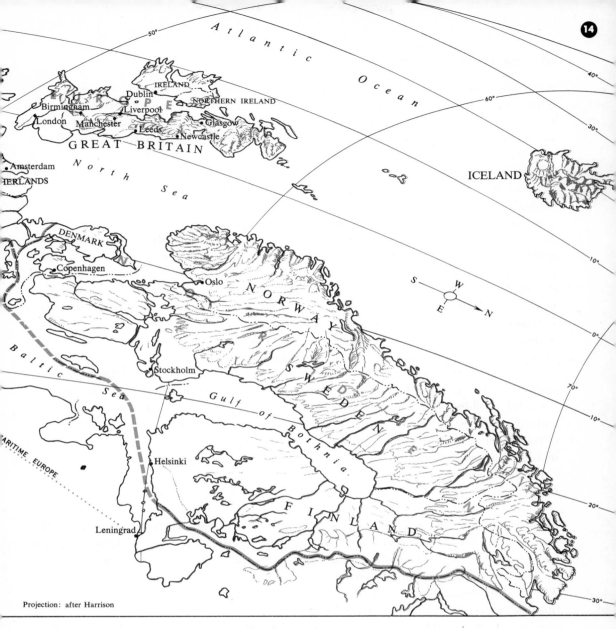

14

Projection: after Harrison

half of the whole surface which includes the largest proportion of the world's inhabited lands, we find that the center of this hemisphere is near Nantes in France (Map 12).[1] The *Land Hemisphere* contains 90 per cent of the land area of the world outside Antarctica. On these lands are 94 per cent of the world's people, and more than 98 per cent of the world's economic production. No other hemisphere can be

[1] The concept of the Land Hemisphere was first presented by Carl Ritter.

drawn to include so much of the inhabited land, so many of the people, or such a volume of economic production. The other half of the world is mostly water (Map 13), and the countries that occupy this half of the world are remote. Events that take place near the center of the world's Land Hemisphere inevitably affect more people than do events in more remote locations.

Location near the center of the Land Hemisphere became a significant geographic fact only in the second half of the twentieth century. It became significant when airplanes gave man the freedom to follow the shortest routes from place to place without regard to land and water distribution, storms, ice, and high mountains. In ancient times when the Early Civilizations appeared, the most centrally located countries were in southwestern Asia because of the pattern of land routes and the areas of dense population. Later the most centrally located parts of the world shifted to eastern Asia and to the eastern part of the Mediterranean Sea. When the exploration of the continents in the fifteenth and sixteenth centuries made the land and water outlines familiar to the Europeans, and European colonists migrated to distant parts of the world, the most central location shifted to the parts of Europe that were accessible to ships. Man was still tied to the surface of the earth, and the easiest lines of travel were spread over the oceans of the middle and low latitudes.

It was early in the twentieth century that the political geographer, H. J. Mackinder, shocked the military strategists of Britain by pointing out the rising significance of land power.[2] Western Europe, he showed, had reached its commanding position through the supremacy of sea power, but with the improvement of land transportation the states occupying the great heartland of Eurasia could deny access to sea power, and could also extend their conquests over the "rimlands" of the continents. He recognized the great strategic importance of Eastern Europe in his famous statement: "Who rules East Europe commands the heartland: who rules the heartland commands the world-island: who rules the

world-island commands the world." The world-island, according to Mackinder, was the great land mass of Eurasia and Africa. In restating his concept after World War I, Mackinder saw land-based air power as giving additional strength to the rulers of the heartland.

It is now necessary to reassess the significance of the arrangement of the world's inhabited lands. Airplanes and rockets have changed the dimensions of warfare, which now requires a truly global view of world strategy. We might paraphrase Mackinder: *Who controls the center of the Land Hemisphere controls the world.*

The States. The European Culture Region occupies the center of the Land Hemisphere. It is divided among nineteen separate states and five small political entities more or less controlled from outside. The arrangement of these states in Europe, as viewed from the east, is shown on Map 14. The culture region has three subdivisions: 1, Western Europe (including the part of Central Europe not under the rule of the Communist Party); 2, Southern Europe; and 3, Northern Europe, or Norden. The eight countries of Eastern Europe, which were a part of the European Culture Region until after World War II, are now more closely connected to the Soviet Culture Region. The European Culture Region, as here defined, makes up 5 per cent of the area of the world's inhabited lands, and is occupied by 14 per cent of the world's population.

THE HABITAT

(Maps 5, 6, 8, 15, and 16) The idea that Europe is a separate continent is a geographic fallacy inherited from the ancient Greeks. On any world map it is clear that Europe is only a peninsula on the western

---

[2] H. J. Mackinder, 1904, and 1919. See also Hans Weigert, 1957.

end of Eurasia. The people who occupy this peninsula are in closer contact with the world ocean than are those who occupy the continental interior: but the dividing line marking the eastern limit of maritime Europe is more realistically drawn from Leningrad to Trieste (Map 14), than along the Ural Mountains which form the conventional boundary between Europe and Asia.

Surface Features. The surface features of Europe are arranged in an intricate pattern (Map 15). A more or less connected series of high mountain ranges run east and west across the southern part of Europe. These ranges include the Carpathians, the Pindus ranges, the Dinaric Alps, the Alps, the Apennines, and the Pyrenees. In the same system are the Atlas ranges of northwestern Africa. Placed as they are these ranges form a barrier along the northern side of the Mediterranean lands, and give special emphasis to the breaches and passes where routes converge. A major breach is formed where the Bosporus and the Dardanelles provide a water passage from the Black Sea to the Aegean Sea. There is a large gap, also, in southern France where the Rhône Valley offers an easy north-south land route. The passes over the mountains, such as the Brenner Pass over the Alps between Italy and Austria, are followed by the major routes of travel.

North of the Alps and west of the Carpathians, the surface features of Europe are made up of an array of hilly uplands and low mountains. These features are not so high as the Alps. They are characterized by massive, rounded outlines, and when man first came upon them they were covered with very dense forests. These are the low mountains that surround the hilly upland of Bohemia on the border between Czechoslovakia and West Germany, and that

divide Germany into separate pockets of lowland. These are the uplands that stand on either side of the valley lowland of the Middle Rhine—the Vosges Mountains and the Schwarzwald (or Black Forest). Across the Rhône from the western margin of the Alps is the Massif Central of France. Low hills and cuestas are arranged in a concentric pattern around the Paris Basin. Hills and low mountains, too, make up much of Scandinavia and a large part of Great Britain and Ireland. The Iberian Peninsula, on which Spain and Portugal are located, is made up of a high plateau, the Spanish Meseta—an upland surmounted in a few places by high mountains.[3]

The plains of Europe are also arranged in a distinctive pattern. From the vast Russian plains of Eurasia a lowland extends westward, narrowed between the Carpathians and the Baltic Sea. Near the North Sea this plain turns southward to extend into what is now Belgium. Low hilly divides separate a series of small lowlands: the Paris Basin, the Valley of the Loire, the Aquitaine Basin, and the Saône-Rhône Trench. From the upper Saône it is an easy matter to cross over to the head of the Seine, or to the Rhine at its great bend near Basel. From Basel the Rhine flows northward between the Schwarzwald and the Vosges Mountains over a wide valley plain before passing through the Ardennes in a narrow gorge. All these rivers draining out from the central part of Europe—the Vistula, the Oder, the Elbe, and the Rhine— give access to the North Sea or the Baltic.

All of northern Europe, as far south as the mouth of the Rhine, was covered by a vast continental ice sheet during the glacial

[3] For definitions of these terms see Appendix B, p. 441.

15

Reykjavik

Norwegian Sea

UPLAND

SCANDINAVIAN

Trondheim

Atlantic Ocean

Bergen

Oslo

Stockholm

Helsinki

KJÖLEN

Edinburgh

North Sea

Copenhagen

Baltic Sea

Belfast

Dublin

London

WESTERN

Hamburg

Bremen

Berlin

Warsaw

Vistula R.

Oder R.

Amsterdam

Rotterdam

Elbe R.

EASTERN

Calais

Brussels

Cherbourg

Le Havre

BRITTANY

ARDENNES

Frankfurt

THÜRINGERWALD

ERZGEBIRGE

SUDETES

Prague

MORAVIAN GATE

Brest

Seine

Paris

Reims

VOSGES

SCHWARZWALD

BOHEMIAN MASSIF

EUROPE

Danube R.

CARPATHIANS

Loire R.

Saône R.

Rhine R.

München

Vienna

Bordeaux

MASSIF CENTRAL

Dordogne R.

Lyon

Berne

Budapest

HUNGARIAN PLAIN

Tisza R.

Garonne R.

Rhône R.

Milano

Trieste

Zagreb

Drava R.

SPANISH

Douro R.

Salamanca

Ebro R.

Marseille

Torino

Genova (Genoa)

Venezia Venice

Po R.

DINARIC ALPS

Belgrade

EUROPE

WALACHIAN PLAIN

Bucharest

Tagus R.

Madrid

MESETA

Toulon

Livorno

Bologna

Firenze (Florence)

Adriatic Sea

Danube R.

Lisbon

Barcelona

APENNINES

Sofia

Guadalquivir R.

Valencia

SOUTHERN

Rome

Tirane

PINDUS RANGES

Sevilla

Cádiz

Napoli

EUROPE

Aegean Sea

Mediterranean Sea

Palermo Messina

Catania

Kalámai

Athens

Sea

SURFACE FEATURES OF EUROPE

0 — 400

Scale of Miles

period. All of Great Britain, except the southernmost part, and all of Ireland were covered. Scandinavia was heavily glaciated, and the rounded knobby hills interspersed with bogs now remind one of the Laurentian Upland of Canada.

Climate and Vegetation. The climate of Europe is strongly influenced by its exposure to the relatively warm North Atlantic Ocean. The North Atlantic Drift brings warm water to bathe European shores, even around the northernmost tip of Norway (Map 8). Upwelling cold water appears along the coast of Portugal. Furthermore, the absence of mountain barriers parallel to the coast, as one finds at a similar latitude in western North America, permits the marine influence to penetrate far inland. The prevailing westerly winds constitute the northern part of the North Atlantic oceanic whirl.[4] As they pass onto the western margin of Eurasia they turn to the right, sweeping as north winds over the eastern part of the Mediterranean. Coming over the open Atlantic water, these westerlies are mild in temperature, even in winter, and carry much moisture. As a result rainfall is heavy and temperatures are moderate all along the western side of Europe. At London, located at latitude 51°31′N, the average temperature for January is 38.5°[5]. Farther inland, where the moderating effect of the open ocean becomes less, temperatures are somewhat lower in winter. Paris, for example, has a January average of 36.1°, and Bucharest (Bucureşti), Romania, averages 24.4°. Even Reykjavík in Iceland, at latitude 64°N, is warmer than this—averaging 30.9° in January. In winter the isotherms cross Western and Central Europe

[4] For an outline of these physical characteristics see Appendix A, p. 434.
[5] Temperatures throughout are given in degrees Fahrenheit; rainfall is in inches.

running north and south—which means that the quickest way to reach places with lower temperatures in January is to travel east, not north. Another, even quicker way is to climb into the uplands or mountains. Even in summer there are snow-covered surfaces in the Alps.

Another result of the sweep of maritime air is that the summers, also, are moderate. Hot summers are found only in the Mediterranean area, and in the protected Wallachian Plain of Romania. At London the average temperature for July is 63.9°, at Paris 67.8°, at Bucharest 73.6°, and at Reykjavík 52.5°. At Rome (Roma), on the other hand, the July temperature averages 78.3°.

The average temperatures, however, do not tell the whole story. The prevailing westerly winds are frequently interrupted by cold air masses of polar origin, the so-called polar outbursts, which are especially strong and frequent in winter. These burrow under the stream of mild, moisture-laden air forming the northern part of the oceanic whirl, and produce cyclonic storms and heavy rain or snow along the advancing cold fronts. The cold air masses in winter reach Europe from three directions: from the Greenland Ice Cap, from the Arctic Ocean, and from the snow-covered interior of Eurasia. As a result European weather is notoriously changeable.

The interaction of warm and cold air masses brings copious rainfall, especially to the western margins of the land. Almost all of Norway, and all but a fringe of eastern Great Britain, receive more than thirty inches of average annual rainfall. Where temperatures are so low there is relatively little evaporation, so that more than thirty inches of rainfall is too much for the best growth of grains, although it is excellent for pasture grasses. Rainfall decreases toward the east, but nowhere, except for a small area in Spain, is there a semiarid climate. Throughout most of Europe there is ample rainfall in all months; but in the Mediterranean area the rains are concentrated in winter, and the summers are dry and sunny. Severe winters, with a long, continued snow cover, are experienced only in Scandinavia and in Eastern Europe (Map 16). The southern fringe of Norway and Sweden has about two months of snow cover, and two months are also found in Poland. Most of the remainder of Europe gets less than ten days of snowfall in the average year, and no continuous snow blanket.

These climatic conditions have not been the same throughout the long course of man's settlement in Europe. The climate changed four times from warm and dry to cool and wet, and each cool wet period resulted in the formation of continental ice sheets over Scandinavia and Finland that then spread out in all directions. Over the ice, cold air accumulated, and the polar outbursts became stronger and more frequent than they are now. The violent wind, descending from the ice, picked up large amounts of fine dust from the bare surfaces around the ice margins and deposited this farther away in the form of *loess*, a soil material that was easily worked by primitive tools and proved highly productive for shallow-rooted crops.

The cover of wild vegetation reflects the climatic conditions (Map 8). Forests advanced northward or retreated southward with the changes in climate. Since the last retreat of the ice, forests have returned to most parts of Europe. The densest of these are located on the hilly uplands and low mountains: the forests are less dense on the sandy or chalky lowlands. In the far north there are some areas of tundra, and much of

Scandinavia is covered with woodland, made up of spruce, fir, and pine. Southern Europe, with its winter rains and summer droughts, was originally covered with an evergreen scrub woodland and maquis. Where the forests and woodlands have been cleared by human action, there are now only poor grasslands and heaths.

THE COURSE OF SETTLEMENT

For something like 500,000 years there have been human beings in Europe. This is about a quarter of the time that man has existed on the earth. Paleolithic man supported himself by hunting, fishing, and collecting the seeds and fruits of wild plants. As the great glaciers advanced southward, he also moved southward, even back into what is now the Sahara; but as the ice melted and the climate became more comfortable, the hunters spread northward again. It was not until the Neolithic peoples made their appearance, however, that any important man-made changes were introduced into the original habitat. Neolithic culture, with grain farming and domestic animals, spread into Europe from Southwest Asia. The first impact in Europe of the Early Civilizations of Mesopotamia and the Nile Valley was made by the Minoan Civilization on Crete about 2800 B.C. From Crete the concepts of civilized living spread to mainland Greece, which became one of the major source regions, or *culture hearths,* for the distinctively European way of life. Later the Roman Empire introduced many changes into Europe north of the Alps and, with the collapse of Rome and with the resulting invasions, the European Culture Region took on additional diversity. Out of the Medieval Period there emerged the great explorations, and the rise of the colonial powers in Western Europe. But it was in Great Britain, and around the shores of the North Sea that the two great contemporary revolutions originated.

The First Farmers. The new technology of farming and of pasturing domestic animals spread into Europe from Southwest Asia between 6000 and 3000 B.C. It was brought by sea along the Mediterranean to the southern part of Europe, and over the North European Plain into the forested country north of the Alps. The grains were wheat, barley, rye, and oats. In the wetter lands there were dairy cattle and hogs, while in the Mediterranean area there were sheep and goats.

Agriculture and the pasturing of animals led the Neolithic peoples to seek land of quite a different quality from that which had attracted the Paleolithic hunters. In the Mediterranean lands water became a matter of prime importance—one of the mythical heroes of ancient Crete was Hercules, a hydraulic engineer. In the forests north of the Alps clearing the land was not easy, especially in the very wet, densely covered areas. The first farmers occupied the porous sandy lands on the glacial outwash plains, the easily worked loess lands, and the chalk uplands of France and southern England where the forest was not very dense.

The coming of the bronze age in Europe again changed the meaning of the habitat. Bronze is made from copper and tin: copper had long been used, but for the first time the sources of tin became important. Both copper and tin were mined in the Erzgebirge (Ore Mountains) on the borders of Bohemia; copper and tin were mined in Spain; and tin was mined in Brittany and on the Scilly Isles off the southwestern tip of England. There was a considerable movement of trade in these ores, not only through the Mediterranean countries, where the Phoenicians held a monopoly of the tin

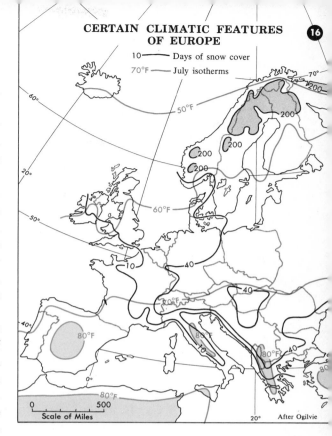

CERTAIN CLIMATIC FEATURES OF EUROPE

10——— Days of snow cover
70°F——— July isotherms

Scale of Miles

After Ogilvie

trade, but also northward through the Irish Sea to Scandinavia. The widespread application of bronze tools made possible the use for agriculture of new lands that had been considered marginal before.

The Germanic tribes were agriculturists. About 2000 B.C. they were occupying the southern part of Scandinavia, and the plains between the Rhine and the Oder. The sandy soils of much of this area were apparently so overworked that they lost what little natural fertility they may have possessed. It is thought that the large areas of treeless heath in this part of Europe may have resulted from man's destruction of the land base. Whatever the reason, Germanic farmers migrated southward, seeking better agricultural lands, which they found in the protected basins and valleys farther south. They formed relatively dense farm settlements along the Rhine and the upper Danube, and in the valley lowlands of France.

In addition to the development of agriculture and mining two other important culture elements were introduced into Europe at this time. One was the horse, introduced from the grasslands north of the Black Sea and the Caspian. The other was the establishment, all over Europe, of a common language of Indo-European origin.

The Greek Culture Hearth. It would be impossible here to specify the many traits of occidental culture that originated with the Greeks. Of all the source regions of the distinctive culture features of the Europeans, the Greek culture hearth is by far the most important (Map 17). From the Greeks came the basic concepts of the scientific method, many of the ideas that have now been incorporated in the Democratic Revolution, many of the techniques of agriculture that were in use until very recently, such basic procedures of commerce as banking, insurance and systems of credit. The Greeks were the first people in history to bring the major part of the food supply for a city from distant places by sea, and so to make the city both more prosperous and more vulnerable to attack than it would otherwise have been. Athens brought its wheat supply from the northern side of the Black Sea. Athens and other Greek city states established colonies around the Black Sea, and at several places in the western Mediterranean—notably Syracuse on Sicily and Marseille near the mouth of the River Rhône.

Not all the theories formulated by the Greeks are still useful, even if their method of formulating and evaluating theory remains valid. Aristotle's Temperate, Torrid, and Frigid zones, defined in terms of latitude, were shown to be inadequate as a basic classification of climate many centuries ago. However, the idea of an uninhabitable Torrid Zone had the effect of hindering exploration and colonization for a long time; and these categories are presented in some schools as if they were still acceptable. From the Greeks, also, came the ideas about the continents that have continued to retard world understanding up to the present time.

Let us see how the idea of the separateness of the continents originated. The word Europe is derived from a Semitic word meaning "toward the setting sun" which the Greek sailors applied to the western shore of the Aegean Sea at a very early date. The word Asia is derived from a word meaning "toward the rising sun," and it was applied to the eastern shore of the Aegean. Later, after the Greeks had learned to know the whole Mediterranean and its bordering lands, they recognized the distinctive character of the three shores. The northern shore was much indented with many harbors, with short rivers, and with high moun-

CULTURE HEARTHS

Cultures of antiquity

Industrial and Democratic Revolutions

Vikings

0   500
Scale of Miles

**EXTENT OF
THE ROMAN EMPIRE
395 A.D.**

Roman Empire in the West
Roman Empire in the East
Imperial territory lost in Third Century

0   500 Miles

After East

tains close behind the coastal regions. In this "temperate" region the Greek civilization had been built. This shore, and the land behind it, they called Europe. The eastern side of the Mediterranean was very different. It had few harbors or indentations, its climate was semiarid, but it did contain two great alluvial valleys watered by large rivers, and in these valleys two of the Early Civilizations had developed. This land they called Asia. Different again was the southern side of the Mediterranean, west of the Nile Valley. This was a very hot desert region, with little vegetation, and only a few oases. The inhabitants were primitive Negro farmers. This land they called Libya. Based on the world known to the Greek geographers, this division into three continents, each a distinctive habitat with a distinctive people and culture, was a useful and, indeed, a brilliant generalization. But carried into the modern world, when geographic horizons encompass the whole globe, the continental divisions are no longer useful for they obscure rather than illuminate the essential regional contrasts. North Africa, for example, is more like Southwest Asia than it is like Africa south of the Sahara; and the division between maritime Europe and continental Europe is more meaningful than the conventional separation of Europe from Asia along the Ural Mountains. To include a part of the Soviet Union in Europe and a part in Asia can only obscure the real unity of the country.

The Roman Culture Hearth. The European Culture Region derived many elements more directly from the Roman culture hearth. Roman conquests had the effect of introducing the fundamental diversities that have been a problem to Europe ever since. The Roman Empire included not only the Mediterranean, but also Europe as far north as the Danube and the Rhine, and

Great Britain as far as the Scottish Lowland. Map 18 shows the extent of the Empire in A.D. 395, after there had been some retreat in the middle valley of the Rhine, and from across the Danube in what is now Romania. The empire had been divided into a western part, ruled from Rome, largely pagan, and Latin in language; and an eastern part, ruled from Constantinople, largely Christian, and Greek in language.

To the scattered tribes of Western Europe the Romans brought a wholly new kind of life. They brought a new language, Latin. They maintained order through the use of military force. They founded many towns in the midst of farming communities where towns and urban populations had never existed before. To be sure the town, with a population engaged in commerce, manufacturing, administration, and other urban pursuits, had first appeared in the Greek culture hearth, but it was the Romans who introduced the town north of the Alps. Among the towns that were founded by the Romans are London, at the head of navigation on the Thames, Köln (Cologne), Koblenz, and Mainz on the Rhine, Bordeaux, at the head of navigation on the Garonne, Lyon, at the junction of the Saône and the Rhône, Belgrade (Beograd), at the junction of the Sava and the Danube, and many others. The Romans also built a system of roads to connect their cities and fortifications.

The Romans introduced certain new concepts regarding land ownership and political power. For the first time in Europe north of the Alps prestige and political power went to the owners of land. The officers of the army, who supported the system with the only organized force, administered political power subject to the directives of the landed aristocracy. The great majority of the people were peasants—illiterate, hard-working farmers on whose incessant toil the whole system rested.

Medieval Europe. The collapse of the Roman Empire in the fifth century after Christ was followed by invasions, and by the destruction of the Roman system of communications. Each community was isolated and self-sufficient. The landlords grouped together under kings who fought each other for control of the better lands. Much of the diversity of language and custom that makes Europe so interesting for the tourist, but makes European unity so difficult to attain, had its origin in this period of collapse, invasion, and political chaos.

Some of the invaders came from the north and east, some from Africa. The barbarians who poured across the Rhine were Germanic tribes that had not been exposed to Roman civilization. They swept across what is now France, and into the Italian and Iberian peninsulas. The Angles, Saxons, Jutes, Danes, and Norwegians invaded the British Isles, pushing the original Celtic peoples into the western parts of Great Britain and Ireland (Map 19). In 711 a new kind of invasion began when the Muslims or Moors, crossed from Africa into the Iberian Peninsula. The Muslims ruled most of the area south of the Pyrenees for some seven centuries, leaving a distinctive impress on the institutions of Spain and Portugal.

Meanwhile Charlemagne, whose empire lasted only from 800 to 843, also set a stamp on the geography of Europe. Charlemagne's empire extended to the Pyrenees, and south of the mountains along the northeast corner around Barcelona. His empire extended eastward as far as the River Oder, and along the valley of the Danube beyond Vienna. When Charlemagne died in 843 his empire was divided among his three sons: the western part, marked off along the Alps, the Jura, the Vosges, and the Ardennes, later became France; the eastern part later became Germany; but the middle part, extending from Italy, across the Alps, and along the Rhine Valley to the North Sea, was the wrong shape to be easily unified, and long remained a zone of conflict between the two giants on either side. In this middle zone several small countries made good their claim to national territory: Switzerland, Luxembourg, Belgium, and the Netherlands.

In Italy the barbarian invasions, and the collapse of Rome, resulted in the appearance of many tiny states. When the barbarians entered the Po Valley many of the Latin-speaking inhabitants fled for protection to the string of marshy islands off the mouth of the Po along the Adriatic shore. Where only poor fishing people had lived before, the city of Venezia (Venice) was built. Venezia, which lacked supporting territory around it, had to live by trade. The Venetian merchants sent their ships to Alexandria where they gained a monopoly on trade with the Arabs, and, through the Arabs, with the countries of southern and eastern Asia. Charlemagne in 810 gave Venezia the right to trade with the communities on the European mainland. As a result it became a center of wealth. Its chief rival was the other Italian port, Genova

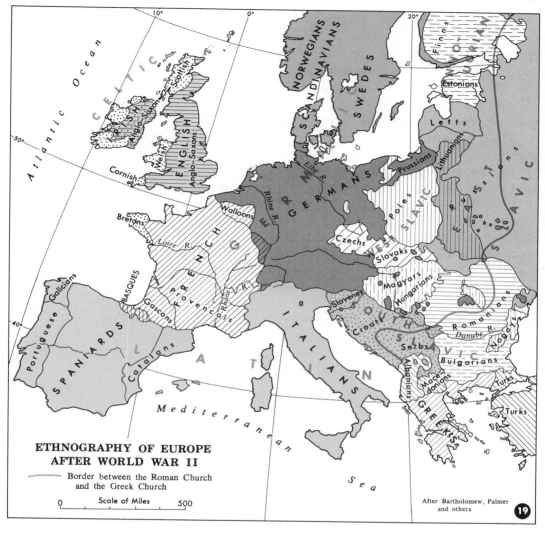

**ETHNOGRAPHY OF EUROPE
AFTER WORLD WAR II**

—— Border between the Roman Church
and the Greek Church

0   Scale of Miles   500

After Bartholomew, Palmer
and others

(19)

(Genoa), which also enjoyed a strategic position to carry on trade between the Mediterranean shores and Europe north of the Alps.

The development of market towns throughout Europe north of the Alps continued rapidly, especially after the twelfth and thirteenth centuries. These small centers of commerce were in some cases established by decree close to the castles of the lords. Many grew at the heads of navigation on the rivers, or at river crossings, such as Paris. In 1317 a sea route from the Mediterranean to the North Sea was established, and port cities thereafter began to grow rapidly. Annual trade fairs at certain European cities attracted merchants from great distances.

From the eleventh to the thirteenth centuries Christian Europe was engaged in a struggle with the Muslim infidels, and these wars had the effect of expanding geographic horizons. There were the Crusades, organized to wrest the Holy City of Jerusalem from the infidels; and there were the wars in Spain and Portugal to free the

Iberian Peninsula from Muslim rule.

After Portugal was freed from Muslim domination, it was the first country to organize a nationally-conscious group under one government. The nucleus from which the liberation proceeded was at Pôrto in the north. Lisbon (Lisboa) was captured in 1147, and in 1254, when the whole national territory was freed, a Portuguese state came into existence—the first of the nation-states.

It was at Sagres, at the southernmost tip of land, that Prince Henry the Navigator founded his geographic institute in 1419. Could Portugal achieve such prosperity as Venezia had once enjoyed? This would depend on finding a sea route that avoided the Arab-held Red Sea and reached around the Muslim countries to India and beyond. At Sagres, maps and documents concerning the unknown parts of the world were brought together, and both Christian and Jewish scholars were assembled to study and interpret them. Portuguese and other sea captains were given instruction in the arts of navigation. But could the "Torrid Zone" be crossed? Aristotle had said that no one could live so close to the sun; Ptolemy had agreed, and had added that the Indian Ocean was enclosed on the south and could not be reached by sailing around Africa. It was not until 1473 that a Portuguese ship, sailing southward along the west coast of Africa, crossed the equator. Then in 1498 Vasco da Gama sailed all the way around Africa to India—proving that the "authorities" were wrong. By this time Columbus had sailed across the Atlantic to America, and the age of exploration had started.

The Rise of the Colonial Powers. The next stage of European development began with the age of exploration, and continued into the period of overseas colonization and the formation of empires based on sea power. The first countries to build colonial empires were Portugal and Spain. In 1494

these two powers divided the world between them, drawing a line 370 leagues west of the Azores (about longitude 50°W) to separate the Spanish world to the west of the line, and the Portuguese world to the east of it. In 1500 it was discovered that South America extended eastward into the Portuguese hemisphere, and the Portuguese promptly started to colonize Brazil. But the chief aim of Prince Henry and his successors was to reach the wealth of southern and eastern Asia: after the voyage of Vasco da Gama, the Portuguese sent ships all the way to the coasts of China and Japan. They were the first to see and name Formosa. Even today a few remnants of this once great empire remain in Portuguese possession, for instance Macao near Hong Kong. Meanwhile Spain had been colonizing in America, and even sent an expedition across the Pacific Ocean from Mexico to claim the Philippines.

It was almost a century later when three other European countries entered the race to carve out colonial empires. Great Britain, France, and the Netherlands directed their attention chiefly to those parts of the world that Spain and Portugal did not want, or that were held too loosely by these earlier powers. All three of the newcomers laid claim to parts of forested, eastern North America, to parts of the Guianas and the Antilles. All three made major conquests in southern and eastern Asia, and in Africa. The greatest of these colonial empires was that of Great Britain.

All of these countries were located on the western side of Europe, where. they had unimpeded access to the open ocean. And all of them except the Netherlands built their national territories in Europe by a process of conquest. Portugal was created by expansion from the original nucleus around Pôrto in the north. Spain succeeded in bringing under one king all the scattered nationalities of Iberia with the exception of Portugal. France was built up around Paris, and was finally rounded out in the eighteenth century within the same barriers that had protected the western part of Charlemagne's empire. In Great Britain the English established their control over the Scots and the people of Wales, and then over the people of Ireland. But it was the overseas possessions that brought prosperity to the home countries—prosperity from the importation of varied raw materials and the export of manufactured goods.

Pre-Industrial Europe. Such was Europe in the eighteenth century. The terrain, cut up into many small basins and plains, was occupied by people speaking a variety of languages, and with contrasting traditions and customs. Not always were the people of one group to be found comfortably nestled into one of the naturally defined regions. Rather, land and culture were intricately associated, a result of the long history of conquest and migration. The map (Map 19) shows the chief ethnic groups of Europe in the period before World War II. A close examination of this map in relation to the basic patterns of the surface features shows the complex areal relations of these features.

The pre-industrial societies, however, did have certain elements in common. Inherited from Rome was the idea of dividing the land into large private estates, with the owners of land enjoying positions of prestige. Army officers and churchmen dominated the political life, and merchants were recognized as necessary but were not admired. Most of the people were poor, illiterate, and often hungry.

There were three chief kinds of towns in pre-industrial Europe. There were commercial towns, such as London and Paris, where the products of many lands were brought together by sea; and many smaller commercial towns that served relatively small communities. There were also religious towns, dominated by huge cathedrals—towns such as Köln, in which religious activities and commerce were combined, or such as Canterbury which was almost purely a cathedral town. And there were administrative towns, each built around the castle of a lord. At first, before gunpowder was introduced, the castles occupied commanding heights that were not easily attacked by men with arrows. But later when masonry walls were no longer useful as fortifications, the administrative functions were moved to new buildings that were more easily accessible. In most of the towns there was some home manufacturing, which produced goods for the townspeople and those in the nearby rural areas. But in some towns there were large factories, where skilled workers were housed, and paid to manufacture a surplus of goods over the needs of the immediate locality—for instance the woolen textile industries of Flanders (now Belgium).

Agriculture had been changed very little since the grains had first been brought into Europe thousands of years before. But population had increased since the early Neolithic period, and there was a mounting demand for foods. The European soils were not very fertile, and soon declined in productivity with continued cropping. To cope with the low yields the farmers made use of the "three field system." Rye or wheat was planted in a field in the fall and harvested late the following spring. Then barley or oats were planted in the same field. In the third year the field was permitted to stand idle, or in fallow. Yields of wheat were scarcely six to ten bushels to the acre; only in a few areas of especially good soils, such as those of the loess lands, could a relatively dense population be supported, and even in the better areas crop failure meant famine. The Dutch at an early date started to reclaim land from below sea level to provide food for their crowded commercial ports.

These several pre-industrial nation states were most of the time in conflict with each other. It was out of this conflict that the national boundaries of the European countries emerged. To be sure, the British, after they had finished their civil wars, enjoyed a certain measure of freedom from constant warfare at home because of the protection afforded by the Channel. Instead they fought most of their wars on the continent, or in distant parts of the world, using small armies of professional soldiers. France enjoyed an especially favored position on the continent. There certainly were gaps in the "natural defenses" that surrounded the country—such as the plain of Flanders—but it was not always easy for an invading army to reach the vulnerable spot. Within the bordering uplands there were several areas of better than ordinary soils, and there was a variety of climatic conditions that permitted varied products. France, alone among the countries of this period, was essentially self-sufficient in terms of basic foods. As a result, it had the densest population and the strongest armies.

Beyond the reach of ships the rest of Europe was not at all prosperous. Kings and dukes ruled over small states, and the process of unification through conquest had only just started. Germany and Italy did not exist as states; Austria, Hungary, and Poland included large territories; in the north there were two kingdoms, those of Denmark and of Sweden, and in the east was the edge of the Russian Empire. The southeast was occupied by the Turks. Map 20a shows the political make-up of Europe in 1721.

The Industrial Revolution. There is a sentence inscribed on the National Archives building in Washington, D.C. that says: "All that is past is prologue." In the European Culture Region the whole 500,000 years of human occupance is, in a sense, prologue to the contemporary world. To be sure the processes of change in Europe during the Paleolithic period were almost exclusively natural processes—that is they were physical, chemical, or biotic processes that went on essentially without interference by human action. The distribution of people at any one time was closely related to the distribution of wild game, fish, and edible plants. When agriculture and domestic animals were introduced into Europe a major revolution in human living took place, and for the first time there were certain areas in Europe where the most significant changes taking place were those introduced by human action. The clearing of the forest, the use of porous soils for farming until the mineral content of the soil was exhausted, the abandonment of land for new clearings, and the replacement of the former grain fields by heath—this was a process of change essentially human in origin. Still, most of the area of Europe remained little touched by the presence of man. The introduction of bronze, and later of iron, increased the impact of man on the landscape; and a still greater impact resulted from the Roman conquest, the establishment of towns, and the building of roads. Nevertheless, the basic methods of making a living from the earth resources remained unchanged: power was supplied by human or animal muscles, and this meant that large numbers of individuals had to labor for the support of the well-to-do few; the same three-field system of grain farming was used, and although animals were pastured in the agricultural areas, their manure was not used as a fertilizer, except in a few places; transportation of bulky goods—for example coal and wheat—was very difficult, and as a result each community had to be self-sufficient in regard to basic products. Communities that were located on navigable water had a very great advantage over other places because bulk shipments could reach them. All of these statements had been true for thousands of years: although changes in the way of life had certainly taken place, no fundamentally new technology had appeared in Europe since the rise of the Minoan civilization about 2800 B.C.

Then things began to happen in Great Britain. It was in England in the second quarter of the eighteenth century that the first change in the techniques of grain farming was adopted—the first change in some 5,000 years. The English farmers invented a system of crop rotation that included feed crops and the pasturing of cattle. A field was used one year for wheat, a second year for a cultivated forage crop, and a third year for hay. Cattle were kept in fenced enclosures where the manure could be collected—something which could not be done when they were kept on open pastures. With the use of more fields for feed crops rather than directly for human food, the acreage of wheat dropped, but because the fields were fertilized and the soil was enriched through the cultivation of forage crops (especially clover which returns nitrogen to the soil) the yield of wheat rose to between ten and twenty bushels to the acre. The use of animals for meat as well as milk greatly enriched the diet of the people of Britain, and the cost was low enough so that meat was available to a large part of the population, not to the wealthy alone. More recently the use of chemical fertilizers has raised the yield of wheat in Europe to over forty bushels to the acre.

Changes were also taking place in the use of fuel. In England, even as early as the thirteenth century, the forests that were close to the towns had been cleared for firewood, so that wood had to be brought from greater and greater distances. It was in that century that the mining of coal was started near Newcastle. Resistance to the use of coal for heating and cooking was strong, especially in places like London where the coal smoke was obnoxious and was considered a danger to health. But as firewood became more and more difficult to find, coal gradually replaced wood. In 1650 two sailing ships were used regularly in shipping coal from Newcastle to London, and English coal was exported to Scotland, Belgium, and France. By 1700 there were some six hundred ships engaged in carrying coal to London, and mining at Newcastle was employing more and more workers.

Meanwhile the demand for fuel was increased because of the increasing need for iron—to be used in ships' fittings, weapons, and implements. The English iron ores had long been smelted with charcoal—with the disastrous result of destroying the forests. Anthracite coal was used successfully in smelting, but charcoal remained cheaper. It was in 1709 that Abraham Darby, living in Coalbrookdale, a little to the west of Birmingham, where good quality bituminous coal was available near the surface, was successful in making coke that could be used for smelting iron. Still, not all the iron smelted with coke turned out well, and charcoal continued to be the more popular fuel.

The steam engine brought about the final victory of coal over charcoal. In Glasgow, Scotland, a young mechanic named James Watt had been trying to repair a new kind of engine that ran with steam. As he tinkered with the machine he suddenly realized

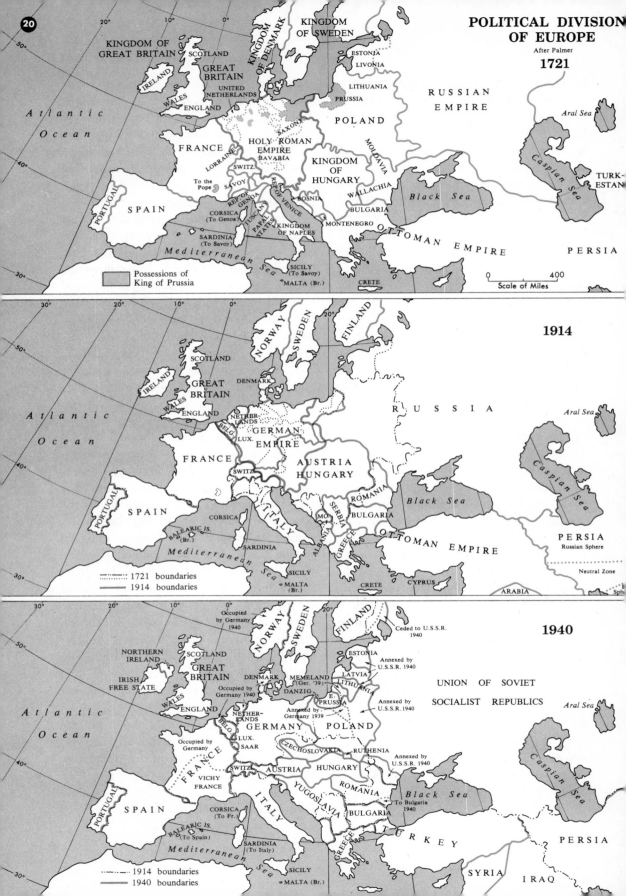

POLITICAL DIVISIONS
OF EUROPE
1964

------- 1940 boundaries
———— 1964 boundaries

0   400
Scale of Miles

that what was needed was a method of maintaining the heat in the cylinder. After some experimental work he took out a patent on a new kind of engine in January, 1769. He had been financed in his experimental work by a landowner named Matthew Boulton, and when Watt's engine proved a success Boulton raised the money to build engines by selling his estates. The firm of Boulton and Watt was established in Birmingham in 1774, and the first engine was placed in operation in 1775. The first engines were used to run pumps: to pump water out of coal mines; to pump water from below a mill wheel back up above it again; and to pump air through a mixture of coke, iron ore, and limestone in order to smelt iron.

Then John Wilkinson, the operator of a cannon factory near Birmingham, invented a method for improving the bore of his guns. Applied to the manufacture of cylinders for the steam engines, the new technique greatly increased the reliability and efficiency of Watt's engine. The finest Swedish wrought iron was imported to make pistons that could stand the strain. Finally, in 1781, Watt took out a patent on a steam engine that would turn a wheel. The Industrial Revolution had been launched.

It is important to know more about Matthew Boulton. One of the essential conditions in England, that made this technological revolution possible, was the existence of men like Boulton who were not against introducing fundamental changes and breaking long standing traditions, and who were willing to postpone the use of money available to them for the sake of future gain. Boulton was the owner of a large estate on which the work was done by tenants. As one of the landed gentry, Boulton had profited from the changes in farming methods that produced more wheat and meat for sale. But, in order to provide the funds necessary for the development of the new steam engine, Boulton sold his estate. In fact England in the eighteenth century was occupied by many Boultons. Agriculture was successful enough to provide an initial source of wealth; some of the landowners were willing to make a clean break with the established way of life, and to postpone the consumption of wealth for the sake of acquiring more wealth later; such non-conformists were not penalized by public opinion or by government action. In their midst, also, there were skillful inventors who approached the machine age with imagination. This potentially explosive mixture occupied a habitat well endowed with just those raw materials essential for a manufacturing industry—iron ore sufficiently pure so that it could be smelted by the crude methods of the time; coal that could be made into coke; limestone; and an abundance of water. The result was the beginning of a revolution in human living.

One of the first applications of steam power was to the cotton and woolen textile industry. In the same year that Watt had patented his first steam engine, Richard Arkwright had patented a new spinning jenny that made possible a vast increase per worker in the production of textiles. The first steam engine to turn the wheels of a textile plant was set up in 1785 at Popplewick, near Nottingham, in England. The result of this new capacity to produce cotton and woolen textiles was a very large increase in the need for raw cotton and wool. Woolen textile plants had been built on either side of the Pennine Hills in England because of the availability there of an abundant supply of wool. The hills had for a long time been cleared of their forests and were used to pasture sheep. But with the new machinery this source of raw wool became quite inadequate. The importation of raw wool and cotton from distant parts of the world took a sudden jump. In the decade from 1751 to 1761 cotton and wool imports had increased a little more than 20 per cent over the previous decade. Be-

tween 1771 and 1781, however, the imports were more than 75 per cent greater than those of the preceding decade; and between 1781 and 1791 the increase was nearly 320 per cent. England had the merchant ships and the colonies to accomplish this.

At this same time there were also prosperous and imaginative people in Europe outside England. In the Netherlands and Flanders much wealth had been accumulated through the development of colonies, and there was a tradition of non-conformity. But in the Netherlands there was no iron ore, no easily accessible coking coal, and no limestone. In France much wealth had been accumulated, because in the pre-industrial world this was the most powerful and most densely populated state, and it also had colonies. But in France non-conformists were treated harshly, and in fact invited to go elsewhere. The social climate was not ready for change. Yet change came. The Industrial Revolution spread to the mainland of Europe. The first railroad on the continent was built in France in 1830, to haul coal from St. Étienne to Lyon. The first railroad in the Netherlands was built in 1839. Bavaria, in southern Germany, had a railroad in 1835, but Spain not until 1848.

The Industrial Revolution came first to Great Britain, and later spread to other parts of the European Culture Region. The process of economic development, and the other changes associated with this revolution, have been described in the Introduction. It is important to keep in mind that Britain went through the stages of development and reached a mature economy in 1850; and thereafter for half a century this one country dominated the world of business and finance.

The Democratic Revolution. The Democratic Revolution also had its origin around the shores of the North Sea, as we have pointed out. England and Scotland contributed much to these revolutionary changes in the status of the individual. In England the power of the aristocracy, backed by armed force, had been destroyed in the fifteenth century, and the acts of the king had been restricted by law. The English inheritance of individual rights, including the right to protection from arrest without warrant, the right to free speech and the free public discussion of political questions, is a part of Common Law, which forms the basis of legal systems in most parts of the English-speaking world.

The idea of popular sovereignty came from France. In the French Revolution of 1789 the ruling aristocracy was eliminated by violence, and a system was established of government by the people. For a time the liberals of Europe saluted Napoleon as the champion of "liberty, equality, and fraternity."

The people of the Netherlands also made their contribution to the concepts of democracy. The flag under which the Dutch fought to gain freedom from Spain in the sixteenth century had horizontal red and white stripes: such a flag was known, even before it was adopted in America, as a symbol of the struggle for liberty. Liberty was not always for the individual—often it was liberty for a conquered nation, freedom from outside interference.

The Subdivisions of Europe. It is small wonder that Europe is notable for the diversity of its landscapes and its peoples. At the beginning of the eighteenth century this culture region was already made up of many contrasting parts, the inheritance of centuries of settlement and conquest carried out against a diverse background. But this inherited diversity has now been compounded by the revolutionary changes of the past two centuries, and by the reactions to these revolutions. Europe is not only the hearth where democracy was forged: it is also the home of fascist and communist reactions. The enormous new power conferred by the changes in technology, combined with the pre-industrial and pre-democratic concepts of the nation-state, are at least partly responsible for two world wars, neither of which could be confined to Europe.

During this time the political map of Europe has been revised several times. The pattern of states that prevailed in 1914 was inherited from the accumulation of past events, especially the Roman conquests and the empire of Charlemagne (Map 20b). Many new states appeared for the first time after World War I, created at the Peace Conference of 1919 (Map 20c). But after World War II some of these states again disappeared from the map, and the boundaries of others were considerably revised (Map 21).

It is convenient, in discussing the characteristics of the European Culture Region, to divide it into three groups of countries. First there is Western Europe, including Great Britain and Ireland (which are sometimes treated separately from the continental countries), and Germany and Austria (which are sometimes included in Central Europe). Western Europe is the core of this culture region, the area in which European characteristics are most typically developed. The second of the divisions is Southern Europe—the Mediterranean countries—where Greece and Rome once flourished, and from which the explorers of the fifteenth century set out to discover what the earth was like. This is a part of Europe that has long been settled and used up, and into which the two revolutions are only now beginning to sweep. The third is Norden —the Scandinavian countries and Finland— the part of Europe where the democratic ideas have advanced at the fastest rate, and are even preceding the modern development of the economy.

THE COUNTRIES OF WESTERN EUROPE

GREAT BRITAIN[6]

For more than half a century—between 1850 and 1900—Great Britain was the world's only example of a mature economy. The initial stages of the Industrial Revolution had been supported by the rapid expansion of the cotton and woolen textile industries. This expansion, as we have seen, was triggered by a series of inventions which radically altered the technology of textiles. It resulted in the creation of a new demand for improved transportation facilities, and this, in turn, created the need for a vast expansion of the steel industry. On the island of Great Britain the earth re-

[6] Officially called *The United Kingdom of Great Britain and Northern Ireland.* Great Britain includes England, Scotland, and Wales. The present title was adopted in 1927, after Ireland had gained its independence from the United Kingdom. In this book the shorter term, Great Britain, is used to refer to the United Kingdom.

sources to support the initial stages of economic expansion were readily available. During the latter part of the nineteenth century the British economy expanded faster than the population, so that there was a steady over-all rise in the income per capita. To be sure not everyone shared equally. The owners of capital were amply rewarded, but, as is usually the case in the initial stages of economic growth, the necessary postponement of consumption was achieved through low wage rates. After 1850 wages were improved and an enlarged domestic market supported the establishment of a great variety of consumer goods manufacturing. Raw materials came to Great Britain from all over the world, and British manufactured goods were sold in the most remote countries. British coal was sent to coal-poor countries on many continents, and vast amounts of British capital were in-

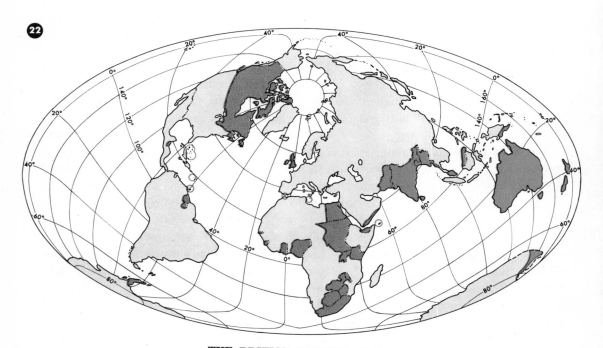

THE BRITISH EMPIRE - 1910

vested in economic development—especially in railroad building. By 1910 the British Empire embraced possessions on all the inhabited continents, and the British Navy controlled access to these possessions (Map 22). The one great center of the world economy was London.

Since 1910, Great Britain's economic and military position in the world has been fundamentally altered. In the first place Britain ceased to be the one great source of manufactured goods. By the end of the nineteenth century the Industrial Revolution had started to spread, and British factories began to run into competition from newer and technologically more efficient factories all over the world. To keep the British industries operating it has been necessary to shift from the production of standard consumer goods to high-cost, high-quality specialties. In the second place the island of Great Britain was no longer safe from enemy attack: submarines, airplanes,

and guided missiles have changed Britain's strategic position. And in the third place the ideas of the Democratic Revolution also spread across the world. Empires administered from Europe have fallen apart, and have been replaced by associations and federations of independent states. The British government has adopted a policy of leading the former British colonies and possessions to self-governing status as quickly as possible. The independent members of the Commonwealth may now accept the Queen as a symbol of authority, but essentially each is attached to London only by ties of sentiment or the advantages of a jointly operated economy. Map 23 shows the status of the various parts of the Commonwealth of Nations in 1964.

What have these changes meant to Great Britain? Can the dense urban populations of the little island of Great Britain, and of the associated part of Northern Ireland, be supported by the national economy? Is

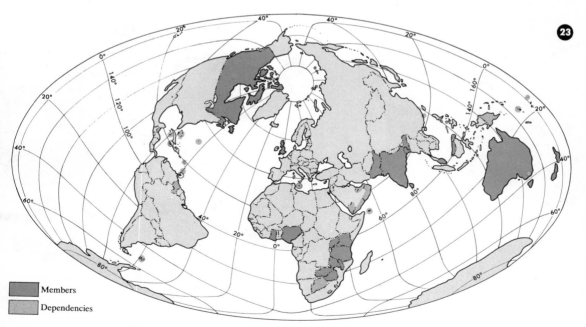

Members

Dependencies

THE BRITISH COMMONWEALTH OF NATIONS - 1964

24

BRITISH ISLES
AGRICULTURE
AND INDUSTRY

Orchards and gardens

Chief farming areas

Predominantly pastoral

Mixed farming and grazing

Non-agricultural

Coal

Steel industry

Industrial center

0   Scale of Miles   100

RAINFALL
Over 30 in.
av. annual

56°

0   100
Miles

0°

OUTER HEBRIDES

SCOTTISH

SCOTLAND

Skye

Aberdeen

Mull

HIGHLANDS

Dundee

Islay

Firth of Forth

Glasgow   Clyde R.   Edinburgh

North   Sea

Atlantic

Ocean

NORTHERN
IRELAND

Belfast

Newcastle

Middlesbrough

Isle of
Man

Barrow-
in-Furness

Irish   Sea

IRELAND

Leeds   Hull

Humber R.

Dublin

Liverpool   Manchester

Kildare

Mersey R.   Sheffield

Limerick

Nottingham   The Wash

Kilkenny

Shrewsbury   Leicester

Tipperary

Aberystwyth

Ouse R.

Cork

W A L E S

Severn R.

Birmingham   Cambridge

Avon R.

E N G L A N D

Oxford

Swindon   London

Swansea

Thames R.

St. George's Channel

Southampton   Brighton

Portsmouth

Isle of Wight

Plymouth

8°   4°   0°

the United Kingdom in the second half of the twentieth century a viable state? These are the questions we need to examine if we are to understand the position of Great Britain in the European Culture Region.

The Habitat. The British Isles (Great Britain and Ireland) lie fully exposed to the weather of the North Atlantic Ocean. No part of the islands is far from the sound of the pounding surf; no part is sheltered from the moisture-laden air. Rainfall on the western sides of the islands is more than sixty inches a year, coming usually in the form of drizzle rather than of violent rains. On the eastern side of the islands the average annual rainfall is less than thirty inches, but no part of the islands suffers from lack of moisture. There are seldom floods or droughts, or very severe winter snows, or long spells of summer heat.

The surface of the British Isles can be divided into two chief types: highlands and lowlands. The northern and western part of Great Britain is made up of highlands and is relatively wet; the southern and eastern part is lowland and relatively less wet (Map 24). The Scottish Highlands are composed of rounded low mountains, related geologically to the highlands of Scandinavia, with a notable linear structure trending from northeast to southwest. The Scottish Lowland is a down-faulted block or graben, bounded by steep fault scarps. This continues in the Ulster Lowland of Ireland. The hilly upland of Wales belongs to this same geologic area. The hilly uplands of southwestern England, southern Ireland, the southern part of Wales, and of the Pennines in England are geologically related to the hilly areas of Europe, such as the Brittany Peninsula (Map 15). The lowlands are similarly related to the lowlands of the continent, being composed of gently folded sedimentary rocks, including layers of chalk that hold up prominent cuestas.

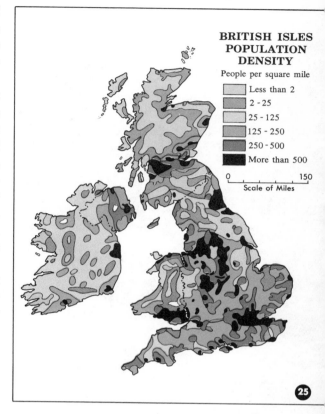

BRITISH ISLES
POPULATION
DENSITY
People per square mile

	People per square mile
	Less than 2
	2 - 25
	25 - 125
	125 - 250
	250 - 500
	More than 500

0   150
Scale of Miles

25

Population. More than 52,000,000 people occupy the 94,000 square miles of Great Britain and Northern Ireland. The pattern, however, is far from uniform (Map 25). There are several areas within which the density of population is over five hundred per square mile; on the other hand there are large areas of the Scottish Highlands where there are fewer than two people per square mile. Furthermore, the thinly populated areas are losing population to the more densely populated areas: the fastest growing populations of Great Britain are in London and Birmingham; since World War II there has been a net loss of population in Scotland and northern England.

More than 80 per cent of the people of Great Britain are concentrated in cities. There are seven large clusters of cities, or conurbations, each with more than a

The valley of the River Wye in England, near the Welsh border. It was in this area that the Hereford breed of cattle originated.

million inhabitants. These are: London (with more than 8,000,000 people in a metropolitan area of 722 square miles), Manchester, Birmingham, Glasgow, Leeds-Bradford, Merseyside (Liverpool and the other cities along the lower River Mersey), and Tyneside (Newcastle and the other cities along the River Tyne). As one would expect in a population so predominantly urban the British birth rate is relatively low (about

eighteen per thousand) and the death rate is also low (about twelve per thousand). The population today includes a larger proportion of older people than it did a century ago.

The people of Great Britain are mostly Anglican or Presbyterian in religion. In England the major religious denomination is Anglican, in Scotland, Presbyterian. In Ireland the separation of Northern Ireland from the Republic of Ireland is based on the concentration of Protestants in Ulster County around Belfast. The remainder of Ireland is almost solidly Roman Catholic. English is the universal language, but in Wales there are a few people who speak Welsh only, and in Scotland and Northern Ireland there are some who speak the old Celtic language known as Gaelic.

Political Organization. The United Kingdom refers to a union of once independent monarchies. On the island of Great Britain there are three national units—England, Scotland, and Wales. England and Wales were united in 1536; England and Scotland in 1707—for which reason the Scots are very insistent that the present Queen is Elizabeth II only in England and Wales, not in Scotland. Just as London is traditionally the political center of England, so Edinburgh is the focus of political life in Scotland, and Belfast in Northern Ireland. Wales, on the other hand, has no traditional focus to its political life. The basic political authority for all four parts of the United Kingdom is in the Parliament which meets in London.

Agriculture, Stock Raising, and Fishing. Although only a small proportion of British workers are employed in agriculture and stock-raising, and although Britain has been dependent on outside sources of food since early in the nineteenth century, agriculture in Great Britain is not without importance. The map (Map 24) shows that most of the agricultural land is located in the lowlands of southeastern England, in areas that receive less than thirty inches of average annual rainfall. In this climate of cool summers and mild winters, where evaporation is never very high, an average rainfall of more than thirty inches is too much for the best growth of wheat and other grains. But such a climate is ideal for the lush growth of pasture grasses. The periods of sunshine are so few that farmers long ago learned "to make hay while the sun shines." The wetter parts of the islands, where the rainfall is more than thirty inches, are mostly used for the pasture of sheep or dairy cattle. In the drier east, especially on the productive soils of the peninsula of East Anglia between the Wash and the Thames estuary, the farmers raise grain, sugar beets, and fruit.

British farmers are among the world's most efficient agriculturists. Most of the British farms are mechanized, and yields of crops are phenomenal. The farmer on the best lands of East Anglia produces eighty or more bushels of wheat to the acre, and the national average for wheat production is thirty-four bushels to the acre. British dairy cattle lead the world in the production of milk per cow, and since World War II there has been a major increase in milk yield due to new methods of animal breeding. British bulls are sought all over the world to up-grade dairy and beef stock; and British sheep are among the world's best producers of mutton and wool.

In spite of all these accomplishments, however, the people of Great Britain can not be fed adequately from the island. To provide a balanced diet, including plenty of meat, would require a minimum of 1.5 acres of crop and pasture land per person. But the total area of Great Britain provides only 1.2 acres per person, and only 31 per cent of the total acreage is suitable for plow

cultivation. This means that there is only about .5 acres of crop and pasture land per person. Or, putting it another way, the farms of Great Britain can provide adequate food for only twenty to twenty-two million people. The greater part of Britain's food supply has to be imported, and paid for with exports.

Another important source of food in Great Britain is from deep-sea fishing. Britain stands about sixth among the sea-fishing countries in the world. British steam trawlers, sailing out of many ports in England and Wales, and out of Aberdeen in Scotland, operate in all the chief fishing grounds of the North Atlantic, from Greenland to North Africa. The herring fisheries of the North Sea were for a long time the source of one of Britain's exports—cured herring. Fish, to supplement the British diet, are derived from widespread fishing operations. Of all the fishing areas the North Sea is the most important, and the major ports are Hull, nearby Grimsby, and Aberdeen.

Raw Materials, Industries, and Commerce. The process of change from a pre-industrial to a mature industrial economy has changed the relative importance of farming and fishing. Only about 5 per cent of the British working force is employed in agriculture and stock raising, and those employed in the fishing industries are much less than this, and are becoming fewer. Employment in manufacturing industries has climbed steadily, but the largest category of employment is in the various service occupations. One of the characteristics of a mature economy is the great variety of kinds of employment.

This process of economic transformation, in which Great Britain has reached an advanced stage, requires a reappraisal of the resource base. The resource endowment of the island of Great Britain was exceptionally favorable to the beginnings of the Industrial Revolution. There was an abundance of wool, and plenty of soft water; there were easily accessible coal measures, iron ores, and limestone. In fact there was one mine shaft in England from which coal, iron ore and limestone could all be brought to the surface. Very early in the initial stages of the Industrial Revolution the domestic sources of raw materials became insufficient. Now, not only must a large part of the industrial raw materials be brought in from outside, but also modern industry requires a great number of new raw materials never previously of importance. Manganese, nickel, chromium, tungsten, and many other minerals are needed for the production of special kinds of steel. And now about 39 per cent of the iron ore needs of Britain are imported—chiefly from Sweden and North Africa. The mines of the Scilly Isles which were once a major source of tin for the ancient world have been completely worked out, and now Britain has to import its tin from Malaya. The diversified manufacturing industries of a mature economy are dependent on supplies of raw materials flowing without interruption from all over the earth.

Coal was basic to the industrial growth of Great Britain during the nineteenth century. Map 24 shows the arrangement of the British coal fields. The coal is mostly bituminous of good quality, with some anthracite in the south of Wales. It is estimated that the reserves of workable coal in Great Britain amount to about forty-four billion metric tons, or enough to last for two hundred years at present rates of production. But present rates and methods of production are not likely to remain unchanged even for the next decade. Already the costs of producing coal have mounted until coal is no longer a major export. Although about 72 per cent of the coal mines are now mechanized, costs remain high for three chief reasons: first, the more accessible and thicker of Britain's coal seams have been worked out; second, British coal seams are thin, and much folded and faulted, which makes them more difficult to work than those of North America; and third, although labor costs have risen, pay is not high enough to attract an adequate number of young men to the industry. The production of coal per miner is only about 20 per cent of that of the average miner in the United States. British coal production was 225,000,000 tons in 1900, and 244,000,000 tons in 1930. But after World War II it dropped to 192,000,000 tons, and by 1958 it had been increased again only to about the level of 1930. British coal is no longer adequate to provide power and raw materials for British industries. Although coal is still the chief source of fuel for the electric generating plants, other less expensive ways of generating power are being sought by the British engineers. One suggestion is to burn the coal in the ground. Great Britain is also the first of the western powers to build an operating thermonuclear power plant. It is estimated that by 1975 half of Britain's electric power will be generated by nuclear reactors.

The steel industry is basic to all other kinds of industrial development. As with all British industries, war damage greatly reduced the productive capacity, and the return to high levels of production has been slow. In 1957 the British steel capacity was about 25,000,000 tons per year, which was a little less than the steel-making capacity of West Germany. Nevertheless, British engineers are among the foremost in the world in terms of technological skill and inventiveness. To be sure there has been some resistance to the adoption of new methods, both by labor and by management; but during the 1960's a definite upturn in production can be seen.

The map (Map 24) shows the arrangement of Britain's major concentrations of steel plants. There are five such concentrations: (1) along the River Clyde in Scotland; (2) along the River Tees near Middlesbrough; (3) on the eastern side of the Pennine Hills around Sheffield; (4) around Birmingham; and (5) in South Wales, near Cardiff. All these steel centers are located on, or close to, the coal fields. Two other steel centers are located on iron ore bodies: Scunthorpe and Northampton. Each of these districts is known for its own distinctive kind of production. Sheffield, for example, is world famous for its stainless steel and for other kinds of alloy steels. The British industries turn out a high-cost, high-quality product for a variety of specialized uses.

The other centers of British manufacturing industry are also highly specialized. Birmingham is known for its manufacture of articles of brass and aluminum, for its bicycles and automobiles, its refrigerators and washing machines. The largest concentration of small consumer-goods manufacturing is around London. Along the River Clyde, downstream from Glasgow, is Britain's largest shipbuilding area. Other shipbuilding facilities are to be found at Newcastle and Belfast. Woolen textiles are grouped around Bradford and along the eastern base of the Pennines; cotton textiles center on Manchester on the western side of the Pennines; Belfast has long been known for its linen textiles. Wool from the Pennines gave Bradford an initial advantage in this industry. Similarly flax grown in Ireland gave Belfast its start. But today less than 10 per cent of the flax for Belfast factories comes from local sources. The cotton

has to be imported, chiefly from America; this flow of raw materials enters Britain through Liverpool, which is easily accessible to Manchester. In all these textile centers there has been a notable increase, since World War II, in the manufacture of textiles from artificial fibers.

It is this enormous development and diversification of manufacturing industry that is the essential earmark of a mature economy. After a few years of slow recovery from the destruction of World War II, the British economy is again showing signs of new vitality. In 1960 some 16 per cent of the gross national product was devoted to new capital formation. There has been a rise in the income per capita, which means that a large proportion of the total population is sharing in the rewards of economic development. This kind of economic society has been called an "affluent society," a society characterized by high mass consumption, and by a high level of social security. The British people have adopted a policy of asking their government to provide a variety of services—health insurance, medical care, old-age compensation, and a number of other measures, which make up the "welfare state."

The British economy survives only on the basis of a large volume of commerce. Anything that restricts the free flow of goods diminishes British prosperity. Interdependence, not self-sufficiency, is the accepted goal.

The huge volume of commerce is reflected in the development of ports and systems of transportation. Six ports handle more than 75 per cent of British commerce. Pre-eminent among the ports is London itself, which handles more than 30 per cent of the total. Southampton is London's "outport," to which can come the larger ships that are too big for the crowded Thames.

Hull is Britain's largest fishing port. Glasgow handles a large part of the exports of Scotland. The second British port, in terms of the volume of commerce, is Liverpool. And among the big six is Manchester, the inland city that is connected to the sea by a thirty-five-mile-long canal capable of carrying ships with a draft of up to twenty-eight feet. These ports are connected with the hinterlands they serve by a web of railroads and highways. No parts of the densely occupied areas of Great Britain are more than five miles from a railroad; and the density of the highways is the greatest in the world. Yet both railroads and highways are in need of modernization. In 1960 programs to rebuild both railroads and highways were being started.

The focus of British life is London, the primate city of Great Britain. It is more than twice the size of the second city, Birmingham. London is not only a great manufacturing center, but also the place where most British firms have offices. This is one of the world's largest centers of banking, insurance, and finance. Here the greatest variety of goods and services can be found, and the most numerous kinds of employment. To London come the leaders not only of business and government, but also of the professions and the arts. In the whole geographic city there are about 8,500,000 people crowded into 722 square miles.

The Commonwealth of Nations. An essential aspect of modern Britain is its relation to the Commonwealth of Nations. This is a community of independent states and their dependent territories, loosely tied together by certain common traditions and interests. All the members inherit the political institutions of democracy, including parliamentary government and, except for Ceylon, the Common Law. Each enjoys economic benefits through access to the Commonwealth market and the use of currency based on the pound sterling. The recognition of the British monarch as the titular head of the Commonwealth is a purely formal arrangement, but it nevertheless symbolizes an association that is all the closer because it is voluntary. The Commonwealth covers an area of 9,500,000 square miles, scattered throughout the world (Map 23), and is occupied by about 691,600,000 people. The existence of the Commonwealth adds greatly to the power position of Great Britain, but also greatly complicates Britain's association with the European Economic Community. The problem is whether Britain is better off if it maintains close association with Europe, or with this widely scattered and diverse group of states. Can Britain find a way to join with other European countries to form an economic community without giving up its position as leading power in the Commonwealth?

In 1963 the Commonwealth was made up of three groups of states. First, the United Kingdom of Great Britain and Northern Ireland. Second, the states which recognize the British monarch as their own sovereign: Canada, Australia, New Zealand, Ceylon, and Nigeria. And third, the remaining countries which recognize the British monarch as head of the Commonwealth: India, Pakistan, Ghana, the Federation of Malaysia, Cyprus, Sierra Leone, Tanganyika, Kenya, Uganda, Jamaica, and Trinidad.

The Viability of Great Britain. Is Great Britain a strong state or a weak one? Do the forces for integration outweigh those for disintegration? How viable is Great Britain? These are the questions that summarize the position of Britain in the modern world.

Britain enjoys both advantages and disadvantages of position. Insularity, even in modern warfare, gives some measure of protection; nevertheless modern technology makes Britain far more vulnerable to attack than it ever was before. Still, an island placed directly athwart the major sea routes, connecting the most productive part of the European continent with the rest of the world, is in a distinctly favorable position for commercial growth. In the modern world Great Britain enjoys a position in close proximity to the center of the Land Hemisphere. Certainly, in time of peace, insularity is a great advantage.

Within this island there is a basic tradition of unity, resting fundamentally on unity of language and of the traditions that are preserved in language. To be sure there are separatist tendencies in both Scotland and Wales which could lead to disintegration if they continued to spread. In so far as economic well-being is a desirable national goal, both Scotland and Wales stand to gain by maintaining close ties with England. But nationalist sentiment is not always guided by economic advantage.

Britain's greatest resources are in the skill, the capacity for hard work, and the emotional stability of the people. The people of this country led in the Industrial Revolution, and the inventiveness of British engineers has not diminished. The survival of the British people through two world wars called for a tremendous national effort. The transfer of emotions from Empire to Commonwealth was itself no small task of national reorientation. If the United Kingdom were to disintegrate into its component parts it would probably not be from outside pressures, but rather from the affluence its people have achieved.

IRELAND[7]

The Republic of Ireland, and Northern Ireland—a part of the United Kingdom—occupy the island to the west of Great Britain. The republic occupies 85 per cent of the total area of Ireland and includes 68 per cent of the population. The division of

[7] In Gaelic the name for Ireland is Eire.

the island into two parts, which occurred in 1921, was based on religious differences —Northern Ireland is predominantly Anglican and Presbyterian, the Republic of Ireland is almost 95 per cent Roman Catholic.

The Irish people have developed an intense antagonism toward the people of England, to whom they are intimately tied, however, by the facts of geography. Ireland was brought under English control during the reign of Henry VIII, who introduced the English system of large private estates with tenant workers. In the late sixteenth century, under Queen Elizabeth I, Scottish Protestant settlers were brought to Ulster, the area around Belfast, thus setting the stage for the difficulties of the modern period. In 1800 the United Kingdom of Great Britain and Ireland was established, but by the late nineteenth century a strong popular demand for independence had developed, and there was almost constant warfare. In 1921 independence was granted, and the Irish Free State was set up as a member of the Commonwealth, separate from Northern Ireland. In 1949 the Republic of Ireland was proclaimed, and all ties with the Commonwealth and with the British monarch were broken.

The population of the Republic of Ireland has been decreasing for more than a century. In the 1840's there were 8,500,000 people in Ireland, but by 1854 the population had been reduced to 6,500,000. This was the result of a blight that attacked the basic food crop, the potato. At least 1,000,000 persons died of starvation, and there was a very large movement of emigrants to the United States. A census in 1951 counted 2,960,000 inhabitants; another in 1961 counted 2,815,000. The population continues to decrease as a result of emigration.

Ireland is a good country in which to pasture animals, but it is a poor country for crops. Only a small area around Dublin averages less than thirty inches of rainfall per year (Map 24); and in this area is found the densest population (Map 25). The remainder of Ireland's central lowland receives more than thirty inches, and where the hilly lands border the western shore rainfall is very heavy. The winters are mild and wet, the summers cool and wet. As a result pasture grasses grow so luxuriantly that the Irish like to refer to their homeland as "the Emerald Isle."

The Irish economy is based on stock raising and agriculture. About 59 per cent of the people are rural, most of them living on farms of less than thirty acres each. Only in the area of relatively light rainfall around Dublin are there large farms—of more than a hundred acres—on which beef cattle are fattened for export to England, and fine Irish horses are raised. Throughout the rest of Ireland most farmers raise beef or dairy cattle, hogs, sheep, and poultry. Each farmer also raises some crops—potatoes and vegetables for food, flax for sale to the linen manufacturers, and potatoes, grain, and turnips as feed for his livestock.

In Dublin, the capital and chief city, there are some manufacturing industries. There are a few factories producing linen and woolen textiles. One of the largest breweries in the British Isles is in Dublin (Guinness Stout). There are also distilleries and shoe manufacturers.

From an economic point of view Ireland is a poor country. It lacks any important minerals, and although some coal is mined, the major fuel is still peat. The climate does not permit a flourishing agriculture. Most of the products of the island are sold in Britain, and most of the industrial establishments have been built with British capital. Unemployment remains persistently high,

The old and the new in Ireland. Cutting peat by hand and with a modern machine. Peat is still the fuel most widely used in Ireland.

and there is a steady current of emigration to England, to the United States, and to many other parts of the world. Irish people in foreign countries tend to send money back to relatives in Ireland, and this is an important source of income. Another major source of income is from tourists, and much attention is devoted to providing visitors with all kinds of facilities. Nevertheless most of the people remain very poor.

The people of Ireland share one common sentiment—the desire for complete independence. They are happy to be completely free from political ties with England. The Republic of Ireland claims Northern Ireland, and there are occasional conflicts along the border. In the absence of external pressures, Ireland remains a poor, but viable state.

FRANCE

Of all the countries of Western Europe France is the one that has suffered the greatest relative decline in national power as a result of the technological changes of the Industrial Revolution. France has a common Latin language but is nevertheless made up of numerous strongly contrasted regions, in each of which differences of habitat are reinforced by contrasted political traditions. In the medieval period the territory was divided among numerous dukes, each controlling the politics and economy of a distinctive habitat. The nation-state that we call France developed as a result of the gradual extension by the kings in Paris of their power over the separate duchies. Each of the French provinces still remains distinctive today, yet all have been welded into one of the most closely knit and self-conscious states of Europe. In the pre-industrial period France, made up of diverse but well integrated parts, was economically strong. But with the techno-logical revolution it became clear that the habitat lacked certain key resources, especially coal. The result has been the decline of France in terms of its power position.

The Habitat. (Maps 15 and 26) Something of the diversity of the French landscape can be seen on the maps. It is important to appreciate the ease of travel within France. In spite of the varied features of the terrain there are no serious internal barriers; the only low mountain area wholly within France is the Massif Central, and movement all around this area is easy. Furthermore, most of the French rivers are deep and gently flowing—navigable for small boats throughout the year almost to their sources.

The Paris Basin has become the core of France. Paris itself is almost in the center of a structural basin. The rocks are arranged in alternating layers of limestone, sandstone, and shale, that are piled on top of each other like a stack of saucers. The up-turned edges of the strata form a circular pattern around the Paris Basin extending from the edge of the Vosges Mountains on the east, across the Strait of Dover to the cuestas of the English lowlands. The more resistant strata stand out boldly, with steep faces looking away from Paris, and with gentle back slopes. These are the so-called "natural defenses of Paris" which force an army, invading from the east, to advance against a series of steep slopes. It was the presence of some eight such cuestas east of Paris that led the Germans, in 1914, to invade France through Belgium, where the cuestas are not so well developed. Each cuesta, with its distinctive soil and its own peculiar kind of local climate, has been used for a distinctive kind of agriculture.[8]

[8] The cuestas are known as *côtes* in French. In wine-growing areas, each côte has its distinctive type of wine.

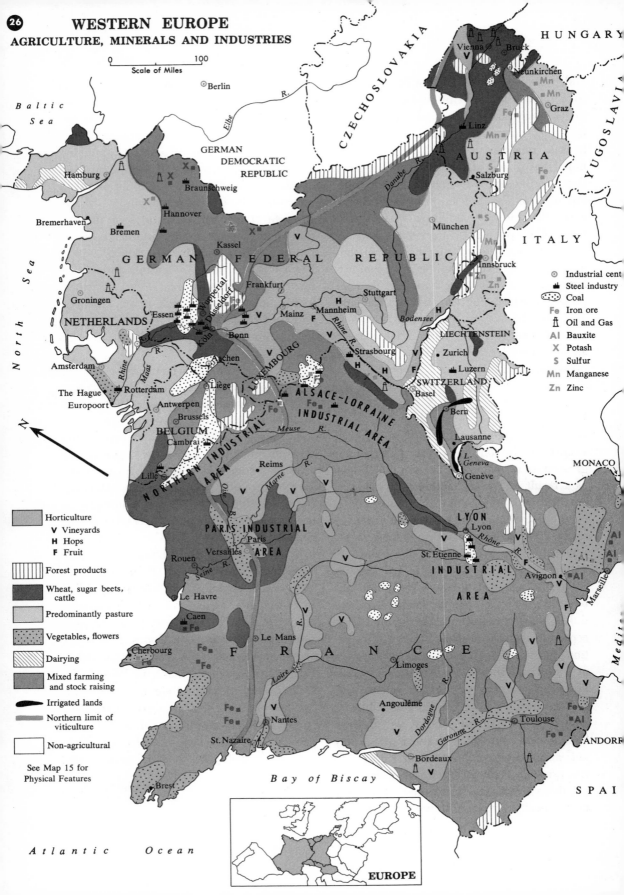

0   100
Scale of Miles

Baltic Sea

North Sea

CZECHOSLOVAKIA

HUNGARY

⊙ Berlin

Elbe R.

GERMAN
DEMOCRATIC
REPUBLIC

Hamburg
Bremerhaven
Bremen
Braunschweig
Hannover
Kassel

GERMAN FEDERAL REPUBLIC

AUSTRIA

Vienna   Bruck
Neunkirchen
Graz
Mn
Mn
Fe
Linz
München
Salzburg
S
S
Mn
Mn

ITALY

YUGOSLAVIA

Groningen
NETHERLANDS
Essen
Wuppertal
Düsseldorf
Köln
Bonn
Aachen
Frankfurt
Mainz
Mannheim
Stuttgart
Strasbourg
Bodensee
Zn
Innsbruck

LIECHTENSTEIN

Amsterdam
The Hague
Europoort
Rotterdam
Antwerpen
Brussels
BELGIUM
Cambrai
Lille
Liège
LUXEMBOURG
Fe
ALSACE-LORRAINE
INDUSTRIAL AREA
NORTHERN INDUSTRIAL AREA
Reims
Marne R.
Oise
Meuse R.

SWITZERLAND
Zurich
Luzern
Basel
Bern
Lausanne
L. Geneva
Genève
Geneva

MONACO

⊙ Industrial cent
⚒ Steel industry
Coal
Fe Iron ore
⛏ Oil and Gas
Al Bauxite
X Potash
S Sulfur
Mn Manganese
Zn Zinc

PARIS INDUSTRIAL AREA
Paris
Versailles
Rouen
Seine R.
Le Havre
Caen
Fe
Cherbourg
Fe
Fe
Le Mans
F R A N C E
Limoges
Angoulême
Dordogne R.
Garonne R.
Toulouse
Bordeaux
Nantes
St. Nazaire
Loire R.
Brest
Fe
Fe
Fe
Fe

LYON
Lyon
Rhône R.
St. Etienne
INDUSTRIAL AREA
Avignon
Al
Al
Al
Al
Marseille
Fe
Fe
Al

ANDORR
SPAI
Mediter

Bay of Biscay

Atlantic Ocean

Horticulture
V Vineyards
H Hops
F Fruit

Forest products

Wheat, sugar beets, cattle

Predominantly pasture

Vegetables, flowers

Dairying

Mixed farming and stock raising

Irrigated lands

Northern limit of viticulture

Non-agricultural

See Map 15 for Physical Features

EUROPE

Population. (Map 1) This diversity of terrain is reflected in the pattern of population. Except for a few places where there are high mountains, as in the Alps and the Pyrenees, and in the dry limestone plateaus south of the Massif Central, the rural population is nowhere less than a hundred people per square mile. On the other hand the coasts of Brittany, the fertile limestone plateau of Picardy, the French part of the middle Rhine Valley in Alsace, and the fertile, broad valleys of the Loire and the Garonne, have rural densities of more than two hundred and fifty people per square mile. On the whole, the population density reflects the agricultural productivity of the soil.

France as a whole is one of the less densely populated countries of Western Europe. This has not always been the case. In 1800, before the Industrial Revolution had made much impact on the continent, France was the most populous country of Europe. At that time France had a population of about 28,000,000, while Germany had 22,-000,000, Italy 17,000,000, and Great Britain only 10,000,000. But the German population overtook that of France about 1870. Between World War I and World War II the population of France would actually have declined had it not been for a considerable immigration from North Africa and from other parts of Europe. The birth rate in 1938 was only 14.6 per thousand, and although it rose to more than 20 per thousand for a few years after World War II, it has since decreased again. France is a demographically mature country—characterized by low birth and death rates. Its total population was estimated to be a little over 46,000,000 in 1962.

Agriculture and Fishing. The tradition of the small, independent farmer, which was well established in pre-industrial France, remains strong. Although the majority of the workers are no longer employed in agriculture, as they were even as late as 1860, the proportion is much higher than in Great Britain (26 per cent of all employed people). Almost half of the agricultural workers are women. As a result France is more nearly self-sufficient in terms of basic foods than any other European country. Whether the variety and quality of French-grown foods is a cause or a result of the high quality of French cooking it is difficult to determine.

French agriculture varies in the detail of its crops, farm practices, and farm layout, in each locality. This amazing variety of landscapes is a part of the charm of rural France. The map (Map 26) shows only a few of the more important areal contrasts. In the north, from the Belgian border southward through the Paris Basin almost to the Loire, is France's chief wheat-growing area. Here wheat and other grains are planted in rotation with sugar beets. Crops are rotated with pasture, and an important part of the farm income is derived from the sale of beef cattle and milk. This productive farming area is developed on the loam-covered limestone uplands of Picardy and the fertile plains of Flanders. Vineyards are found in certain locations as far north as the eastern part of the Paris Basin. Champagne comes from the eastern slopes of the Côte de Brie between the Marne and the Seine, Alsacian wines from the western slopes of the Rhine Valley, Burgundy from the slopes overlooking the upper Saône, Bordeaux from the vineyards along the lower Garonne. From the Loire Valley, and from the Mediterranean shores, come the common wines that form so important a part of the French diet. Similarly there are specialized areas devoted to the production of vegetables, for instance the area around the outskirts of Paris, the coastal areas of the Brittany

The medieval walled city of Carcassonne in southern France, built to defend a twelfth-century castle.

Peninsula, the middle Garonne Valley, and the lower Rhône Valley. Normandy, parts of the Massif Central and of the French Alps, are used chiefly for dairy cattle, and from these places come some world-famous kinds of cheeses—such as Camembert from Normandy, Gruyère from the French Alps. Roquefort is made from the milk of goats pastured on the dry limestone plateau south of the Massif Central. Normandy, too, is known for its apples, and for a famous kind of apple brandy from the orchards of Calvados.

In addition to agriculture, France derives a part of the food supply from fishing. There are numerous small ports in southern Brittany, and along the English Channel, from which French fishermen sail to all the major fishing grounds of the North Atlantic —as far as the cod fishing grounds off Newfoundland and Greenland.

Minerals and Industries. Pre-industrial France was already noted for certain high-quality manufactures in which individual craftsmanship was of major importance. These traditional products have not been dropped as a result of the Industrial Revolution but remain as a distinctive part of the French economy. They include such things as lace and silk goods, glass and chinaware, articles of wood, perfumes and cosmetics.

France still stands in the forefront of the world of fashion, a position based on long experience with clothing design and tailoring.

But the Industrial Revolution has diversified French industry. The initial period in France took place later than in Great Britain—between 1830 and 1860. After 1860 there was a notable diversification of industry, and by 1910 when France achieved maturity, there were numerous large-scale manufacturing plants. About a third of the workers in France are now employed in mining and manufacturing, which is almost the same as the proportion employed in agriculture. However, industrial employment is increasing while agricultural employment is declining.

French industrial growth has been handicapped by the lack of certain essential raw materials, and the poor geographic arrangement of resources. Since World War II France has had to import about 38 per cent of its requirements of fuel and power. Although the country has some coal—notably along the Belgian border, in Lorraine on the border of the Saar, and around St. Étienne southeast of Lyon—almost none of this is suitable for coking (Map 26). About a third of the coal has to be imported. Moreover there is almost no oil. It is because of this lack of fuels that France has had to develop its hydroelectric resources, especially in the Alps and the Pyrenees. The country is abundantly supplied with low-grade iron ore, but this also is located in Lorraine on the borders of Luxembourg. In the case of both coal and iron, French sources are only just within the national boundaries, and the coal measures and ore bodies extend into Belgium and Luxembourg. More than 60 per cent of all French industries, therefore, are located north and east of the Seine.

There are four major centers of manufacturing industry (Map 26). The largest is in and around Paris. Here, in an area lacking all of the basic raw materials, are the country's chief engineering industries. The factories manufacture automobiles, airplanes, and a great variety of small machines for household use. The second industrial area is in Lorraine, where most of the steel-making capacity of the country is concentrated. Here also are important textile and rubber industries. The third area is in the north, along the Belgian border, where coal as a fuel, and as a raw material, is easily accessible. Here there are metallurgical and food-processing industries, about half of the French textile industries, plastics and chemical industries. The fourth industrial area is in the Rhône Valley around Lyon, extending into the valleys of the Massif Central around St. Étienne, and also eastward into the valleys of the Alps. Here metallurgical industries and textiles are of chief importance, but there are also numerous chemical industries and food-processing factories. Bauxite is one of the raw materials with which France is well endowed, located in the lower Rhône Valley and near the Pyrenees. It is smelted into aluminum in the places nearby where there is an abundance of hydroelectric power. Potash is another

important French resource, located in the southern part of the Rhine Valley near Mulhouse. Shipbuilding is important at St. Nazaire at the mouth of the Loire, at Rouen and Le Havre along the lower Seine.

Although France has to import large quantities of oil and coal, and other raw materials, the country is not so dependent on trade as is Great Britain. Most of the French manufactured products are consumed in France. The country is also largely self-sufficient in terms of food. A dense web of railroads and highways connects all parts of the country with Paris. This primate city, with its population of nearly 7,000,000, is the focus of all aspects of French life, not only political, but also economic and social. The ports of France are not so important as those of Great Britain. The chief ones are Marseille, Le Havre, Rouen, Dunkerque, St. Nazaire-Nantes, and Bordeaux.

The French Community. France, like Great Britain, once controlled a far-flung empire, including possessions in Asia, Africa, and the Americas. To be sure, French Canada was taken by the British in 1763, and French Haiti threw off French rule and gained its independence in 1804. But colonialism has met its greatest challenge since World War II, and it is in this latest period that the French possessions have broken apart into a large number of sovereign states. In 1958 the government of France established the French Community (*Communauté française*), a more closely knit international organization than the Commonwealth of Nations. The president of France is now also president of the French Community, and there is an executive council, a senate, and a court of arbitration. The Community administers all matters pertaining to foreign policy, national defense, economic and financial policy, policies regarding the use of natural resources, and the supervision of higher education. The Community in 1961 included the French Republic, nineteen overseas *départements,* and six overseas territories—all but four located in Africa. The Community has decreased in size, however, as one after another of the African states has asked for a larger measure of independence of action. Most of the African states have joined a loose federation known as the French *Entente.* In 1962 the Community consisted of the French Republic; the overseas departments of Martinique, Guadeloupe, Réunion, and Guiana; the overseas territories of French Polynesia, New Caledonia, French Somaliland, Comoro Archipelago, Saint-Pierre and Miquelon, Southern and Antarctic Territories, and the Wallis and Futuna Islands; the member states of the Central African Republic, the Congo Republic, the Malagasy Republic, and the republics of Chad, Gabon, and Senegal. The Entente included the Ivory Coast, Dahomey, Upper Volta, and Niger.

The Viability of France. France is one of the world's outstanding examples of a strongly unified nation-state. The French tradition is so strong that France remains closely integrated in spite of the existence of a bewildering array of small political parties, all in violent disagreement over policy.

The French national territory, however, no longer provides the basis for a self-sufficient economy. Not only is France dependent on outside sources of oil and coal, and other raw materials, but the resources that it does possess are so arranged that the greater part of French industry has been built in a vulnerable position close to the borders. In World War II, moreover, when warfare became mechanized, the traditional natural defenses of France no longer served as a barrier to invasion. Instead, the pattern of paved roads formed the basis for military movements, and the small villages and towns where the roads converge were more

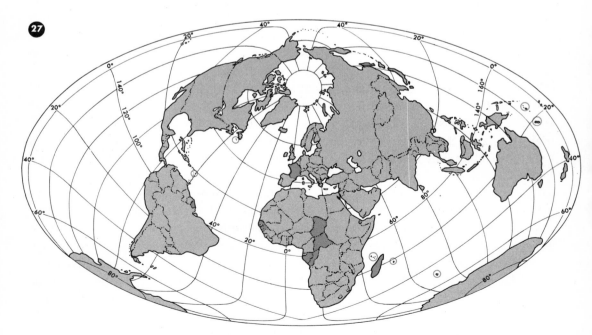

FRENCH COMMUNITY - 1963

important as strong points of defense than the slopes of the cuestas or the hilly uplands.

No country can gain more from giving up the idea of economic self-sufficiency in favor of international interdependence. This is exactly what the European Economic Community is achieving: a reduction of tariff barriers, a removal of restrictions against the movement of labor and capital from country to country. France with its complementary resources, and its skilled labor, can play a major role as a part of a larger European region. We shall discuss the European Economic Community later.

Another recent development of great importance to France is the discovery of what appears to be a large oil field in the Sahara. The strategic picture would be greatly changed if France had access to abundant supplies of fuel close at hand.

THE BENELUX COUNTRIES

The Benelux countries—Belgium, the Netherlands, and Luxembourg—are of an importance in the European Culture Region which is out of all proportion to their size. Europeans have fought over this territory for many centuries. Because of the arrangement of surface features and rivers the inhabitants of the "Low Countries" have always found themselves the focus of attention. The low, marshy plains that they occupy form a route of passage from the western apex of the Eurasian plains southward into France, and also a route of passage along the rivers from Central Europe to the North Sea. In the first instance the rivers, running across the direction of human movement, become defense lines and boundaries; in the second instance the rivers are the axes of circulation, uniting the people who live on either side. As long as man remains tied to the surface of the

earth, the control of this little area affects commercial and military affairs over a wide area. Because no one of the great powers that have arisen from time to time in Europe has ever gained permanent possession of the Low Countries, the liberty-loving people within the area have been able to assert and maintain their independence. The three small states are what political geographers describe as *buffer states*.

The pattern of surface features and rivers provides a stage on which many important historical events have been enacted. The western end of the once densely forested hilly upland, known as the Ardennes, crosses northern Luxembourg and southeastern Belgium, leaving a lowland gap of less than one hundred miles between the upland and the sea along the Franco-Belgian border (Map 15). This is Flanders. Through this gap Germanic tribes once poured into France, and those who remained to settle on the productive loess soils had to fight to keep out those who pressed on them from all sides. Caesar called the Belgians "the bravest of all the Gauls." The Romans established the limits of their empire along the Rhine (Map 18), but the Latin language did not survive the breakdown of Roman rule in the northern part of what today is Belgium (Map 19). The dukes who came to own large feudal estates in this area maintained their independence from the growing French state to the south; and numerous towns were established that were strong enough even to defy the dukes. Essentially independent commercial towns developed near the river mouths. In Flanders several free towns engaged in commerce and the manufacture of woolen textiles. During the religious wars of Europe the King of Spain inherited the Low Countries from his parents and hoped to establish the Roman Catholic faith in them. He met the determined opposition of the Calvinist Netherlanders, who, as early as 1581, managed to push out the Spanish garrisons. In the Netherlands the demand for the right to select its own form of government was born of conflict; and since 1648 this country has been recognized as independent by all the much stronger powers which have coveted control of the Rhine mouth. The boundary between the Netherlands and Belgium is based on the battle-lines of the seventeenth century: the area south of the border remained in Spanish hands and became predominantly Catholic, while the area north of the border became predominantly Protestant. At the time that Belgium was recognized as an independent country in 1830, the northern part of the country was occupied by people who spoke Flemish

(related to the Dutch language), and the southern part by French-speaking Walloons. The Duchy of Luxembourg, a remnant of a large feudal estate, was recognized as independent in 1839.

The land that these countries occupy is strongly diversified. In the south is the upland of the Ardennes, and in Luxembourg there is even a small piece of the Paris Basin (Map 15). Between the northern edge of the Ardennes and Brussels is a continuation of the fertile limestone area of northern France, deeply covered with loess, the wind-blown dust that had been carried away from the front of the ice sheet by outpouring cold air masses. Just north of the Rhine is the terminal moraine of the ice sheet, and much of the surface of Belgium and the western Netherlands, as well as northern Germany, is made up of sandy outwash plains (Map 28). The coastal area from Calais in France to the northern part of the Netherlands is low and marshy. This part of the coast has been sinking since long before the dawn of history, but the invasion of the sea has been held back by the deposition of a vast amount of sand and silt, brought down by the rivers and dropped in the shallow water at their mouths. The line on Map 28 shows the approximate position of the shore about 5000 B.C., and gives a measure of the amount of new land gained since that time.

The construction of new land by the rivers along the low coast is a complex process. Three rivers—the Rhine, the Meuse, and the Scheldt—form a maze of interconnected channels. These rivers drop sand and silt along the bottoms and sides of their channels, so that in the course of time these channels have been built up higher than the level of the plain over which the rivers are flowing. As the land sinks, the rivers continue to pour into the sea running along the raised channels. The North Sea has a large tidal range—fourteen feet at Antwerp. There are some places along the coast where the water recedes as much as two miles at low tide, leaving an expanse of sand. The wind picks up this sand and blows it into mammoth dunes just beyond the high tide line. These dunes serve to stabilize the shore, for the sea does not break through them except during unusually heavy storms. Owing to the gradual sinking of this whole area the land behind the dunes is now below sea level.

Over many centuries the inhabitants of the Low Countries have developed techniques for reclaiming land that lies below sea level and below the level of the rivers. First they constructed earth dikes to keep the flood waters out of the towns. It was not until after 1400 that the first success was scored in pumping water out from the marshes. At that time returning Crusaders brought back the idea of the windmill for pumping water. By 1612 an area near Amsterdam had been drained and was kept dry by the windmills. Between 1839 and 1856 an area between Amsterdam and Rotterdam was drained, but by this time the windmill was obsolete and pumping was done by steam engines. The major effort today is being devoted to the draining of the Ijsselmeer (Zuider Zee), a project which began with the completion of the great dike across its mouth in 1929. The lands thus reclaimed and put to use are known as *polders*. In modern times the pumping of the water is done with diesel engines.

In addition to the draining of the Ijsselmeer to provide more farm land, another major engineering project is to control the water where the three rivers enter the North Sea. In 1953 there was a disastrous flood resulting from exceptionally heavy gales from the west, coming just at the time of a very high tide. It was the worst flood disaster since 1421. In the late 1950's a project was started to build dikes across all but one of the river channels, and to keep open just the one deep canal to reach the ports of Rotterdam and Antwerp. Near Rotterdam a huge new port—Europoort—is under construction, and is planned for completion between 1975 and 1980. It will make possible a vast increase in the tonnage of goods carried in and out through this route.

The use of this reclaimed land for crops and animals has often been described. Most of the polders, even when drained and when the salt is flushed out of the soil, remain too wet for crops (Map 26). Usually they are seeded with meadow grass on which high-grade dairy cattle are pastured. Dutch cheeses are famous, and both butter and cheese are exported. Near the dune belt along the shore of the North Sea, where sand has been blown into the polders creating a relatively porous soil, the land is used for the intensive production of flowers and vegetables.

The other major agricultural area of the Benelux countries is on the loess lands of Belgium, between Brussels and the edge of the Ardennes. This is a continuation of France's important wheat and sugar beet area. In Belgium the farmers grow oats, along with wheat and sugar beets, and raise cattle and horses.

In these countries the proportion of people engaged in farming is higher than in Great Britain, but not so high as in France. In the Netherlands 19 per cent of the workers are farmers, in Belgium, 12 per cent. Although farming is intensive and yields are high, both countries have to import a large part of their food supply.

The Benelux countries are now largely industrial. Belgium entered the initial phase of the Industrial Revolution after gaining independence in 1830, and the Netherlands followed soon after. For a time the large-scale steel plant at Liège in Belgium was the only such integrated steel plant in the world, and in 1845 Belgium was second only to Great Britain in coal production. Iron ore was supplied from the Ardennes. But as the economy became diversified, more and more of the raw materials were imported. Both Belgium and the Netherlands have now reached the stage of high mass consumption—a form of economic prosperity that began, for these countries, with the formation of a customs union (including Luxembourg) in 1922. Belgium is now one of Europe's leading producers of goods made from lead, zinc, copper, and aluminum. The industries of the Netherlands include shipbuilding, food processing, tin smelting, fertilizer manufacturing, and oil refining. Amsterdam has long been known for its diamond cutting, and Rotterdam has become the headquarters of such world-wide industrial enterprises as the Royal Dutch Shell Company. In 1962 the largest field of gas in Europe was discovered in the eastern part of the Netherlands. The gas is exported to other countries and will be used for the development of chemical industries at home.

Both Belgium and the Netherlands, before World II, had large colonial empires. The Dutch East Indies, now the Republic of Indonesia, once supplied many raw materials for Dutch industries, and absorbed Dutch manufactured products. The Netherlands' overseas territories now include only two: the Netherlands Antilles, and Surinam. Belgium lost the Belgian Congo in 1960, and granted independence in 1962 to the kingdoms of Rwanda and Burundi, former trust territories. A new phase of economic

development has been reached: the old idea that resources and markets must be controlled politically has given way to the new idea of international cooperation within the frame of the European Economic Community, and the result has been a wave of new prosperity.

The little Duchy of Luxembourg has long recognized the need for cooperation with its neighbors. Its mines of iron ore have for a century yielded the major export product, half of which now goes to Belgium. Some of the ores are used to manufacture iron and steel in Luxembourg itself. There are also tanneries, flour mills, breweries, and other industries.

The three Benelux countries are well-integrated, viable states with mature economies. Each has a strongly developed sense of national identity. This is true even in Belgium where nearly half of the people speak only Flemish, about a third speak only French, and less than a quarter speak both languages. Belgium is predominantly Roman Catholic; the Netherlands, formerly Protestant, is now about 40 per cent Roman Catholic. All three countries gain from the elimination of economic restrictions to commerce, and the free movement of workers; and all three are now enjoying a condition of high mass consumption, with domestic markets more and more capable of consuming the products of industry.

GERMANY

Of all the countries of continental Europe, the one that has gained the most from the technological changes of the Industrial Revolution is Germany. The greater part of what is now Germany was never included in the Roman Empire. While France was being given the benefits of Roman civilization, the German tribes remained barbarians. When France was united as one of the first pre-industrial nation states, Germany remained only a complex pattern of independent kingdoms and duchies. In the early nineteenth century France was the strongest state of continental Europe. France entered the initial stage of the Industrial Revolution between 1830 and 1860; for Germany the initial stage took place between 1850 and 1870. When Germany was finally united under the Kaiser in 1871 it was made up of four kingdoms—of which the strongest was Prussia—five grand duchies, thirteen duchies and principalities, and three free cities. By contrast the political structure of France was simple and integrated.

With the technological changes of the Industrial Revolution came the need for a reappraisal of the resource base of these two states. It was an inescapable fact of geography that Germany possessed the coal and France possessed the iron. And these were two very different states, one declining in strength, the other gaining, which spoke different languages, were moved by quite different values and purposes, and were traditionally antagonistic. The new technology demanded either that the one conquer and subjugate the other, or that they accept interdependence and cooperation as a way of life. Rivalries between states have occurred in many places and at many times; but such a rivalry located in Europe, at the center of the world's Land Hemisphere, is of basic concern to all mankind.

The Habitat and the Pattern of Settlement. Germany and France are also contrasted in the relation of the settlement pattern to the habitat. Whereas France, in the pre-industrial period, was surrounded by upland barriers but enjoyed relatively easy movement within the national territory, Germany found more serious obstacles to movement within its territory than along its borders. When the Germanic tribes, migrating southward from the North German Plain along the shores of the Baltic Sea and the North Sea, entered the uplands of Central Europe they found a complex arrangement of hilly uplands and low mountains separating low-lying basins and valleys. The uplands were once covered with dense forests—a fact reflected in the frequent use of the German word *wald* (meaning forest) in the proper names of uplands and low mountains (Schwarzwald, or Black Forest; Böhmerwald, or Bohemian Forest; Thuringer Wald, or Thuringian Forest). In contrast, no physical barrier impeded German movement eastward into slavic territory along the southern shore of the Baltic Sea or down the valley of the Danube. Within the territory that became Germany, agricultural settlement was concentrated in the basins and valleys which were less densely forested than the uplands, and which enjoyed milder winters.

Germany's rivers, which have been of importance as lines of travel throughout the long history of settlement in Europe, tended to diverge rather than to provide for a focus of routes within the national territory. The Rhine, which became Germany's "stream divine," runs along the western border, and since it is navigable throughout the year as far upstream as Basel, provides a major route of travel from Europe north of the Alps to the North Sea. The Danube, navigable as far as Ulm, provides an outlet for all of southern Bavaria eastward to the Black Sea. In north-central Germany the Weser leads out to Bremen, and the Elbe to Hamburg. In contrast to the river pattern the railroads, which were largely developed after Germany became one country in 1871, focus on the capital city of Berlin.

The Population of the Two Germanies. Before World War II, Germany had an area of 181,699 square miles and a population of about 67,000,000. This large population was the result of a very rapid net rate of growth which took place after 1850. Until 1910 Germany had the highest birth rate of any country in Northern and Western Europe; but by 1933 it had one of the lowest. At the conclusion of World War II Germany lost 24 per cent of its pre-war territory—all of the territory east of the Oder River and its tributary the Neisse was taken over by the Soviet Union and by Poland, and Germans in this area moved westward. Furthermore, Germany was divided into two separate parts, one occupied by the Soviet Union, the other by the British, the Americans, and the French. The capital, Berlin, was similarly divided into occupation zones and access to it guaranteed by the occupying powers. East Germany became the German Democratic Republic, with an area of about 42,000 square miles and a population estimated in 1962 to be a little over 17,000,000 (including East Berlin). West Germany became the German Federal Republic with an area of nearly 96,000 square miles (including the Saar) and a population, including that of West Berlin, of about 57,000,000. The population map (Map 1, pp. 4-5) shows that the greatest densities are in the urban-industrial areas, along the northern edge of the uplands from Leipzig and Hannover to the Ruhr, and then southward along the Rhine and its bordering uplands.

The Economy. The German people stand among the world's leaders in their scientific knowledge, technical skill, and willingness to work hard. Their skills appear not only in manufacturing industry, but also in agriculture. Before World War II Germany was able to increase the yield per acre of wheat, and to lead the world in the per acre yield of sugar beets and potatoes. By 1937 Germany was producing almost 85 per cent of its food requirements—and much of this on soils of only moderate fertility. But much of Germany's food supply came from east of the Oder River. The 12 per cent of the

German population living in the territory which was lost as a result of World War II raised about 25 per cent of Germany's food. They also mined 16 per cent of the German coal and produced 7 per cent of the manufactured goods—chiefly in Upper Silesia, now a part of Poland.

The pattern of agriculture in modern Germany is shown on Map 26. The areas devoted chiefly to livestock are on the sandy glacial soils of the north and northwest, and in the hilly uplands and low mountains of the center and south. Agriculture is concentrated on the more productive loess soils along the margin of the uplands, and in the warmer lowlands. In the north the farms produce rye, potatoes, and livestock; farther south they produce wheat, barley, sugar beets, and livestock. Along the middle part of the Rhine Valley and its tributaries there is an important area devoted to wine, fruit, and grain. In the south, especially along the shores of the Bodensee (Lake Constance), there is an area of concentrated agriculture producing fruit and hops.

Since 1860, however, the German economy has been based primarily on manufacturing industries. And with the application of the new technologies to the steel industry, the Ruhr District has become the chief center of development. At first two tons of coal were needed to produce steel from one ton of iron. As a result the steel industry was located on the coal fields, and the iron ore was imported. The Ruhr became not only the economic heart of Germany, but also of the whole of Europe. The Ruhr was found to have about 90 per cent of the bituminous coal of Germany, and about half of all such coal in Europe. Of the coal mined in the Ruhr before World War II, 48.5 million tons a year were used in the manufacturing industries of the Ruhr itself; 39.6 million tons were sent to other parts of Germany; and 39.6 million tons were exported to the Netherlands, Belgium, Luxembourg, France, Italy, Switzerland, the Scandinavian countries, the Balkans, Spain, and other countries outside Europe.

The great industrial complex of the Ruhr was created after 1860. Before that it was only a poor grazing area, with sandy infertile soils. Coal had been mined, but could not be sold in competition with wood more than twenty miles from the mines. When the technological changes were introduced, railroads and canals made it possible to ship Ruhr coal out to distant places, and to bring in iron ore, and the hardeners of steel, and other raw materials. In the Ruhr itself vast concentrations of industry and of urban residences appeared (Map 29). On the map the white areas are now almost empty of human inhabitants. In the black areas residences are crowded around the huge industrial plants. There are coke ovens, blast furnaces, steel-rolling mills, and a vast complex of industries that make things from steel. Based on the large supply of good-quality coal there are industries making synthetic fibers, plastics, pharmaceuticals, and other chemicals.

Germany's pre-war industries were not limited to the Ruhr. The Central Industrial District, between Hannover and Leipzig, produced a variety of consumer goods, including optical instruments and china. Extensive seams of low-grade lignite were used to provide fuel for steam-electric plants, and as a raw material for chemical industries. There was also an important center of heavy industry in Upper Silesia, now a part of Poland (Map 42), and in the Saar on the French border.

During World War II Germany's industrial plants were largely destroyed, and for a time after the war there was some support for the idea that Germany should never be permitted to rebuild them. But the facts of geography outweighed even the fear of

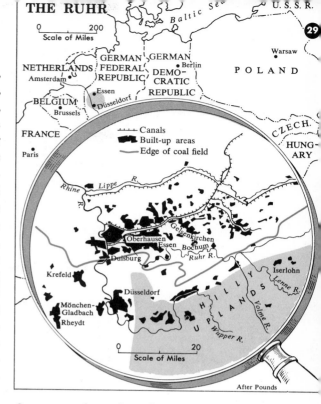

Germany. The Ruhr industrial complex and Ruhr coal were too firmly established as the industrial core of all Europe. As a result the Ruhr industries have been rebuilt, with aid from the United States, and are now equipped with the latest technical improvements. Once again the Ruhr is functioning as the economic heart of the European Culture Region.

East Germany, occupied by the Soviet Union, has also been rebuilt, but with its economy oriented eastward. Its agriculture has been collectivized, and its industries are now operated under state control. In 1958 East Germany produced only 3,000,000 tons of steel, compared with West Germany's 26,300,000 tons. But the Central Industrial District does continue to produce optical and precision instruments, some of which are exported to the West.

The Viability of Germany. Germany, even the Germany of the 1930's, was not nearly so unified around a common state-idea, as was France. There were still great contrasts in the political attitudes of the

The junction of the Ruhr River and the Rhine at Duisburg—the industrial heart of the European Economic Community.

people of the North German plains and of those of Bavaria. There was a major difference between the industrially-minded people of the Ruhr and the pre-industrial people of eastern Germany, where a landed aristocracy still persisted, and where political control was in the hands of military leaders. In spite of a common language and literary tradition, there were still profound differences of religion and of political attitudes. The occupation of East Germany by the Soviets has served greatly to increase the differences that separate Germans from Germans, and to make more difficult the eventual reunification of Germany, which all Germans so strongly desire.

THE MOUNTAIN COUNTRIES[9]

Between Central Europe and the Mediterranean lie the rugged Alps, crossed by only a few relatively easy pass routes which

[9] Among the mountain countries of Western Europe should also be included two small principalities: Andorra in the Pyrenees between France and Spain, which used to derive its income from sheep grazing and smuggling operations, and which is now rapidly developing its tourist business; and Liechtenstein, in the Alps between Austria and Switzerland, which has an economy very similar to that of its neighbors, and which now derives a considerable income from the sale of postage stamps to collectors.

have been used since the dawn of history. Astride the Alps are the two mountain countries—Austria and Switzerland. Like the Low Countries, Austria and Switzerland owe their independence, in part, to the positions that they occupy on major routes of travel between powerful neighbors. But while Austria and Switzerland are alike in terms of the positions that they occupy in the European Culture Region, in every other respect they are different. Austria has been involved in all the conflicts of

Europe: Switzerland, at least in the present century, has been able to maintain its neutrality, and to make the maintenance of neutrality a part of its state-idea.

AUSTRIA

Austria is the remnant of the Empire of Austria-Hungary (Map 20b, p. 54). Before World War I, Vienna was the administrative and commercial center of an empire that extended from the borders of Germany eastward along the River Danube to Serbia and Romania, northward to what is now Czechoslovakia and southern Poland, and southward to the Adriatic and what is now Yugoslavia. Over the diverse peoples of this area—Germans, Magyars, Slavs, (Map 19, p. 49)—the emperor in Vienna was the supreme ruler. The Austro-Hungarian Empire was characteristically pre-industrial and pre-democratic: it had a landed aristocracy, a politically powerful army to keep diverse social and political groups in order, and a vast population of peasant farmers working on land they did not own. World War I broke this empire into its component parts, each national group being awarded independence (Map 20c).

Austria included the part that was almost solidly German in language and Roman Catholic in religion. But the resulting state included two very different parts that were brought together by the chance relationships of geography: the mountain area with its relatively simple, almost self-sufficient economy; and Vienna, the former capital of the Austro-Hungarian Empire, the chief commercial center of the Danube Valley, a city which in 1910 had a population of more than 2,000,000. The story of Austria since 1918 has been concerned with the struggle to rebuild a viable state out of such diverse elements.

Vienna itself has been a major problem.

In 1918 it was a great city suddenly cut off from the hinterland that it had served. New kinds of economic activity had to be found, such as the manufacture of fancy leather goods, jewelry, and art objects. It became an important tourist center. By 1938 the city had recaptured much of its transit trade between Central Europe and the Mediterranean. But once again in World War II the established patterns of trade were broken apart, and Vienna now stands on the very edge of the Soviet-dominated territory, from which it is cut off by the "iron curtain." It has developed a greater and greater variety of consumer-goods manufacturing to provide as much employment as possible for its people. But it is still dependent on aid from outside, and since 1918 has steadily lost population.

Austria as a whole, however, has emerged from World War II stronger than it was before the war. Resources within the national territory have been developed: extensive forests support the export of timber, and also the manufacture of many products made from wood; small supplies of bituminous coal, and iron-ore bodies, support an iron and steel industry, which is, however, dependent on imports of coal from the Ruhr; bauxite deposits and hydroelectric power have been developed for an aluminum industry. New industries include textiles, chemicals, ceramics, paper, and machinery. But Austria remains dependent on imports for about 75 to 80 per cent of its food supply, and for a large part of its industrial raw materials. A small oil field in the Danube Valley supplies domestic needs. The new industries are mostly in the western part of the country, which gives a better balance between the two parts of Austria.

Austria is succeeding in the reconstruction of a viable economy. That it should succeed in this effort is a matter of vital concern to the western nations, if only because of its geographic position, as an exposed bastion of the non-communist world.

SWITZERLAND

Switzerland is also a closely integrated and viable state. Moreover it is the world's outstanding example of how the formulation of a powerful state-idea can overcome the disintegrative effect of geographic diversity.

The Swiss territory is made up of three contrasted parts. The southern 58 per cent of the national territory is in the high Alps, where snow-capped ranges rise to more than 15,000 feet above sea level, separated by deeply carved longitudinal valleys which run parallel to them. In this region are 18 per cent of the Swiss people. These mountains, unlike those of Austria, contain no mineral resources. The economy includes the raising of grapes and grains in the valleys, and the pasturing of dairy cattle in the summer on the high alps above the tree line—where the famous Swiss cheeses are produced. This is one of Europe's major tourist regions, visited now by great numbers, both in summer and winter. The northwestern part of the country is made up of the parallel limestone ridges of the Jura Mountains, including about 10 per cent of the national territory and occupied by 13 per cent of the people. Lumbering and dairying are two major occupations of this region, but it is also the chief area for the making of watch parts, based on the presence there of generations of skilled craftsmen. Between the Alps and the Jura is a hilly upland which extends from Lake Geneva to the Bodensee (Lake Constance). This includes 32 per cent of the national territory and is occupied by 69 per cent of the population. This is a region of prosperous farms raising wheat, rye, oats, barley, tobacco, sugar beets, and, on the sunnier slopes, grapes. Cattle are pastured in the higher valleys. This is also the area that is predominantly industrial, and in which all the major cities are located.

Manufacturing industries provide employment for about 57 per cent of the Swiss workers. This includes about 10 per cent who are engaged in watchmaking. Most of the workers are employed in the manufacture of textile machinery, diesel engines, machine tools, precision instruments, typewriters, and calculating machines. There are also chemical industries, textile factories, metal-processing plants, and many others. The contrast in attitudes is very great between the mountain people of the Alps, the watchmakers of the Jura, and the industrial workers of the central area.

But there are other contrasts within the Swiss territory. About 56 per cent of the people are Protestants, concentrated chiefly in the industrial cities; about 42 per cent are Roman Catholics, chiefly in the Alps and the Jura Mountains. Furthermore, the national territory is sharply divided into four areas in each of which a different language is spoken. For the Swiss people as a whole 72 per cent speak German, 20 per cent speak French, 6 per cent speak Italian, and 1 per cent speak Romansh. The important point is that these diverse components are not intermingled. For the most part each separate group occupies a separate part of the national territory—a situation recognized by political geographers as most likely to produce disintegration.

How did the Swiss produce a strong viable state out of these geographically separate components? The nucleus of the Swiss state, the three cantons bordering the Lake of Lucerne, became independent in 1291.

At this time the citizens were guaranteed equal treatment before the law, and representative government. As new cantons were added these principles were maintained, so that each part of the Swiss Federation remained essentially autonomous, yet all were closely integrated in loyalty to a common state-idea. A part of this state-idea is the principle of neutrality in Europe's conflicts; another part is the principle that democracy should permit a maximum of local autonomy where such diverse groups are to be welded together in a single state. From the beginning the Swiss economy has been dependent on commerce—as it was when the three original cantons profited from the transit trade between Central Europe and the Mediterranean. Now most raw materials have to be imported, and

most of the products are sold outside Switzerland. The Swiss industries are in large measure dependent on coal, iron, and steel from the Ruhr, and on free access to the raw materials and markets of the whole world. To insure continued access to the outside world, the Swiss have built a fleet of some four hundred river boats, operating on the Rhine between the Swiss port of Basel and Rotterdam. Neutral Switzerland, with its stable government and strongly united people, has become the world's banker and has provided the headquarters for numerous international agencies, such as the Red Cross. Although Switzerland has not joined the United Nations, it has provided the home for several United Nations agencies, and for numerous international conferences.

THE COUNTRIES OF SOUTHERN EUROPE[10]

Many of the attitudes, objectives, and technical skills that we think of as distinctively European had their origin in the culture hearths of Southern Europe (Map 17, p. 46). The Minoan Civilization developed on the island of Crete about 2800 B.C., and from there the center of civilized living moved to the mainland of Greece. Later the center of the civilized world shifted to Rome. But after the great explorations, which began in the fifteenth century, had opened geographic horizons to the whole

world, the focus of events moved to Western Europe, leaving the Mediterranean countries behind.

The countries of Southern Europe—Portugal, Spain, Italy, and Greece—share certain characteristics in common. In all of them are the memories and the monuments of past glory; in all of them the people today struggle with poverty on land long ago ruined by archaic agricultural methods and pre-industrial technology; in all of them the population is increasing rapidly because the widespread application of modern health measures, since World War II, has produced a sharp drop in the death rates. Nothing but a massive injection of new capital investment, along with a program of land redistribution and agricultural improvement, can rescue the people from deepening poverty. Actually, these meas-

[10] In Southern Europe there are five small states: Monaco, on the Riviera, noted for its gambling casino; San Marino, in the Apennines southeast of Bologna, which makes a major part of its income from the sale of postage stamps; the Vatican State, in Rome, seat of the Roman Catholic Church and residence of the Pope; Cyprus, in the eastern Mediterranean, became independent in 1960; and Malta, the little island between Sicily and Africa, became independent in 1964.

ures are being taken, and Italy, greatly stimulated by membership in the European Economic Community, has entered the initial phase of the Industrial Revolution.

THE HABITAT

(Maps 5, 6, 8, and 15) The three peninsulas of Southern Europe are mostly mountainous. Rugged ranges of mountains form the axes of the peninsulas of Italy and Greece, rising to elevations just under 10,000 feet; on these peninsulas there are only narrow patches of coastal lowlands or intermont basins—the largest area of plain in Southern Europe is the Po Valley of northern Italy. Three famous volcanoes are occasionally active in Italy: Vesuvius near Napoli, Etna in Sicily, and Stromboli off northeastern Sicily. The third peninsula —the Iberian Peninsula—is separated from the rest of Europe by the rugged Pyrenees. It is made up of an extensive plateau known as the Meseta, which stands about 2,000 feet above sea level. The Meseta is surmounted by several ranges of mountains, and drops off sharply around its margins to narrow belts of coastal lowland on the east, and to the valleys of southern Spain and southern Portugal on the southwest. A belt of low mountains forms a westward continuation of the Pyrenees along the northwestern coast of Spain.

The climate of Southern Europe is distinctive. This region has the so-called Mediterranean climate, characterized by winter rains and summer droughts—a type of climate that is to be found between latitudes 30° and 40° on the western continental margins both north and south of the equator. The largest area of such climate is found along the shores of the Mediterranean Sea, from northwestern Africa to Israel and Turkey, and even in the southern part of the Soviet Union on the shores of the Black Sea. Throughout this area the winters are mild. The dry summers are hot except along the exposed Atlantic coast of Portugal and Morocco, where cold water keeps summer temperatures relatively low. On the mountain slopes, where rainfall is heavy in winter and where some rain falls even in summer, the surface was originally covered with forest; and the Po Valley and northwestern Spain, which lie far enough north to escape the summer droughts, were also forested. But most of Southern Europe was once covered with an evergreen, broadleaf woodland and brush. The characteristic brushy vegetation of this region is known as *maquis*.

Man as an Agent of Destruction. The Mediterranean habitat has been profoundly modified by human action. Today very little of the original forest or woodland cover remains (Map 30). Where there were forests even in historical times, there are now vast areas covered only with maquis, or even entirely bare. On steep slopes the clearing

FORESTS OF THE MEDITERRANEAN AND SOUTHWEST ASIA

Present forests

Ancient forests

of the vegetation results in a rapid run-off of the water during rain. Water, which under natural conditions is retained by the soil and soaked up in the litter of organic matter on the forest floor, now descends the rivers in torrents, causing rapid soil erosion on the slopes, and depositing coarse sand and gravel on once fertile lowlands. Streams which once flowed gently all the year round, now dry up completely during the summer droughts. With more and more people to be fed, and with a slow but continuous decline in crop yields due to the destruction of the resource base, more and more marginal land has to be cleared and plowed. As pastures support fewer and fewer animals, grazing is extended to the steeper slopes. Nothing is so utterly destructive of the vegetation cover as are sheep and goats, yet these animals alone can survive on poor pastures. The widespread grazing of goats has created deserts where once there were still waters and green pastures. It is thought that the extensive grass-covered surfaces on the Spanish Meseta, which are now used for the grazing of sheep, once supported woodlands. Destructive human action has created poverty in many parts of the world —but in the Mediterranean lands the penalty for misuse of the land is especially severe because of the nature of the climate. The great seasonal contrast between heavy winter rains and summer droughts increases the danger of soil erosion when the protective cover of plants is broken.

The Food and Agriculture Organization of the United Nations (FAO) has a program for the rehabilitation of agriculture in these countries. The farmers must be moved away from the steeper lands, and agriculture concentrated on the small areas of lowland. On these small areas crop yields must be greatly increased through irrigation, the use of fertilizers, and the substitution of modern farm machinery for the traditional agricultural implements. A considerable part of the agricultural land is to be used for feed crops, so that grazing animals can be removed from the steeper slopes. Meanwhile the watersheds are to be replanted with trees, and the lower slopes terraced not only to protect them from erosion, but also to regularize the flow of water through the rivers. But, the key element in the program is the integration of farming and animal husbandry, which traditionally have been carried on by different people in separate areas.

SPAIN AND PORTUGAL

Spain and Portugal are the countries that occupy the Iberian Peninsula. Portugal was the first of the European nation-states, and both Portugal and Spain at one time had large overseas possessions. In 1494, by the Treaty of Tordesillas, Portugal and Spain divided the whole globe into a Portuguese hemisphere and a Spanish hemisphere (approximately along the present longitude 50°W). Today these great colonial empires have collapsed, and the countries which sent out their sons to conquer the world are now very poor. Both countries are under the personal rule of fascist dictators supported by military and police power.

The Iberian Peninsula has been occupied by many different peoples. The early Celtic inhabitants were first subjugated, at least at places along the coast, by the Phoenicians, who founded a naval base at Cádiz to guard the Strait of Gibraltar. The Carthaginians made use of the peninsula for an invasion of Europe and the march on Rome during the Punic Wars. The Roman defeat of the Carthaginians was followed by the conquest of Iberia, and the establishment of numerous Roman settlements. The Romans brought the Latin language, and many basic culture traits—including the idea of the large private estate. With the collapse of Rome came the invasions of Germanic tribes, including the Vandals, the Suevi, and the Goths. It was these barbarians who introduced Christianity. Then came the invasions of the Muslims, known as Moors, from Africa, who conquered all but Galicia in the northwest corner of the peninsula. The Muslims introduced many new crops—such as sugar cane, citrus fruits, and rice—and new techniques of irrigation. Their university at Córdoba became a major center of learning. Over a period of some seven centuries the Christians gradually reconquered the peninsula. By the end of the thirteenth century Portugal had become a strongly unified nation-state, embracing the Portuguese-speaking people of the Atlantic coast. In 1492 the last of the Muslim strongholds in southern Spain fell to the Christians.

As a result of all these migrations and conquests the people of the Iberian Peninsula are diverse, even speaking different languages. Not only is Portuguese distinct from Spanish, but so also are Galician, Catalan, and Basque (Map 19). The Spanish spoken around Sevilla and Cádiz is quite different from the "pure" Castilian of the central Meseta around Madrid. The Portuguese were able to assert and maintain their independence, with the help of the British, but the other separate groups were all brought under the central authority of Madrid—which had the strategic advantage of a central position, from which the conquest of the peripheral parts of the peninsula could be carried out. The characteristics of the people of the Meseta remained quite distinct from those of the coastal areas. Where the Portuguese, exposed to all the exciting new contacts with distant peoples and cultures, learned the art of compromise and adjustment, the

Castilians took pride in uncompromising devotion to tradition. The economic, social, and political institutions of Spain remained relatively inflexible and unchanging, even in the face of the demands imposed by the administration of a vast colonial empire.

Population. Within the area of the Iberian Peninsula there are notable contrasts in the density of population (Map 1, pp. 4-5). The margins of the peninsula support several concentrations of people: in Portugal north of Lisbon (Lisboa); in Galicia; in the mountains south of the Bay of Biscay; in Catalonia around Barcelona; on the east coast around Valencia; and along the lower valley of the Río Guadalquivir. On the Meseta the only concentration is around Madrid itself; otherwise it is thinly populated, especially along the Spanish-Portuguese border. There are three cities of more than a million inhabitants each: Lisbon is the primate city of Portugal; but in Spain, Madrid and Barcelona are of about equal size.

Agriculture, Stock Raising, and Fishing. Nearly half of the workers of both Spain and Portugal are employed in agriculture, yet the agriculture is far from prosperous. In some places the farmers work as tenants on large estates, the owners of which probably live in Madrid or Lisbon. In other places, where estates have been broken up by inheritance, an individual farmer may own several separate fragments of land located at considerable distances from each other. Farm techniques are archaic: much of the wheat is still sown, harvested, and threshed by hand, and yields are very low.

The economic map of Southern Europe (Map 31) shows an important contrast in the agriculture between the cooler and wetter northwestern part of the Iberian Peninsula and the hotter and drier southeastern part. In the northwest of Spain the grains include maize and wheat, and feed

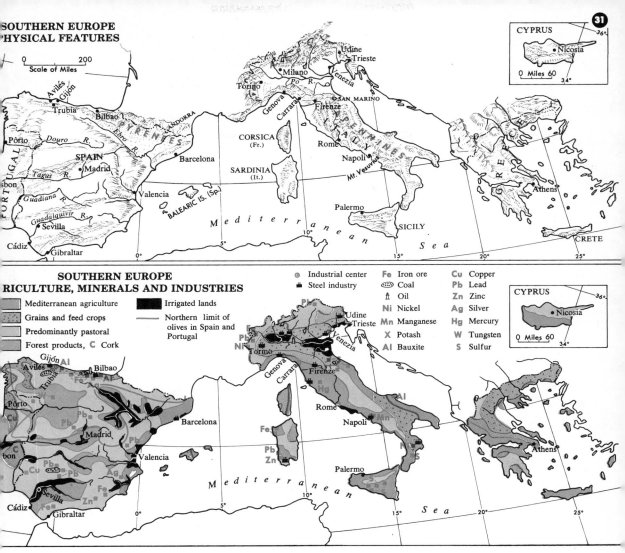

31

SOUTHERN EUROPE
PHYSICAL FEATURES

0 — 200
Scale of Miles

CYPRUS
36°
Nicosia
0 Miles 60
34°

Avilés
Gijón
Trubia • Bilbao
PYRENEES
ANDORRA
Pôrto
Douro R.
SPAIN
Madrid
Tagus R.
sbon
Guadiana
Guadalquivir R.
Sevilla
Cádiz
Gibraltar

Torino
Milano
Po R.
Genova
Carrara
CORSICA (Fr.)
Barcelona
SARDINIA (It.)
Valencia
BALEARIC IS. (Sp.)

Udine
Trieste
Venezia
SAN MARINO
Firenze
ITALY
APENNINES
Rome
Napoli
Mt. Vesuvius
Palermo
SICILY

GREECE
Athens
CRETE

Mediterranean   Sea
10°   15°   20°   25°

SOUTHERN EUROPE
AGRICULTURE, MINERALS AND INDUSTRIES

Mediterranean agriculture	Irrigated lands
Grains and feed crops	Northern limit of olives in Spain and Portugal
Predominantly pastoral	
Forest products, C Cork	

Industrial center   Fe Iron ore   Cu Copper
Steel industry   Coal   Pb Lead
Oil   Zn Zinc
Ni Nickel   Ag Silver
Mn Manganese   Hg Mercury
X Potash   W Tungsten
Al Bauxite   S Sulfur

CYPRUS
36°
Nicosia
0 Miles 60
34°

Gijón
Avilés   Al   Bilbao
Trubia
Pôrto   Cu
Pb
Madrid   Pb
Cork   Pb
bon   Cu
Pb   Ag
Sevilla   Zn
Cádiz   Fe
Gibraltar

Barcelona
Valencia
Fe
Pb
Zn

Pb
Udine
Trieste
Pb
Ni   Torino   Venezia
Genova
Carrara   Firenze
Hg
Al
Rome
Napoli   Mn
Palermo

Athens

Mediterranean   Sea
5°   10°   15°   20°   25°

crops are used to support herds of beef and dairy cattle. Toward the south maize disappears, and the cattle are replaced by sheep. In the area included in the category of "Mediterranean Agriculture" there are large areas of vineyards and orchards. As far as the red line on the map the chief acreage in this category is used for olive trees—Spain is the world's largest producer of olive oil. Among the olive trees grains are often interplanted—wheat in the north and on the better soils, barley in the south and on the thinner soils. The grapes are made into wine, or exported as fruit or raisins. There are many famous kinds of wine, each of which comes from a small, distinctive

area: for instance port wine from the valley of the Rio Douro above Pôrto; and sherry from Jerez de la Frontera inland from Cádiz. Along the sunny southeastern coast around Valencia there are large acreages of irrigated land devoted to oranges and dates. The irrigated areas are also used to grow summer vegetables and rice.

The map also shows that an important area of the Iberian Peninsula is used for "forest products." From northern Portugal come rosin and turpentine derived from pine plantations. In southern Portugal and Spain there are millions of acres of cork oak (*quercus suber*), from which comes about 70 per cent of the world's supply of

Vineyards—from which Port wine comes—on the steep slopes of the Rio Douro in Portugal, inland from Pôrto.

natural cork. Portugal is the world's leading producer of cork.

There are also large tracts of poor grassland on the Meseta that are useful today only for the grazing of sheep. British-bred Merino sheep provide the wool for which Spain is famous. It has long been the custom to feed sheep on the Meseta in winter when there is enough rain to make the grass green. During the dry summers the flocks are driven up into the mountains that stand above the surface of the Meseta (Map 15). Here there is enough moisture, even in summer, to support the pasturing of sheep. This is a form of seminomadic grazing known as *transhumance.*

Fishing is an important occupation, especially in Portugal. From numerous small ports along the Portuguese coast fishing boats go out as far even as the fishing grounds off Labrador. From the coastal waters of the Atlantic the fishermen take sardines, tuna, anchovies, and mackerel. One of Portugal's well-known products is canned sardines in olive oil.

Minerals and Industries. The Iberian Peninsula is not well endowed with minerals. To be sure, there are some ore bodies that were first opened up by the Phoenicians, such as the copper mines north of Cádiz; and there are small bodies of silver ore that have been mined for many centuries. But none of these are of more than local significance. The mines of coal, lead, and zinc north of the Guadalquivir Valley are not of much importance either. The major mineral resources are in the mountains south of the Bay of Biscay: high-grade iron ores south of Bilbao, and both iron ore and coal south of Avilés. The iron ore of Bilbao used to be exported, chiefly to the Ruhr, but now there are new steel plants built at both Bilbao and Avilés, to use the Spanish ores. A variety of new industries has been developed at the ports along this coast.

The major manufacturing center of Spain, however, is Barcelona. Here one finds urban industries using large-scale technology, wage workers, and an active economic life, which make it clear that Catalonia, at least, has felt the impact of the Industrial Revolution. Barcelona produces metal and leather goods, paper, chemicals, textiles, and a variety of other consumer goods. The city is supplied with electricity from a hydroelectric plant nearby. There is nothing else like this in Spain or Portugal.

Viability. In spite of poverty and widespread illiteracy, Portugal is a viable and well-integrated state. The use of the Portuguese language, and the literary tradition of that language, give the Portuguese people a distinctive state-idea. Yet Portugal might not have been able to withstand pressures from Madrid had it not been for the traditional support of British sea power.

The Spanish state, on the other hand, is both poor and poorly integrated. The Spanish Civil War of 1936 to 1939 brought devastation to an already impoverished country, and thereafter the European states that might have aided in the reconstruction of the Spanish economy were engaged in World War II. Even in the 1960's much of the industrial equipment and the transportation facilities are still old and inefficient. But, starting in 1961, new investment in manufacturing industries began to provide for more employment, and there was a rise in the gross national product per capita.

Nevertheless there remains a lack of balance among the parts of the country. Catalonia and Barcelona were making rapid industrial progress before 1936, and this progress continues. Now a second industrial district has been created along the coast of the Bay of Biscay. The rest of the country is still much less progressive and remains chiefly rural and agricultural. The democratic ideas that had taken root in Catalonia before the Civil War still characterize the northern fringe of Spain, but these ideas are strictly controlled by a dictatorship based on the power of the army. Perhaps the Spanish state could not have survived intact without a strong central authority to hold the diverse parts together.

ITALY

Among the countries of Southern Europe Italy is by far the strongest from an economic point of view, and by far the most important from a strategic point of view. The economic strength of Italy is concentrated in the north, in the great industrial centers of the Po Valley: south of Firenze (Florence) the country still struggles with problems of rural poverty. The strategic importance of Italy results from its position in relation to the major pass route from Eastern Europe to the Mediterranean Sea. The one relatively easy route from the middle part of the Danube Valley ascends the valley of the Sava River by way of Zagreb, and descends to the head of the Adriatic at Trieste (Map 15). After World War II Trieste was made a free territory under the protection of the United Nations, because the interests of so many states converge upon it.

Population. Italy is much more densely populated than any of the other South European countries (Map 1, pp. 4-5). The greatest densities are found in the Po Valley; on the peninsula the population is concentrated along either coast. Probably the densest rural population in Europe is found on the small plain of Napoli (Naples) at the base of Mount Vesuvius. In Italy as a whole only a little more than 30 per cent of the people live in cities of over 20,000; but this figure is misleading since the proportion of urban people is much higher in the north, and much lower in the south.

Agriculture. The agriculture of northern Italy is quite different from that of the south. On the fertile alluvial soils of the Po Valley there are modern, mechanized farms, raising wheat, rice, maize, hemp, sugar beets, fruits and vegetables, and on the wet meadows of the river floodplain there are fine pastures for beef and dairy cattle. Around Firenze there are large areas of vineyards from which the Italians make their famous Chianti wines. Toward the south, however, the length of the summer dry period increases, and agriculture becomes less prosperous. Soil erosion has ruined much land. The farmers are handicapped by the fragmented farm properties, and by the prevailing poverty which makes the use of modern farm techniques impossible because of the lack of capital. Nevertheless, there are certain areas intensively used for specialty crops: the fine volcanic soils of the Napoli plain, for example, where the farmers raise vegetables, fruit, wheat, and rice. Along the Adriatic coast the usual combination includes wheat, olives, almonds, and grapes. Agriculture is intensive, also, in Sicily where the crops include citrus fruits, grapes, wheat, and olives.

Since 1950 the Italian government has been carrying out a major program of economic development. Land has been redistributed to break up large and inefficiently operated estates, and to bring fragmented holdings together in one place. New irrigation systems have been built, and drainage works started along the wet coastal lowlands. As always when programs of economic development are properly applied, there is a reduction in the number of people engaged in farming. By 1957 the proportion of workers employed in agriculture had dropped to almost 30 per cent.

Minerals and Industries. An important part of Italy's development program, therefore, is focused on new capital investment in industry. Italy is not rich in mineral resources, and has to import almost all of its coal, and half of its oil needs. There are small ore bodies of iron, copper, lead, zinc, and others; but Italy's only abundant minerals are sulfur and mercury. In the Alps Italy has abundant water power potential, and hydroelectric plants produce power for the industrial cities, and to operate the railroads. Italy is the largest producer of hydroelectric power in Europe.

The manufacturing industries are concentrated in the north. These produce foodstuffs, textiles, and machinery. Italy designs and manufactures some of the popular small automobiles now being sold widely throughout the countries of the European Economic Community. Italian sewing machines, typewriters, and calculating machines are reaching markets all over the world. Italy is challenging France in the design of ladies' dresses, and in the production of motion pictures.

Viability. The Italian state was not established until 1871. Like Germany it was formed by combining several long-independent kingdoms. Italy resembles Spain in that its industrial development is concentrated in one part of the country. But in Italy these political contrasts are not re-

Milano, a city of a million and a half, is Italy's second city and major center of manufacturing industries. The Pirelli Building in foreground.

inforced by differences of language, as they are in Catalonia. The energetic effort to do something about the widespread poverty, through a balanced development of agriculture and industry, has the enthusiastic support of the people, and thereby strengthens the feeling of Italian unity.

GREECE

During the many centuries from the Roman conquest of Greece in 146 B.C. until the liberation of Greece from Turkey in 1829, the Greek people were under foreign rule. That they maintained their sense of nationalism is a tribute to the strength of the Greek tradition. The map on page 245 (Map 60) shows the Ottoman Empire at its greatest extent, when the authority of the Sultan reached westward as far as the Adriatic Sea, and northward to include Hungary, Romania, and the northern shores of the Black Sea. The capital city, Constantinople, was also the center of Greek influence, and of the Greek Orthodox Church. Gradually the Turks were pushed back from Europe until, after World War I, they retained only a small piece of territory west of the straits. But all around the shores of the Aegean Sea Turkish Muslims and Greek Orthodox Christians were intermingled, and there were Greeks outnumbering Turks along parts of the eastern Aegean shores, and on Cyprus. In 1922, the Turks defeated an invading Greek army, and an agreement was reached to exchange populations. About 1,500,000 Greeks moved out of what is now Turkey, chiefly into the parts of Greece, vacated by the Turks, along the northern shore of the Aegean. As a result both Greece and Turkey became more homogeneous.

The mountainous peninsula of Greece, which seemed so well-endowed as a habitat to the Greeks of antiquity, now hinders rather than aids the formation of a modern state. The long misuse of the steep highlands for the grazing of sheep and goats has resulted in much land destruction, and in an intensification of winter floods and summer droughts. After World War II the Greeks were the poorest of the peoples of Europe, and more than two thirds of them were living in small, isolated rural villages, dependent on the continued destructive grazing of goats.

The position of Greece on the map, separating the communist controlled territory of Eastern Europe from the Mediterranean, is too important from a strategic point of view to permit neglect by the non-communist countries. Since 1950 Greece has received large amounts of financial and technical aid, and in 1961 was started on the process of becoming a full member of the European Economic Community. The Greek economy is being rebuilt. New paved roads, new electric power facilities, new irrigation and drainage works, new ports, and new factories are all providing the foundations for economic development. Greece is no longer Europe's poorest country.

Greek agriculture is also being improved. In the southern part of the country where the small lowland plains are used to grow wheat, barley, and cotton, yields of all these crops have been increased through the use of better farm techniques. The lower hill slopes, especially near the sea, are used for olive groves and vineyards. In the north, where the summer droughts are not so long, the land is used to grow wheat, tobacco, rice, cotton, and feed crops for dairy and beef cattle. An effort is being made to reduce the dependence on goats in the highlands, and to provide greater economic opportunities for the pastoralists away from their highland villages. By 1975 it is planned to increase the area under irrigation by nearly 75 per cent.

The Greek economy is also supported by other kinds of activity. There are few mineral resources, but the sea is rich with fish. Greek merchant ships, which make up one of the world's largest merchant fleets, sail to ports all over the world, and the money these ships earn is sent back to help those who remain at home. The government is also making a great effort to increase the already considerable income from tourists.

The Greek state is strong and viable in spite of its economic problems. The people are fully conscious of their great literary and political traditions. The long periods of foreign rule, and the threat of re-newed domination from the north, serve to strengthen their sense of nationalism, and the will to support their own independence.

THE COUNTRIES OF NORTHERN EUROPE

The northern part of Europe, known as Norden,[11] includes the four Scandinavian countries (Denmark, Norway, Sweden, and Iceland), and Finland. The people of Scandinavia are of Germanic origin and speak a group of related languages. The Finns, on the other hand, are descendants of a people who migrated from farther east in Eurasia and who speak a Finno-Ugrian language. Denmark and Sweden were for a long time rivals for control of Norden, and Sweden, at the beginning of the eighteenth century, controlled a large part of the coast-line of the Baltic Sea. In 1721 the Swedes were pushed back from the southern and eastern part of the Baltic, and in 1809 they lost Finland to Russia. Since that date Sweden has never been involved in a war. Sweden and Norway were separated in 1905. The Republic of Iceland, first estab-lished in A.D. 930, was re-established in 1944 after many years of control by Den-mark. The people of all these countries are predominantly Lutheran.

Both the Industrial Revolution and the Democratic Revolution came rather late to Norden. Economic development in Den-mark and Sweden has now, however, reached the stage of maturity, and many elements of the new technology have been adopted in the other countries. Not only did Iceland have the world's first parliament, but throughout Norden there has never been any such reaction against the sweep of democratic ideas as has appeared in parts of Southern Europe. Today the countries of Norden are among the most thoroughly democratic countries of the world.

THE HABITAT

There is no other place in the world with a habitat like that of Norden. The only other continental west coast, in either hemi-sphere, lying poleward of latitude 55° is in Alaska; but the Alaskan west coast is bathed by the cold Bering Sea, and the coastal cli-mate is polar (Maps 5 and 8, pp. 10-11 and 16-17). By contrast the western part of Nor-den is bathed by the relatively warm water of the North Atlantic Drift, with the result that the average temperatures of the warm-est month are above 50°, even north of 70°N. At Tromsö in Norway, a little south of 70°N, the average temperatures in both July and August are about 51°; and the coldest month, February, averages 25°— about the same as Chicago. The coast of Norway is ice-free all the way around the northern tip of the Scandinavian Peninsula. The Gulf of Bothnia, on the other hand, is frozen for nearly seven months each year.

The Scandinavian Uplands make up the major part of Norden (Map 15, p. 42). These uplands are formed on very ancient, massive, crystalline rocks that are among the oldest rocks exposed anywhere at the earth's surface. During the Ice Age, continental glaciers, fed by heavy winter snows, formed over this area and spread out in all direc-tions. The bedrock was scraped bare of soil, and the glacial debris was dumped into the valleys. Almost all of Finland and Swe-

[11] Norden is the regional name given to North-ern Europe by the Scandinavian geographers.

den is made up of knobby, rock hills and a labyrinth of bogs and lakes. The surface rises toward the border of Norway and, northeast of Bergen, it reaches altitudes of more than 8,000 feet above sea level. As the ice descended through pre-glacial valleys westward toward the sea it scoured great U-shaped troughs which, invaded by the sea, now form long, narrow, steep-sided, and very deep, embayments known as *fiords*. The great Sogne Fiord, north of Bergen, is 125 miles in length, and more than 4,000 feet deep near its mouth. Norway's outer coastline is about 2,100 miles long; but the whole coastline including the fiords measures 12,500 miles.

There are only small areas of lowland. These include the southern rim of Finland, a part of southern Sweden, the Oslo Lowland of Norway, and a narrow lowland area near Trondheim. Denmark is entirely a lowland. These low-lying areas include marine terraces, moraines, outwash plains, and other features of glacial deposition.

Iceland, on the other hand, is a volcanic island, with more than 150 volcanoes. Mount Hekla, about seventy miles east of Reykjavík, has erupted more than twenty-three times since 1104. Much of the surface not covered by glaciers is made up of lava flows and accumulations of ash. There are many varieties of hot springs and geysers.

All but the northern part of Scandinavia, and the higher altitudes, were originally covered by seasonal forest (Map 8, pp. 16-17). As far north as about 60°N, the predominant trees were beech. This is the region that has been cleared and planted with crops and pasture-grasses. Along the margins of the open tundra birch trees are predominant. But in between are extensive coniferous forests, composed largely of pine and spruce.

DENMARK

Denmark is the only country of Norden in which agriculture is of major importance. Before World War II, Denmark was the world's leading exporter of butter, bacon, and eggs. Yet more than half of Denmark's population is urban, and there is a major concentration of manufacturing industry around Copenhagen. Denmark, accepting the principle of economic interdependence among states, has developed a mature economy. Its people enjoy a high standard of living, and by long tradition are devoted to democratic procedures.

The economy of Denmark was radically changed after 1870. Before that date the land was used chiefly for the production of grains for human consumption, and most of the workers were employed in agriculture. But in the decade of the 1870's the European market was reached by wheat and maize from the United States and Argentina, which were sold at prices that the Danes could not meet. Denmark proceeded, then, to import its grain. At present about 30 per cent of the wheat required for the domestic food supply is imported. So also is the maize to feed poultry and hogs, and the fodder for dairy cattle. The Danish farms still grow wheat, barley, sugar beets, and feed crops, but their chief effort is focused on the low-cost production of butter, bacon, and eggs for export. Rather than reduce the supply of butter for export, the Danes import vegetable oil, and manufacture margarine for their own use. About 64 per cent of Denmark is under cultivation, yet only about 23 per cent of the workers are now employed in agriculture.

Denmark's economy has been diversified. A large fleet of fishing boats operates in the North Sea; and because of Denmark's position most of the catch can be sold fresh in

European markets. Around Copenhagen, especially, there are many kinds of manufacturing industries. In addition to the food-processing plants, which introduced the Industrial Revolution into Denmark, Danish industries now include the manufacture of diesel marine motors, automobiles, and many kinds of household utensils. The necessary raw materials and steel are imported—the steel and coal from the German Ruhr—and the finished products are sold abroad.

Denmark still administers two island possessions. The Faeroe Islands, midway between Scotland and Iceland, are occupied almost entirely by fishing people. Similarly Greenland, the world's largest island, is occupied along its southwest coast by people whose economy is almost entirely devoted to catching and processing fish. The Eskimos, who once inhabited this part of the world, have all but disappeared as a culture, although the descendants of the Eskimos now work as fishermen alongside the Danes, or are employed as workers on the air bases in the far north.

Denmark is a strong, tightly knit, and viable state. Its people are united by the use of a common language, by the practice of the Lutheran faith, and by the traditional struggle to wrest a good living from a habitat that is not naturally productive.

SWEDEN

Sweden is one of the most progressive countries in the world in terms of the two great revolutions. Since the 1920's its economy has reached the stage of maturity, supported by manufacturing industries of extraordinary diversity. In spite of poor soils and a short growing season, Swedish farmers hold the world records for the yields per acre of several crops. Although the

Swedes maintain the form of a monarchy, their's is one of the countries in the world that most nearly approaches a complete democracy, as this term is defined in the introduction. Furthermore, they have gone the farthest of any large country in the development of a "welfare state." The Swedish birth rate is the lowest in the world: before World War II it had dropped to about 14 per thousand, and although it rose after the war it has now fallen again to the pre-war level. The population is between 50 and 60 per cent urban, and less than 15 per cent of the workers are employed in agriculture.

Most of the people and the economic production of Sweden are concentrated in the south (Map 1, pp. 4-5). The greatest concentration is between Stockholm and Göteborg in the Central Lowland, where there are more than 250 people per square mile. The great north country, on the other hand, has a very thin population, especially in the far north where the Laplanders pasture their reindeer. Agriculture and industry are also concentrated in the south. In Sweden as a whole only about 9 per cent of the land is cultivated, but in the Central Lowland about 70 per cent is cultivated. Industries are similarly concentrated in the south, except for the paper and pulp plants along the coast of the Gulf of Bothnia farther to the north.

The Swedish farmers—less than 15 per cent of the working force—have done an amazing job. The transformation of agriculture began in the 1890's with the break-up of large rural properties. At this time the rural population moved out of the villages in which most of the farmers lived, and established a settlement pattern of individual farmsteads. But in more recent times, especially since World War II, there has been a strong tendency to combine the family-sized farms into larger and more efficiently operated units. More than three quarters of the farm income is now derived from meat, milk, butter, cheese, and eggs; less than one quarter comes from the small grains, hay, potatoes, and sugar beets. By making use of machinery, fertilizer, improved seed, and other new techniques, the yields per acre of Swedish crops are among

In summer the rivers of Sweden are used to carry logs from the upland forests to paper factories at the river mouths.

the highest in the world. Before World War II the farms could supply only about 90 per cent of domestic needs for food: by 1960 the farms were producing about 110 per cent of these needs. Considering the climate, the soil, and the nature of the surface this is a remarkable achievement. Even in the northern part of the country, where only barley, hay, and potatoes can be grown, yields were improved during the 1950's and crops were pushed farther north.

Sweden had two natural resources that supported the initial steps of the Industrial Revolution. One of these resources was timber, chiefly spruce and pine. About 1860 markets for Swedish timber were opened up in Great Britain and France, and since that time Sweden has continued to supply a large part of Europe's needs. The first stage of the Industrial Revolution took place between 1870 and 1880, and one of the first changes to be introduced was a shift from the export of all the timber, to the use of a part of it in the manufacture of pulp and paper. The manufacture of paper requires a very large supply of pulp-wood, and a large volume of water; but the finished product is very much less bulky than the raw materials. For this reason pulp and paper mills are commonly located close to the forests, on rivers. In Sweden the paper industries were built near the river mouths where the streams reach the Gulf of Bothnia. In winter the trees used to be cut and dragged over the snow to the rivers, and in spring the logs were floated downstream to the factories. But because of the long frozen period in the Gulf of Bothnia, the product could only be shipped out in summer. Since World War II, more and more of the logs have been carried to the mills on motor trucks. And the factories now make many things beside pulp and paper. Although Sweden has now virtually lost its match industry (until 1932 Sweden had almost a world monopoly in the manufacture of matches), many other wood-working industries have appeared, manufacturing furniture, pre-fabricated homes, plywood, wallboard, and a variety of mill goods. The world's largest concentration of wood-using industries, including chemicals, is at Sundsvall, about 200 miles north of Stockholm.

The Swedes have now reached an important stage in the use of timber. The virgin stands of trees are gone, and the wood industries are making use of second-growth forests. Although growth at these latitudes is slow, the quality of the wood is still high. But the drain on the resource base has exceeded the annual growth: the result is a critical shortage of this basic material.

The second of the two natural resources on which the Swedish economy relied for its initial development was iron ore. The Bergslagen ores, located about 120 miles northwest of Stockholm, were used as early as the thirteenth century for the smelting of high-quality iron. The fuel was charcoal. Swedish iron was sold all over Europe, and was prized for its special strength. In the seventeenth century Sweden was the world's largest producer of iron. But when the method of using coke had been perfected, Sweden could no longer compete with coal-rich countries, except in the production of high-quality iron and steel. Swedish iron ore was in great demand in the iron-poor Ruhr. Around 1900 a body of iron ore (about 70 per cent iron) was discovered in the far north. The Kiruna District is 165 miles from the head of the Gulf of Bothnia, with which it was connected by rail. But Kiruna is only 80 miles from the ice-free Norwegian port of Narvik, and a large part of the Swedish ore is now exported by this route.

Sweden's manufacturing industries are highly diversified. Near the Bergslagen mines, and near the ports where German coal can be brought in, the Swedish steel plants make high-quality steel. From this steel all kinds of high-quality goods are made: knives, scissors, tools, surgical instruments, refrigerators, cream separators, vacuum cleaners, calculating machines, and telephones. Sweden is the world's largest exporter of ball bearings, most of them manufactured near Göteborg. But even this long list fails to mention more than a few of Sweden's many kinds of manufacturing plants.

Although Sweden has very little coal, and no oil, its rivers carry a large potential of hydroelectric power. Some 80 per cent of this potential, however, is on the rivers of the thinly peopled northland, north of the Bergslagen area. The harnessing of the great rivers of the northland has necessitated the construction of unusually long transmission lines to bring the power to the industrial centers. The world's longest and most highly charged transmission line runs for 590 miles from the northernmost, and largest, of the hydroelectric stations on the river above Luleå to the Swedish Central Lowland west of Stockholm. It carries a charge of 380,-000 volts.

The Swedish people can be very proud indeed of the technical achievements of their engineers. The lack of a naturally productive habitat has not kept the Swedes from developing a very high standard of living. They have been similarly imaginative in the building of economic, social, and political institutions. The five basic principles of democracy are guarded with fervor, and when the voters decided to support the development of a "welfare state" the government responded promptly. The Swedes now devote nearly 30 per cent of their national budget to pay for welfare benefits, which include such items as payments to mothers for children, free school lunches, free tuition at schools and universities, free hospitalization, and many other things. Now an old-age pension system has been adopted, to guarantee every worker at age 67 an income about 66 per cent of his average earnings during his fifteen most profitable years. To be sure, the cost of supporting such a welfare program has begun to counterbalance the desire for security. But even if there should be some opposition to additional benefits it is not likely that the voters would give up any major part of the system. There are no rebels to attack so comfortable a set of institutions, and the Swedish economy shows no sign of becoming less productive.

FINLAND

Finland is a country of rocky hills, and swamps, and many lakes, of dark spruce and pine forests, of long snowy winters and short cool summers, and of hardy, industrious, liberty-loving people. The Finns are not Germanic, like the Scandinavians, and their language is not even Indo-European in origin. They were conquered by the Swedes and were ruled by them for many centuries. Even now about 9 per cent of the population—mostly along the southwestern coast—speaks Swedish. The Swedish influence is reflected, also, in the fact that about 95 per cent of the Finns are Lutherans. From 1809 to 1917 Finland was a province of the Russian Empire, a province in which the tsars had the greatest difficulty in maintaining order. Although independent since 1917, the Finns are still under constant pressure from the Soviet Union.

The population of Finland is concentrated in the south, and along the eastern shore of the Gulf of Bothnia (Map 1, pp. 4-5). About 75 per cent of the people are rural; and in the vicinity of the large cities of Helsinki, Turku, and Tampere, the rural population is more than 125 people per square mile. North of the Gulf of Bothnia, however, there are less than 10 people per square mile.

Most of the Finns make a living from agriculture, combined with the cutting of timber. More than 35 per cent of the workers are employed on farms. In Finland as a whole only about 7 per cent of the area is under cultivation, but the proportion varies from the southwest, where nearly 25 per cent is cultivated, to the far north where less than 1 per cent is cultivated. Hay is the crop that occupies more than three quarters of the cultivated land, followed by oats, rye, wheat, and barley. The hay is mostly fed to dairy cattle, which have to be kept in barns for seven to eight months of the year. In the years before Finland was attacked by the Soviet Union in 1939, a great effort was being made to achieve self-sufficiency in the food supply. Actually the Finns did produce enough for their needs of dairy products, meat, eggs, and potatoes. Then in 1939 the Soviet armies took away some of Finland's best agricultural land—between the head of the Gulf of Finland and Lake Ladoga (Map 32). The Finns were able to resettle the persons thus displaced, and between 1939 and 1949 they more than doubled the acreage of spring wheat. This was done largely by pushing the crop limits farther north than had ever been possible before. But Finland can now produce only about 80 per cent of its food requirements.

Almost the only great natural resource in Finland is timber. Forests still cover about 71 per cent of the area of the country, and lumber is Finland's major export. Many people engaged in farming are also employed part-time during the winter as timber cutters. In addition to the lumber exported, wood is now the raw material used in many kinds of wood-working industries. Finland is the world's largest exporter of

NORDEN
AGRICULTURE, MINERALS & INDUSTRIES

32

Forest products
Predominantly pastoral
Grains and feed crops
Non-agricultural

Coal
Fe Iron ore
Cu Copper
Au Gold
Ag Silver
Mn Manganese
Mo Molybdenum
Ni Nickel
Zn Zinc
Industrial center
Steel industry

GREENLAND
(To Denmark)

Ice free areas

Kane Basin
Thule
Baffin Bay
Upernavik
Godthaab
Umivik
30°
40°
50°
0   300
Miles

Atlantic Ocean

LOFOTEN ISLANDS

Narvik
Bodö
Cu Sulitjelma
Zn **Cu**
Fe Mo-i-Rana
Fe
Cu

Kiruna
Fe
Fe Gällivare
Fe
Fe Kemi
Cu Luleå
Cu Boliden
Fe Skellefteå
Oulu

U. S. S. R.

70°

Kirkenes **Fe**

Kristiansund
Trondheim
Løkken
Cu Röros
Ålesund

N O R W A Y
S W E D E N

Umea
Gulf of Bothnia
Härnösand
Sundsvall

Otanmaki
Kajaani
Fe

F I N L A N D

Kuopio
Outokumpu **Cu**
Joensuu

Vaasa

Mikkeli
Vouksenniska
Lake Ladoga

Cu Bergen
Odda
Rjukan
Cu
Mo
Ag
Ni
Kongsberg
Drammen
Oslo
Mo
Fe
Mo
Stavanger
Fe
Sandefjord
Moss
Sarpsborg
Fredrikstad
Kristiansand

Cu
Fe Falun
Cu
Ludvika
Sandviken
Gävle

BERGS LAGEN

Karlskoga
Fe Västerås
Karlstad
Eskilstuna
Örebro
Ammeberg
Stockholm
Södertälje
Zn
Norrköping
Trollhättan
Linköping
Motala
Jönköping
Huskvarna
Boras **Mn**
Orrefors
Göteborg
Aalborg

Pori
Tampere
Rauma
Lahti
Hämeenlinna
Turku
Kotka
Fiskars
Porvoo
Helsinki
Gulf of Finland

Baltic Sea

SWEDISH INHABITED AREAS
Discontinuous
Continuous
Settlement boundary

0   150
Miles

From Kirk Stone

DENMARK
Aarhus
Copenhagen
Odense
Hälsingborg
Malmö
Trelleborg

GERMANY

0   100
Scale of Miles

24°   20°   16°
66°
Isafjördhur
Siglufjördhur
Sandhárkrókur
Húsavik
Akureyri
Breidha Fjörd
Seydhisfjördhur
Faxa Bay
64°
Reykjavík
GLACIER
Mt. Hekla

Sheep
Cattle

0   50
Miles

After Focus

A Norwegian whaling ship in the Antarctic. These ships are floating factories which can process all parts of the whale while still at sea.

plywood. Finnish factories make spools, and pre-fabricated houses—mostly exported to the Soviet Union. Wood is used to make paper and pulp; and as by-products of the paper industry, Finland also produces rayon, fodder cellulose, turpentine, pine oil, and chemicals. Finland is second only to Canada in the export of newsprint.

In terms of numbers of workers employed, other manufacturing industries are more important than are those using wood. The largest source of employment is in the factories manufacturing metal goods. Except for copper, of which Finland has a small supply, all the other metals are imported. Pig iron is made from scrap iron at Turku; steel rails and locomotives are manufactured at Tampere; and at Helsinki there are shipbuilding yards. Around Tampere there are numerous textile factories.

Finland is a country with a strongly developed state-idea. To be sure, its national territory is not well endowed with resources, other than timber; but what Finland lacks in resources it makes up in skill and determination. Loss of territory and the payment of reparations to the Soviet Union have slowed economic development. Yet these outside pressures have fostered the feeling of nationalism, and strengthened the spirit of independence. Finnish national self-consciousness is based on certain distinctive characteristics: the Finnish language, the distinctive music, literature and art, the devotion to the principles of democracy, the high percentage of literates and the emphasis on education. Located as it is on the border of the Soviet Union, only a determined people with a strong sense of nationalism could survive.

NORWAY

Norway, also, has felt the full sweep of both of the great revolutions. The Norwegians by long tradition have been a seafaring people. From their protected fiords, the Vikings set out to raid the coasts of Europe and the British Isles. They sailed boldly westward across the open ocean and established colonies in Iceland and Greenland; and about A.D. 1000 they visited the shores of North America. Yet the Norwegian habitat does not offer the space for any large concentrations of people. The country was ruled first from Denmark, later from Sweden. Only in 1905 was Norway separated from Sweden, and an unguarded frontier established between them. Since that date the two countries have gone their separate, but quite friendly, ways.

The population of Norway is strongly homogeneous in culture, but diverse in geographic arrangement. Except for the nomadic Lapps (who range across the whole northern part of Norway, Sweden, and Finland), the people of Norway speak a common language, Norwegian, and profess a common religion, Lutheran. Like the Finns and Swedes, they have a strong sense of national consciousness. But, to a much greater degree than either Finns or Swedes, they are clustered into separate areas of concentrated settlement. Over half of the Norwegians live on the lowland at the head of the Oslo Fiord, about 500,000 of them in the city of Oslo. About a quarter of them

form a narrow band of settlement along the southwest coast, focusing on Bergen. Another small area of concentrated settlement is found on the lowland around Trondheim. Elsewhere there are only small, scattered villages clinging to the margins of the fiords.

Norway is not a good farming country. Only 3 per cent of the national territory is under cultivation, and most of this is around Oslo. Less than 30 per cent of the workers of Norway are employed on farms. On the largest lowland area around Oslo the farmers raise wheat on the better soils, and elsewhere raise potatoes, oats, barley, and hay. Hay and grains cut for fodder are grown on most of the farms, and occupy the land almost exclusively in the meat and dairy areas along the southwest coast, and around Trondheim. In the country as a whole, hay occupies 75 per cent of the cultivated area.

Fishing is more important than farming from an economic point of view, although less than 10 per cent of the workers are employed in it. The Norwegian fishermen catch more fish each year than are caught by the fishermen of any other European state. However, the value of the fish exports is not large. Two thirds of the annual catch is made up of herring, which are caught along the coast south of Trondheim from December to March. A major problem is involved in handling such a large volume of fish in so short a time. Much of the herring catch is marketed as fish meal for fertilizer, and as oil for margarine. The other major type of fish is the cod, which is caught from January to April along the northern coast, especially off the Lofoten Islands. Because of the remote position of these fishing grounds, the cod must be dried or salted—which reduces their value on the European markets.

The Norwegians are the world's leading whalers. In 1955 the whaling fleet consisted of a hundred and thirty ships and ten factory ships, which was more than the fleets of all other nations combined. Whaling is done exclusively in the ocean off the Antarctic Continent. The chief product is whale oil, used in the manufacture of margarine.

About a third of the workers of Norway are employed in manufacturing industries. Industries did not get an early start in Norway due to lack of fuels, but development took place rapidly after 1900 when the first hydroelectric installations were built. Norway has more potential hydroelectric power than any other European country; and, in contrast to the situation in Sweden, something like 80 per cent of Norway's potential is located in the south where the people and industries are concentrated. Although only about a quarter of the potential has been harnessed, Norway today uses more hydroelectric power per person than any other country in the world. Since 1900 numerous industries have been developed that require large quantities of low-cost electricity. There are metal refineries producing copper, nickel, aluminum, manganese, chromium, and zinc. Pig iron is made in electric furnaces. The process of extracting nitrogen from the air was pioneered in Norway, and this was the first country to develop the method of heating houses by electricity.

Norway is also endowed with some resources useful in industry. There are iron and copper mines—and enough coal for domestic needs is now brought from Spitsbergen (Svalbard) in the Arctic Ocean about four hundred miles north of Norway. Norway also has spruce and pine forests, similar to, but not so large as, those of Sweden.

A very important support for the Norwegian economy, however, is derived from the earnings of the merchant fleet. Norway stands third among the nations of the world in terms of the tonnage of its cargo vessels, nearly half of them oil tankers. Something like 80 per cent of the operations of this fleet are carried on between foreign ports, but the earnings permit Norway to import a much greater quantity of goods than can be paid for by exports alone. Norway's high standard of living could not be supported without the merchant fleet.

ICELAND

Iceland, located in the North Atlantic Ocean about six hundred miles west of Norway and just south of the Arctic Circle, was for a long time isolated from the conflicts that troubled the European Culture Region. Settled originally by Vikings, it was left to govern itself when regular communications across such a large expanse of stormy ocean proved impossible. The Norwegians returned to claim possession in the thirteenth century, and then in the fourteenth century Iceland came under Danish rule. In 1918 Iceland's independence was again recognized, and it formed a union with Denmark. In 1944 complete independence was reestablished. But Iceland is no longer isolated. In the modern world Iceland's position, close to the most direct air route between Europe and North America, gives it a new and disturbing strategic importance.

The population of Iceland is concentrated in the southwestern part, around the city of Reykjavík. About half of all the Icelanders live in the city or its immediate suburbs. The remainder are scattered in small villages and towns around the coast. With a high birth rate (27.4 per thousand in 1960) and the lowest death rate in Europe (6.6 per thousand) the net rate of increase is high, which places a severe strain on an economy that is still underdeveloped.

Nevertheless, a major effort is being made to promote the economic development of the country. As late as 1880 more than 70 per cent of the workers were employed in agriculture, but now only 20 per cent are so employed. In spite of the short cool summers, some land in the southwest is used to grow hay, potatoes, and turnips. Cultivated farm land forms only 1 per cent of the total area, and another 10 per cent is used for grass pasture for sheep, cattle, and horses. More than 40 per cent of the workers are employed in the fishing or food-processing industries. Industrial plants in Reykjavík can fish and mutton, and manufacture such products as fish meal, herring oil, cod-liver oil, and butter. The relatively small population has the highest level of foreign trade per capita of any country in Europe.

SUMMARY

It was in the European Culture Region that what we call Occidental Civilization had its beginnings. From the culture hearths of Crete, Greece, and Rome the basic ideas and techniques of the European way of life were introduced. In successive periods the centers of power shifted westward along the Mediterranean and northward into Europe north of the Alps.

By this time, however, the latest of the great revolutionary periods of human history had started. The new center of culture change was around the shores of the North Sea, and from this nucleus the new technology and the new concepts of democracy began to spread. In Europe the pre-industrial and pre-democratic institutions were strongly developed. Both technological change, and change in the status of the individual, were resisted, and reaction inevitably brought conflict. After two world wars, both of which started in Europe, it became clear that whatever happens in this central part of the Land Hemisphere is of deep concern to people everywhere.

The reactions against the two revolutions have restricted the full development of institutions suitable to the new conditions of life. The new techniques of production and transportation have created a condition of potential abundance instead of a condition of scarcity. Yet nations have continued to act as if the traditional scarcities still existed. The policy of Germany under Hitler was to expand the national territory by military force, in order to gain more *lebensraum*. This was the time-honored principle that in order to be strong, states must have control over the earth resources on which they are dependent—an objective inherited from the Early Civilizations. But the result in the European Culture Region has been that the new productivity has not always been used to provide people with better living conditions. The concept that self-sufficiency and strength can no longer go together has been difficult to accept.

The five basic elements of the Democratic Revolution have also been resisted. Many reformers have been disillusioned by the compromises and delays inherent in the democratic process, and have turned to dictatorship and armed force to hasten the granting of what they called "social justice" to the common man. Both fascists and communists talk about the rise of the common man to power, and the communists call their states "people's democracies." But the people are not trusted with the power of the ballot, nor are they given equality before the law, nor free access to knowledge until that knowledge has been carefully edited. The communists now hope to make rapid technological progress by government decree, but along with industrial growth they deny all five principles of what we call democracy.

The Rise of the European Economic Community. After World War II events in Europe began to necessitate a search for new institutions to accommodate the new technology. There is only one solution for the stubborn geographic facts that the new technology requires a much broader resource base than has previously been true, and that resources are very unevenly distributed over the earth. As soon as the necessity for economic interdependence is accepted it becomes clear that poverty and underdevelopment in any one state have the effect of lowering, or threatening, the economic well-being of other states. In the modern crowded world a new approach to international cooperation is essential, and such an approach is especially needed in Europe, where a relatively small area is divided into nineteen sovereign states, including Cyprus, and five small principalities.

At this critical moment in history the leadership has been found to build the necessary institutions. In 1952 six states agreed to pool their coal, iron, and scrap metal and to send these commodities freely, without tariff restrictions, into any of the participating countries. The six were France, Germany, Italy, and the three Benelux countries. In 1954 steel was added to the list, and in 1957 the same six countries set up the European Atomic Energy Community (Euratom) and agreed to pool atomic resources and knowledge.

In 1957, also, a second revolutionary step was taken. This was the ratification, by the same six countries, of the European Economic Community. This new institution embraced both of the previous organizations, but went farther toward the establishment of an area of unrestricted trade. It was agreed to eliminate tariff barriers and other trade restrictions over a fifteen year period, and to permit the free flow of raw materials, manufactured goods, capital, and workers among the member states.

The results have been nothing short of spectacular. The gross national product per capita of the participating countries has taken an upward jump (7 per cent in 1960 alone), and the market for consumer goods has begun to expand at a rate unprecedented in the European area. It has already given rise to the development of an entirely new port, known as Europoort, at the mouth of the Rhine, to handle the anticipated increase in imports and exports (Map 26). Among other changes has been the increased ownership of private automobiles, and the resulting traffic jams. Private automobiles change living habits profoundly: they permit families to seek new homes in suburban areas; to extend the range of movement not only from day to day, but also at vacation time; they undermine long-established customs and principles of morality. But they give the individual a new feeling of freedom in a crowded world. After World War II the United States was producing about 84 per cent of the world's automobiles and Europe was producing 14 per cent. By 1959 the proportion of automobiles produced in the United States had dropped to 53 per cent, while that of Europe had risen to 42 per cent. The automobile age has introduced the demand for an almost endless list of other goods. The investment of new capital in consumer goods industries has created new jobs; new jobs have created an expanded market for consumer goods; and for every person now employed in a manufacturing industry there are at least two employed in a long list of service occupations. Suddenly the economies of the six countries have reached a stage of high mass consumption.

The success of the European Economic Community has created a variety of reactions. There were those outside it who were worried about a decrease in exports to these countries; but in fact the increase in purchasing power has had the result of increasing imports. It is a principle of economic geography that the largest volume of trade is between two highly industrialized countries with mature economies, not between an industrial country and its suppliers of raw materials.

Within Europe the countries that were left out of the Economic Community began to reconsider their policies. They organized the so-called "Outer Seven"—Great Britain, Denmark, Norway, Sweden, Switzerland, Austria, and Portugal—into the European Free Trade Association (EFTA). Plans were made to reduce tariffs and promote the exchange of goods within this other group. In 1961 Greece applied for admission to the Economic Community.

The admission of Great Britain to the Community raises serious problems based on certain facts of geography. Among the original six members, France produces nearly half of all the foods raised within the Community. Since World War II French farmers have been increasing their production of foods and they hope to find expanded markets within the new organization. But Great Britain receives much of its food supply from Canada, Australia, New Zealand, and other members of the Commonwealth. If Britain should enter the Economic Community what would be the effect on these members of the Commonwealth? And if Commonwealth countries could send their foodstuffs to the European market what would this mean for the French farmers? The solution of such problems requires a clear understanding of the facts and issues, and adroit statesmanship to find the necessary compromises.

What the European Economic Community can do for Europe and the world is important. The Community has become the fastest-growing large area of any part of the world, and the world's most active trading area. As the volume of economic production rises, so also does the level of living, and so also does military power. The whole picture of raw material strategy in the world will require revision. And in a world divided between two opposed powers, and therefore constantly exposed to the danger of armed conflict, a third great power has appeared. Europe, devoted to the concept of international cooperation, has the resources, the capital, and the skills to become a major nucleus of economic power; and located at the center of the Land Hemisphere, it is in a position of dominant strategic importance.

3

THE
SOVIET
CULTURE REGION

Country	Political Status	Latest Estimate Population	Capital City
Union of Soviet Socialist Republics Incl. SSRs:	Federal Soviet Republic	221,000,000 ('62)	Moscow
Armenia		1,768,000 ('59)	Yerevan
Azerbaydzhan		3,700,000 ('59)	Baku
Byelorussia		8,226,000 ('60)	Minsk
Estonia		1,196,000 ('59)	Tallinn
Georgia		4,049,000 ('59)	Tbilisi
Kazakh		9,301,000 ('59)	Alma-Ata
Kirghiz		2,063,000 ('59)	Frunze
Latvia		2,094,000 ('59)	Riga
Lithuania		2,713,000 ('59)	Vilnius
Moldavia		2,880,000 ('59)	Kishinev
Russian SFSR		117,494,000 ('59)	Moscow
Tadzhik		1,982,000 ('59)	Dyushambe
Turkmen		1,520,000 ('59)	Ashkhabad
Ukraine		43,091,000 ('60)	Kiev
Uzbek		8,113,000 ('59)	Tashkent
Albania	People's Republic	1,700,000 ('62)	Tiranë
Bulgaria	People's Republic	8,000,000 ('62)	Sofia
Czechoslovakia	People's Republic	13,900,000 ('62)	Prague
Germany, East	Democratic Republic	17,200,000 ('62)	E. Berlin
Hungary	People's Republic	10,100,000 ('62)	Budapest
Poland	People's Republic	30,400,000 ('62)	Warsaw
Romania	People's Republic	18,800,000 ('62)	Bucharest
Yugoslavia	Federal People's Republic	18,800,000 ('62)	Belgrade

The Soviet Culture Region occupies the heartland of Eurasia, extending across the northern part of the world's largest land mass from the Baltic Sea to the Bering Strait and the shores of the Pacific Ocean. The core of this culture region, and also the core of the Union of Soviet Socialist Republics—the Soviet Union—is between the Baltic Sea and the Ural Mountains. The region is distinguished by two basic facts: that it was organized into political units by pre-industrial and pre-democratic East Europeans, and that it is now under the control of the Communist Party.

There are three outstanding characteristics of this region as a human habitat. First is its isolation from the rest of the world.

If the European Culture Region can be described as maritime, the Soviet Culture Region merits the adjective continental. It includes the part of Europe that is least accessible to the world ocean—the part east of a line drawn from Leningrad to Trieste (Map 14); but it also includes the vast interior of Eurasia, isolated on the south by great expanses of arid lands and by ranges of rugged mountains, and on the north and east by ice and fog. Only in Eastern Europe is the border of the region crossed by numerous lines of transportation (Map 10, pp. 24-25). The people of this culture region, locked in the continental interior, long remained isolated from direct contact with ideas emanating from Greece and Rome.

◄ *Mayakovsky Subway Station, Moscow.*

The second fact is that the greater part of this area is poorly suited for agriculture. Most of the good cropland is in the west, on the margins between seasonal forest and grasslands: toward the east the cropland is pinched out between the dry lands to the south and the cold lands to the north. The greater part of the region is either too dry, too cold, or too mountainous for crops.

The third fact is that this huge continental area contains an extraordinary wealth of industrial minerals, fuels, and sources of power. It holds the world's largest reserves of iron ore; it has major supplies of copper, nickel, manganese, lead, zinc, platinum, gold, and silver. It has ample reserves of oil, and an abundance of coal. Its rivers offer almost half of the total hydroelectric potential of the world.

Since 1917 the Soviet Union has been organized under the control of the Communist Party, and since World War II this control has been extended to the countries of Eastern Europe. The Communist Party is the ultimate source of political power, for within the party all decisions of public policy are made, and all officials to administer the policy are selected. The Communist Party is not easy to join: candidates are carefully screened for complete loyalty to communist doctrine as set forth by Marx and Lenin, and for complete obedience to Party leaders. Within the Party there are discussions of policy issues; and to a certain extent the opinions of the vast majority of the people who are not members of the Party cannot be ignored. But once a decision has been reached, no further consideration of alternative policies is permitted. The Party stands outside the government, supervising the officials and public administrators, who are responsible to the Party rather than to the people.

The Communist Party follows the doctrines presented in the writings of Marx and Lenin. The causes of poverty and warfare, according to the communists, are to be found in the private ownership of land and capital. Marx, observing conditions in London during the early stages of the British Industrial Revolution, concluded that the owners of capital would always resist paying labor more than a bare subsistence wage. The benefits of the new technology would be collected by a smaller and smaller number of monopolists, until, eventually, the industrial workers would rise up and seize power by force.

Lenin, writing in 1916, elaborated on the Marxist doctrine in his explanation of the great war then raging. The owners of capital, he said, invest more and more of their surplus savings in new machinery and new factories, in order to secure more private gain, until the volume of production vastly exceeds the capacity of the domestic market to absorb it. This leads to imperialism—the seizing of colonies in order to gain possession of new sources of raw materials, and new markets for manufactured goods. The industrialized countries soon find themselves competing for colonies, and this competition leads to imperialist wars. A believer in the doctrines of Marxism-Leninism, as every member of the Communist Party must be, harbors no doubts concerning the coming collapse of capitalism and the ultimate victory of communism.

From the point of view of the non-communist world, these explanations overlook two essential facts. First, that in a free society, where a majority can determine policy through the use of the ballot, laws are formulated to insure that the national income is widely spread among the people. In countries with mature economies, the workers receive a sufficiently large share of the income from goods and services so that the domestic market can absorb a vast increase in the volume of production. The second fact is that trade is most profitable when it is between countries with mature economies, and not when it is between one industrial country and its economically underdeveloped colonies.

Why, then, does communism exert an attraction as a means of reducing poverty, and of avoiding warfare? Clearly, the greatest attraction is felt, not by urban-industrial workers, but by land-hungry peasants in pre-industrial countries. To these people communism offers a rapid and ruthless program of modernization and economic development, and an immediate liquidation of the owners of land or capital. To people long accustomed to hopeless poverty, the communists offer hope for a better future. Within the Soviet Union, where the workers have been accustomed to working hard for meager rewards, living conditions are now improving, and hope is held out for rapid gains in housing, clothing, and food. To be sure, the whole program of technological change has been planned and controlled by the state; but the Soviet people have never known an economic or political system that was not bureaucratic and despotic. The communists have imposed no

harsher restrictions on the freedom of the individual than did the tsars. Although all five of the basic elements of the Democratic Revolution are denied, and although the members of the Communist Party occupy positions of power and prestige that make them a new elite, it is important to remember that these developments have taken place in a culture region where the institutions of a free society have never taken root in the past.

The Soviet Culture Region is made up of two chief parts. The core of the region, where its characteristics are most clearly developed, is in the Soviet Union. The Soviet Union forms by far the larger part of the total area. In Eastern Europe there are eight countries, known as People's Democracies, which are in many ways transitional between the European Culture Region and the Soviet Culture Region, but are included in the latter. These are the German Democratic Republic, Czechoslovakia, Poland, Hungary, Romania, Bulgaria, Yugoslavia, and Albania. The culture region as a whole comprises about 18 per cent of the inhabited area of the earth, and is occupied by 7 per cent of the world population.

THE UNION OF SOVIET SOCIALIST REPUBLICS

The Union of Soviet Socialist Republics embraces about one sixth of the whole inhabited land surface of the earth. It stretches in an east-west direction more than half way around the world. If the westernmost part of the Soviet Union were placed at the same longitude as the westernmost tip of Alaska, the easternmost part of the Soviet Union would touch Norway. The inset on Map 34 shows the relation of Soviet territory to that of the United States, with each placed at its proper latitude. Within the vast area of the Soviet Union there are over 221,000,000 people. Of these only 55 per

cent are Russians, and the remainder are made up of more than one hundred different nationalities.

THE HABITAT

(Maps 5, 6, 8, and 34) The habitat of the Soviet Union is not well favored for agriculture. In spite of its vast area, a large part of the national territory is not suited to support a dense population under present conditions of technology. The inset on Map 34 shows that although the Soviet Union is very large, it lies farther north than the midcontinent part of the United States.

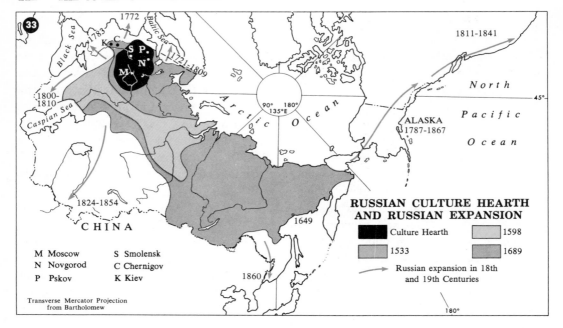

RUSSIAN CULTURE HEARTH
AND RUSSIAN EXPANSION

Culture Hearth   1598

1533   1689

Russian expansion in 18th
and 19th Centuries

M Moscow   S Smolensk
N Novgorod   C Chernigov
P Pskov   K Kiev

Transverse Mercator Projection
from Bartholomew

Surface Features. The plain that touches the shores of the North Sea in Europe and extends along the southern side of the Baltic Sea (Map 15, p. 42), opens out east of the Baltic until it extends all the way from the Black Sea to the Arctic Ocean (Map 34). In the European part of the Soviet Union, between the Baltic and the Ural Mountains, this plain is varied by belts of low hills and moraines, culminating in the Valday Hills between Moscow and Leningrad. The Urals, too, are a belt of hilly upland and low mountain extending from Novaya Zemlya almost to the Aral Sea. Between the Urals and the hilly upland of Central Siberia is the world's largest area of almost flat land, imperfectly drained by the Yenisey and Ob-Irtysh rivers. The channel of the latter river drops only 298 feet in 1,864 miles, or about two inches a mile. Since both the Ob and the Yenisey flow northward, the mouths are the first parts of these rivers to freeze in winter, and the last parts to thaw out in spring. This means that each year there are vast floods covering thousands of square miles of the swampy West Siberian Lowland. The rivers that flow southward, such as the Dnepr, the Don, the Volga, and the Ural, are filled with water during the spring thaw, but since their mouths remain open the floodwaters do not back up over such wide areas.

The greater part of Siberia is hilly or mountainous. Immediately to the east of the Yenisey floodplain is the sharp western border of the Siberian Upland which extends eastward to the Lena River. East of the Lena the whole northeastern part of Siberia, including the peninsula of Kamchatka, is made up of ranges of mountains, intermingled with hilly uplands. There are only a few valley lowlands: chiefly along the middle course of the Lena, and along the Amur Valley. The Amur Lowland is connected southward by a long narrow valley to Vladivostok. In the far north the Arctic Coastal Plain slopes gently into the Arctic Ocean.

Much of the southern border of the Soviet Union is drawn along the crests of

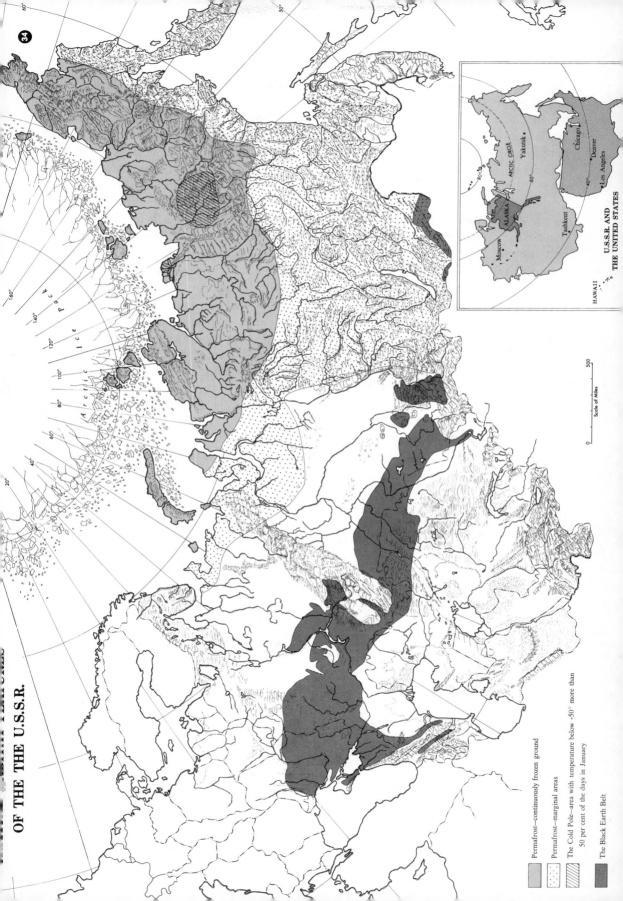

OF THE THE U.S.S.R.

Permafrost—continuously frozen ground

Permafrost—marginal areas

The Cold Pole—area with temperature below -50° more than
50 per cent of the days in January

The Black Earth Belt

U.S.S.R. AND
THE UNITED STATES

HAWAII

Scale of Miles

0   500

towering ranges of mountains. Soviet territory includes some of the country south of the Caucasus Mountains; but from Afghanistan eastward to the Amur Valley, the border runs along such high ranges as the Pamirs, the Tien Shan Mountains, and the Altai Mountains. Passes through these mountains exist, and between the Tien Shan and the Altai ranges there is a wide, easy pass route into China—though this route leads only into the vast desert area of inner Asia.

In the midst of the high mountains is Lake Baykal. This long, narrow lake (395 miles long and 49 miles wide) occupies a rift depression, down-faulted between towering ranges. Baykal is the world's deepest lake—5,712 feet deep. It is drained northward from near its southwestern end by the Angara River, a tributary of the Yenisey. Lake Baykal is frozen over for four months each year, from January to April.

The southernmost part of the Soviet Union in Central Asia, between the Caspian Sea and the Tien Shan Mountains, is a great desert region. Water pours from the bordering ranges, some draining into Lake Balkhash, some draining through the two great rivers—the Syr Darya and the Amu Darya—into the Aral Sea. The Caspian, the southern shore of which is in Iran, receives water chiefly from the Volga and the Ural rivers. The average level of this sea is ninety-two feet below the level of the world ocean.

The line on Map 36 shows that a large part of the Soviet territory was never reached by the continental glaciers. The ice that formed over Scandinavia moved out in all directions from that area of deep winter snows. Toward the southeast the ice pushed as far as Kiev and almost to the middle valley of the Volga. But most of Siberia, where winter snowfall is very light, was never glaciated.

The Climates. The interior of Eurasia is noted for the severity of its climates. Far from the moderating effect of open ocean water the winters are extremely cold, and there is very little rainfall or snow (Map 6, pp. 12-13). In the desert of Soviet Central Asia winters are cold and summers are hot.

The world record for low temperatures (outside Antarctica) is held by stations in northeastern Siberia. On still, cloudless nights in January, 1885 and again in February, 1892, a temperature of —89.7° was recorded at Verkhoyansk, and more recently —89.9° was reported from nearby Oymyakon. In this part of Siberia temperatures below —50° are experienced frequently in January (Map 34). At Verkhoyansk the average temperature for January is —52.6°, and the average for July is 59°—the world's greatest range of average temperatures. The average annual rainfall at Verkhoyansk is only 5.1 inches, which, in a region of such low temperatures, is enough to support woodlands (Map 8, pp. 16-17). In winter northeastern Siberia receives only a thin cover of snow. This was also true during the glacial period, and as a result, glaciers never formed here. Without the protection of snow the ground water is frozen solid. In summer only the surface thaws out, and water remains permanently frozen underneath—a condition described as *permafrost.* A large part of eastern Siberia is included in the permafrost area (Map 34).

As a result of the extreme, low temperatures developed in winter through night radiation under cloudless skies, the air in contact with the cold earth is chilled. Cold air accumulates until it is deep and heavy enough to slide off, which it does in the form of cold waves, or polar outbursts (see Appendix A, p. 436). These are the cold air masses that produce the offshore winter monsoons of eastern Asia, and the winter storms of the North Pacific Ocean. They also slide westward out of inner Asia, bringing winter cold waves to Europe even as far as Great Britain. On the unobstructed Russian plains these frigid blasts from the northeast bring very low temperatures.

But the Russian farmers are more concerned with drought than with cold. The cold air masses of winter are made up of very dry air which can evaporate most of the snow cover, thus depriving the soil of much-needed water in places that are on the semiarid border. With the snow cover gone, even the moisture in the soil may be evaporated, and this will have serious effects on the harvests of the following summer. The summers, when most of the rainfall comes, can be unexpectedly dry as blasts of hot, desert air come out of Central Asia east of the Caspian Sea. Records for the area north of the Caspian Sea indicate that periods of summer drought, long enough to produce crop failure, were felt thirty-four times in the eighteenth century, and forty times in the nineteenth century. In other words, serious summer droughts come on an average every second or third year—sometimes for two or three years in succession.

The average climatic conditions are shown on Map 5 (pp. 10-11). The plains north of the Black Sea and the Caspian Sea, and north of the Aral Depression, are on the margin between humid climates with severe winters (D), and climates that are deficient in moisture (B). Between the arid and semiarid climates of southern Russia and the polar climates (E) of northern Russia (where the average temperature for the warmest months is less than 50°) there is a belt of humid climates with severe winters. The northern part of this belt, where only one to three months average over 50° (Dfc), is marginal for agriculture because of the shortness of the growing season. The re-mainder of the area, where there are at least four months averaging over 50° (Dfb), extends in a narrowing belt, interrupted by the Urals, that reaches eastward as far as Novosibirsk. Mild winters occur nowhere in the Soviet Union except to the south of the Caucasus Mountains, and on the steep, south-facing slopes of the Crimean Peninsula. The latter area has a small bit of Mediterranean climate (Csa) with winter rains and summer droughts.

Vegetation and Soils. These climatic features are reflected in the arrangement of the natural vegetation (Map 8, pp. 16-17). The dry lands, characterized by the existence of bare ground between the plants, extend from the eastern and northern side of the Caspian Sea eastward to Lake Balkhash, including the whole of Soviet Central Asia. North of this region are successive belts running more or less west-east, reflecting the climatic pattern: first, park grassland consisting of prairie with scattered patches of woodland; then seasonal forest, consisting largely of broadleaf deciduous trees in the south (reaching about as far north as Leningrad), and north of that chiefly spruce, fir, and pine, together with hardy deciduous species, such as larch, birch, and aspen. This latter is the forest described by the Russians as *taiga*. Toward the north the taiga thins out into a poor woodland with small, widely-spaced, stunted trees. In the polar area the taiga gives way to tundra—a treeless expanse of moss, lichens, and coarse sedges.

Russian soil scientists were the first to recognize that these belts of vegetation and climate correspond to differences of soil. The Black-Earth Belt is a zone of dark-colored soils formed under the grasslands on the margin between the humid and semiarid climates (Map 34). Under the prairie the soil is a *chernozem*, one of the world's most productive grain soils. This is a deep soil, rich in organic matter, and containing in its lower horizons, some two to three feet below the surface, unleached concretions of carbonate of lime. In wetter climates these accumulations are dissolved and carried away by percolating water. Where the climate is drier, under the short-grass steppe, a *chestnut-brown* soil is formed, a little less rich in humus, but with a larger amount of carbonate of lime. These two soils, taken together, form the Black-Earth Belt.

These are the features of the Soviet habitat. These are features characteristic of the higher middle latitudes and the high latitudes of the Northern Hemisphere, features which are closely similar to those found in Canada and parts of Alaska. Yet Canada was mostly glaciated, and where glaciers were once active the present surface is dotted with lakes. The many lakes and bogs of the Laurentian Upland of Canada are similar in origin to the many lakes of the Scandinavian Upland, Finland, and the western margin of the Soviet Union where it adjoins Finland. The unglaciated surfaces of Siberia resemble the similarly unglaciated Yukon upland of Alaska. What were the conditions and what were the incentives that led the Russians to move into and settle this vast expanse of northern Eurasia, and then to move on eastward even into North America?

THE ORIGIN AND GROWTH OF MODERN RUSSIA

At an early date the Slavs had occupied the forests of the hilly area between Moscow and Kiev. They were essentially an inland people, cut off from the sea by the Balts, the Lithuanians, the Swedes, and the Germans who lived along the shores of the Baltic Sea. They made a living by herding swine in the forests, and by collecting honey

and other wild products. They were a gifted people, inventive and musical. From the reeds growing in the marshes on the edge of the forest northwest of Kiev they had fashioned some nine different musical instruments.

It was the Slavic peoples of the forests and the bordering steppes who were first known as Russians. Those who cultivated the grasslands around Kiev became known as Little Russians, and those who made clearings in the forest farther north around Novgorod became known as Great Russians. In addition to Kiev and Novgorod, other Slavic towns of that early period were Pskov, Smolensk, Chernigov, and Moscow (Map 33). As early as the ninth century A.D., the Slavs around Novgorod came into contact with the Vikings, who were seeking a route overland to Constantinople. Viking traders followed the rivers southward through the forests, using the Dnepr to carry them across the steppes from Kiev to the Black Sea. The dukes who ruled the Slavic communities lived apart from the peasants. The farm villages paid taxes collectively, in return for which the dukes gave them a measure of military protection; but the peasants were left to run their own village affairs with little interference from the "government." The ruling group carried on an active trade with Constantinople exchanging furs, honey, and slaves for silks, wine, and gold.

Christianity came to the Slavic communities in the tenth century. From Rome missionaries brought the Roman Catholic religion to the Slavs of Poland; while from Constantinople they brought the Greek Orthodox religion to the Slavs of Russia.

Then, for nearly four critical centuries, the Russians were cut off from the rest of Europe. In 1054 nomadic horsemen from Central Asia began to push westward along

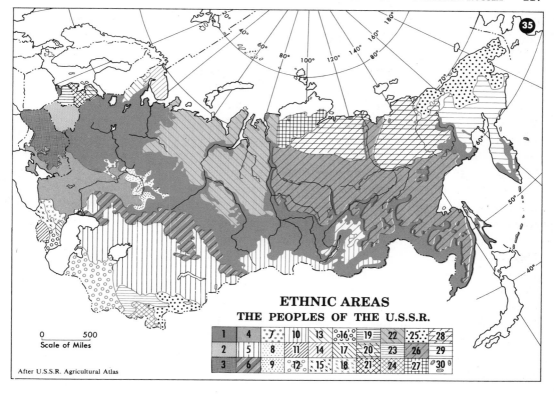

ETHNIC AREAS
THE PEOPLES OF THE U.S.S.R.

Scale of Miles
0   500

After U.S.S.R. Agricultural Atlas

KEY TO THE ETHNIC AREAS OF THE U.S.S.R.

1. Great Russians
2. Byelorussians (White Russians)
3. Ukrainians
4. Russians and Ukrainians
5. Kazakhs
6. Russians, Ukrainians, and Kazakhs
7. Mordvinians
8. Tatars
9. Bashkirs
10. South and Southeast Siberians
    Ahais
    Khahoss
    Skorians
    Touvinians
    Buryats

11. Armenians
12. Turkmens

13. Karelians
14. Finns
15. Georgians
16. Azerbaijanis
17. Dagestanis
18. Seven North Caucasus groups
19. Lithuanians
20. Estonians
21. Latvians
22. Khantis, Komis, and Selkups
23. Uzbeks
24. Tadzhiks
25. Khirgiz
26. Evenks
27. Dolganis
28. Yakuts
29. Koryaks
30. Nivkhis and Ainus

the zone of grassland north of the Black Sea. They disrupted trade along the Dnepr and brought it almost entirely to a stop, so that Kiev declined in importance. Only the Slavic communities deep in the forests could prosper—for instance Novgorod and Moscow. Even there the invaders came to exact tribute. The Golden Horde of Tatars reached the Volga River in 1237, and by 1240 they had taken Kiev, and moved on westward farther into Europe. From 1240 to 1480 the dukes who ruled over the Slavic communities were appointed by the Tatars.

The dukes who ruled over Moscow, the Dukes of Muscovy, were the ones who gradually rebuilt the power of the Russians. First they extended their control over the other Slavic towns. Then in 1480 Ivan III was able to regain Russian independence from the Tatars by refusing to pay tribute. Ivan IV (known as Ivan the Terrible) was the first ruler to adopt the title "Tsar," meaning Caesar, in 1547, and the first to extend control over non-Russian peoples. Between 1552 and 1590 his armies pushed eastward to the Volga River, which at that time became the well-defined eastern boundary of Russia.

From this base, the expanded Russian culture hearth, the conquest of the whole vast extent of Siberia took place. The cossacks, horsemen from the steppes who enlisted in the service of the tsars, led the attack on the crumbling Tatar fortresses. One of the first centers they captured was a place called Sibir (from which came the name Siberia) on the lower Irtysh River. Using the tributary streams wherever possible, Russian fur traders pushed on eastward with little hindrance from the primitive forest tribes, eventually founding a trading post on the shores of the Sea of Okhotsk in 1640.

Meanwhile the Russians were also expanding westwards. Peter the Great (1689-1725) sent his armies against the Swedes, who controlled the territory between Russia and the Baltic coast, and gained possession of what is now Estonia and Latvia. In 1703 he founded the city of St. Petersburg (now Leningrad) at the end of the Gulf of Finland, and "opened a window to the west" by making this city, rather than the more isolated Moscow, his capital.

The tsar stimulated the economic development of two parts of his territory. The beginnings of an iron industry, for the production of armaments, were made through the use of iron ores from the Urals, smelted with charcoal. And he found an export product that could be sold in the countries of Western Europe, along with Russia's traditional export—furs. This was wheat. Wheat was raised with the labor of serfs on vast estates in the Black-Earth Belt north of the Black Sea. It was hauled by wagon to the Volga River, and then pulled upstream as far as the river was navigable. From 1709 to 1722 Russian workers were engaged in digging one of Russia's most important canals, connecting the head of navigation on the Volga with the port of St. Petersburg. For nearly two centuries wheat was transported over this route to provide Great Britain with an important part of its wheat supply.

After the death of Peter the Great his aims of territorial expansion, and of economic development, were continued. Russia extended its territory westward to include Poland, and southward to the northern shores of the Black Sea. In the far east Russian traders moved on into Alaska, and southward along the Pacific Coast into California. In 1812 a Russian settlement was established only forty miles north of

San Francisco. In 1867, however, the United States purchased Alaska for $7,200,000, and Russian expansion into North America came to an end.

Economic development continued with the adoption of the new technology of the Industrial Revolution. The first railroad was built between St. Petersburg and Moscow in the 1850's. More were then built radiating from Moscow, which provided the country west of the Urals with a rather widely spaced web of railroads. The new technology also resulted in a shift of the iron and steel industry from the Urals, where the only fuel was charcoal, to the Donbass (the Donets Basin), where iron ore, manganese, and coal could be assembled at lower cost than elsewhere. As usual at that stage, heavy industry was located close to the sources of coal.

The ideas generated in the European Culture Region regarding the status of the individual also filtered back eastward. Democratic ideas, which elevated the individual to a position of dignity and importance, were totally alien to the Russian culture. The freeing of the serfs in 1861 was a revolutionary step, even if it failed to solve the problems of widespread poverty, illiteracy, and inequality of status. As soon as the serfs were free to move there was a demand for new land, but in the older settled parts of Russia all the land was already held in private estates. The government offered free land for pioneer farmers east of the Volga River, in the eastern part of the Black-Earth Belt which extends into Siberia. Between 1860 and 1880 there were about 110,000 new settlers moving into this area, and between 1880 and 1892 the number of migrants rose to 440,000. These were voluntary settlers, in contrast to the many political prisoners who were exiled to Siberia, and who

were usually sent to the more remote areas to engage in such arduous tasks as lumbering and mining. The voluntary farm colonists had, by 1900, occupied the greater part of the Black-Earth Belt.

The problem of maintaining communications with the eastern part of the Empire worried the tsars. After the initial settlements had been made on the Sea of Okhotsk, it became clear that Russia would have to expand southward to reach ports that were free from ice in winter. In 1860 Russia annexed the country north of the Amur River and extended its territory southward to Vladivostok (Map 33). But the journey overland to Vladivostok took so long that most communications between St. Petersburg and the far east were made by ship, by way of Suez and Singapore. In 1891 the tsar started to construct a railroad line extending all the way across Eurasia; and by 1902 it was completed except for a gap at Lake Baykal. It was a long, single-track line, and the trip across took ten days, but it was faster than the long sea voyage. Finally, in 1904, the difficult construction of the connection around the mountainous southern end of Lake Baykal was completed. By this time the Russians were involved in a disastrous war with Japan over Manchuria (1904-1905), and the railroad made possible the movement of troops and supplies to this distant theater of war. Later the railroad became the axis of a long string of pioneer farm settlements stretching all the way across southern Siberia to Vladivostok.

The Revolutions of 1917. Russia on the eve of World War I was a vast and loosely articulated country. Its railroads were inadequate to serve so vast an area, and highways scarcely existed. Except for the heavy industries of the Donbass, and the numerous factories of Petrograd (St. Petersburg) and Moscow, most of the country remained rural and agricultural. Oil from Baku on the Caspian, manganese from Chiatura in Georgia, gold from the valley of the Vitim River, a tributary of the Lena in Siberia, provided the chief mineral exports. But politically and socially the country remained in a poor condition. The aristocracy lived quite well, and those who were grouped around the tsar enjoyed a cosmopolitan life not unlike that elsewhere in Europe. Furthermore, in Moscow and Petrograd there were many brilliant Russian scientists and engineers, many outstanding writers and composers. But the middle class was very small, and most Russians were poor and illiterate, with little hope of bettering their condition. The tsar held final and complete authority; and his government was corrupt and inefficient. The country was held together by the operations of a secret police, by the transfer of thousands of troublemakers to Siberia, and by the power of the army.

The spirit of revolt against the established form of government and against the whole system of privilege and inequality had been boiling beneath the surface for decades, until it broke out on the defeat of the Russian army by the Germans in World War I. In March,[1] 1917, liberals, who believed in the ideals of democracy, assumed leadership of the movement of popular discontent and set up a provisional government. But the liberals were confronted by the collapse of the tsarist system into many conflicting parties, each with its own program for political change. The Bolsheviks called for the formation of a socialist state, but there were other groups working for the preservation of the monarchy, and there were many who

[1] The old Russian calendar, still in use at that time, dated the first revolution in February rather than March. The second revolution which took place on November 7 is still known as the "October Revolution."

merely watched events but took no part in them. This was the situation on November 7, 1917, when Lenin, with the support of the Congress of Soviets, declared that the government was in the hands of the "people's commissars," appointed from the ranks of the Bolshevik party.

Since 1917 the Russian Empire has been transformed into a modern socialist state. Many of the policies adopted by the leaders are based on old Russian traditions that go back to the culture hearth of the ninth century; but many others are derived from the writings of Marx and Lenin. Since 1928 the industrial sector of the economy has been built up rapidly under a succession of "five-year plans."

Population. The population of the Soviet Union is enormous, and it is still in the process of rapid growth. According to the census of 1939 the population was 170,467,-000; the census of 1959 counted 208,826,650; and in 1962 estimates gave the Soviet Union 221,000,000. The distribution of the population over the national territory is shown on Map 1 (pp. 4-5). Most of the population is concentrated in the triangle between the Black Sea, the Gulf of Finland, and the southern part of the Ural Mountains, which constitutes the core of the Soviet state. Outlying clusters of people are found on either side of the Caucasus Mountains, in the oases of Central Asia, and are spread out eastward in a long string of settlements all the way to the Pacific. A very large part of the national territory is empty, or very thinly populated.

The sweep of the Industrial Revolution into this country is reflected in the increased proportion of the population grouped together in cities. The census of 1926 showed only 18 per cent of the total living in cities; but by 1939 the proportion of city people had reached 32 per cent, and by 1959 it had reached 48 per cent. In 1959 there were three

Government operated open-air book shops are common in the U.S.S.R.
This one is in Kiev in the Ukraine. (Photo by E. Demarest Peterson)

great conurbations of more than a million each. These were Moscow (Moskva), with 7,300,000 in its metropolitan area, Leningrad (formerly Petrograd), with 3,500,000 and Kiev, with about 1,000,000. Other cities of nearly a million included Baku, Gorkiy, Kharkov, Tashkent, Novosibirsk, and Kuybyshev (Map 36). In 1961 it was decided to prevent the further growth of these very large cities by surrounding the urban areas with "green belts" in which very little building is to be permitted. Further growth is to be directed into satellite cities, the optimum size of which is conceived to be 100,000.

Four chief clusters of cities can be seen. The largest cluster includes both Moscow and Leningrad together with 143 other smaller cities. A second cluster centers on Sverdlovsk in the Ural Mountains, including about 100 urban centers. A third cluster of about 50 cities is in the Donbass between Dnepropetrovsk and Rostov. And a fourth cluster, with 14 cities, is in the Kuznetsk Basin around Novosibirsk and Novo Kuznetsk. The remainder of the Soviet cities are more widely scattered.

Included in the population of the Soviet Union there are more than sixty different ethnic groups, speaking eleven major languages (Map 35). Great Russians form almost 55 per cent of the total (53 per cent in 1926). Ukrainians form nearly 18 per cent (21 per cent in 1926), and Byelorussians nearly 4 per cent (3 per cent in 1926). These chief Slavic groups form 77 per cent of the total. The other 23 per cent includes

SOVIET CULTURE REGION
SURFACE FEATURES AND POLITICAL DIVISIONS

80°   10°

North Sea

N O R W A Y

S W E D E N

GERMAN
FEDERAL
REPUBLIC

GERMAN
DEM. REPUBLIC

•Berlin

Baltic   *Sea*

Gulf of Finland

F I N L A N D

•Murmansk

NOVAYA ZE

•Prague

AUSTRIA

CZECHOSLOVAKIA

P O L A N D

Klaipėda

Ventspils

Riga

LITHUANIAN S.S.R.

LATVIAN S.S.R.

ESTONIAN S.S.R.

Lake Ladoga

White Sea

•Arkhangelsk

•Warsaw

BYELORUSSIAN
S.S.R.

•Minsk

Leningrad

Zagreb•

Budapest•

HUNGARY

•Split

YUGOSLAVIA

•Belgrade

UKRAINIAN S.S.R.

•Kiev

•Moscow

R U S S I A N

•Gorkiy

•Tiranë
ALBANIA

ROMANIA

MOLDAVIAN S.S.R.

•Sofia

BULGARIA

•Bucharest

•Odessa

Dnepr R.

•Kharkov

•Kazan

•Perm

•Sverdlovsk

CRIMEAN
PENINSULA

•Donetsk

Saratov

•Kuybyshev

•Ufa

•Chelyabinsk

T U R K E Y

Black Sea

•Sochi

•Rostov

Don R.

Volga R.

•Volgograd

•Magnitogorsk

KAZAKHSTAN   S.S.R.

•Pyatigorsk

•Astrakhan

GEORGIAN

Ural R.

•Batumi

•Ordzhonikidze

Tbilisi•

ARMENIAN S.S.R.

Yerevan

SYRIA

AZERBAYDZAN S.S.R.

AZERBAYDZAN
S.S.R. •Baku

*Aral
Sea*

Lake Balk

I R A Q

Caspian Sea

UZBEKISTAN
S.S.R.

•Tashkent

KIRGHIZIA S.S.R.

TURKMENISTAN
S.S.R.

•Samarkand

Amu Darya

•Dyushambe

I R A N

TADZHIKISTAN S.S.

– – – – Southern limit of Glaciation

AFGHANISTAN

many national minorities with distinctive languages or religions—such as the Muslims of Uzbek, the Georgians and Armenians south of the Caucasus Mountains, the Baltic nationalities, and the numerous tribes of Siberia.

During World War II the non-Russians who were accused of giving aid to the invading Germans were moved eastward. A colony of Germans on the Volga River, groups of Tatars still in the Crimea, and several tribes of formerly nomadic peoples from the Caucasus Mountains, were transferred to Siberia or to Central Asia. Some Russians from the densely populated parts of the country were sent to the part of East Prussia from which the Germans were expelled, or to the southern part of Sakhalin Island from which the Japanese were driven out.

The non-Russian minorities have generally been granted "cultural autonomy" and have formed their own political units. These are "national in form and socialist in content," which means that they make use of their own language (although Russian is also taught in the schools), and encourage local artistic productions, but must conform politically to the policies laid down by the Communist Party of the Soviet Union.

The political subdivisions which give expression to these various ethnic and national groups are shown on Map 36, and listed at the beginning of this chapter. Although Byelorussia and the Ukraine are members of the United Nations, they are recognized by the United States as constituent members of the Soviet Union. The United States does not recognize the incorporation of Estonia, Latvia, and Lithuania into the Soviet Union.

Agriculture. To provide food for such large numbers of people has called for tremendous effort. Actually the agricultural problems are still far from solved, and it is commonly recognized that this sector of the economy has been the least successful. To understand the existing situation, we need to go back to the period before World War I, and to trace the changes in the geography of agriculture that have been made since then.

Changes in the Agricultural System. Agriculture, in 1914, was still inefficient. To be sure, the tsars had long been exporting large amounts of timber and furs, wheat, flax, hemp, potatoes, and sugar beets. One of the chief reasons why so poor a country could export so much wheat was because the peasants were too poor to eat wheat bread, and lived, instead, on rye bread. Only around Kiev in the Ukraine had new ideas in agricultural practices been adopted: here wheat crops were rotated with potatoes, sugar beets, and hay crops, and some animal manure was used. Elsewhere in the Black-Earth Belt it was common to plant winter wheat and spring wheat in sequence and then leave the field fallow for a year. In poorer areas it was usual to cultivate wheat for two to six years, and then leave the field fallow for five to twenty years. Furthermore, most of the farm areas were so poorly served by railroads that they remained isolated. The large landowners did little to improve the use of their vast estates, and the collective farm villages, where the land was used in common as it had been in the ancient Slavic culture hearth, had neither the capital nor the skills to improve farming methods. Land redistribution programs before 1914 had divided some of the communal village lands among the peasants, so that by the beginning of World War I there were millions of small privately-owned farms. About half of the peasants in the European part of Russia owned their

Workers threshing wheat on a Kolkhoz (collective farm) in the Ukraine. (Photo by E. Demarest Peterson)

own farms. But only in the Ukraine did they start to adopt new farm practices to increase yields.

After the Revolution of 1917 the Communist Party undertook to reorganize the agricultural system. The confiscation of large estates received great popular approval, but the first attempts to establish collective farms were resisted. A compromise had to be reached, and the continuation of the system of private peasant farms was permitted—the peasant proprietors were known as *kulaks*. The continuation of the system of private ownership did not last long; as soon as the government felt strong enough to carry through a revision of the agricultural system it did so. By 1938 the kulak class had been liquidated, and the peasants had been grouped together in government-operated state farms (*Sovkhoz*) and large

collective farms (*Kolkhoz*). In 1938 there were 3,961 state farms; by 1958 the number had been increased to 5,905. Most of the new state farms were located in areas of special climatic hazard, for instance on the dry margins or in the far north. In 1938 there were 242,400 collective farms, but by 1958 the number had been reduced to 76,535, partly by combining them into larger units. On state farms the directors were appointed by the government and the workers were paid wages. On collective farms the directors were elected by the members, and each farmer received a share of the profits in proportion to the amount of work he had performed. In 1961 the Communist Party announced its intention of taking the next step from socialism to communism: namely to require work from each member of a collective in proportion to

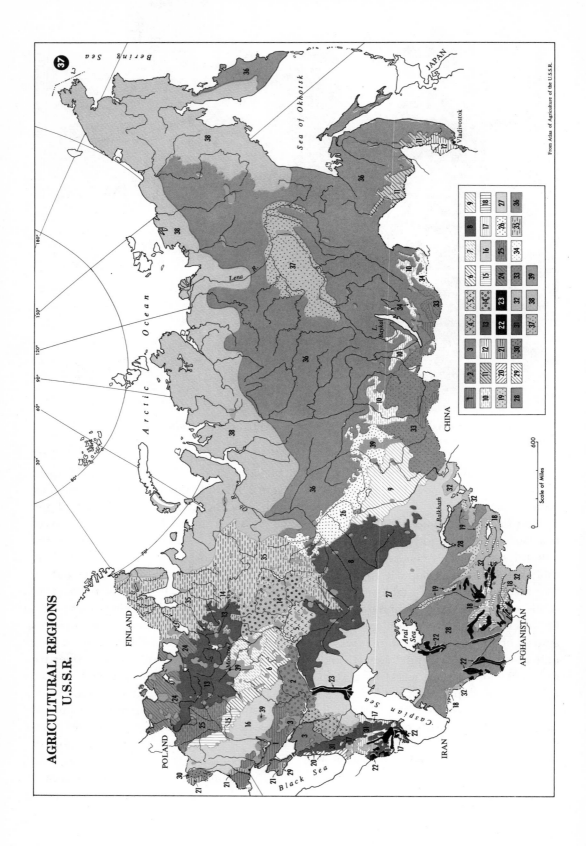

AGRICULTURAL REGIONS
U.S.S.R.

From Atlas of Agriculture of the U.S.S.R.

Scale of Miles

0   600

THE AGRICULTURAL REGIONS OF THE U.S.S.R.

1. Grain, sunflower, and other oil crops, together with hemp, tobacco, sugar beets, fruits, and vegetables; dairy and beef cattle, and wool-sheep in the Moldavian and Ukrainian S.S.R.S.

2. Grain and sunflower, together with leguminous crops and rice; beef and dairy cattle, hogs, and wool sheep along the Volga.

3. Grain, sugar beets, and sunflowers, together with hemp, tobacco, rice, fruits and vineyards; beef and dairy cattle, hogs, poultry, and wool sheep in the northern Caucasus.

4. Grain and cattle, together with sunflowers; meat and dairy cattle, and wool sheep in the northern Caucasus.

5. Grain and cattle, together with legumes, potatoes, sugar beets and vegetables; beef and dairy cattle, and hogs in the woodland steppe east of the Volga.

6. Grain, sugar beets, and hemp, together with sunflower and other oil crops, vegetables and fruits, beef and dairy cattle, hogs, and poultry in the chernozem zone.

7. Potatoes, vegetables, dairy cattle, hogs, and poultry, together with flax, hemp, sugar beets, fruits, and berries north of the chernozem zone.

8. Spring wheat, together with oil crops, meat and dairy cattle, and wool sheep in the black-earth belt.

9. Spring wheat, together with sugar beets, sunflowers, beef and dairy cattle, and wool sheep in western Siberia and eastern Kazakhstan.

10. Grain and beef cattle, with small areas of sugar beets and flax.

11. Grain, soy beans, beef and dairy cattle, together with potatoes and vegetables in eastern Siberia.

12. Wheat, rice, soy beans, sugar beets, livestock, combined with hunting, reindeer herding, and bee-keeping.

13. Flax and dairy cattle, together with potatoes, vegetables, and hogs in the non-chernozem zone of Byelorussia and Russia.

14. Flax and livestock, together with grains, potatoes, vegetables in the upper Volga and northern Urals.

15. Flax and hemp, together with potatoes, hogs, beef and dairy cattle in the Ukraine.

16. Sugar beets and winter wheat, together with other grains, hemp, flax, tobacco, fruits and vegetables, beef and dairy cattle, in the central chernozem zone.

17. Fruit, vineyards, vegetables, together with grain, tobacco, sugar beets, and livestock in the northern Caucasus and south of the Caucasus.

18. Fruit, vineyards, and livestock in central Asia.

19. Meat and wool sheep, Astrakhan fur, and grains, in central Asia.

20. Tea and citrus fruits on the Black Sea and the Caspian coasts.

21. Vineyards, fruits, vegetables, and some tobacco in Moldavia, the Ukraine, and the Crimean Peninsula.

22. Irrigated cotton, together with fruits, vineyards, and silk production.

23. Irrigated vegetables along the lower Volga.

24. Beef and dairy cattle, and hogs, together with flax, sugar beets, potatoes, and vegetables along the Baltic coast.

25. Dairy and beef cattle, and hogs, together with potatoes, sugar beets, flax, and hemp in Byelorussia.

26. Dairy cattle and spring wheat, together with other grains, flax, hemp, and saffron in western Siberia.

27. Semiarid grazing land with beef and dairy cattle, meat and wool sheep, and some small areas of grain farming.

28. Arid grazing land with meat and wool sheep.

29. Mountain pasture for meat and wool sheep in the Crimea.

30. Mountain pasture for meat and wool sheep, beef and dairy cattle, and small areas of vineyards in the Carpathians.

31. Mountain pasture for meat and wool sheep, beef and dairy cattle in the Caucasus.

32. Mountain pasture for meat and wool sheep, beef and dairy cattle in central Asia.

33. Mountain pasture for meat and wool sheep, beef and dairy cattle in eastern Siberia.

34. Meat and wool sheep, beef and dairy cattle, with some agriculture in Siberia.

35. Fur and sea animals, hunting, some dairying, and small areas of barley, hay, and potatoes in northern Europe.

36. Hunting of fur and game animals, reindeer herding, fishing, and small areas of dairying and crop farming in Siberia.

37. Beef and dairy cattle, horses, grains, and the Yakut fur industry of Siberia.

38. Reindeer herding on the tundra.

39. Intensive agriculture (potatoes, vegetables, fruits, and berries), beef and dairy cattle.

individual ability, and to reward each member in proportion to his needs. Meanwhile, to keep the farmers in a cooperative mood, individuals are being permitted a piece of land on which to grow crops and pasture a cow or a pig; and the products of these small plots can be used by the family or be sold in local markets to provide additional income. There are reports which suggest that these privately-operated plots of land are among the most productive of the Soviet agricultural areas.

The Distribution of Agriculture. Map 37 shows the distribution of agriculture in the Soviet Union. The best conditions for grain farming are to be found in the Black-Earth Belt which extends eastward from the Ukraine in a narrowing zone, squeezed between aridity to the south and the shortness of the growing season to the north. The agricultural heartland of the Soviet Union is a little smaller than the major agricultural area of the United States (386,000,000 acres under crops compared with 440,000,000 acres in Anglo-America). But even in this most favored region natural disasters recur at unpredictable intervals. In 1921-1922 something like 5,000,000 people died of starvation, and famine conditions came again in 1932-1933. The effect of droughts is worsened, moreover, by the fact that the fundamental revision of the agricultural system is not yet completed.

Communists do not accept the idea that man is limited by his natural surroundings, or that science and engineering cannot transform the habitat so that natural disasters are reduced or eliminated. One step toward this transformation has been the mechanization of the farms. Collective farms are easier to mechanize than smaller privately-owned farms would be, especially when the fields are not fenced and there are no property lines to consider. In 1938 there were already 483,500 tractors in operation on Soviet farms, and by 1958 this number had been increased to 1,699,700. Machines make possible the cultivation of large areas where yields per acre are small, and help to make droughts less disastrous.

Another, less successful, effort to minimize the effect of climatic hazards has been the program to develop strips of forest as shelter belts in the treeless steppes and prairies. Such a program proved ineffective when it was tried in the United States in 1934, and it has proved equally ineffective in the Soviet Union. The plan, as adopted in 1948, was to plant a complicated pattern of forest strips covering a total of 15,000,-000 acres. These were to give protection from the drying, cold air masses of winter, and also from the hot winds of summer, over about 300,000,000 acres. In addition, it was planned to build 4400 ponds and small reservoirs to conserve water. In fact shelter belts do not shelter beyond the immediate vicinity of the trees, and the trees take so much water from the soil that the crops near them suffer.

Much more spectacular is the project to reverse the flow of the Ob River. The divide between the headwaters of the Irtysh, and of the rivers that drain southward toward the Aral Sea, is very low. The proposal is to build a long earth dam behind which the spring floods of the Ob and its tributaries would be caught. Then, by dredging a shallow channel through the divide this large volume of water would be turned southward into the dry region north of the Aral Sea, where potentially productive soils, now used only for dry farming and sheep grazing, could be put to better use. The technical and economic feasibility of such a gigantic scheme is still under study.

Within the agricultural area certain localities are developing in which specialized farming is concentrated. Such specialization in land use is found around the larger cities, where the farmers grow cabbages, potatoes, and beets, and pasture dairy cattle. Along the Black Sea coast from the south-facing slope of the Crimea eastward there is a narrow fringe of vineyards, and to the north of the mountains there are specialized areas devoted to fruit orchards. Near the eastern end of the Black Sea in Georgia there are tea plantations.

The greatest development of irrigated agriculture has been in Central Asia. Since the beginning of the first five-year plan in 1928 the Soviet government has greatly expanded the irrigated area. The ancient oasis towns which were trading centers on caravan routes thousands of years ago, such as Tashkent, Samarkand, Kokand, and Bukhara, have been revitalized and given a modern appearance as a result of the expansion of irrigated crops. Large dams and irrigation canals have been built. The Great Fergana Canal, two hundred miles long, brings water to the important Fergana oasis around Kokand. The oasis of Tashkent is supplied with water from a tributary of the Syr Darya. Both the Syr Darya and the Amu Darya support oases far out across the desert almost as far as the Aral Sea. The major crop in Soviet Central Asia is cotton, but there are also large acreages of wheat grown on land that is not irrigated. Other irrigated crops include sugar beets, sesame, fruits, flax, tobacco, rice, and alfalfa. The irrigated area of Uzbek around Tashkent produces about 60 per cent of the cotton in the Soviet Union. There is one place, where the Amu Darya forms the border between the Soviet Union and Afghanistan, that the Soviet tourist guides delight in visiting to point out the advantages of communism. On the Soviet side of the river the landscape reminds one of southern California—rich plantations of cotton, extensive orange groves, productive vineyards, and thriving towns; just across the river is Afghanistan with its rude villages of Afghan shepherds, whose only prized possession is their freedom.

Apart from these irrigated areas, and the spots of specialized agriculture, the different crop combinations occupy broad bands, more or less corresponding to the zones of climate and soils. In the south, among the spots of specialized agriculture, the crop combination includes oranges, grapes, tobacco, cotton, and winter wheat. To the north of this, on the former grasslands, is the zone of mixed farming: winter wheat, maize, sunflowers, hemp, sugar beets, and tobacco, together with pasture for beef and dairy cattle. Within the zone of park grassland and the southern part of the seasonal forest the crops include spring wheat and winter rye, and also maize, barley, and oats, together with some hemp. Here agriculture is combined with the raising of hogs. Farther north, where the summers are too cool and the growing season too short for the best crop yields, there is a zone of flax and grass pasture for dairy herds. In the taiga there are only scattered agricultural clearings used to raise barley, hay, and potatoes, and to feed beef cattle.

Farm settlements have also spread eastward along the Trans-Siberian Railroad, even as far as Vladivostok. In the narrowing agricultural area that extends along the Black-Earth Belt beyond the Urals as far as the Kuznetsk Basin, the farms are used to pasture beef and dairy cattle, and to grow such crops as spring wheat, rye, barley, oats, and flax. Farther to the east, in the Amur Valley east of Lake Baykal, pioneer settlers grow spring wheat and rye. The formerly nomadic peoples of Siberia who once moved their sheep from lowland to mountain with the seasons, and the reindeer herders of the far north who moved from taiga to tundra in the summer, and back again in winter— all have now been established in fixed settlements. Sheep, cattle, and reindeer are still pastured, but during the winter the animals are fed on hay raised during the summer. Vegetables, including cabbages and potatoes, are grown along the river valleys, even north of the Arctic Circle. In the valley lowland that extends north of Vladivostok the chief crops are spring wheat, rice, soybeans, sugar beets and vegetables, and the pastures are used to feed beef and dairy cattle.

Considering the climatic handicaps, even of the best agricultural lands, the Soviet government has made important strides toward increasing the supply of food products and fibers. The irrigated lands have been greatly extended, and although serious problems of salt accumulation have arisen in some places, the productivity of the dry lands has been significantly increased. The agriculture of the grasslands has been diversified to permit crop rotation, and animals are combined with agriculture to provide manure for fertilizer. Farming has been largely mechanized, which allows for the cultivation of large areas where yields are low. Still, the climatic hazards remain: desiccating winds dry out the land, and dust storms blow away the good top soil; crop failures due to summer frosts or droughts bring food shortages. The Soviet scientists have not yet learned how to control the weather.

Mining and Industry. In the transformation of the economy the most spectacular successes have been made in the mining and industrial sectors. The transformation was recognized as essential when Stalin, in 1925, stated that the basic purpose of government would be to make the country a major

industrial producer as rapidly as possible. Stalin gave heavy industry priority over consumer goods. In 1928 the first of a succession of "five-year plans" set production goals in mining and industry. Under Stalin's direction the Industrial Revolution, which had been started before 1917, was completed, and the economy of the Soviet Union advanced to a stage of maturity.

Russia entered the initial phase of the Industrial Revolution about 1890. However, credit for recognizing the need for economic development goes to Peter the Great, who turned the attention of his people westward to the more advanced European countries. One of the preliminary steps, toward the introduction of the new technology, was taken when the iron and steel industry was shifted from the Ural district, where the fuel was charcoal, to the Donbass. Russia was well along in the process of technological change when World War I began. By 1914 the country was producing some 4,000,000 tons of iron and steel per year, and some 40,000,000 tons of coal. After the communist take-over in 1917 there followed a decade of reconstruction and reorganization before the drive to maturity could be started again.

Since 1928 the production of both coal and steel has been increased rapidly. In 1928 the Soviet Union produced only about one tenth as much coal as was produced in Great Britain and Germany combined. By 1959, however, Soviet production reached 558,320,000 tons, which was greater than the production of both Great Britain and Germany, or the production of the United States. During the same period the Soviet Union changed from being a very minor producer of steel, to a major producer, second only to the United States. In 1959 the Soviet Union produced 19 per cent of the world's steel and 20 per cent of the world's

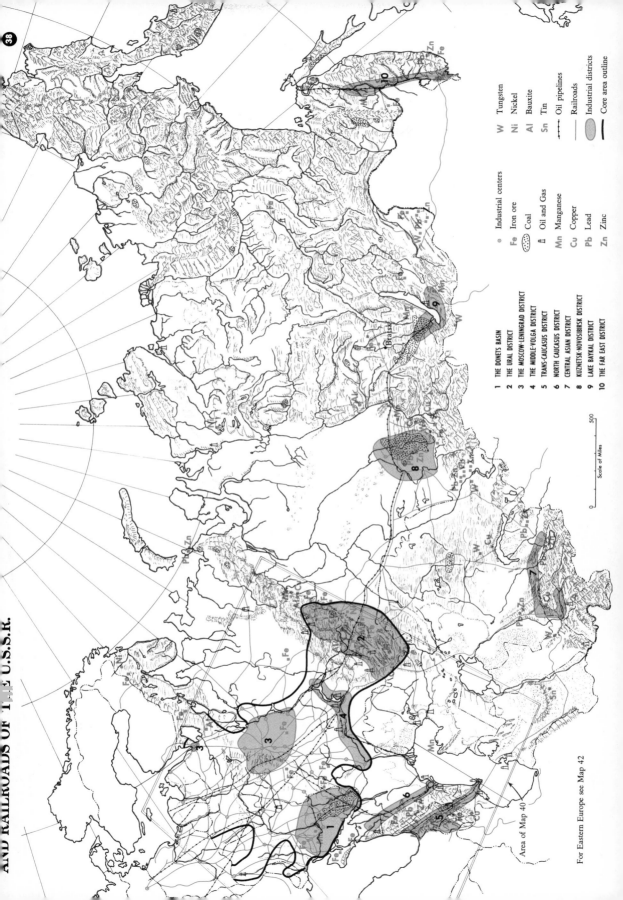

INDUSTRIAL CENTERS AND RAILROADS OF THE U.S.S.R.

Industrial centers
Fe Iron ore
Coal
Oil and Gas

Mn Manganese
Cu Copper
Pb Lead
Zn Zinc

W   Tungsten
Ni Nickel
Al Bauxite
Sn Tin

Oil pipelines
Railroads
Industrial districts
Core area outline

1 THE DONETS BASIN
2 THE URAL DISTRICT
3 THE MOSCOW-LENINGRAD DISTRICT
4 THE MIDDLE-VOLGA DISTRICT
5 TRANS-CAUCASUS DISTRICT
6 NORTH CAUCASUS DISTRICT
7 CENTRAL ASIAN DISTRICT
8 KUZNETSK-NOVOSIBIRSK DISTRICT
9 LAKE BAYKAL DISTRICT
10 THE FAR EAST DISTRICT

Area of Map 40

For Eastern Europe see Map 42

Scale of Miles
0   500

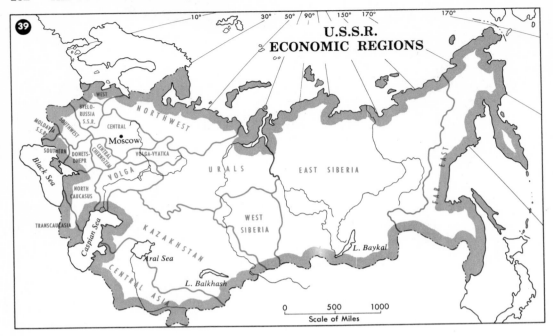

coal (as compared with the United States which produced 27 per cent of the steel and 16 per cent of the coal). From an economic point of view, the Soviet Union achieved the status of a mature economy about 1950.

It is important, however, to observe the contrasts between the process of economic growth in the Soviet Union and in Western Europe or Anglo-America. In both cases the postponement of consumption was a necessary aspect of development, together with the investment of a portion of the gross national product in new capital formation. In Great Britain this phase of development was carried out during the first half of the nineteenth century, and was possible because the owners of capital preferred to invest money in new capital rather than spend their profits for personal pleasure, and because the workers were paid wages as low as conditions permitted. This was the situation described by Karl Marx, on

which he based his predictions about the collapse of the capitalist system. In the Soviet Union, by decree rather than persuasion, some 25 to 30 per cent of the gross national product has been invested in new capital formation. This represents a very great postponement of consumption, and the ones who are being asked to carry the economic burden are the farmers and the industrial workers.

According to Soviet plans the standard of living of the industrial workers is to be raised substantially during the 1960's. In every city there is a large amount of new construction—of standard apartment buildings housing sixty families. By 1970 it is planned to provide every family with a private apartment, allowing two rooms to each family of three or four people. The investment of new capital is to be diverted from the heavy industries into consumer goods, so that there will be a large increase in the use of vacuum cleaners, refrigerators,

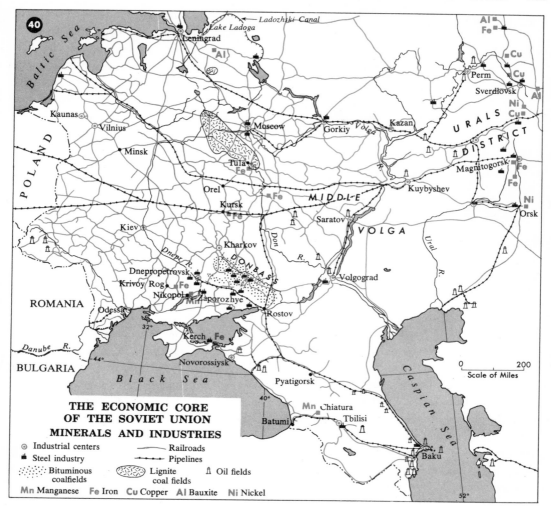

40

THE ECONOMIC CORE
OF THE SOVIET UNION
MINERALS AND INDUSTRIES

⊙ Industrial centers   Railroads
▪ Steel industry   Pipelines
⋰⋱ Bituminous   Lignite   ⌂ Oil fields
     coalfields   coal fields
Mn Manganese   **Fe** Iron   **Cu** Copper   **Al** Bauxite   **Ni** Nickel

Scale of Miles — 0 ... 200

and other household gadgets which up to now have been priced beyond the reach of the average worker. But even if the plans are carried through, the Soviet workers will achieve, by 1965, a standard of living (as measured by the purchase of food, clothing, and housing) about half that of the workers of the European Economic Community.

Economic Regions. In 1957 the process of economic planning in the Soviet Union underwent a fundamental change. Instead of planning by industry for the country as a whole, with decisions on all important

questions being made in Moscow, the program of development was decentralized. The national territory was divided into seventeen economic regions (Map 39), each with a planning council to direct its development. The whole planning operation was co-ordinated at the national level. Each region is now to make its own distinctive contribution to the national economy, based on its endowment of resources; but each will be able to supply itself with a sufficient diversity of products—including steel, textiles, and processed foods—so that it can be

Skilled workers turn out precision instruments in a Kiev factory. (Photo by E. Demarest Peterson)

operated as a more or less self-sufficient and independent unit. Furthermore, the various regions will be tied together by a network of electric power lines, and by pipelines for the shipment of oil and gas.

It is, nevertheless, important to note that this development of outlying regions was still in the planning stage in the early 1960's. In 1959 about 72 per cent of the manufacturing industry of the country was still concentrated in the core area shown on Map 40.[2]

The Industrial Districts: The Donbass. Russia's first modern steel industry was developed late in the nineteenth century in the Donbass. Although it is now known

[2] The percentages quoted on the following pages are from Richard E. Lonsdale and John H. Thompson, "A Map of the USSR's Manufacturing," *Economic Geography*, Vol. 36, 1960; pp. 36-52. The ratio of each industrial center to the total manufacturing of the Soviet Union was calculated by the use of a formula in which the number of workers employed in industry and the amount of fixed capital were balanced.

The formula: $M = \dfrac{En + Cn}{2}$ where M is the magnitude of manufacturing, En is employment as a percentage of the Soviet total, and Cn is the fixed capital as a percentage of the total. Data are from Soviet sources.

that this basin contains only 5 per cent of the coal in the Soviet Union (Map 38), this was, in the 1890's, the only accessible area where all the necessary raw materials were located close together. Iron ore of good quality came from Krivoy Rog, about three hundred miles to the west, and manganese was mined at Nikopol on the lower Dnepr River. Because more coal than iron ore was used in those days, the first steel plants were located at the coal fields. In modern times steel plants have also been built at Krivoy Rog, and at Kerch on the Crimean Peninsula where a large volume of low-grade ore has been found. Recently a major iron ore body—perhaps the largest in the world—has been discovered in a belt about ninety miles long by ten miles wide southeast of Kursk.

The industrial district built around the Donbass extends from Krivoy Rog to Rostov. A large dam on the Dnepr River at Zaporozhye, which was damaged by the Germans in World War II, has been rebuilt. From this and other dams comes an abundance of electric power. In 1959 the Donbass produced 40 per cent of the steel in the Soviet Union, and was responsible for 14 per cent of all Soviet manufacturing. The steel from this region is used to manufacture a variety of products.

The Ural District. The second of the great steel districts is in the Ural Mountains, where Peter the Great built Russia's first iron industry. In the nineteenth century the lack of coking coal in the Urals resulted in the decline of the old charcoal-based industry. But in this century, with the new technological skills, the steel plants are no longer so closely tied to the sources of coal. The Ural District is supplied with lignite, and is a major source of an amazing variety of minerals: iron ore, copper, nickel, chromium, manganese, tungsten, lead, zinc, bauxite, platinum, gold, asbestos, magnesium, and potash. At Magnitogorsk, Chelyabinsk, Sverdlovsk, and other small cities, there are steel plants, chemical plants, and many factories that make use of steel. Coking coal, however, has to be brought to this district all the way from the Kuznetsk Basin and Karaganda. The Ural District was responsible for 11.75 per cent of all Soviet manufacturing in 1959.

The Moscow-Leningrad Districts. The largest concentration of manufacturing industry in the Soviet Union is in, and around, the great city of Moscow. In this area are some 10 per cent of the people of the Soviet Union. These urban people provide the largest market for consumer goods, and also the largest reservoir of skilled workers. The manufacturing industries are varied: textiles, precision machinery, chemicals, tools, foods, and many others. Gorkiy is a center for the manufacture of automobiles and farm machinery. The whole Moscow District is abundantly supplied with electric power from both hydroelectric and steam-electric stations, now attached to a grid of transmission lines extending over the whole of the economic core area. Oil and gas are piped from the new Volga-Ural oil field. This district has 18.1 per cent of the country's manufacturing.

The city of Leningrad is also a major industrial center. When the first five-year plan was put into operation in 1928, the factories of Leningrad provided most of the industrial goods; but since the 1930's its share of the total has declined. Leningrad is still an important producer of tractors and other farm machines, textiles, tobacco products, and other consumer goods. More important, it is the major center for research and development, on which the future strength of the country depends. In 1959 it had 4.9 per cent of Soviet manufacturing.

The Middle Volga District. The long-neglected Middle Volga is now the Soviet Union's most rapidly expanding industrial district. For a long time, after the rise of Russian power under Ivan the Terrible, the Middle Volga was the eastern boundary of the state. In the centuries that followed, the land to the west of the Volga was divided into large private estates, with villages of serfs who worked on them. The country to the east of the Volga, on the other hand, remained sparsely occupied by nomadic herders. Under Peter the Great the steppes west of the Volga became the chief export-wheat region. When the serfs were freed in 1861, many pioneer farmers crossed the Volga to settle on the virgin land beyond the old frontier. This was the beginning of the great eastward sweep of farm settlement along the Black-Earth Belt. On the Volga near Saratov a colony of German farmers was established. The Volga itself was used only for navigation. Because of its low gradient, its high annual floods in April and May, the rapid drop of the water level to low-water stage in summer, and the fact that it freezes over for four months every winter, the Volga posed serious problems, both for navigation and for hydroelectric development. Even in 1937, at the end of the second five-year plan, nothing had been done about the Volga except to draw up plans. The rapid development of the Middle Volga District only began after World War II.

There are two elements in the development of this new industrial district; and one is oil. With the approaching exhaustion of the Caspian oil fields around Baku, Soviet geologists undertook an intensive search for new fields. They found and began the development of a new source of oil in the area between the Urals and the Middle Volga, known as the "Second Baku." In 1950 this area was still producing only about 25 per cent of Soviet oil, but by 1956 it was producing more than 66 per cent. Furthermore, it is now known that this field contains a very large reserve, perhaps the largest in the whole national territory. As a result of increased oil production from this new field the Soviet Union is now an oil exporter. In 1960 coal was still providing some 66 per cent of the fuel requirements of the country, but by 1972 it is planned to satisfy a major part of these requirements with oil. Oil from Kuybyshev and gas from Saratov are now piped to Moscow and other industrial areas. Oil is pumped from Kuybyshev to oil refineries on the Caspian Sea which were formerly supplied from Baku. And it is now also being brought to the new industrial district along the Angara River north of Irkutsk.

The industrial development of the Middle Volga District is not based on oil alone. It is also supported by a vast electric power supply derived from the Volga River. In 1954 the first dam was completed on a Volga tributary near Perm. In 1958 the big dam on the Volga itself, just upstream from Kuybyshev, was completed—a huge structure 2,300 feet long and more than 260 feet high. The Volga is being transformed into a continuous string of artificial lakes extending all the way from Volgograd (formerly Stalingrad) to north of Moscow. The water thus stored will be used to generate a tremendous amount of electric power, and then to irrigate the semiarid steppe country to the east of the lower Volga.

The new industrial development along the Middle Volga, centering on Volgograd and Kuybyshev, includes almost every kind of manufacturing except steel. There are cement plants, factories making huge turbines, machinery for boring wells, pumps, excavators, machine tools, automobiles, synthetic rubber and fibers, and alcohol. A new aluminum industry is served by the abundant electric power. As a result of all this growth, the population of the area has increased: between 1939 and 1959 the population of Kuybyshev more than doubled. In the latter year the Volga District was responsible for 5 per cent of Soviet manufacturing, but already this figure requires substantial revision.

Outlying Industrial Districts. In 1959 the economic core of the Soviet Union was responsible for 72.3 per cent of the manufacturing in the country. The rapid industrial growth of the Middle Volga District is producing an increase in this concentration. However, Soviet policy, as we have said, calls for economic development of the outlying regions. In 1959 there were six chief industrial concentrations outside the core area (Map 38).

The largest of the outlying districts is the Kuznetsk Basin, which, in 1959, was responsible for 4.05 per cent of Soviet manufacturing. A field of good bituminous coal has supported the development of a large steel industry at Novo Kuznetsk (formerly Stalinsk). In nearby cities, notably Novosibirsk, there are numerous industries that make use of steel in the manufacture of metal goods and machinery. There are also chemical plants, food-processing plants, and others.

Another very large concentration of manufacturing is located south of the Caucasus Mountains around Baku, the chief city and capital of Azerbaydzhan, and Tbilisi, the chief city and capital of Georgia. This district also extends westward to the eastern shore of the Black Sea. Within it are several sources of mineral raw materials, most important of which is the world's largest supply of manganese at Chiatura. Baku was already at the center of Russia's largest oil field. But there are also supplies of both coal and iron ore. At Rustavi, about twenty miles southeast of Tbilisi, a new steel plant has been built to provide support for further industrial development in this

A dam and hydroelectric plant that is being built on the Volga River, ten miles upstream from the center of Volgograd (formerly Stalingrad). (Photo by E. Demarest Peterson)

economic region. In 1959 this district as a whole included 4.0 per cent of Soviet industry.

A third outlying district is located north of the Caucasus Mountains. There are two oil fields in this region, and Groznyy, at the eastern end of the area, is another major oil refining center. In addition to refining, the industries of this area include machinery, textiles, and food processing. In 1959 the district embraced 2.1 per cent of Soviet industry.

A fourth industrial district is located in Central Asia, centering on Tashkent in Uzbek. Along with the development of irrigation in this area, hydroelectric power is being generated; and manufacturing industries have been built which make use of local raw materials. There are sugar refineries and other food-processing plants, factories making cotton and wool textiles, leather and metal goods, and agricultural machinery. This manufacturing formed 2.65 per cent of the Soviet total in 1959.

The fifth outlying district, and the one with the greatest potential for growth, is located on either side of Lake Baykal, centering on Irkutsk on the west, and Ulan-Ude on the east. In 1959 this district was only beginning to be developed, and accounted for only 1.35 per cent of the Soviet total. The economic planners, however, have recognized the enormous resource endowment of the Angara Valley. The Angara River, which is the outlet for Lake Baykal, is characterized by a remarkably even flow of water, and none of the seasonal extremes common with other Soviet rivers. Furthermore, the descent from 1,486 feet above sea level at the outlet of the lake to about 700 feet at Bratsk, 400 miles away, means that along this river are some of the finest potential water power sites in the whole Soviet Union. Electric power is now generated at Irkutsk and Bratsk, and these places are connected by transmission lines with the largest hydroelectric station of all at Krasnoyarsk on the Yenisey River. The

Angara Valley has other resources also. One of the Soviet Union's major coal fields has been discovered along this valley. On both sides of Lake Baykal there are ores of iron, manganese, tungsten, lead, zinc, and tin. On the hills bordering the Angara Valley are fine stands of pine and larch that have scarcely been touched. An oil and gas pipeline from the Volga-Ural oil field has been built to Irkutsk. This city, long famous as the outfitting point for gold miners on their way to the gold fields along the Lena Valley, is rapidly becoming a center of diversified manufacturing and the heart of a developing economic region.

The sixth of the outlying industrial districts is in eastern Siberia, along the lower Amur Valley and around Vladivostok. There are coal mines, steel industries, and a variety of other kinds of manufacturing. In 1959 this district formed 1.85 per cent of the Soviet total.

All these areas of industrial concentration, including the core area comprising 72.3 per cent of Soviet industry, accounted for 86.4 per cent of the manufacturing in the Soviet Union in 1959. The balance of 13.6 per cent was scattered throughout the national territory.

Transportation. The vast distances which separate these various industrial districts place a heavy burden on the systems of transportation. In fact the very isolation of one district from another in terms of distance forces the policy of building self-contained, and more or less self-sufficient, economic units. The internal transportation facilities are quite inadequate to the task of providing the kind of economic integration which is found within the United States and Western Europe.

Highways in the Soviet Union are poorly developed. In the Russia of the tsars the country roads became almost impassable during spring and early summer, even for horse-drawn wagons. Only in winter, when sleighs and sleds could move easily over snow-covered, frozen surfaces, was land travel even relatively easy. There were, and still are, two chief difficulties: first, is the great distance between villages; and second, is the general lack of road-building

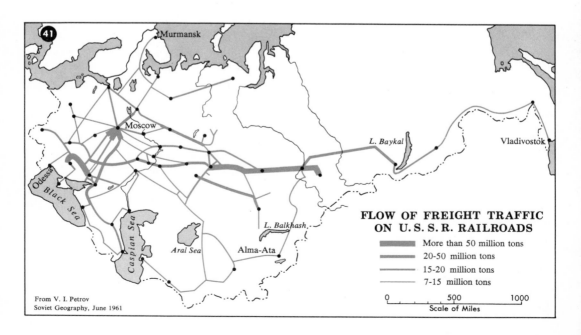

FLOW OF FREIGHT TRAFFIC
ON U.S.S.R. RAILROADS

	More than 50 million tons
	20-50 million tons
	15-20 million tons
	7-15 million tons

From V. I. Petrov
Soviet Geography, June 1961

Scale of Miles

materials, including gravel. During the period of rapid economic growth since 1928, the government has built dams, power lines, and other facilities, but has scarcely touched the highway problem.

Railroads have been of special importance in providing distant connections within the Soviet Union, yet they, also, are quite inadequate. The tsars built railroads in the western part of the country, radiating from Moscow over most of the area west of the Urals. In order to guard against the use of the railroads by invading armies from Europe, a broad gauge of five feet was adopted and became standard throughout the country (standard gauge in Western Europe is 4 ft. 8½ in.). After World War I a large part of the Russian rail system had to be entirely rebuilt. In 1917 there were only 35,000 miles of railroad that could be used, including the 4,268 miles of the Trans-Siberian Railroad which was double-tracked. By 1955 the Soviet government had nearly 75,000 miles in operation, but even this was not enough. The rail density in the Soviet Union is eleven times less than that of the United States and the railroads are not adequate to carry all the freight that needs to be transported.

The Soviet waterways are, therefore, a vital part of the economy. The chief development of these waterways has been in the area west of the Urals, where it is possible to ship goods by boat all the way from the Caspian Sea and the Black Sea to Leningrad on the Baltic, or to Arkhangelsk on the White Sea. To be sure the rivers, and the canals that tie them together, are navigable for only 150 to 200 days each year because of ice.

The Soviets have been successful in developing more or less regular navigation on the Arctic Sea route. In the west ice-free conditions extend around the northern tip of Norway as far as Murmansk, and ice-breakers can keep the channel open through the White Sea to Arkhangelsk. The ocean into which the Ob and Yenisey rivers empty has an open season, extending usually from July to October, because it is protected from the Arctic ice pack by islands (Map 34). To the east, all the way to the Bering Strait, the ice pack is driven onto the shore by the north winds, and prevents all navigation except during a brief summer period between July and September. Nevertheless, during this period ships, with the aid of a new nuclear-powered ice breaker, make trips along the Arctic coast, picking up lumber and other products sent down the rivers.

The Viability of the Soviet State. The Soviet Union is a strong and viable state. Its economy has reached maturity, and its people can hope for an improvement in living conditions and a decrease in work requirements. Although the state embraces numerous separate nationalities there is little or no demand for independence. To create a strong, viable state under these conditions, and in a habitat that does not yield easily to human effort, has been no slight accomplishment.

Communism is the state-idea that links the Soviet people together. An anthropologist would recognize the unchallenged faith in Marxism-Leninism as a kind of secular religion—a religion with its own prophets, scriptures, missionaries, and shrines (like the tomb of Lenin on Red Square in Moscow). Several generations of Soviet people have been brought up to embrace the new faith without question, and to serve the Communist Party without hesitation. The prophets tell of the impending collapse of the capitalist countries, and of the threat these countries pose to Soviet security. These people, whatever their nationality, have little doubt that the surest road to peace and security is through the complete spread of communism over the whole earth.

The Soviet state is also viable because it is strong economically, and growing stronger. The Soviet leaders have rebuilt the damage done in World War II, and have achieved a mature economy, which is varied and self-sustaining. The inadequacy of the transportation facilities has been compensated by the development of more or less self-contained parts, each with a capacity for continued growth. Economic growth is now moving ahead faster than population growth, with the result that the people can begin to feel relief from poverty.

A very large amount of thought and effort has gone into the educational system, with its emphasis on the training of scientists and engineers to carry on the work of research and development. The results are visible in the great dams, the huge electric plants, the new weapons, and the astronauts flying through space. All these accomplishments, too, form a part of the state-idea. What if the diet is a little monotonous; what if conditions are a little crowded in the one-room-per-family apartments; what if the lines are long at the meat counters, or at the stores where a few vacuum cleaners have been put on sale. These privations are made to seem temporary and worth while.

An important part of the analysis of the viability of the Soviet state is concerned with the barriers that isolate it from neighbors. In a more exposed geographic position the influence of the outside world could scarcely have been so minimized, and con-quests and invasions might have come from many directions, not only from the west. Along the whole long boundary that extends from the Caspian Sea to the Pacific Ocean there are only five railroads that cross into neighboring countries (Map 38): one enters China from the west, but has not yet been built across the vast deserts of inner Asia; one connects the Trans-Siberian Railroad with Ulan Bator in Mongolia, and continues on into China; another enters the eastern part of Mongolia; the other two are where the southern branch of the Trans-Siberian Railroad cuts across Manchuria to Vladivostok. There are no all-weather motor highways that cross the border. There are two air routes: one that connects Tashkent with Afghanistan, Pakistan, and India; and one that crosses from Irkutsk into Mongolia, and thence on into China. The fact that the Soviet Union borders China and the countries of Southwest Asia does not mean that there are close contacts.

Furthermore, the long coastline of the Soviet Union does not give the country easy access to the world ocean. Between Vladivostok and Murmansk every port is frozen for all but a few months in each year.

Only on the European side is the Soviet Union in close contact with bordering states, and from this direction have come repeated invasions. Now this vulnerable western border is sealed off from what the Soviets think of as the "unfriendly capitalist world" by a *cordon sanitaire* of communist-controlled states.

THE COUNTRIES OF EASTERN EUROPE

Eastern Europe is a zone of transition between maritime Europe, now included in the European Culture Region, and continental Eurasia, in which the Soviet Culture Region developed. It has long been a zone of conflict between the Germanic peoples and the invaders from the east—such as the Slavs, Magyars, and Turks. Before the eighth century A.D. the Slavs had moved westward beyond the River Elbe and had come into contact with the Germanic tribes. But over the centuries the Germanic peoples grew stronger and more numerous, and for a time they pushed eastward at the expense of the Slavs. German settlers moved down the valley of the Danube and along the plains south of the Baltic Sea (Maps 15 and 19, pp. 42 and 49). They even sent a colony far out to the east to settle in the midst of Slavic territory along the Volga River. The Slavs were able to resist the German pressure in places that were protected by barriers—marshes, swamps, densely forested mountains, or tracts of poor sandy soils. The Poles held on east of the swampy valley of the Vistula while the Germans pushed by them along the Baltic to the north, and along the Carpathian forelands to the south. The forested Erzgebirge and the Böhmerwald protected the salient of the Czechs in Bohemia. World War II reversed this trend, and the Slavs have moved westward again at the expense of the Germans.

Eastern Europe is the region where the Eurasian plains lead into maritime Europe. Where they lead toward the North Sea the plains are narrowed between the Carpathians and the Baltic. The plains along the Black Sea lead into the Wallachian Plain of Romania, and on up the valley of the Danube through the Plain of Hungary almost as far as Vienna. In the east, north of the Black Sea, these plains are grass-covered, and the grasslands point fingers of open land toward Poland and along the Danube through the Wallachian Plain and the Plain of Hungary (Map 8, pp. 16-17). The mountains were, and generally still are, densely forested—not only the high mountains such as the Carpathians, but also the low mountains and hilly uplands such as Transylvania, the Bakony Forest, the Bohemian Upland and its low mountain borders.

The division of this part of Europe into political units has gone through a succession of complicated changes. The maps on pages 54 and 55 show the political boundaries and states in 1721, 1914, 1940, and 1964. In 1721 most of Eastern Europe was claimed by four countries: Poland, Hungary, Turkey, and the Holy Roman Empire. By 1914 Poland had been gobbled up by Germany, Austria, and Russia, the Empire of Austria-Hungary embraced numerous contrasted ethnic groups, and the Balkan countries had appeared in the part of Europe then recently evacuated by the Turks. The boundaries of 1914 bore scant relation to the ethnic patterns or to the underlying terrain.

It is important to understand the distribution of the major religious faiths in Eastern Europe. In addition to relict groups of Muslims in the Balkan countries that were once part of the Ottoman Empire (for example, in Albania), there are two distinct forms of Christianity, one that spread from Rome and the other from Constantinople (Map 19). The Roman Catholic faith reached the Croats and Slovenes, the Magyars, the Czechs and Slovaks, the Poles, and the Slavic peoples along the eastern shore of the Baltic Sea. The Greek Orthodox faith reached the Serbs, the Bulgarians, the Romanians, and the Russians. The people in the area reached by the Greek Orthodox church generally use the Cyrillic alphabet, and those to the west use the Roman alphabet. The one exception is Romania, which uses the Roman alphabet but practices the Greek Orthodox faith.

After World War I the political boundaries in Eastern Europe were largely redrawn. With the breakup of the empires the numerous nationalities pressed their claims to independence, following the principle, so eloquently set forth by Woodrow Wilson, that well-defined national aspirations should be accorded the utmost satisfaction possible. Geographers made large-scale maps to show in detail the distribution of people speaking different languages. And an effort was made to draw boundaries in such a way that people of one language and nationality would find themselves included within the territory of one state. This did not prove to be as simple as it may sound. On the border of Germany and Poland it was found that the Germans were the more numerous in the cities, even in the midst of an almost solidly Polish rural population. Furthermore, East Prussia was clearly German, and Germans, intermingled with Poles, extended all along the Baltic coast. To give the new Polish state access to the sea, the so-called Polish Corridor was drawn across territory where Germans and Poles were mixed, separating East Prussia from the rest of Germany. The border between Germany and Czechoslovakia was also troublesome because Czechs were in a majority in the Bohemian Upland, but Germans were more numerous in the forested, mountain country around it. It was decided to give Czechoslovakia the advantage of a boundary drawn along the crest of the mountains. The Germans who were thus left inside Czechoslovakia provided an excuse for the German demand for a revision of the boundary in 1938.

In spite of every effort the new states inevitably included numerous and sometimes restive minorities. Germans were left inside Poland, and Poles inside Germany. Romania included small areas that were almost solidly German, and others, especially in Transylvania, where there were large numbers of Magyars. Both Czechoslovakia and Yugoslavia brought together different ethnic groups that had never developed a common sentiment of nationality. The Czechs, influenced by the Germans, had developed certain traits that did not mix easily with those of the Slovaks, who had been under Magyar influence. In Yugoslavia the Croats and the Slovenes were Roman Catholic and used the Roman alphabet, but the Serbs were Greek Orthodox and used the Cyrillic alphabet.

There was another purpose that led to the formation of these new states of Eastern Europe. The countries of Western Europe wanted a buffer zone—a *cordon sanitaire*—to separate their own territories from the developing communist society of the Soviet Union. The new states served to give political expression to long-smoldering nationalist feelings; but they also served to wall off the communists from the "free world."

However, when Germany under Hitler threatened the continued existence of some of these states, the other countries of Western Europe failed to give them protection. Germany's invasion of Poland started World War II; and in the course of the war German armed forces occupied all of Eastern Europe. Afterwards it was the Soviet army that liberated these countries from the Germans—except for Yugoslavia and Albania. And in all the Eastern European countries, except for Yugoslavia and Albania, the Communist Parties gained control of the post-war governments under the protection of the Soviet army. Germany was deprived of all of its territory east of the Oder River and its tributary the Neisse. The Polish national territory was moved westward: Poland lost territory in the east to the Soviet Union, but was compensated with new territory in the west, including the Upper Silesian industrial area. The small independent states east of the Baltic—Estonia, Latvia, and Lithuania—were incorporated in the Soviet Union as autonomous soviet socialist republics. Under Soviet control the old perplexing problem of ethnic distribution was attacked by forcing minorities of one nationality to move out of territory assigned to another state. The Germans were forcibly removed to what remains of Germany, and the Poles in the east were moved into the homes and onto the farms evacuated by the Germans. The *cordon sanitaire* is now maintained by the Soviet Union as a defense against the West.

In the period since World War II other profound changes have taken place in Eastern Europe. There had long been small groups in these countries, especially in Bohemia, that were devoted to democratic principles, and that were working to overthrow the system of autocratic government, of privileged landowning classes, and of military and police control. The establishment of the Soviet system has brought some of these changes rapidly, but it has also replaced one form of autocracy with another—the so-called dictatorship of the proletariat. Furthermore, all of these countries except Yugoslavia and Albania are now strictly controlled by the Soviet Union. As the revolt in Hungary in 1956 made quite clear, there are many people in these countries who would willingly break away from Soviet domination if they could.

Yugoslavia and Albania, at some distance geographically from the Soviet Union, have been able to maintain an independence of action and of policy not permitted in the other satellite states. Yugoslavia has developed a unique blend of communist control and free, but not private, enterprise. Albania, in its remote position not easily accessible from the Soviet Union, has been able to defy the dictates of Moscow, and to develop its own distinctive brand of communism.

THE GERMAN DEMOCRATIC REPUBLIC

At the conclusion of World War II Germany was divided into sectors, each occupied by one of the victorious powers. There were American, British, and French sectors in the west, and a Soviet sector in the east. In 1949 the western sectors were combined in the German Federal Republic with its capital in Bonn, and the Soviet sector was organized as the German Democratic Republic with its capital in East Berlin (Map 21).

It should be noted that the Soviets use the word "democracy" in a sense quite different from western usage. Democracy in western terms refers to a system of government that has been selected by the people of a state, and in which the supreme power has been retained by the people and delegated to representatives, whose authority is periodically renewed in accordance with established law. Furthermore, in a democracy there is an acceptance of majority rule, and an agreement to promote the adoption of policy by persuasion and not by force. A western democracy is one in which citizens accept the responsibilities of sovereignty, and in which there is free access to knowledge. In a Soviet-inspired "People's Democracy," on the other hand, the supreme authority remains with the Communist Party and its appointed administrators who act in the name of the people. The Soviets maintain that western freedom leads to control by those who have money, and that the workers in such a system have no real freedom of action. However the members of the Communist Party, who are selected for their devotion to the communist cause, reserve to themselves all ultimate decisions of policy, and expect unquestioning obedience to Party policies. The basic issue is whether the individual citizen may exercise equal rights and responsibilities, or whether these rights and responsibilities are to be exercised for him by an authority he did not select. Furthermore, in the Soviet system there is no freedom of access to knowledge, for news is carefully withheld or edited by those who are responsible for the destinies of the people.

The two systems confront each other along the line that separates the European

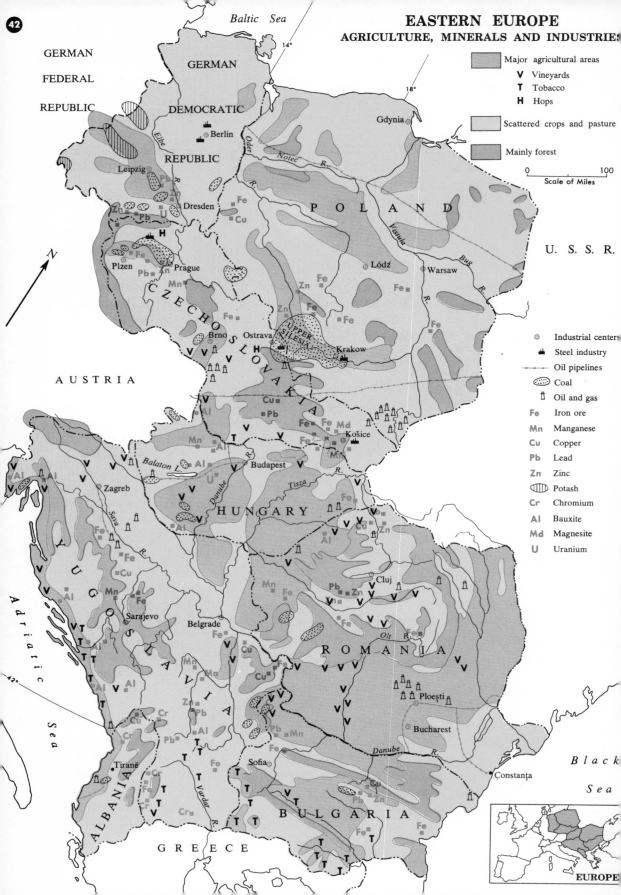

42

Baltic Sea

EASTERN EUROPE
AGRICULTURE, MINERALS AND INDUSTRIES

GERMAN

FEDERAL

REPUBLIC

GERMAN

DEMOCRATIC

● Berlin

REPUBLIC

Leipzig

Pb
Zn

Zn
Pb ○ Dresden

Fe

Cu

U

H

Plzen

Pb Zn ○ Prague

Mn

Fe

C Z E C H O S L O V A K I A

Fe

Brno ● Ostrava

UPPER
SILESIA

Krakow

Zn

Fe

AUSTRIA

V V V

V

Al

Cu
Pb

Fe Fe Md

Fe

Košice

Mn

Mn

Al

Fe

Balaton L.

Al

U

Danube

Budapest

Tisza

Fe

Zagreb

Al

H U N G A R Y

Al

Cu Zn

Al

Al
Al

Sava R.

Fe

Mn

Fe

Cu

Cu

Fe

Cluj

Pb Zn

Y U G O S L A V I A

Mn

Al

Fe

Sarajevo

Belgrade

Fe

Cu

R O M A N I A

Olt R.

Fe

Fe

V

Cu

Ploești

Mn

Al
Cr

Zn
Pb

Bucharest

Al

Pb

Cr

Cu

Al

Pb Mn

Cr

Tiranë

Fe

Fe

Sofia

Danube R.

Constanța

A L B A N I A

Fe

Cu

Pb Zn

Cr R.

Vardar R.

B U L G A R I A

T T T T T

Fe

Fe

G R E E C E

Gdynia

P O L A N D

Vistula

Lódź

Warsaw

Bug R.

U. S. S. R.

Fe

Fe

Fe

Legend

▨	Major agricultural areas
V	Vineyards
T	Tobacco
H	Hops
░	Scattered crops and pasture
▓	Mainly forest

Scale of Miles
0 — 100

⊙ Industrial centers
🏭 Steel industry
〜 Oil pipelines
⬭ Coal
⛽ Oil and gas
Fe Iron ore
Mn Manganese
Cu Copper
Pb Lead
Zn Zinc
▥ Potash
Cr Chromium
Al Bauxite
Md Magnesite
U Uranium

Adriatic Sea

Black Sea

EUROPE

Culture Region from the Soviet Culture Region. The line, marked by barbed wire and plowed ground, slashes across Germany: in Berlin it is marked by the famous wall erected in 1961 to stop the flood of refugees seeking escape to the west.

The 17,000,000 people of East Germany are not sharing in the prosperity of West Germany. In fact the population of East Germany declined by more than 1,000,000 between 1950 and 1960 due to the flight of refugees to the West. East Germany, once a major producer of food for pre-war Germany, is now faced with food shortages, and the government is wrestling with the usual difficulties found wherever farmers are forced into collectives and denied the right to work their own land. The communist government has made a great effort to increase industrial production. Apart from Berlin, which was a major industrial center before World War II, East Germany's chief industrial area is the triangle between Leipzig, Dresden, and the West German border (Map 42). Leipzig was once famous the world over for its printing and publishing houses, and Dresden was equally famous for its china. Factories still turn out products ranging from cameras and optical goods to textiles and machinery. The lignite deposits of this area furnish fuel for steam-electric plants, and raw material for a chemical industry. A large part of the minerals and fuels for industry are imported from the Soviet Union, and of the exports 45 per cent go to the Soviet Union and 32 per cent to other communist countries.

The fact remains that the German Democratic Republic is not a viable state. It can be maintained as long as Soviet military power supports it, but its people remain restive and discontented. On both sides of the line the demand for the reunification of Germany is strong.

POLAND AND CZECHOSLOVAKIA

East of Germany there are two quite different states in which the people speak Slavic languages. Poland is a state with a strong nationalist sentiment, and one that has been repeatedly conquered by Germans and Russians over the past several centuries. Czechoslovakia is a creation of the international conferences that followed World War I, and is a state that had never previously existed as a unit.

Poland. A Slavic people who speak the Polish language, who are predominantly Roman Catholic, and whose traditions include a long-continued struggle for independence, occupy the plains north of the Carpathian and Sudetes Mountains and south of the Baltic Sea. Warsaw (Warszawa) on the Vistula River has remained the urban center of this strongly nationalistic ethnic group. From the fourteenth to the eighteenth centuries the Polish kingdom was one of the largest states of Europe, extending at one time almost to the Black Sea and eastward to the Dnepr River (Map 20). But by 1914 there was no country named Poland, for the Polish territory had been partitioned among neighboring empires. After World War I, it again became independent and its territory was given exact definition. Then after World War II the Soviet Union took about 45 per cent of the pre-war Polish territory where there were Byelorussian majorities. In compensation about a third of the territory of the new Polish state was taken from East Germany, and the foreign minorities were forcibly removed, so that now Poland is much nearer to being solidly Slav than ever before.

The communist government that was established in Poland after World War II undertook two major economic reforms. The first was in the farm system. Before the war the extensive plains of Poland were divided into large private estates owned by a small number of landlords. The great majority of the people of Poland were illiterate, and very poor, tenant farmers. Under the communists the landlord class was wiped out, and the large estates were divided among the tenants. The new government could command the enthusiastic support of the people, because land is what the tenant farmers had long demanded. But in 1949 the communist government took the next step, which was an attempt to combine the small private farms into collectives on the Soviet model. The farmers were to work the collectives with government-owned machinery and to be paid according to the amount of work they performed. The Polish farmers rebelled at this, and the program for establishing large collective farms was postponed. However, the abolition of privately-owned farms still remains an essential goal of communist policy.

The plains of Poland offer a large area of good farmland. Less than 10 per cent of the present territory of Poland is too wet, too sandy, or too steep to be used for crops. About 20 per cent of the territory, chiefly in the mountains, is covered with coniferous forests from which a regular supply of lumber is cut. The rest of the country is used to grow rye, potatoes, wheat, oats, barley, and sugar beets, and to pasture cattle (Map 42). Crop yields are not high in comparison with similar habitats in other countries, but this is due chiefly to the illiteracy of the peasants, and to the continued resistance to the new farming techniques that require large-scale operations with machinery. About half of the workers in Poland are employed in agriculture.

The second major economic reform introduced by the communists was the nationalization of industry. The industrial core of Poland is Upper Silesia, where Poland now has possession of the second largest supply of good coking coal in Europe—second only to the Ruhr. Poland has sources of iron ore nearby, to supplement necessary imports of iron from the Soviet Union, for the development of a steel industry. Nearby also are copper mines, and the largest lead and zinc mines in Europe. At Nowa Huta, a suburb of Kraków, the Polish government has built a huge new steel plant; there are also new textile factories in several cities, and in Warsaw new automobile and electric motor plants.

Poland today is economically more viable than it was pre-war. The rapid development of its industry is reflected in an increase in the gross national product per capita. Nevertheless, living standards are not high in comparison with those of Western Europe. Housing is still far short of the needs of the urban population, and consumer goods are not available in adequate quantities to meet the demands of the people. Since the people never really did enjoy the rights and responsibilities of a western-type democracy, it is doubtful if the lack of this kind of democracy is being felt; but the traditional demand for national independence, which is so distinctive a part of the Polish state-idea, still burns in spite of the existence of a police state.

Czechoslovakia. Czechoslovakia, unlike Poland, never did exist as a separate state before World War I. The Kingdom of Bohemia was a part of the Austrian Empire and was oriented economically and politically toward Vienna. Slovakia, on the other hand, was a part of the Kingdom of Hungary and was oriented toward Budapest. Czechs and Slovaks both speak Slavic languages and are predominantly Roman Catholic. However, the Czechs enjoy the highest standard of living and have the lowest rate of illiteracy of any part of Eastern Europe. In Czechoslovakia as a whole the Czechs form about 66 per cent of the population, and the Slovaks about 28 per cent. After World War II a minority problem was solved by the evacuation of some 3,000,000 Germans.

The habitat of the Czechs is the hilly upland of Bohemia (Map 15, p. 42). This gently rolling terrain of moderate relief is drained by the headwaters of the Elbe, and is bordered on the north, northwest and southwest by ranges of low mountains. The hilly lands terminate sharply in the east at the base of the western end of the Carpathians. Just west of the Carpathians there is a relatively easy route of passage, known as the Moravian Gate, connecting the valley of the Danube to the south with the plains of Poland along the Oder River to the north.

The people of Bohemia have for a long time been progressive and prosperous. Bohemia was the industrial core of the Austro-Hungarian Empire. After World War I when the Industrial Revolution came to Bohemia, the Czech people were thought to be the most firmly democratic of any people in Eastern Europe. Nevertheless, in 1948 the Communist Party took over control of the government, and Czechoslovakia became a satellite of the Soviet Union.

The Czechs are primarily urban and industrial; the Slovaks are primarily rural and agricultural. In the country as a whole the proportion of workers employed on farms is about 38 per cent, but in Slovakia the proportion is much higher. Although there is very little level land the farms are highly productive, and the land is intensively and effectively used. More than 80 per cent of the agricultural land is now in collectives on the Soviet model, operated with machinery supplied by the state. The crops include barley, rye, wheat, oats, hops, grapes, and sugar beets. Hops from Bohemia are used in the manufacture of beer at Plzeň. Large areas are also used for dairy cattle. In the mountainous regions pine forests provide a supply of lumber.

Czechoslovakia is well supplied with minerals. Coal around Ostrava in the Upper Silesian district, close to the Polish border, supports a steel industry, which at one time was adequately supplied with iron ore from ore bodies between Prague and Plzeň. Now most of the iron ore comes from Krivoy Rog in the Soviet Union. Lignite is available for fuel and to support a chemical industry. Kaolin and graphite are mined in Bohemia. In the Erzgebirge there are mines of lead and zinc, antimony, mercury, magnesite, tin, and uranium.

Industrial development is still greatest in the western part of the country. Prague has a wide variety of industries, chiefly manufacturing consumer goods. Plzeň is not only a center for breweries, but is also the location of the famous Skoda armament works. Brno manufactures chemicals, machinery, and wool textiles.

But the communist government, here as in the Soviet Union, is attempting to provide industrial development in all parts of the country, in order to decrease the concentration of industries and so the differences in economic well-being between primarily urban and primarily rural areas. A huge new iron and steel plant is being built at Košice in the eastern part of Slovakia. Since the iron ore is shipped by rail from Krivoy Rog this will represent a considerable saving in transportation. The coal will come from Ostrava. When the plant is completed, about 1965, the steel will support the development of steel-using industries in hitherto rural areas.

HUNGARY, ROMANIA, BULGARIA

Three countries that are described as the "Danubian Countries" border the Danube east of Austria. These are Hungary, Romania, and Bulgaria. Each has a distinctive language, historical tradition, and sense of nationality; but all three share the common fate of subordination to the economy and to the national interests of the Soviet Union. They occupy the two extensive grass-covered plains—the Plain of Hungary and the Wallachian Plain—and the bordering mountains (Map 15, p. 42).

Each of these countries possesses a unique personality. At the end of World War I the boundaries of independent Hungary were drawn to include the areas almost solidly occupied by Magyars. These were Asian nomadic people who migrated during the ninth century A.D. from the Russian plains, across the forested Carpathians, to the grassy plains to the south. Now 97 per cent of the Hungarians are Magyars, and Magyar minorities are found within the bordering territories of Czechoslovakia, Romania, and Yugoslavia. About 70 per cent of the Hungarians are Roman Catholic. The Romanians, on the other hand, are the descendants of the Romans who occupied the land north of the Danube until A.D. 271, mixed with the native Dacians. Their language is closer to Latin than is Italian. In religion they are more than 80 per cent Greek Orthodox, the faith derived from Constantinople. The Bulgarians speak a Slavic language that is close to Russian, and are also predominantly Orthodox. Both Romania and Bulgaria were formerly under Turkish rule, and achieved independence in 1878.

The Danubian Countries have long been primarily agricultural. Each had developed a characteristic pre-industrial type of society—with the land divided into vast private estates owned by an aristocratic minority, the majority of the people working as tenant farmers, and the political system largely controlled by the army. Some 60 per cent of the population is still rural, and is mostly grouped in small villages. When, in each of these countries, the Communist Party seized control of the government after World War II, the landlord class was liquidated, and the private estates were distributed among the peasants, much to the delight of the latter whose traditional demand had been for land redistribution. The next intended step was to group the peasants together in collectives, and then eventually to group the collectives into large state-owned units in which the workers would be paid wages. In this way the benefits of large-scale operations with machinery would be brought to these countries. Yet, for one reason or another—chiefly resistance on the part of the peasants—agricultural production has remained static, or has slightly declined, since the period before World War II.

The crops of this area reflect the climate of mild winters and hot rainy summers. Winter wheat and maize are grown in all three, with wheat occupying first place in Bulgaria. In Hungary and Romania the maize is fed to domestic animals. These countries are large producers of hogs, cattle, sheep, horses, and poultry. Between 10 and 15 per cent of the cropland is devoted to sunflowers, for oil and feed, and to tobacco. Bulgaria follows Turkey and Greece in the production of "Oriental" tobacco. Bulgaria is also famous for its roses—used in the manufacture of perfume.

The major effort of the communist governments, however, has been devoted to the increase of industrial and mineral production. Much has been accomplished in spite of the relatively modest endowment of the region. Romania has the best list of resources, including, in Transylvania, one of the largest natural gas reserves in the world, and a small oil field at Ploeşti. Hungary possesses about 12 per cent of the world's known reserves of bauxite, located near Lake Balaton in the western part of the country. Because of the lack of an abundant supply of low-cost electric power to support an aluminum industry, only about 10 per cent of the bauxite is processed in Hungary. In all three countries there are small supplies of lead and zinc, copper, manganese, iron, and lignite. But there is a deficiency of coking coal and iron ore. As a result, the establishment of basic heavy industries, as demanded by the Soviet planners, means that most of the raw materials have to be imported. Some of the steel is used in the manufacture of machinery, especially in Budapest, and some is exported to the Soviet Union. A new chemical industry has been developed in Hungary, based on local sources of lignite. Consumer goods still comprise the greater part of all manufacturing, although the Soviet managers have given such products little attention. In Bulgaria and Romania the largest proportion of industrial workers are employed in food-processing plants.

Each of the three Danubian Countries is now separately, but closely, attached to the economy of the Soviet Union. Whereas, formerly, these countries traded up and down the Danube with Western Europe, now foreign trade is mostly with the Soviet Union and the other satellite countries: 80 per cent of the trade of Bulgaria, 75 per cent of that of Romania, and a little less than 66 per cent of that of Hungary is with the commu-

nist countries. The Communist Council for Economic Mutual Aid looks forward to the development of each country toward somewhat separate goals: Bulgaria is to concentrate on lead and zinc mining, on light industries and food processing, and on the development of the Black Sea coast for tourists; Hungary is to increase its production of bauxite and aluminum, precision machinery, and domestic animals; and Romania is to produce more oil and gas, more equipment for oil refineries, more petrochemicals, steel, and food products. Less attention is to be given to the manufacture of consumer goods for domestic markets.

YUGOSLAVIA AND ALBANIA

Yugoslavia and Albania are the two countries of the Soviet Culture Region that are the most remote from Moscow, not only in terms of distance but also in terms of the flow of communications. Neither country was occupied by Soviet troops after World War II, but both became communist under the leadership of those who had resisted the German and Italian occupation during the war. This spirit of resistance to outside domination is now directed at the Soviet Union.

Yugoslavia. Yugoslavia, like Czechoslovakia, was created after World War I by bringing together several neighboring but quite separate groups of people. The contrasts within Yugoslavia are based on language, religion, and tradition. The somewhat less than 20,000,000 people are divided among four groups: Serbs, 43 per cent; Croats, 34 per cent; Slovenes, 7 per cent; and Macedonians, 7 per cent. The remainder includes a variety of nationalities—Germans, Italians, Turks, Romanians, Bulgars, Greeks, and others. Most of the people speak Serbo-Croatian, a Slavic language; but the Serbs use the Cyrillic alphabet, and the Croats the Roman alphabet (Map 19, p. 49). The people of Serbia are Greek Orthodox, and form 47 per cent of the total; the people of Croatia and Slovenia are mostly Roman Catholics, forming 36 per cent of the total. In addition, in the mountainous country of southern Yugoslavia, in Bosnia and Hercegovina, there are numerous Muslims comprising 11 per cent of the total. Superimposed on these culture contrasts, and partly the cause of them, are the divisions of the country created as it came under foreign domination from various directions. In the

Dubrovnik, on the Adriatic coast of Yugoslavia, has many buildings that date back to the fourteenth and fifteenth centuries.

north, including Belgrade and Zagreb, the country was once under the influence and political control of Hungary, and later of the Austro-Hungarian Empire. The long narrow strip on the Adriatic coast, on the other hand, was under the domination of Venezia from 1420 to 1797—at which latter date it was brought under the political control of Austria. Most of southern Yugoslavia, as far west as the line on Map 19, was long influenced by Constantinople, and was controlled by Turkey until 1878. The southeastern part of the country, including Macedonia, was ruled by Turkey until 1912, except for some small protected spots in the mountains of Montenegro that the Turks could never effectively control.

Each of these different groups of people, occupying different parts of a rugged terrain, developed a strong sense of nationalism as a result of the long periods of foreign domination. After World War I they were all grouped together in the Kingdom of the Serbs, Croats, and Slovenes, which after 1929 became Yugoslavia. Invaded in World War II by the Germans and Italians, they again resisted fiercely. The resistance forces were violently anti-fascist, and after the liberation of the country in 1945 they established their own communist-style government. Only the urge for independence from foreign domination, from whatever source, has been strong enough to counteract the disintegrative effect of differences of language, religion, and tradition.

Yugoslavia is a poor country. Some 66 per cent of its workers are employed in agriculture, yet the only good cropland is in the north, in the valley of the Danube and its tributaries the Sava and the Drava, where Yugoslavia shares a portion of the Plain of Hungary (Map 15, p. 42). Agriculture is intensive, especially on the rich black soils of the Vojvodina (the area north of the

Sava-Danube rivers). Here the crops include wheat, maize, hemp, potatoes, sugar beets, sunflowers, and fruits. In Macedonia there is cotton; and along the Adriatic shores there are vineyards. Domestic animals, especially in the north, include cattle, horses, hogs, and poultry. Sheep and cattle are pastured in the mountains; in the area of Mediterranean climate where the government is attempting to replant the forests, goats are prohibited. The basic fact remains, however, that there are too many farmers to be supported on the small area of good farm land.

Yugoslavia is building new manufacturing industries, and attempting to increase its production of minerals. It has some good coal, and some oil; and its industrial minerals include copper, chromium, manganese, lead, zinc, bauxite, iron, and antimony (Map 42). Manufacturing industries are concentrated in Belgrade, Zagreb, and Sarajevo.

Yugoslavia is a viable state, largely because its leaders have known how to take special advantage of the feeling for independence that is the one common characteristic of all the peoples included in it. At first glance one might say that the forces for disintegration must surely win out over anything but military force, and that sooner or later the state must disintegrate into its component parts. But there is little demand for such disintegration: the state-idea, of independence for Yugoslavia, outweighs the desire for separation by Serbia, Croatia, and the other national groups. Perhaps in a geographic position less remote from the borders of the Soviet Union, or in a habitat more easily penetrable from the Adriatic, the maintenance of Yugoslav independence would have been more difficult. As it is the Yugoslav leaders have developed their own distinctive kind of communism—subservient neither to the Soviet Communist Party nor to the great powers of Western Europe. The effort to establish collective farms on the Soviet model has been abandoned, and 90 per cent of the cropland is now in private hands. Industry, on the contrary, is publicly owned, but is organized into separate companies that compete with each other: each has its own sales force promoting the use of its own products. The workers elect their own boards of directors; the managers are selected by the boards and are responsible to them, not to the government. The results of this distinctive form of communism, with its mixture of free competitive enterprise, can be seen in booming industrial cities, and in a notable rise in the gross national product which is widely shared among the people. The popularity of the system is reflected in the considerable degree of free public discussion of political issues permitted in this one East-European country.

Albania. Albania is even more isolated than Yugoslavia. Not only is it difficult to reach overland because of the rugged terrain, but also this part of the Adriatic coast offers no good harbors for anything larger than fishing boats. The people speak a number of related dialects which are Thracian rather than Slavic. About 65 per cent of the population is Muslim. More than 70 per cent of the people gain a meager living from growing maize on the 10 per cent of the land that is arable, or from pasturing sheep and goats on the steep mountain slopes. There is a small oil field, some lignite, and there are also some ores of chromium and copper; but industrial development has yet to make a start. Like the people of Yugoslavia, the Albanians love liberty enough to support any government that will defy foreign attempts to dominate them. The Communist Party of the Soviet Union has little control over this remote country.

SUMMARY

The two great revolutions of the contemporary world, spreading eastward from the center of origin in Western Europe, were brought to peoples with quite different cultural traditions from those of the maritime west. These were people who had had only indirect contact with the culture hearths of Greece and Rome, and to whom the ideas of democracy were alien. These were people who had been conquered again and again by outsiders, and among whom the almost fanatical desire for independence had long been frustrated. Among the separate ethnic groups were the Great Russians, originally from the forests between the Urals and the Baltic. The Great Russians had had their share of conquest and dominance by foreigners, but they had learned from Ivan III that the best defense is attack—and this lesson they have never forgotten. The Russians built a vast empire through the conquest of other national groups—an empire that embraces not only Slavs, but also many other kinds of people, not only Greek Orthodox Christians, but also Muslims and others. Since 1917 these various nationalities have enjoyed a high degree of cultural autonomy, within the general limits prescribed by the Communist Party; and one non-Russian has risen to the highest office in the Soviet system (Stalin was a Georgian). These separate nationalities, as we have pointed out, no longer constitute forces of disintegration. But the Russians have been less successful in establishing Marxism-Leninism as a substitute for nationality among the countries that had once been directly influenced by Rome. Generally, to the west of the line shown on Map 19 (p. 49) the desire for independence continues to burn fiercely under the watchful control of the Soviet army. The core of the Soviet Culture Region is in the Soviet Union, and the countries of Eastern Europe, since the communist take-over of the late 1940's, constitute a zone of transition in which the characteristics of the European Culture Region and of the Soviet Culture Region are intermingled. The countries of this transitional area are potentially explosive, and require the constant vigilance of the Soviet Union to keep them under control.

The Industrial Revolution has been eagerly accepted by the communists. A large proportion of the gross national product in each of the Soviet countries is being devoted to new capital formation—at the expense of the workers. During the initial phase of technological change new capital is devoted to building up the basic industries, such as steel, and to the construction of what the economists call "social overhead"—electric power facilities, transportation, ports, and the other things required by industrialized countries. Consumer goods come later, after the economies have achieved maturity; and for the early stages of growth the levels of living are conspicuously lower than those of neighboring mature economies of Western Europe. Furthermore, the Communist Party of the Soviet Union is deeply conscious of the possibility of invasion, especially from the west, and a large part of the new productivity has been devoted to the construction of armaments. During the early 1960's the Soviet Union has begun to insert new capital into the manufacture of consumer goods, but the countries of Eastern Europe are, with some exceptions, still chiefly concerned with building the basic heavy industries.

The Soviet Culture Region has not made conspicuous economic gains in agriculture as it has in industry. There are certain places, to be sure, where agricultural improvement has transformed the local economies, as in the irrigated, cotton-growing areas of Soviet Central Asia, or the fruit-orchard areas of the Crimea. In general, however, the most successful farming has been on state farms, operated with wage workers like large-scale industrial plants. The modernization of farming along these lines requires a large reduction in the proportion of the working population employed in agriculture, and this, again, cannot be achieved without a large increase in the number of jobs in industry—especially in the Soviet system where the proportion of people in service occupations is not so large as in capitalist countries. The farmers who work on the collective farms, with some exceptions, are not inclined to make the much needed extra effort for the good of the state. In fact, in 1961, small plots of land were set aside on each collective farm for the use of individual farmers—small plots that added up to something like 3 per cent of all cultivated land. And from this 3 per cent now comes a very large proportion of such things as potatoes, meat, eggs, vegetables and fruit. These privately-grown products can be used by the farmer's family, or can be sold for individual profit in nearby markets. Part of the food problem of the Soviet Union is certainly a reflection of such climatic hazards as drought and cold, but part, also, is a reflection of the failure of the communist system in the agricultural sector of the economy.

For the rest of the world the major question regarding the Soviet Culture Region is whether, or not, the Soviet leaders will embark on a program of further imperial expansion, either through fear or miscalculation. It is a military axiom that the best defense is offense, and there is no doubt that the Soviet leaders are concerned about the possibility of invasion—the historical record includes numerous such invasions, starting with the Vikings and the Swedes, including Napoleon and the French armies, the Japanese in the Far East, the Germans during World War I, the allied armies that invaded Soviet territory after the Revolution of 1917, and finally invasion by the Germans under Hitler. Fear of invasion is surely justified by the record; and if the powers opposed to the Soviet Union were weak enough to make a Soviet attack successful, it is likely that the Soviet leaders would press for every advantage. It is important that they should make no miscalculations on this score. In the course of time fears and enmity may be reduced through patient negotiation, so that this aspect of our divided world may not loom so menacingly on the eastern horizon.

4

THE
ANGLO-AMERICAN
CULTURE REGION

Country	Political Status	Latest Estimate Population	Capital City
Canada	Federal State	18,600,000 ('62)	Ottawa
United States	Federal Republic	185,822,000 ('62)	Washington, D.C.
St. Pierre & Miquelon	French Overseas Territ.	5,000 ('60)	

The Anglo-American Culture Region is made up of two countries—the United States of America, and Canada. It occupies the northern part of North America and lies within the area of the Land Hemisphere. This region includes 14 per cent of the inhabited land area of the earth, and is occupied by 6 per cent of the world's population.

This is the part of the world in which the two great revolutions of modern times have had the maximum effect on the lives of the largest numbers of people. There are other parts of the world in which the principles of democratic living have gained more complete acceptance, and there are other parts of the world in which the new technology has led to an even more advanced stage of economic development. But never before in the history of mankind have so many individuals enjoyed both such a high degree of political and economic freedom, and such high standards of material well-being. The people of the United States and Canada are far ahead of the rest of the world in economic productivity, and in the use of energy. They are, moreover, among the chief custodians of the concepts of equality before the law, of government with the consent of the governed, and of the principles of responsible citizenship.

The dynamic society that has produced these achievements has been built by individuals who have brought skills and ideas to America from all over the world. The first European settlers in eastern North America were British, French, Dutch, Swedish and German; but since early colonial times there have been many others who have come to settle in Anglo-America, including Italians, Irish, Poles, Russians, Austrians, Mexicans, and Puerto Ricans. About 10 per cent of the population of the United States today is made up of Negroes whose ancestors were brought as slaves from Africa. There are numerous native-born Americans whose ancestors came from China, Japan, and the Philippines. Each of these racially and culturally diverse groups has made its own unique contribution to the character of Anglo-American society.

The continent to which all these diverse peoples came proved to be remarkably well-endowed with resources. It had been a good hunting ground for the Indians, and in some places, when the forests were cleared, the soils yielded good crops for European farmers. But it was the new technology that made the resources of the continent important. Coal was of no significance as a resource to the Indians; in fact, bituminous coal was not a major fuel in the steel industry until after 1856. The productive black soils of the Midwestern prairies were not highly rated for agriculture until a whole series of mechanical inventions had

◄ *United States Steel Corporation, Clairton Coke and By-Product Plant.*

been made, mostly after the Civil War. The important geographic fact is that resources were so located within North America that as settlement and economic development spread across the continent, and as the technology of production continued to be improved, the resources needed at each period of economic history were easily accessible to the places where they were to be used. The large area with no internal tariff restrictions made it possible to seek raw materials from the sources which could be used at lowest cost. The very large gross national products per capita of both the United States and Canada can be explained on the basis of an interplay of technology, economic and political institutions, and amazingly well-arranged habitats.

To understand the strategic position of Anglo-America in the modern world it is necessary to look at the map of the Land Hemisphere (Map 12, p. 36). To earthbound people, who must cross the oceans in ships, the oceans that separate Anglo-America from Europe and eastern Asia are the Atlantic and the Pacific. But in an age of high-flying airplanes and missiles it is important to understand that the major centers of the European Culture Region are to the northeast, and that the most direct route from New York passes over eastern Canada. The major centers of the Soviet Culture Region and of the East Asian Culture Region lie north and northwest. The ocean that lies between Anglo-America and the other centers of economic and military power is neither the Atlantic nor the Pacific. It is the Arctic Ocean.

THE HABITAT

(Maps 5, 6, 7, 8, 43, and 44) The European colonists in eastern North America found a habitat not unlike that of Western Europe. The forests included many familiar

ANGLO-AMERICAN CULTURE REG
SURFACE FEATURES AND
POLITICAL DIVISIONS

———— Physiographic boundary

•••••••••• Line of 200 frost free days
    from Texas eastward

– – – – – Mid-Canada line

▬▬▬▬ DEW line

━━━━ Southern limit of tundra

━ ━ ━ Southern limit of glaciation
    east of the Rockies

0   500
    Scale of Miles

GREAT LAKES - ST. LAWRENCE PROFILE

Sault Ste. Marie
L. Superior
ELEV. 602′
L. Huron and L. Michigan
ELEV. 578.5′
Lake St. Claire
L. Erie
ELEV. 572′
International Rapids
L. Ontario
ELEV. 246′
St. Lawrence R.
ELEV. 20′
SEA LEVEL
WELLAND CANAL
SOULANGES CANAL
LACHINE CANAL
From Focus

43

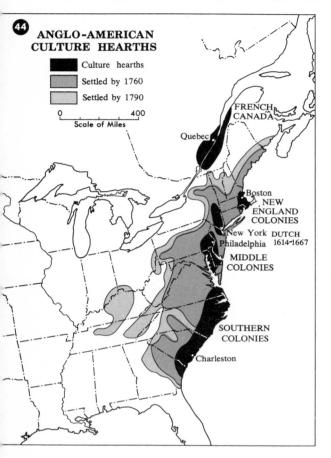

44 ANGLO-AMERICAN CULTURE HEARTHS

- ■ Culture hearths
- ▨ Settled by 1760
- ▨ Settled by 1790

0   400
Scale of Miles

Quebec

FRENCH CANADA

Boston
NEW ENGLAND COLONIES

New York   DUTCH
Philadelphia   1614-1667

MIDDLE COLONIES

SOUTHERN COLONIES

Charleston

dinavian Upland of northern Europe. There are similar glaciated surfaces with knobby, rock hills, and many lakes and bogs. Both are built on some of the oldest crystalline rocks exposed at the earth's surface, which contain many ore bodies of such minerals as iron, nickel, copper, and uranium. The arrangement of lakes—the Great Lakes, Lake Winnipeg, Lake Athabasca, Great Slave Lake, and Great Bear Lake—around the margin of this upland is a notable feature of North American geography. The Laurentain Upland has its southern border along the northern side of the St. Lawrence Valley, except where it extends to include the Adirondacks, which also belong geologically to the Canadian area.

South of the St. Lawrence, and trending in a northeast and southwest direction, are the Appalachian Highlands. In eastern Canada and New England the hilly uplands and low mountains border the sea. This part of the Appalachians was scraped and polished by the glaciers of the Ice Age, and moraines and outwash plains fill the valleys. The rivers have been pushed out of their pre-glacial courses, and as a result they are frequently interrupted by falls and rapids. The line on Map 43 shows the southern limit of glaciation. From the St. Lawrence Valley south of Montreal a narrow lowland extends southward through the Lake Champlain-Hudson River Valley, and then southwestward through the heart of the Appalachians all the way to Alabama. To the east are the crystalline rocks of the Blue Ridge and the Piedmont (named on Map 43), and of the massive and rounded low mountains known as the Great Smokey Mountains. From Pennsylvania to Alabama the great valley is bordered on the west by long, more or less parallel ridges formed by the erosion of folded rock strata, through which the rivers pass in water gaps. The

species of trees, and the climate was suitable for the cultivation of the familiar European crops. To be sure, the summers were hotter and the winters colder than those of Europe, but not enough so to cause any serious problems of adjustment. The surface features had been formed by processes similar to those operating in Western Europe. There were many "New World" landscapes that reminded the pioneers of the homes they had left.

Surface Features. The surface features of eastern North America are arranged in a simple pattern. The whole northeastern part of the continent is made up of the Laurentian Upland, where the landforms bear a striking resemblance to those of the Scan-

whole western side of the Appalachians is made up of hilly uplands formed on horizontal or gently dipping rock strata, which are known as the Allegheny Plateau in the north (in New York, Pennsylvania, eastern Ohio and northern West Virginia), and the Cumberland Plateau (from southern West Virginia southward). The eastern edge of the plateaus forms an almost unbroken escarpment that constituted a major barrier to westward movement for the early pioneers. This escarpment stands high in the Catskill Mountains west of the Hudson; it is called the Allegheny Front in Pennsylvania and Maryland, and the Cumberland Front farther south. In the west the hilly uplands extend fingers of hills out into the Central Plains, and into the western parts of Kentucky and Tennessee where they border the Blue Grass Basin and the Nashville Basin. The uplands cross the Mississippi south of St. Louis to form the Ozark Highlands.

Coastal plains border the sea all the way from New York to Texas. The Piedmont upland forms the inner margin of the Atlantic Coastal Plain. East of the Piedmont the resistant crystalline rocks are covered by much younger sedimentary strata. The rivers descend from the Piedmont to the Coastal Plain over falls and rapids, so that this eastern edge has come to be known as the "Fall Line." A string of colonial cities was established along the Fall Line, not only because of the water power available there, but also because this marks the inner limit of navigation on the rivers of the Coastal Plain. The cities include Trenton, Philadelphia, Wilmington, Baltimore, Washington, Richmond, Raleigh, Columbia, Augusta, Macon, and Columbus. The Coastal Plain swings around the southern end of the Appalachians, along the Gulf Coast, and on through Texas into Mexico. The Mississippi,

after passing through the uplands near its junction with the Ohio, crosses the Gulf Coastal Plain on a wide floodplain—bordered by steep valley bluffs—and enters the Gulf through its delta south of New Orleans.

The whole central part of the continent is made up of extensive plains. The Central Plains start on the western side of the Appalachians, and lie roughly between the Great Lakes and the Ohio and Missouri rivers. The line on Map 43 shows that the glaciers moved as far south as these rivers, leaving the Central Plains marked with moraines, outwash plains, and old lake beds. The Great Plains lie farther to the west, where the climate is semiarid and where the original vegetation was mostly grass. The plains rise over almost imperceptible steps to the front of the Rocky Mountains. Denver, which is on the plains some twenty miles east of the mountains, is at an altitude of 5,280 feet. The plains sweep all the way from the Gulf of Mexico northward through the Mackenzie Valley of Canada to the Arctic Ocean.

The western part of North America is strikingly different from the east. It is made up of towering ranges of high mountains, separated by valley lowlands, basins, and plateaus. There are two separate chains of mountains: the easternmost one is known as the Rocky Mountains and reaches from New Mexico into Canada, then continues on to form the Brooks Range of northern Alaska; the western ranges border the Pacific, and include the Sierra Nevada, the Klamath Mountains, the Cascade Mountains, the Cordillera of British Columbia, and the Alaska Range of southern Alaska. Between these two systems are a series of plateaus and basins: the Colorado Plateau, the Great Basin, with its basin and range landscape, the Columbia Plateau, and in the north the Yukon Valley. Among the Pacific coastal ranges there are several important lowlands, such as the Puget Sound Lowland, the Willamette Valley, and the Great Valley of California.

Climate and Vegetation. The eastern part of North America is covered with forest (Map 8, pp. 16-17), and, in Canada, forest extends westward to the Rocky Mountains north of the Great Plains. Toward the north, where the summers are shorter and the winters are very cold, the forest gives way to a stunted woodland, and then to a treeless tundra. Between the Great Lakes and the margins of the tundra the climate is one of severe winters and short, cool summers (Dfc on Map 5, pp. 10-11, defined in Appendix A, p. 437). The winters west of Hudson Bay are dry and cold, similar to those of Siberia, but because of the smaller width of the continent, Canada does not have such extreme low temperatures. Severe winters are experienced, on the average, as far south as Boston and Cleveland and a line running westward from Cleveland across the middle part of the Central Plains (between C and D climates on Map 5). The severe winter climates have several weeks of continuous snow cover each winter; the mild winter climates to the south may experience cold waves with snow even as far south as Florida and Texas.

This whole eastern part of the United States and Canada has variable weather in summer and winter like that of Western Europe. Warm, moist air is brought to the land from the Gulf of Mexico and the warm Atlantic Ocean by winds circulating around the oceanic whirl (Appendix A, and Map 6). These winds, which come from the southeast, south, and southwest, are interrupted at frequent intervals by cold air masses, or polar outbursts, coming from Greenland or northern Canada. Along the cold fronts there are heavy storms and much rain or snow. In summer the oceanic air predominates, and the average wind direction along the east coast is from the southeast, south, and southwest; in winter the cold air masses predominate, and the average wind direction along this coast is offshore from the northwest. Summer is the rainy season, but the winters are by no means dry. Along the Gulf Coast the average wind direction in summer is from the south, and in winter from the north. From the Great Lakes eastward over New England and the St. Lawrence Valley the weather is extreme in its variability, with storms and clear skies alternating at short intervals.

The inner part of the North American continent, between the Great Lakes and the Rocky Mountains, and north of latitude 40°N, has a continental type of climate. Here the summers are hot and rainy and the winters cold and dry. Map 7 (p. 14) shows that the belt within which temperatures reach 110° on at least one day in the average summer extends northward from Mexico almost to the border of Canada. Fargo, in North Dakota, is the weather station in the United States with the greatest average range of temperature—from an average of 71.3° in July to an average of 7.1° in January. Ranges between summer and winter are even greater farther north in Canada. The winters in the Mackenzie Valley are very cold, but because of the smaller size of North America compared with Eurasia, and the presence of Hudson Bay, the lowest temperatures in winter are not quite so low as those of Siberia.

The central part of the United States, and south-central Canada, were covered with grass when the European settlers first reached these regions. The eastern edge of the prairie was well within the area of humid climate (compare Maps 5 and 8, pp. 10-11 and 16-17), which leads geographers to believe that the forest had been pushed back toward the wetter east by Indian burnings. Along the forest-prairie margin, fingers of forest extend westward along the river valleys. Farther west, however, forests almost entirely disappear, and the surface is covered with a carpet of short steppe grass. This is the semiarid land known as the Great Plains.

The western part of North America differs from the eastern part not only in its surface features but also in its climates and vegetation. Southern California, south of Los Angeles, is dry. Typical dry-land vegetation covers all but the mountainous parts of Arizona, New Mexico and western Texas, and extends northward, east of the Sierra Nevada, as far as southern Oregon and Idaho, and as far east as the Wyoming Basin. The dry-land vegetation extends east of the Rocky Mountains in the south: the dry margin passes close to Forth Worth and San Antonio, and reaches the Gulf of Mexico a little to the north of the Mexican border. Most of the southwestern states are dry, except for the mountains which receive abundant rains in summer and are snow-covered in winter. The Pacific coast from southern California to Puget Sound has a Mediterranean type of climate, with winter rains and summer droughts—cool summers along the coast, hot summers inland.

The weather of the western part of the continent is produced by air masses circulating around the North Pacific oceanic whirl and by the polar outbursts that push into the oceanic whirl. Cold air masses in winter come usually from Siberia, across the North Pacific—which, like the North Atlantic, is very stormy in higher middle latitudes. Cold

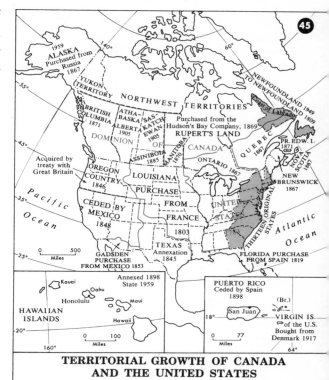

TERRITORIAL GROWTH OF CANADA AND THE UNITED STATES

air masses from Canada also affect the weather of the Rocky Mountain states, and occasionally may even push on into southern California.

THE CULTURE HEARTHS

(Map 44) When the European colonists first came upon the continent of North America it had already been occupied for more than 10,000 years by the so-called Indians. They were a Mongoloid people who had crossed from easternmost Siberia into Alaska at a time during one of the glacial periods when the sea level was some 400 feet lower than it is today. These primitive hunters, fishers, and collectors migrated southward, eventually reaching the southern extremity of South America. In the course of time they learned how to cultivate certain distinctively American crops, chief among which were maize, potatoes, beans, squash, tomatoes, and tobacco. In the part of the hemisphere that later became Latin America there were concentrations of Indians in the areas where the two early civilizations had developed in Central and South America. But in the northern part of North America which later became Anglo-America the Indians were hunters, fishers, collectors, and migratory farmers, with only a loose attachment to the land. The scanty population of Indians had, however, made a number of fundamental changes in the original vegetation cover through the use of fire. Fires in the grasslands swept out of control and had the effect of pushing back and sharpening the western edge of the forest. Within the eastern forests, also, there were grassy openings which the early settlers identified as "Indian oldfields." The Indians could offer no real resistance to the invasions of the Europeans.

The distinctive character of Anglo-America was derived from four chief culture hearths. These were (1) French Canada; (2) New England; (3) the Southern Colonies; and (4) the Middle Colonies. The Dutch, who occupied the Hudson Valley only from 1614 to 1667, nevertheless left an imprint on this area that is visible even today. In the southwest of the United States traits derived from the Spanish culture hearth in Mexico are important; and there are still traces of Russian influence in Alaska and along the Pacific coast almost as far as San Francisco. But the major source regions for the distinctive ways of life in the United States and Canada were the four culture hearths.

French Canada. The culture hearth of French Canada occupied the lower St. Lawrence Valley downstream from Montreal. The first French settlement was made in 1608 at Quebec, and from there French missionaries, trappers, and fur traders spread out inland over a vast area of interior North America. Traveling in their canoes the French occupied the shores of the Great Lakes, and by easy stages reached the headwaters of the Mississippi system and of the rivers draining northward to the Arctic. They held a vast area in a loose grip through trading posts established at such strategic spots as Detroit, Chicago, and St. Louis.

There were other French settlers, however, who came as farmers rather than as missionaries or traders. They laid out their farms along the St. Lawrence in the original area of the culture hearth, and although some emigrants moved from there to other parts of Canada and into northern New England, most of these people remained firmly and solidly settled in the original French area. Here they now form one of the distinctive parts of Canada: a community of farmers, self-sufficient, politically conservative, and Catholic, perpetuating the way of life of rural France in these new surroundings.

New England. The northernmost of the three British culture hearths was in New England. The Pilgrims came to this area in 1620 by mistake, for they were intending to settle in the northern part of Virginia. These were the people who left England and the Netherlands at a time when the first concepts of equality before the law, and of government by consent of the governed, were being formulated. The Plymouth Compact, by which the members of the colony set up their own government and pledged their support to it, was the first written statement of these principles.

The New Englanders took steps to carry out these principles. In the early years of settlement they built their houses close together in villages. The citizens of the community came together periodically for "town meetings," at which the problems of public policy were discussed and decisions were made based on the opinions of the majority. The idea of a veto or of the use of force by a minority were discarded, yet the majority learned to respect the rights of a minority. The people of New England recognized the need for popular education, and they established public schools and colleges. The first college to be established in Anglo-America was Harvard in 1636.

New England was, however, a harsh habitat for these early settlers. Its stony or sandy soils, its many ledges of bare rock, its severe winters and cool summers made farming difficult. Yet, with great labor, fields were cleared of trees and the stones were used to make walls. The farmers learned from the Indians how to grow the Indian crops, maize, beans, and squash; and they also tried the familiar European grains, wheat, barley, rye, and oats. The chief source of wealth, however, was the sea, in which there was an abundance of fish—including the cod which was familiar to the fishermen of Western Europe. The New England forests provided masts and timber for ships. Little by little the economy of New England shifted from farming to seafaring, and the New England merchants sent their ships to trade in the ports of the whole world.

The Southern Colonies. Very different were the ideas developed in the culture hearth of the Southern Colonies. The first settlement in Virginia, in 1607, was soon followed by others which spread along the navigable rivers of the Coastal Plain from Maryland to South Carolina. The land was divided into large private estates, and the owners enjoyed the status of "landed gentry." They developed a way of life which was both genial and civilized. There was music, literature, and dancing; the children of the well-to-do were educated at home by tutors.

The Southern Colonies developed a plantation economy. It happened that at about this time the Indian crop, tobacco, and the Indian method of smoking it in pipes, met with great favor in England. When the tobacco plant was introduced into Virginia it did very well in the hot, rainy summers, and there was an expanding market for all the tobacco that could be sent home. But there were not enough workers available to clear the land, to plant, cultivate, and harvest the crop, and to prepare the leaf for shipment. At first indentured servants from England were tried, but then the landowners turned to Negro slavery as a solution to the labor problem. In the Carolinas the landowners tried various other kinds of commercial crops—such as cotton, rice, and indigo.

In the culture hearth of the Southern Colonies there was strong support for the concept of liberty. Liberty, however, meant the right of the free citizens to elect their own government without arbitrary interference from England. Yet, at the same time, the idea that Negro slaves might have the right to equal treatment before the law was disturbing and subversive, for slavery had become the necessary basis for the economic life.

The Middle Colonies. The culture hearth of the Middle Colonies was located on the hilly Piedmont of eastern Pennsylvania, and the adjoining parts of New Jersey and western Maryland. Here the yields of tobacco were not enough to make these products commercially profitable. But wheat and maize, and other food crops, did much better than on the stony farms of New England. To this culture hearth came Europeans from many different countries: first the Dutch and the Swedes, but soon there was a strong incoming tide of English, Scottish, and Irish; and there were also many Germans. All established themselves on the land as small farmers, each family building a home on its own farm. Several different kinds of religious beliefs were introduced. There were the Dutch Reformed and Lutheran churches, the Roman Catholic and Quaker, the Presbyterian from Scotland, and the Anglican from England. All learned to live together in mutual tolerance. Because most of the people lived on separate farms rather than in compact village communities, education was carried on in the family; but because the families were not well-to-do commercial farmers, there were no tutors. The children learned from their parents to read from the Bible, to write, and to do simple arithmetic. The immediate family, grouped around the hearthside, was the basic unit, and it was usually a self-sufficient one.

From this mixture of peoples of different origins came an amazing series of innovations. These were the farmers who first made use of the Indian grain, maize, to feed the European domestic animal, the hog. Maize was raised as a feed as well as a food, and bacon, ham, and lard were produced for sale. These people were the first to build the sturdy four-wheeled wagons, drawn by teams of horses or oxen, which later were known as "prairie schooners." These people invented the long rifle. They adapted the Scandinavian log cabin to American conditions. They invented the pot-bellied stove that heated the cabins much more efficiently than open fireplaces. Here also there was democracy. The self-educated frontiersmen were not so much interested in ideas as were the Southerners, nor in methods as were the New England-

ers; but they did learn to practice a system of equality and tolerance among their neighbors and equals. From this culture hearth came the restless pioneers who were the most vigorous in pushing westward across the Appalachians into Kentucky and Tennessee, then northward into Canada, and later across the mountains and deserts to the Pacific coast.

THE UNITED STATES OF AMERICA

The United States of America was fashioned from the mixture of attitudes, objectives, and technical skills of the three British culture hearths. When the newly independent country brought together a group of its leading men to write a constitution they came from all three culture hearths, and the compromises they worked out made national existence possible. The world's first systematic statement of the ideals of the Democratic Revolution are contained in the Declaration of Independence, the Constitution, and its first ten amendments.

How has it happened that the people from these diverse culture hearths, and the millions of immigrants from other culture regions, have been able to achieve such a high degree of freedom, security, and material comfort that they have become the envy of the rest of the world? Are they more skillful, more intelligent, more resourceful than other people? Are they willing to work harder? Do they occupy lands more abundantly endowed with resources than other lands? To find the answers to these questions it is necessary to go back to these three culture hearths and trace the changes that have led step by step to the formation of the modern nation.

The growth of population and the expansion of the area of settlement started as soon as the earliest colonies were established. At first growth was lateral, hemmed in by the Appalachians. By 1700 the settlements formed an almost complete belt all the way from what is now Maine to Virginia. Map 44 shows that by 1760 the pioneers had pushed across Pennsylvania to Pittsburgh, by 1790 they had started down the Ohio River, and had occupied the fertile limestone basins of Kentucky and Tennessee. The map also shows the parts of the country most directly reached by influences from each of the three British culture hearths.

The process of population growth, settlement expansion, and economic change, by which the struggling nation of 1783 grew into the modern giant, involved a series of stages. In each stage there was a different balance between technical skills, economic institutions, political attitudes, and the resource base—the land. At each stage, moreover, the national territory was marked off into more or less clearly defined sections which differed in the nature of the resource base, in economic development and orientation, and in political attitudes. It is possible to identify five stages in the development of the United States: (1) the period of adjustment to independence (1783-1840); (2) the initial phase of the Industrial Revolution (1840-1860); (3) the development of a mature economy (1865-1910); (4) the achievement of high mass consumption (1910-1950); and (5) new revolutions in technology (since 1950).

The Adjustment to Independence (1783-1840). During the time when the newly federated states were becoming adjusted to national independence, and when the national territory was being expanded westward toward and beyond the Mississippi (Map 45), the states tended to group into three distinctive sections (Map 46a). The

New England culture hearth and the Middle Colonies developed strong common interests which served to differentiate the Northeast from the rest of the country. Beyond the Appalachians was the frontier, which after 1787 was known as the Northwest Territories. The third section, in the south, was distinguished by the existence of slavery, and a cotton and tobacco economy.

The Northeast. Manufacturing industries appeared first in the Middle Colonies and in southern New England. The poverty of the soil in hilly New England was evident even by the middle of the eighteenth century when this part of the colonies became a net importer of basic foods and fibers. In the port cities the chief industries included handicrafts, rum distilling, and shipbuilding; and the New England merchants sent ships to trade or fish all over the world. In the Middle Colonies agriculture was more successful in producing the basic foods, and a better balance between farming and urban industries was established. New York became the chief port, with Philadelphia second, and Baltimore not far behind. Philadelphia, with its "Fall Line" water power, had developed a variety of industries, manufacturing textiles, hats, food and wood products, hosiery, paper, and printing. Sugar refining, iron founding, and toolmaking were also carried on. These were all small-scale enterprises, easily supplied with raw materials by the small sailing ships of that day, or by horse-drawn wagons overland.

The late eighteenth century was the time when the British inventors were starting to produce their new machines. In 1769 Richard Arkwright patented his machines for weaving yarn; but the British were not at all willing to permit the new machines to be exported. The Philadelphians offered a prize to any one who would build a spinning ma-

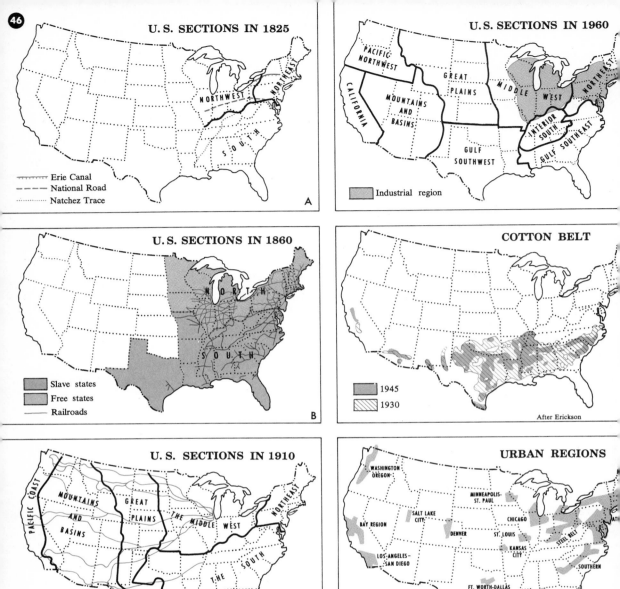

U. S. SECTIONS IN 1825

NORTHWEST
NORTHEST
S O U T H

⊥⊥⊥⊥⊥⊥ Erie Canal
‑‑‑‑ National Road
········· Natchez Trace

A

U. S. SECTIONS IN 1960

PACIFIC NORTHWEST
CALIFORNIA
MOUNTAINS AND BASINS
GREAT PLAINS
MIDDLE WEST
NORTHEAST
INTERIOR SOUTH
GULF SOUTHWEST
GULF SOUTHEAST

▨ Industrial region

U. S. SECTIONS IN 1860

N O R T H
S O U T H

▨ Slave states
▨ Free states
— Railroads

B

COTTON BELT

▨ 1945
▨ 1930

After Erickson

U. S. SECTIONS IN 1910

PACIFIC COAST
MOUNTAINS AND BASINS
GREAT PLAINS
THE MIDDLE WEST
NORTHEAST
THE SOUTH

— Transcontinental railroads

C

URBAN REGIONS

WASHINGTON OREGON
BAY REGION
SALT LAKE CITY
LOS ANGELES‑ SAN DIEGO
DENVER
MINNEAPOLIS‑ ST. PAUL
CHICAGO
ST. LOUIS
KANSAS CITY
STEEL BELT
ATH
SOUTHERN
FT. WORTH‑DALLAS
GULF REGION
FLORIDA

0   500
Scale of Miles

chine in America, and in response a young mechanic named Samuel Slater came to Philadelphia with the plans of the Arkright frame in his head. The Philadelphians, however, did not wish to risk their capital on such a speculative proposition, and Slater went to Rhode Island looking for backers. The New England merchants were not afraid of speculative ventures: Slater built the first thread mill in Pawtucket, near Providence, in 1790. In consequence New England, rather than Pennsylvania, became the chief textile manufacturing region of the United States.

Slater's knowledge of the new machinery did not extend to the steam engine. Power for the new mills, therefore, was supplied by falling water—and all through the interior of New England were many small water-power sites, which had been created when the glaciers disarranged the pre-glacial drainage. Textile factories, and manufacturing towns sprang up in small units along the New England valleys.

The Northeast became industrialized. By 1840 this section had more than 30 per cent of its workers employed in manufacturing industries, while the average for the whole country was only about 20 per cent. The Northeast also became interested in tariffs to protect its new industries from imported products. This part of the country was not at all sympathetic to the system of slavery since this would have been quite unprofitable in an industrial or a small farm economy.

The Northwest. The second of the three sections at this early stage of national growth was the Northwest—the newly colonized land west of the Appalachians. From Pittsburgh the settlers had gone down the Ohio River, and spread outwards from it. The Ordinance of 1785 provided for a survey of all the unsettled parts of the national territory in accordance with a rectangular system of section, township, and range; and the lands thus marked off were put up for sale. The pioneers who moved onto the new lands, cleared the forest, and started farming, came mostly from the Middle Colonies (Map 44). They brought with them many of the features that continue to characterize the farming of the United States, such as a dispersed pattern of population on family farms worked by the owners, and the practice of growing maize and feeding it to hogs or cattle. They also brought with them the log cabin and the four-wheeled wagon.

The people in the Northwest were isolated from the potential markets of the Northeast. They could not ship their lumber, bacon, lard, and tobacco back east. In-

stead they built rafts and floated these products down the Ohio and Mississippi rivers to New Orleans where they sold rafts and all. They would then walk home again over the famous Natchez Trace (Map 46a). From the original settlers of the Middle Colonies these people inherited an urge to pioneer in new lands, to carve new farms out of the forest. It was their influence in the government that led to the expansion of the national territory westward in the Louisiana Purchase of 1803 (Map 45).

The South. The third section, the South, differed notably from the other two. Here tobacco and cotton were grown as commercial crops with Negro slave labor. Cotton had been introduced from the tropics through Charleston. In the hot, rainy summers the plant grew well, but each winter it was killed by frosts. Whereas the plant would continue productive for several years in the tropics, here new varieties of the cotton plant had to be developed as annuals. In 1793 Eli Whitney invented the cotton gin, a device which permitted one worker to do the work of two hundred in separating the seed from the fiber. With the advantage of the new, high-yielding varieties of cotton, and the cotton gin, the South was able to compete with the tropical countries in the production of low-cost fiber for the English textile mills. Since the South had no industries to protect and wanted access to a foreign market for its export product, this section of the country opposed the idea of protective tariffs as advocated by the Northeast.

Cotton plantations appeared first in several separate localities where soils were especially favorable. These were the Piedmont of South Carolina, the Black Belt of Alabama west of Montgomery at the southern extremity of the Appalachians, the country around Natchez on the valley bluff overlooking the Mississippi floodplain, the western part of Tennessee around Memphis, and the Nashville Basin of Tennessee. But the expansion of English textile manufacturing at this time created an increasing demand for cotton, and soon plantations were carved out of the forests from the Carolinas around the southern end of the Appalachians as far as the Mississippi. It was found profitable to grow cotton as far north as there was a growing season of two hundred days (Map 43): where frosts reduced the growing season to less than two hundred days the yields were not high enough to make cotton planting profitable at the prices then paid. Just north of this line tobacco could be planted. South of the two-hundred-day line, cotton swept westward across the Mississippi, into Arkansas, southern Oklahoma, and eastern Texas.

The Initial Phase of the Industrial Revolution (1840-1860). The initial phase of the Industrial Revolution took place in the United States between 1840 and 1860. It was supported by the construction of railroads, and by the steel industry which developed as a result of the need for rails. It was made possible by a considerable investment of foreign capital, notably from Britain and France.

The effort to provide transportation between the Northwest Territories and the Northeast, and so to reorient the flow of trade toward the Northeast, rather than down-river to the south, began as early as 1800. The "National Road" was started about this time, to run from Washington across the Allegheny Front, through the hilly country and into Ohio (Map 46a). It was planned eventually to extend the road to St. Louis, but it was never completed as a wagon road. At present the old National Road is followed almost exactly by US 40. In 1825 the Erie Canal was completed between Albany and Buffalo, and at once the products of the Northwest began to move eastward instead of down the Mississippi. The pre-eminence of New York was established at the end of the Hudson-Mohawk route. Railroads soon replaced canals for most shipments. The first twelve miles of the Baltimore and Ohio Railroad were opened for business in 1830. In 1831 railroads started operations out of New Orleans, and between Albany and Schenectady. In 1833 the Southern Railroad started running trains out of Charleston, South Carolina. The first railroads in New England, in 1835, connected Boston with Lowell, Worcester, and Providence. By 1840 there were 2,799 miles of railroads in the United States, and by 1850 there were 8,683 miles. Between 1850 and 1860 the mileage jumped to 30,283. This was a period when rail connections with the old Northwest Territories completely reoriented the economy of that area. The two sections became complementary in their economies, and cooperative in politics (Map 46b).

It was the need for better rails in the period after 1850 that provided the initial impetus for the development of the steel industry. The new railroads of the 1830's and 1840's were built with iron rails; but even with the relatively light traffic of that period it was found that the rails would wear out and require replacement in about two years. Modern steel rails last for as much as eighteen years on main lines. In the 1850's no one knew how to make good steel in large quantities and at low cost per unit. As late as 1855 the chief fuel used in making pig iron was charcoal, although there were some furnaces in Pennsylvania that made use of anthracite coal from the Scranton area. Pennsylvania was the chief source of the iron ore. After 1856 technological improvements made possible the use of bituminous coal converted into coke, and rapidly increased the capacity to produce steel. As a result of these changes, the iron and steel industry shifted to the Pittsburgh-Cleveland area where bituminous coal was in abundance, and where, in the course of time, lake steamers could bring iron ore from Minnesota (Map 48).

As settlement proceeded toward the west, the issue over slave-states and free-states was sharpened. Ever since 1800 it had been customary to admit new states to the Union in pairs, so that the balance in Congress between slave states and free states could be maintained. West of the Mississippi, however, the continuation of this policy did not seem possible. The Louisiana Purchase clearly included more land in the north than in the south (Map 45). The westward expansion of the southern section was blocked for a time by territory belonging to Mexico. Pioneers, however, paid little attention to political boundaries, and moved on into new country when they found it attractive and only thinly occupied. After many years of friction with the Mexican authorities in Texas, the English-speaking settlers declared the independence of Texas from Mexico, and in 1836 defeated the Mexican forces. From 1836 to 1845 Texas was an independent country. Then it agreed to join the Union in 1845 as a slave state, and it looked for a time as if the balance in Congress might be maintained.

In fact, however, the territory into which the pioneers were moving was very different in its physical character from the eastern part of the country. It was clear that before long cotton planting in the traditional manner would be blocked by inadequate rainfall—and when cotton was blocked, so was slavery. Furthermore, the settlement of the west was coming from the old Northwest rather than from the South.

In 1847 the Mormons established their colony at Salt Lake City, and the state that they outlined included much of what is now Utah, Nevada, and southern California. Pioneers were moving also into the Oregon Territory, which Great Britain agreed to relinquish to the United States. As a result of the War with Mexico, California was ceded, and almost immediately thereafter gold was discovered near Sacramento. The result was a rush of new settlers into this far western territory. When California was admitted as a state in 1850 there was no mention of slavery in its constitution.

By 1860 there was a strong political split in the United States between the North and the South (Map 46b). The issue of slavery was one fundamental cause of the division, but there were also other important differences between the two sections. The South was rural, with a land-owning aristocracy, and with an economy based on the export of cotton and tobacco. The North was rapidly changing toward an urban industrial society, with an economy based on manufacturing industries. Agriculture was carried on by small landowners, who lived and worked on their own farms. To them slavery was not only abhorrent but also unprofitable. This part of the United States had entered the initial phase of the Industrial Revolution. With the more densely settled part of the national territory thus divided into two rather than three sections, each with a distinctive state-idea, and with the west still too remote to act as a balance, the stage was set for the Civil War.

The Development of a Mature Economy (1865-1910). During the half century between the Civil War and the beginning of World War I the United States went through the transition period from the initial phase of the Industrial Revolution to the development of a mature economy. In general, this process of economic growth was similar to that described in the Introduction, and similar to the process of growth already completed in Great Britain and to that going on at the same time in France and Germany. But in the United States there was one basic difference—a difference that made the development of the United States unique in world history: the process of development of a mature economy was carried on in a period of vast expansion—expansion of population, expansion of the gross national product at a rate greater than that of population, expansion of the market for all kinds of products, expansion of the national territory and of the resource base provided by the physical habitat. Of course there were business recessions, and prosperity seemed to go up and down in cycles; but the trend was generally upward. Everywhere there was growth; and from this atmosphere of growth the American character became stamped with an attitude of confidence and optimism which, in itself, promoted further growth. A mature economy was reached sometime during the first decade of the twentieth century, and embraced an area of continental proportions.

In this process of growth the old alignment of North and South ceased to be important. In fact a new major division of the country appeared, which for a time threatened to break the growing nation apart. This was a division of economy and political attitude between the humid east and the dry west. This dangerous two-fold division, however, was blurred and balanced by the appearance of six distinctive sections (Map 46c). The processes that led, step by step, to the pattern of sections observable in 1910 may be described under four headings: (1) the forging of effective connections with California; (2) the building of new indus-

trial capacity in the Northeast and the Middle West; (3) the settlement of the grasslands; and (4) the appearance of areas of specialized economic production.

Connections with California. In 1865 there was great danger that the Union might be split apart in a new direction. The forces for disintegration had been overcome by war; but now a new challenge arose with the settlement of California. The settlements along the Pacific coast were not only remote from the settled eastern parts of the United States; they were also facing quite new and different problems in an unfamiliar habitat. Here was a land of rainy winters and dry summers where agricultural practices differed from those of the east. Here was a dry land where irrigation had to be developed and where the flow of water in the rivers had to be conserved. Here was mountainous country, rich in gold, silver, timber, and furs.

The basic challenge was to tie these remote settlements with the long-settled east. The form of government, with its structure of separate states, permitted a large amount of local autonomy; yet never before in history had so large and varied an area been under one government without a strong central authority backed by military force. Was it possible to build the necessary physical facilities for communication and for the transport of products over such vast dis tances? Before the Civil War mail sent westward from the Mississippi by stage took at least three weeks to reach San Francisco. It took just about the same length of time to send mail by ship to Panamá, across the isthmus, and by ship again to California. The Pony Express, started in 1860, could carry small loads of urgent mail in eight days. On the other hand, bulky shipments had to go by water all the way around the southern tip of South America. A telegraph

DEVELOPMENT OF RAILROADS IN THE UNITED STATES

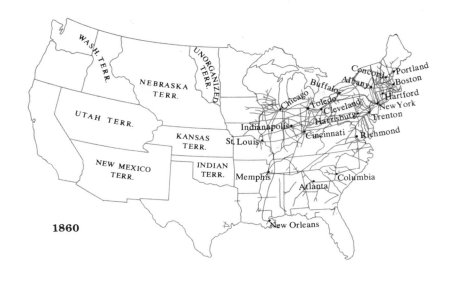

1860

47

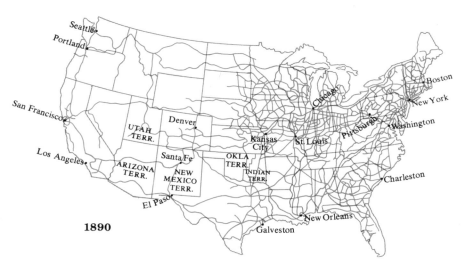

1890

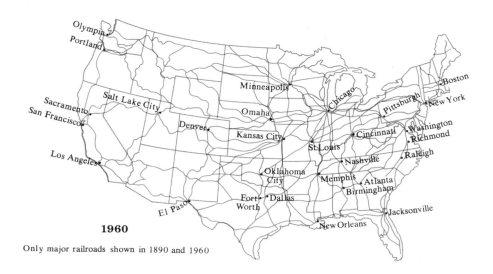

1960

Only major railroads shown in 1890 and 1960

line, opened in 1861, helped to speed the sending of messages.

The preservation of the Union, which permitted the United States to grow up to embrace its immense national territory, was achieved because it became technically and financially possible to build transcontinental railroads. The railroad itself had only been known in America for a few decades, and the use of steel rails had started just before the Civil War. By the end of the war there was enough new steel-making capacity in the Northeast and the Middle West to turn out steel rails fast enough and cheaply enough to permit their use on the transcontinental lines. There were also immigrant Irish workers numerous and hardy enough to do the job of laying the rails across thousands of miles of deserts and mountains. And there were financiers who could command capital, and whose business vision was broad enough to plan and direct the whole incredible operation.

The first of these transcontinental railroads was built between Omaha and San Francisco. It was started at both ends in 1863, and on May 10, 1869, the Central Pacific and the Union Pacific lines were joined near Ogden, Utah. Within the next two decades railroads were built to connect Chicago, St. Louis, and New Orleans with the Pacific Northwest and with southern California; and additional lines in between connected the country east of the Mississippi with Denver and Salt Lake City (Map 47).

Industrial Development. Meanwhile the extension of railroads and the construction of new manufacturing industries went on rapidly in the older, eastern part of the United States. The total mileage of railroads in the nation as a whole jumped from 53,878 in 1870 to 163,597 in 1890, and by 1910 reached 240,293. It was this rapid extension

of the railroads that not only made possible the transportation of bulky goods at low cost, but also provided a steadily increasing market for steel. The new transcontinental lines opened up the previously little settled country between the Mississippi and the Pacific coast. From this vast territory came not only gold and silver, but also many industrial raw materials needed by the eastern factories. With the expansion of the national income, the market for consumer goods of all sorts increased steadily; and millions of immigrants came to America to take advantage of the increasing number and variety of jobs. They came because they heard that America was prosperous, and because they came America was prosperous. In addition to people, there was a strong flow of capital investment into the United States; although, even so, about 95 per cent of all investment was derived from savings in the United States. Between 1870 and 1910 the gross national product averaged a 10 per cent growth each decade.

Basic to all this economic growth was the increase in the capacity to produce steel. During the period of great railroad expansion, nearly 70 per cent of the steel was used to make steel rails; but later there was an increase in the use of steel to manufacture an increasing variety of consumer goods. This shift from the use of steel for rails to the use of steel for other manufactures marked the achievement of maturity.

During the period from 1865 to 1910 the steel industry became concentrated in new areas. After the development of the beehive coke oven in 1859, bituminous coal became the chief fuel used in the manufacture of steel, replacing anthracite coal and charcoal. The industry began to move away from Scranton, and because more coal than iron ore was required in the steel-making process, the mills were located near the bitu-

minous coal fields (Map 48). In 1879, some 2.10 tons of coal were needed to produce one ton of pig iron. By 1910, technological progress, and differences in the composition of the iron ore used, resulted in a drop in the coal requirements—only 1.62 tons were needed to produce a ton of pig iron. But by this time the industry had become established close to the coal sources, and the steel centers were attracting other steel-using industries to the same areas. These major industrial concentrations were at Buffalo, in the triangle between Pittsburgh, Youngstown, and Cleveland, and around Gary at the southern end of Lake Michigan.

This shift to the southern shores of the Great Lakes was accompanied by the start of mining operations on the great Mesabi Range, located a little northwest of Duluth near the western end of Lake Superior. The Mesabi iron ore body was remarkable for its purity. Furthermore it was near the surface, with only a thin covering of glacial drift, which permitted mining by open-pit methods rather than with expensive shafts and tunnels. And it was close to the shore of Lake Superior. When mining started at Mesabi in 1892, the Sault Ste. Marie canal was already in operation, connecting Lake Superior with the lower lakes. The canal had been built in 1855, and enlarged in 1881. The Michigan and Minnesota ores could be shipped only during the summer because of ice; but during the shipping period a vast tonnage of ore was carried by lake steamers through the canal, and thence

A cattle roundup in Arizona. In spite of the development of modern techniques for fattening beef cattle, the herding is still done largely on horseback.

to the industrial centers along the southern shores of the lakes. Nowhere else in the world was industrial growth so aided by the geographic arrangement of raw materials and markets.

Early in this period a belt of concentrated manufacturing activities appeared in the Northeast and the Middle West. By 1870, about 80 per cent of all industrial employment was in the area extending from southern New England to Baltimore, and across Pennsylvania and New York to the southern shores of the Great Lakes. In 1870, about 44 per cent of the people of the Northeast lived in cities: by 1910 more than 70 per cent did so. In the Middle West the urban population of 1870 was a little over 20 per cent; but by 1910 the proportion had increased to 53 per cent.

The Settlement of the Grasslands. The growth of manufacturing industries, however, was only a part of the story of expansion in the period between 1865 and 1910. The spread of farm settlement onto the grasslands was another epic. Before the Civil War the prairies west of Chicago did not have a high value, since, in the absence of timber, settlement on them was not easy. After the Indians and the buffalo had been eliminated, the grassy plains, which extended as far as the front of the Rocky Mountains, from Canada to Texas (Map 8, pp. 16-17), were used chiefly for pasturing cattle on the unfenced range. As the railroads advanced across the plains, the railheads became places to which the animals were driven for shipment east. Around the margins of the grasslands a string of great commercial cities became established. These included Edmonton and Winnipeg in Canada; and in the United States Minneapolis-St. Paul, Chicago, Indianapolis, St. Louis, Kansas City, Dallas and Fort Worth.

The spread of farm settlement onto the grasslands was made possible by a series of inventions. As a result of these the American grasslands were transformed from low-value range lands to high-value farm lands excellently suited to the production of grain and meat. The first invention that made all this possible was the railroad itself, for without low-cost bulk transport the products of the farms could never have been brought to the eastern markets. Another important invention of the 1830's was the steel plow, for the traditional iron-shod plow could not turn the thick prairie sod.

At the time of the Civil War the grasslands were still not developed for the kind of farming now characteristic of the Middle West. However, from the Middle Colonies the farmers who pioneered across the Appalachians brought the system of raising wheat and maize, and feeding the maize to hogs and cattle. This combination of grains and livestock on the same farm had been found remarkably profitable, in part because the animal manure could be used to maintain the productivity of the soil. On the open range, however, the manure was lost. And, on the grasslands where timber was scarce, it was not possible to fence the fields to keep grazing animals away from the growing crops, so that friction was produced between farmers and cattlemen.

This problem was solved by the invention of barbed wire. This new kind of wire was invented in 1873, and its manufacture in large quantities was immediately undertaken by the nearby steel industries. Within a decade barbed wire had been sent to the other areas of midlatitude grasslands throughout the world. Barbed wire made low-cost fencing possible, and for the first time in history cattle and grain could be raised on the same farm in the world's prairies. For the first time the rich black soil under the tall grass could be used for grain farming without excluding cattle from the region.

The fences, however, created new problems. On the range cattle could easily walk to a nearby stream to get water; but when the pastures were fenced water had to be provided. Digging a well was possible but not easy until the invention of well-drilling machinery. Then there was the problem of how to bring the water to the surface. Windmills had been known since antiquity, and had been brought back to the Netherlands by the crusaders who found them in use in the Holy Land. But the Dutch windmills were cumbersome affairs which had to be turned toward the wind by hand, and could only be stopped by furling the sails. Furthermore, on the prairies there was no material available with which to build these windmills. In 1854 Daniel Hallady of Connecticut built a new kind of mill which would turn automatically toward the wind, and which could be stopped by turning the fan blades. The new mills, built of wood, were produced in quantity by a manufacturer, and shipped to the prairie farms to be assembled. Along with drilling machines and windmills came other inventions: the large harvesting combine, first used in California, made it possible for one farmer to harvest a large acreage where yields per acre were low; new and more efficient plows and harrows raised productivity per farmer; silos made possible the storage of feed for the winter feeding of animals in a severe-winter climate; new varieties of wheat raised the yield per acre in semiarid country.

The movement of farmers onto the grasslands began after the Civil War. In 1862 the Homestead Act provided that any one who was willing to develop a farm could take possession of 160 acres of the public domain with no payment other than registry fees. After 1870 the spread onto the prairies continued rapidly. As land values increased, farmers profited not only from producing and selling farm products, but also from the "unearned increment"—the increased value of their lands. This increased value, collected by a vast number of small farmers, was spent to purchase the products of the factories. And in this region there began to appear a phenomenon unique in world history—farmers who retired to live on income from mortgages.

As the wave of farm settlement continued toward the west, a new kind of habitat was entered. The short-grass steppe was a reflection of reduced, and less dependable, rainfall. In the semiarid climates new techniques of farming had to be developed, and farms had to be much larger than in the humid east. By 1890 all the first-class public land in the United States had been occupied, and the frontier of new settlement had essentially disappeared. Thereafter new settlement only filled in the empty places, bringing into use poorer and poorer soils. In 1909 the Homestead Act was revised to permit settlers to take out 320 acres, and in 1916 as much as 640 acres, of land.

Specialized Economic Regions. As settlement spread over all the empty area between the Mississippi and the Pacific coast, many diverse habitats were occupied. With reductions in the costs of transportation, and an increase in the demand for varied products, many areas of specialized production appeared. For example, in the Salinas Valley of California farmers came to specialize in growing lettuce, and from this one valley now comes about 80 per cent of the lettuce consumed in the whole United States. Because of especially favorable physical conditions, or because of the presence of farmers with special skills, certain small areas could be devoted almost exclusively to the production of one kind of vegetable or one kind of fruit. And because there were no trade barriers within the vast territory of the country, these specialized products could reach the national market. By 1910 the agricultural regions of the United States had been highly diversified, with numerous small areas devoted to specialized products. This kind of national interdependence allows for the widest variety of goods at the lowest possible costs.

The Six Sections. As a result of this process of growth and diversification, the territory of the United States in 1910 was marked off into six sections (Map 46c). The Northeast and the Middle West were primarily industrial; but in these sections, especially in the Middle West, there were areas of very productive agriculture and also of mining. The Great Plains included the drier parts of the farming and ranching country; and because of the recurrence of drought, and the uncertain nature of the agriculture, the farmers of this section had to face problems quite different from those of the Middle West, and to seek quite different political solutions. This was the region that was represented by the so-called "Farm Block" in Congress.

The Mountain and Basin section included a vast expanse of varied country, towering ranges of high mountains, sunlit desert basins, forests and barren lands. The basic support for the economy came from mining —not only mining for gold and silver, but also for copper, lead and zinc, and other industrial metals. Near the railroads the forests of the wetter mountains could be cut and shipped east as lumber. Range cattle and sheep were driven above timber line in summer to feed on the rich grasses of the mountains, and were driven back to the lowlands in winter to be fed on alfalfa. This characteristic form of transhumance was developed throughout the section. And in a few favored spots where water could be provided for irrigation, there were areas

Vineyards at San Bernardino in southern California.

of intensive agriculture. The Mormons had been the first English-speaking settlers to develop irrigation. But they were soon followed by many other settlers whose chief interest was in agriculture. By 1890 irrigated areas dotted the mountain piedmonts throughout the area. When railroads made them accessible to eastern markets these oases came to specialize in such crops as potatoes, sugar beets, fruits, and vegetables. In the Columbia Plateau of eastern Washington and Oregon the land was used for vast wheat farms. Throughout the area, also, many places were set off as national

*Land ruined by erosion in the hills of northern Alabama. Rural poverty is
the result of poor farm technology. Such lands are now being redeveloped.*

parks or national monuments to preserve especially striking pieces of scenery. The first of these was Yellowstone National Park, established in 1872 to preserve the geysers and hot springs. More and more people were attracted to the region as tourists.

Meanwhile the Pacific Coast section continued to thrive, as new farm settlement spread around the Puget Sound Lowland, and the Willamette Valley in Oregon; throughout the Central Valley of California, and around Los Angeles in Southern California. In this varied section, with its mild rainy winters and hot dry summers, many specialized districts appeared, sending products all the way across the continent to the eastern markets.

The sixth section was the South. This region, in the period from 1865 to 1910, hardly shared in the economic growth characteristic of the rest of the country. In 1880 the South had 27 per cent of the population of the United States, but produced only 14

per cent of the national income. The farmers continued to struggle with an obsolete agricultural system. The slaves were replaced by tenants and sharecroppers, working for the white owners. There seemed to be no way of escape from the cotton-planting system in the presence of large numbers of illiterate, untrained, and very poor Negro and white workers.

Cotton planting proved disastrous to the land. Even as late as 1910 the planting, cultivation, and harvesting was done by hand. The system was based on the employment of an abundant low-paid labor force. But cotton farming on hilly land caused serious soil erosion. On the cleared and plowed land of the Southeast the typical summer cloudbursts cut immense gullies, and stripped the top soil from the whole cotton-growing area. By 1910 there were parts of the Cotton Belt that had been so eroded that they had become useless. An outstanding example was the Black Belt of

Alabama. So great was the destruction of this once-productive land, that a dense Negro population was left stranded on it, reduced to the level of subsistence farmers struggling for survival.

In the South there were almost no alternative forms of employment. To be sure, there was a steel industry at Birmingham, Alabama, based on nearby sources of coal, iron ore, and limestone. There were a few places where lumber was cut, and some manufacturing plants using wood as the raw material. On the Coastal Plain a few people were employed in the production of tar, pitch, turpentine, and rosin from the pine forests. But mostly there was no place for the poor tenant or sharecropper to go— nothing to do but go on raising more cotton on land that yielded poorer and poorer harvests.

United States Overseas. By 1910 two other changes had appeared. The supply of first-class, free land ready for farm colonists was at an end. And the United States had expanded overseas. After the war with Spain, the United States came into possession of Puerto Rico, the Hawaiian Islands, and the Philippines, as well as some smaller island bases in the Pacific Ocean. In 1903 the newly independent Panamá leased a strip of land to the United States "in perpetuity" for the purpose of building a canal. Work on the canal started in 1903, and was completed in 1915. The United States had become a world power—almost before its citizens knew what had happened.

The Achievement of High Mass Consumption (1910-1950). The achievement of an economy of high mass consumption took place, in spite of two wars and a depression, between 1910 and 1950. The mature economy was further diversified by the appearance of many new kinds of consumer goods, notably automobiles, and by the continued elaboration of service occupations. The national wealth was spread widely among the people, and the gross national product continued to increase—until in 1950 the United States produced nearly half of the world's total of goods and services.

The achievement of high mass consumption was accompanied by a further diversification of the national territory. The eight sections that have characterized the geography of the United States since 1950 are shown on Map 46d. The processes that produced these changes can be described under three headings: (1) the growth of the automobile industry; (2) the transformation of the South; and (3) the industrialization of the West Coast.

The Automobile Industry. The invention of the automobile started a new phase of the Industrial Revolution. The internal combustion motor was developed in Germany and France between 1874 and 1894; and inventors, like Henry Ford in the United States, started working with new models of the motor between 1890 and 1900. But the big growth of the automobile industry took place around Detroit, and in nearby parts of Ohio and Indiana, after 1910. In 1908 there were 194,400 automobiles registered in the United States, but by 1914 there were 1,664,000. The economies resulting from the new large-scale manufacturing operations— the beginnings of automation—brought the prices of automobiles down to what large numbers of people could afford to pay. By 1948, about 54 per cent of the families in the United States owned an automobile, and by 1958 the proportion had reached 73 per cent. The result was the development of a huge new industrial concentration which included the manufacture of many new kinds of products related to the automobile. New kinds of raw materials were needed, and this stimulated mining operations throughout the world. Tin, which is used in bearings, regained a strategic significance it had not enjoyed since the bronze age.

The automobile brought about many changes in the patterns of settlement and the distribution of population. Old wagon roads had to be rebuilt, and new highways laid out; and along the highways many of the economic activities once found only in the cities began to spread away from the old urban areas. Population began to migrate from the central cities into the sprawling suburbs. A radically different way of life appeared as more and more people began to live close to the highways rather than on the land.

The Transformation of the South. The South began its spectacular economic growth about 1930. By 1950 two distinct sections had appeared—the Southeast and the Gulf Southwest.

The first attack on the economic problems of this region came with the development of the hydroelectric potential of the Southeast. As early as 1916 a power plant had been built on the Tennessee River at Muscle Shoals, and the power used to manufacture nitrate for fertilizer. But the major development of this area took place after 1933, under the direction of the Tennessee Valley Authority. A new concentration of manufacturing industries developed in response to an abundant supply of electric power. A similar development of the hydroelectric potential of the Piedmont in North Carolina resulted in a new concentration of the cotton textile industry in that area. Many of the companies which formerly operated in New England moved to these new southern manufacturing districts.

The second cause of the transformation of the South was the mechanization of cotton growing. During World War II the new mechanical cotton pickers, along with new machines for planting and cultivating the cotton, made it possible for one skilled worker to do the work that once required hundreds of low-paid, unskilled field hands. Former tenants and sharecroppers were forced in large numbers to seek employment in the new factories of the region, and large numbers also were forced to move to the cities of the Northeast and the Middle West. Mechanization made it necessary to give up growing cotton in hilly areas: cotton is now concentrated on the level lands of the Coastal Plain, the Mississippi floodplain, and the black prairies of Texas (Map 46e). There has been a large increase in cotton growing in the irrigated areas of Arizona and California. On the old cotton plantations of the Southeast some of the land is used for other crops such as peanuts, much of it is used to grow feed for cattle, and much has been replanted with forests for the production of lumber and pulpwood.

The third cause of the transformation of the South is the development of new petrochemical industries in the Gulf Southwest, especially around Houston and Dallas in Texas (Map 48). The Texas and Oklahoma oil and gas fields, along with sulfur and salt from the Gulf coast, provide the raw materials for the manufacture of synthetic rubber and a variety of industrial chemicals. Gas from this region is now piped to California and to the cities of the Middle West and the Northeast.

The Industrialization of the Pacific Coast. The third of the major shifts in economic development during the period up to 1950 has been the development of manufacturing industries, and the further differentiation of agriculture, along the Pacific Coast. In the Pacific Northwest the changes are based on the huge power potential of the Columbia River, and the extension of irrigation as a by-product of power development. In California, new concentrations of heavy industry have appeared along the shores of San Francisco Bay and in the Los Angeles area. However, nearly half of the industrial expansion of California, during and since World War II, has been in the manufacture of airplanes and other transportation equipment. As a result, and also partly as a cause of this economic development, there has been a notable increase of population in California. Between 1939 and 1954 the population of this one state increased by 6,000,000, which is three times greater than that of the second most rapidly growing state—Florida.

New Revolutions in Technology (since 1950). These various processes of growth, stimulated by the resources of a richly-endowed habitat, have produced the United States of the modern period. By 1950 the United States accounted for nearly half of the value of the goods and services produced in the whole world. Since 1950 the proportion has dropped—due to the revival of the economies of the European countries and of the Soviet Union—but the gross national product per capita of the United States rose from $1,491 in 1950 to over $2,000 in 1957. Nowhere else in the world have so many people reached such a high level of material well-being. The conditions that have contributed to this achievement include human skills and ingenuity, most happily combined with a favorable habitat. They include the large investment of new capital in war industries. They include suitable political and economic institutions, especially the existence of a mass market to

The cure for soil erosion is contour plowing and strip cropping. This is modern agriculture in Iowa.

which the whole continent has access, and which permits the development of areas of specialized production (Maps 48 and 49).

As a result of the achievement of such a high degree of economic growth, and the widespread acceptance of growth and change as normal, the stage is set for the appearance of new revolutions in technology. Not all of the applications of science and engineering are devoted to probing outer space: highly effective efforts are being devoted to improving agricultural and industrial production, and to the preservation of the resource base on which the economy must rest. The modern United States can be examined in terms of four recent trends: (1) the revolution in agriculture; (2) the changing relations of raw materials and industries; (3) the continued development of transportation; and (4) the rise of great urban regions.

The Revolution in Agriculture. The revolution in technology reached the agricultural sector of the American economy during and after World War II. To be sure, agricultural machinery has been replacing human and animal muscles for many decades. Before 1940 the replacement of horses with tractors resulted in a major shift of crop acreages—large areas that had been used to grow feed crops for work animals could be turned to growing food crops for human beings, or feed crops for animals to be fattened. The production of foods and fibers was greatly increased through the process of mechanization. Already the yield of crops per farmer was high by world standards. But a major breakthrough in the technology of agriculture took place in the 1940's and 1950's. Yields per acre of maize have been more than doubled through the widespread use of "hybrid corn." Beef cattle and hogs can be fattened on less feed than ever before through the application of new methods of animal breeding. Better breeds of dairy cattle, hogs, poultry, and sheep, have increased production and decreased the feed requirements. New kinds of insecticides have brought many insect pests under control for the first time in history; and new chemical fertilizers and soil conditioners have converted poor, sandy soils into high-yielding soils—so much so that with modern agricultural techniques the natural character of the soil is no longer so critical. Soil conservation practices have returned worn-out lands to production, and are enormously reducing the rate of new destruction.

An essential fact, however, about the agricultural revolution is the reduction in the number of farmers. More food is produced by fewer farmers. In the years 1910 to 1914 it took 135 man-hours of work to produce a hundred bushels of maize; by 1950-1953 it took only 34. In 1940 some 20 per cent of the workers of the United States were employed on farms, and one farm worker produced enough farm products for himself and ten or eleven other persons. In 1962 only about 7.5 per cent of the working force was employed on farms, and one farm worker produced enough farm products for himself and twenty-seven other people. Since World War II there has been a 12 per cent increase in the consumption of food per capita, and yet food surpluses have continued to pile up in warehouses throughout the country. Clearly the money invested in scientific research and development is paying off, and the technical knowledge now exists to permit a real attack on the problem of human hunger.

Raw Materials and Industries. Since 1910 the United States has become progressively more dependent on foreign sources of industrial raw materials. As the economy has reached maturity, and then continued its ad-

THE UNITED STATES AND
SOUTHERN CANADA
AGRICULTURE **49**

Atlantic Ocean

Pacific Ocean

ALASKA

Pacific Ocean

200 Miles

S P R I N G   W H E A T

C O R N   B E L T

W I N T E R   W H E A T

Pacific Ocean

Pacific Ocean

Scale of Miles
0   500

Irrigated crops
Fruit and truck crops
C Cotton
Co Coffee
P Pineapples
R Rice
S Sugar cane
Dairy
Tobacco
Mixed farming and stock raising
Grains and feed crops
Predominantly pastoral
Forest products
Non-agricultural

PUERTO RICO

HAWAIIAN ISLANDS

Pacific Ocean

HAWAII
MAUI
MOLOKAI
LANAI
OAHU
KAUAI

0   50 Miles

vance to a condition of high mass consumption, there has been a demand for a huge increase in both the volume and the variety of raw materials. To make available just the right quality of material at the lowest possible cost it has become necessary to reach out to places outside the national territory for ninety-seven industrial raw materials, in addition to certain foodstuffs. The modern automobile requires the importation of three hundred different commodities, supplied by fifty-six different countries. The telephone includes forty-eight different materials supplied by eighteen countries. Even a can of ordinary shoe polish includes eight ingredients that come from outside the United States. There are thirty-nine industrial commodities for which the United States is more than 80 per cent dependent on foreign sources, including tin, nickel, manganese, chrome, natural rubber, coconut and other vegetable oils, tanning materials, jute and burlap, carpet wool, raw silk, and industrial diamonds. There are fifteen commodities for which the United States is between 50 and 79 per cent dependent on foreign sources, including newsprint, uranium, bauxite, fluorspar, lead, mercury, tungsten, and zinc. In 1959 the United States was estimated to have only about 15 per cent of the world's proven oil reserves; and it was predicted that by 1980 the country would be dependent on foreign sources. The United States has long had sufficient supplies of copper, but since 1946 it has been less costly to import between 20 and 30 per cent of the requirements from outside than to use domestic ores. The situation is similar in regard to iron ore. The high-grade ores of the Mesabi Range were exhausted by the end of World War II, and now the United States depends for more than 25 per cent of its ore on foreign sources—chiefly Canada and Venezuela. The remainder of its iron ore needs come from the exploitation of low-grade ores in the Lake Superior region and other places. The only industrial raw materials in which the United States is self-sufficient, or nearly so, are coal, sulfur, phosphate rock, and potash.

Changing technology is also responsible for a major shift in the sources of power. In 1860, wood was still the chief fuel of the United States, supplying more than 80 per cent of the energy. Between 1860 and 1910 wood ceased to be of importance as a source of energy, and coal supplied something like 75 per cent of the energy requirements. In the 1960's the share of coal in the production of energy has dropped to only 23 per cent, and oil and gas together supply 73 per cent. Hydroelectric power supplies 4 per cent.

Meanwhile, the continuing revolution in technology, which created the need for many new industrial raw materials, has decreased the dependence of the steel industry on coal. No longer is twice as much coal as iron ore required. It was estimated, about 1950, that of the total transportation costs in producing and marketing steel, about 26 per cent was for coal shipments, 21 per cent was for iron ore shipments, and 53 per cent was for the shipment of finished steel products to the consumer. If the steel industry were being located today without reference to any pre-existing facilities, the greatest economy would be gained by placing it close to the market for steel rather than close to the sources of coal or iron ore. The raw material required in the greatest volume is actually water—used to cool the furnaces. Only the inertia resulting from the heavy investment in existing equipment keeps the steel industry from shifting away from the coal fields, closer to the markets. In the United States since 1950 the largest development of new steel-producing capacity has been along the Delaware River, near the head of Chesapeake Bay, and at the southern end of Lake Michigan near Chicago.

There has been a similar shift in other industries since 1950 away from the manufacturing belt (Map 46d, and Map 48). The most rapid industrial growth is now no longer in the traditional manufacturing centers, although these centers still lead in the proportion of total production. The greatest gains are being made in the Pacific Northwest, California, Texas and the Southwest, and Florida. The older industrial areas are not growing as fast as is the national average.

Transportation. The economic development of the United States has been accompanied by an amazing elaboration of the facilities for transportation. The greatest concentration of all forms of transport is in the industrial region. Here, three major east-west lines of communication connect the Middle West and the Northeast. The heaviest volume of freight moves between Pittsburgh and New York City, in spite of the heavy grades over the Allegheny Front. The route through the Mohawk Valley and the Hudson Valley requires fewer grades but is longer. The route from the Ohio River to Baltimore is shorter but steeper than the other two. Both rail and road traffic moves on all three routes, but the greatest concentration is through Pennsylvania. For the country as a whole, some 47 per cent of all freight transport was carried by rail in 1959.

The railroads now face competition with several other forms of transportation. Motor trucks carry about 20 per cent of the country's freight, and the rapid construction of new limited-access highways makes long-distance truck hauls, as well as short hauls, advantageous for some products. A dense network of airlines serves the country, but the planes carry chiefly passengers and mail, and only about 1 per cent of the freight. Coastal shipping and canal boats carry some 15 per cent of the freight. The latest transportation facility is the pipeline, which in 1959 carried about 17 per cent of the nation's freight. The first long-distance pipelines were built during World War II, yet the total mileage now exceeds that of the railroads. Oil and gas from the Gulf-South-

A complex of pipelines for transporting oil at Port Arthur, near Beaumont, Texas, a major oil refining and industrial center.

west now reach the urban centers of the Northeast, and Canadian oil and gas are piped to the western United States as well as to the cities of eastern Canada. Even coal, pulverized and mixed with water, moves through pipelines.

A major new transportation development was the completion, in 1959, of the St. Lawrence Seaway. This canal made it possible for ocean ships to pass the rapids on the

High-speed, limited-access highways serve modern American cities. This is Sacramento, California.

St. Lawrence River to reach the Great Lakes (inset on Map 43). The larger part of the tonnage in the first year of operation carried freight from Canadian ports on the Great Lakes to Montreal; but an important item was the shipment of iron ore from Labrador to the steel plants in the United States along the southern shores of the Great Lakes.

The Great Urban Regions. The United States is a nation that is still growing in all its parts. The rate of population increase was maintained at a high level by immigration until World War I. Since then immigration has been limited to quotas, and the greater part of the increase is due to the excess of births over deaths. The net rate of increase was notably less during the depression decade from 1930 to 1940, but between 1940 and 1950 the population increased 14.5 per cent, which was the greatest numerical increase for any decade in the nation's history. Between 1950 and 1960 the rate of increase was even higher, reaching 19 per cent.

The pattern of population has been changed during the period since World War II. There have been major migrations of people, especially to California and Florida. But all over the country there has been a continued movement of people from rural areas into the cities. In 1870 only 25 per cent of the population was urban, but by 1960 the figure was 64 per cent. In the Northeast the urban population formed about 75 per cent of the total. City people are spreading away from the central cities into great sprawling suburbs, thus creating serious problems of metropolitan government.

The suburban sprawl is now rapidly filling in the intervals between major cities with the homes of people who work in the cities, and who travel back and forth mostly in private automobiles. This suburban sprawl is in the process of creating some fifteen major urban regions. The largest of these extends all the way from Maine to Virginia, and reaches an arm westward through New York to Buffalo (Map 46f). It is in these fifteen major urban regions that the greatest proportion of the population increase will take place in the years ahead. And these fifteen regions are rapidly becoming the sections into which the future United States will be divided—for already life in Connecticut is more nearly like that in New Jersey than it is like that of northern New England. Old sectional differences are in the process of dissolving into the new super-concentrations of urban people.

The great industrial region of the Northeast and the Middle West (Map 46d) remains the core area of the United States. In spite of the rapid growth of other areas, including the fifteen urban regions, this core area still contains 43 per cent of the population, 52 per cent of the national product, and 68 per cent of manufacturing employment. There is now less difference in income per capita between the core area and other parts of the country than existed before 1910, but it still remains the heart of the national economy, and the largest market for goods and services. It represents the greatest concentration of purchasing power in the whole world.

The Outlying States. In 1959 Alaska and Hawaii became, respectively, the forty-ninth and fiftieth states of the United States. If it was the railroad that made possible the consolidation of the whole breadth of North America under one government, it is the jet airplane that makes possible the extension of the national territory to these outlying places. From Seattle to Anchorage, Alaska, is 1,425 miles, or about three hours of flying time; from San Francisco to Honolulu, Hawaii, is 2,392 miles, or about five hours of flying time. The overland route to Alaska,

extending from Dawson Creek to Fairbanks —the Alcan Highway—is 1,982 miles long.

Alaska is huge and varied, but small in population and economic development. Along the Pacific coast the climate is one of mild winters and cool summers (Map 5, pp. 10-11), with much storminess and heavy rainfall. North of the Alaska Range, on the other hand, the climate is similar to that of Siberia, which it faces, only fifty-two miles away, across the Bering Strait. The small population of less than 300,000 is concentrated chiefly in the south, around Anchorage, the chief city, and Juneau, the capital. The only agricultural areas are around Anchorage (the Kenai Peninsula and the Matanuska Valley), and in the Tanana Valley around Fairbanks, where the farmers grow potatoes, truck crops, and hay, and feed dairy cattle. In the Kenai Peninsula and the Yukon Valley there are mines producing coal, chromite, lead, gold, and silver —long ago Alaska produced enough gold to repay the $7,200,000 paid to Russia as the purchase price in 1867. In addition to gold the other chief products are timber and canned salmon which come from the coastal area south of Juneau. The strategic position of Alaska is reflected in the fact that about 25 per cent of the population is made up of people in the armed services.

The Hawaiian Islands, by contrast, are small, but have a relatively high density of population. Located in the low latitudes in the mid-Pacific, they enjoy the temperate tropical climate of the trade-wind zones. The northeast winds bring heavy rainfall to the windward sides of the volcanic mountains; but on the lee sides there is so little rain that crops have to be irrigated. The abundant sunshine and the freedom from cold weather and violent storms makes the islands ideal spots for comfortable living. The original Polynesian inhabitants were living quite comfortably when they were discovered by Captain Cook in 1778. Even as late as 1878 they made up 76 per cent of the population. But by that time whalers and missionaries from New England had landed on the islands, and thereafter people of many races were brought to work on the plantations of sugar cane and pineapples. In 1950 only 17 per cent of the population was native Polynesian. The rest of the population included: Japanese, 37 per cent; Americans and Portuguese, 23 per cent; Filipinos, 12 per cent; Chinese, 7 per cent; Puerto Ricans, Koreans, and Samoans, 4 per cent. There are large areas devoted to sugar cane and pineapples, and these products are sent to Honolulu for processing and canning. A considerable income is brought to the islands by tourists; and, as in Alaska, about 25 per cent of the inhabitants are in the armed services.

Viability. The United States of America is a strong, viable state. How was this achieved? Step by step people of diverse origins, with institutions developed in diverse culture hearths and diverse habitats, have built the traditions and purposes which now unite them in support of a common state-idea. The process by which the modern United States was built has not been easy, nor have the problems of the continued development of a society, dedicated to the dignity and responsibility of the individual, been entirely solved. There are differences of attitude about race relations; there are challenging problems related to the building of new institutions and new attitudes in the presence of rapid and unsettling technological change. But none of these problems defies solution. There is no tendency toward a split into two major sections offering conflicting solutions. Faced with a threat of attack from outside, the overwhelming majority of the people would not shrink from defense of the American way of life.

CANADA

The second great nation into which the Anglo-American culture region is divided, is Canada. The total national territory of Canada covers an area second only to that of the Soviet Union. Furthermore, there are many close similarities of terrain, climate, and vegetation between these two countries. However, a large part of Canada is empty, or only thinly occupied: the effective national territory is limited to a narrow belt along the southern border, with a break north of Lake Superior (Map 2, p. 6).

Canada has made notable contributions to the progress of the great contemporary revolutions. When the federation was established in 1867, people of diverse languages and attitudes were brought together under one government—people whose ways of life were derived from the French culture hearth, and from the British culture hearths of New England and the Middle Colonies. The Canadians have succeeded in accommodating the differing ideas of the French and English-speaking groups, and they have done so within the framework of a free society. The Industrial Revolution has given Canada a mature economy, with a gross national product per capita which is second only to that of the United States. For better or for worse, Canada is intimately tied to the colossus along the southern border, if only because of the geographic position of its effective national territory. But Canada is also tied to the Commonwealth, and to the Queen as the symbol of Commonwealth unity. Lying, as Canada does, between the United States and the antagonistic countries of Eurasia, there is no possibility of avoiding involvement if conflict should come, nor can the United States fail to provide for mutual defense.

The Habitat. The greater part of the national territory of Canada is not suitable for agricultural settlement. More than half of the area is included in the Laurentian Upland (Canadian Shield), a heavily glaciated hilly land on some of the earth's oldest rocks (Map 43); and another part is taken up by the Rocky Mountains. The northern 25 per cent of the country is covered with tundra, and has a polar type of climate (Maps 5 and 8, pp. 10-11 and 16-17). More than 50 per cent of the country is covered with forests of spruce and fir, and experiences a climate of severe winters and short, cool summers. To be sure, because of the long hours of sunlight in summer, crops can be ripened even at the mouth of the Mackenzie River; but the northernmost outpost of agricultural settlement based on grain farming is in the Peace River Valley. Only 16 per cent of Canada can be classed as potential farmland, and only about 7 per cent is under cultivation. The land used for farms is mostly in the mixed coniferous and broadleaf forest area of the south, on the prairies between Winnipeg and the eastern front of the Rocky Mountains where the rainfall is not very dependable, and in the valleys of southern British Columbia (Map 49).

The Formation of Canada. The earliest, permanent European settlements in what is now Canada were made by the French at Quebec in 1608, and by the British on the eastern side of Newfoundland in 1610. The British colony was only a base for the use of fishing fleets and had almost no connections with the land behind it. The French colony became the nucleus of the French culture hearth, previously described (p. 162). From Quebec French missionaries and fur traders spread so thinly over the interior of North America that, although they were the first settlers, they could never make good their claims for possession. On the other hand, French farmers along the lower St. Lawrence Valley, downstream from Montreal, became so solidly entrenched on the land that they could never be dislodged. France gave up all claims in Canada by the Treaty of Paris in 1763 (except for the small islands of St. Pierre and Miquelon, off the south coast of Newfoundland).

Settlement by English-speaking people during the colonial period, other than at the fishing base on Newfoundland, was chiefly in three places. The early French settlers in Nova Scotia were expelled by the British, and in 1713 Nova Scotia came under the control of Great Britain. Between 1760 and 1763, and later during the Revolutionary War, many settlers from New England came to Nova Scotia because they preferred to remain loyal to the King. They brought with them many of the traits developed in the New England culture hearth. They settled solidly, also, in the new colony of New Brunswick. Meanwhile people from the Middle Colonies culture hearth, with their somewhat different characteristics, moved into Ontario where their settlements bordered the western end of the French country. In 1670 the whole northern interior of the continent was placed under the control of the Hudson's Bay Company, which was granted a monopoly of the fur trade. This monopoly was held until 1859. Meanwhile, however, in 1825, the Company gave up to Russia its claim to the Pacific coast north of British Columbia and to the whole area west of the 141st meridian.

Canada did not exist under a single government until the British Parliament established the federation in 1867 and gave it autonomy as a Dominion. Canada at that time included four provinces: Nova Scotia, New Brunswick, Quebec, and Ontario. Map 45 shows the steps in the spread of Canadian jurisdiction westward across the prairie provinces to British Columbia. It was in 1867, also, that the United States purchased Alaska from the Russians. In 1869, Canada purchased the whole northern part of the continent from the Hudson's Bay Company. But Canada did not finally achieve its present boundaries until the inclusion of Newfoundland in 1949.

The basic concepts of the Canadian state were derived from the three northern culture hearths of the colonial period—the French, the New England, and the Middle Colonies (Map 44). English-speaking settlers migrated into Canada in large numbers during and after the Revolutionary War—especially into Ontario from the Middle Colonies. However, the present population of Canada includes not only elements from these three sources, but also immigrants from Europe. The great wave of immigration took place between 1901 and 1913, when Canada's transcontinental railroads were opening the prairie region for farm settlement. Canadians of French or British origin made up about 88 per cent of the population in 1901, but by 1911 the proportion was down to 84 per cent. Another wave of immigration took place after World War II. As a result the population today includes many from Eastern and Southern Europe. Germans, Italians, Poles, and Netherlanders are especially numerous; and the movement of people from Great Britain to Canada continues in strength.

The Sections. Canada offers a notable illustration of the principle that handicaps of a geographic nature do not inevitably condemn a country to poverty or to disintegration. The study of historical geography provides numerous examples of the effect of dividing a state into two antagonistic sections, where the forces of disintegration have become intolerably great; and it also offers numerous examples where the threat of disintegration has been met by the development of a strong central authority under a dictator—a police state. But Canada has brought the French community

and the English-speaking community together in a strongly integrated state within the framework of a free democratic government.

The French section of Canada coincides closely, but not exclusively, with the Province of Quebec. This province includes about 15 per cent of the total area of Canada; but the settled part—the part that can properly be described as the French section of Canada—is limited to a narrow belt along the lower St. Lawrence Valley in the south. In this belt as a whole about 82 per cent of the population is of French origin, and in the rural areas the proportion is well over 90 per cent. The French Canadians act as a unit in the national politics of Canada; their basic objectives are the preservation of the ideals of a Catholic society and their French traditions.[1] Although Quebec is occupied by only 29 per cent of the people of Canada, its representatives, voting as a unit, play an important role in the formulation of Canadian national policy.

The other major section of Canada is Ontario. This province, like Quebec, includes a large area north of the limits of settlement. Its total area is about 11 per cent of the national total, and it is occupied by 33 per cent of the Canadian population. The southern part of Ontario, lying just north of Lake Ontario and Lake Erie, is more than 75 per cent British; but in the rest of the province people of French and

[1] The political attitude of the French section is described by Gustave Lanctot in the following words: "Comme, par instinct et par volonté, il entend se garder français et catholique, le but de la politique pour lui, ce n'est ni la prospérité, comme pour l'Américain, ni même la liberté, comme pour l'Anglais, mais la survivance ethnique. C'est sous ce seul angle qu'il envisage tout le problème national." Quoted by N. L. Nicholson in W. G. East and A. E. Moodie (eds.), *The Changing World, Studies in Political Geography,* George G. Harrap & Co., London, 1956; p. 325.

British origin are intermingled, along with many immigrants from other sources.

These two contrasting sections are occupied by about 62 per cent of the population of Canada, and contain the chief cities. Actually this is a country which has no primate city: metropolitan Montreal has a population of about 1,900,000 (1960), and metropolitan Toronto one of about 1,650,000. Quebec is much smaller. The latter is the center of French Canada, while Toronto is the urban focus of British Canada. Montreal stands on the border between the two parts, and about 65 per cent of its inhabitants are French. The capital, Ottawa, is also in this border zone.

The English-speaking part of Canada includes three other sections in addition to Ontario. There is the eastern section, known as the Maritime Provinces, made up of Nova Scotia, New Brunswick, Prince Edward Island, and Newfoundland—comprising 5 per cent of the area, and 12 per cent of the population of Canada. There is the section known as the Prairie Provinces, made up of Alberta, Saskatchewan, and Manitoba—comprising 20 per cent of the area, and 18 per cent of the population. And there is British Columbia, with about 9 per cent of the area and 8 per cent of the population. Each of these sections has its own distinctive approach to national public policy, based on differences of economy and resources.

The remainder of the national territory, some 40 per cent of the total, is occupied by only about 0.2 per cent of the people. This includes Yukon Territory and the Northwest Territories. The Territories lie mostly outside the area of effective settlement, as do the northern parts of the provinces. Over 90 per cent of the people of Canada live within two hundred miles of the border of the United States.

Agriculture. (Map 49) In Canada as a whole, agriculture is much less important than other forms of employment. Only about 11 per cent of Canadian workers are employed in agriculture, and some of these work part-time in industries, in logging operations, or as fishermen. In the predominantly British parts of Canada agriculture is in the process of going through a revolution, similar to that in the United States. Since the period before World War II agricultural production has increased more than 50 per cent, along with a decrease in the number of farmers.

In French Canada, farming has changed little since the early years of settlement. Along the shores of the St. Lawrence River and the estuary most of the land is used for dairy farming. The animals have to be kept in barns and fed for many months each year, but feed is supplied in large part from locally produced hay. Most of the farmers also fatten hogs. Close to Montreal there is a belt of vegetable farming, and downstream from Montreal a small area devoted to tobacco—here the farms are small and worked intensively.

The Maritime Provinces are generally too cool and rainy to allow much agricultural use, but there are a few spots of intensive farming. One of the more important such areas is the Annapolis Valley of Nova Scotia. For a long time this valley has been noted for its apple orchards; but in recent years the orchard area has been decreased to make room for dairy cattle and poultry. The largest continuous area of farmland in the Maritime Provinces is on Prince Edward Island, where potatoes are the chief crop, and where dairying and poultry raising are also important. In New Brunswick, along the border of Maine, there is an area of specialized potato farming, similar to that of Aroostook County.

Wheat field and grain elevators at Indian Head, forty miles east of Regina in Saskatchewan.

The most productive agricultural area of eastern Canada is in the southern part of Ontario. The cooler parts of this area are used for rearing beef cattle, mostly on feed grains brought from western Canada by lake steamer and railroad. Dairy cattle are found along the St. Lawrence River west of Montreal, and also to the west of Toronto. In the Niagara Peninsula, between Lake Ontario and Lake Erie, there is a district of intensive fruit production—grapes, apples, peaches—and of other specialized crops. Apples are grown, also, in a narrow belt along the northern shore of Lake Ontario. There is a small area devoted to the production of tobacco north of Lake Erie. And at the extreme southwestern end of Ontario there is an area where maize is raised to feed hogs and cattle, and where sugar beets are important.

Quite different is the agriculture of the Prairie Provinces. These grasslands were opened up between 1901 and 1913, in part by immigrants from the United States, and in part by settlers from various parts of Europe. This area became one of the world's most important sources of hard, spring wheat. For a time during World War II it greatly increased its herds of cattle and its hogs; but after the war, with the increased use of mechanical equipment, there was a return to almost exclusive wheat production. This area is still one of the major sources of wheat in the world, but because of its dependence on one major crop, has a vulnerable economy. In the drier parts wheat is less important than are the range cattle. Generally speaking agriculture has pushed northward as far as the border between the grasslands and the forest (Map 8, pp. 16-17); but there is an isolated area of agricultural settlement at Peace River, about a hundred and fifty miles north of Edmonton. Here the farmers raise grain, and feed cattle. This is the northernmost outpost of agricultural settlement.

In mountainous British Columbia there are only small areas suitable for farming. An intensive truck and dairy farming district is located along the lower part of the Fraser River Valley, and on the eastern side of Vancouver Island, close to the city of Vancouver. There is an important concentration of apple, peach, and apricot orchards in the Okanagan Valley, just north of the border of the United States. Still farther north there is an area of well-developed transhumance—cattle are fed on the high mountain pastures in summer, and on hay in the lowlands during the winter.

Forests and Minerals. (Maps 8 and 48) About a third of the total area of Canada is covered with forests. These are mostly composed of spruce, fir, larch, and pine, mixed in places with aspen, birch, beech, maple, and willow. On the rainy west coast there are stands of hemlock, cedar, and Douglas fir. The forests are thicker and more valuable as a source of lumber where the rainfall is heavier, for instance in British Columbia. In the zone of woodland near the northern limit of the forest the trees become smaller and more widely spaced. It is estimated that only about 35 per cent of the total forest area is accessible enough, and has sufficient growth, to be considered economically productive. A considerable part of the forest, especially in the east, is of chief value as a source of pulpwood for the manufacture of newsprint.

These forests provide Canada's most valuable exports. In 1960 about 15 per cent of the value of all exports was newsprint, and another 6 per cent was pulp to be manufactured into newsprint elsewhere. It is estimated that about half of all the newspaper pages in the world are printed on Canadian paper. Quebec is the leading producer of pulpwood, but Ontario, New Brunswick, Newfoundland, and British Columbia are also important producers. Lumber, most of which comes from the forests of the Pacific coast, formed another 8 per cent of Canadian exports.

Canada is one of the free world's major sources of minerals. There has been a very large development of oil and natural gas from the Prairie Provinces since World War II; and pipelines now make the gas available in the western United States, and in the large cities of eastern Canada. In these same provinces there are also vast stores of lignite. The Laurentian Upland, however, is the great treasure-house of industrial and precious metals. One of the great mining areas is at Sudbury, northeast of Lake Huron, where mines produce nickel (this is the world's chief source), copper, and platinum. A new, major source of iron ore has been developed northwest of Lake Superior, only a little north of the Mesabi Range. Another major iron ore source is at Schefferville, 360 miles north of the St. Lawrence estuary, to which it is now linked by railroad. Just north of Lake Huron there is a major source of uranium. Besides these there are many other mining areas, some not easily accessible, where silver, gold, uranium, and cobalt are extracted. Canada leads the world, also, in its supply of asbestos, from mines located a little to the east of Montreal. There are lead and zinc mines in Newfoundland, and in northern Nova Scotia there is an important source of bituminous coal. It may well be that with further exploration still more mineral sources will be discovered in the ancient rocks of the Laurentian region.

Industrial Development. (Map 48) Canada's economic development, reaching a gross national product per capita second only to that of the United States, has been supported by a series of export specialties. The exports of codfish and fish products were important at an early period. Later the fur trade brought a substantial income. Furs are now less important than timber, wheat, minerals, and paper pulp. Capital from the United States has developed more than half of Canada's productive capacity in these commodities.

The initial phase of the Industrial Revolution reached Canada in the period between 1890 and 1914. This period was marked by a great expansion of the railroads, by the opening up of the prairie lands for grain, by a large influx of immigrants, and by a rapid increase, during the 1890's, in the price of grain. Large investments of foreign capital backed domestic capital to provide the initial impetus for sustained growth. In 1929 the ratio of new capital formation to the gross national product was 23 per cent, which was ample to keep the Canadian economy ahead of the increase in population.

Canada is unusual among the economically more advanced countries in that a condition of high mass consumption was reached during the 1920's, although the development of a mature and diversified economy was not achieved until about 1950. This was possible, it seems, because of the exceptional value of Canada's raw material exports. Canada was not afraid of accepting a status of "economic colonialism," and profiting from it.

Canada is no longer exclusively an exporter of raw materials. But there is no other independent country in the world in which such a large proportion of the capital investment is owned by foreigners. Non-Canadians own 40 per cent of the manufacturing industry, 45 per cent of the mining and smelting industry, 42 per cent of the railroads, and 50 per cent of the oil industry. But this investment of capital, in large part from the United States, has allowed Canada to become one of the world's leading industrial countries. All but 6 per cent of the manufactured products are consumed in Canada. The two great industrial centers are Montreal and Toronto, but there has been a rapid spread of industries across the whole length of the country, and especially in Vancouver. The major support for these has come from new hydroelectric developments—chiefly from the St. Lawrence River, the northbank tributaries, and from Niagara Falls. A very large hydroelectric potential in British Columbia and in Labrador has, as yet, been only slightly developed.

Canadian industries now produce a great variety of products. Some make use of Canadian raw materials, such as the paper and pulp industries of Quebec, the industries smelting and refining non-ferrous metals at Sudbury, the food processing plants, the oil refineries, the saw mills, and the industries manufacturing tobacco products, chemicals, and wood products. But many other Canadian industries make use of imported raw materials. Of major importance are the new aluminum industries: one at Shipshaw near Arvida on the Saguenay River northeast of Quebec; the other at Kitimat on the coast of British Columbia, where water from east of the coastal mountains has been diverted to a power plant near sea level. The bauxite and semi-refined alumina are imported from Jamaica and British Guiana. Also based on imported raw materials or semi-manufactured products are the textile and clothing factories of Montreal, and the factories in Toronto and neighboring towns which make machinery, automobiles, agricultural implements, airplanes, rubber goods and electrical apparatus.

As Canadian industries have grown, the ties with the United States have become closer rather than weaker. The development of a mature economy never increases self-sufficiency, and it has not done so here. For example, it proves less expensive to import coal to Montreal and Toronto from the eastern United States than from the coal fields of Alberta; and it is more profitable to export gas by pipeline from the oil and gas fields of the Prairie Provinces to the western United States than to send it all the way to the big cities of eastern Canada—although oil from western Canada is now brought by pipeline to Ontario for refining.

The Steep Rock Mine, west of Port Arthur, Ontario, one of the major sources of iron ore in Canada.

More than half of Canada's oil needs are imported from Venezuela or from the Persian Gulf region, rather than from western Canada. An effort has been made to tie the east and the west more closely together, and so to diminish the economic dependence on connections across the border. Such transcontinental connections are being provided first by the railroads, then by the pipelines, and most recently by the paved Trans-Canada Highway which runs from Newfoundland to British Columbia. The Alcan Highway, which reaches Fairbanks in Alaska, connects with the Canadian highways at Dawson Creek, north of Edmonton.

The most important transportation development of recent years has been the building of the St. Lawrence Seaway, completed in 1959 (inset on Map 43). This permits the passage of ships, drawing twenty-seven feet or less, from the ocean to the whole Great Lakes system. Other links in the system are the Welland Canal between Lake Ontario and Lake Erie, and the Sault Ste. Marie Canal between Lake Huron and Lake Superior. The St. Lawrence Seaway has been of great importance in bringing iron ore from Labrador to the

steel plants of the United States, but by far the larger share of the tonnage passing through this Seaway is of Canadian products moving from western Canada, and from Toronto, to Montreal.

Viability. Canada is economically strong because it has accepted the necessity and the desirability of international interdependence. The Canadian economy, to a much greater degree than that of the United States, is dependent on exports and imports. Although the greatest movement of goods is across the border with the United States, Canada also has essential connections with the rest of the world, and is, therefore, like any modern state with a mature economy, vulnerable to any interruption in the free flow of commerce.

The Canadians have been able to form a strongly integrated state out of widely divergent ingredients. Not only is there the very fundamental contrast between the traditions and purposes of French and British Canada, but also there is the great difference in outlook between the people of eastern Canada and those of the west. And the Canadians, who form only a narrow fringe of settlement along the whole northern border of the United States, have always been concerned to preserve their own distinctive characteristics. They have succeeded in building a bridge between America and Britain. This is no small accomplishment. Still, Canadians feel deeply the steady pressure of American ways of life and thought, and their reaction is to join in resisting this pressure. Canadians of whatever background, of whatever religion, and of whatever political attitude on domestic issues, are drawn together in support of the Canadian state precisely because of the desire to preserve their own distinctive ways from the overwhelming impact of America.

SUMMARY

Although both of the great revolutions of the contemporary world had their beginnings in the European Culture Region, both have had their greatest development in the Anglo-American Culture Region. The European colonists who came to what they called the "New World" found a land only thinly occupied by native peoples, none of whom could make protracted resistance against the newcomers. In the absence of restrictions from other established societies, the colonists were free to find new solutions to old problems and to experiment with ideas generated in many different parts of the world. Even communism was tried in the Plymouth Colonies in 1620, and later by another group of pioneers in Ohio. Many ideas were put into operation, and some proved useful. It is important that Anglo-America sprang from four distinctive culture hearths, and that ideas, especially in the Middle Colonies, came from many different parts of Europe. Anglo-America is a blend of many origins.

Amazingly fortunate, also, has been the changing relationship of Anglo-American society and the habitat. At each stage of development there have been resources at hand, so located that they could be utilized at low cost. When timber was needed for ships in New England, or water power for factories, these resources were close by. When iron was needed to make anchors, cannons, and other equipment for ships, the raw materials at hand included bog-iron ore (a bacterial deposit in the bottoms of the glacial lakes of New England), oyster and clam shells for lime, and forests for charcoal. Later, when steel was needed for rails, and the charcoal had to come from greater distances because the nearby forests had been cut away, the steel makers found the anthracite coal of the Scranton area not too difficult to mine. Then, when bituminous coal, transformed into coke, became the basis for steel making, the market for steel and the workers to make steel were already west of the Appalachians, easily reached from Pittsburgh and Cleveland. At the same time, when a vastly increased volume of high-quality iron ore was needed, and when poorer and more limited ores were no longer profitable, the vast ore body of the Mesabi Range became available, and the Great Lakes provided a low-cost route of transportation to the steel mills. Still later, when steel, and a series of mechanical inventions together with barbed wire, made the use of the prairies possible for the production of grain and meat, the settlers found themselves on the margins of some of the world's most productive grassland soils, hitherto but slightly used and still almost unoccupied. The story can be elaborated at length: the amazing fact is that Anglo-America has enjoyed a happy relationship between the stages of settlement and the stages of economic development. The Industrial Revolution has proceeded, step by step, to create unprecedented material comfort and well-being, and to provide a security from natural disasters never before known.

The kind of advanced technological and democratic society found in Anglo-America is sometimes grouped with other similar societies around the world and described as "Neo-European." In Australia-New Zealand, for example, the new forms of technology and the institutions of a free, democratic society have also been developed in the absence of pre-existing societies, perhaps not in so favorable a habitat but certainly in a region that has permitted the greatest possible freedom of development. Anglo-America, however, occupies a very different geographic position. This culture region is situated close to the center of the Land Hemisphere, whereas Australia-New Zealand is very remote from it. The Arctic Ocean and the North Atlantic Ocean are wide enough to give some freedom from potential invasion in the modern world, yet not so wide as to isolate Anglo-America from the focus of world strategy in Western Europe. Just as the English Channel gave protection in the days of sailing ships to the people of Great Britain, so now the wider world ocean in the age of airplanes and missiles gives America some protection without the handicap of isolation. In this position, the people of the United States and Canada share responsibility for insuring the survival of the concepts of human society which they have done so much to create.

5

THE
LATIN AMERICAN
CULTURE REGION

Country	Political Status	Latest Estimate Population	Capital City
Argentina	Federal Republic	21,300,000 ('62)	Buenos Aires
Bahama Islands	British Colony	105,000 ('60)	
Bermuda	British Colony	42,640 ('60)	
Bolivia	Republic	3,600,000 ('62)	Sucre
Brazil	Federal Republic	70,528,625 ('61)	Brasília
British Guiana	British Colony	600,000 ('62)	
Brit. Honduras	British Colony	90,381 ('60)	
Chile	Republic	7,900,000 ('62)	Santiago
Colombia	Republic	14,800,000 ('62)	Bogotá
Costa Rica	Republic	1,300,000 ('62)	San José
Cuba	Socialist Republic	6,800,000 ('62)	Habana
Dominican Republic	Republic	3,200,000 ('62)	Santo Domingo
Ecuador	Republic	4,600,000 ('62)	Quito
Incl. Galápagos Is.	Dependency		
El Salvador	Republic	2,800,000 ('62)	San Salvador
Falkland Islands	British Colony	2,191 ('59)	
French Guiana	Fr. Overseas Department	31,000 ('60)	
Guadeloupe	Fr. Overseas Department	270,000 ('60)	
Guatemala	Republic	4,000,000 ('62)	Guatemala
Haiti	Republic	4,300,000 ('62)	Port-au-Prince
Honduras	Republic	2,000,000 ('62)	Tegucigalpa
Jamaica	Republic	1,647,000 ('62)	Kingston
Martinique	Fr. Overseas Department	277,000 ('60)	
Mexico	Federal Republic	37,200,000 ('62)	Mexico City
Netherlands Antilles	Integral part of the Netherlands Realm		
Incl. Curaçao		190,000 ('60)	
Aruba		124,000 ('60)	
Bonaire		56,000 ('60)	
Saba		6,000 ('60)	
St. Eustatius		1,016 ('60)	
St. Martin		1,094 ('60)	
		1,537 ('60)	
Nicaragua	Republic	1,600,000 ('62)	Managua
Panamá	Republic	1,100,000 ('62)	Panamá
Panama Canal Zone	U.S. Military Reservation	42,122 ('60)	
Paraguay	Republic	1,900,000 ('62)	Asunción
Peru	Republic	10,600,000 ('62)	Lima
Puerto Rico	Self-governing Commonwealth of U.S.	2,500,000 ('62)	San Juan
Surinam	Integral part of Neth. Realm	308,000 ('60)	
Swan Islands	U.S. Possession	28 ('60)	
Trinidad & Tobago	Republic	900,000 ('62)	Port-of-Spain
Turks & Caicos	British Colony	5,716 ('60)	
Uruguay	Republic	3,000,000 ('62)	Montevideo
Venezuela	Federal Republic	7,800,000 ('62)	Caracas
Virgin Islands	British Colony	7,338 ('60)	
Virgin Islands	U.S. Unincorporated Ter.	32,099 ('60)	
St. Croix		14,973 ('60)	
St. Thomas		16,201 ('60)	
St. John		925 ('60)	
West Indies	British Colony		
Antigua		54,354 ('60)	
Barbados		232,085 ('60)	
Cayman Islands		7,616 ('60)	
Dominica		59,916 ('60)	
Grenada		88,677 ('60)	
Montserrat		12,157 ('60)	
St. Kitts-Nevis & Anguilla		56,658 ('60)	
St. Lucia		86,108 ('60)	
St. Vincent		79,948 ('60)	

◄   *Brasilia, Esplanade of the Palacio Alvarado.*

Latin America occupies that part of the American hemisphere which is relatively remote from the center of the Land Hemisphere. It is separated from Anglo-America by the Florida Strait and by the United States-Mexico border. Most of South America lies east of the longitude of New York, and the east-coast countries are closer to Europe than they are to the United States. A large part of South America, however, lies beyond the horizon of the Land Hemisphere—as Richard Edes Harrison put it: "pointing like a dagger at the dead heart of Antarctica" (Maps 12 and 13, both of them on p. 36).

In 1956 the populations of Anglo-America and Latin America were about equal, with a little more than 185,000,000 in each. But by 1960 the population of Latin America had increased to 207,000,000, while that of Anglo-America was only about 197,000,000. It was estimated, in 1960, that by the year 2000 Latin America would be occupied by 593,000,000 people, while Anglo-America would have only 312,000,000 inhabitants. Within Latin America, in 1960, there were 129,423,000 people in the eighteen countries of Spanish origin; there were 66,302,000 people in Portuguese Brazil; 3,097,304 in French Haiti; 4,780,000 in two small island-states that soon thereafter became independent; and 6,847,000 divided among one self-governing commonwealth, and the possessions of Great Britain, the Netherlands, France, and the United States. Latin America includes about 15 per cent of the inhabited land area of the world, and is occupied by about 7 per cent of the world's population.

Latin America is in process of rapid and fundamental change. It is feeling the full impact of both revolutions: the traditional pre-industrial and pre-democratic institutions are crumbling, and until a new order can be created the situation is filled with danger as well as opportunity. In the midst of the chaos of a collapsing dictatorship the Communist Party, as the instrument of the Soviet Union, has gained control of Cuba, and similar developments are threatened elsewhere. The situation, in which interference from outside can be threatened, is created by the revolutionary changes currently affecting this culture region. Nowhere else in the world is a predominantly rural society so rapidly becoming predominantly urban. The rate of population increase—126 per cent between 1920 and 1960 —is greater than the rate of increase in any other major region of the world. As health and education are improved there is an insistent clamor for a wider distribution of income, and for an end to the system of special privilege.

Compared with Anglo-America, Latin America embraces sharper contrasts in habitat and in settlement from place to place. To be sure, all the Latin American countries are facing similar problems of economic development, and in all of them there is a mounting concern with the status of the common man. But the variety of habitats in which these problems are faced, and the different stages reached in the processes of change, have combined to produce great contrasts in the conditions of life. There are some countries where the great majority of the people are of unmixed Indian ancestry, and here the inherited culture traits of the Indians are important in an understanding of current attitudes (Map 50). There are other countries in which the population is more than 90 per cent unmixed European—Spanish, Portuguese, Italian, German, Polish, and others. In some areas there is a large proportion of Negroes in the population. And in others the population is a mixture of Spanish and Indian—

mestizo. There are some countries already well advanced in industrial development, and others that have yet to develop the attitudes that are a prerequisite for industrialization. There are some countries still under the traditional rule of military dictators, and one that is under the control of the Communist Party; but there are also at least two countries that can be classed among the most complete democracies in the world.

It is significant that the traditional ways of life with which the Spanish countries started were forged not in the New World, but in Spain; and similarly the Brazilian culture had its beginnings in Portugal. One finds primary settlement centers in Latin America, where the first Spanish and Portuguese colonies were established, and one can trace the process of spread by which the present states were created. But one finds few genuine culture hearths in which new

ways of life were forged, except perhaps in the Central Area of Mexico, in Middle Chile, and in the Northeast of Brazil. In a sense each of the modern states was built around a settlement nucleus which, in a small way, was a culture hearth. But in Latin America the culture hearth concept is of less importance than in Anglo-America, and the connections with the European homeland are much more direct.

THE HABITAT

(Maps 5, 6, 7, 8, 51, and 52) The diversity of the Latin American habitat results from the pattern of the surface features, climates, and vegetation. High mountains extend southeastward from northern Mexico through Central and South America to Tierra del Fuego. East of the mountains in South America there are extensive plains, and two geologically similar areas of hilly

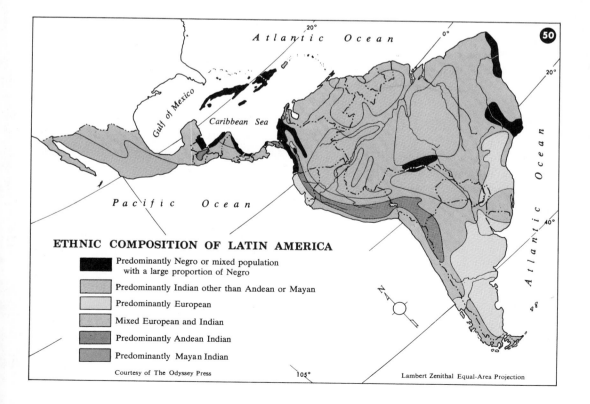

ETHNIC COMPOSITION OF LATIN AMERICA

- Predominantly Negro or mixed population with a large proportion of Negro
- Predominantly Indian other than Andean or Mayan
- Predominantly European
- Mixed European and Indian
- Predominantly Andean Indian
- Predominantly Mayan Indian

Courtesy of The Odyssey Press

Lambert Zenithal Equal-Area Projection

upland and low mountains—the Brazilian Highlands and the Guiana Highlands. In northern Venezuela and the Antilles the high mountains make a wide eastward arc bordering the Caribbean Sea. These surface features are given additional variety by the climate and the vegetation cover. No other culture region extends over such a range of latitude: from north of 32°N on the California-Mexico border to almost 56°S at Cape Horn. As a result there are many different climates in this region, and this is reflected in the variations in the vegetation cover. In the Atacama Desert of Northern Chile is one of the few places on earth where no rain has ever been recorded; but there are other areas where the rainfall is very heavy, and the Amazon carries the greatest volume of water of any river in the world.

The climatic position of Latin America should not be misinterpreted. A large part of the region lies within the low latitudes— and quite commonly the low latitudes are thought to be unbearably hot, with "steaming jungles." This is far from the truth. There are, to be sure, small pockets protected from the winds where high humidity produces a "hot house" climate; but for the most part tropical climates are never very hot and never cold—rather they are truly temperate in that they are never extreme. Map 7 (p. 14) shows the parts of the world where temperatures of more than 110° are experienced at least once a year. The only parts of Latin America where such temperatures occur are in northern Mexico and northern Argentina. Along the Amazon temperatures as high as 100° have never been recorded.

Latin America never experiences severe winters of the kind found in the northern hemisphere. Cold air masses do pour out of Antarctica and produce exceptionally stormy conditions over the southern oceans. These air masses move northward across South America, even across the equator, but by the time they reach South America passage across the open ocean has raised the temperature of the lower layers of air. The tapering of the continent toward the south means that the increase in latitude is compensated by a decrease in the distance from the sea. As a result, even in southernmost South America where the average temperature for the warmest month is below 50°, the average for the coldest month is above 32°.

Caribbean Sea

SOUTH AMERICA
SURFACE FEATURES
52

0   250   500   750
Scale of Miles

VENEZUELA
Caracas
Orinoco R.
Georgetown
Paramaribo
Cayenne
GUIANA HIGHLANDS
BR. GUIANA
SURINAM
FR. GUIANA
COLOMBIA
Bogotá
EQUATOR
Quito
ECUADOR
Rio Negro
Amazon
Marañón R.
Madeira R.
B R A Z I L
Recife
Ucayali R.
PERU
BRAZILIAN HIGHLANDS
São Francisco R.
Lima
Salvador
La Paz
BOLIVIA
Brasília
PARAGUAY
Paraguay R.
TROPIC OF CAPRICORN
Asunción
Rio de Janeiro
São Paulo
CHILE
Tucumán
Atlantic
Paraná R.
ARGENTINA
Ocean
Rosario
Pacific
URUGUAY
Valparaíso
Buenos Aires
Santiago
Montevideo
Ocean
HUMID
PAMPA
Concepción

Comodoro Rivadavia

MIDDLE
AMERICA
SOUTH
AMERICA

LATIN AMERICA
CULTURE REGION

50°   90°   80°   70°   60°   50°   40°   30°   20°

There are certain important differences between the geographic arrangement of the habitat in Anglo-America and Latin America. In Anglo-America, as we have seen, the physical resources that were needed at different stages of technological development were so located that they could be used at relatively low cost. In Latin America there are many resources, great in volume and superlative in quality; but the distribution is extremely unfavorable. For example, although the continent is rich in high-grade iron ore it has only 0.1 per cent of the world's coal. Most of the potential water power sources are at a great distance from the areas where electricity is needed. Where the population density necessitates a free flow of transportation, as in southeastern Brazil, the Great Escarpment on the eastern edge of the Brazilian Highlands imposes a major obstacle to railroad development. And where the Amazon and its tributaries provide a vast length of potentially navigable waterways, there are very few people (Map 2) and only a small volume of production. Poorly arranged resources do not prohibit economic development, but they do make that development more expensive in terms of capital and labor.

POPULATION AND SETTLEMENT

(Maps 2, 50, and 53) People of diverse racial and cultural origins came to these habitats. The first were the so-called Indians, a Mongoloid people who came to the American hemisphere from Asia by way of the Bering Strait, and thence migrated southward until they reached the southern tip of South America. The Fuegian Indians of southern Chile remained among the world's more primitive people. But others of the Indian groups advanced much farther in terms of cultural development. In the Andes around Lake Titicaca the potato was domesticated, and in the same general region the llama and the alpaca were first used as domestic animals. In Colombia the guinea pig was domesticated. The Indians of Central America were probably the first to develop the wild grain, teosinte, as the cultivated crop, maize.[1] Two of the world's six Early Civilizations appeared in the Americas: the Mayan Civilization in what is now Guatemala and southern Mexico; and the Andean Civilization, in what is now Peru and Bolivia. The Indians were concentrated in these two areas, and in a few smaller clusters elsewhere—such as the highlands of Colombia (the Chibchas), and Paraguay (the Guarani). The Mayas were conquered by the Toltecs from the dry area of northern Mexico, and these again by the Aztecs from the same area. When the Spaniards first arrived, the capital of the Aztec Empire was in the Central Area of Mexico, on the site of the present Mexico City. With the exception of these more advanced cultures, the Indians were widely scattered, as they were in North America. The countries in which Indians make up a majority of the people today include Mexico, Guatemala, Ecuador, Peru, and Bolivia.

There were certain characteristics which were common to all the Indians of the Americas. Although some Indians, such as the Mayas, were advanced in mathematics and astronomy, none of them had any written language. Although the more advanced Indians built pyramids and temples, none of them understood the principle of the arch. Although the Indians of Peru had invented every known method of weaving textiles, none of the Indians understood the principle of the wheel, even the potter's

[1] See footnote, p. 18. Other distinctively American crops include manioc, beans, squash, tomatoes, tobacco, and cacao.

wheel. The dog was common to all Indian groups, and there were llamas and alpacas in Peru, guinea pigs in Colombia, and turkeys and ducks in Mexico; but the native Americans had never seen cattle, sheep, goats, horses, pigs, or chickens before the arrival of the Spaniards. The Indians had no concept of private property in land: land was held in common and worked collectively. The Incas developed what has been perhaps the world's only example of pure communism—a system in which each member of the community worked according to his ability and was rewarded according to his needs. The Inca was the supreme ruler of an empire that extended from southern Colombia all the way to Argentina and Chile. In the other great Indian empire— that of the Aztecs in Mexico—the emperor, and the nobles who made up the aristocracy, had assumed the right to collect tribute from the Indian communities of specified areas. In other parts of the Americas political organization was primitive and chiefly tribal in scope. These were the peoples that the Europeans found living in the "new world" that Columbus discovered in 1492; and they were called Indians because Columbus thought that the land he had discovered was a part of India.

The first Europeans to establish colonies in the Americas were the Spaniards and the Portuguese. The Spaniards came not only seeking quick wealth, but also eager to spread the Catholic faith among the pagan Indians, and to establish their own Spanish institutions in what was to them a "new world." They were attracted primarily to the areas where there were large numbers of Indians, and where there were sources of gold and silver. They avoided the dense forests where the Indians were few. The

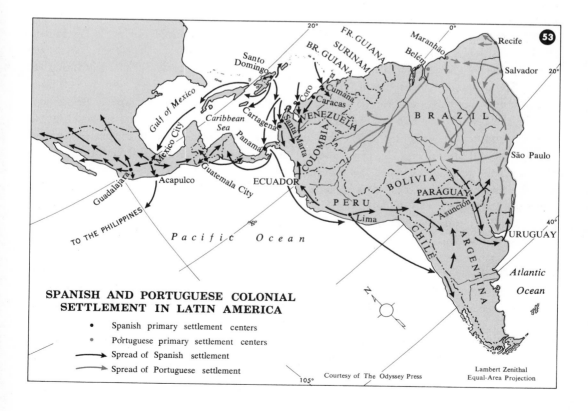

SPANISH AND PORTUGUESE COLONIAL SETTLEMENT IN LATIN AMERICA

- • Spanish primary settlement centers
- • Portuguese primary settlement centers
- → Spread of Spanish settlement
- → Spread of Portuguese settlement

Courtesy of The Odyssey Press

Lambert Zenithal Equal-Area Projection

Portuguese were much less concerned to convert Indians or to implant institutions; but they did look for ways to make profitable investments of capital that would repair the weak finances of Portugal. The Portuguese brought with them the desire for speculative profits—for quick returns on money invested. In the Treaty of Tordesillas (1494) with Spain, the world was divided into a Portuguese and a Spanish hemisphere at what is now approximately longitude 50°W. The Portuguese primary-settlement centers were all east of that line. Both Spaniards and Portuguese spread from their first settlements to the parts of the country that attracted them, leaving the densely forested areas for the most part unsettled and unclaimed. It was to these areas that the British, the Dutch, and the French came a century later.

Spanish Colonial Society. The Spanish settlers came to America with purposes and attitudes quite different from those brought, about a century later, by the British settlers in Anglo-America. The idea of individual equality before the law had not reached Spain. Spanish society was sharply divided into classes, each with a different relationship to the law. At the top was an aristocracy of landowners, enjoying a position of prestige essentially outside the law. Associated with the aristocracy were the Church and the army. Because the only organized force was the army, the officers controlled political affairs, subject only to the veto of the ·aristocracy. But together these politically powerful groups made up only a small fraction of the total population. The great majority of the people were tenant farmers on whose constant toil the whole system rested. They raised their own food and fibers on land they did not own. They earned a miserable additional wage tending

the landowner's cattle, raising his commercial crops, or working in the mines to produce gold, silver, and other valuable metals. The majority of the people were poor, illiterate, sick, hungry, and hopeless.

The clusters of concentrated settlement remained isolated from each other. The landowners were not interested in the spread of pioneer settlements; and because they derived a good living from their large properties they were not concerned to increase the volume of food production. The tenant farmers were allowed to use some of the poorer land on the vast estates to raise food for themselves. This led to the clearing of steep slopes to plant maize, and resulted in such excessive soil erosion that large areas were utterly destroyed. Where Indians were concentrated before the arrival of the Spaniards, people of Indian ancestry—sometimes mixed with Spanish blood—now make up most of the population.

Portuguese Colonial Society. The Portuguese colonists in the Northeast of Brazil were highly successful in establishing a profitable economy in the new world. The Portuguese landowners, unlike the Spaniards, were much concerned to make good use of their lands, and if properties ceased to be profitable, they did not hesitate to move elsewhere. In the Northeast they started to plant sugar cane, which, for the first time in history, was produced in large quantities for a mass market. They set up a plantation system for the first time in America, and imported Negro slaves from Africa to do the work. The first slave market in the Americas was held in Salvador in 1538. Negroes did all the work of preparing the land, planting and cultivating the cane, harvesting and grinding, and extracting the raw sugar for shipment. The Portuguese

A Mayan temple at Chichén-Itzá, in Yucatán, Mexico. The Mayan people were highly skilled, with an advanced knowledge of astronomy and mathematics.

owners handled the business affairs, the operation of the ships, and the protection and administration of the territory. So prosperous were the cane growers that in 1624 the Dutch invaded the area. They were pushed out of Salvador almost at once, but they gained hold of the whole coastal area from the São Francisco River to the Amazon until they were finally forced out in 1654. From the Negroes of the Northeast they learned how to operate a sugar cane plantation, and they passed on this skill to other European colonial powers.

At São Paulo there was no such prosperity. In 1554 a mission was established on the highlands, and the poorer people from Portugal, who could not compete as workers with the Negro slaves, settled around the mission. Semi-military groups, known as *bandeira,* were organized to explore the whole interior of South America, looking for sources of quick wealth, especially gold. They pushed southward to the shores of the Plata River, opposite Buenos Aires, and north and west over the whole of the Brazilian backlands as far as the edge of the forest. They had no way of knowing when they had passed the western limit of the Portuguese hemisphere, nor did they care. Between them and the Spaniards—except in the south—was a belt of dense forest occupied by few Indians. Since the forest was not attractive to either the Spaniards or the Portuguese, it was left unsettled. Finally, near the end of the seventeenth century, they did find gold in the country north of Rio de Janeiro, known as Minas Gerais. From 1700 to 1800 this was the main focus of Portuguese interest and wealth: in fact, since the sugar from the Northeast was no longer able to hold a monopoly of the European market, many cane growers moved south with their slaves and started panning for gold. Soon they found diamonds in the same area. As in the cane area of the Northeast, this part of Brazil also has a large proportion of Negroes in its present population.

Other European Colonies in Latin America. About a century after the arrival of the Spaniards and the Portuguese, other European countries began to look for space in the Americas. After the Dutch had been pushed out of the Northeast of Brazil, they settled in the Guianas and the Antilles. They started planting sugar cane and importing Negro slaves. The Spaniards did the same, especially in Venezuela and in the Cauca Valley of Colombia. The French established a sugar cane colony in the western part of Hispaniola, and the British started growing cane in Jamaica and Barbados. The Negro slave and the single commercial crop appeared wherever sugar cane could be grown profitably. The crop, which requires eighteen months to ripen, could not survive in areas where there were annual frosts.

The Appearance of the Independent States. The present-day states of Latin America made their appearance after 1804. The success of the American Revolution and the French Revolution made a deep impression on the educated people of Latin America, and there were a few liberal-minded leaders who became sincerely devoted to the ideals of democracy. But most of those who led their countries to independence did not define freedom in terms of individual equality before the law, nor did they accept the principle of majority rule. Freedom, for most of them, meant freedom to control the government of their

area without interference from outside. So far as most of the people were concerned, independence meant only a change of rulers.

The independence movement in Latin America started with Haiti in 1804. The leaders in this case were mulattoes, sons of French planters and Negro women, who had been educated in Paris and exposed to the ideas of the French Revolution. The slaves, who formed the great majority of the people of Haiti, were encouraged to rise against the small minority of French masters; and in a short time they established control, not only over the former French colony in the western part of Hispaniola, but also over the Spanish colony in the eastern part. Not until 1844 did the Spanish colony gain its independence from Negro Haiti and become the Dominican Republic.

Throughout the Spanish colonies the demand for political independence from Spain mounted rapidly. When the revolts were successful, new independent states were set up, which at the beginning, at least, embraced territory formerly administered by one of the Spanish colonial units. For example, when Mexico became independent in 1821, the new state included all the territory formerly administered by the Viceroy in Mexico City—from thinly peopled California and Texas to remote Costa Rica. The routes of travel over so large an area were poorly developed. And, although the separate clusters of people in the Central Area of Mexico were so close to the capital that they could not break away, Guatemala, on the other hand, was far enough away so that after a few years it was able to declare its independence from Mexico. It took with it all the communities strung along the isthmus that were still more remote from Mexico. Then in a short time El Salvador and Nicaragua broke away from Guatemala, and the small highland communities of Honduras declared their independence. Finally Costa Rica, at the end of the line, found itself independent.

The story in other parts of Spanish America was a similar one. At first Colombia, Venezuela, and Ecuador were liberated as one country by Simón Bolívar, and became the United States of Colombia. But the demand for independence in the outlying areas of settlement was so strong that they broke away to form Venezuela and Ecuador. Close to the Spanish administrative center of Lima the separate clusters of people were held together to form Peru; but "Upper Peru" broke away as Bolivia, and the single cluster around Santiago formed the nucleus of Chile. Several separate clusters were united in Argentina, but remote Asunción formed the core of independent Paraguay. Uruguay was established as a buffer state between the Spanish and Portuguese settlements.

By contrast the numerous separate clusters of population in Portuguese Brazil were held together to form a single country. To be sure, the southernmost cluster, in the state of Rio Grande Do Sul, attempted to withdraw from the rest of Brazil, but the revolt was put down. Until 1889 Brazil was a monarchy.

Spain was able to hold on to its colonies in the Antilles until the Spanish-American War of 1898. At this time Cuba was given its independence, and Puerto Rico became a possession of the United States. In 1903 Panamá seceded from Colombia, and was promptly granted protection by the United States in exchange for the lease "in perpetuity" of the Canal Zone. In 1952 Puerto Rico became a self-governing commonwealth, "freely associated" with the United States;

and in 1962 the former British colonies of Jamaica and Trinidad became independent members of the Commonwealth of Nations.

The Industrial Revolution and the Democratic Revolution. When the several countries of Latin America gained their independence they were still pre-industrial and pre-democratic. Furthermore, the state-ideas that provided the necessary political integration were, at first, purely negative—the desire by the politically powerful people to administer their own countries free from any outside interference. This is still a powerful underlying purpose throughout Latin America. The economies of the several states were based on mining and agriculture, but in the region as a whole probably more than 80 per cent of the people were engaged in subsistence farming. They consumed only what they themselves produced, and they produced only for their own basic needs. The great majority of the Latin Americans were outside the economic system of buying and selling, of money and credit. Most of them were illiterate, poorly housed, poorly fed, and in bad health.

Since about 1920 Latin America has been changing at a more and more rapid rate. The old traditional, agrarian Latin America, with its landed aristocracy, its petty army revolts, its great contrasts between rich and poor—all this has been fast disappearing. Latin America is now feeling the full force of the Industrial and the Democratic Revolutions, and as a result the traditional institutions are crumbling, and a new Latin America is emerging.

The Latin American countries have long been producers of raw materials for export. In 1960 sixteen of the twenty countries depended on the export of just two commodities for more than 60 per cent of their national income. Furthermore, fourteen of the

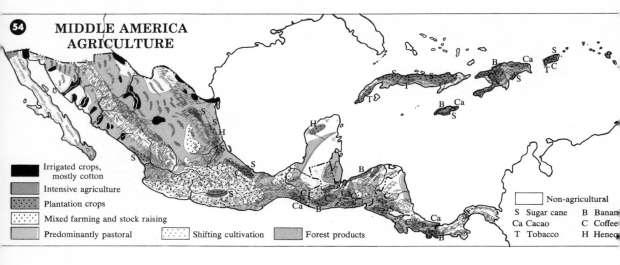

MIDDLE AMERICA AGRICULTURE

- ■ Irrigated crops, mostly cotton
- Intensive agriculture
- Plantation crops
- Mixed farming and stock raising
- Predominantly pastoral
- Shifting cultivation
- Forest products
- □ Non-agricultural

S Sugar cane   B Banana
Ca Cacao   C Coffee
T Tobacco   H Heneq

countries depended on one export product for over 50 per cent of their national income. This is a highly vulnerable situation, for such countries are at the mercy of market changes in distant places that can scarcely be predicted, let alone controlled. The following table illustrates the problem:

PROPORTION OF TOTAL EXPORTS IN 1960

Bolivia	Tin, lead	72.5%
Brazil	Coffee, cacao	61.6%
Chile	Copper, nitrate	77.1%
Colombia	Coffee, oil	89.0%
Costa Rica	Coffee, bananas	77.3%
Cuba (9 mos.)	Sugar, tobacco	89.0%
Dominican Republic	Sugar, coffee	64.8%
Ecuador	Bananas, coffee	76.4%
El Salvador	Coffee, cotton	79.4%
Guatemala	Coffee, bananas	81.6%
Haiti	Coffee, sisal	64.0%
Honduras	Bananas, coffee	63.6%
Nicaragua	Coffee, cotton	63.4%
Panamá	Bananas, cacao	72.7%
Uruguay	Wool, meat	75.4%
Venezuela	Oil, iron ore	97.5%

The impact of economic development on these pre-industrial countries has been very uneven. In some places there has been a rapid expansion of manufacturing industries —notably in São Paulo and in Mexico. At several places there have been new steel plants—built with capital in part derived from outside sources—the largest of which is the Guilherme Guinle National Steel Plant (formerly Volta Redonda) in Brazil (Maps 56 and 57). The countries that seem to have entered the initial phase of the Industrial Revolution include Argentina, Chile, Mexico, Venezuela, and Puerto Rico. The pre-eminence of São Paulo in economic development is obscured by the averages for Brazil as a whole. But in most parts of Latin America even the conditions necessary to start the process of development have yet to be met. In 1962 the economy of Latin America as a whole was described as stagnant. In the years from 1957 through 1961 the annual rate of increase in the production of goods and services amounted to only about 4 per cent. But since population was growing at a rate greater than 3 per cent per year, the net growth of production per capita amounted scarcely to 1 per cent. Economists estimate that a growth per capita of at least 2.5 per cent per year is necessary to start the initial phase of development. Furthermore, so unstable were the economic and political conditions in 1962 that a steady outflow of domestic

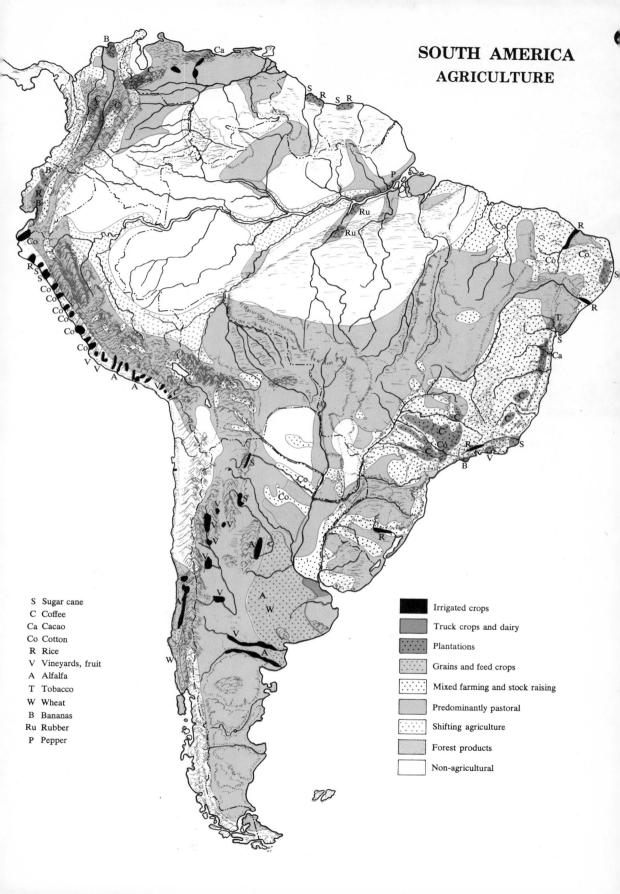

SOUTH AMERICA
AGRICULTURE

S   Sugar cane
C   Coffee
Ca Cacao
Co Cotton
R   Rice
V   Vineyards, fruit
A   Alfalfa
T   Tobacco
W   Wheat
B   Bananas
Ru Rubber
P   Pepper

Irrigated crops

Truck crops and dairy

Plantations

Grains and feed crops

Mixed farming and stock raising

Predominantly pastoral

Shifting agriculture

Forest products

Non-agricultural

The market at Pátzcuaro, an old Tarascan Indian community in the state of Michoacán, Mexico.

print more currency. But without a corresponding increase in the volume of goods offered for sale this has led, inevitably, to price increases. Between 1957 and 1962 prices climbed 212 per cent in Argentina, 158 per cent in Bolivia, 146 per cent in Brazil, 133 per cent in Uruguay, and 111 per cent in Chile.

Meanwhile each of the Latin American countries has undertaken a major attack on ill-health and illiteracy. As a result of new medical and sanitary techniques the death rates have been lowered in spectacular fashion. More children survive, life expectancy is increasing, and for the population as a whole there is more energy due to the decrease in disease. Schools have been built, even in rural areas, and the number of illiterate people has been very greatly reduced. The results of all of this are first, a very rapid net increase in population; and second, a mounting popular demand for a wider share of the rewards of the economy, and for an end to the system of privilege and inequality. There is a wave of resentment against the whole system of economic colonialism under which economic policies are decided in distant and foreign cities. There is an increasing demand that resources be kept for exploitation by the inhabitants of a country, not by foreigners. There is a demand for an end to colonialism, regardless of cost.

These revolutionary changes are taking place so rapidly that development has become very uneven. Economic development is focused on a few areas, and a majority of the people are still poor. In some countries democratic institutions and attitudes have been successfully developed—notably in Uruguay and Costa Rica; but in other countries the ideas of democracy have scarcely been felt.

savings, chiefly to the United States and Switzerland, had set in. It seemed that there was a widespread lack of popular demand for economic development, and of a willingness to undertake the necessary postponement of consumption in order to start the growth process.

No other culture region, in the early 1960's, was suffering more from an inflation of prices. There was a world-wide decline in the prices offered for exports, and in the European market increased competition with the products of other countries was being felt. In addition the flow of new capital from outside the region was somewhat slowing off. In order to support domestic industries and provide work for the increasing numbers of people, the Latin American governments have been forced to

THE SPANISH COUNTRIES OF THE MAINLAND

Sixteen of the eighteen countries in which Spanish is the official language, are located on the mainland of the American continents. Since these countries gained their independence each has developed distinctive characteristics, and each now poses special problems of continued growth.

MEXICO

Mexico was one of the first countries in Latin America to do something about the problems of poverty and inequality. Before 1910, under the dictatorship of Porfírio Díaz, Mexico was a typical example of the results of the Spanish agrarian tradition. About 80 per cent of the Mexicans have some Indian ancestors, and only 15 per cent are pure Spanish in origin. In 1910 barely 15 per cent could read and write, and more than 90 per cent of the people were trying to eke out a miserable living by growing crops on land they did not own. Most of the wealth was in the hands of less than 3 per cent of the people. But between 1910 and 1915 Mexico initiated a genuine revolution —not just a change of power from one group to another. The constitution of 1917 provided a legal basis for changing the whole concept of private property in land, and it became illegal to hold property that was not effectively used. Large acreages of land were expropriated, especially in the period between 1935 and 1940, and turned over to farm-village communities, known as *ejidos*. The landed aristocracy as a class was wiped out—not by violence, but by a rapid process of economic and social change. The foreign oil properties were also expropriated in 1938, and are now operated by the Mexican government. For many decades these changes reduced the production of food and of money-earning exports; but since 1950 the Mexican economy has been booming.

All of this has been carried out in a difficult habitat. Most of Mexico is mountainous, with slopes that should never have been cleared of forest cover. About half of the national territory is deficient in moisture throughout the year, and only 12 per cent gets adequate rainfall at all times. To be sure, Mexico is supplied with certain important reserves of coal and oil, and of minerals useful in industry. But in 1910 over 90 per cent of the people were farmers, and even today over 50 per cent of the working force is employed in agriculture. Furthermore, the population is concentrated in the Central Area of Mexico, between Mexico City and Guadalajara; and here there is a concentration of farmers growing maize, although this is an area too dry and too cool for good maize yields. As a result of this emphasis on maize, the Mexicans live poorly in their chief area of concentration.

The government has been trying to improve the economy in a variety of ways. In fact Mexico is a good example of the beneficial results of balanced economic development. Since 1950 there has been an important increase in the irrigated area, used for growing cotton. There has been a movement of maize growers from the Central Area to the Gulf Coastal Plain, where the climate and soil are well-suited for this grain. In the highlands there is an effort to change from maize farming to the production of wheat and the pasturing of dairy cattle. Mexico continues to be an important producer of cotton, coffee, sugar cane, and henequen, but these products no longer make up so large a proportion of the total agricultural production as they did even so late as the 1930's. The proportion of agricultural workers dropped from 70 per cent in 1930 to 58 per cent in 1956.

Agricultural improvement has been balanced with industrial growth. The steel industry, centering at Monterrey, has been enlarged; but the largest and most diversified of the industrial centers is in and around Mexico City. Mexico continues to supply a major part of the United States needs of fluorspar, lead, antimony, bismuth, and cadmium, as well as smaller amounts of copper and zinc. But the oil fields now produce only for Mexican refineries, and the oil products are distributed by the government for use in Mexico. Whether this system costs less than it would to export the raw material and import the manufactured products is not a relevant question: to the Mexicans it is important that they now make their own policy decisions. Accepting Mexican policies, there has, since 1950, been a vast increase in manufacturing establishments—mostly branches of United States plants. Electric power projects are being built to give additional support to the new industries, and all over the country new paved highways are improving the transport situation. Subsistence farmers are decreasing rapidly in numbers, and as a result there is a considerable increase in retail trade and employment in service occupations. Mexico, in 1960, had a population increase of 3.4 per cent, which is just about as high a rate of increase as is possible: but in that same year its gross national product was increased 5.7 per cent.

Mexico is a strongly integrated state. The great majority of the people support their one-party system—the *Partido Revolucionario Institucional.* They are ready to work hard in support of its economic policies, and to assist in the building of a distinctively

Mexican society. Mexico is well on the road toward a solution of some of its traditionally insoluble problems.

THE CENTRAL AMERICAN COUNTRIES

The Central American countries (Guatemala, El Salvador, Nicaragua, Honduras, Costa Rica, and Panamá) are all small. In Guatemala about 60 per cent of the population is of unmixed Mayan Indian ancestry (Map 50); in the highlands of Costa Rica, on the other hand, the population is of unmixed Spanish ancestry. Elsewhere Spanish and Indian are mixed in varying proportions; but along the Caribbean lowlands of Panamá, Costa Rica, and Nicaragua the population includes a large proportion of Negroes.

Most of the people of Central America are poor subsistence farmers, or wage workers on plantations of commercial crops. Of all crops, maize occupies the largest acreage. It is grown on steep mountainside farms from which yields per acre are small. There are two major commercial crops—coffee and bananas. The coffee is grown in the mountains at elevations between about 2,000 and 6,000 feet above sea level.[2] The subsistence crops and the pastures for beef and dairy cattle are on the higher slopes above the coffee plantations. The banana plantations were developed by two large companies owned in the United States—the United Fruit Company and the Standard Fruit Company. The plantations were

[2] The people of this part of Latin America recognize contrasting zones of different altitude: *tierra caliente* up to about 2,000 feet, where average annual temperatures are between 75° and 79°; *tierra templada*, between 2,000 and 6,000 feet, with average temperatures between 65° and 75°; and *tierra fría*, between 6,000 and 10,000 feet, where average temperatures are between 55° and 65°. Above 10,000 feet are the grass-covered meadows and the zone of permanent snow.

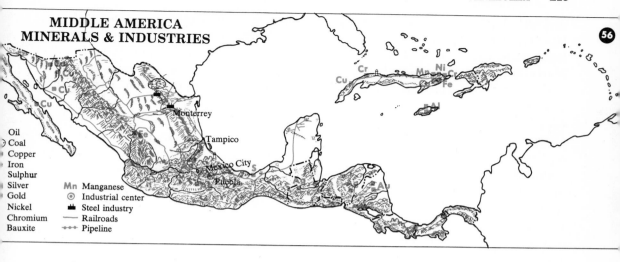

MIDDLE AMERICA
MINERALS & INDUSTRIES

Oil
Coal
Copper
Iron
Sulphur
Silver
Gold
Nickel
Chromium
Bauxite

Mn Manganese
⊙ Industrial center
⚒ Steel industry
— Railroads
+++ Pipeline

Monterrey
Tampico
Mexico City
Puebla

carved out of unoccupied forest land, mostly since 1900. The chief crop is still the banana, but on a few of the plantations other crops are now produced, such as abacá (hemp), cacao, and sisal. In Honduras there is some cutting of pine timber from the higher mountain forests; and from El Salvador comes Peruvian balsam, used in the manufacture of perfumes. In the lowlands of Nicaragua and El Salvador there are areas devoted to growing cotton. There is no large-scale industrial development in this area. In Panamá, the relatively high income per capita results from retail sales in the Canal Zone and nearby cities.

A plan to organize at least some of the countries of this area into a common market has been making important progress. In 1960 four countries were included—Guatemala, El Salvador, Nicaragua, and Honduras. It was agreed to reduce or eliminate tariffs and to provide for the free movement of trade across the once tightly-sealed borders. New manufacturing industries are to have access to the whole market—for example a paper manufacturing plant in Honduras will sell throughout Central America, and a tire manufacturing enterprise in Guatemala will have a similar range. This is the beginning of a relaxation of trade restrictions that could have important results in the decades ahead.

Most of the Central American countries remain pre-democratic, with a small group of landowners in control (fourteen families in El Salvador), and with the army running the governments. Costa Rica stands in striking contrast to its neighbors. Here democratic institutions are traditional. The small, independent coffee planters of the highlands are not in competition with a landed aristocracy, and the only armed force is provided by the police—there is no army. The Costa Ricans are more than 80 per cent literate.

VENEZUELA

Venezuela has the highest gross national product per capita in all Latin America. The reason for this is the income derived from the export of oil. Large amounts of foreign capital have been invested in the exploitation of Venezuela's oil (Map 57), which was first exported in 1918. Since 1930 Venezuela has stood in either second or third place in world oil production each year.

The population of Venezuela is not large, but it is increasing at a rate faster than that of Latin America as a whole. The largest concentrations of people are in the highlands around Caracas, and south of Lake Maracaibo (Map 2, p. 6). In 1900 the city of Caracas was occupied by less than 5 per cent of the population, but in 1960 it was occupied by 17 per cent of the population. Caracas is still growing rapidly. The people of Venezuela are mostly a mixture of Indian and Spanish, with perhaps 20 per cent of unmixed Spanish origin. Along the Caribbean coast there is a high proportion of Negroes.

Most of the people of Venezuela are still very poor. Scarcely 2 per cent of them enjoy sufficient income to purchase more than the bare necessities of life. For a long time after 1918 this condition of widespread poverty was preserved by government policy. Most of the people were tenants on large landed estates, and their incomes consisted of meager wages for work on the commercial crops of coffee, cacao, and sugar cane, and from their own subsistence crop of maize which was grown on the land not suited for other uses. The income from oil was used to build luxurious clubs and office buildings in Maracaibo and Caracas, and to maintain a well-paid army. The dictator ran Venezuela as if it were his own personal estate. Since 1958 Venezuela has had a liberal government which has been attempting to establish such democratic procedures as the secret ballot and majority rule. It is now the policy of the government to use oil income to build roads, pipelines, and new manufacturing industries, so that when the oil is used up the Venezuelan economy will not collapse. A new development of iron ore mining south of the Orinoco River has taken place, and on the river a new steel plant is being built. In the core area of the country, inland from Caracas, many new manufacturing industries are being established, some of them

making use of oil and gas as raw materials. Venezuela is reinvesting a very large proportion of its annual income in new capital formation, which, before many years, will pay off in an increased number and variety of jobs.

At the start, however, this policy is running into difficulties. The first industrial wage workers, with real money in hand for the first time, are not finding enough of the basic foods in the markets. As a result prices are going up, and the workers are unable to realize the better living that was promised. The contrast between wealthy and poor is strikingly visible in and around Caracas, where beautiful new homes are bordered by shack-towns. The integration of Venezuela, in spite of its national wealth, is not yet assured.

COLOMBIA

Colombia contains more geographic contrasts than any other area of similar size in the world. This is due to the existence of very high mountains in which there are intermont basins and valleys at all different altitudes. Since the country is not far from the equator there is a maximum variety of altitude zones;[3] and the introduction of Spanish domestic animals and Spanish crops made all these contrasted habitats potentially productive. There is also diversity of population and economy. There are numerous separate clusters of people that are made up of unmixed Indians; but the cluster of people around Medellín is predominantly Spanish in origin. In many parts of the country the population is mixed Indian and Spanish, but in parts of the *tierra caliente* there are large proportions of

[3] See footnote, p. 214. The upper limit of the *tierra caliente* in Colombia is about 3,000 feet, and of the *tierra templada,* about 6,500 feet. The mountain grasslands are called *páramos.* The snow line is about 14,500 feet.

Harvesting potatoes in highland Bolivia, where the Indians still use traditional farming methods. The first cultivation of the potato was in this region.

Negroes (Map 50). Furthermore, the contrasts in economic development among these diverse clusters of people are very great. The economic core of the country is in the area around Medellín, where coffee is the chief export crop, and where there is an important new development of manufacturing industry.

The Colombian economy is not well balanced. Coffee is the one large export, which leaves the country vulnerable to changes in world demand. The government is now attempting to balance the rapid growth of the Medellín area by new economic developments elsewhere—a new steel plant in the remote highlands north of Bogotá; the industrial development of Cali; and a river basin development, like that of the Tennessee Valley Authority in the United States, for the Cauca Valley. A major problem has always been transportation, due to the mountainous nature of the terrain. The airplane can provide quick access for mail and

passengers; but bulky shipments have to rely on motor trucks and railroads.

From the point of view of political geography the question is whether it is possible to change the diversity of Colombia from a liability to an asset. If local loyalties outweigh national support, diversity is a disaster; but if the country can be integrated, as Mexico is, by a powerful state-idea, then diversity is a source of strength.

THE ANDEAN COUNTRIES

The Andean countries (Ecuador, Peru, and Bolivia) occupy the parts of Latin America that were once ruled by the Inca. In each of these countries the population is still more than 70 per cent Indian. Furthermore, most of the Indians remain subsistence cultivators, essentially outside the economic system of buying and selling. The gross national products of these countries are low: the lowest in all Latin America is that of Bolivia.

Ecuador is sharply divided into two parts. In the mountains, with the exception of the city of Quito, the population is very largely Indian. Along the Pacific there are a few Indian communities, but most of the people are a mixture of Indian and Spanish. There are some Negroes in the northern part of the coastal area. A large proportion of the national product of Ecuador originates in this Pacific region. There are plantations of bananas, rice, cacao, and on the lower mountain slopes, coffee. There is a small oil field west of Guayaquil, the chief city.

Peru is also divided into two chief parts. The highlands, as in Ecuador, are largely occupied by Indian farming communities; but there are also some important highland mining areas—especially the area inland from Lima, from which come copper, vanadium, silver, gold, and other metals. Inland from the newly developed industrial town of Chimbote (Map 57) there are some sources of good-quality coal. Hydroelectric stations provide the power for making steel. Iron ore comes from southern Peru by ship. The coastal region of Peru, unlike that of Ecuador, is very dry, so that all agriculture is based on irrigation. Irrigated commercial crops include chiefly cotton and sugar cane. Peru also has an oil field.

The part of Peru that lies east of the Andes has long suffered from difficult accessibility. Since 1940, however, several motor highways have been built across the mountains, and where these roads extend onto the eastern lowlands there are some new pioneer settlements. A small oil field has been found, and there is hope that a much larger reserve will be discovered.

Bolivia is the poorest of the three countries. Its Indian population is concentrated around the shores of Lake Titicaca, where the land is used to grow subsistence crops and to pasture sheep and alpaca for their wool. All through the highlands there are small isolated Indian communities that remain mostly self-sufficient. The national economy is supported by mining: Bolivia is a major source of tin, and produces tungsten, bismuth, lead, silver, and copper. Under the lowlands, east of the Andes, there is oil.

Since 1950 Bolivia has been engaged in a program of land redistribution, but, as in the case of Mexico, there is not nearly enough arable land to satisfy the needs of the farmers. Bolivia, unlike Mexico, has very little industrial development, and no large inflow of capital into manufacturing development. So far the Bolivian revolution has increased the poverty of the people.

CHILE

Chile can be compared and contrasted with Mexico in many ways. In both countries the agrarian tradition inherited from Spain had resulted in a great concentration of land in the hands of a minority of the people. Mexico had its revolution: Chile has been redistributing its land, but through the operation of economic processes and without recourse to revolution.

Most of the people of Chile are concentrated in the Central Valley between Valparaiso and the beginning of the embayed section of Southern Chile. Between latitude 30°S and Concepción the climate is one of winter rains and summer droughts, similar to that of California—a Mediterranean climate. South of Concepción the climate resembles that of British Columbia and southern Alaska in North America. North of 30°S, Northern Chile—the Atacama—is one of the driest parts of the world. The extremities of Chile are thinly populated, but they produce an important part of the national wealth. In Northern Chile, nitrate and copper; in Southern Chile, oil (from Tierra del

Fuego), and wool from Patagonia, north of the Strait of Magellan.

The core of the Chilean state is the middle part. Here the population is composed of a mixture of Spanish and Indian, with the Spanish inheritance predominant. As in Mexico, the land used to be held in huge properties by some 3 per cent of the people. Because the landowners were interested in cattle, much of the best land in this area was used for irrigated alfalfa, leaving the poorer land for wheat—the basic food crop of Chile. But the Chilean landowners, unlike the Mexicans, were not reluctant to become businessmen. There has been a strong movement to sell the large estates in small lots, and to reinvest the profits from land sales in manufacturing industries. Already Chile uses far more electric power per capita than any other Latin American country. A steel plant has been built near Concepción, supplied with coal from nearby sources, and iron ore from Northern Chile and Peru. A large development of industries is taking place in and around Santiago, Valparaiso, Concepción,

and Valdivia. Chile, along with Mexico, is one of the few Latin American countries that has entered the initial phase of the Industrial Revolution. It is also one of the few in which democratic processes are being rapidly adopted.

ARGENTINA

Unlike any of the other countries of Latin America previously discussed, Argentina is a relatively new creation. During most of the colonial period this part of South America was remote from the centers of Spanish settlement, and remained thinly populated. At the time that independence was gained from Spain, the center of Argentine life was Tucumán. For several decades civil war raged between those who wanted to have a loose federal structure, and those who wanted a closely integrated state with Buenos Aires as the center. The supporters of a closely integrated state were victorious. With the adoption of a new constitution in 1853, modern Argentina began to emerge. Between 1853 and 1914 there was a large inflow of British capital, invested in rail-

Chuquicamata, Chile's great copper mine in the Atacama, and one of the world's chief sources of copper.

roads, docks, cattle ranches, and packing plants. The Argentine state developed the largest volume of exports and imports of any Latin American country, but its economy was closely tied to the economy of Great Britain. Since 1914 the demand for an end to economic colonialism has become progressively stronger, and the ties with Great Britain have been loosened. The result has been a decrease in the gross national product per capita, but an increase in the sense of independence.

The Argentine national territory embraces four notably contrasted habitats. First, in the west are the towering ranges of the Andes, dry in the north where they border Bolivia and Northern Chile, wet and forest-covered in the south. Second, in the whole northern part of the country is a low-latitude region mostly covered with a scrub woodland, interrupted here and there by grassy openings—a region across which the Río Paraná sprawls in shifting meanders. Along the eastern base of the Andes there are several spots of settlement based on irrigation; and there are clusters of settlement along the Paraná and between the Paraná and the Uruguay, but most of this region is thinly populated. Third, the southern part of Argentina, south of about latitude 40°S, the area known as Patagonia, is mostly dry and cool, with only a very few spots of settlement. The fourth of the major habitats is the Humid Pampa—a mid-latitude grassland, exceptionally level, covered with a wind-blown dust or *loess*, of extraordinary natural fertility. This is a region of mild winters, with cool summers near the ocean and hot summers elsewhere (Map 5, pp. 10-11).

The Humid Pampa has become the core of Argentina. The story of the settlement and development of this region in many ways parallels that of the settlement of the North American prairies, which took place at about the same time. When the Spaniards first settled at Buenos Aires in 1536, they found an endless expanse of tall grass, and a scanty population of nomadic Indian hunters. When the Spaniards introduced horses and cattle, the Indians quickly adopted them and revised their way of life accordingly. The horses made the killing of game much easier, but soon the supply of game animals was inadequate. For centuries the Indians lived by raiding the Spanish settlements and stealing cattle. The Spaniards found little to interest them in this area: there were no large numbers of Indians to be converted to Christianity, no minerals, and no farm tools that made easy the clearing of the tall grass. During the whole colonial period the Humid Pampa remained thinly occupied by Spaniards along the Plata-Paraná shore, where large unfenced ranches were used to feed mules and scrubby cattle. Buenos Aires was known as the back door to Peru, because the chief route of connection between Lima and Spain went by way of Panamá.

The modern development of the Humid Pampa began after 1853. The first railroad was built out of Buenos Aires in 1857. But in this treeless region, even more than in North America, modern cattle and grain farming could not be successfully combined until barbed wire made fencing possible. By 1880, for the first time, the Humid Pampa could be developed for both cattle and crops. Two events followed: first, the army was used to eliminate the Indians in a campaign lasting from 1879 to 1883; and second, the whole of the Humid Pampa was quickly divided into vast private estates or *estancias*. Most of the area of the Humid Pampa came into the possession of some three hundred families. Instead of 160-acre farms, as in the United States, the properties here were more likely to be 100,000 acres.

The British did not want the lean beef obtainable from the scrubby cattle already present in the region: instead they wanted fat beef, and to get this they sent breeding stock to rebuild the herds. But the big clumsy beef animals did not do well on the native Pampa grasses. They needed a feed crop, and the crop that was found to be ideally suited to this region was alfalfa. This was a plant that had been first grown in Southwest Asia and brought into the Mediterranean region even as early as 400 B.C. The Spaniards introduced it into South America in the sixteenth century, but, in Argentina, it had not been able to compete with the native Pampa grasses. In order to prepare alfalfa pastures it was necessary to eliminate the grass by planting wheat or maize for three or four years. And to do this kind of farm work, the landowners needed labor—much more labor than was available in this part of the world. In response to this need there was a flood of immigrant colonists from Europe—Italian, Spanish, German, and others. The immigrants were employed as tenant farmers on the large estancias. For four years a tenant would plant and harvest wheat or maize, then plant alfalfa and move away. Argentina became one of the world's lowest-cost producers of wheat, and the world's leading exporter of maize. But the basic purpose of this agricultural development was the preparation of alfalfa pastures. After five years or so the alfalfa would begin to decline in yield, and a new tenant would be employed to plant another series of grain crops followed by a new alfalfa seeding. By World War II about half of all the alfalfa acreage in the world was in the Humid Pampa.

It was at this time that the outlines of the Humid Pampa as a region emerged. Before 1880 there was no sharp line to distinguish the Humid Pampa from the Dry Pampa to the west. Agriculture could expand westward as long as the yields per acre of grain and alfalfa made this type of farming profitable. One might assume that if the price of wheat on the world market had been higher such farming might have been profitable farther west. The whole concept of the Humid Pampa, it may be argued, was derived from the balance of costs and prices involved in grain farming in the late nineteenth century, not by any nature-given quality of the climate. This is a further illustration of the principle that the significance to man of the physical features of a habitat is a function of the attitudes, objectives, and technical skills of man himself.

Before 1914 there were few manufacturing industries in Argentina. Even wheat was sent to Great Britain to be milled and then sent back again as flour. Industrial development in Argentina began during World War I; and since World War II the rate of development has been rapid. Manufacturing enterprises include flour milling, meat packing, leather working, and many others that utilize Argentine raw materials. But there is perhaps no other country in the world which is so poorly supplied with fuel or industrial raw materials. Argentina has only small supplies of low-grade coal, and only a part of its requirements in oil. From Comodoro Rivadavia, in Patagonia, a pipeline now brings gas to Buenos Aires, but the city still depends in large part on imported coal. There is no potential source of hydroelectric power within range. Furthermore, Argentina has only poor supplies of iron ore and other industrial metals. Nevertheless, a steel plant has been built on the Río Paraná near Rosario; and oil and gas from oil fields along the eastern Andean piedmont in the Northwest will supply raw materials for a petro-chemical industry a little up-stream from Rosario. Buenos Aires is the largest industrial city, with about 30 per cent of the total population of Argentina; but manufacturing is also important in the smaller cities. Argentina today has the largest value of manufacturing production per capita of all Latin America.

Argentine politics reflect a continued struggle to formulate an acceptable state-idea. There is a strong sentiment in favor of national, economic self-sufficiency, which was given its greatest expression during the rule of Juan Perón. But in a country so notably lacking in the basic raw materials for industry, a policy of economic self-sufficiency can only bring disaster. The government must steer a course between complete dependence on a foreign economy, such as that of Great Britain, and complete economic independence. There is a similar conflict between those seeking solutions through the operation of a strong military dictatorship, and those attempting to build the institutions of a free democracy. Resistance to the ideas of the Democratic Revolution is still strong. Until these basic conflicts of policy are resolved, Argentina can scarcely enjoy to the fullest degree the benefits of a rich soil and a mild climate.

URUGUAY AND PARAGUAY

Uruguay and Paraguay, both small neighbors of Argentina, are vastly different from each other. The Paraguayan state was built around a single cluster of people near Asunción, and is now mostly a mixed population of Spanish and Indian. Uruguay was long a no-man's-land between the Spanish and Portuguese colonies, and was only granted independence in 1828 to create a buffer state between Argentina and Brazil. Its population is mostly European. In the twentieth century Uruguay has achieved the largest degree of democracy of any Latin American country, and stands among the few with more than 80 per cent literacy. Paraguay remains a military dictatorship. Uruguay is second only to Argentina in the per capita value of manufacturing production, and its wealth is widely distributed among the people. Paraguay's small income per capita derived from exports of beef, lumber, quebracho, and other minor items is concentrated in the hands of a small proportion of the population. Neither country possesses mineral resources; but Uruguay has become one of the world's major producers of wool, and Uruguayan industries manufacture many products based on the vast herds of sheep and cattle.

PORTUGUESE BRAZIL

Each of the sixteen Spanish-speaking countries just discussed has distinctive characteristics and problems. Yet all the Spanish countries as a group stand in sharp contrast to Portuguese Brazil. This is more than just a contrast of language: it is also a contrast in attitudes, in national characteristics, and in the possibilities of development. Brazil, the largest Latin-American country and the one with the greatest variety of resources, probably enjoys the greatest potential for economic development. Yet this country, also, faces difficult political and economic problems. The settled part of the country lies mostly within the zone of seasonal forest near the eastern coast (Maps 2 and 8), and a large part of the huge national territory (Brazil is the fifth largest country in the world) is either empty or very thinly occupied.

Brazil varies considerably in population and economic development from one part

The River Amazon, near Belém, Brazil. Houses are built on stilts to safe-guard them from floods; and the dug-out canoe is the common form of transportation.

of the country to another. There are parts where the population includes a large pro-portion of Negroes; on the other hand São Paulo and South Brazil are occupied by a population of almost purely European origin—Portuguese, German, Polish, and Italian (Map 50). And in the state of São Paulo, and in places along the Amazon, there are colonies of Japanese. Brazil, like Canada, has no primate city, for São Paulo and Rio de Janeiro are almost the same size. The capital is the new city of Brasília, which was only begun in 1956. It is situated in the thinly peopled backlands of the country.

The Habitat. The greater part of Brazil is hilly (Map 52). Only narrow strips of low-land are found along the Atlantic coast. The largest areas of plain are in the remote

forests of the upper Amazon, or in the upper Paraguay Valley—both areas of very thin population. From Salvador in the Northeast to the southern part of Brazil, the eastern edge of the Brazilian Highlands is marked by a sharp drop of more than 2,000 feet—a feature known as the Great Escarpment. Almost unbroken by river val-leys it constitutes a serious barrier to rail transportation. In the part of the country where the Brazilian national life comes to focus on Rio de Janeiro and São Paulo, the hilly uplands are surmounted by groups of low mountains, none of which reach 10,000 feet above sea level, but which contain only minute areas of level land. It is important to note, also, that many of Brazil's great rivers rise in the highlands just north of Rio de Janeiro: the headwater tributaries

57

SOUTH AMERICA
MINERALS AND INDUSTRIES

Legend

- ⊙ Industrial centers
- 🏭 Steel industry
- ⛽ Oil
- Coal
- Fe Iron
- Au Gold
- Ag Silver
- P Platinum
- Al Bauxite
- Mn Manganese
- Cu Copper
- V Vanadium
- Sn Tin
- Hg Mercury
- ⬥ Nitrate
- ♦ Diamonds
- W Tungsten
- Pb Lead
- ⋯ Pipeline

SOUTH AMERICA RAILROADS

Barranquilla
Caracas
Medellín
Bogotá
Quito
Manaus
Belém
Lima
Salvador
La Paz
Brasília
Corumbá
Antofagasta
Asunción
Rio de Ja[neiro]
Santos
Valparaíso
Montevideo
Buenos Aires
Valdivia
Bahía Blanca

0   600
Scale

of the Paraná rise on the very crest of the Great Escarpment and flow westward to form the main stream, which finally reaches the sea near Buenos Aires; the São Francisco also rises in this area, flowing northward for a thousand miles before turning east to plunge over the Paulo Affonso Falls toward the sea; the southern tributaries of the Amazon also rise in this central part of the highlands.

The Amazon, itself, flows through the world's largest expanse of tropical rain forest (Map 8, pp. 16-17). This is a very thinly populated region, parts of which lie outside Brazil's effective national territory. Along the eastern side of the highlands, from the Northeast to the south of Brazil, there is a belt of seasonal forest; but for the most part the interior is covered by a woodland savanna—a grassland with scattered scrubby trees and thickets.

Very little of Brazil suffers from a deficiency of moisture (Maps 5 and 6), and very little is rendered unproductive because of excessive rainfall. Only in the south are frosts experienced during the winters; yet no part of the national territory experiences excessively high temperatures (Map 7). Brazil is truly moderate in climate. But even so, the population is by no means uniformly spread over the vast area.

Agriculture. Since the first Portuguese settlement in Brazil, in 1500, agriculture has been largely confined to the area of seasonal forest. Between 1538 and about 1700 the Portuguese developed the world's first large-scale plantation economy in the Northeast—the labor was supplied by Negro slaves brought from Africa, and the crop was sugar cane. Sugar cane is still grown in this area (Map 55), but it is no longer such a profitable business as it was in the seventeenth century. Near Salvador there is a small area that has been used for tobacco growing for more than four hundred years. Between 1700 and 1800 attention shifted to the country north of Rio de Janeiro, where gold and diamonds had been discovered. The forest lands nearby were cleared to produce food for the miners. Between 1830 and 1930 Brazil's wealth was derived largely from coffee planting in the country back from São Paulo—where immigrant tenants from Italy and other parts of Europe provided the labor. Since the beginning of the present century cacao plantations have been carved out of the forest south of Salvador; and there are now small rubber plantations near Salvador and in the Amazon region. Outside these major areas of commercial crops, the seasonal forests have been cleared for the production of food crops and for pasture for cattle. As a result most of this kind of forest is now gone.

Agricultural methods have not changed much in four centuries. On the large private properties, tenant farm families are established on a temporary basis. The tenant farmer clears perhaps ten acres by cutting and burning. In the clearing he plants maize, rice, and beans, and perhaps cotton or manioc. Yields are profitable for two or three years, after which the farmer plants pasture grass and moves to a new part of the forest. The landowner then pastures beef cattle on the land that the tenant has relinquished. After a few years the second-growth forest recaptures the land, and the cattle are moved to new pastures. If the forest can remain on the land for fifty years or so, the soil is rebuilt and the cycle of farming and pasturing can be repeated. But close to the cities the clearing has taken place at much shorter intervals, partly to supply the city people with charcoal, with the result that today there are large areas, once forested, to which the trees will not return because of soil erosion. In the course of four centuries a small population has managed to destroy the agricultural potential of a vast area.

Modern farm techniques, however, have come to Brazil since World War II. The Brazilian agronomists had long recommended better farming methods, but without much success. As long as new land was plentiful there seemed no need to apply conservation methods. But now Brazil's supply of seasonal forest land is almost used up. New farm techniques require the use of machinery, better quality seeds, improved breeds of animals, the terracing of sloping land (most of Brazil's territory is hilly), and the reconstruction of worn-out soils by organic and chemical conditioners and fertilizers. In the progressive state of São Paulo, and in a few spots elsewhere, the farms have been modernized; but the production of food still lags behind population growth in Brazil as a whole, and the price of food in the city markets has been rising at an alarming rate.

Two quite different solutions to the food problem have been advocated. One is to promote the westward movement of small-farmer pioneers onto the lands covered by woodland savanna. The other is to promote the further spread of new agricultural techniques. The small farmer cultivating a ten-acre clearing is a high-cost producer, and it is doubtful whether this traditional system can in fact be employed in the backlands where soils are very poor. The poor savanna soils can be made productive through the use of machinery, soil conditioners, and other new techniques. If the purpose is to supply more food to the cities at steady prices, these new methods might be applied more effectively, however, to worn-out lands close to the urban centers. But when agriculture is modernized, as in the United States, the number of people employed in farming must be decreased. If large numbers of people now engaged in farming are no longer needed, it is clear that many new jobs must be provided in urban occupations.

Industrial Development. Unlike Argentina, Brazil does possess a wealth of industrial raw materials. In the highlands north of Rio de Janeiro there are large bodies of high-grade iron ore (Map 57). Ore from this region is being exported, even to distant Japan. In this same area, and also in other parts of Brazil, there are important sources of manganese. Other minerals available in the Brazilian Highlands, but not shown on Map 57, include zirconium, chromium, molybdenum, nickel, tungsten, titanium, industrial diamonds, beryl, mica, quartz crystals, and semiprecious stones. To be sure, Brazil lacks adequate supplies of both coal and oil, but it does have a large hydroelectric potential.

Brazil has developed a large concentration of manufacturing industry in São Paulo and Rio de Janeiro, and in the area between and to the north of these two metropolises. The largest steel plant in Latin America is the Guilherme Guinle Plant at Volta Redonda, about midway between these two cities, which together form Brazil's largest market for steel. The steel plant, and another smaller plant near São Paulo, are supplied with iron ore, manganese, and limestone from the mining area a short distance to the north; and with some of the coal from the southern part of Brazil, which has to be mixed with imported coal.

The state of São Paulo, with its great urban center, is in a relatively advanced stage of economic development. Although the textile industry is still predominant, a great variety of other kinds of manufacturing have been built, which suggests that São Paulo, at least, has passed through the initial phase of the Industrial Revolution and is on the way toward maturity. The difficulty is that São Paulo is so far ahead of the rest of Brazil. São Paulo alone accounts for over half of Brazil's industrial production: it pays 40 per cent of the production tax, 50 per cent of the consumption tax, and 60 per cent of the import tax levied by the Brazilian treasury. São Paulo is by far the largest industrial center in all Latin America. It is sometimes described by the Brazilians as a locomotive pulling twenty empty freight cars (the other states). When the industrial development of Rio de Janeiro and the zone between the two cities is added to the figures for São Paulo it appears that this core area accounts for about 76 per cent of Brazil's manufacturing production.

The Viability of Brazil. This rapid development of the city and state of São Paulo does, in fact, create a serious problem. Between 30 and 40 per cent of the gross national product originates in this one state. The income per capita in this area is perhaps even greater than that of Venezuela. By contrast, the level of living in other parts of Brazil, especially the Northeast, compares with the poorest parts of Latin America.

This striking contrast in economic development, and in the attitudes acompanying economic development, has produced a sectional division in Brazil that might well threaten the viability of the nation were it not for the geographic arrangement of these sectional differences. São Paulo occupies a central position within the national territory. If it were located on the periphery of the country, the forces for disintegration might indeed be overwhelmingly strong: but in political geography there are few if any examples of the withdrawal of a centrally-located section from the rest of a country. The unity of the Brazilian state is given support by a distinctive language, by a historical tradition that stands in striking contrast to that of Spanish America, and by an active flow of domestic commerce.

Another important element in the Brazilian state-idea is the new capital, Brasília (see the illustration at the chapter opening). Brazilians of all political parties take pride in the imaginative architecture, the ultramodern plan, and especially the building, of this distinctively Brazilian creation. It has been situated in the midst of the thinly-peopled backlands, near the stream divide where three of Brazil's great rivers rise—the Paraná, the São Francisco, and the Tocantins. The hope that the establishment of a city will lead to a movement of pioneers into the backlands is perhaps not justified; for Brazilian experience shows that when state capitals have been located in similar situations, the result has been a movement of people out of the rural areas and into the cities. But as an integrating factor in Brazilian political life, Brasília is a major triumph.

THE ANTILLES AND THE GUIANAS[4]

The countries and colonies of the Antilles and the Guianas share a common historical background. Except for the Spanish colony established by Columbus on the island of

[4] The islands of Caribbean America include the Greater Antilles (Cuba, Jamaica, Hispaniola, and Puerto Rico), the Lesser Antilles, and the Bahamas. The Bahamas are not properly included in the Antilles. Many geographers prefer the name West Indies instead of the Antilles.

Hispaniola, and except for thinly spread Spanish settlements on the other parts of the Greater Antilles, the rest of the Antilles, and the Guiana region on the continent of South America (between the Amazon and the Orinoco), were at first left unoccupied. But after the Dutch had learned from the Negroes of Northeast Brazil how profitable it might be to raise sugar cane, the Dutch,

Hill slopes in Puerto Rico, badly eroded as a result of clearing of the natural forest cover. These slopes have been replanted since the photograph was taken.

the French, and the British moved into these empty areas. Negro slaves were brought to the Antilles in large numbers. French sugar cane planters in Haiti (then Saint Domingue) became enormously wealthy, as also did the British planters in Barbados and Jamaica (after the British took it from the Spaniards). When the independence movement came to Latin America early in the nineteenth century, the first country to gain independence was Haiti (1804). A French-speaking Negro republic was set up, and until 1844 the Haitians controlled the whole island of Hispaniola. In 1844 the eastern two-thirds of the island

became the Dominican Republic. The Spanish colony of Cuba became independent as a result of the Spanish-American War of 1898, at which time, also, Puerto Rico became a territory of the United States. The Virgin Islands were purchased by the United States from Denmark in 1917. In 1962 Jamaica and Trinidad became independent members of the Commonwealth. The other islands of the Antilles and the Bahamas were divided among Great Britain, France, the Netherlands, the United States, and Venezuela.

The tremendous prosperity of the period of sugar cane planting came to an end long ago. When the slaves were emancipated, after 1834, the economy had to be rebuilt with free labor. After 1900 the spectacular rise of Cuba as the world's chief producer of sugar was the result of four chief factors: (1) the existence in Cuba of an ideal soil and climate for growing sugar cane; (2) a supply of cheap labor; (3) location close to the world's largest market for sugar; and (4) a large investment of capital from the United States in the land and machinery needed to produce sugar. Most of the other islands remained poor, with large populations crowded on the small areas of potentially productive land. The chief products of the Antilles and the Guianas today include sugar, molasses, rum, cotton, limes, tomatoes, coconuts, cacao, arrowroot, and bananas. On the higher areas of the larger mountainous islands there are coffee plantations. The only mineral resources of the Antilles and the Guianas are oil and asphalt in Trinidad, oil, chromium, manganese, and nickel in Cuba, and bauxite in Jamaica, British Guiana, and Surinam. This is the world's chief source of bauxite. Large oil refineries on the islands of Curaçao and Aruba refine some of the Venezuelan oil. But for the most part the economy of the Antilles and the Guianas fails to support the population adequately. On the other hand, important changes have taken place in Cuba, in Puerto Rico, and in Jamaica and Trinidad.

CUBA

Since 1959 Cuba has been a matter of special concern, both to Anglo-America and to Latin America, because of the establishment there of a Soviet-controlled dictatorship of the Communist Party. The people of Cuba had been demanding independence from outside interference for a long time. When Spanish rule was ended in 1898 the United States reserved the right to exercise police powers in Cuba for the purpose of maintaining order. Meanwhile, investments from the United States in sugar cane plantations and mills, in mines and ports, and in tourist facilities, became very profitable. But the profits went largely to a few large corporations, to a few wealthy Cubans, and to the officials of the Cuban government. A military dictatorship was firmly established, and a large number of Cubans found themselves with what they felt was less independence than they had enjoyed under Spain. Meanwhile, the sugar cane workers, most of them employed only during the harvest season from January to June, lived miserably in slum districts within sight of the new luxury hotels, and were kept in order by a well-organized police force.

This was the unhappy situation when Fidel Castro and a small band of followers took refuge in the mountains of eastern Cuba. The struggle to overthrow the dictatorship gained much sympathy not only in other countries of Latin America, but also in the United States. But when the revolution was successful, and then was transformed into a Soviet-style dictatorship, much of this support fell away. The old economy based on sugar cane, tobacco, and tourists, with some mineral exports, was largely destroyed as industries were taken over by the government, and agriculture was organized into collectives. Some of the sugar cane workers were given new homes and lands on which to grow food crops, but for most of the Cubans there was less food, not more. Many Cuban liberals fled into exile.

Meanwhile, those who support the sweep of the great revolutions over Latin America, especially the Democratic Revolution, are deeply concerned about Cuba. Not only does Cuba offer a Soviet-controlled base close to the borders of the United States, but also the communists in Cuba can menace the continued advance of democratic ideals in Latin America.

PUERTO RICO

In marked contrast is the situation on the island of Puerto Rico. Before 1940 Puerto Rico was an almost classic example of the evils of economic colonialism. The application of health measures had greatly reduced the death rate and caused a sudden upsurge in the net rate of population increase. The density of population on this mountainous and purely agricultural island rose to 670 people per square mile. Yet the best third of the island was owned by two large sugar companies. The land was used in part to grow cane, but a large part of the company properties was held in pasture for future cane expansion. The Puerto Ricans, like the Cubans, were employed only during the harvest season, and in between harvests the majority of them had no source of income. On the steep mountain slopes of interior Puerto Rico small farmers cleared the protecting forest, and planted maize and tobacco.

Since 1940 the political and economic life of Puerto Rico has been transformed. Under the inspired leadership of liberal-minded statesmen, Puerto Rico gained, in 1952, the status of a self-governing commonwealth "freely associated" with the United States. Its people are citizens of the United States, but pay no federal income tax on money earned in Puerto Rico. Corporations owned outside the commonwealth may not possess more than five hundred acres of land. The large sugar companies now restrict their activities to grinding the cane and preparing sugar for shipment. Cane is grown on cooperative farms, and on small privately-owned plantations. Large acreages of Puerto Rico's best land have been taken out of pasture and used to produce food. After a survey of the quality of the land throughout the island, a new plan for the better use of the soil was worked out and the farmers were persuaded to adopt it. The steeper slopes are now no longer used for maize and tobacco, but rather for coffee or other tree crops which protect the surface from erosion. The modernization of agriculture has resulted in a reduction of the number of farmers. To provide new jobs the government has encouraged the development of new manufacturing industries, by granting a ten-year period with no taxation until the new firms can become established. The income per capita in 1956 placed Puerto Rico third among the Latin American countries; and it was more widely distributed than in Venezuela. Puerto Rico has clearly entered the initial phase of the Industrial Revolution.

An important fact about Puerto Rico is that this transformation of the island economy has been accomplished by democratic processes, not by decree enforced with arms. To be sure there are still too many people in Puerto Rico, and some sixty thousand each year migrate to the mainland, chiefly to New York City. But Puerto Rico can demonstrate to the world that it is possible to provide economic development without losing basic freedoms, even in an over-populated, and under-developed country. Puerto Rico stands as the major challenge to Cuba.

JAMAICA AND TRINIDAD

The newest independent states in the Latin American region are Jamaica and Trinidad. For many decades Great Britain has been following a policy of preparing its colonial possessions for self-government, and of pushing them toward independence as rapidly as possible. In 1958 the British islands of the Antilles were organized into a Federation of the West Indies, which after a few years of preparation was to become independent. The Federation included Jamaica, Trinidad, Barbados, the Windward Islands, and the Leeward Islands. The proposal soon ran into two chief difficulties: the better developed islands were reluctant to accept the burden of the less prosperous ones; and loyalties on each of the three major islands were too strong to permit the easy formulation of a state-idea for the Federation as a whole. In 1961 Jamaica voted to withdraw. In 1962 Jamaica and Trinidad were both granted independence, and the other islands remained as British colonies.

SUMMARY

Of all the major regions of the world, the Latin American Culture Region is now receiving, in the second half of the twentieth century, the most direct impact of both the Industrial and the Democratic Revolutions.

Before World War II these revolutionary changes had reached only a few parts of Latin America; by 1955 only a few places remained untouched. It is important to understand that the vast surge of popular support for the principles of democracy is not communist inspired. Rather the opposite; for where the communists have taken control of a revolutionary movement they have reacted vigorously against the Democratic Revolution, denying all five of the principles involved.

What is happening in Latin America can be described quite simply. The pre-industrial and pre-democratic institutions have become intolerable to large numbers of people. They are intolerable because they deny equality of status and opportunity, because they fail to make a serious attack on poverty, ill-health, illiteracy, and an in-adequate diet, and because they fail to provide the individual with a decent living. But even more important, they do not provide any large numbers of people with the opportunity to participate in the formulation of policy, the intangible but essential element in political stability. More and more Latin Americans are finding out through education that the second half of the twentieth century is a period of "rising expectations" all over the world, when the common man can demand a larger share of the fruits of industry, and when he can demand a larger responsibility for the shaping of the future.

6

THE
NORTH AFRICAN-
SOUTHWEST ASIAN
CULTURE REGION

Country	Political Status	Latest Estimate Population	Capital City
Afghanistan	Constitutional Monarchy	13,800,000 ('60)	Kābul
Algeria	Republic	11,700,000 ('62)	Algiers
Bahrain Islands	Sheikhdom; British Protectorate	147,000 ('60)	
Ifni	Spanish Colony	54,000 ('60)	
Iran	Monarchy	21,200,000 ('62)	Tehrān
Iraq	Constitutional Monarchy	7,500,000 ('62)	Baghdad
Israel	Republic	2,300,000 ('62)	Jerusalem
Jordan	Constitutional Monarchy	1,800,000 ('62)	'Ammān
Kuwait	Sheikhdom; Brit. Protect.	300,000 ('62)	Kuwait
Lebanon	Republic	1,700,000 ('62)	Beirut
Libya	Monarchy	1,200,000 ('62)	Al Bayḍā'
Morocco	Independent Kingdom	12,300,000 ('62)	Rabat
Muscat & Oman	Sultanate (In close treaty relationship with Brit.) Incl. enclave in Trucial territory	544,000 ('60)	Muscat
Qatar	Sheikhdom; Brit. Protect.	45,000 ('60)	
Saudi Arabia	Monarchy	6,000,000 ('62)	Riyadh
South Arabia, Federation of Incl. Aden	British Colony & Protect.	155,000 ('60)	
Spanish Sahara Incl. Río de Oro Saguia el Hamra	Spanish Territory	25,000 ('60)	
Sudan	Republic	12,400,000 ('62)	Khartoum
Syrian Arab Republic	Republic	5,100,000 ('62)	Damascus
Trucial Coast	Seven Sheikhdoms; British Protected	86,000 ('60)	
Tunisia	Republic	4,300,000 ('62)	Tunis
Turkey	Republic	29,200,000 ('62)	Ankara
United Arab Republic	Republic	27,200,000 ('62)	Cairo
Yemen	Monarchy	5,000,000 ('62)	San'a

The North African-Southwest Asian Culture Region is an area of conflict and boiling antagonisms. It is, indeed, ironic that so much hatred should have been generated in a region that cradled three of the world's great religions—Judaism, Christianity, and Islam—in each of which the faithful are exhorted to treat all men as brothers. Yet the record of man's inhumanity to man, of conquest and reconquest, of ruthless destruction and of deep-seated resentments, goes back before the dawn of written history. Conflict and antagonism still complicate the solution of problems in the modern

◄ *Nejd, Saudi Arabia: Settlement of Khats Daghrah*

period, only now the situation is further aggravated by the impact of the great contemporary revolutions.

This culture region corresponds roughly, but not exactly, with the world's largest area of aridity. Water spells the difference between life and death; and in the desert landscape the sharpest possible line separates the rich green of the oases from the brown and empty land beyond the last irrigation canal. Since time immemorial the people who live in the desert have been lean and hungry, accustomed to hardships, devout and uncompromising in religion; and the people who live in the midst of the lush luxury of the oases have sometimes become fat, lazy, and contented when they have forgotten their desert origins. The lean, God-fearing son of the desert looks with disgust on the pleasure-loving oasis dweller, learns to envy him, and then to conquer and to subjugate him. The contrast is vividly portrayed by comparing the long epic poem of the Persian historian, Firdausi (Abu'l Kasim Mansur), of the tenth century, with the Rubaiyat of Omar Khayyam who lived some two centuries later, also in Persia. The Rubaiyat is a protest against the narrowness, bigotry, and uncompromising austerity of the desert people. The antagonism of these two contrasted people runs like a theme with variations through the long course of man's experience in this area.

This is a land of innovation. Here we find evidence of some of the earliest domestication of plants and animals. In this region two of the world's Early Civilizations appeared, one in the valley of the Tigris-Euphrates which we call Mesopotamia, the other in the valley of the Nile in Egypt. Distinctive ways of life were also forged in four other culture hearths: in the mountainous desert between the Caspian Sea and the Persian Gulf, which was formerly called Persia and is now Iran; in the coastal area on the eastern side of the Mediterranean, which was once Phoenicia, and is now Lebanon; in the hilly uplands on the desert margin at the eastern end of the Mediterranean, formerly Palestine, and now divided between Israel and Jordan; and in the desert oases of Arabia. The innovations developed in these culture hearths included not only religious and ethical ideas, but also techniques for living in the desert habitat, techniques for controlling water and for administering its use, techniques for domesticating a long list of crops and animals, and also many basic ideas in the realm of mathematics and astronomy.

This region must also be seen as a crossroads. Extending, as it does, from the Atlantic Ocean across North Africa into the southwestern part of Asia between the Indian Ocean and the Caspian Sea, it lies athwart all the most direct routes of travel between the European countries on the one hand, and the non-European countries of Africa and southern and eastern Asia on the other. Since these parts of the world became occupied by man there has been a need for routes of travel and trade across the intervening belt of deserts. There have been overland routes; and sea routes taking advantage of the arrangement of the Red Sea and the Mediterranean; and now the air routes from Europe to the "Far East" are bunched together over this same area to avoid the mountains to the north and the vast expanses of the Indian Ocean to the south. The strategic importance of these routes of crossing was important even in ancient times; in the modern world their importance has increased.

The whole pattern of internal diversity, and of intersecting crossroads, has been complicated, since 1908, by the discovery

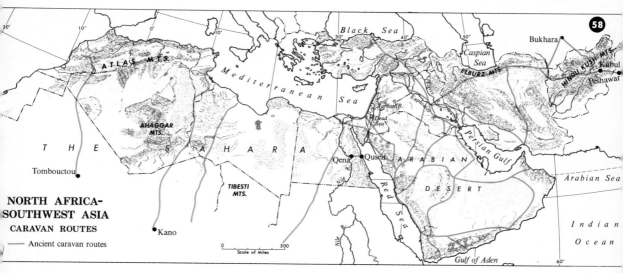

**NORTH AFRICA-
SOUTHWEST ASIA**
CARAVAN ROUTES

—— Ancient caravan routes

and exploitation of vast stores of oil. The greatest reserve of oil in the world is around the Persian Gulf, and now new oil pools have been found under the Sahara. Oil gives the region a new dimension of strategic significance.

The North African-Southwest Asian Culture Region covers about 10 per cent of the inhabited land area of the earth, and is occupied by only about 5 per cent of the world's population. The inhabitants, for the most part but not exclusively, speak Arabic and practice the religion of Islam.[1] To be sure, there are more Muslims outside this region than there are within it; and in Turkey, Iran, and Afghanistan, although the religious practices are carried on in Arabic, the people speak other languages. Moreover, in the midst of this region is the Jewish state of Israel, the people of which speak Hebrew. Nevertheless, the region as a whole is characterized by the distinctive association of aridity, the Arabic language, and the religion of Islam.

[1] *Islam* is the name of the religion first preached by Muhammad and written down in the holy book known as the Koran. The people who practice Islam are called *Muslims*. They are not properly described as Mohammedans.

THE HABITAT

(Maps 5, 6, 7, 8, and 61) The greater part of the area of the North African-Southwest Asian Culture Region is deficient in moisture throughout the year. Most of it receives an average annual rainfall of less than ten inches. With high rates of evaporation it means that this is the world's largest area of dry land. Nevertheless, there are certain places where water is available. There is a fringe of Mediterranean climate along the northern coast of Africa, around the coasts of Turkey, and along the eastern side of the Mediterranean into southern Israel. Here the summers are hot and dry, but there is some rainfall in winter. Furthermore, there are numerous ranges of high mountains bordering this region, or standing as isolated groups of peaks in the midst of the deserts. The mountains receive much more rain than the neighboring lowlands, and provide abundant run-off. The Highlands of Ethiopia receive heavy rains in summer, supporting floods in the Nile from May to September. The high ranges of eastern Turkey and western Iran receive heavy rains in winter, and the higher slopes are deeply covered with snow. Winter rains, and melting snow in spring, support floods in the Tigris and Euphrates rivers from November to May. In a smaller way the mountains of Syria and Lebanon support the flow of the Jordan River into the Dead Sea. Apart from these rivers, however, there are only a few scattered spots were water is available at the surface.

These climatic features are reflected in the cover of natural vegetation. The Mediterranean areas were originally covered with evergreen woodlands, now largely destroyed by the grazing of sheep and goats. The high mountains, where moisture is abundant, were once covered by dense forests—such as the famous cedar forests of Lebanon which furnished the Phoenicians and the Egyptians with wood for shipbuilding. Most of these forests, also, are now gone—with a resulting increase in both floods and drought on the bordering lowlands. The semiarid climates in North Africa, and in what is now eastern Syria, Jordan, and the northern part of Arabia, once supported a short-grass steppe, useful for the grazing of animals during the winters. Large parts of this region, however, are now entirely barren, or have only scattered, drought-resistant plants.

This is also the world's largest area of very high summer temperatures (Map 7, p. 14). A belt, within which there is at least one day in the average year that reaches 110°, extends from Morocco eastward across the Sahara to the Red Sea, and on across Arabia to the Persian Gulf. Hot days are experienced in Central Africa around Lake Chad, and along the coast of Somalia. There is an eastward continuation of this belt in the Indus and the Ganges valleys. In the central part of the Sahara there may be more than twenty-nine such hot days in the average year. Al'Azīzīyah in Libya, twenty-five miles south of Tripoli, had a temperature of 136.4° on September 13, 1922. This is the highest air temperature ever officially recorded. Such very high temperatures, especially when combined with high humidity as they are along the shores of the Red Sea and the Persian Gulf, form the world's most uncomfortable climates.

In contrast, however, are the very low temperatures of parts of this region. Throughout the dry lands, where the loss of heat by radiation under clear skies at night is very rapid, there is a sharp drop of temperature after sunset. A drop of as much as forty or fifty degrees is not uncommon. The world record for range of temperature within a twenty-four-hour period is held by In-Salah, an oasis settlement in southern Algeria (a drop from 126° to 26°).

The surface features of this region are by no means uniform. The popular impression that deserts are made up largely of vast areas of shifting sands is far from the truth. The areas of sand dunes (stippled on Map 61) make up only about 10 per cent of the surface of the Sahara. The largest such area in the world is located in southern Arabia, south of the Persian Gulf. Most of the desert surface is a rocky platform, where the underlying geologic formations are only thinly mantled by angular rock fragments. These are described by the Arabic word *hamada.* In Iran there is a large area of basin and range desert, similar to the dry lands of the southwestern United States and northern Mexico. The surface features associated with the wetter climates include hilly uplands, some small coastal plains, and the high mountains. The great alluvial plains are formed by rivers descending from the wetter mountains to cross the bordering deserts.

The hamadas must be differentiated into those cut by numerous dry watercourses, or *wadis,* and those that remain almost uncut. Where the hamadas border high mountain ranges, as happens south of the Atlas

Mountains in North Africa, or where they are surmounted by high peaks as in the Ahaggar of the western Sahara, or the Tibesti Mountains north of Lake Chad, the water draining from these mountains cuts numerous valleys. It is believed that there was surface water in these valleys during the wetter glacial periods. Now the typical wadi has steep, evenly cliffed sides, and a flat, gravel-filled bottom. Water is seeping through the gravel and can be brought to the surface by means of ordinary wells. But where there are no mountains to catch the rain, the hamadas may be quite smooth, with very little surface water, as in the Libyan desert west of the Nile.

THE COURSE OF SETTLEMENT

This varied habitat has been continuously occupied by man for a very long time. Archaeologists think that the great revolution in human living conditions that marks the change from Paleolithic to Neolithic, probably made its start in the highlands east of Mesopotamia, and then spread down the rivers to the alluvial plain. Many basic innovations came from here. It was in Mesopotamia that people first learned how to make and use the wheel, the plow, and the loom. Scholars in this area were the first to chart the pattern and movements of the stars, and to make use of a form of arithmetic based on multiples of six and sixty. From this arithmetic comes our division of the calendar and of the day, and the division of the circle into 360°. Furthermore, many of our well-known food, feed, and fiber crops were first developed in Southwest Asia, or in nearby parts of northeast Africa. Most of the species of animals that have been domesticated—such as horses, sheep, goats, cattle, and pigs, were probably introduced into Southwest Asia from India or from Central Asia. But some animals were originally domesticated within

this region—notably the single-humped camel in Arabia, the ass in Ethiopia, and the cat in Egypt.

ORIGIN OF CERTAIN CROPS
(after George P. Murdock and others)

Southwest Asia	Egypt Mediterranean
wheat	clover
barley	beet
alfalfa	parsnip
pea	artichoke
onion	asparagus
radish	cabbage
lettuce	celery
chive	dill
garlic	rape
leek	flax
cucumber	olive
grape	
melon	*Ethiopia*
apple	castor bean
fig	cress
pomegranate	coffee
cherry	
mulberry	*Sudan*
opium poppy	
rose	cotton
saffron	gourd
	watermelon

Southern Arabia

date palm

The beginnings of civilization, also, appeared first in this part of the world. Archaeologists, using the breakdown of carbon-14 as a method of dating, have shown that some of the structures at Jericho, near the northern end of the Dead Sea, were built about 7000 B.C. Jericho is perhaps the world's oldest town. One of the six Early Civilizations described in the introduction to this book developed in Mesopotamia around 4000 B.C.; another developed in the Nile Valley, and still another in the Indus Valley, just east of this region.

Over the many thousands of years of continuous settlement the record includes repeated invasions and conquests. The underlying theme—of conflict between oasis dwellers and desert people—runs through the whole story. Yet the kinds of life that have been possible in the oases and in the desert have changed from time to time with changes in the skills of the people. Without the camel there could be no nomadism except on the desert margins, and without the date palm the oases could not support such large numbers of people. Without government and law, and without military force to support the law, there could be no permanent and ambitious irrigation works; and when governments have collapsed, so have the engineering works that effective public administration made possible. Without modern engineering techniques, and without the needs created by the internal

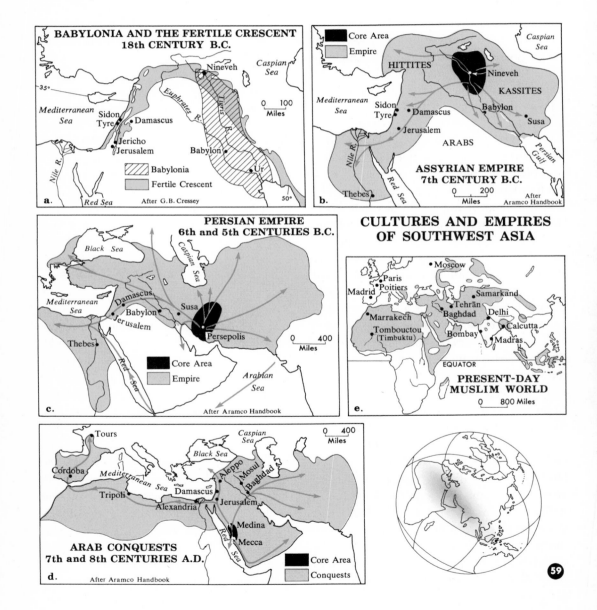

CULTURES AND EMPIRES OF SOUTHWEST ASIA

a. BABYLONIA AND THE FERTILE CRESCENT 18th CENTURY B.C.
After G. B. Cressey

b. ASSYRIAN EMPIRE 7th CENTURY B.C.
After Aramco Handbook

c. PERSIAN EMPIRE 6th and 5th CENTURIES B.C.
After Aramco Handbook

d. ARAB CONQUESTS 7th and 8th CENTURIES A.D.
After Aramco Handbook

e. PRESENT-DAY MUSLIM WORLD

combustion motor, the long-known oil seeps of the Persian Gulf area had little significance except as natural curiosities.

Nevertheless, throughout the long course of settlement, the geographic framework of mountains and water has provided an underlying continuity of pattern. The two great exotic river systems—the Tigris-Euphrates and the Nile—have supported powerful and antagonistic states ever since human knowledge has permitted the cultivation of crops, and concepts of government have brought large numbers of people under a single ruler. And between these two great valleys, a crescent-shaped area with relatively abundant water from the high mountains has provided a channel of communication and a route for conquering armies. This is the so-called *Fertile Crescent*, with its eastern point along the west-facing mountain piedmont on the border of Mesopotamia, and its western point along the eastern side of the Dead Sea depression in what is now Jordan (Map 59a). Within this crescent are such ancient market centers as Mōsul, Aleppo, Damascus, and Jericho.

The Rise and Fall of the Empires in Antiquity. Six areas have been of major importance as culture hearths, and some have been, from time to time, the cores of empires. These six areas are Mesopotamia, Persia, Phoenicia, Palestine, Egypt, and Arabia.

Mesopotamia. The oldest of the culture hearths is Mesopotamia—the Tigris-Euphrates Valley. Here the hot, dry climate, the abundant sunshine, and the absence of frosts permits crops to grow luxuriantly wherever there is water. And water in abundance is delivered by the two great rivers, draining the high mountains to the north and east. The rivers carry large amounts of silt, produced by the erosion of the highlands, and they deposit this silt on the alluvial plain where it creates a soil of high potential productivity. The largest silt accumulation takes place along the channels of the rivers, and these are gradually raised until the rivers flow along the highest part of the floodplain. In times of high water the rivers may break through their banks and follow new channels, leaving the abandoned channels as curved "ox-bow" lakes and marshes. The building of irrigation canals, and the provision of drainage systems so that the fields will not become impregnated with salt from the evaporation of water, requires a high degree of engineering skill. Skill of this kind, together with an effective government to regulate the use of the water, was first developed around 2500 B.C. in Sumeria, the capital city of which was Ur (Map 59a).

The oasis people of Mesopotamia occupy a land notably vulnerable to invasion. People living downstream are always at the mercy of those upstream from them, provided the latter have the necessary skills to divert the water. The Sumerians were in constant trouble with the Akkadians who lived upstream. Finally the Babylonians, who lived still higher upstream, succeeded in establishing control over the whole of Mesopotamia (from 1894 to 1594 B.C.). It was during that period that the world's first written code of law was prepared, by Emperor Hammurabi who ruled Babylonia between 1792 and 1750 B.C. (see the table on pp. 240-241).

Mesopotamia is also vulnerable to invasion from outside. No barriers prevent the mountain people to the north, or to the east, from descending onto the fertile plains; and no barriers impede the desert people to the west from looking covetously at the rich green fields of the irrigated lands. Babylonia was at one time invaded by the Hittites, coming from the highlands of what is now

HISTORICAL DEVELOPMENTS OF

EGYPT

Declared a Republic, 1953
Titles of Bey and Pasha abolished
Kingdom of Egypt, 1922-1952
British Protectorate, 1914-1922
British and French Sphere of Interest, 1801-
Suez Canal, 1869—Aswan Dam, 1902
British Defeat of French, 1801
French Occupation, 1798-1801
Ottoman Rule, 1517-1914 _

Ayyubids and Mamelukes, 1250-1517
Syria and Egypt linked

The Fatamids, 969-1171
Control of N. Africa, Sicily, Syria,
Hejaz, and Yemen; Cairo the capital
Turkish Dynasty, 868-905
Muslim Rule, 642-868
Baghdad, 750-868
Damascus, 661-750
Byzantine Rule, 324-640
Roman Rule, 30 B.C.-A.D. 324

Ptolomies, 323-
Alexander's Conquest, 332-323
Alexandria, 332
Persian Rule, 525-332 _

Assyrian Rule, 670-654 _

Ethiopian Kings, 720-663

Breakdown into Upper and Lower Egypt, 1075
Re-establishment of Central Rule, 1570-1075
Invasion of Palestine and Syria, 1490-1436
Invasion of Sudan
Breakdown into Separate Kingdoms, 1785-1570
Hyksos invade the Delta, 1730-1570

Re-establishment of Central Rule, 2050-1785
Capital at Thebes
Authority extended to Sudan and Syria
Breakdown of Central Rule
Feudal Lords Supreme, 2154-2052
Establishment of Central Rule, 3110-2200
Capital at Memphis

Prehistoric Neolithic Culture, 4500

LEVANT*

Israel, 1948
British Mandates:
Jordan, 1920-1946
Palestine, 1920-1948
French Mandates:
Syria, 1920-1944
Lebanon, 1920-1944

_ _ _ _ _ _ _ _ _ _ Ottoman Rule, 1517-1918 _ _ _ _ _ _ _ _ _ _ _ _

Crusades, 1097-1291
Saladin, 1174-1193

◀ ◀ ◀

Ommiad Caliphate (Damascus) 661-750   ▶ ▶ ▶
Muhammad, c.570-632

Palmyra, 42 B.C.-A.D. 292
Queen Zenobia
Jesus Christ, 4 B.C.-A.D. 31

Pompey captured Jerusalem, 63
Seleucid Empire, 312-64 _
_ _ _ _ _ _ _ _ _ _ Persian Rule, 539-332 _ _ _ _ _ _ _ _ _ _ _ _ _ _ _
Jewish Exile, 586-538
Judean Kingdom, 933-586
Hezekiah, 715-687
Solomon, 973-933

David, 1013-973

Hebrews in Palestine,
Aramaeans in Syria
Moses, c.1200
Philistine Invasions from Sea, 1200
Abraham, c.1650-c.1550

Caucasian and Semitic Cultures, 2500

Jericho, 7000

* Reproduced with permission from George B. Cressey: *Crossroads,* published by J. B. Lippincott Company, Philadelphia, Pa., copyright 1960; pp. 50-51.

NORTH AFRICA AND SOUTHWEST ASIA

MESOPOTAMIA*

British Mandate: *Iraq, 1920-1932*

------Ottoman Rule, 1534-1918
Mongol Rule, 1258-1534
  Hulugu captured Baghdad, 1258

◀ ◀ ◀ Abbasside Caliphate (Baghdad), 750-c.1100
  Al-Mamun, 813-833
▶ ▶ ▶
Arab Invasion, 636 _____

------ Seleucid Empire, 312-138

------Persian Rule, 539-331
Chaldean Empire (Babylon), 625-539
  Nebuchadrezzar II, 605-562
  Nabolpalassar, 626-605
------Assyrian Empire (Nineveh & Nimrud),
  2025-606
  Ashurbanipal, 668-630
  Tiglath-pileser III, 745-727

  Tiglath-pileser I, 1114-1076
Mitanni Kingdom (Hurrians) c.1520-1350
Kassite Conquest, 1590-1167
Hittite Invasion from North, 1594
First Babylonian Dynasty, 1894-1594
  Hammurabi, c.1792-1750
Amorites (Mari), 2000
Third Dynasty of Ur, c.2118-2010

  Ur-Nammu, 2118-2101
Akkadian Dynasty (Semites), 2336-2156
  Sargon I, 2336-2281

First Dynasty of Ur, c. 2500-c.2400

  Sumerian culture, c.3400
Jarmo, 4750

IRAN*

Pahlavi Dynasty, 1926
Qajar Dynasty (Tehrān), 1794-1925
D'Arcy Oil Concession, 1901
Safawid Dynasty (Isfahan) 1500-1794
  Shah Abbas I, 1586-1628

Mongol Rule, *Tamerlane, 1380-1393*
  Genghis Khan, 1219-1227
Hafiz, c.1325-1388
Marco Polo, 1271 and 1295
Saadi, c.1184-1291

Firdausi, 999

_____Arab Invasion, 641
Sassanian Empire, c.226-651
  Shapur I, 241-272
Nestorian Church founded, c.489
Parthian Empire
  (Ctesiphon) 250 B.C.-A.D. 229

◀ ◀ ◀ ◀ ◀ ◀ *Arsaces VI, c.171-138*
Achaemenid Dynasty, c.700-331
  (Persepolis and Susa)
  Xerxes, 486-465
  Darius I, 522-486
  Cyrus II, 550-530
Media (Ecbatana-Hamadan) c.675-550

  Zoroaster, c.630
Mannean Kingdom (Hasanlu) 1000-800

Elamites (Susa), c.2850-635

Caspian culture, 5000

Turkey, and then by the Kassites from the east, from what is now Iran. Then after these invasions the warlike Assyrians, who occupied the country above the alluvial plain and had their capital at Nineveh, established control not only of the whole of Mesopotamia, but also of the Fertile Crescent, and even of Egypt (Map 59b). But the Assyrians, in turn, were conquered by their neighbors, and in 612 B.C. Nineveh was completely destroyed. The Chaldean Empire, which followed, brought all of Mesopotamia and the Fertile Crescent under one administration, with its capital at Babylon. This was the great age of Babylon, with its hanging gardens and its obvious comfort and luxury. But in 539 B.C. the Persians managed to take Babylon without a fight, and established the greatest empire the world had seen up to that time (Map 59c).

Persia. The culture hearth of Persia adjoins Mesopotamia on the east, and extends southward along the eastern side of the Persian Gulf. But near as the two culture hearths are to each other, they offer the most striking contrasts in many respects. In the basin and range desert of Persia there is no great alluvial valley abundantly supplied with water. Persia's largest river is a tributary of the Tigris-Euphrates (actually of the Shatt al Arab through which the two great rivers drain to the Gulf). On the mountain piedmont where this river emerges onto the lowland, was one of the two chief centers of Persian culture—Susa, near modern Dezfūl. Most of Persia is divided into compartments by the mountain ranges, and settlement is restricted to the piedmont alluvial fans that form the margins of the desert basins. Persepolis, the second of the great Persian centers, occupied such a site.

In many respects the way of life developed in Persia differed from that in Mesopotamia. Since the Persian oases were located along the main caravan routes connecting the Mediterranean with India and China, many ideas and skills were brought to Persia from outside the region. Into the Persian culture hearth came horses, sheep, and goats from Central Asia, and cattle from India. Rice came from Southeast Asia by way of India. Within Persia, where irrigation was just as essential as in Mesopotamia, the problem was not how to control a large river on its floodplain, but how to tap the underground sources of water. This was done—and still is—with a distinctively Persian type of well, the *qanat.* Tunnels were dug into the alluvial fans, each starting near the base of the fan and sloping gently toward the apex. Water seeping through the fans was tapped high on the fan slope, and carried through the tunnels to the oases lower down. In addition to these technical innovations, the Persians developed one of the world's earliest religions—that of Zoroaster.

In the sixth century B.C. the Persians began to develop an empire. The Achaemenid Dynasty lasted from 700 to 331 B.C., and at its height the Persians controlled a vast area extending into Egypt and Thrace (where the Persians and Greeks came into conflict), northward into the desert of Central Asia, and eastward to the Indus Valley (Map 59c).

The Persian Empire finally fell as a result of invasion by a Greek army led by Alexander the Great, the pupil of Aristotle. Alexander led his troops around the coast of what is now Turkey, southward to Egypt, and then through the main part of Persia, all the way to the Indus River. He destroyed Persepolis in 325 B.C. When he died in Babylon in 323 B.C., the Persians re-established control over their own homeland; and were strong enough to prevent the Romans from pushing east of Mesopotamia, but they never again were able to recapture the vast area that they once had controlled.

Phoenicia. The Phoenicians established one of the world's earliest states based on long-distance trade, in the area now known as Lebanon. Their ports—Tyre and Sidon— were the commercial centers of the ancient world. Phoenician sailors steered their ships the length of the Mediterranean, and even into the open Atlantic to reach the tin mines of the Scilly Isles off Great Britain. The bronze that they manufactured was made from copper, which probably came from Cyprus, and tin from Britain. They also took their ships through the Red Sea and the Persian Gulf, and eastward to India. They founded colonies at strategic places along the coasts: the greatest of these was Carthage (near the present city of Tunis), which was a major trading center from the time of its establishment in 550 B.C. until its destruction by the Romans in 146 B.C.

Palestine. Palestine, adjoining Phoenicia on the south, was another separate culture hearth. This was the Land of Caanan, the Promised Land of the Old Testament, the well-watered country bordering the desert into which Moses led the Hebrews. Here the Hebrew prophets formulated the principles of Judaism, to be incorporated later in the teachings of Jesus, and in Christianity. These same teachings were also incorporated by Muhammad in the religion of Islam. When, in later times, the Jews in Palestine and Arabia refused to follow certain of the religious practices prescribed by Muhammad, the Muslims drove them out, and occupied the whole area themselves. Jeru-

salem remained the Holy City of three faiths, but by the end of the seventh century A.D. was in Muslim hands.

Egypt. The Nile Valley is another great alluvial plain, like the valley of the Tigris-Euphrates. The Nile brings water and silt to its valley, and crops there grow luxuriantly. But Egypt is quite different from Mesopotamia in certain fundamental characteristics of its geography. Egypt has never been exposed to invasion and conquest from the east or west along its middle course: on the east the Red Sea forms a barrier impassable to invading armies; and on the west the vast unbroken surface of the Libyan hamada provides only scattered and minute spots where settlement is possible. Egypt was only vulnerable at either end. The valley could be, and has been, invaded from the Sudan and Ethiopia, and from the delta, which is separated from the western end of the Fertile Crescent by only a narrow belt of desert. However, in its position of relative isolation, Egypt in the very early period could develop its own distinctive culture, and work out its own problems of government.

The table (pp. 240-241) shows that from the first appearance of irrigated agriculture around 4500 B.C., until about 1000 B.C., the Egyptians fought only among themselves. There was an alternation of periods of strong central government with periods of collapse when each feudal lord administered his own lands. The capital was either at Memphis in lower Egypt, or at Thebes in upper Egypt. Then between 720 and 670 B.C. the whole valley was under the control of the Ethiopian kings; but in 670 the Assyrians appeared in the delta region, and by 663 they had conquered the whole valley as far as the first cataract at Syene (now Aswan). From that date until

A.D. 1953 Egypt was never entirely free from outside control.

Arabia. The sixth of the major culture hearths is Arabia, the great desert area that lies between the Red Sea and Mesopotamia. Since the land is made up of hamadas and ergs there are no large areas where irrigation is possible, although there are many small wet spots. The time when the desert people first used the date palm to make the oases productive, and the camel to give mobility and to make the nomadic life possible, is lost in antiquity. During all the long periods of empire building that we have described, Arabia remained unconquered. It had no focus, no core of settlement: and yet the widely scattered people of the Arabian desert developed a coherent and distinctive culture.

Arab culture finally gained a focus in both a spiritual and a geographic sense as a result of the work of the great religious leader, Muhammad, who was preaching in Mecca in the seventh century A.D. Muhammad brought together in the Koran the accumulated insights of the Arabs; and this book has ever since provided the followers of Islam with a guide to all aspects of life.

Conquests in Later Times—The Spread of the Muslims. As a result of the teachings of Muhammad, the Arabs started on a wave of conquest that carried them far from the original culture hearth. This was conquest inspired by an aggressive faith, the chief purpose of which was to increase the number of Muslims in the world. As the Arabs carried their faith to other lands they took with them, also, their distinctive way of life, especially the use of the camel and the date palm, and the elaborate skills needed for survival in the desert and for making the oases productive. In A.D. 632 they burst from Arabia into the Fertile Crescent and

Mesopotamia. In 641 they conquered Persia, and in 642 they took over control of Egypt. Here they came into contact with the pastoral Berbers whose homeland was the semi-arid coastal zone to the west of the Nile. The Berbers, who had been familiar with the date palm and the camel for at least two centuries, now embraced the faith of Islam and fanned out ahead of the Arabs all across the Sahara. By 732 all of the western Sahara was Muslim. The Negro farmers, who had been living in isolation in the small desert oases, were overrun by the Berbers who took over the most remote pastures and wet spots. The Arabs pushed on across the Sahara into the rainy country to the south, and established the great caravan routes across the desert over which they brought African products and Negro slaves to the Mediterranean coast. The Arabs also crossed the Strait of Gibraltar to the Iberian Peninsula, and continued on across the Pyrenees into France. Their progress was halted when they were defeated by Charles Martel at the Battle of Tours in 732 (Map 59d). Thereafter the Muslims withdrew south of the Pyrenees, and for many centuries maintained their hold on all but the northern parts of Spain and Portugal. They did not entirely lose control of this part of Europe until the Battle of Granada, in southern Spain in 1492.

The Muslims did not confine their missionary efforts to Europe, Africa, and Southwest Asia. They also spread the faith far to the east. There are Muslim populations today in Pakistan, Indonesia, and even the Philippines (map 59e). The Caliph was both the religious leader of the followers of Islam and the administrative head of the vast territories controlled by the Muslims. The center of the Muslim world was Damascus, from 661 to 750, and Baghdad, from 750 to 868. During the Caliphate of Al-Mamun (813-833) Baghdad was the focus of the intellectual world, where the works of the ancient scholars were translated into the Arabic language. It was during this time that the Hindu system of arithmetic, with its use of the decimal system, was introduced into Baghdad, and eventually carried on into Europe.

Reaction. The success of the Muslim conquest set up the usual reactions. Invasions of Muslim-held territory came from various directions, and piece by piece the vast empire was broken apart—but not until after many centuries of conflict between Christians and Muslims. One reaction came from Europe. Between 1096 and 1291 a series of armed pilgrimages, or actual military expeditions, were launched in Europe for the purpose of recovering the Holy Land from the Muslims. These were the crusades. In the end the Holy Land remained firmly in Muslim hands.

Another effort to break the strength of the Muslims was made by the Portuguese. Ever since the establishment of Muslim control over the greater part of this culture region, Europe had been effectively isolated from the populations of India, Java, and China. The Muslims controlled all the crossroads. The traders of Venice and Genoa had to deal with the Arabs if they wished to profit from the importation into Europe of the exotic products of the Orient. The Portuguese, however, were not content to leave the Arabs in control. In 1415 they crossed the Strait of Gibraltar and captured the Muslim fortress at Ceuta, thus becoming the first Europeans to claim territory outside Europe. Under the direction of Prince Henry the Navigator, the Portuguese sailors learned the arts of navigation, and step by step explored the route southward along the

THE OTTOMAN EMPIRE AT ITS GREATEST EXTENT
■ Core area   □ Empire

west coast of Africa, seeking a way to India that would outflank the Muslim strongholds on the Red Sea. Eventually, in 1497-1498 Vasco da Gama sailed around the southern extremity of Africa and across the Indian Ocean to India. The Portuguese were the first to break the Arab monopoly over trade between Europe and Asia.

The Muslim world was also attacked from the east. In the thirteenth century, mounted warriers under Jenghiz Khan poured out from the Mongolian grasslands of Central Asia in waves of conquest. They invaded China to the east, and Europe to the west; and they also invaded and conquered Mesopotamia, which they ruled from 1254 to 1534. The Mongols were more interested in pasture for their animals than in land for crops; and so they almost completely destroyed the ancient system of irrigation in that area. Mesopotamia, always vulnerable to attack, was reduced to ruins and its population scattered.

The Ottoman Empire. Late in the thirteenth century still another conquest made its start. This time the empire was built by the Turks, and its core was on the straits that connect the Black Sea with the Aegean. The Turks were a nomadic people who had moved out of Central Asia into the interior of what is now Turkey. They had become

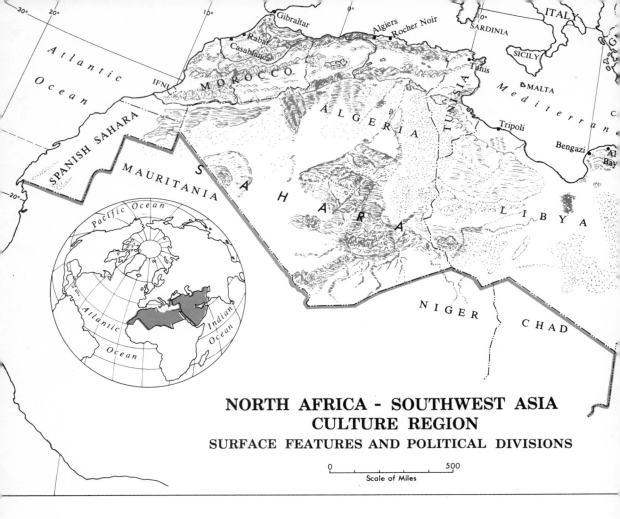

NORTH AFRICA - SOUTHWEST ASIA
CULTURE REGION
SURFACE FEATURES AND POLITICAL DIVISIONS

0   500

Scale of Miles

Muslims, but with religious forms that were distinctively Turkish. In 1453 the Turks captured Constantinople from the Christians and made it their capital. From there they pushed their conquests out in all directions. They were able to extend their rule over Greece and the Balkans and up the Danube Valley almost as far as Vienna. They controlled almost the entire shore line of the Black Sea. In 1517 they took Egypt, and moved westward through North Africa. In 1534 they took over what was left of Mesopotamia, and they controlled all the margins of the Arabian desert—the Hejaz, the Yemen, and the western side of the Persian Gulf (Map 60). However, they never succeeded in conquering the Persians, nor were they able to subdue the Arabs in their desert habitat.

The European Period. In the nineteenth century a new strategic dimension was added to the already complex picture of strategy in the North African-Southwest Asian Culture Region. At this time revolutionary changes were taking place in Europe, and the European countries were reaching out to distant parts of the earth for raw materials and markets. The old idea, derived from the Early Civilizations, that to be strong a state must be self-sufficient and must actually possess its own resources, was still leading ambitious rulers to plan the

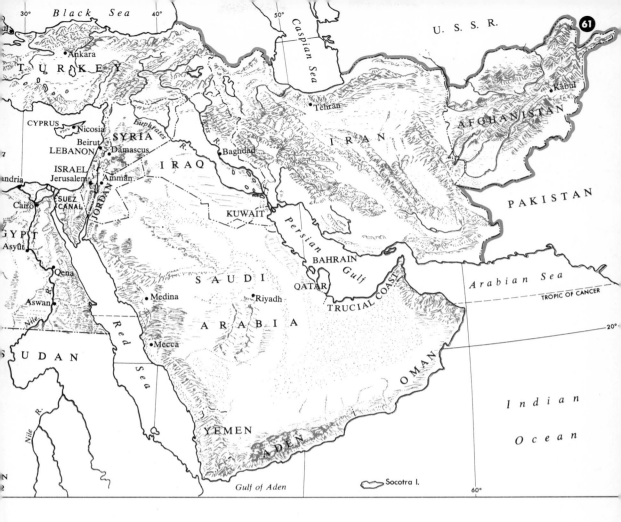

conquest of other people's territory—even though the Industrial Revolution had already rendered these ideas obsolete. In 1830 France started the invasion of Algeria, and the French and the Spanish gradually gained control of all the western Sahara and of the country to the south of it. France, Great Britain, and the Netherlands had all gained possession of colonies in southern and eastern Asia, and this raised again in a more acute form the old problem of developing and securing an easier route across the belt of deserts.

The development of a sea route through the Mediterranean and the Red Sea, by way of Suez, was made possible through the technological changes of the Industrial Revolution. The Red Sea was by no means an easy route for sailing ships. Even after keels made it possible for ships to tack against the wind, it was dangerous to do so against the strong northerly winds of the Red Sea because of the coral reefs along the coasts, especially in the narrow northern arm of the Red Sea, the Gulf of Suez. But with the invention of steamships the Red Sea route suddenly took on a new strategic value that it had never had before. It took ten years to dig the sea-level canal, 107 miles long, across the Isthmus of Suez, under the direction of the French engineer, Ferdinand de Lesseps. When the canal was opened in 1869 the world patterns of trade and military strategy were fundamentally altered. The British developed their "life-line of the Empire," defended by a string of fortresses and naval bases: Gibraltar, Malta, Cyprus, Suez, and Aden. The protection and maintenance of this route became a major purpose of British strategy; it became increasingly important after 1908, when the first productive oil well was drilled in the Persian Gulf region.

Meanwhile the decline of the Ottoman Empire left a dangerous power vacuum in this critical crossroads area. When the Russians, in the course of expanding their national territory, looked covetously at Constantinople and the command of the straits that gave access to the Black Sea, the French and British joined with the Turks to defeat the Russians—in the Crimean War of 1855-1856. But in 1911-1912 Italy invaded and gained possession of Libya, and in the Balkan War of 1912-1913 Serbia, Bulgaria, Greece, and Montenegro attacked the defeated Turkey.

World War I completed the dismemberment of the Ottoman Empire. Before the war Germany had been building a land route to parallel the British sea route to the Persian Gulf—the famous Berlin to Baghdad Railroad. When the war started Turkey came in with Germany, and shared defeat at the hands of the Allies. France assumed a mandate over Syria and Lebanon, and Great Britain over Palestine, Trans-Jordan, and Iraq. It was during the war, in 1917, that the British government announced its plan to provide land in Palestine for the resettlement of the Jews, in an area that had been in Muslim hands for more than a thousand years.

Such have been the processes of change in this region; processes that have created striking contrasts in attitudes and ways of life from place to place, and have led to the present-day conflicts that constitute so serious a problem in this critical area. This region is usefully subdivided into four parts for further discussion (Map 61): (1) The Persian Gulf countries; (2) the countries of the Eastern Mediterranean and the Nile; (3) the countries of North Africa; and (4) the countries of the Eastern Border.

THE PERSIAN GULF COUNTRIES[2]

The Persian Gulf countries hold underground the world's largest reserve of oil. In 1961 it was estimated that nearly 62 per cent of the proved reserves of oil in the world were concentrated around the Persian Gulf. The presence of such a large proportion of the world's oil in this one relatively small area gives this region a strategic importance out of all proportion to its population or to its previous economic status. The international conflicts and rivalries resulting from the sweep of the Indus-

trial Revolution are now focused on the Persian Gulf.

These countries have five things in common. First, they occupy a desert habitat where the search for a supply of water is the single most important problem in maintaining life. Second, the great majority of the people are farmers or nomadic herdsmen. Third, the great majority of the people are also Muslims, for whom the patterns of economic, social, and political behavior are spelled out in the Koran, and who have never experienced either security or justice outside their tribes. Fourth, in each country there is a vast gap between the small

[2] Include Iraq, Iran, Saudi Arabia, Kuwait, Bahrain Island, Qatar, the Trucial Coast, Oman, the Federation of South Arabia, and Yemen.

minority of wealthy people and army officers who control the government, and the huge majority of very poor, illiterate farmers and herders. And fifth, enormous financial resources have become available to the politically powerful minorities as a result of the export of oil.

The development of the oil fields by the large oil companies has introduced the most advanced engineering concepts, and the newest ways of life of the European and Anglo-American culture regions, into countries quite unprepared to receive them. Some of the hereditary rulers of the Persian Gulf area have become incredibly wealthy. Governments have taken on new functions, and in order to perform these functions have employed a large number of new "white-collar" workers. Cities have started to grow rapidly; and in the cities people have heard about demands for equality and liberty, and about rising expectations for a better living. These are people who are acutely conscious of the inequities of the traditional society, who are envious of the high standard of living of the foreigners, and who are violently nationalistic.

The three chief independent countries of the Persian Gulf area are Iraq, Iran, and Saudi Arabia. Iran is also one of the Eastern Border countries. Along the edge of the Persian Gulf are several small oil kingdoms: Kuwait, Bahrain Island, Qatar, and the kingdoms of the Trucial Coast. Also bordering Saudi Arabia but not important as sources of oil are Oman, the Federation of South Arabia, and Yemen (Map 61).

IRAQ

Iraq is the country that occupies most of the area formerly known as Mesopotamia. This is the land that the Hebrews knew as the "Garden of Eden" where the empires of antiquity flourished. Baghdad, during the Abbasside Caliphate, was the intellectual center of the world. This is also the land that lies open to invasion and conquest, especially from upstream. In the thirteenth century the Mongols largely destroyed the ancient systems of irrigation and reduced Mesopotamia from a land of growing crops and dense population to a pastoral one occupied by nomadic tribes. Mesopotamia became a zone of conflict between neighboring powers—between the Ottoman Empire and Persia. When the British established a protectorate over the area in 1920 the population was probably less than it had been in antiquity. The people today speak Arabic and are mostly Muslim: those of northern and central Iraq, who came under the influence of the Turks, are predominantly orthodox (Sunni), whereas those of the south, who were closer to Persia, are mostly members of another Muslim sect (Shiite).

Under Ottoman rule, Mesopotamia remained poor and neglected. The people were mostly pastoral nomads, with camels, sheep, and goats. They were grouped together in tribes, each under the control of a sheikh. When these wandering pastoralists gave the Turkish authorities much trouble in maintaining order, the Turks attempted to solve their administrative problems by attaching each tribe to a specific area of land. As a result pastoral nomadism had to give way to settled farming. When the British took control of Mesopotamia after World War I, they were unhappy about the collective ownership of land within each tribe, and they assigned ownership to the sheikhs, leaving the people as tenant farmers. Agriculture remained primitive, dependent largely on the natural floods of the rivers. When Iraq became independent in 1932, the great majority of the people were poor and illiterate, suffering from a variety of

An irrigation system in Iraq. Water is drawn from the canal simply by making a gap in the banks; this then has to be closed up again afterwards, as is being done here.

diseases which resulted from bad hygiene and malnutrition, and unhappy about the system of landlord and tenant that had been imposed on them.

In 1962 it was estimated that the population of Iraq was about 7,500,000—still not very large in relation to the area and its potential productivity. More than two thirds of the people were rural, and were employed in agriculture. However, Baghdad had become a thriving modern city with a rapidly increasing population of literate urban workers.

Agriculture. Farming without irrigation is possible only along the southwest-facing piedmont of the mountains that separate Iraq from Iran and Turkey (Map 62). This is the eastern side of the Fertile Crescent, watered in part by streams descending from the highlands, in part by rainfall concentrated in the winter months. Where the average annual rainfall is over twelve

inches it is possible to grow wheat and barley. On the lower slopes of the mountains there are vineyards, and orchards of peaches, apricots, and nut trees.

Elsewhere in Iraq all crops have to be irrigated. The Tigris River is filled with water from November to May, the highest floods being in April. The Euphrates River, which drains snow-capped mountains farther to the north, has its highest water level in May. In some places the land is moistened by the natural spread of the water from the river channels, but in other cases irrigation works carry the water away from the rivers and control its use. Between the two rivers wheat, barley, and millet are grown, and close to the rivers rice is important. Conditions are ideal for the production of long-staple cotton, and the cultivation of this crop is steadily increasing.

A very intensive and unusual kind of agriculture is found along the channel that drains both the Tigris and the Euphrates waters to the Persian Gulf—this channel is the Shatt al Arab. The tides in the Persian Gulf make the fresh water back up and overflow the banks of the channel. Twice daily the alluvial lands along the Shatt al Arab are flooded, and twice daily at low tide the water is drained off. There is a narrow ribbon of flooded land, partly in Iraq and partly in Iran. From this well-watered and sun-baked strip, about a hundred and twenty miles long and one or two miles wide, come about two-thirds of all the world's dates.

Oil. The major source of wealth in modern Iraq, however, is the production and export of oil. From the earliest times the presence of oil, asphalt, and natural gas has been known in Mesopotamia. Bricks from the ancient cities of Ur and Babylon were made of sun-dried mud held together with asphalt. Aladdin's Lamp, we may presume,

PERCENTAGE OF WORLD
OIL RESERVES AND PRODUCTION, 1961[3]

Country	Reserves	Production
Iran	9.4	5.3
Iraq	8.7	4.5
Kuwait	21.6	7.4
Neutral Zone	1.7	0.8
Qatar	0.8	0.8
Saudi Arabia	19.1	6.2
Totals	61.3	25.0

was lighted with oil from one of the natural seeps. Gas seepages have been burning for many thousands of years, and are described in the Old Testament. But it was not until 1908 that the first oil well was brought into production in Iran. Within a few years the major European and American oil companies had gained concessions and the main outlines of the Persian Gulf oil region had been defined. But because of the difficulty and expense of developing these fields in the desert habitat, production was slow to expand. As late as 1948 the whole Persian Gulf area produced less than 5 per cent of the world's oil. However, by 1958 it was producing over 23 per cent of the total. The table shows the proportion of proved oil reserves in the Persian Gulf countries in 1961, and the proportion of world production in the same year.

Within Iraq there are six developed oil fields (Map 63). Until 1956 the largest production came from Kirkūk in northern Iraq, but since that time large oil reserves have been found in the south in the Basra area. The oil from Kirkūk is pumped through pipelines across the desert westward to ports on the Mediterranean shores of Syria and Lebanon. The oil from Basra is piped to the head of the Persian Gulf.

Oil revenues are creating major changes in Iraq. The first to benefit from the new

[3] From *World Oil*, August 15, 1962; p. 85.

wealth were those who were already well-to-do, with the result that the contrast between the standard of living of the landowners and the political leaders, and that of the tenant farmers, became all the wider. But the government has been devoting a part of the oil revenues to the development of permanent improvements. There is an ambitious program of irrigation works. Several large dams on the Tigris and the Euphrates are under construction; and a new system of canals will greatly enlarge the area that can be irrigated. Drainage projects will remove some of the marshes, and after the soil has been flushed out with fresh water to remove the accumulation of salt, still larger additions to the cropland can be expected. The government is also taking steps to improve the transportation system. Highways passable for motor trucks will make many small rural villages accessible for the first time to the outside world. Airfields at Baghdad and Basra are being improved. New housing and office buildings are being constructed in Baghdad. A major effort has been started to eliminate illiteracy, and to reduce disease.

The Spirit of Revolt. These steps toward economic and social betterment have given rise to a spirit of revolt. The ideas of the Democratic Revolution as they sweep over Iraq are not exactly the same as those that developed around the shores of the North Sea, but they are nevertheless related to all

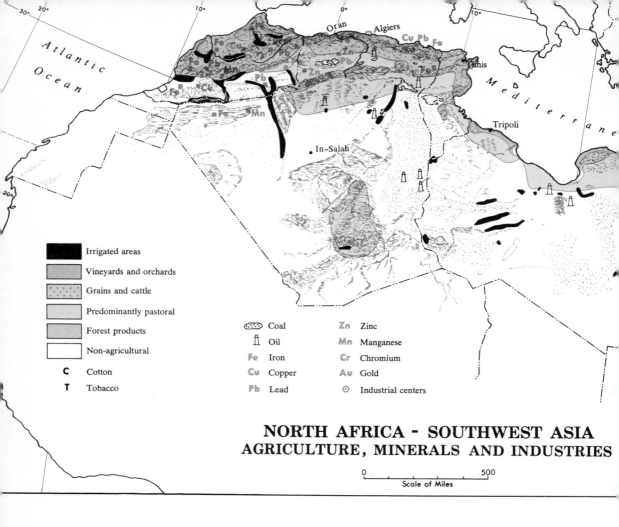

Legend

- Irrigated areas
- Vineyards and orchards
- Grains and cattle
- Predominantly pastoral
- Forest products
- Non-agricultural

C Cotton
T Tobacco

Coal
Oil
Fe Iron
Cu Copper
Pb Lead

Zn Zinc
Mn Manganese
Cr Chromium
Au Gold
⊙ Industrial centers

NORTH AFRICA - SOUTHWEST ASIA
AGRICULTURE, MINERALS AND INDUSTRIES

0   500
Scale of Miles

---

the world's movements toward liberty. The demand among the newly educated urban people is for equality of status for Iraq among the nations of the world, and for the right of a duly constituted Iraqi government to administer the country without interference from outside. There is a demand for an end to the system of privilege for landowners and foreigners. The increasing dissatisfaction resulted, in 1958, in the overthrow of the monarchy, and the establishment by the army of a republican form of government, under centralized control. There is a strong feeling of nationalism. The need for foreign financial and technical assistance is accepted, but even the sug-

gestion of foreign control is bitterly resented. This oil-rich country has a great opportunity to raise the level of its economic life. The problem is to educate the people so that they will not destroy what the government is building for the future.

IRAN

Iran cannot be omitted from a discussion of the Persian Gulf countries because its territory is endowed with one of the world's important reserves of oil. However, Iran, as a whole, is one of the countries of the Eastern Border and will be discussed later in that part of the North African-Southwest Asian Culture Region (p. 271). The

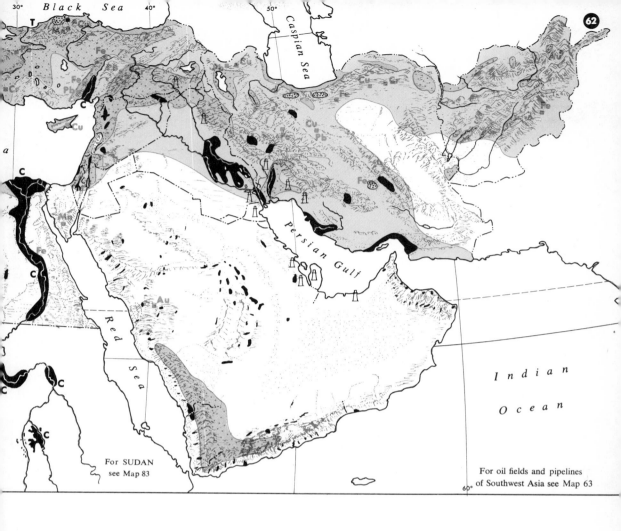

Black Sea

Caspian Sea

Persian Gulf

Red Sea

Indian Ocean

For SUDAN
see Map 83

For oil fields and pipelines
of Southwest Asia see Map 63

small corner of the national territory that extends from the mountain piedmont onto the alluvial plain at the head of the Persian Gulf is the part that holds most of Iran's oil (Map 62). This area has been Persian for a long time: the ancient city of Susa, near Dezfūl, was one of the culture hearths of ancient Persia (Map 59c). The area along the mountain piedmont, southeast of Dezfūl, has now become Iran's most productive oil field. At Ābādān, on the Shatt al Arab, one of the world's largest oil refineries has been built with British capital. Iran produces about as much oil as Iraq does each year—yet, as we shall see, Iran is not always aligned politically with the oil countries.

SAUDI ARABIA AND ITS NEIGHBORS

Saudi Arabia is the country that occupies the greater part of the Arabian Peninsula. This thinly peopled desert is the culture hearth in which the Muslim religion and the Arabic language originated. Mecca is still the holy city of Islam, the city toward which all Muslims face in prayer, and to which many still make pilgrimages.

The population of Saudi Arabia is widely scattered, and there are vast areas that still remain entirely empty. There never has been a census, but it was estimated in 1962 that the population might be about 6,000,-000. All the small, isolated oasis settlements,

An oil pipeline connecting the Persian Gulf oil fields with a port in Lebanon.

Crops—dates and other fruits, millet, wheat, and rice—grow luxuriantly wherever water can be found. In addition there are nomadic herders—Bedouins—who manage to make a living from a vast area of scanty pasturage.

Around the southern border of Arabia there are three countries that remain independent of the king of Saudi Arabia. These are separated from the center of political authority in Saudi Arabia by one of the world's largest areas of shifting sand dunes (stipple on Map 61). Along the southern coast are a series of more or less independent sheikhdoms grouped together in the British Protectorate of Oman, and the Federation of South Arabia. The Federation is made up of the former British colony of Aden, together with twenty-three sheikhdoms, sultanates, and emirates that occupy the dry coastal land of Arabia. The scattered population of more than 600,000 makes a poor living from the small patches of irrigable land where well water is available near the coast. In the southwest is the independent kingdom of Yemen, occupying the highlands near the southern end of the Red Sea. In the highlands of Yemen, and in the highlands west of Muscat in Oman, there is enough rainfall to support crops without irrigation. Farmers raise dates and grains, and on the higher slopes, coffee.

The Oil Fields, and the Oil Kingdoms. Life in Saudi Arabia has been transformed by the development of the oil fields. Instead of facing west through Mecca and its Red Sea port, Saudi Arabia now faces east to the Persian Gulf. All along the gulf there are small sheikhdoms that have remained independent of the king of Saudi Arabia, and some of these produce vast quantities of oil. But within Saudi Arabia itself are about 19 per cent of the world's known oil reserves. The income from the oil provides the king with ample funds to support a

and the encampments of nomadic Bedouins, are closely integrated under a hierarchy of rulers. Each oasis village and each nomadic tribe is ruled by a local chief, or sheikh, who has absolute authority over his subjects. The sheikhs, in turn, are under the authority of the king, whose capital is in the oasis town of Riyadh.

The great majority of the people of Saudi Arabia are farmers. There can be no large concentrations of population since there is not a single river in Arabia that has enough water to flow regularly to the sea. The miniature wet spots in the desert are places where wells tap underground water in sufficient quantities to support some irrigation.

strong army. At Riyadh a modern city has been built adjoining the old Arab stronghold, and a railroad connects the capital with the port of Ad Dammān on the Persian Gulf. Some of the king's income has been spent on schools and hospitals, on highways, airfields, and port improvements. But the great majority of the people of Saudi Arabia still remain almost untouched by the spectacular changes around them.

One of the most remarkable of the independent sheikhdoms on the Persian Gulf is Kuwait, a small area of desert about the size of Connecticut. Kuwait has the best harbor along the coast of the Gulf; and in former times was an important commercial port and center for pearl fisheries. In the modern world, however, Kuwait is important because it holds, beneath its surface, about 22 per cent of the oil reserves of the whole world. The ruler of this little piece of land has an income of more than a million dollars a day. When the exploitation of oil made the precise demarcation of boundaries necessary in 1922, agreement could not be reached regarding the ownership of two areas. These were set up as "neutral zones" —one between Saudi Arabia and Iraq, the other between Saudi Arabia and Kuwait. In the case of the latter, the sheikh of Kuwait and the king of Saudi Arabia share equally in the oil royalties. Kuwait itself has been independent since 1961. Bahrain Island, Qatar, and the seven separate sheikhdoms

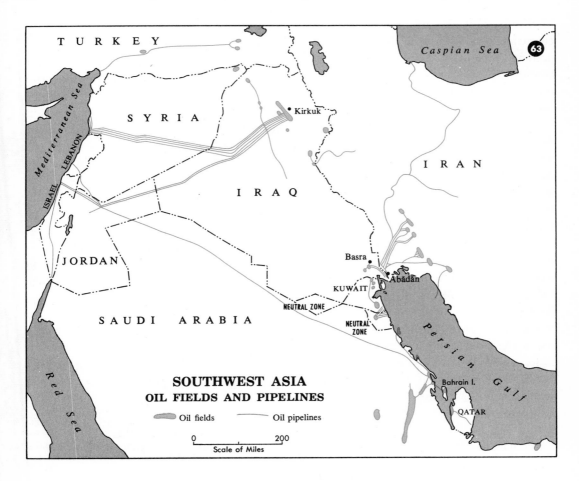

SOUTHWEST ASIA
OIL FIELDS AND PIPELINES

Oil fields   Oil pipelines

0   200
Scale of Miles

of the Trucial Coast are under British protection.

Most of the oil that is exported from Kuwait, Bahrain Island, Qatar, and Saudi Arabia is sent to Europe by tanker through the Suez Canal. Some from Saudi Arabia, less than a third of the total, is shipped through a pipeline to the Mediterranean coast (Map 63).

The settlements along the Persian Gulf have had to face the problem of finding enough fresh water not only for drinking, but also for the refineries, and for the operation of air-conditioning equipment. In Kuwait, for example, the wells are brackish, and cannot be used even for irrigation. Until 1950 drinking water had to be brought by barge from the Shatt al Arab, sixty miles away. Now Kuwait is supplied with about five million gallons of water a day from the world's largest salt-water distillation plant.

THE COUNTRIES OF THE EASTERN MEDITERRANEAN AND THE NILE[4]

The second of the four parts of the North African-Southwest Asian Culture Region is composed of the countries of the Eastern Mediterranean and the Nile (Map 61). These countries have little or no oil within their national territories; but they include the countries through which the oil must pass on its way from the Persian Gulf to the European markets. The crossroads theme, which runs all through the historical geography of this whole culture region, is strong and persistent along the eastern side of the Mediterranean. This, the western end of the Fertile Crescent, was the chief passageway between Mesopotamia and Egypt. This was the western end of the long overland caravan routes that connected Asia with Europe in ancient times. This was the route between the Mediterranean and the Indian Ocean, by way of the Red Sea, that has been fought over by interested powers since the invention of steam ships. Since the opening of the Suez Canal, and the development of its importance as a route for the transportation of oil to Europe, the interests of the whole world have come to a focus on this strategic area.

THE UNITED ARAB REPUBLIC[5]

Egypt differs in one important respect from Mesopotamia. Whereas the latter could be invaded and occupied by conquerors from almost any direction, Egypt was vulnerable only at either end—and since ancient times there has been little threat from the people up-stream. Egypt has been brought under foreign domination again and again by people who held control of the mouth of the Nile, leaving the Egyptian people to develop their own distinctive culture along the Nile Valley. The majority of the Egyptians, crowded in the ribbon of irrigated land from the head of the delta to the first cataract, protected from the east by the Red Sea and from the west by the almost empty stretches of the Libyan Desert, felt only remote contacts with their conquerors. Yet foreign powers controlled or "protected" the government of Egypt for thousands of years. Egypt came successively under the rule of the Greeks, the Romans, the Muslims, the Turks, the French, and the British. Yet dur-

---

[4] Include the United Arab Republic (Egypt), Sudan, the Syrian Arab Republic, Lebanon, Jordan, and Israel.

[5] The United Arab Republic is the name officially adopted in 1958 to include both Egypt and Syria. Syria withdrew from the republic in 1961. In 1963 an Arab Federation was formed, consisting of Egypt, Syria, and Iraq.

ing all this time the Egyptian farmers were hardly disturbed by the changes in government, or by the conquests from outside. The Egyptian countryman, the *fellah* (plural *fellahin*), is racially and culturally distinctive, the product of thousands of generations of life in an isolated habitat.

Since 1952 Egypt has declared and made good its sovereign independence. And since 1956 the Egyptians have proclaimed their leadership of the Arab world and of the revolutions that now so deeply stir that world. Not only have foreign influences been excluded from Egypt, but the monarchy also has been overthrown, and the landlords have been deprived of their traditional dominance in politics. The Egyptian state is not yet ready to enter the initial phase of the Industrial Revolution, but it is taking steps in that direction. There is no tendency to endorse the basic ideas of the Democratic Revolution as these ideas were formulated in Europe and Anglo-America. But this revolution is coming to Egypt in the form of rising demands for an end to the system of privilege, and for an acceptance of the principle of individual dignity.

The Population of Egypt. The central position of Egypt in the North African-Southwest Asian Culture Region is more than a fact of geography. Egypt's population of more than 27,000,000 represents almost 20 per cent of the population of the whole culture region. By contrast, Iraq and Saudi Arabia, Egypt's rivals for Arab leadership, have only about 7,000,000 each.

The first modern census of Egypt was taken in 1882. In that year there were 6,804,000 Egyptians. Almost all of them lived on the 13,500 square miles of irrigated land along the Nile Valley between Aswan and the Mediterranean, giving that area a population density of about five hundred per square mile. Earlier estimates of the population density are not very reliable.

It would seem to have been about the same at the time of Christ; in 1800 however, after some three centuries of Turkish rule, the density was probably only two hundred per square mile. During the whole period of history the birth rate was high (between 40 and 50 per thousand), but so also was the death rate. The area of irrigated land remained more or less the same, varying only with the height of the annual flood. When the Nile flood was higher than normal there would be more food and more people could be fed; when it was lower than normal there would be less food, and many people would die of starvation. This uninterrupted process of birth and death and of struggle for survival formed a grim background to all the conquests and all the changes of dynasty over thousands of years.

With the opening of the Suez Canal in 1869, Egypt became a major concern of the British. Maintenance of the sea route to India and Australia depended on Egypt's friendliness toward British interests. This meant that Britain needed to gain the support of the Egyptian government and those with political power. They did so by giving assistance to Egypt in the form of medical services; and in 1902 British engineers completed the Aswan Dam. For the first time the Nile floods could be controlled; and the irrigable area was enlarged to cover about 13,700 square miles. Periodic famines also could be limited.

Immediately the population began to increase rapidly. By 1907 it had passed 11,000,000. The census of 1947 counted over 19,000,000; and that of 1960 counted 26,059,000. The population density in the inhabited area of the Nile Valley now averages more than 1800 per square mile, and there are parts of the valley where the density of the rural population is more than 3,000 per square mile—a figure exceeded only in parts of China.

The rural population, the fellahin, constitutes Egypt's major problem. Most of the farmers are tenants on large properties; a few have their own farms which are usually less than half an acre in size. The homes are two-room mud huts, infested with flies. Their water supply comes from the Nile, and their fuel is dried dung. The birth rate among these people is one of the highest in the world—about 50 per thousand in rural areas, 45 per thousand for Egypt as a whole. For a long time a population increase was checked by a very high death rate, especially among babies; but since World War II the application of modern health measures, including the use of DDT, has cut the death rate from over 35 per thousand in 1945 to less than 20 per thousand. The result has been a sudden jump in the rate of increase. "Egypt," writes the geographer George B. Cressey, "seems like a nation smothered by itself."

The Nile. This concentration of rural people in Egypt is completely dependent on the Nile. Herodotus (484-425 B.C.) was one of the earliest writers to recognize that in a very real sense "Egypt is a gift of the Nile." The Nile water makes life possible in the desert; and the river brings to its narrow floodplain and delta a load of silt, derived from the erosion of the Highlands of Ethiopia, which has proved to be extraordinarily fertile. The water that drains from the mountains of equatorial Africa, and collects in Lake Victoria and Lake Albert, gives rise to the main stream of the Nile—known as the White Nile. As the river reaches the southern margin of the Sahara it spreads out in a vast marsh, covered with floating vegetation, where much volume is lost by evaporation. But after the White Nile is joined by the Blue Nile and the Atbara River, draining from the Highlands of Ethiopia, the river has enough volume to

continue its flow all the way across the desert to the Mediterranean. Before the construction of the Aswan Dam the lower Nile rose and fell with a regular rhythm. In summer there are torrential rains in Ethiopia, and the water flows into the Nile through the two major tributaries. Below Aswan the first rise in the water level is felt in May, and by September the river has reached its highest stage. At this time of year about two thirds of the water in the lower Nile comes from Ethiopia. After September the flood subsides, and the lowest stage is reached in April or early May. At low-water stage about 85 per cent of the water in the lower Nile is brought by the White Nile.

Agriculture. Few places in the world have been so continuously cultivated over so many thousands of years as has the Nile Valley. Each year the flood waters used to be directed onto diked fields and allowed to drop their load of mud. Then when the flood waters drained away the rich, moist earth lay exposed to the hot sunshine. The floods had the additional effect of flushing out the salt, which always threatens to accumulate in irrigated areas where drainage is slow and some of the water is allowed to evaporate. In Mesopotamia parts of the alluvial plain have been ruined by salt accumulation; but this problem did not exist in Egypt. Year after year the land used to produce bumper crops, of which wheat was the most important.

When British engineers completed the Aswan Dam in 1902 there followed a series of major changes in Egyptian agriculture. In the first place the old system of basin irrigation, based on the Nile floods, had to be abandoned. It was replaced with perennial irrigation—water being brought great distances in canals and directed to the fields through ditches. The area of irrigable land was increased, especially in the low-lying section to the west of the lower Nile, known as the Faiyum Basin. Since the floodwaters were held back in a reservoir, the differences in the amount of water coming from Ethiopia each year were no longer important. However, the soil was no longer replenished each year with fresh silt, for the load of silt was caught in the reservoir. Furthermore, landlords were encouraged to use some of their lands for the production of a crop that could be sold in Great Britain. This was long-staple cotton—a valuable type of cotton that can be grown only in desert oases, where temperatures are high, and where there are no other kinds of cotton growing nearby. Egypt thus became one of the major sources of long-staple cotton for the British textile mills.

Meanwhile, Egypt's food production has failed to keep pace with the increase in mouths to be fed. To be sure, agriculture has become more intensive. With perennial irrigation there are three crop seasons each year. From February to May is the planting season for cotton, maize, rice, sugar cane, millet, peanuts, sesame, and vegetables. In July rice and millet are sown in flooded areas near the river. In November a third series of crops is sown on the same land—consisting of wheat, barley, flax, and vegetables. Cotton is still the chief commercial crop of Egypt; but the chief food crop is now maize—and corn bread challenges the traditional wheat bread in the Egyptian diet. Yet in spite of this intensive agriculture, total production has lagged behind. This is due, in part, to the declining productivity of the heavily worked soil. Since 1902 the Egyptians have become major users of fertilizer. For a long time Egypt was an important purchaser of Chile's nitrate; but now it has developed its own phosphate deposits, and makes use of guano

from a vast number of pigeon towers. Even this is not enough, and increasing amounts of fertilizer have to be imported at high cost. Most farm methods are still primitive: the land is worked with wooden plows; weeds are cut down with hoes; crops are harvested with hand sickles, and threshed on threshing boards. The new government is trying to do something about the poverty of the people. The large landowners are being urged to decrease their acreage of cotton to allow for the production of more food. Cotton harvests can be maintained on smaller acreages with the use of machinery, including the mechanical cotton picker. The government is building schools, and is broadening the application of modern medical services—all of which has the unfortunate effect of increasing the net rate of population increase. And the fellahin are poorer than they were before the completion of the Aswan Dam.

With financial and technical assistance from the Soviet Union, Egypt is starting the construction of a new dam. The High Dam, as it is called, is being built across the river a short distance above Aswan. It will be more than three miles long, and three hundred feet high. The reservoir behind the dam will be the largest man-made lake in the world, extending far back into the territory of Sudan. These engineering works will mean that the irrigated area can be increased by almost one third, and the value of agricultural products by one half. From the dam the Egyptians will also be able to generate electric power. The power can be used to support the development of much-needed manufacturing industries, including a nitrate plant. Nevertheless, simple arithmetic shows that these developments will not be nearly enough to take care of the inevitable increase in population in the decades ahead.

Cities and Industries. Cairo is a city of over three million, and Alexandria has a million and a half. The people in these cities enjoy opportunities for education, and many are employed in jobs for which education is a prerequisite. Egypt is better off than Iraq, and much better off than Saudi Arabia, in having a well-trained and efficient group of public administrators. Factories are being built, and new jobs in manufacturing industries are being made available to people with the necessary skills. There are textile factories, food-processing plants, oil refineries, cement, glass, and chemical works.

It is from these city people, however, that there comes the chief demand for an end to colonialism and any form of interference from outside. Although they recognize that foreign financial aid and technical assistance will be needed for a long time, they do not want such aid to be followed by controls of any sort. They are people who feel deeply the kind of indignity that comes from an inferior position—for centuries, they believe, Egypt has occupied an inferior position as a result of foreign domination. There is a great rise of popular hatred among these people for anything foreign, especially for anything British. And the United States has also incurred their hatred for its part in the establishment of the Jewish state of Israel.

The Suez Canal. The Suez Canal is perhaps the world's most important strategic prize. This narrow body of water provides shipping with the lowest-cost connection between the European countries and the countries of the Orient. In 1953 the shipping passing through the Suez Canal amounted to about eighty-nine million tons, compared with thirty-six million tons passing through the Panama Canal. The only canal in the world that carries a larger tonnage is the Sault Ste. Marie Canal between Lake Superior and Lake Huron, where iron ore is the major cargo. At Suez 75 per cent of the tonnage northbound through the canal consists of oil.

The canal has proved to be highly profitable. For many years it was operated by an Egyptian corporation, in which the controlling financial investment was British. Most of the officials who collected the tolls and managed the day-to-day business of the canal were French. This arrangement was based on a concession granted by Egypt that was due to expire in 1968. In 1956, however, the Egyptian government yielded to the rising demand for an end to foreign control of the canal. If the other Arab states of the Persian Gulf area could become wealthy on oil, it was felt that Egypt too should be able to gain an income from the shipment of oil. The canal was seized, and has since been operated entirely by Egyptians. Those Europeans who feared that the Egyptians would not be able to operate the canal efficiently were proved to be wrong. Each year the canal now yields a profit to the Egyptian treasury, which is an important source of funds for the much needed economic development.

SUDAN

To the south of Egypt is the Republic of the Sudan, which has gained independence since World War II. Sudan is one of those marginal states that can be included in either of two neighboring culture regions. The whole southern part of Sudan is occupied by Negro herdsmen whose way of life closely resembles that of the people in the Central African Republic and the bordering parts of the Republic of the Congo (see Map 81). This part of Sudan is definitely a part of the African Culture Region. The northern part of Sudan, however, is predominantly Muslim and Arabic-speaking. Furthermore, the use of the water for irrigation in the area around Khartoum raises legal and engineering problems that are intimately connected with Egypt. In the minds of the political leaders Sudan is an Arab state, and therefore definitely belongs in the North African-Southwest Asian Culture Region.

Sudan was the name given by the Muslim geographers to the savannas south of the Sahara. In the Arabic language "Bilâd-es-Sudan" means "the Land of the Blacks." Most of the people in the new state of the Sudan are Negro herders whose cattle, camels, sheep, and goats feed on the grasslands of the southern part of the country. But the Arabic-speaking Muslims of the central Sudan, who make up 30 to 40 per cent of the total population, are the ones who control the government. Most of the export products also originate in the same central area.

The territory now included in the Sudan came under the control of the Egyptians in a series of military campaigns started in 1820. Arabic-speaking Muslims, who were friendly to Egypt, were placed in control. For many years they profited from the sale of Negro slaves, and of ivory elephant tusks which were collected by the Sudanese Negroes for their new masters. When Great Britain gained control of Egypt, the British put an end to the slave trade in spite of strong resistance on the part of the Muslims. The area was placed under a joint administration and became the Anglo-Egyptian Sudan.

During the period of joint control much was done to increase the agricultural production of the Sudan. A dam was built on the Blue Nile, and the water held by this dam was used to irrigate a large area between the Blue Nile and the White Nile. This area, with plenty of water, much sunshine, and a fertile soil became an important producer of long-staple cotton. The

capital, Khartoum, located on the northern edge of the irrigated area, became a thriving commercial town.

In 1953 Britain and Egypt agreed to withdraw their claims to the Sudan and to permit the people of that country to decide their own political future. The government declared the independence of the Sudan in 1956.

THE SYRIAN ARAB REPUBLIC

Syria is a poor, mountainous and desert country that occupies a part of the coast of the eastern Mediterranean. Immediately back from the coast are high ranges of mountains, which in ancient times were heavily forested, but which are now entirely denuded as a result of overgrazing by sheep and goats (Map 30, p. 86). Rivers descending from these highlands support irrigated agriculture along the east-facing piedmont which is a part of the Fertile Crescent. On Syria's good irrigated agricultural land, the crops include cotton, maize, wheat, millet, apricots, plums, figs, apples, oranges, grapes, pears, olives, walnuts, melons, and mulberry trees on which to feed silkworms. On the lowlands of northwestern Syria the famous Latakia tobacco is grown. There is little industrial development; but some income is derived from the shipment of oil to the Mediterranean ports by pipeline from the Iraqi oil fields (Map 63).

The Syrian Arab Republic has only recently become an independent country. This part of the Ottoman Empire was placed under the administration of France after World War I. It became independent in 1944, but from 1958 to 1961 formed part, with Egypt, of the United Arab Republic. This arrangement was not new, for Syria had been many times under Egyptian rule, and many times also under the rule of Mesopotamia or Turkey.

A grove of the famous cedars in the mountains of Lebanon.

LEBANON

Lebanon is the modern state that occupies the ancient culture hearth of the Phoenicians. The mountain ranges along the eastern side of the Mediterranean reach their greatest elevations in this country. Watered by ample winter rains these mountains were once clothed with the famous "cedars of Lebanon," which were used by both the Phoenicians and the Egyptians to build their ships. Only a few protected groves of cedars now remain. Along the coast, and in the longitudinal valley between the ranges of mountains, there are excellent soils where a Mediterranean agriculture flourishes.

Lebanon is a relatively prosperous country. Its gross national product per capita is more than twice that of Syria. Since ancient times the ports on this part of the coast have handled trade between Europe and the Orient. The overland caravan routes came to Tyre and Sidon, much as the modern transport routes come to Beirut. Lebanese banks handle the business of much of the Arab world. Beirut has become an educational center and carries on a large tourist business. The Lebanese population includes both Christians (50 per cent) and Muslims (42 per cent); and 80 per cent of the people are literate. Since gaining its independence from France in 1944, Lebanon has maintained a democratic form of government.

JORDAN

Jordan is a strip of territory that was left over when the map of Southwest Asia was redrawn after the collapse of the Ottoman Empire. After World War I the country to the west of the Jordan River was called Palestine, while the country to the east, a thinly populated zone between the former Turkish and Arab territories, was called Trans-Jordan. Both were placed under British administration. The kingdom of Trans-Jordan was granted independence in 1946. In 1948 Palestine was divided again between the Jewish state of Israel and Jordan. which was expanded to include the almost solidly Muslim part of Palestine (Map 61).

This desert and steppe country is still very thinly peopled by nomadic shepherds. When Israel and Jordan were separated, many Muslims fled from Israel and now form colonies of displaced people in Jordan. Since they have no jobs, and no land that they can farm, these refugees are cared for by the United Nations. The problem of resettling them is not easy, for Jordan has very little land suitable for agriculture, and its grazing lands are already occupied to capacity.

ISRAEL

The Jewish state of Israel was recognized as an independent country in 1948. Until that date the Jews had no homeland to give them status as a nation. However, when Israel was established in the midst of the Arab states a major focus of conflict was created. Jerusalem, the holy city of Christians, Jews, and Muslims, was divided between Israel and Jordan, and became the capital of Israel.

Very little of the land included in the territory of Israel is flat. The Jordan River drains southward from the mountains on the border of Syria and Lebanon into Lake Tiberias (Sea of Galilee), and continues southward through a wide rift valley to the Dead Sea, 1,292 feet below sea level. The same depression continues southward to the Gulf of Aqaba, an arm of the Red Sea. Most of the land on either side of the Jordan Valley is a hilly upland, which in the past used to be covered in part with trees. There are two plains near the coast. The Plain of Esdraelon extends inland from the port of Haifa; and a coastal plain extends southward from Tel Aviv along the edge of the Mediterranean.

Israel is on the dry margin of the Mediterranean climate (Map 5, pp. 10-11). On the coastal plain as far south as the Egyptian border the climate is one of mild, rainy winters and hot, dry summers. There is more rain in the hills than in the lower areas. The Dead Sea depression is very dry, and so also is the whole triangle of territory, known as the Negev, which extends to the Gulf of Aqaba.

Population. The long history of conquest by outsiders brought a variety of peoples to the more accessible parts of Palestine. During the lifetime of Jesus, the area was a Roman province. In A.D. 636 Palestine was invaded and conquered by the Muslims. For nearly thirteen centuries, from 636 to 1917, Palestine was a Muslim country, except for a brief period of Christian rule during the Crusades. In 1917, during World War I, the British army invaded Palestine in the campaign against Germany's ally, Turkey; and after the war the League of Nations assigned Palestine to the protection of Great Britain.

In 1917 the British government issued the so-called Balfour Declaration, encouraging the establishment of a national home for the Jewish people in Palestine. The Declaration read as follows:

His Majesty's Government view with favor the establishment in Palestine of a national home for the Jewish people, and will use their best endeavors to facilitate the achievement of that object, it being clearly understood that nothing shall be done which may prejudice the civil and religious rights of existing non-Jewish communities in Palestine or the rights and political status enjoyed by Jews in any other country.

In response to this declaration some Jews from various parts of the world did migrate to Palestine, but after Hitler came to power in Germany a very large number of refugees sought a new life in this Jewish haven. By 1940 the population of Palestine was nearly 1,500,000. Of these, 60 per cent were Muslims, and 31 per cent were Jews. The Jews had built a beautiful modern city, Tel Aviv, and had introduced modern agricultural methods and new systems of irrigation. In 1948 the British withdrew from Palestine, granting independence to both Jordan and Israel. The United Nations attempted to draw a boundary between the two states that would separate predominantly Jewish and Muslim populations, but this boundary has still not been accepted by the interested parties.

The census of 1961 showed that Israel had a population of 2,170,082, of which the Jews made up 90 per cent. Since 1948 the movement of Jews to Israel has been greatly increased, bringing immigrants from seventy different countries. And about 650,000 Arabs have left their homes in Israeli territory and fled to Jordan. The population of Israel is now 76 per cent urban, for even those Jews who have taken up farming make their homes in the towns and go out each day to work in the fields.

Agriculture. Israel faces a difficult task in building a viable economy on a land so lacking in basic resources. Much of the agricultural potential of Palestine had been destroyed by ruinous farming and grazing methods of the past. As elsewhere in the Mediterranean region much of the land, once forested, now stands barren and deeply eroded as a result of overgrazing by sheep and goats. The hilly parts of Palestine are among the most desolate. This also has the effect of increasing the severity of floods and droughts in the bordering

An Israeli village in the hilly country near Jerusalem. The much-eroded slopes are being reconstructed through the planting of trees.

lowlands. One of Israel's major problems is to find enough water to make summer irrigation possible. The Jordan River water is shared by Jordan, Lebanon, and Syria. Furthermore, where it borders Israeli territory the river is deeply entrenched below the surface. On the coastal plain wells are used to tap the ground water; but where the wells have been pumped too much, salt water from the sea actually seeps back inland. This has already happened around Tel Aviv and Haifa.

The Israelis have made a great effort to increase commercial crop production and to decrease costs. They have protected the watersheds with reforestation, and have reduced soil erosion by replacing sheep with cattle—mostly dairy cattle selected from the world's finest stock. On the lower hill slopes they have planted orchards of oranges and olives. Oranges are Israel's leading export,

mostly sent out through the newly-constructed port of Ashdod. On the plains the farms are mechanized, and fertilizer is used to restore and maintain the soil. On some irrigated areas three crops a year are harvested, and yields are high. The crops include wheat, oats, barley, peanuts, cotton, and vegetables.

Manufacturing Industries. Israel could not survive as a purely agricultural state. Manufacturing industries provide the backbone of the economy. Most of the raw materials have to be imported, and the finished products exported, so that any profits to Israel must be derived from "value added by manufacture." The capital for the initial industrial development has been furnished by Jewish people in Europe and America. Today Israel has a much larger industrial capacity than any other state in this culture region. Electric power is provided by a hydroelectric station on the Jordan River, and by diesel oil stations. Israel has built its own oil refinery at the head of the Gulf of Aqaba. The factories turn out optical instruments, precision tools, watches, cosmetics, pharmaceuticals, cut diamonds, and a variety of forms of machinery. A steel plant is located near Haifa.

The Viability of Israel. In a world at peace there is no reason why a skillful people, abundantly supplied with capital from abroad, should not develop a prosperous economy in spite of a lack of local resources. Israel could, under the right circumstances, put up stiff competition with Lebanon for the commerce and financial leadership of Southwest Asia. But the very success of the Israelis in establishing a workable economy, and in gaining the highest gross national product per capita of any state in this part of the world, has only increased the hatred of the Arab neighbors. No ships are allowed to carry oil to Israel through the Suez Canal. No pipelines from the Persian Gulf area are allowed to pass through Israeli territory. No Arab state can do business with Israeli merchants. The Arab states do not even recognize Israel politically.

This surrounding sea of animosity has had two results in Israel. First, it has made the continuation of outside financial assistance essential. But second, it has had the effect of creating a strongly cohesive state out of the most varied ingredients. The one thing the Israelis have in common is the Jewish religion. Coming from seventy different countries they have brought to Israel many different languages, many different standards of living, many different attitudes and objectives. In Israel, survival depends on the acceptance of common principles and purposes—the creation of a Jewish state, the use of the Hebrew language, the support of the Israeli form of government. Outside pressure has been a major factor in creating and maintaining the necessary cohesion within the state.

THE COUNTRIES OF NORTH AFRICA[6]

The countries of North Africa form an extension of the North African-Southwest Asian Culture Region. This area includes most of the Sahara, and the fringe of somewhat wetter country along the Mediterranean coast. The great majority of the people are Muslims who speak Arabic or Berber. The countries included are Libya, Tunisia, Algeria, Morocco, and two small Spanish possessions (Map 61).

The great desert that extends across the northern part of Africa was little known to the Egyptians, the Greeks, or the Romans in ancient times. The Greek geographers were familiar with the desert margins. They

[6] Include Libya, Tunisia, Algeria, Morocco, Ifni, and Spanish Sahara.

knew of the intense heat of the northern part of Africa, and reasoned from this that if such high temperatures were encountered so far from the equator, the regions still closer to the equator must be uninhabitable. The people of the Sahara were Negroid farmers, clustered in the few spots where water could be found. The Mediterranean fringe, where there is enough rain to support grass, was the homeland of the Berbers.

By A.D. 732, within a century after the death of Muhammad, the Muslims had swept across the whole of the Sahara. The invasion was led by the Berbers, who had become Muslims; and was supported and carried even beyond the desert by the Arabs. Today the Berbers are found in the more remote parts of the Sahara, and also in the Mediterranean port cities where they form a restless minority, reluctant to accept almost any kind of authority. The Arabs, who followed closely behind the Berbers, promptly laid claim to ownership of all the oases, and set the Negroid people to work for them as tenant farmers. The oasis agriculture was enriched by the addition of the date palm, which had been brought from Arabia. But the Muslims—both Arabs and Berbers—remained nomadic, pasturing their animals wherever the rains supported an adequate growth of grass, and returning to the oasis settlements at harvest time to collect the rent. With the mobility given them by the use of the camel, they were able to travel across great distances of arid country, even across the desert to the wetter country to the south.

The Arabs found a major source of profit in bringing valuable articles from south of the Sahara to sell in Europe. Their caravans crossed the desert by several routes (Map 58), and over these routes they brought Negro slaves, gold, ivory, ostrich plumes, and other goods of high value. They sold these exotic things in the bazaars of the Mediterranean coastal cities, or in Arab-controlled Spain and Portugal. The Berbers, who were pushed away from the most desirable oases by the stronger Arabs, often made a good living by raiding the Arab caravans or by collecting tolls for safe passage. A major Berber stronghold was in the rugged mountains of the Ahaggar in the western Sahara.

The European invasion of the Sahara came during the nineteenth and twentieth centuries. The Spanish, the French, and the Italians crossed the Mediterranean and established colonies on its southern shore, bringing with them their distinctive kinds of agriculture. The exploits of the French "Foreign Legion" in subduing the rebellious Berbers of the Sahara are well known. The whole of the desert country came into the possession of the Europeans, although actual settlement by them was mostly restricted to the Mediterranean coastal zone. Since World War II, Libya, Tunisia, Algeria, and Morocco have all gained their independence.

LIBYA

Libya is the former Italian colony that occupies the north-central Sahara to the west of Egypt. The Libyan desert is the driest part of the Sahara, and since its rocky and sandy surfaces have no highlands standing above them the hamadas are almost unbroken by wadis. Only a few miniature wet spots in the Libyan desert are habitable. The major farming areas, and the chief concentrations of population are along the immediate Mediterranean coast—in the west on either side of Tripoli, and in the east extending eastward from Bengasi. About three quarters of the population of Libya are living along the coast near Tripoli. The Libyan capital, however, is at Al Baydā', 135 miles northeast of Bengasi.

Most of the Libyans earn a living from farming and herding. The agriculture includes barley and wheat, olives, dates, figs, almonds, and tobacco. On the steppes nomadic herders tend sheep, goats, camels, horses, and cattle.

Since 1960 Libya has been experiencing the kind of sudden transformation that was once found only in the Persian Gulf countries. Major new oil fields have been discovered in the Sahara. One of the first oil sources to be brought into production was at Zelten, located in the midst of the desert some two hundred miles south of Bengasi. In 1962 a pipeline was put into operation to bring this new flow of oil to the Mediterran-

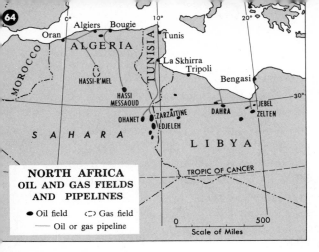

**NORTH AFRICA
OIL AND GAS FIELDS
AND PIPELINES**

● Oil field   ⊂⊃ Gas field
— Oil or gas pipeline

0   500
Scale of Miles

ean coast at El Brega (Map 64). A second major field has been developed more recently at Dahra, to the northwest of the Zelten field. As is true elsewhere in this culture region, the development of the oil fields is creating even more startling contrasts between the well-to-do city people, and the majority of rural inhabitants who have not shared in the new prosperity.

ALGERIA, TUNISIA, AND MOROCCO

The three countries of North Africa, to the west of Libya, were largely developed by the French. Algeria, after 1830, became a major area of French colonization, and in 1902 it was included as an integral part of the French Republic. Tunisia and Morocco were ruled by Muslim sultans under French protection. Actual settlement by immigrants from France was restricted to the coastal area of Algeria where French and Muslim farmers were intermingled, and where French merchants and administrators formed the majority of the population in such places as Algiers, Bône, and Oran. In Algeria as a whole Arabs and Berbers made up 89 per cent of the population at the conclusion of World War II. The only non-French areas in this part of Africa were Spanish Morocco, the international settlement at Tangier, near the Strait of Gibraltar,

and the Spanish possessions along the Atlantic coast of the Sahara—Ifni and Spanish Sahara.

The three countries have now become independent. In 1956 French and Spanish Morocco, and the international settlement at Tangier, were united in one independent Morocco; and Tunisia, also, was granted independence. In 1962 Algeria became independent, in spite of the bitter opposition of the people of French ancestry who hoped to keep it as a part of France.

Agriculture and Herding. In each of the three countries agriculture gives employment to about 70 per cent of the workers. The chief farming areas are along the Mediterranean coast and on the lower slopes of the Atlas Mountains, where the climate is one of mild, rainy winters, and hot, dry summers. Wheat and barley are the important grains; and on the mountain slopes there are olives, grapes, citrus fruits, and plantations of cork oak. Vegetables are concentrated near the cities. On the dry side of the mountains and in the wet spots of the desert the chief crop is the date palm.

The nomadic herders are found chiefly on the desert margins, or in the highlands that stand above the general desert level. Camels, sheep, goats, cattle, and horses are, for these people, the chief source of wealth. Because of the numerous wadis that cross the hamadas of the western Sahara, there are many small habitable spots in this area. Some of the wadis that lead southward from the Atlas Mountains support ribbons of date palms that reach, almost unbroken, for hundreds of miles into the desert. The nomadic herders still come and go between the date plantations and the grassy pastures. Dates, from these Saharan oases, are used chiefly as food by the herders.

Minerals and Industries. The French engineers and geologists found a wealth of minerals in North Africa. In Algeria there are mines producing phosphate rock, manganese, lead, zinc, copper, and other metals (Map 62). But the new major sources of wealth in North Africa are oil and gas, which were discovered in the Sahara, south of the Atlas Mountains, in 1957. Gas is now brought by pipeline to Oran and Algiers, and oil pipelines connect the Sahara fields with ports on the Mediterranean (Map 64). The Sahara, according to some reports, is another major source of oil, comparable to the Persian Gulf. Even if it proves to be somewhat less than these optimistic estimates indicate, the strategic picture of Europe's oil supply has already been substantially altered.

French plans for investment in independent Algeria include not only the continued development of oil as an export, but also the development of manufacturing industries. A steel plant is to be built at Bône, a petroleum refinery is to be set up at Algiers, and a petrochemical industry is to be built in a suburb of Oran. There are also plans for new pipelines, new highways, electric generating plants, expanded irrigation works, and other forms of economic development. Whether these plans will be carried out remains to be seen.

THE COUNTRIES OF THE EASTERN BORDER[7]

From the central part of the North African-Southwest Asian Culture Region another arm extends eastward between the Black Sea and the Caspian on the north, and the Persian Gulf and the Indian Ocean on the south. The countries of the Eastern Border include Turkey, Iran, and Afghanistan (Map 61). These are Muslim countries, but the people speak languages other than Arabic. Pakistan, which is also a Muslim country, shares many things in common with the countries of the Eastern Border, but is included in South Asia because of its even more intimate connections with India.

These three countries share in the crossroads character of this culture region. Turkey, because of its position astride the narrow sea connection between the Black Sea and the Aegean, is closely watched by many nations that would like to be sure of unhindered use of this route. Iran, because of its position across the land connection between the Caspian Sea and the Indian Ocean, has long been a major route between the East and the West (Map 58). Afghanistan is crossed by the ancient caravan route between the oases of Central Asia and the Indus Valley. But these three countries are of strategic importance for another reason as well: the Soviet Union has established communist-controlled states around its borders from the Baltic Sea to Korea; the only non-communist states bordering the Soviet Union, apart from Finland, are Turkey, Iran, and Afghanistan.

TURKEY

The site at the southern end of the Bosporus where it joins the Sea of Marmara has for a long time been the focus of international interest. The first city on this site was Byzantium, a Greek colony. In A.D. 328 the Emperor Constantine enlarged Byzantium and named the new city Constantinople; and in 330 this became the capital of the Eastern Roman Empire, and later the

[7] Include Turkey, Iran, and Afghanistan.

A Muslim mosque in Turkey, built in the 17th century. This style of architecture is distinctively Turkish.

center of the Greek Orthodox Church. In 1453 Constantinople was captured by the Turks and became the capital of the Ottoman Empire, and the seat of the sultan.

The sultan was not only the ruler of an empire, but also the religious leader of the Muslims. Constantinople attracted wealthy and gifted people from a wide area of the old world. But the people over whom the sultan ruled were mostly very poor, illiterate peasant farmers, striving to make a living from farms that were too small, on a land that was too steep and too dry. The wealthy people were not landlords, for in Turkey there were few large estates: the wealthy people were merchants and administrators who lived in the capital. The contrast between the splendor of Constantinople and the squalor of the country was enormous.

The first revolt against the privileges of the wealthy was led by a group of young army officers. In 1876 these young officers, their own promotion blocked by an excess of generals, tried to force the sultan to give up his absolute powers. They failed. In 1908, however, another similar revolt was successful, and a constitutional government was established, in which the powers of the sultan were limited. These younger officers had been trained in German military schools, and when World War I started they sided with Germany. The result was the complete defeat of Turkey and the breakup of the Ottoman Empire.

After the war the straits were placed under international control, although they were left nominally within Turkish territory. New Turkish leaders appeared who were able to arouse a spirit of Turkish nationalism and to re-establish a viable state on the ruins of the empire. The new Turkish government was able to negotiate a treaty with the Soviet Union over their common frontier, and also to establish new frontiers with Greece and Bulgaria. In 1923 Ankara became the capital of the new Turkey, and in 1930 the name of Constantinople was officially changed to Istanbul.

Population. At the time that Turkey became a republic its territory was occupied by people of many different nationalities. Around the Aegean Sea, Greeks, Turks, and Bulgarians had been thoroughly mixed over the centuries. In 1923 a new approach to the solution of territorial problems was tried. A wholesale exchange of people was carried out: Bulgarians moved back into the territory assigned to Bulgaria, Greeks moved back into Greece, and Turks moved into Turkey. Perplexing minority problems were eliminated, and Turkey became very largely a country occupied by Muslims who spoke the Turkish language. Christians and Jews were permitted to practice their own religions, but most of these non-Muslims were in Istanbul.

The Economy. Turkey is still primarily an agricultural country. Over 76 per cent of its workers are employed in agriculture. Most of these farmers own their farms—a situation that is distinctly unusual in a pre-industrial country.

Turkey makes good use of the small arable area. A large part of the national territory is mountainous (Map 61), and a large part also is too dry to be used for crops without irrigation. Most of the farmland is along the coasts where the climate is Mediterranean (Map 5, pp. 10-11). On the small alluvial plains the land is used intensively to grow cotton and tobacco in summer, and perhaps a winter crop of wheat or barley. On the steep valley sides that face toward the sun there are vineyards, and on those that face away from the sun there are orchards of fig and nut trees. The wetter parts of the interior plateau are used for wheat and other grains. The greater part of the interior, however, is useful only for the grazing of sheep and goats.

Turkey has been trying to establish manufacturing industries, and to begin the large-scale development of its mineral resources. Turkey is better off than many countries in terms of basic minerals. It has the best coal in Southwest Asia, and it even has a small oil field (Map 62). There are also mines producing iron ore, copper, chromium, manganese, antimony, sulfur, and salt. A new steel plant has been built at Karabuk, fifty miles to the south of the coal fields. With continued financial and technical assistance from outside, Turkey may be able to raise the standard of living and take some of the pressure off the hard-worked land.

IRAN

Iran was mentioned previously (p. 252) as one of the Persian Gulf oil countries. It does share some of the characteristics and problems of these countries; but it is more than just an oil country, and in many ways it does not share the attitudes and policies of the other Persian Gulf states.

Population. There are over 20,000,000 people in Iran—many more than in neighboring Iraq, almost as many as in Turkey. Most of them are Muslims, but they adhere to a different sect than do the Turks. Most of them, also, speak Persian, but there are several million Iranians who speak other languages, including Kurdish, Baluchi, and Armenian.

The chief concentration of people today is in and around the capital city of Tehrān.

But there are small concentrations of population scattered throughout the country. Some are along the mountain piedmont facing the Persian Gulf and on the alluvial lowland. Some occupy the many scattered oases of the interior—a basin and range desert with small irrigated areas on the alluvial fans.

The Economy. Most of the Iranian workers are employed in agriculture, although Iran is a poor country for raising crops. Irrigated land, and land that gets enough rainfall to be used for crops occasionally, amounts to only about 4 per cent of the national territory. This means that there is less than one acre per capita of food-producing land. Only about 6 per cent of the total area can be used for grazing. Much the greater part of Iran is unproductive desert or mountain.

The agricultural lands of Iran are mostly owned by well-to-do landlords, many probably resident in Tehrān. A wealthy man may own several villages. It is an accepted principle that there are five elements involved in crop production: land, water, seeds, animals, and labor. The person who provides each of these elements receives one-fifth of the profits. The farmer, whose one contribution is the labor, gets one-fifth to the landowner's four-fifths. If he can produce two hundred bushels of grain on his farm, his share is forty bushels: he has to support himself and his family on an income of approximately $100 a year. The landowner derives a substantial income from his large holdings, and is not seriously interested in increasing crop production through the adoption of new farm methods. The peasant farmer himself is too poor to buy a modern plow or other mechanical equipment; he is usually too poor to buy his own ox, yet if he could do this he would be able to double his income. Here is a situation in which nothing short of a vast injection of new capital in the form of irrigation works, schools, and new machines, could have any real effect in raising the miserably low standard of living.

The crops most commonly grown in Iran are wheat and barley, although there are certain parts of the country where other crops are concentrated. Rice, for example, is the favorite crop along the low coastal fringe at the southern end of the Caspian Sea. Along the Persian Gulf and the Shatt al Arab there are large areas devoted almost exclusively to date palms. Other crops include cotton, tobacco, sugar beets, and fruits. Along the southern side of the Elburz Mountains around Tehrān the farmers produce a fine quality of apricots, and melons, and also grapes for raisins and for wine making.

Most of the grazing of sheep and goats is carried on by nomadic tribes in the traditional manner. The animals are driven up into the mountains in the summer and are returned to the lowlands in winter. The sheep of northwestern Iran produce the wool that supplies the famous Persian rug industry. The weaving of rugs is still carried on in the villages by skilled weavers, and the world still offers a market, although a shrinking one, for these beautiful products.

Iran is fortunate in having oil, since the income from oil may some day provide the necessary source of capital. Iran has an estimated 9 per cent of the total proved oil reserves in the world. The largest developed field is in the Persian Gulf area (Map 63); but explorations in 1960 revealed new and promising oil fields in other parts of the country. In 1909 a huge oil refinery, at one time the largest in the world, was built with British capital at Ābādān on the Shatt al Arab. In addition to oil there are sources of other minerals: coal, iron, lead, and copper (Map 62).

Modern Iran. Modern Iran is still a very poor country. Because of the scattered arrangement of the settlements, and the internal diversity of the population, the development of a cohesive state is not easy. The great majority of the people are illiterate, and remain essentially ignorant of political pressures from the world outside. The new urban population, chiefly in Tehrān and Ābādān—including oil workers, small shopkeepers, traders, government workers, and students—is the segment which is in close touch with the revolutionary ideas of the modern world. These are the people who subscribe to the more violent forms of nationalism, and who look for radical solutions to the problems of poverty. However, for the most part the people of Iran do not believe in majority rule, nor even in the public discussion of political policy. Policy is in the hands of the shah and the officers of his army.

Iran does not share the attitudes and policies of the Arab countries. Only a small minority speak Arabic, and the Muslim sects have little sympathy for the beliefs of the more traditional Muslim of the Arab states. Moreover, Iran has granted *de facto* recognition to Israel, which no Arab state would consider doing.

AFGHANISTAN

East of Iran are two other Muslim countries—Afghanistan and Pakistan. Pakistan is one of those transitional countries that might be included in either of two bordering culture regions. It is here included with India in South Asia. Afghanistan belongs in the North African-Southwest Asian Culture Region (Map 61).

Afghanistan is a land of high mountains and deserts, occupied by many different groups of people speaking different languages. In the northeast is the towering range of mountains known as the Hindu Kush. In the southwest is a desert basin so dry that it remains almost uninhabited. Scattered and diverse tribal groups occupy this rugged land. Although the people are mostly Muslim, the different tribes adhere to what are sometimes antagonistic sects. There is no national language, although the tribes that think of themselves as "true Afghans" speak Pushtu. About a third of the people speak Persian. Most of those who can be called "true Afghans" live in the mountainous western part of Pakistan.

The formation of the Afghan state can only be explained in terms of centuries of migration and conquest. In this territory people of diverse origins have come into conflict. Greeks, Persians, Mongols, Muslims, and more recently Russians and British, have all invaded this mountainous area. The present boundary between Afghanistan and Pakistan is the so-called Durand Line, drawn in 1893 to mark the innermost limit of British control. It cuts right through the middle of territory occupied by certain tribes, and leaves to the east people whose closest connections used to be with Kābul.

One of the world's oldest caravan routes crosses Afghanistan. It connects Bukhara and Tashkent with Peshawar on a tributary of the Indus River. From the Amu Darya and the piedmont oasis of Mazār-i-Sharīf, the route crosses several smaller ranges, finally surmounting the Hindu Kush by way of the Hajikhak Pass at 12,188 feet. The route then crosses the Paghman Mountains to Kābul by the Unai Pass at 5,740 feet. From Kābul to Peshawar the route follows the narrow gorges of the Kābul River and crosses the Khyber Pass at 6,825 feet. Over this, and neighboring routes, have come repeated invasions of India by people from Central Asia. For many thousands of years the Afghan tribesmen have made a living by collecting tolls from passing traders. Fiercely independent, they have fought the invaders who have attempted to bring them into submission.

The greater part of Afghanistan is too steep or too dry to support any very dense population. But in some of the valleys, deep set among the spectacular ranges, there are spots of extraordinary beauty where irrigation permits the luxuriant growth of crops.

Most of the people—estimated at about 14,000,000—who occupy Afghanistan, are herders who pasture sheep and cattle on the high mountain meadows in summer, and seek the shelter of the valleys in winter. On the irrigated land the crops include wheat, barley, cotton, sugar beets, sugar cane, and alfalfa. The country is self-sufficient in terms of food, and also in terms of the wool and cotton from which textiles are woven.

SUMMARY

In spite of the variety of conditions found within the North African-Southwest Asian Culture Region, there are certain common characteristics which give unity to this area. This is the largest continuous area occupied by peoples of the Muslim faith. It includes one of the world's largest deserts. The belt of deserts that extends from the Atlantic coast of North Africa eastward to the Indus Valley of Pakistan has long constituted a barrier between the dense and commercially active populations of Europe and the dense populations of southern and eastern Asia. For a long time the Muslims controlled the routes by which trade between Europe and Asia passed across the desert barrier. In the late fifteenth century the Portuguese outflanked the Muslims by establishing a sailing route around southern Africa. Later again, when the new technology of transportation made it possible, the French and the British developed a sea route through the Mediterranean, the Suez Canal, and the Red Sea, establishing military control of strategic points, and lining the route with fortresses and naval bases. For the most part the Europeans left the native peoples of this region alone except when they were needed as laborers or troops.

All this was changed after 1908 when the first oil well was brought into production. Even by World War I the importance of the region had become apparent—not just as a region of transit, but as a region richly endowed with a resource of vital concern to the European countries. By World War II, when oil had become essential for industry, for heating, for transportation, and for operating the mechanized equipment essential for warfare, the region had gained a position of major strategic significance. After World War II, the rise of the spirit of militant nationalism resulted in the formation of newly independent states. These states could be divided into two groups: those that produced the oil, and those that controlled the routes by which oil was taken to the European markets. By 1955 the European countries were getting 70 per cent of their oil from the Persian Gulf region. The rulers of the oil countries became enormously wealthy; but the countries through which the oil was exported were not sharing in the profits. This situation stimulated further successful revolts against European domination, leading in 1956 to the seizure of the Suez Canal. The discovery of new oil sources in Algeria in 1957, and in Libya in 1960, has forced a revision of the strategic picture.

Meanwhile, all over the Muslim world there have been new attacks on traditional authority, both foreign and domestic. Wherever a new class of educated city people has appeared, it has provided the focus for a demand to end colonial rule from Europe. There has been much sympathy for the economic program offered by the Soviet Union; and Egypt's "high dam" project was financed by that country. People unaccustomed to such democratic ideas as majority rule and the secret ballot, have been little impressed by the concepts developed by the Democratic Revolution in parts of Europe and in Anglo-America. At the same time, any government, however strongly centralized, could not long survive if it failed to demand and secure as much independence as possible from outside interference. There has also been an increasing demand for the kind of economic development that will reduce the widespread poverty. But such economic development requires engineering and technical skills not commonly possessed in the Muslim countries. The geographer, W. B. Fisher—a penetrating student of this region—suggests that the Arab has "a mentality which does not always view with favor the exact and numerical approach to reality." The Industrial Revolution will make slow headway in this culture region without the application of a large amount of technical assistance from countries where the use of the scientific method is widespread.

In the midst of this complex pattern of conflict is the new Jewish state of Israel. The use of advanced technology has already permitted the Israelis to attain a higher gross national product per capita than any other state in this region, and to advance boldly into the initial phase of the Industrial Revolution. But the antagonism of its Arab neighbors necessarily restricts the potential economic development of this country.

7

THE
SOUTH ASIAN
CULTURE REGION

Country	Political Status	Latest Estimate Population	Capital City
Bhutan	Formal Protectorate of India	700,000 ('62)	Punakha Tashi Chho Dzong
Ceylon	Republic	10,500,000 ('62)	Colombo
India	Republic	434,807,245 ('61)	New Delhi
Incl. Andaman & Nicobar Is.	Owned by India		
Laccadive, Minicoy, & Amindivi Is.	Dependencies		
Excl. Kashmir-Jammu		3,583,585 ('61)	
Maldive Is.	Sultanate; Brit. Protect.	89,000 ('60)	
Nepal	Constitutional Monarchy	9,500,000 ('62)	Katmandu
Pakistan, E. & W.	Republic	96,600,000 ('62)	Rawalpindi
Incl. W. Pakistan		37,396,000 ('58)	
E. Pakistan		46,500,000 ('56)	
Sikkim	Formal Protectorate of India	161,080 ('61)	Gangtok

The South Asian Culture Region includes the countries of the Indian subcontinent. There are four independent states—India, Pakistan, Nepal, and Ceylon—and three protectorates—Bhutan and Sikkim in the Himalayan borderland, and the Maldive Islands in the Indian Ocean southwest of India. This is a region with very large densities of population: among the three clusters of people in Eurasia (Map 1, pp. 4-5), South Asia stands second in total numbers. With a little more than 3 per cent of the area of the earth's inhabited land this region is occupied by nearly 18 per cent of the world's population. And with a continued high birth rate of more than 40 per thousand, and a decreasing death rate, the dimensions of the impending population explosion stagger the imagination. Although the Latin American Culture Region has a higher rate of increase, the total number of people involved in the South Asian situation makes the demographic crisis of this region more critical.

The people of South Asia are culturally diverse. In 1947 the whole area was occupied by something like 250,000,000 Hindus and 92,000,000 Muslims, along with numerous other religious groups. That year India and Pakistan were created as separate states, and an attempt was made to draw the boundaries between them so that most of the Hindus would be in India and most of the Muslims in Pakistan. But so great was the actual intermingling that many Muslims and many Hindus were left on the wrong sides of the border. After the partition there was a large migration of Muslims from India into Pakistan, and of Hindus from Pakistan into India. As a result, Pakistan is now about 85 per cent Muslim, and India has about the same proportion of Hindus. Buddhists are concentrated in Ceylon, and in the mountains of the northern border. There are a large number of small religious sects in this culture region, and—in addition to the Hindus and Muslims—nine other major religions with millions of adherents each.

The language situation is even more complicated. The only common language that is spoken by the educated people almost everywhere is English. Map 65 shows the language patterns in South and Southeast Asia, considerably simplified. In South Asia the main language group is described as Indo-Aryan, but this includes at least a dozen languages. In the southern part of India, and northern Ceylon, there are four major languages which are grouped together as Dravidian. On the northern border there are several Sino-Tibetan languages, and on the northwest border of Pakistan there are languages related to those of Afghanistan. The languages of India, and the proportion of the total population speaking each, are given in the following table.

LANGUAGES OF INDIA[1]

Indo-Aryan Group	(Per cent of population)
Hindi	39.2
Marathi	7.8
Bengali	7.0
Gujarati	4.6
Oriya	3.6
Rajasthani	3.5
Punjabi	3.3
Assamese	1.0
Dravidian Group	
Telegu	9.2
Tamil	7.4
Kanarese	4.0
Malayalam	3.7

Both India and Pakistan face a serious problem in establishing a national language. Hindi is the literary language of India, and the one in which political affairs are conducted—yet millions of people, especially among the Dravidians, do not understand Hindi, and are proud to preserve their own languages. Urdu is the most widely understood language in West Pakistan; but in East Pakistan the language is Bengali, which

[1] After David Sopher in *Focus*, American Geographical Society, Vol. 6, No. 6, 1956.

is also spoken by the people in the neighboring parts of India. A major question is whether the ties of religion are more enduring than those of language.

India, with its nearly 450,000,000 people, is struggling to find a solution to the problem of hunger and economic development. Whether the restless millions of Indians can be led to take the steps necessary to start the process of economic development, and whether the gross national product can be raised faster than the rate of population growth, are questions of vital concern to the western nations.

THE HABITAT

The South Asian Culture Region is built on relatively simple lines. Its surface features include some of the world's loftiest mountains, and some of the world's widest alluvial plains. In the south, there is a triangular-shaped hilly upland bordered on either side by coastal lowlands. This is the classic region of the monsoons.

Surface Features. (Map 66) South Asia is separated from the rest of Asia by some of the world's most spectacular mountains. The several ranges of the Himalayas extend in an arc from the headwaters of the Indus River, near the border of Pakistan and Afghanistan, for about 1,500 miles to the great bend of the Brahmaputra River. The mountains are from 100 to 150 miles wide. The crest of the northernmost range of the Great Himalaya is about 20,000 feet above sea level; and there are about forty peaks that rise more than 25,000 feet. Mount Everest, the world's highest mountain, has an elevation of 29,028 feet. The snow line is between 15,000 and 19,000 feet, and mountain glaciers descend through the valleys as low as 11,000 feet. No wheeled vehicle can cross this range, and no military invasion has ever passed southward across the Hima-

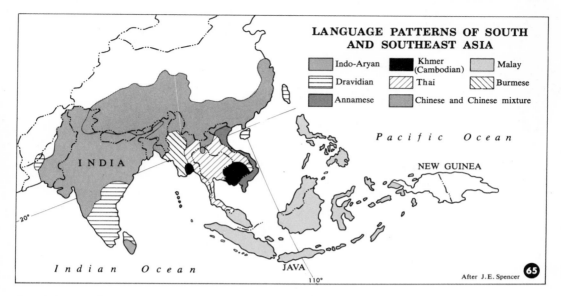

LANGUAGE PATTERNS OF SOUTH AND SOUTHEAST ASIA

Indo-Aryan   Khmer (Cambodian)   Malay
Dravidian   Thai   Burmese
Annamese   Chinese and Chinese mixture

Pacific   Ocean

INDIA

NEW GUINEA

Indian   Ocean   JAVA   After J.E. Spencer   65

layas from Tibet to the lowlands of India; although a Chinese army did invade Nepal in 1791, and the Chinese have ruled the southern slopes.

At either end of the Himalayas there are lower mountains, trending more or less north and south, which also form barriers that are difficult to cross. In the northwest is the famous Khyber Pass, connecting Peshawar in Pakistan with Kābul in Afghanistan, and, beyond Kābul, leading over the Hindu Kush Mountains to the deserts and plains of Central Asia.

Immediately south of the high mountains are the alluvial plains, built through the deposition of material worn from the mountains and brought down by the headwaters of the Indus, the Ganges, and the Brahmaputra. The great rivers sprawl across the vast level expanses of the plains which extend about 1,800 miles east and west, with a width of nearly 200 miles. The Indus flows 900 miles through the desert to the ocean. The Ganges drains all the country from near Delhi eastward, and with the Brahmaputra, pours into the Bay of Bengal through one of the world's large deltas. It is

significant that the eastern part of the delta, now included in Pakistan, is the part which is actively growing, enriched each year by the floodwaters of the great rivers. The western part of the delta no longer receives the floodwaters, and its soils are not so productive as those of the eastern part. The Hooghly River, on which Calcutta is situated, does not even receive the overflow from the Ganges, and its channel is only kept from silting up by the ebb and flow of the high tides (nine to fifteen feet) at the head of the Bay of Bengal.

South of the Ganges Plain is Peninsular India, made up of hills and plateaus that rise sharply from coastal lowlands on either side. The upland country is known as the Deccan—a land of ancient crystalline rocks, cut by streams into a region of hills between 2,000 and 4,000 feet above sea level. East of Bombay the Deccan becomes a plateau, made up of deep accumulations of lava which has weathered into a distinctive black soil known as *regur*. On the west the edge of the Deccan rises to the Western Ghats, a range of mountains between 4,000 and 8,000 feet above sea level. In the north around

SOUTH ASIAN CULTURE REGION
SURFACE FEATURES AND
POLITICAL DIVISIONS

INDIA 1963

Claimed by China

PAKISTAN
KASHMIR
PUNJAB
RAJASTHAN
UTTAR PRADESH
NAGALAND
ASSAM
GUJARAT
MADHYA PRADESH
BIHAR
MANIPUR
ORISSA
WEST BENGAL
MAHARASHTRA
GOA
MYSORE
ANDHRA PRADESH
KERALA
MADRAS

0   300
Miles

0   300
Scale of Miles

Khyber Pass
Peshawar
Islamabad
Rawalpindi
KASHMIR

C H I N A

HIMALAYAS
Mt. Everest

Lahore
Amman
Quetta

PAKISTAN
Indus
THAR DESERT

IRAN

Delhi
Bilari
Jaipur
Ganges R.
Lucknow
Varanasi
Allahabad

NEPAL
Katmandu
SIKKIM
BHUTAN
Brahmaputra R.
Patna
PAKISTAN
Dacca

Karachi

I N D I A

Ahmadabad

Damodar R.
Calcutta
Hooghly R.

BURMA

Nagpur
Mahanadi R.

—20°

Bombay
Hyderabad
Godavari R.

Bay of Bengal

I n d i a n

WESTERN GHATS

—15°

O c e a n

MALABAR COAST
COROMANDEL COAST

Madras

—10°

LACCADIVE ISLANDS
(To India)

65°   70°

85°   90°

CEYLON
Colombo

—5°

MALDIVE ISLANDS
(Br. Protec.)

Pacific Ocean

Indian Ocean

—0°

75°   80°

**BRITISH IND
AFTER 1857**

Diu (Port.)
Damão (Port.)
Goa (Port.)
Yanam (Fr.)
Mahe (Fr.)
Pondicherry (Fr.)
Karikal (Fr.)

British area

Bombay the Western Ghats border the sea, but in the south there is a coastal lowland, from five to seventy miles in width, known as the Malabar Coast. The Eastern Ghats are not so prominent as those that mark the western edge of the Deccan, but they also drop to a coastal lowland. The eastern coast is known as the Coromandel Coast. The island of Ceylon belongs geologically to the mainland, from which it is separated by a narrow strait, so shallow that ocean ships cannot pass through it. The highest peak on Ceylon reaches 8,291 feet above the sea.

The Climates. (Maps 5, 6, and 7) The climates of South Asia are dominated by the monsoons. During the winter the winds are predominantly from the northeast; and except in the southernmost part of India and Ceylon the air is stable and brings little rainfall (see Appendix A, p. 436). During the summer, on the other hand, the flow of air is generally from the southwest, and this air is very unstable and brings heavy rainfall, especially to places where the air is forced to rise along windward mountain slopes. This seasonal shift of wind directions is described as the winter and summer *monsoon*.[2]

[2] The classic explanation of the monsoon was based on the temperature relations of land and water, and the flow of air from relatively cool to relatively warm places. It is now recognized that this explanation is not adequate. The winter monsoon is in part produced by the piling up of air on the right of the jet stream and the resulting general subsidence southward. The jet stream in winter is bifurcated by the Himalayas and the Tibetan Highlands, one arm passing to the south over northern India. At this season, moreover, the southern part of the Pacific trade winds crosses Southeast Asia and southern India, moving generally from the northeast (inset on Map 6). In summer the jet stream moves north of the Tibetan Highlands, and air from the Indian Ocean flows across India from the southwest—and all the way on into East Asia. For an up-to-date explanation of these seasonal winds, and of the related pattern of rainfall in South Asia see Glenn T. Trewartha, *The Earth's Problem Climates*, University of Wisconsin Press, 1961; pp. 151-170.

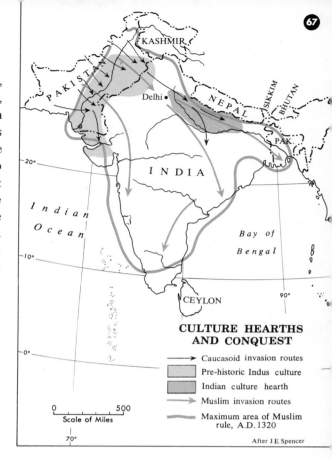

CULTURE HEARTHS AND CONQUEST

→ Caucasoid invasion routes

▨ Pre-historic Indus culture

▨ Indian culture hearth

→ Muslim invasion routes

━ Maximum area of Muslim rule, A.D. 1320

Scale of Miles 0 — 500

After J.E. Spencer

The people of South Asia think of the year as divided into three seasons. From October to March is the cool season, during which the southwest monsoon is gradually replaced by the flow of dry air from the northeast. From March to June is the season of hot weather, during which temperatures over 110° are regularly experienced in Pakistan and the Ganges Valley of India (Map 7). The maximum temperatures of the year come at this time, usually during May. The replacement of the dry air from the northeast with the moisture-laden and unstable southwest monsoon results in cloudiness, which has the effect of reducing somewhat the high temperatures of summer. The period from June to September is the rainy season, during which time rainfall is very heavy. These seasonal characteristics are illustrated by the climatic data for Bombay.

AVERAGES OF TEMPERATURE AND RAINFALL AT BOMBAY

	Jan	Feb	Mar	Apr	May	Jun	Jul	Aug	Sep	Oct	Nov	Dec	Year
Temp.	75.5	75.7	79.5	83.1	85.8	84.0	81.4	80.8	80.9	82.4	80.6	77.4	80.6
Rf.	0.1	0.1	0.0	0.0	0.7	19.9	24.2	14.5	10.6	1.9	0.4	0.0	72.4

(*World Weather Records,* Smithsonian Miscellaneous Collections, 1947)

The pattern of moisture availability in South Asia ranges from arid to superhumid (Inset on Map 68). Something like half of this region is deficient in moisture for at least part of each year, and marginal areas that are described as dry subhumid suffer frequently from droughts due to less than normal rainfall. In the northwest is the Thar Desert which is deficient in moisture throughout the year: even in summer when a thin stream of moist air from the southwest moves in from the Indian Ocean the area is overlain by dry continental air which comes from Iran. The result is low rainfall, and this, combined with the high temperatures of that season, produces a large moisture deficiency. The other large area of deficiency is on the Deccan to the east of the Western Ghats. This is a "rain shadow" effect due to the subsidence of air in the lee of the Ghats. On the other hand the parts of South Asia that receive too much moisture are on the windward slopes of the mountains. The west-facing slopes of the Western Ghats receive very heavy rainfall in the season of the summer monsoon, and so also do the south-facing slopes of the mountains on the India-Burma border and on the northern side of East Pakistan. There is one station in the hills north of the Ganges-Brahmaputra delta—Cherrapunji (altitude 4,000 feet)—which, during the period from 1906 to 1940, had an average rainfall of more than 106 inches in June, with very little or no rain in November, December, and January, and an average annual rainfall of 425.2 inches—the second highest in the world.

POPULATION AND SETTLEMENT

(Maps 65 and 67) To understand how this habitat came to be occupied by a population of such cultural diversity, it is necessary to go back to origins. Man's history in South Asia is not so well known as his history in Southwest Asia. The Indus Civilization, one of the six Early Civilizations, is known to have existed as an urban culture in the Indus Valley at about the same time as the rise of civilization in Mesopotamia. In fact archaeologists point out that there must have been a considerable amount of communication between them, since Indian artifacts have been unearthed in Mesopotamia. For reasons not clearly understood, the Indus Civilization declined, and by 2500 B.C. the cities of the Indus Valley had been abandoned. However, many of the distinctive traits of that early civilization were preserved by the scattered inhabitants of India—one of these was the decimal system of arithmetic.

Although South Asia is protected by a barrier of high mountains, invasions have nevertheless swept repeatedly into this region—usually from the northwest, through what is now Afghanistan, but sometimes from the northeast. The native Dravidian peoples, with their distinctive languages, with a knowledge of rice and wheat cultivation, of domesticated cattle and other advanced skills, were thinly scattered over all the parts of South Asia that were neither too wet nor too arid. But about 1500 B.C. Aryan tribes from Central Asia began to ·move across the mountains into India, at about the same time that other Aryan tribes were moving into what is now Iran. The Aryans were superior to the native peoples in terms of political organization and the techniques of warfare, and by 1000 B.C. they had gained control of the upper Ganges and the upper Indus. This is the area in which the Indo-Aryan culture had its origin, and from which it spread over the whole of South Asia. The population was at first a mixture of Aryan and Dravidian, the Dravidian traits surviving with the least admixture in the southernmost parts of the peninsula. There are still some people of almost unmixed Dravidian ancestry in that part of the region, and others whose darker skin color is perhaps due to the mixing of Dravidians with still more primitive Negritos. But the population of modern India as a whole has been mixed, as a result of numerous other invasions, with Muslims, Mongols, and other more recent groups.

The Indian Culture Hearth. The Indo-Aryan languages, and many other characteristic traits of Indian culture, originated in the Indian culture hearth. This was located in the part of South Asia where the Aryans first established control, and where they found the native inhabitants already advanced in technical skills (Map 67). Here, in the period between 1000 and 500 B.C., many distinctive, Indian traits were formed. It was during this time and in this specific setting that the Hindu religion developed, and with it the caste system which is so characteristic a feature of Indian culture. We may speculate that originally the conquering Aryans wished to maintain their racial purity, and that for this purpose they developed taboos against marriage outside their group. The priests and political leaders came to form a hierarchy of Brahmans, the people of the highest caste and the unchallenged rulers of Indian society. Below

the Brahmans there developed some 2,300 other castes, each made up of individuals who were born into the group and who were never permitted to leave it or to marry outside it. Each caste was responsible for the performance of certain kinds of work. At the bottom of the whole system were the "untouchables," people who performed the most menial and unclean tasks, who were not allowed to enter any public buildings, and for whom separate wells were dug so that the water used by other castes should not be contaminated. Not until the time of Mahatma Gandhi (1869-1948) was any serious attempt made to accept the untouchables as members of Indian society.

In addition to the caste system there are other distinctive traits of Indian culture and of the Hindu religion that originated in this culture hearth. Hindus treat cattle as sacred, and believe that it is wrong to kill animals or to eat meat: some Hindus carry ritual to such an extreme that they use brooms to sweep the ground that they are about to walk on in order to avoid killing insects. There are many Indians whose attitude toward life and its problems is to seek oblivion from care, pain, and external reality. Such people may achieve a condition of spiritual peace that brings intense personal satisfaction, but they do not make good scientists and engineers.

Buddhism developed in this culture hearth during the fifth century B.C., largely as a protest against the rigid ritualism of the Hindu priests. The Buddhists also seek to overcome the passions and anger that move human beings, but they do not insist on such a close adherence to traditional practice as do the Hindus. At the present time in South Asia Buddhism is only of major importance in Ceylon and among the Himalayan peoples—in fact it is more important now in other parts of Asia than it is in its place of origin.

The peculiar combination of circumstances that made this specific location favorable to the forging of a new culture should be noted. The upper Ganges Valley around Delhi is far enough west to avoid the dense rain forests of the lower Ganges, and far enough east to avoid the aridity of the Indus Valley (Map 8, pp. 16-17). This area on the border between the seasonal forest and the scrub woodland, in a position abundantly supplied with water from the rivers pouring southward from the mountains, and endowed with potentially productive alluvial soils, offered certain physical advantages. Furthermore, it was neither so isolated that outsiders could not bring in the varied alien traits that are needed for culture growth, nor was it so readily exposed to invasion that life could not achieve a certain stability. Closer to the pass routes over the mountains to Afghanistan the communities were exposed to frequent raids, but these unsettling events did not bother the communities farther to the east. There were invasions which did reach this culture hearth, it is true. Yet such a tremendous military movement as the invasion by the Greeks under Alexander (327-325 B.C.) carried only as far as the Indus, leaving the Indian culture hearth still beyond the Greek world. From the first to the third centuries A.D. the greater part of northern India was included in the Kushan Empire, that extended far into Central Asia; yet this period was not marked by any slowing down of cultural development in India. In fact the political leaders of the Central Asian empire were perhaps responsible for the spread of Buddhism into Central Asia and on into China.

The Muslim Conquest. The tide of Muslim conquest that began in Southwest Asia in the seventh century A.D., reached the borders of South Asia some two centuries later. Between 900 and 1300 the Muslims swept over most of South Asia except for Ceylon and the southernmost part of Peninsular India. They settled mostly in the dry western part of South Asia, which was, for them, a familiar kind of habitat. There were, therefore, large parts of the region in which the Hindus remained in the majority, and where Muslim control was only loosely applied.

The impact of these two dissimilar religions could almost be used as an example of what happens when an irresistible force meets an immovable object. In India the Muslims were impelled by a militant faith to kill or convert those who remained unbelievers. The Hindus, on the other hand, were not at all concerned to force their beliefs on others—in fact they sought an escape from such worldly conflicts and passions. The Muslims had to learn to accept the fact that the Hindus could not be converted, and that there were too many of them to kill.

India was also conquered by the Mongols. As part of a widespread pattern of invasion and conquest originating in the grasslands of Inner Asia, the Mongol leader Tamerlane led his army into India, from Kābul in Afghanistan, in the late fourteenth century. Muslim rule had by this time collapsed and South Asia had become a complicated pattern of independent states each ruled by a prince—some of them Muslim, some Hindu. The Mongol invasion brought anarchy. However, in the sixteenth century a Mongol ruler succeeded in rebuilding Muslim control of India, with Delhi as the capital. A succession of emperors, the Moguls, controlled varying extents of territory, and were constantly at war with the lesser rulers of the region.

The Europeans. Meanwhile a new kind of invasion had started. The European conquest was begun by the Portuguese, who reached Ceylon in 1505 after discovering a sailing route around southern Africa. In 1510 the Portuguese captured one of the best harbors on the Indian west coast—Goa—which was retained as a Portuguese possession until 1961. Portugal was too small a country to hold the vast extent of African and Asian territory that its navigators had claimed, and after the middle of the sixteenth century the Portuguese monopoly of trade in the Indian Ocean was broken by the Dutch, the French, and the British. Today Portugal has lost all but a few trading posts in Asia. The Dutch, the French, and the British all established posts at various places around the shores of India, but the British at Calcutta were the most strategically placed to control Bengal, which was India's richest area at that time. The French, therefore, turned their attention to Indochina, and the Dutch shifted to Java and Malaya. After 1759 the British had a free hand in India.

From 1600 to 1858 British contacts with India were in the hands of the East India Company. Trade with India was enormously profitable for the company, and there is no doubt that certain benefits were enjoyed by the Indians. Indian products—chiefly iron and steel goods, and fine textiles—were able to reach a wider market than ever before. The company maintained a police force and kept the peace among conflicting interests in India. But it made almost no capital investments in India, and it attempted to preserve the traditional ways of life rather than to bring change. One step of fundamental significance was taken by Lord Macaulay in 1835 when he initiated the idea of selecting a few Indian students each year to be educated in England, with the hope that they would later return to India and interpret to the Indians the meaning of British institutions and attitudes. This policy has had major results in the modern period.

The Taj Mahal at Agra, on the bank of the Jumna, a tributary of the Ganges. This fine example of Mogul architecture was completed in 1650.

After 1784 parts of India were included in a British colony. The East India Company was not abolished until 1858, but the British government gradually took over the administration of India. India was still not treated as a unit. The part of the country under direct British control is shown on Map 66; the remainder was governed by more than six hundred independent rulers, with territories that ranged in size from one of 15 acres in Bilbari to one of 82,313 square miles in Hyderabad.

It is difficult to assess the results of nearly four centuries of British influence in South Asia. It would be a mistake to follow the communist line which condemns all forms of colonialism as evil. On the other hand it would also be a mistake to see British rule in India as an unmixed blessing. The British government, unlike the East India Company, has invested vast sums of money in the construction of irrigation systems, hydroelectric plants, railroads, highways, and other forms of so-called "social overhead." British technicians have attempted to diversify and increase the yields of crops, and they have assisted in the construction of manufacturing industries and mining enterprises. In the process Indian trade has been radically changed. When the East India Company was in operation India was an exporter of manufactured items of high unit value. As a British colony in the nineteenth century India became an exporter of raw materials, and an importer of manufactured goods. British cotton textiles were sold at prices far below those necessary to support the home weaving of textiles. British factories took the foundations from under the whole Indian economic system. Major British achievements in India were in the fields of medicine and hygiene; but medicine and hygiene have served to lower the death rate in relation to a continuing high birth rate,

with disastrous results on the net rate of population growth. It can scarcely be denied that the Indian peasant has a poorer house, poorer clothing, and less to eat than he had before the arrival of the Europeans.

South Asia is a land of villages. In 1941 there were 450,000 villages, of less than five hundred inhabitants each, in the area that later became India and Pakistan. The average village had about a hundred mud houses, bordering narrow, unpaved lanes which became impassable during the rainy season. Even during the dry season wheeled vehicles could not reach the average village, which remained, therefore, largely self-sufficient and remote from the outside world. The variety of castes provided a variety of products for home use.

The Modern States. In 1947 India and Pakistan were separated, and granted independence and membership in the Commonwealth (Map 66). Ceylon became an independent country, and a member of the Commonwealth, in 1948. As previously indicated, the partition of the South Asian mainland between India and Pakistan was intended to separate populations which were largely Muslim from those which were largely Hindu. As we shall see, the lines of division cut across the developed lines of trade, and had the effect of separating farmers from their markets, and manufacturers from their sources of raw materials.

THE REPUBLIC OF INDIA[3]

The Republic of India, or Bharat, is the second largest country in the world in terms of total population. In 1962 there were about 448,300,000 Indians. The areas of

[3] The Hindi equivalent of the English word "India" is Bharat. As Hindi replaces English as the national language, the name Bharat will be more and more widely used.

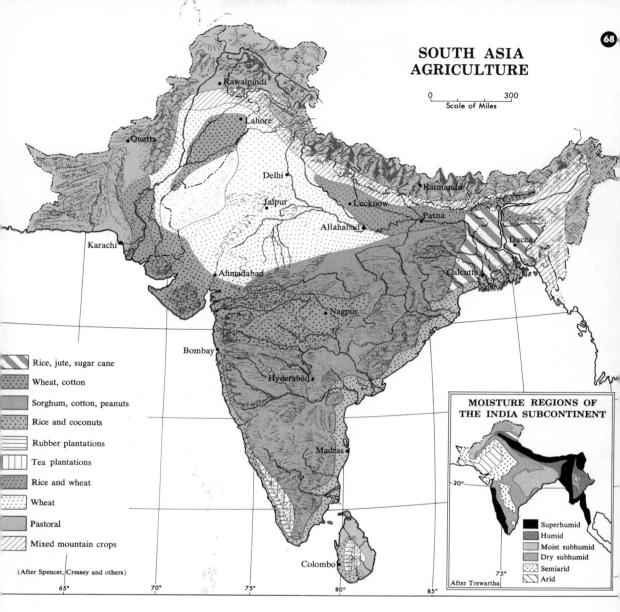

SOUTH ASIA AGRICULTURE

0   300
Scale of Miles

Legend:

- Rice, jute, sugar cane
- Wheat, cotton
- Sorghum, cotton, peanuts
- Rice and coconuts
- Rubber plantations
- Tea plantations
- Rice and wheat
- Wheat
- Pastoral
- Mixed mountain crops

(After Spencer, Cressey and others)

65°   70°   75°   80°   85°

Cities: Rawalpindi, Lahore, Quetta, Delhi, Jaipur, Katmandu, Lucknow, Patna, Allahabad, Dacca, Karachi, Ahmadabad, Calcutta, Nagpur, Bombay, Hyderabad, Madras, Colombo

MOISTURE REGIONS OF THE INDIA SUBCONTINENT

- Superhumid
- Humid
- Moist subhumid
- Dry subhumid
- Semiarid
- Arid

After Trewartha

20°, 75°

greatest density now are the same areas that have been relatively well populated since the earliest historical times—the Ganges Plain, and the coastal lowlands on either side of Peninsular India (see the maps inside the back cover). The density is much lower on the hilly uplands and plateaus of the Deccan, and among the Himalayan foothills.

Although 82 per cent of the people of India are rural, there are some large urban centers. The largest city is Calcutta, with a population in the census of 1961 of nearly 4,500,000 in the metropolitan area. Bombay, the second city had more than 4,400,000. India has no primate city, for these two cities are of almost equal size. Calcutta and Bombay still rival for primacy within the Indian state. Three other cities have more than a million inhabitants each —Madras, Hyderabad, and Ahmadabad— and Delhi, the capital, has only a little under a million. Nevertheless, the population of India remains predominantly rural, grouped

Harvesting millet by hand in one of the dry parts of India.

in small, isolated villages, connected with the urban world only by footpaths.

India stands among the very poor countries of the world; and its rural people are getting still poorer. This means that millions of people in this country are eating less, are living in poorer homes, and are less adequately supplied with clothing. With a gross national product per capita of only $72 in 1955, India stood eighty-fourth among the ninety-six countries for which data were available in that year. Yet the government of India, under the leadership of Jawaharlal Nehru, was making prodigious efforts to launch an effective attack on the problem of poverty. During the 1950's, when India's investment in new capital was about 7 per cent of the gross national product, the econ-

omy could be described as entering the initial phase of the Industrial Revolution. The question remains whether this country can increase its production, and the number of jobs, at a rate faster than the increase in population.

Agriculture. (Map 68) The agricultural sector of the economy is the one most difficult to push forward. Just about 70 per cent of the working force is employed in agriculture, and contains the most conservative elements of the population, the individuals least in contact with new ideas, and the ones least likely to accept new ideas. Since 1950 the production of food has not kept pace with the increase in the numbers of people to be fed.

The greater part of the food supply is provided by three grains: rice, wheat, and sorghum. Rice produces more food per acre than any other grain, but with Indian farming methods it can only be raised where there is an abundance of water, where the land slopes gently enough to permit the flow of water through the paddies, and where the soil is not so porous that the water is lost through seepage. These conditions are found in only a small part of India—on the Ganges Plain, and on the coastal lowlands on either side of Peninsular India—and in these places rice gets priority. On the extraordinarily productive lands of the Ganges-Brahmaputra delta it is possible to harvest two rice crops each year. Rice is replaced by wheat on the better lands where rice cannot be grown. The wheat area is in the upper part of the Ganges Valley, on the rich lava soils of the Deccan plateau, and around the margins of the Thar Desert. In the middle Ganges Valley there is a transitional area where rice is grown in summer and wheat in winter on the same land. Sorghum, the least productive of the grains, and yet the one that can be grown on the poorest soils, is found on the hillier and drier parts of the Deccan. The largest densities of population are associated with rice cultivation, and the lowest densities with sorghum.

Commercial crops are variously combined with the three grains. In the Ganges-Brahmaputra delta region jute and sugar cane are planted in rotation with rice. Cotton is the crop usually associated with wheat, especially on the regur soils of the lava plateau east of Bombay. Cotton and peanuts are associated with sorghum.

In addition to the major crop combinations, there are smaller areas of specialized commercial crops. Along the fringe of the coastal lowlands from the delta near Calcutta to the southern end of the Coromandel Coast, and on the Malabar Coast as far north as Goa, there is an almost continuous belt of coconut palms. On the southern part of the Malabar Coast, behind the fringe of coconuts, there are rubber plantations. On the higher parts of the Western Ghats, and on the very rainy slopes of the mountains north of the Ganges-Brahmaputra delta, there are tea plantations.

Generally speaking, Indian agriculture is characterized by low yields per acre. The average yield of rice per acre is only twenty-four bushels, compared with fifty bushels in China, and seventy-one bushels in Japan. The yields of wheat are also low—less than half those of the United States.

There are a number of reasons for this poor showing of Indian agriculture. Certainly one cause is the large area with a moisture deficiency and uncertain rainfall. Another factor is the widespread illiteracy of the farmers. It is also important that most of the wheat soils of India are so deeply leached that they are not naturally productive, and the yields of crops decline rapidly under heavy use. A century ago it

was possible for the farmers to shift their croplands from place to place so that each field could lie fallow for a period of years and regain some of its productive capacity. But the mounting pressure of population on the land base has gradually shortened the fallow period until widespread soil destruction has taken place. Furthermore, until recently, there has been no fertilizer easily available. The animal manure, which in other countries is used to maintain soil fertility, is not available as a fertilizer in India because it is used as fuel. Long ago the supplies of firewood were exhausted, and dried dung became the traditional fuel.

Animals occupy a very special place in Hindu agriculture. Because of the religious taboos against killing animals and eating meat or fish, the major use of animals has been for draft purposes, or for wool or leather. Yet India has the largest number of domestic animals of any country in the world—160,000,000 cattle, compared with about 100,000,000 in the United States. There are also vast numbers of goats, sheep, horses, donkeys, water buffalo, camels, and elephants. These animals consume an enormous amount of feed. Although the Indian farmers can spare little land for the growing of feed crops, large areas, that could be used for human food, are left as poor grazing lands. India's animals constitute a serious drain on the already overworked resource base.

Manufacturing Industries and Raw Materials. (Map 69) India's industrial growth since 1951 is a major accomplishment, when viewed against this background of an unchanging rural society, even if its success has yet to be demonstrated. Entry to the initial phase of the Industrial Revolution has required fundamental changes in the Indian culture. In the first place manual work has had to be made respectable. It has not been at all easy to get young Indians to study engineering, chemistry, or physics, or to learn the skills which would permit them to take jobs as welders or automotive mechanics. Furthermore, among the members of many castes there has been a deep-seated disdain for those who earned a living by trade. And besides making such a fundamental attack on inherited attitudes, it has been necessary to find a vast amount of new capital to invest in machinery, factories, railroads, highways, and power plants —all the complex equipment required for the modernization of an economy.

That India has been able to find the resources of skill and capital to start the Industrial Revolution is in part a legacy of the British colonial administration. When, in 1835, Lord Macauley started sending Indians to England to be educated, he began something that has proved to be critically important. India has found the leaders who have been able to combine the skills and ideals of the Occident with the ethical insights of Indian society.

The Indian habitat does provide many of the raw materials required for industrial growth. There is a vast store of high-grade iron ore. India stands second to the Soviet Union in the production of manganese, and it has large reserves of high-grade bauxite to support an aluminum industry. India leads the world in the production of mica, and is among the world leaders with monazite. However, there is a lack of such non-ferrous metals as tin, copper, lead, and zinc.

India is fairly well supplied with sources of power. There is enough coal for a considerable expansion of production, although almost all the good coking coal is concentrated in one area—along the valley of the Damodar River west of Calcutta (inset on Map 69). There are indications that small quantities of oil and gas may be developed

in the Brahmaputra Valley and north of Bombay. India also has a large hydroelectric power potential; and the work of harnessing the rivers has been started.

India's rapidly expanding iron and steel industry is located near the sources of good coking coal and iron ore. The Damodar Valley is rapidly becoming the "Ruhr of India." The great Tata steel industry at Jamshedpur is located midway between the iron ore and the coal supplies; another large plant is located at Asansol in the midst of the coal mines. A little downstream from Asansol a new integrated steel plant is being built at Durgapur. New steel centers are also being built with British, German, and Soviet backing at Rourkela, southwest of Jamshedpur, and at Bhilai, about 150 miles east of Nagpur. The increased supply of steel is being used to produce agricultural implements, hardware, locomotives, diesel engines, railroad cars, machine tools, telephone equipment, scientific equipment, and a variety of consumer goods. The economic core of the Indian state extends westward from Calcutta to the Damodar Valley within the hilly upland.

The Industrial Revolution made its start in India with the textile industry. In the mid 1950's, of all the investment in manufacturing industries about 44 per cent was in cotton and jute textile factories. The largest concentration of cotton textile factories is in Bombay, easily accessible to the major area of cotton production in the Deccan. The largest concentration of jute textile factories is in Calcutta, supplied in part by jute raised in the western part of the Ganges-Brahmaputra delta, and in part by imports from East Pakistan. Other textile factories, scattered in small towns all over India, make use of wool, rayon, and imported silk. Coir textiles (made from coconut fiber) are manufactured in the cities of the Malabar Coast.

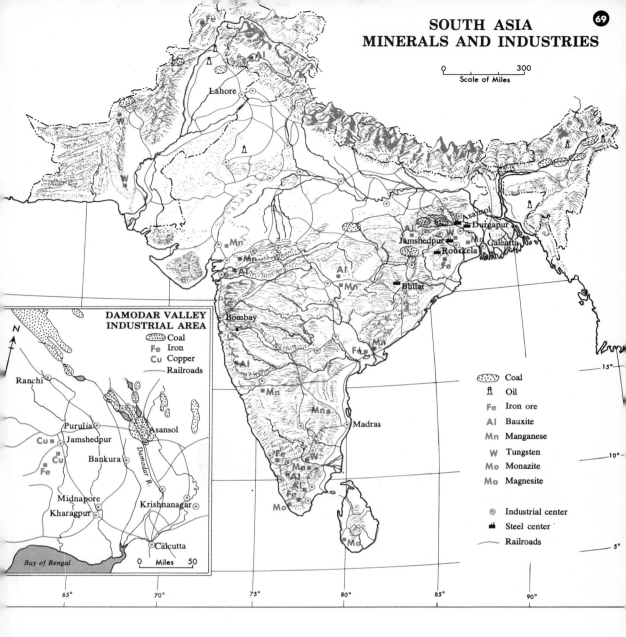

DAMODAR VALLEY
INDUSTRIAL AREA
Coal
Fe Iron
Cu Copper
Railroads

Coal
Oil
Fe Iron ore
Al Bauxite
Mn Manganese
W Tungsten
Mo Monazite
Ma Magnesite

Industrial center
Steel center
Railroads

The Program of Economic Development.
The people of India are discovering in larger and larger numbers that something can be done about hunger and poverty. As they make pilgrimages to distant shrines, and as they move into the great cities, they see that some people are enjoying a better standard of living. The government is responding to the mounting demand for economic development. The program to accelerate the Industrial Revolution, as formulated in 1961, has seven parts.

The first part of the program calls for an increase in the production of food. This cannot be accomplished in India by using the same methods that have brought such spectacular results in the United States. To increase the use of machinery poses serious problems in a country where the average farm family has less than two acres of land, and this often scattered in miniature fragments. The basic problem in India is to increase the area under cultivation, and to increase the yields per acre. An increase in the cultivated area involves the invasion by farmers of some of the land left aside for animals to graze on. It also involves the extension of irrigation. During the ten-year period from 1951 to 1961 there was a 36 per cent increase in irrigated land, and an even larger increase is planned for the next decade. The increase in yields per acre is to be gained through better education in farm practices, through soil conservation measures, through the increased use of fertilizers, and through an increase in the area on which two crops can be harvested each year. A new fertilizer plant in the Damodar Valley has already enormously increased the availability of cheap fertilizer. In 1951 only 55,000 tons of nitrogenous fertilizer were available; but by 1961 there were 360,000 tons.

The second part of the program of economic development involves the construction of high dams. The irrigation works built by the British, when India was a colony, were barrages which diverted the floodwater from the rivers into irrigation ditches; but these barrages did not store water in reservoirs. During the 1950's it was estimated that only about 6 per cent of the volume of water in India's rivers was being used. It is important to remember that throughout Peninsular India the rivers are in flood during the summer rainy season, but that many of them almost dry up during the dry season. High dams will store the water that has been running off in torrents during the rainy part of the year, and will permit the use of this water during the dry season, not only for irrigation but also for the generation of electric power.

The third part of the program is concerned with the construction of motor highways. There is a need for new trunk roads to tie the country together, but there is an even greater need for secondary roads to give access to the small, isolated villages. At present a village only ten miles from Calcutta would not be able to send its products to that market even if its farmers could produce a surplus over their own needs, because there is no road passable to wheeled vehicles. The construction of all-weather motor roads will be enormously expensive, and cannot be undertaken without large amounts of financial aid from foreign sources.

The fourth part of the program is land redistribution. Excessively large private properties are to be broken up, and fragmented holdings consolidated. Even so there is not nearly enough land to provide farms for all the peasants, and agricultural improvements must coincide with an increase in the number of non-agricultural jobs.

The fifth part is an attack on illiteracy. Instead of spreading the educational effort evenly over the whole country, the plan is to concentrate on groups of about seventy villages at a time, so that each group can be given schools and teachers in sufficient numbers to reach all the people.

The sixth part is an effort to increase the production of raw materials. There will be a drive to discover new mineral sources, and an effort to increase the efficiency of mines already in operation.

And the seventh part involves the investment of new capital, much of it from private sources, in manufacturing industries. Many new industries are needed to provide jobs for those who must leave the rural areas. And the efficiency of the workers in industries already established must be increased through better machinery, better training, and better management. The plan calls for an increase of 14 per cent in the gross national product per capita between 1961 and 1966.

The Viability of India. India, the world's largest non-communist country in terms of population, is in the midst of revolutionary change. It has yet to be demonstrated that economic development can be advanced rapidly enough to catch up with the massive, deepening poverty of the Indian people. And even more significant is the question of whether this can be done within the framework of a democratic society.

Can a modern, viable state be built out of such varied ingredients? There has already been a rearrangement of India's political subdivisions to give clearer political expression to the separate language groups. Can ties of religion be made strong enough to counteract the disintegrative effect of diversities of language? Hinduism does provide a basis for national integration, at least among Hindus. There are certain common traditions that override the diversities of language, such as the feeling of respect for Brahmans, for certain rituals in honor of the five chief deities, for the belief in reincarnation and the sacredness of cattle, for participation in religious festivals, and for pilgrimages to bathe in the water of the Ganges or to worship at mountain shrines. But these common Hindu experiences could not have served as a basis for the spread of democratic ideas if it had not been for the amazing leadership of Gandhi. As Barbara Ward reports: "he brought millions upon millions of simple, conservative, religious souls into a vast movement of mass politics without once using the slogans of hatred or pumping the bellows of angry exclusive nationalism. He combined the deepest inspiration of Hindu asceticism and renunciation with the most modern sense of human and national equality."[4] It was Gandhi who delivered the first effective blow against the caste system. The ideas so eloquently expressed by him constitute a strong integrating factor for his many followers.

The whole free world watches with deep concern for the outcome of the revolutionary changes now sweeping over India.

[4] Barbara Ward, 1961.

A crowded slum district on the outskirts of the modern capital city of New Delhi, India.

The Sukkur Barrage on the Indus River in Pakistan. Built between 1923 and 1932 it controls one of the largest irrigation systems in the world.

PAKISTAN

Even Gandhi could not prevent the separation of India and Pakistan in 1947. The partition has been described as an economic and political disaster; but the Muslims had feared that as a minority group within a Hindu state their needs would fail to get effective political expression. Since 1947 the two governments have been seeking ways to effect the necessary compromises if the economy of South Asia is to be rebuilt.

A major problem of political geography has been created by the separation of the national territory of Pakistan into West Pakistan and East Pakistan. East Pakistan, which has 55 per cent of the population, is located on the rich, eastern part of the Ganges-Brahmaputra delta, 920 miles across Indian territory from West Pakistan. West Pakistan is an area, largely deficient in moisture, which was originally settled by Muslims migrating from desert lands farther to the west. East Pakistan, by contrast, is one of the wettest parts of South Asia, and

the people who live there face entirely different kinds of problems. In many ways the people of East Pakistan resemble their Hindu neighbors, even in their use of a modified caste system of hereditary occupations. The people of West Pakistan eat wheat and mutton; those of East Pakistan eat rice and fish.

One of the most fundamental of the internal contrasts within Pakistan has to do with language (Map 65). Although in Pakistan as a whole about 86 per cent of the people are Muslim, they have no common language other than English. The official national tongue is Urdu, a language that makes use of many words of Persian and Arabic origin, but that is otherwise related to Hindi. Urdu is the literary language, especially in the part of West Pakistan that adjoins India where the plains of the Indus and the Ganges come together. As we have noted previously (p. 278), the language spoken in the western part of West Pakistan is the same as that spoken in eastern Afghanistan (Pushtu). Nevertheless, Urdu is tending to replace Pushtu and other local languages in West Pakistan. But it is making no headway at all in East Pakistan, where Bengali is almost universal. The people who use Bengali have a rich literature of their own—and their second language is apt to be either Hindi or English, but not Urdu. It is uncertain whether the ties of language or those of religion are the stronger —if the former, then it is even possible that the people of East Pakistan and those of the neighboring parts of India, where Bengali is also the language, may consider the creation of an independent Bengal state.

Compared with India, Pakistan is even more predominantly rural and is even poorer. Only 8 per cent of the people of Pakistan live in cities of 20,000 or over. The only city with a population of over a million is

Karachi, once the port for a large part of what is now northern India. The capital has temporarily been removed to Rawalpindi, while an entirely new capital city nearby—Islamabad—is being built. Lahore is the second city of Pakistan, and the capital of West Pakistan. Dacca is the largest city and the capital of East Pakistan. About 65 per cent of the Pakistanis are employed in agriculture, and the gross national product per capita is only $66.

Agriculture. (Map 68) The agriculture of the two parts of Pakistan is quite different. In East Pakistan, where there is a rural population of more than one thousand people per square mile, about 75 per cent of the cultivated area of the Ganges-Brahmaputra delta is used to grow paddy rice. This is the part of the delta that is annually enriched by mud brought by the floodwaters, and that has been used for intensive farming for a long time without the need of fertilizer. The parts of the delta that are deeply flooded at high water, and are therefore not suitable for rice, are used to grow jute, a fiber plant that became enormously important in the world when cheap containers were needed for bulk shipments of such things as coffee. Each farmer has two to four acres of land, usually scattered in miniature fragments. Rice is the basis of the food supply, and jute is the money crop. Formerly the jute from the eastern part of the delta was sent to the textile factories of Calcutta, and much of the crop is still exported to these factories. But Pakistan now wants to build its own jute textile factories. From this area the world still gets almost 80 per cent of its jute fabrics. Other crops include sugar cane, cotton, and tobacco.

West Pakistan grows wheat, millet, and cotton. Enough wheat is usually raised to provide a small surplus for export. But the chief export crop is cotton, which once had the same relationship to the cotton textile factories of Bombay that the jute in the east had to the jute textile factories of Calcutta. The irrigated areas also grow a variety of fruits.

Agriculture in West Pakistan is dependent on irrigation. The Indus itself rises far to the north among the Great Himalaya, and is joined by four large tributaries on the plain south of the mountains. In summer when the snow is melting in the mountains, and when the summer monsoon is bringing rain to the mountain slopes, these rivers are in flood. With the world's largest complex of barrages, canals, and other irrigation works, an area of about nine million acres is being irrigated; and further engineering works will add several more millions of acres. With plenty of water, and the intense summer sunshine, crops grow luxuriantly. Nevertheless, the farmers of Pakistan get only a slightly higher yield of wheat per acre than do the farmers of India.

Minerals and Industries. (Map 69) Pakistan is not well endowed with minerals, and it has few manufacturing industries. Large bodies of iron and chromite ores are known to exist in the mountains of the west, near the border of Afghanistan, and both coal and oil are found in the Indus Valley. Exploration for oil along the Indian border is being pushed. Recently gas has been discovered in East Pakistan.

At the time that Pakistan and India were separated in 1947, most of the industrial development was in India. India had 857 cotton textile factories, whereas Pakistan had only 15. To be sure, there were some industries in small towns near the base of the mountains within Pakistan territory—where manufactures included a variety of consumer goods. Plans have been drawn up calling for the investment of new capital in

The elephant, here being used in Ceylon, is an important work animal throughout parts of South and Southeast Asia.

manufacturing industries, but Pakistan will still remain predominantly agricultural for a long time.

Pakistan as a State. There are many problems to be solved before Pakistan can be formed into a strong and viable state. Some of these problems are domestic. Something must be done about the concentration around Karachi of many Muslims who moved to Pakistan after the partition, and for whom there are not nearly enough jobs in the city. In 1959 a land-reform program was started, which may bring yet more people to Karachi. Individual holdings in irrigated areas are to be restricted to five hundred acres, in non-irrigated areas to a thousand acres; and the large private properties, which will be broken up, are to be redistributed among the peasants. But there is not enough good farmland to accommodate the farm population, and jobs in non-farm occupations will have to be created.

Some of the problems of Pakistan involve dealings with neighbors beyond the borders.

Negotiations with India over the use of the Indus and its tributaries were started in 1952; and in 1960 a treaty was signed, which permits India to use the water of the eastern tributaries, and at the same time guarantees the free flow of water in the main stream and its western tributaries for use in Pakistan. The already large system of irrigation canals in the Indus Valley is to be enlarged much further, for the benefit of both India and Pakistan. A major political obstacle has now been removed, which will permit a direct attack on the engineering problems involved.

There are problems, also, where people speak the same language on both sides of the border. In the Northwest Frontier area people speak Pushtu, and identify themselves as Pukhtun (Pathan). The border between Pakistan and Afghanistan (the Durand Line) represents the farthest limit of British control, and bears no relation to the geographical contrasts of language and political loyalty. Some of these people have even talked of setting up a new state—Pukhtunistan—carved out from the territory of the two neighbors. Another area with a similar problem is in East Pakistan, where Bengali is the language.

The border dispute with India over Kashmir is one that still remains to be solved. Kashmir is the territory in the northwestern corner of South Asia where some of the world's highest mountains come together. In the midst of the towering ranges of snow-capped mountains is the Vale of Kashmir, a valley about eighty-five miles long and twenty miles wide, where the city of Srinagar is located. Kashmir is crossed from east to west by the upper Indus River. The dispute arose in 1947, when the Hindu ruler of Kashmir decided to join India, but the largely Muslim population rose in arms against this decision. In 1949 the United Nations arranged a truce and temporarily divided the territory along the cease-fire line. Pakistan administers the western and northern part of the country, and India administers the southern and eastern part. Both sides agree that the decision should be based on a plebiscite, but the method for administering the plebiscite has yet to be worked out.

To find a state-idea acceptable to all the parts of Pakistan, and strong enough to overcome the forces of disintegration, will not be easy. And to find solutions for the economic problems of a country abruptly cut off from its markets will also be difficult.

THE STATES
OF THE NORTHERN BORDER

In addition to Kashmir there are three small political units along the northern border of India, which form a transition between Hindu India and Buddhist Tibet. These are the independent Kingdom of Nepal; the Indian protectorate of Sikkim; and the semi-independent Kingdom of Bhutan (Map 66).

Nepal has the lowest per capita income of any country in the world ($40). Its population is a mixture of Caucasoid and Mongoloid elements in the south, and is largely Mongoloid in the high mountain country to the north. In the south the people practice a modified form of Hinduism: in the north they practice Lama Buddhism. There are three distinct agricultural zones in Nepal. On the plains south of the mountains and the lower foothills the crops are similar to those of neighboring India—rice, wheat, jute, tobacco, linseed, and mustard seed. Parts of these plains are swampy, and the land is still covered with uncleared jungle in which are found elephants, rhinoceroses, tigers, leopards, and wild boars. The second zone includes the lower and wider Himalayan valleys between 3,000 and 6,500 feet above sea level. The greatest concentration of both population and crops is in the Katmandu Valley, which comprises about 230 square miles of good farmland where rice is grown in summer, and where the same fields yield harvests of wheat, barley, potatoes, linseed, and vegetables in winter. The overgrazed pastures of the mountain slopes in this zone are used to feed cattle (which are used for work and milk, but not for meat), and buffalo, sheep, goats, and hogs (which are used for both milk and meat). Still higher, in the high valleys and basins between 7,000 and 14,000 feet, there are scattered areas growing wheat, barley, and potatoes, and pastures where the yak is the common animal (used for work, and for milk and fiber). This high part of Nepal, above which tower the world's most lofty peaks, is essentially Tibetan in culture.

Sikkim and Bhutan are even less developed economically. No motor road enters Bhutan at all; but the Sikkim capital can be reached by automobile, and a railroad reaches Darjeeling, in India, near the Sikkim border. Sikkim is under the protection of India, and is of strategic importance because through this little state passes the one caravan route over the high Himalayas to Lhasa in Tibet.

CEYLON

The island of Ceylon occupies a strategic position midway across the Indian Ocean. In ancient times Chinese and Arab merchants met here, and this was the first objective of the Portuguese navigators when they found a route around South Africa. Ceylon was a colony of different European powers from 1505 to 1948—first of Portugal, then of the Netherlands, and lastly of Great Britain. The population is a mixture of native inhabitants, who came originally from northern India, and Tamil-speaking invaders from southern India, together with Europeans and many others. Its population is 61 per cent Buddhist, 22 per cent Hindu, 9 per cent Muslim, and 7 per cent Christian.

The course of settlement was marked at one time by a notable shift of population. The earliest settlements were concentrated in the northeastern part of the island, where rainfall is light and where crops have to be irrigated. The much wetter southwestern side was originally covered with a dense rain forest and was not attractive to the first settlers (Map 8, pp. 16-17). However, when the Tamil invasion ruined the irrigation system, the northeastern area was largely abandoned. Today it offers a thinly-peopled frontier into which settlers may again spread using modern methods of irrigation. Meanwhile the much wetter southwestern part of Ceylon provides good land for the production of rice.

The long period of European control has resulted in a well-developed commercial agriculture. The first product to make Ceylon famous was cinnamon, which was formerly collected from the forests of the mountain zone, and which had attracted the attention of the Dutch. Now only about 26,000 acres of cinnamon plantations remain. Between 1835 and 1878 the British developed plantations of coffee, also in the mountain zone. The coffee grew very well and brought the colony considerable prosperity, until competition with Brazil caused a decline. For a brief period plantations of cinchona (for the production of quinine)

were tried, but they could not compete successfully with the cinchona plantations developed by the Dutch in Java. Starting in 1875 the British developed plantations of tea on the wet mountain slopes, and to this day Ceylon is the chief source of British tea. Rubber plantations were developed at the base of the mountains below 2,000 feet, and are still productive. The southwestern coastal zone is used intensively for food crops; and since it has two rainfall maxima each year—in May and October—can produce two rice harvests per year from the some paddies. There are also large acreages devoted to coconuts interspersed among the rice paddies. Even with this intensive rice production, however, and with a yield per acre well ahead of that of India, Ceylon has to import more than a third of its needs in rice.

The government of Ceylon, independent since 1948, is trying to increase the amount of food grown on the island. With assistance from Great Britain and other countries, new irrigation systems are being developed to make settlement possible again in the northeast. Manufacturing industries are being built in Colombo, and hydroelectric power stations are being put into operation in the mountains. Ceylon's population density is relatively low in relation to its agricultural potential; therefore programs for economic development seem to hold more hope of success than they do in the more densely crowded countries.

SUMMARY

The South Asian Culture Region was the main focus of British colonialism in the eighteenth, nineteenth, and twentieth centuries. In this respect South Asia differs notably from Southeast Asia and from East Asia. Over the diverse native cultures there was thrown a superstructure of British administration, which had the superficial effect of creating a kind of unity in South Asia as a whole. Actually, however, because economic development under British auspices was focused on a few places, and because large parts of India were outside the area of British colonial administration, the pre-British diversity of the region was only reinforced, and the contrasts from place to place were made more sharp.

The idea that the British had an over-all plan in their contacts with South Asia is quite misleading. They did not come to India to invade and conquer: they came to trade. For a long time the only contacts the British had with the Indians were through the three trading ports—Calcutta, Bombay, and Madras. Later, when step by step they assumed the responsibilities of administration and the maintenance of order, they did establish certain British institutions, such as the legal system, and the courts before which individuals were given equality of treatment. And the students who were sent to England to be educated became advance agents for the revolutionary new ideas being formulated in Western Europe.

The British did carry out a number of projects, some of which have proved beneficial to India, some harmful. They invested money in mines and commercial plantations, and they offered the Indians employment in these business undertakings. They built the most extensive network of railroads in Asia; and in the Indus Valley they built the world's largest irrigation system. They taught the Indians how to carry on the business of running a country—they established a Civil Service. They gave India a medical program, and, in the fields of hygiene and sanitation, actually tried to introduce changes in the Indian way of life.

One clear result—an unexpected one—has been the population explosion. A reduced infant mortality rate has meant more people to feed; yet the British had concerned themselves with commercial agriculture, not with the production of food crops, and some of the best lands had been used to grow products for export and not to grow rice. Furthermore, the British factories could produce consumer goods at a much lower cost than could the skilled Indian workers in the villages. British manufactured goods cut the market from under the skilled artisans of India, and left millions of them without employment.

The British started industrial development in India, but left it incomplete. The Indians themselves were not ready to advance into the new economic world: the poor people were illiterate and unskilled in the technology of factory production; the wealthy people were interested in luxurious living for themselves, not in postponing consumption for the sake of future gain. There were a few Indians who adopted these British attitudes, and did establish businesses—such as the Tata family which made investments in the steel industry. But there was not nearly enough domestic capital available to carry India on into the initial phase of the Industrial Revolution. The revolution in technology came to India, destroyed some aspects of the traditional economy, but led to no new growth.

The British also brought democratic ideas to India. And it has been through the teaching of Gandhi and his successors that the ideas of the Democratic Revolution, modified to fit the traditions of the Indian culture, have been spread. This is still one of the countries of the non-communist world, a country in which public policy can be publicly discussed, in which the government is responsible to the people, in which there is a government of laws rather than of men.

The results of British colonialism can also be observed, in somewhat different forms, in the other countries—in Pakistan and Ceylon, even in remote Nepal. The results are both good and bad, beneficial and harmful. But the existing reaction to the sweep of the two great revolutions over this culture region can only be understood as the aftermath of this unique form of colonialism.

8

THE
SOUTHEAST ASIAN
CULTURE REGION

Country	Political Status	Latest Estimate Population	Capital City
Brunei	British Colony	83,877 ('60)	Brunei
Burma	Federal Republic	21,700,000 ('62)	Rangoon
Cambodia	Constitutional Monarchy	5,200,000 ('62)	Phnom Penh
Indonesia	Republic	96,600,000 ('62)	Djakarta
Laos	Constitutional Monarchy	2,000,000 ('62)	Vientiane
Malaysia, Fed. of			
Malaya		7,400,000 ('62)	Kuala Lumpur
Sabah		500,000 ('62)	Jesselton
Sarawak		800,000 ('62)	Kuching
Philippines	Republic	29,600,000 ('62)	Quezon City
Portuguese Timor	Port. Overseas Province	502,000 ('60)	Dili
Singapore		1,700,000 ('62)	Singapore
Thailand	Constitutional Monarchy	28,000,000 ('62)	Krung-Thep
Vietnam:			
Republic of			
Vietnam (So.)	Republic	15,300,000 ('62)	Saigon
Democratic Rep.			
of Vietnam	People's Republic	16,600,000 ('62)	Hanoi

The Southeast Asian Culture Region lies between India and China. These two great giants of the Asian world have been indirectly in conflict with each other in this intermediate area for thousands of years. Each has brought to this region its own distinctive attitudes, objectives, and technical skills; and these have been variously superimposed on numerous native cultures. The result is a "shatter belt," a region of unexpected diversity. Even now, in the second half of the twentieth century, India and China offer to the people of Southeast Asia two contrasting reactions to the great revolutions that began in Europe.

The contrast in culture between India and China originated far back in human history. The traditional culture of India, as we have seen, has been characterized by a rigid caste system, by a strict adherence to form and ritual, by a notable inflexibility in

adjusting to local situations, and by a lack of agricultural skill as revealed in the low yields of basic crops. It is characteristically Indian that the treatment of animals prescribed by the Hindu religion should remain unchanged in spite of massive food shortages. In striking contrast, the traditional culture of China has been flexible, adjustable to local situations, and pragmatic in that results have been considered more important than the methods of achieving them. Moreover, Chinese agriculture represents a perfection in pre-industrial skills.

For thousands of years the products of Southeast Asia have been marketed in Europe. The early Phoenician traders brought items of great value back to Europe by way of India. Arab merchants also profited from this trade, acting as middlemen between these remote countries and the merchants of Venice. The Muslims combined commerce

◄ *Fishing junks in the harbor at Singapore.*

with a determination to spread their faith, and carried not only their trade but also the religion of Islam as far east as the Philippines. The Portuguese in the sixteenth century found a way to outflank the Arabs, and thereafter European ships came to Southeast Asia around southern Africa. In modern times rice, rubber, and tin have focused the eyes of the world on this region. Spices have been produced here since Neolithic times, although trade in them is not so profitable now as it once was.

Almost all of Southeast Asia became divided among the great colonial powers. The Portuguese came first in the early sixteenth century, and they are now the last to go. All the countries, except for Thailand, were administered as colonies of one or another outside state: Great Britain, France, the Netherlands, Spain, Portugal, or the United States. The differing colonial policies of these countries produced additional diversity in an already diverse area. During World War II, Southeast Asia was invaded and conquered by the Japanese, with two important results: hatred of the Japanese became violent; and the demand for an end to all forms of colonialism could no longer be resisted. Now a new kind of conquest threatens the newly independent countries —the establishment of communist dictatorships by outside force.

There are nine independent states in this culture region. They are Burma, Thailand, North Vietnam and South Vietnam, Cambodia, Laos, the Federation of Malaysia, Indonesia, and the Philippines. The last two colonial possessions in this region are Portuguese Timor and Brunei (Map 70). The Southeast Asian Culture Region comprises 3 per cent of the area of the world's inhabited lands, and is occupied by a little over 7 per cent of the world population.

THE HABITAT

(Maps 5, 6, 8, and 70) The geographic arrangement of the surface features and climates in Southeast Asia is complicated. Fingers of high mountains spread southeastward from Central Asia, their ends submerged as strings of islands. Between the fingers are lowlands across which great rivers drain the torrential monsoon rains to the sea. Between the islands and the mainland the ocean is relatively shallow—less than six hundred feet in depth—and during the glacial periods, when the sea level dropped several hundred feet because so much water had become locked on the land in the form of ice, the islands formed continuous, or nearly continuous, land bridges. It is an important fact that due to the arrangement of mountain chains, peninsulas, and islands, the shortest sea routes connecting the Orient and the Occident pass through the Strait of Malacca.

Surface Features. The rugged ranges that fan out from the eastern end of the Himalayas serve to divide Southeast Asia into compartments. These mountains are by no means so lofty as the Himalayas, but they constitute major barriers because of the dense cover of rain forest, and the very steep slopes. The westernmost of the ranges, which runs along the India-Burma boundary and along the eastern side of the Bay of Bengal, is continued southward as a string of islands—the Andaman and Nicobar Islands. This chain is continued farther by the islands off the southwest coast of Sumatra. Another range forms the border between Burma and Thailand; and still another runs through Laos and along the western border of Vietnam.

The mountains on the mainland of Southeast Asia are all the result of erosion by rivers on complex geologic structures, but

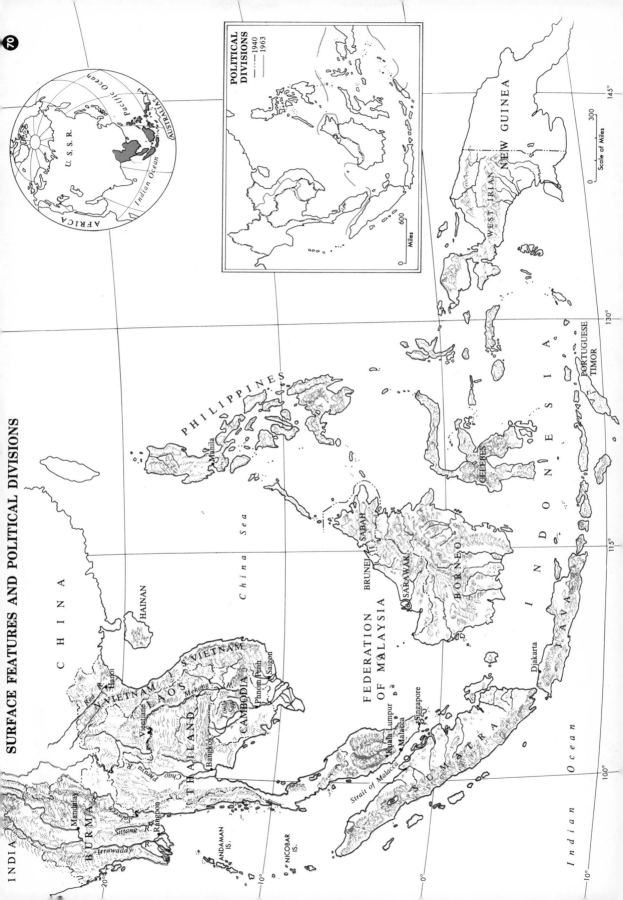

SURFACE FEATURES AND POLITICAL DIVISIONS

70

POLITICAL DIVISIONS
------- 1940
——— 1963

Scale of Miles
300

Miles
0   600

Pacific Ocean

U.S.S.R.

AFRICA

AUSTRALIA

Indian Ocean

INDIA

CHINA

BURMA

Mandalay

Irrawaddy R.

Sittang R.

Rangoon

ANDAMAN IS.

NICOBAR IS.

HAINAN

N. VIETNAM

Hanoi

Red R.

LAOS

Vientiane

S. VIETNAM

THAILAND

Chao Phraya R.

Bangkok

CAMBODIA

Mekong R.

Tonle

Phnom Penh

Saigon

China Sea

PHILIPPINES

Manila

FEDERATION OF MALAYSIA

Kuala Lumpur

Malacca

Strait of Malacca

Singapore

SUMATRA

BRUNEI

SABAH

SARAWAK

BORNEO

CELEBES

INDONESIA

Djakarta

JAVA

WEST IRIAN

NEW GUINEA

PORTUGUESE TIMOR

Indian Ocean

145°

130°

115°

100°

20°

10°

0°

10°

on the islands there are numerous active volcanoes, especially on Java and Sumatra. Java and the Central Area of Mexico are the two parts of the world with the most complete array of volcanic landforms: new volcanoes in the process of growth, massive ones that have long been active, old dead volcanoes in the process of being worn away by streams, and an amazing variety of cinder cones, lava flows, ash accumulations, hot springs, and related phenomena. Because of the deep accumulation of volcanic ash on Java and Sumatra, and because this ash is rich in the minerals that make good plant food, the soils of these islands have long been recognized as exceptionally productive.

Five great rivers fan out from the rugged mountains of inner Asia, and have built extensive alluvial lowlands and deltas along their lower courses. In the west the lowlands of Burma are drained by the Irrawaddy (and its tributary the Chindwin), and by the shorter Sittang that drains the lowland south of Mandalay—at one time occupied by the Irrawaddy. The huge, flat delta of the Irrawaddy, west of Rangoon, begins about 150 miles from the sea. Near the eastern border of Burma is the Salween River, which rises far inland in Tibet. In its upper course the Salween runs parallel to the upper Mekong and the upper Yangtze through enormous, steep-sided gorges in the midst of some of the world's most rugged terrain. Only near its mouth does the Salween Valley broaden out to form an alluvial lowland.

The great river of Thailand is the Chao Phraya.[1] This river rises in the northern part of the country, and flows southward across

[1] The Chao Phraya is sometimes called the Menam. In the Thai language Mae Nam means river: the Thais refer to their river as the Mae Nam Chao Phraya.

a broad alluvial plain to the head of the Gulf of Siam.

The next great river to the east of Thailand is the Mekong—one of Asia's longest rivers. It rises in Tibet and flows for about 2,800 miles through southern China, along the border of Thailand, Laos, and Vietnam, and through Cambodia and southern Vietnam across its vast delta to the China Sea. From June to November the Mekong is swollen with floodwater from the monsoons and from the melting snow of its headwater mountains. When this great volume of silt-laden water reaches the lower river it overflows its banks and covers large areas of floodplain. In Cambodia the river floods into the lake known as the Tonle Sap, which at this season is thirty to forty feet deep and covers an area of about 2,500 square miles. When the Mekong floods subside after November the river occupies only a part of its floodplain, and the Tonle Sap drains out through a tributary that joins the Mekong at the Cambodian capital of Phnom Penh. In the dry season the lake is from three to ten feet deep, and covers only about 1,000 square miles.

The easternmost of the great rivers in Southeast Asia is the Red River (or Song Koi) which rises in the mountains of southern China and flows eastward through deep gorges to the alluvial lowlands around Hanoi in North Vietnam. Like the other rivers of this region, the Red is enlarged by floods from June to October, and during the dry season is greatly reduced in volume.

Climate and Vegetation. The seasons in Southeast Asia are produced by differences in rainfall rather than by differences in temperature. The rains, as in South Asia, are heavy wherever moist, unstable air comes onshore or rises against the windward side of a range of mountains: they are light where stable air is moving offshore, or in the rain shadow of a range of mountains. The picture is complicated by the complex arrangement of the surface features and coast lines.

The whole of Southeast Asia is dominated by the monsoons. In winter, when the jet stream moves south of the Himalayas, the general surface air movement over Southeast Asia, north of the equator, is from the northeast (Map 6, pp. 12-13). Over the Philippines, and westward over Indochina, the northeast winds are an extension of the trade winds of the North Pacific, which at this season reinforce the northeast monsoon. South of the equator the air is moving from the northwest and west: this is the time of the "West Monsoon" in Java; and it is the time of the onshore summer monsoon in northern Australia. During the summer in the northern hemisphere, on the other hand, there is a vast flow of air from the southwest, out of the Indian Ocean, which crosses the western part of Sumatra, Malaya and Indochina, and continues on into China. This flow of unstable air also reaches the Philippines. But at the same time the offshore monsoon is moving out of northern Australia from the southeast and is covering eastern Sumatra, Java, Borneo, and New Guinea. In Java this is known as the "East Monsoon."

As a result the time of the rainy season, and the amount of average annual rainfall, differ from place to place. On the northeast-facing coast of Vietnam, for example, the rainy season is from September to·December when the northeast winds prevail, and the rest of the year is relatively dry. On the island of Java the rainy season on the northern and western sides comes during the West Monsoon from December to March; but on the southern and eastern sides the heaviest rains come during the period of the East Monsoon. An average annual rainfall of more than eighty inches is experienced throughout all the equatorial parts of Southeast Asia, except for the string of islands to the east of Java. Singapore, almost on the equator, has an annual average of ninety-five inches, and during the driest month receives more than six inches. Very heavy rain falls along the eastern side of the Bay of Bengal; but in the rain shadow of the mountains of western Burma, the middle Irrawaddy Lowland around Mandalay is quite dry (Rangoon, average annual rainfall ninety-nine inches; Mandalay, thirty-three inches).

This is a region of high average annual temperatures, but of no extremely high temperatures of the type experienced in northern India and Pakistan (Map 7, p. 14). The range of temperature between the average for the warmest and the average for the coolest month is only a few degrees. Near the equator the average annual temperatures are between 79° and 81°—which, combined with high humidity, create a climate in which European-style clothing is very uncomfortable.

The vegetation of Southeast Asia reflects not only the differences in climate but also the activities of man. Except on a few high mountains, there are never any frosts; and plant growth is interrupted only where there is a long dry season. Where the rainfall is very heavy, and there is no really dry period, the original vegetation used to be a luxuriant rain forest (compare Maps 6 and 8); but in the areas where there is a dry season lasting for several months the original cover used to be a seasonal forest (semideciduous). In the very dry places, such as central Burma and the islands east of Java, the vegetation used to be a scrub woodland.

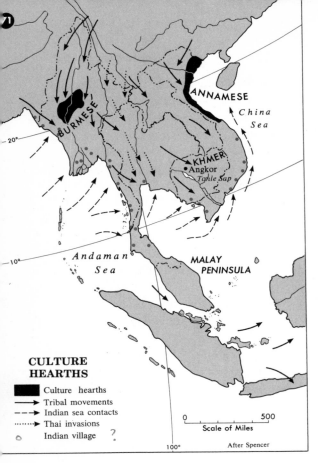

CULTURE HEARTHS

- ■ Culture hearths
- → Tribal movements
- – – → Indian sea contacts
- ········→ Thai invasions
- ○ Indian village

Scale of Miles
0   500

After Spencer

THE PROCESS OF SETTLEMENT

(Maps 1 and 71) Man has been active in Southeast Asia for a very long time. Anthropologists believe that the ancestors of *homo sapiens* first appeared in the tropical zone—extending from Southeast Asia to Central Africa—at a time when the climate was more nearly uniform throughout this area. Man was present in Southeast Asia during the glacial periods, when the now separate islands were more or less continuous land bridges. The most primitive people still present in this region are the Negritos, a dark-skinned, kinky-haired group among whom the adults grow to less than five feet in height. Negritos were probably present in India at an earlier period and were driven southward to the southern extremity of the peninsula by the Dravidians. They are still to be found in small, isolated groups in the Andaman Islands, Timor, and the interior of New Guinea.

The great cultural revolution that marked the advance from Paleolithic to Neolithic—from primitive hunting, fishing and collecting, to agriculture and animal husbandry—took place somewhere in the southern part of Asia. Many of the earliest crops and animals, as we have reported (p. 237), originated in Southwest Asia, either on the border between Iran and Mesopotamia, or in the Fertile Crescent. Many domestic animals were first domesticated in Central Asia. There is also some evidence that certain crops and animals first appeared in Southeast Asia. Sauer speculates that some of the earliest cultivation of crops may have been carried on by fishermen who wanted to grow a fiber crop from which to make nets.[2] The bark of the paper mulberry tree is still widely used to make clothing, as well as for the manufacture of rice paper by the Chinese. Early food crops in Southeast Asia were the taro root (an edible root grown in

[2] Carl O. Sauer, 1952.

In the mountain areas there is the usual vertical zonation, but only in a few places do the mountains rise high enough to reach above the tree line. These types of original vegetation have been much disturbed by human action. Where rice paddies have been developed the original cover of vegetation has been entirely removed. The practice of shifting agriculture, whereby the land is cleared, planted with crops for a few years, and then allowed to grow up again as forest, may have the effect of destroying the original vegetation and replacing it with quite a different type. If the periods of recuperation are too short—as they are apt to be where the population is too dense for this kind of agriculture—the soil is so seriously damaged that the original plant cover will not return. The large areas of savanna in Southeast Asia were probably once covered with seasonal forest.

swamps) and the yam (also a root crop). It is possible that rice was first grown as a grain crop on dry land somewhere in the mountainous country on the border between Burma and India; although some scholars locate the first domestication of rice farther west. It was developed as a wet-land crop, grown in paddies, somewhat later. Other crops that may have been domesticated for the first time in Southeast Asia include bananas, breadfruit, coconuts, ginger, and various spices. Certain domestic animals, too, may have been used by man for the first time in this region—pigs, chickens, ducks, and geese. All of these crops and animals were incorporated in the great cultures of the neighboring areas—India and China.

Into the intermediate area between India and China came migrating tribes who brought with them the more highly developed agricultural and animal technology from outside. The Caucasoids were the first to sweep along the land bridge through what is now Malaya, Sumatra, and Java, meeting and marrying with the Negritos, or pushing them farther out into the more remote areas. Later, the Mongoloids followed the same route, intermingling with the previous inhabitants to produce the present racial types of Indonesia. The Burmese people migrated from the north, perhaps as much as 2000 years before Christ, bringing with them their Tibeto-Chinese language. They became Buddhists as a result of contacts with the Indian culture hearth.

No large culture hearths developed in Southeast Asia comparable to those of India and China (Map 67, p. 281, and Map 75, p. 331). The Burmese culture developed its distinctive characteristics in the relative isolation of the dry zone of the middle Irrawaddy Valley, around Mándalay. The Annamese culture had its beginnings around Hanoi in the valley of the Red River, and spread southward along the coast of what is now Vietnam. The present state of Cambodia includes the core of the Khmer culture, which occupied the alluvial plain of the lower Mekong and the basin of the Tonle Sap. At the height of Khmer power, in the twelfth and thirteenth centuries A.D., the rule of Angkor was extended westward across the Chao Phraya Valley even as far as the borders of Burma.

The Thai people came into Southeast Asia more recently than any of the other so-called natives. They migrated out of southwestern China, driven on by the expansion of the Chinese, and they filtered into the parts of Southeast Asia not already densely populated. They avoided the Annamese communities along the coast, and the Burmese communities of the Irrawaddy Valley, but they found the valley of the Chao Phraya only thinly peopled by Khmers. In the thirteenth century they established the first Thai state in the northern part of the Chao Phraya lowland. They had only just completed their occupation of the whole lowland at the time of the arrival of the Europeans.

Meanwhile both Indians and Chinese had entered Southeast Asia. The Indians came first as traders. They sailed along the shores of the Bay of Bengal, and took advantage of the seasonal shift of the monsoons to make the voyages out and back again. At first they avoided the long voyage around the southern end of the Malay Peninsula by crossing it at the narrowest point, near the present southern border of Burma. On the Gulf of Siam they built new vessels and set sail along the coast of Indochina, going even as far north as the Island of Hainan. By the beginning of the Christian era they had established a large number of city states at the places shown on Map 71, each state a kind of principality ruled by an upper-caste Hindu, where Indian traits were superimposed on the local Khmer or Annamese cultures. The Chinese contacts at that time were largely confined to the Annamese culture hearth around Hanoi, and along the coast south of the Red River.

No one culture hearth can be identified from which the Malays spread outwards. There were dozens of small, more or less distinct Malay communities along the shores of Sumatra, Malaya, Java, and Borneo. The Malays became a seafaring people, who spread as far west as Madagascar, as far east as the islands of the Pacific, and as far north as southern Japan, through the Philippines and along the coast of China. Early in the Christian era Indian traders and missionaries established posts on the islands. From the seventh to the fourteenth centuries these far-flung Malay communities were loosely tied together around a Hindu administrative center in southern Sumatra; and during the next two centuries, after the administrative center had been moved to Java, almost the whole area that is now Indonesia came under one ruler. Starting in the thirteenth century the Arabs and the Indians introduced the religion of Islam, and by the sixteenth century, shortly before the arrival of the Europeans, the Malays had become almost solidly Muslim.

The conquest of Southeast Asia by the Europeans began with the arrival of the Portuguese in the sixteenth century. The Malay communities, scattered along the shores and only loosely tied together, were easily taken over by the Portuguese, starting with Malacca in 1511. But the Portuguese hold on this vast area was not strong enough to survive the pressure of the Dutch, the French, and the British. In Southeast Asia the only remaining Portuguese possession is the trading post on a part of the island of Timor (Map 70). In 1565 the Spaniards be-

gan to occupy the Philippine Islands, coming to them not by way of the Indian Ocean, but across the Pacific from the Mexican port of Acapulco. The other parts of Southeast Asia were similarly divided. The Netherlands established their hold on the Netherlands East Indies, administered from Batavia (now Djakarta). The British claimed the thinly peopled Malay Peninsula, and after 1824, established their great naval base and commercial port of Singapore. They also assumed control of Burma, and administered it as if it were a part of India. The French became involved in Indochina. Although the French included in their colonial possessions numerous Thai communities, in what is now Laos, they stopped at the Mekong River. By agreement between the French and the British, Thailand was left as an independent monarchy, between the British area of interest in Burma and French Indochina (inset on Map 70).

During the period of European colonial rule the immigration of both Indians and Chinese was encouraged. Under British protection Indians came into Burma, where they provided a large part of the labor force needed for the development of commercial rice plantations on the Irrawaddy delta. The Indians also came to Burma as retail merchants and bankers, and before long these "aliens" held a monopolistic control over the Burmese domestic economy. This alien control by Indians and British was deeply resented by the Burmese who felt that their distinctive culture had not been protected—especially in the period between 1886 and 1937 when Burma was administered as a part of India. The French also imported workers to develop commercial plantations of rice. The Mekong delta was included in the French colony of Cochin China, and the previously unoccupied swampy margins of the delta were cleared and converted into commercial rice plantations. The French established protectorates over Annam, Tonkin, Laos, and Cambodia. The Chinese immigrants who entered all the French-controlled areas of Indochina not only performed the hard work necessary to develop plantations and mines, but also gained control over the retail trade and banking. But the Chinese did not arouse such antagonism among the native peoples as did the Indians in Burma—due largely to the greater flexibility of their institutions which enabled them to adjust adroitly to the ways of life of the communities of which they became a part. Although Thailand remained independent, British interests developed commercial rice plantations along the lower Chao Phraya around Bangkok—which only became the capital in 1782—and rubber plantations and tin mines in southern Thailand. Chinese workers were employed in these operations also. At present Indians, the leading minority group, make up 7 per cent of the population of Burma. The Chinese form the leading minorities in all the other countries. And in Singapore they make up nearly three quarters of the population.

During World War II the Japanese invaded Southeast Asia. The only part of the region that the Japanese forces did not control was the more remote and inaccessible part of northern Burma. From northern Burma the famous Burma Road was built, to move essential supplies to the beleaguered Chinese, in Kunming, across some of the world's most rugged terrain. When the Japanese were forced out of Southeast Asia, the former European colonies insisted on their complete independence, and on an end to anything that resembled colonialism. The indignity of having their lives con-trolled by alien administrators, and of having their economies oriented toward those of other countries, produced a reaction of violent nationalism. Their hatred of foreigners embraces not only the former colonial powers but also—and especially—the Japanese. All the countries share these experiences and sentiments; yet each country has certain unique characteristics of its own which reflect a varied cultural background and the diverse conditions of the habitat.

BURMA

There are two ways in which Burma is unique among the countries of Southeast Asia. The first is the simplicity of its geographic arrangement. The core of the Burmese state is the Irrawaddy Lowland, which is surrounded on three sides by very rainy, densely forested, and deeply dissected mountains. Although about sixty different languages are spoken by tribes living in the mountainous areas of Burma, the people of Burmese origin are concentrated in the core area, where they speak a common Tibeto-Chinese language and are devout Buddhists. And the second is the fact that the Burmese national territory includes some potentially productive rice land not now occupied, which can provide for an increase in Burma's population during the foreseeable future.

Burma's more than 21,000,000 people are concentrated in the Irrawaddy Valley (Map 1, pp. 4-5). Only 10 per cent of them live in cities of more than 20,000, the two largest of which are Rangoon (more than 700,000) and Mandalay (over 200,000). There are two areas with more than two hundred people per square mile: one on the Irrawaddy delta; and the other in the dry zone around Mandalay. The lowland area as a whole, including the Sittang Valley and the lower

Salween Valley, has a population of more than fifty per square mile. The whole mountainous border country, and the Chindwin Valley, have less than fifty people per square mile. Compared with those of India or China, or even with those of the other Southeast Asian countries, these densities are relatively low.

Most of the people of Burma are subsistence farmers (Map 72). Although the gross national product per capita is one of the lowest in the world ($53 in 1955), the self-sufficient farm families have much more land on which to support themselves than do those of India. In Burma the average farm is about ten acres, and if more land is needed there is the Chindwin Valley which is still almost empty and undeveloped. In the dry zone the crops include rice, millet, sesame, peanuts, and cotton. In the thinly populated hilly and mountainous areas shifting cultivation is carried on in temporary forest clearings, where upland rice, maize, beans, tobacco, cotton, sesame, potatoes, and vegetables are often grown in the same field. Since there is plenty of land, the pressure of population on the resource base is less severe than it is across the mountains in India and Pakistan.

The development of Burma as one of the world's leading producers of surplus rice for export was carried out by British managers with Indian workers; and it was done almost entirely in the very wet, densely forested Irrawaddy delta. The Burmese had shunned the delta until the British directed the clearing operations and built the rice paddies. In spite of low yields per acre, Burma before World War II produced some three million tons of rice a year to be exported, chiefly to India. One result of the Japanese invasion was the collapse of the commercial rice plantations, in part because

hundreds of thousands of Indians fled from Burma. Rice production dropped to about one million tons. Since the country became independent commercial production has again increased, but not to its pre-war levels. Rice is now exported to Indonesia, Ceylon, Pakistan, India, and the Philippines.

Burma has long been known for its jade and its oil, but there are also numerous other resources that could be developed. For thousands of years Burma has been the world's chief source of jade (Map 72), much of which used to be sent to China. Oil from Burma was used to supply the lamps of India: as early as the ninth century A.D. oil wells had been drilled in the Irrawaddy Valley, and the oil was exported through Indian trading posts. Some increase in oil production is still possible, but Burma cannot be included among the world's major oil producers. Little-used mineral wealth includes sources of coal, iron, tin, tungsten, nickel, lead, zinc, and copper—some of which are almost essential for Indian industries. Before World War II, Burma was the world's leading producer of teak.

The Burmese government has a program for economic development, but the pressure to take immediate action to raise the standard of living is not so strong as in India. New manufacturing industries have been built in Rangoon, the city which handles almost all the foreign trade of the country. But it is significant that although Rangoon is more than three times larger than Mandalay, its population actually declined between 1953 and 1960, while that of Mandalay increased. This is a reflection of the desire among the Burmese to minimize foreign control, even over their economic life. The average Burmese prefers to live in Mandalay, or to have a farm in the relatively sunny dry zone. Efforts to provide

SOUTHEAST ASIA
AGRICULTURE, MINERALS AND INDUSTRIES

72

Irrigated rice
Rubber plantations
Teak forests
Mixed plantations
Shifting cultivation

Scale of Miles
0   400

Coal
Oil
Fe   Iron
Ni   Nickel
Mn   Manganese
Pb   Lead
Zn   Zinc
W   Tungsten
Cr   Chromium
Sn   Tin
Cu   Copper
       Railroads
       Oil pipelines

new farms for subsistence rice production in the delta area have met with little success. The delta, and the city of Rangoon, are densely populated as a result of foreign enterprise—British and Indian. The core of Burma remains in the dry zone up-river, and Rangoon is not as firmly established as the primate city as its relative size would indicate.

THAILAND[3]

Thailand is a more varied country than Burma. The core of the state is the highly productive valley of the Chao Phraya; but there are also major concentrations of people and production outside the core area. Furthermore, the boundaries of Thailand are not based on the spread of Thai settlement in this region, but rather on the limits reached by France and Great Britain in their extensions of colonial power. Because the boundaries bear little reference to ethnic distributions, except that with Burma in the west, they are subject to dispute and possibly revision.

Although Thailand was never the colony of a European power, the British invested both money and technical assistance in the development of resources. The commercial rice plantations of the Chao Phraya delta around Krung-Thep (Bangkok) were developed with British capital and Chinese coolie labor. When exports of rice from Burma decreased during World War II, the crowded rice-deficient countries of Asia had to depend almost entirely on the rice exports of Thailand. British capital also developed rubber plantations and tin mines in

[3] The name Thailand, which in the Thai language means "the land of the free," was officially adopted in 1939, to replace the name, Siam, the Khmer word for this area. In 1945 the name Siam was readopted, but in 1949 it became Thailand once again.

the Malay Peninsula, and built railroads which made possible the shipment of teak from the forests of the northern highlands (Maps 10 and 72). Rice, rubber, tin, and teak are Thailand's chief exports, and these products help to give the country a gross national product per capita that is about double that of Burma.

About 82 per cent of the workers in Thailand are employed in agriculture. The number of wage workers on the commercial plantations are only a small part of the total number of people who derive a living from the land. The great majority are subsistence farmers who cultivate their own small farms. And of all the cultivated area, about 90 per cent is used to grow rice. In Thailand, one of the places where rice was first domesticated, there are hundreds of varieties of rice, each variety especially adapted to a particular kind of habitat. Other crops include maize, sesame, peanuts, beans, coconuts, pepper, and a variety of vegetables. The Thai people are accustomed to eating poultry and pork; and in the Chao Phraya Lowland the network of small river channels provides them with a supply of fish. The rural people of the alluvial lowlands live quite well in comparison with other rural people in Southeast Asia; but those who live in the hilly uplands of eastern Thailand, where soils are poor and overworked, do not do so well.

The people of Thailand, like the Burmese, have a strongly developed sense of nationality, of a state-idea. Their tradition of independence extends back to the time when they migrated from what is now China rather than accept the status of vassals. The Thais are conscious of the threat to their independence that has appeared along their northeast border, and they know that their national territory lies astride the one land route from China to the richly productive rubber and tin lands of the Malay Peninsula.

VIETNAM, CAMBODIA, AND LAOS

Vietnam, Cambodia, and Laos are the three countries into which the former French Indochina was divided after World War II. This region is geographically complex, with a population of diverse origins and traditions, occupying a habitat that is marked off into more or less isolated compartments by the arrangement of the surface features. The populated areas are around the margins of Indochina: along the Annamese coast, with dense concentrations at either end in Tonkin and around Saigon; around the Tonle Sap; and along the valley of the Mekong River. In the center of this region is a very rainy, forested highland in which the population is scanty. When the French captured Saigon in 1859, this ancient Khmer settlement had been in Annamese hands for about two centuries. The French made Saigon the administrative center not only for Cochin China, but also for the protectorates to the north and the west.

The French undertook to develop a profitable commercial agriculture, as the British did in Burma and Thailand. They cleared and diked the Mekong delta, and made it into a surplus rice producing region that rivaled the "rice bowls" of Burma and Thailand—created in the same kind of habitat at about the same time. On the hills north and northeast of Saigon they developed plantations of rubber, tea, coffee, and cinchona; and they tried to relieve the population pressure in the crowded communities of the Annamese coast by opening up a new frontier of settlement in the highlands. They were not successful, chiefly for two reasons:

the first was the presence in the highlands of a malarial mosquito that breeds in turbulent mountain streams; and the second was the unwillingness of the Annamese people to leave the familiar coastal habitat.

The population distribution of the countries of Indochina is very irregular. About three quarters of all the people in the former French colony and protectorates were in the part that has now become Vietnam. The chief concentrations now are in the north, around Hanoi, where the rural density is one of the highest in the world, and where land properties have been subdivided again and again into miniature fields; and in the south around Saigon, where commercial rice planting is associated with larger land properties. A string of densely populated communities runs along the coast of Annam, each community separated from its neighbors by rugged spurs of the highlands which come down into the sea. Another dense cluster of population is in Cambodia, around the Tonle Sap and the Cambodian capital, Phnom Penh. Population clusters are found along the Mekong Valley, even beyond Vientiane, the Laos capital.

The basic crop of Indochina is rice. Except in the Mekong delta where rice is grown for sale, the rice farmers only produce food for their own subsistence. Because of the complexities of the rainy seasons, and because double cropping is possible in some especially favored spots, rice is harvested in different parts of the area in every month of the year. A variety of supplementary crops includes maize, sugar cane, beans, pepper, sesame, taro, betel nuts, and vegetables. There is not much room in the crowded areas for domestic animals, but the Annamese and Khmers regularly supplement their diet with fish. The Tonle

Sap has been described as the world's largest fish pond. And during the dry season especially, when its volume is decreased, fish are taken from it in abundance.

Much of the very considerable endowment of minerals in Indochina is located in North Vietnam, on the margins of the Tonkin Lowland. Here there are mines of anthracite coal, and in the vicinity are sources of tin, lead, zinc, tungsten, manganese and chromium.

Vietnam and Laos have been the first countries of Southeast Asia to experience actual armed attack by communist forces. After the withdrawal of the Japanese, at the end of World War II, the returning French troops soon found themselves involved in guerrilla warfare. In Vietnam the Communist Party joined with natives of the country, many of them non-communists, who were demanding immediate independence from France. The French garrisons in remote mountain posts were, one by one, forced to surrender. When, in 1954, the success of the communists in the whole of northern Vietnam was certain, both sides agreed on an armistice. An arbitrary line was drawn across Vietnam at latitude 17°N. The French withdrew from the north, and the communists took over, forming the Democratic Republic of Vietnam. To the south of this line the Republic of Vietnam was granted independence by France.

The attack on Laos came later. Between 1960 and 1963 communist armed forces entered Laos from North Vietnam and started a war that had no fixed fronts, no battle lines—only skirmishes in forested country—which looked very confusing when plotted on a map. Laos is not a nation. It has no tradition of unity, no experience with independent government. Rather it is made up of Thais and others, living in isolated small communities, practicing shifting agriculture

in a densely forested, hilly upland where only footpaths connect with the outer world. The conquest of Laos brought nothing but trouble for the French, and will do no more for the communists. But it does extend communist-held territory to the Mekong River— and the Mekong is an open road southward into South Vietnam and Cambodia. Moreover, across the river is Thailand and a route to Malaya.

THE FEDERATION OF MALAYSIA

Malaya differs from the other parts of Southeast Asia in that it is largely a creation of British enterprise, in an area that was formerly almost unoccupied except along the coast facing the Strait of Malacca. Malacca, itself, was a Malay community before it was captured by the Portuguese in 1511; and there were other similar communities on this part of the Malay Peninsula. The east coast, exposed to the full sweep of the monsoons and washed by a heavy surf, was not attractive to the Malay sailors. When the British empire builder, Sir Thomas Stamford Raffles, founded Singapore on an uninhabited island in 1819, he was the first to recognize the major strategic significance of this place. Singapore became the pivot of the whole British commercial grasp over the Asian World.

Malaya was created chiefly for the purpose of producing tin and natural rubber. Both of these products became important because of technological innovations associated with the Industrial Revolution in Europe and Anglo-America. There was no substitute for tin in the manufacture of automobile bearings and solder, nor in the making of "tin" cans. Rubber, after 1909, became enormously important in the manufacture of tires. Both tin and rubber are highly speculative products because, at any moment, an inventor in a distant part of the world may find a better way to make bearings, or a way to replace natural rubber entirely with a synthetic product. But until these things happen, tin and rubber will provide the basis for the commercial economy of Malaya.

In order to produce tin and rubber workers had to be imported. The Malays have never been willing, in any large numbers, to undertake work for wages, but have preferred to remain in their village communities growing rice and catching fish. Because of this the British brought in Chinese coolies to wash the stream gravels for tin. When any of these workers managed to save enough money they would cease to work as laborers and become, .instead, retail merchants and bankers. Some made substantial fortunes, and the domestic economy of Malaya is still very largely in their hands. Today large-scale tin mining operations with giant dredges owned by Europeans account

for about 60 per cent of total production; but Chinese-owned operations, using a hydraulic process, account for the remainder. Furthermore, a Chinese merchant was the first to invest in the development of a rubber plantation (near Malacca, in 1895)—at a time when the modern use of rubber had not been conceived. The British and the Chinese own most of the plantations today, while most of the rubber workers are Indians (Tamils from South India) brought in under contract. Malaya produces about 38 per cent of the world's tin, and 34 per cent of the world's natural rubber—both limited by international quota arrangements.

As a result of the immigration of people from China and India, these two minority groups, added together, almost equal the number of native Malays. At the time that Malaya was granted independence as a federation of eleven Malay states in 1957, the Malays made up 50 per cent of the total population, the Chinese 37 per cent, and

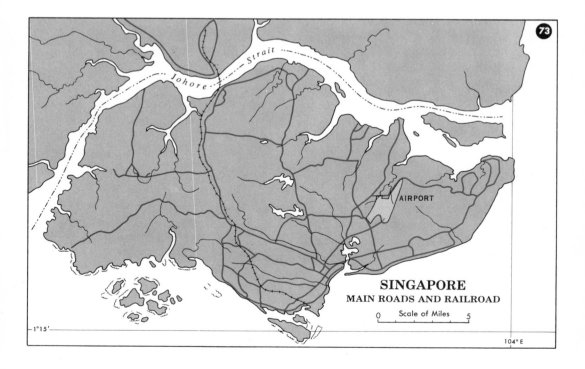

SINGAPORE
MAIN ROADS AND RAILROAD

Scale of Miles
0   5

A village on Java, Indonesia. Bananas and fruit trees are planted around the houses, and the pond is stocked with fish.

the Indians 11 per cent—the remaining 2 per cent consisted of Indonesians and Europeans. The government was in the hands of the Muslim Malays, but the economy was largely controlled by the Chinese and the British. The country was dependent on imports for almost half of its food supply—chiefly imports from Thailand. And there were two major questions for the future to answer: one related to the uncertainty of continued markets for tin and rubber; the other to the probable political attitude of the Chinese.

When Malaya became independent in 1957 Singapore was not included, and the capital of Malaya was placed at Kuala Lumpur. The reason for separating Singapore from Malaya was that the Malays formed only 13 per cent, while the Chinese formed 73 per cent, and the Indians 8 per cent of the population in the city. The political leaders of Malaya were afraid to include

Singapore because this would have given the Chinese a majority. Singapore was granted self-government. But the economic function that fostered the growth of Singapore, into a city of well over a million inhabitants on its little island (Map 73), had been that of commerce. At large part of the business of southern and eastern Asia with Europe was transacted in Singapore; and through Singapore's modern docks passed vast quantities of goods representing the products of many parts of the world. Singapore played this role because the British had become the world's bankers and traders. And its future as a major commercial city would seem to be tied to the future of Great Britain.

In 1963 the political problems and fears of Malaya were surmounted and the Federation of Malaysia was established; but in 1965 Singapore again separated from the Federation, which now includes Malaya and

Terraced rice paddies on Bali. Efforts to use land effectively have transformed the original vegetation and landforms.

two of the British colonies on Borneo: Sabah (North Borneo), and Sarawak (Map 70). The chief purpose of the Federation is to establish a strong democratic state across the line of communist advance toward Indonesia.

The remaining British colony on Borneo—Brunei—chose to remain outside the Federation. Newly discovered oil fields in Brunei make this little area second only to Canada among the oil-producing states of the Commonwealth. Brunei now rivals Kuwait in terms of per capita income.

INDONESIA

The Republic of Indonesia gained its independence from the Netherlands in 1950, after a century and a half of Dutch colonial rule. Since the Dutch, unlike the British, had never trained the Indonesians to be public administrators, the new government faced serious problems in the development of a viable state once independence had

been achieved. The Dutch developed a highly profitable commercial agriculture in the Netherlands East Indies; but this had the effect, as in Malaya, of making the people dependent on imported foods. Chinese workers were brought in, even into densely populated Java. When modern medicine and health measures were introduced, the result was a population explosion. In 1815 the population of Java was about 4,500,000: by 1960 it had reached 60,000,000, producing an over-all density of more than 1,200 people per square mile.

The population is very unevenly spread over the islands of Indonesia (Map 1, pp. 4-5). The very dense population of Java is not able to feed itself. On the other hand Sumatra, which comprises 32 per cent of the area of the national territory, is occupied by only 16 per cent of the total population; and, moreover, this one island produces 70 per cent of the value of all Indonesian exports.

The Indonesian part of Borneo is only effectively occupied by Indonesians along the coasts and at the oil fields; a large part of it is occupied by scattered tribes of migratory farmers. Before World War II the Dutch administrators made serious efforts to develop plantations on the other islands, and to attract workers away from Java. But the Javanese resisted every effort to make them leave their familiar communities. Since independence the new government has continued its efforts to open up new pioneer zones in Sumatra and Borneo, but without success.

The concentration of population on Java is not a new phenomenon. The maps inside the back cover show that even in 1800, shortly after the Dutch established colonial rule at Batavia (now Djakarta), Java was more densely populated than the other islands. To be sure, Java has fine, productive volcanic-ash soils, but so also does Sumatra. It is significant though that the coasts of Java are not bordered by such extensive swamps as are those of either Sumatra or Borneo, and so were more accessible in the past to the Malay navigators. The Dutch made use of Javanese workers to develop plantations of commercial crops which, for a time, were enormously profitable.

The Dutch plantations produced a variety of products. Before World War II Java was second only to Cuba in its production of sugar—mostly grown on the fine soils of the northern coastal plain. In the mountains were plantations of coffee, tea, cinchona, and teak. The largest area was taken up with rice paddies, which were even extended on terraces up the steep mountain sides. The rubber plantations on Sumatra before the war produced more than those in Malaya. The Dutch also developed certain mineral resources, such as tin on Bangka and Beli-

tung; and they developed oil fields on Sumatra, Java, and Borneo.

Since 1950 the new government has greatly decreased the area devoted to plantations of commercial crops, and has tried to increase the acreage of food crops for domestic use. Java is no longer a major sugar producer, and much of the land once used to grow cane is now used for rice paddies (Map 72). Two harvests of rice are taken each year from this productive land. Other food crops grown in combination with the rice include maize, manioc, soybeans, peanuts, and sweet potatoes. On the poorer soils, such as those of Madura, maize is more important than rice. The rubber plantations on Sumatra are still being operated, and so are those in the mountains of Java. But there are large areas, elsewhere than Java, where a small population still practices a shifting cultivation in temporary forest clearings, growing upland rice, taro, yams, sweet potatoes, maize, bananas, sago, and manioc.

Indonesia has found no new mineral sources since it gained independence. But the tin mines are still productive, and the country produces about half as much tin as Malaya. The oil fields have been somewhat expanded.

Independent Indonesia faces many difficult problems, and its people have been poorly prepared to assume the responsibilities of self government. In addition to the technical problems of increasing agricultural productivity, and of providing jobs for a rapidly expanding population, there is the political problem of integrating in one state people who speak many different languages, and whose tradition has been that of community independence rather than national unity. There is no state-idea to bring the diverse groups together—other than the negative one of securing independence from the Netherlands. But a positive state-idea is needed if the many islands, spread over a 3,000 mile arc, are to be united effectively under one government.

THE PHILIPPINES

There are 7,083 islands and islets included in the Philippines, which add up to an area a little greater than that of California. Two thirds of this area, however, is taken up by the islands of Mindanao and Luzon (Map 70). The population of about 29,600,000 is concentrated in three places: on the lowland extending from Lingayen Gulf to Manila on Luzon; on the southeastern peninsula of Luzon; and on the group of four smaller islands in the center of the archipelago. Elsewhere the islands are thinly populated.

The Philippines were for centuries a neglected colony of Spain, the most remote of the Spanish possessions. The islands became a possession of the United States in 1898, at which time programs were started to reduce illiteracy and ill-health, to increase the production of both subsistence and commercial crops, to provide transportation facilities, and in many other ways to prepare the people for independence. In 1934 the United States promised to grant independence after a twenty year period, but plans were upset by the Japanese conquest in World War II. After the islands had been liberated independence was granted on July 4, 1946, and special access to the markets of the United States was provided until 1974.

The economy of the Philippines was changed radically during the period of American administration. Rice and other food crops are still produced, and rice takes up 40 per cent of the agricultural land; but the islands are no longer self-sufficient in

A volcano erupting in the Philippines. There are many volcanic forms on the islands of Southeast Asia, and particularly on Java and Sumatra.

terms of food. On Negros large sugar cane plantations were developed in the past, and before World War II sugar was a major export. Since the war coconut products have been competing with sugar for first place. Coconuts provide whole nuts, copra, coconut oil, husks (for making charcoal to use in gas masks), and tuba (a fermented juice made from the tip of the growing palm). Abacá, the source of Manila hemp, was once grown almost exclusively in the Philippines, but is now grown also in the American tropics. Tobacco used to be important when Manila cigars were widely used. There has been some small-scale development of copper, iron, and chromium mining, but gold is the only mineral which is of major importance among the exports.

Manufacturing industries give employment to a considerable number of Filipinos, especially in and around Manila. During the period of American administration the old handicraft products were largely replaced by manufactured articles, some imported, some made locally. As elsewhere in Southeast Asia, the Chinese retail merchants have profited from the sale of factory-made goods —from the replacement of betel nuts with chewing gum, of palm liquor with beer. Magazines, comic books, radio, and television "sell" the American way of life in a country where most of the people cannot afford it. The Filipinos would like to live the way they see people living in the movies; but there are too many lawyers, and too few artisans and mechanics, to support such a standard of living.

The Filipinos are struggling with the problems of building an integrated state in the face of numerous handicaps. In spite of the considerable attention given to the training of public administrators, the people of the Philippines were scarcely prepared to assume the duties of responsible citizenship. The $218 of gross national product per capita, which is second only to that of Malaya in Southeast Asia, is channeled too exclusively into the hands of an already wealthy and politically powerful minority. However, dishonesty and inefficiency in the government are gradually being reduced. There is the additional problem of trying to build an integrated state out of the widely separated populations of the small islands. In the Philippines, where the contacts with America have created a wave of rising expectations for a better standard of living, a government that hopes to survive must work energetically to increase the tempo of economic development.

SUMMARY

The Southeast Asian Culture Region is receiving its own versions of the Industrial and the Democratic Revolutions. There are still many people in this area who are ignorant of the greater material comforts that the modern world affords. These people are the illiterates, the subsistence farmers who live in isolated rural communities, the people who are in the contemporary world and yet not a part of it. Contact with the European colonists did not lead to the widespread economic betterment of the people, because even where new opportunities for employment were created, wages were not high, and the European health measures resulted in the creation of many more mouths to feed. The individual native was poorer than before because there was less to eat and there were more people to crowd into each house—this being especially true in densely populated Java. Some Europeans talked about democracy and the dignity of the individual, but they did not apply these ideals in dealing with the inhabitants of their colonies. The Europeans lived apart, in luxurious homes, with ample food, with all kinds of comforts and distractions that were quite alien to the region. The Europeans established commercial plantations and mines, to provide goods for sale in Europe that could be produced nowhere else; but the people of Southeast Asia did not share widely in the economic rewards. This form of exploitation was the standard, and almost unchallenged, procedure of the nineteenth century. Exploitation, combined with the practice of white superiority—so eloquently described and justified in the writings of Rudyard Kipling—gave rise to a deep-seated, burning hatred of the colonial powers.

Several things had the effect of bringing this hatred of colonialism to the surface. One was education, and the decrease in illiteracy. Each year more and more people could read about the outside world, and each year the number grew of young people who had received a higher education in Europe or America. The efforts of the British and Americans to train Asians for administrative posts led the Asians to grasp for power now, not ten years from now. Certainly the systems of mass communication in the modern world—radio, television, newspapers and comics, and especially movies—gave larger and larger numbers of people a new view of how life might be. All over the world this led to the "revolution of rising expectations," as Adlai Stevenson termed it. Finally, the defeat of the colonial armies by the Japanese showed that the Europeans were not invincible. After World War II the demand for independence and equality of national status among nations could no longer be resisted.

When independence did not bring the expected results, the newly awakened people began to look for quicker solutions. Since the Europeans have gone the dislike of aliens has begun to shift to the Indians, especially those who are established as traders. The more adjustable Chinese are tolerated. Behind the Chinese, however, are the communists of China, who would like nothing better than to stir up dissent and conflict because, in their view, this hastens the inevitable triumph of their own way of life. In this complex situation, with its many unknown factors, the Southeast Asian Culture Region stands poised, as it has been for a long time, between India and China.

9

THE
EAST ASIAN
CULTURE REGION

Country	Political Status	Latest Estimate Population	Capital City
China:			
People's Republic of China	People's Republic	716,500,000 ('62)	Peking
Republic of China	Republic	11,400,000 ('62)	Taipei
Hong Kong	Colony & Lease of U.K.	3,300,000 ('62)	
Japan	Constitutional Monarchy	94,900,000 ('62)	Tōkyō
Korea:			
North Korea	People's Republic	8,300,000 ('62)	Pyŏngyang
South Korea	Republic	26,100,000 ('62)	Seoul
Macao	Port. Overseas Province	220,000 ('60)	Macao
Mongolian People's Republic	People's Republic	1,000,000 ('62)	Ulan Bator
Ryūkyū Islands	U.S. Military Possession	883,052 ('60)	

The waves of conflict set in motion by the Industrial Revolution reach a special intensity in the East Asian Culture Region. Here the ancient and distinctive culture of China, evolved over thousands of years of continuous development, is now in the throes of violent change. European contacts with China during the nineteenth and early twentieth centuries introduced revolutionary ideas to this ancient society. But it was the events of World War II and the years immediately thereafter that set the stage for the seizure of power by the Communist Party in 1949. Today more than a quarter of all the people in the world are involved directly in the convulsions of a China in the process of change.

Even under the communists, Chinese attitudes, objectives, and skills remain distinctively different from those of any other culture. The basic attitudes were derived from the teachings of such philosopher-scholars as Confucius, who lived six centuries before Christ. These founders of the Chinese way of life did not preach democracy—in fact there are few parts of the world where democratic ideas are more alien. Even within the family there is no democracy: there is complete subservience to the authority of the oldest man; younger sons do not expect to be treated as equals of the eldest son, nor do girls receive the same status as boys. There are quite different codes of conduct for dealing with people outside the family and with those within the family. Over the centuries the Chinese have perfected the art of dealing with strangers. Chinese diplomats are noted for their skill in getting what they want from conquerors and more powerful neighbors, and Chinese merchants have long been recognized as masters of devious business transactions. The Chinese are a pragmatic people for whom results are more important than the means of achieving them.

An important, distinctive feature of the Chinese culture is the style of writing. Instead of using an alphabet to build words, the Chinese use characters to stand for words and combinations of words. There are several quite different languages, as defined by word sounds, which use the same written

◄ Terraced farming in Japan.

characters. Many of the characters used in the Japanese language are derived from the Chinese.

An outstanding element of Chinese culture is the agricultural skill. Within the Chinese culture hearth farmers learned to practice a labor-intensive form of agriculture requiring a vast expenditure of muscle-power. As the population increased and the individual farmer was driven to provide more and more food, he reacted with a further intensification of effort on smaller and smaller plots of land. Only on certain kinds of soils that could be improved by hand methods could the farmer produce enough for himself and his family. Therefore, the mounting pressure of population on the land base has resulted in a greater and greater concentration on the river floodplains. Chinese farmers, using organic fertilizers, were able to secure higher yields per acre than farmers in any other culture area; but in modern times Japanese farmers, using chemical fertilizers and insecticides, and working with small power machinery, now hold the world record for crop yields per acre. Yet, because of the Chinese agricultural methods, large areas of the East Asian Culture Region remain uninhabitable.

The Chinese have a long record of expansion and political conquest, even in areas not suited to their kind of farming. They spread southward into the Yangtze Valley, from their original culture hearth along the Wei Ho and the Hwang Ho,[1] pushing the Thai peoples out of their ancestral habitat in the Szechwan Basin. The Chinese pushed on farther southward, occupying the coastal fringe and the river floodplains as far as Canton and Tonkin. They exacted tribute from the peoples of Southeast Asia, and

---

[1] In the language of North China the word *ho* means river. Hwang Ho means Yellow River. In the language of South China *kiang* means river.

many Chinese businessmen migrated into this region. They also spread northward into Manchuria; and through Korea the Chinese way of life was taken to Japan. Their political control extended westward into Mongolia, Sinkiang, and Tibet.

The chief area of concentrated Chinese settlement along the Hwang Ho was invaded repeatedly, and suffered infiltration by outsiders. For thousands of years the Chinese were the world's most civilized and prosperous people, and the ease and luxury of the Chinese civilization invited conquest. The nomadic peoples of inner Asia swept repeatedly into China—even after the Great Wall had been built in the third century before Christ. Sometimes invasion was in the form of migration, sometimes in the form of military conquest; but the Chinese always managed to assimilate the invaders.

The nature of the traditional Chinese culture left China open and vulnerable to the countries that had been transformed by the Industrial Revolution. During the nineteenth century Chinese territory was neatly set off into spheres of interest claimed by the French, the British, the Germans, and the Russians. The United States insisted on an "open door" policy, which permitted American traders and missionaries access to all parts of China. Finally the Japanese, adopting European notions of imperialist expansion, moved onto the mainland through Korea, seized Manchuria, and then, during World War II, extended control over most of eastern China. China's struggle to throw off foreign control started in 1911 but came to an end with the Japanese conquest.

After World War II, China was in chaos. The Japanese had driven millions of farmers away from their farms, and broken the traditional close ties of the individual with his land. With an increasing population, and a state of economic collapse, vast num-

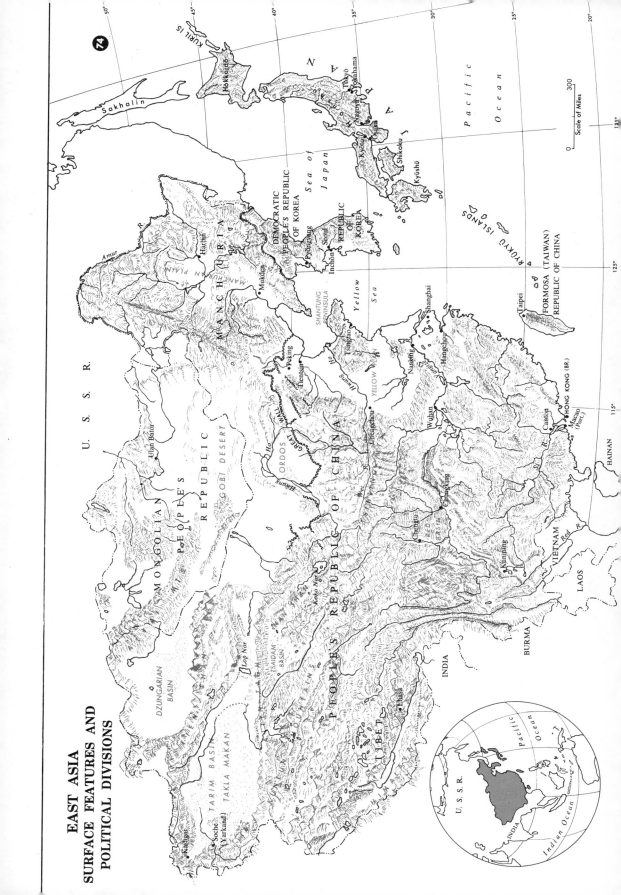

**EAST ASIA
SURFACE FEATURES AND
POLITICAL DIVISIONS**

74

KURIL IS.

Sakhalin

Hokkaido

J A P A N

Tokyo
Yokohama
Nagoya

Kyoto

Shikoku

Kyūshū

Pacific

Ocean

Scale of Miles
0   300

Sea of

Japan

RYUKYU ISLANDS

Taipei

FORMOSA (TAIWAN)
REPUBLIC OF CHINA

Amur

MANCHURIA

Harbin

Mukden

DEMOCRATIC
PEOPLE'S REPUBLIC
OF KOREA

Pyongyang

Seoul
Inchon

REPUBLIC
OF
KOREA

SHANTUNG
PENINSULA

Yellow

Sea

Tsingtao

Shanghai

Hangchow

Nanking

YELLOW R.

U. S. S. R.

Ulan Bator

M O N G O L I A N   P E O P L E ' S   R E P U B L I C

GOBI DESERT

ORDOS

GREAT WALL

Hwang

Peking

Tientsin

Ho

Shihkiachwang

Wuhan

Canton

HONG KONG (BR.)
Macao (Port.)

HAINAN

DZUNGARIAN
BASIN

TARIM   BASIN

TAKLA MAKAN

Lop Nor

TSAIDAM
BASIN

Kashgar
Soche
(Yarkand)

T I B E T

Lhasa

Chengtu

Chungking

Kunming

P E O P L E ' S   R E P U B L I C   O F   C H I N A

BURMA

INDIA

LAOS

VIETNAM

Red R.

Si R.

Wei

90°   45°   40°   35°   30°   25°   20°

135°

125°

115°

U. S. S. R.

Pacific
Ocean

INDIA

Indian Ocean

bers were left hungry and hopeless, and ready to accept the communist program as a quick solution to the problems of poverty. Traditionally the establishment of a new regime in China has resulted in the flight of the defeated parties to the offshore islands, including Formosa (Taiwan). Here the remnants of the Ming dynasty had found refuge from the Manchus in the seventeenth century. Now in the twentieth century the opponents of communist rule have found refuge there too. China has become divided between the People's Republic of China and the Republic of China. Japan, rebuilt after the war with aid from the United States, is the only Asian country to have passed through the Industrial Revolution, and to have exchanged self-sufficiency for interdependence.

The East Asian Culture Region is important in the modern world because of the huge concentration of people involved in it. The region lies at the edge of the Land Hemisphere, separated from the central part of the hemisphere not only by great distances, but also by a vast area of thinly populated deserts and high mountains. The fact that so many people are crowded into the eastern part of the continent of Asia gives this region an importance not suggested by its global position. The East Asian Culture Region includes about 9 per cent of the inhabited land area of the earth, and is occupied by 29 per cent of the world's population. The countries of this region are the People's Republic of China, the Republic of China, Mongolia, North Korea, South Korea, and Japan.

THE HABITAT

(Maps 5, 6, 8, and 74) The East Asian region is made up of strongly contrasted habitats. The greater part of the area is the dry and mountainous interior of the Asian continent,

including the western parts of China (Tibet and Sinkiang), and Mongolia. The eastern margin of the continent and the mountainous islands off the continental shore, on the other hand, receive abundant rainfall in summer.

The Surface Features. From the western end of the Himalayas towering ranges of mountains extend in great loops toward the northeast. There are the Tien Shan and Altai ranges on the border of the Soviet Union; there are the Kunlun and Astin Tagh ranges on the northern side of Tibet. From eastern Tibet numerous ranges extend into Southeast Asia, and the Tsin Ling Mountains point eastward into the wet part of China. The northern face of the Tsin Ling range is one of the world's largest fault scarps (produced by slipping along a break in the earth's crust). Where the Tsin Ling range emerges from Tibet its crest is about 12,000 feet above sea level, but as the mountains descend eastward they become only a string of low hills, all but submerged in the alluvium north of the lower Yangtze. Ranges of high mountains border the Manchurian Lowland on both sides; and a range of high mountains forms the backbone of Korea. The chains of islands in the Pacific Ocean off the coast of East Asia are formed by mountains that rise from the ocean floor, some barely reaching above sea level, others that are more than 12,000 feet above sea level.

Within the embrace of these numerous curving ranges of high mountains are desert basins, plateaus, hilly uplands, alluvial lowlands, and shallow seas. In the continental interior there are dry basins from which the water escapes only by evaporation. Between the Himalayas and the Kunlun Mountains is the high Plateau of Tibet, made up of many discontinuous ranges separating dry basins, the floors of which average between 13,000 and 15,000 feet above sea level. This is the world's largest area of very high elevation. North of the Kunlun and Astin Tagh Mountains is the Tarim Basin, which contains the sandy Takla Makan desert, an area still not fully explored. Streams descending from the bordering mountains combine to form the Tarim River which drains into the Lop Nor, a salt-encrusted and wind-swept flat. The eastern part of the dry interior of Asia is known as the Gobi. A large part of this desert is made up of rocky plateaus, or hamadas; but in the north and east there is a fringe of short-grass steppe between the desert and the high mountains on the Soviet border, extending into western Manchuria.

Hilly uplands on ancient crystalline rocks form a large part of eastern China. Everywhere south of the Yangtze Lowland, as far as northern Vietnam, the surface is made up of rounded hills, surmounted in a few places by low mountains. The uplands reach elevations between 4,000 and 5,000 feet above sea level. These hilly surfaces extend to the coast, hemming in such narrow alluvial valleys as that of the Si Kiang, in which Canton is located. Hills form the surface of Hainan. North of the Yangtze the Shantung Peninsula, and the peninsula in southern Manchuria which points toward Shantung, are also made up of hills.

The alluvial lowlands, on which the population of East Asia is concentrated, are of two types. There are innumerable small delta plains and narrow valley floodplains along the coasts and on the islands. In Korea, with its backbone of high mountains, ridges descend toward the west like ribs. Between the ribs are narrow alluvial lowlands, which are continuous only near the coast. On Formosa the main range of high mountains is near the eastern side, and the slopes descend steeply to a narrow plain along the Pacific. On the western side there is a wider alluvial lowland. On the Japanese islands

there are only discontinuous delta plains where the rivers descend from the mountains, or enclosed structural depressions nestled amid steep ranges. The largest lowland area is the Kanto Plain, on which Tokyo is located.

The other type of alluvial lowland has been built by the great rivers—one, the Yellow Plain, built by the Hwang Ho, and the other, the Yangtze Plain, built by the Yangtze Kiang. Both of these rivers rise in the high mountains of Tibet, close to the sources of the Salween and the Mekong. The two Chinese rivers enter the sea relatively close together after flowing 2,900 miles and 3,430 miles respectively. But in their mid courses, and in the lowlands that they have developed, they differ widely.

The Yellow Plain. The Hwang Ho flows northeastward out of Tibet into the great desert area of inner Asia. It makes a huge bend around the sandy Ordos Desert before it is joined, near the northern base of the Tsin Ling Mountains, by its tributary the Wei Ho. It then crosses the Yellow Plain, the largest lowland of East Asia. The western edge of this plain is bordered by a deep accumulation of wind-blown dust, or loess, brought by the winter winds from the deserts of inner Asia. The loess is yellowish in color, and so fine in texture that it feels like flour when it is pressed between the fingers. The Hwang Ho picks up a vast quantity of this fine dust as it passes through the loess hills, and redeposits this alluvium on the plain to the east, gradually extending the plain out into the Yellow Sea. The alluvium is deposited on the bottom and sides of the river channel which is, in this way, gradually built up higher than the general level of the plain. In times of flood the surface of the water in the Hwang Ho is about twenty-five or thirty feet above the level of the alluvial plain. In an effort to control the floods the

Chinese have, for thousands of years, been building artificial dikes on top of the natural levees which mark the edge of the normal river channel. But the longer the river is confined to its channel, the higher this channel is raised, until eventually a break is made in the dikes at high water, and the river finds a new route to the sea. Since 2300 B.C. the Hwang Ho has made eight major shifts in its course. Between A.D. 1194 and 1853 the river entered the sea south of the Shantung Peninsula, not far from the mouth of the Yangtze. Between 1853 and 1938 it emptied into the sea north of the Shantung Peninsula. In 1938 the Chinese diverted the flow in an effort to stop the Japanese invasion, and made the river return to its old channel south of the peninsula. Now it has been returned again to its northern channel.

The Yangtze Plain. The valley of the Yangtze is very different. The Yangtze emerges from the high mountains of Tibet to enter the Szechwan (Red) Basin, a structural depression among the high mountains once occupied by a lake. The lake has long been drained, and the tributaries of the Yangtze have cut the surface into hills. The one, narrow bit of plain is around the city of Chengtu. The Yangtze leaves the Szechwan Basin to plunge through a narrow gorge in the bordering mountains, and then to emerge at the head of its alluvial lowland. The river meanders in great curves, shifting its course from time to time and leaving the surface of the plain marked with abandoned ox-bow lakes and crescent-shaped stretches of fine silt or sand, or even gravel. The river floods are not so disastrous as those of the Hwang Ho because there are numerous spillways to carry away the excess waters through earlier channels. The river pours into the sea through two mouths near Shanghai.

The Climates and Vegetation. The East Asian Culture Region occupies the eastern side of a continent in the middle latitudes, a position similar to that of the eastern United States in North America. The climates of eastern Asia and of eastern North America are, in fact, remarkably similar, except that, latitude for latitude, the winter temperatures of eastern Asia are about 10° to 20° lower than those of eastern North America. The table compares the average monthly temperatures and rainfall for two places at about the same latitude in each culture region. In both places there is the same prevailing southeast wind of summer and prevailing offshore wind of winter. But in Asia the cold air masses of winter, originating in the very cold area of eastern Siberia, are lower in temperature and more persistent than are the cold air masses in eastern North America. The rainfall is at a maximum in summer—July in Asia, June in North America. In eastern Asia at this time there is a strong inflow of moist air from the Indian Ocean (see p. 281). The dry season is in winter, when the polar outbursts dominate the weather, bringing clear skies and dry cold air.

Where the offshore islands are mountainous there is a tendency for the rainiest time of the year to come when the air is forced to rise against the steep mountain slopes. Thus, the rainy season of western Japan comes in winter when the prevailing wind direction is from the northwest. But the rainy season on the eastern and southern sides of Japan comes in summer, when the southeast winds prevail. In the southern part of Japan, and on the islands south of Japan, there is a tendency for a second rainfall maximum to occur in September as a result of the frequent heavy rains associated with typhoons at that season (a situation similar to that in

COMPARISON OF TEMPERATURE AND RAINFALL AVERAGES
AT SHANGHAI AND CHARLESTON, S.C.

Shanghai (lat. 31° 11′ N)

	Jan	Feb	Mar	Apr	May	Jun	Jul	Aug	Sep	Oct	Nov	Dec	Year
Temp.	37.8	39.4	46.0	56.1	65.5	73.4	80.4	80.2	73.0	63.5	52.0	42.1	59.1
Rf.	2.0	2.3	3.5	3.7	3.5	7.2	6.0	5.7	4.4	3.2	2.1	1.4	45.0

Charleston, S.C. (32° 47′ N)

	Jan	Feb	Mar	Apr	May	Jun	Jul	Aug	Sep	Oct	Nov	Dec	Year
Temp.	49.8	51.2	57.5	63.9	72.1	78.1	80.6	80.0	76.2	67.0	57.8	51.0	65.4
Rf.	3.1	3.3	3.4	2.9	3.4	4.8	7.1	6.6	5.0	3.6	2.4	2.9	48.5

(*World Weather Records*, Smithsonian Miscellaneous Collections, 1947)

North America at the same latitudes, where heavy rains result from the hurricanes).

The climatic types of East Asia occupy positions similar to those of eastern North America. The convergence of Dfa-Cfa-Dfb-Cfb near Boston finds its analogue in the Sea of Japan between Honshū and Korea. The border between A climates and C climates which is found in southern Florida, has its counterpart in southern Formosa and Hainan. But there is no counterpart in eastern North America for the dry winters of Asia (Cwa, Dwa). The summer rainfall is abundant in South China and the Yangtze Valley. But the line of the Tsin Ling Mountains constitutes a major climatic divide: for to the north of these mountains the winters are much drier and the summer rainfall is more uncertain. The Shantung Peninsula forms the southern limit of severe winters—and, unlike North America at these latitudes, there is almost no snow.

The inner part of the Asian continent is not open to the south, as North America is. Warm, moisture-laden air cannot cross the Himalayas, nor can it reach far inland from the east coast. The interior, therefore, is not only cold because of its altitude and its exposure to cold air masses from farther north, but it is also very dry.

These climatic features were at one time reflected in the cover of natural vegetation.

The high mountains, and the rainy hills of South China, are still covered by forests—rain forest along the coast and on Formosa. Forests also once covered the mountains and plains of Korea and Japan, and the mountains of Manchuria. The Manchurian Lowland was a grassland, and grass interspersed with a light forest cover probably characterized the wetter parts of North China, including the Shantung Peninsula. But these parts of China have been used by man over such a long period that the original landscapes have been completely altered. Even the soils are now man made. It is no longer possible to reconstruct with certainty the exact boundary between forest and grassland in North China.

THE ORIGIN AND DEVELOPMENT OF CHINA

It was in the distinctive habitat of North China—the loess lands and the Yellow Plain—that the Chinese culture originated. One of the very old human remains, Peking man, was found in this area, and dates back perhaps half a million years. People of the Mongoloid race have been occupying North China for a very long time. It was in this region that one of the world's six Early Civilizations appeared. Although China's beginnings are not so ancient as those of the civilizations of India, Mesopotamia, and

Egypt, the Chinese culture has the longest record of continuous development of any of the world's great cultures. No part of the world has been so completely transformed by human action as has the landscape of North China during this long period.

The Chinese Culture Hearth. (Map 75) The Wei Ho, 540 miles long, collects the water running down the steep northern slopes of the Tsin Ling Mountains, and drains it away eastward. It empties all this water into the Hwang Ho which, at its junction with the Wei, turns eastward, hemmed in between the loess hills to the north and the eastern ridges of the Tsin Ling Mountains to the south. The loess picked up by the Hwang Ho and deposited along its valley at flood time is enormously fertile for shallow-rooted crops; and although control of the Hwang Ho was beyond the engineering skill of the ancient Chinese, this was not true for the Wei which provided extensive experience in controlling water where the dimensions of the problem were not so overwhelming. The Wei Valley provided an open landscape, with a light forest cover interspersed with grass, which posed no major difficulties for the primitive farmers. Of all the six Early Civilizations, the Chinese seems to have been located in the most clearly favorable habitat.

There were at least two other factors favorable to cultural growth in this habitat. One, was the presence in the area of a number of wild plants that could be easily cultivated. The forests included such fruit trees as the apricot, the white-fleshed peach, pear, plum, and persimmon, and also a variety of nuts. Among the native grasses there were several varieties of millet, and probably buckwheat, all of which were easily brought under cultivation. Even more important, the Wei Valley was not so isolated that it was out of reach of ideas from distant places. There was a steady infiltration of "barbarians" into the civilized part of China from the grasslands of Mongolia, and from time to time there were actual invasions. From the upper end of the Wei Valley an ancient caravan route led westward along the northern edge of the high country of Tibet, around the margin of the Tarim Basin, and on to such ancient market towns in Central Asia as Samarkand and Bukhara, to which merchants brought their products from Southwest Asia and even from the shores of the Mediterranean. The culture hearth of China was enriched with items imported over this ancient route —items such as wheat, that became the major grain of North China. The cultivated plants of China and of Southwest Asia were interchanged along this route. The Wei Valley was also accessible from the south, around the eastern end of the Tsin Ling Mountains; from this direction came many of the distinctive features of Chinese culture, such as rice, bamboo, pigs, poultry, water buffaloes, and other innovations of Southeast Asia. Ivory, and the elephant as an art object if not as a work animal, also came from Southeast Asia. Jade came from Burma. All these alien items were incorporated into the developing Chinese way of life.

The Chinese pattern of settlement was suited to the habitat. The farmers were grouped together in compact villages, not scattered on individual farms. Cities, protected by walls, provided centers for commerce and administration. Meanwhile the farmers developed a complex of related skills: skill in the control of water, skill in the preparation of land for planting and in the use of organic fertilizers, skill in harvesting. All these skills required the use of human muscles on smaller and smaller areas of land. Such a system could only be ap-

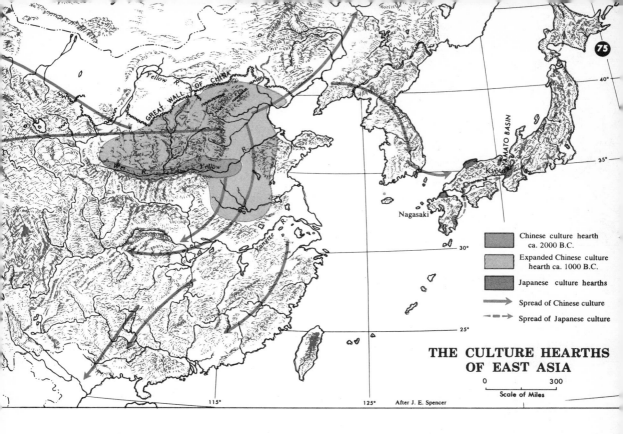

75

Chinese culture hearth
ca. 2000 B.C.

Expanded Chinese culture
hearth ca. 1000 B.C.

Japanese culture hearths

Spread of Chinese culture

Spread of Japanese culture

THE CULTURE HEARTHS OF EAST ASIA

0   300

Scale of Miles

After J. E. Spencer

---

plied on land that could be made highly productive, not on marginal lands where yields per acre were necessarily low. The increase in population resulted in a greater and greater concentration on the river flood-plains.

Chinese society became highly central-ized and authoritarian. The oldest man in the family had undisputed authority, and his special rights and responsibilities were passed on to the eldest son. All sons en-joyed privileges that were not given to girls. The heads of families were further grouped together under the authority of the small group of landowners, and the landowners, in turn, were under the authority of the em-peror whose word on all matters was final. The landlords constituted a group apart from the rest of the Chinese population. These people were carefully educated schol-ars. They were the ones who followed the teaching of Confucius and who maintained

the stability of Chinese culture. No one had the knowledge, or the prestige and power, to dispute the decisions of these philosopher-scholars who were also owners of the land. It was they who developed to a high art the forms of behavior that minimized friction among individuals, and it was they, also, who learned, in dealing with other people, how to secure personal advantages with al-most no show of force. In their hands was the continuity of traditional Chinese cul-ture.

There are numerous other traits of the Chinese culture which are distinctive. The use of chopsticks is one, which is found only in East Asia, or among people from East Asia. Very important, too, is the style of writing. In this culture region there are many spoken languages, but the written characters that stand for words have a basic similarity inherited from the Chinese cul-ture hearth.

The Spread of Chinese Culture. The distinctively Chinese way of life was being forged in the inner hearth before 2000 B.C. (Map 75). By 1000 B.C., Chinese culture, still in the process of formation, had expanded to the outer hearth including the loess hills and the Yellow Plain. Chinese engineers were now ready to wrestle with larger problems on a larger stage. During the next several centuries the Chinese way of life was carried onto the river floodplains of South China, even as far as Tonkin, and also into southern Manchuria and Korea. Through Korea, Chinese traits were brought to the Japanese islands.

Civilized China has a long record of invasion and conquest from neighboring and differing cultures. The earliest historical record tells of the Chou invasion (about 1122 B.C.) from the steppes of Mongolia. The invaders divided the land into large private properties over which they ruled as landlords, collecting rent from the peasants who continued to live in their farm villages, cultivating their ancestral lands. In this way the basic distinction of landlord and tenant was introduced into the Chinese culture. The invaders were soon absorbed and became as thoroughly Chinese as the people who had been in the culture hearth before them.

Political unification under one ruler did not take place in the culture hearth until the Ching Dynasty (221-206 B.C.). It was during this period that the several separate fortifications, built to guard against the raids of the pastoral nomads, were connected to form the Great Wall (Map 75). The main part of the wall reached from north of Peking to the edge of the Tibetan highlands where the Hwang Ho emerges onto the desert. Extensions of the wall were, at a later time, built westward to protect the caravan route from the Mongolians, and eastward to protect southern Manchuria from the Manchurian nomads. But impregnable walls have never proved to be permanently impregnable. The invaders kept coming, even if they had to bribe the gatekeepers to let them through. The Han Dynasty (202 B.C.-A.D. 9, and A.D. 25-220) was troubled by repeated invasions. From A.D. 220 to 589 China was broken into three parts: the old culture hearth of North China, with its capital at Peking; the lower Yangtze Valley with its capital at Nanking; and the Szechwan Basin with its capital at Chengtu.

The Dynasties. The sequence of dynasties is not important for the purposes of this study.[2] However, it is important to understand the relationship of the population to the land base which has been going through a recurring cycle again and again during the past two thousand years. The cycle starts when a powerful ruler succeeds in

[2] The Chinese dynasties include:
Ching 221-206 B.C.
Han 202 B.C.—A.D. 9, and A.D. 25-220.
The three kingdoms 220-589.
Sui 589-618.
Tang 618-906.
Sung 960-1279
Mongol 1279-1368
Ming 1368-1644
Manchu 1644-1911
The Nationalist Revolution 1911
Communist rule 1949

gaining control over the separate parts of China. Strong central authority brings freedom from warfare among lesser authorities. Freedom from warfare means that more food can be raised, and this reduces the death rate. The population increases until the pressure for more food becomes insistent. But, owing to the nature of Chinese agricultural techniques, expansion onto new land in a different kind of habitat is not possible. Instead, the Chinese farmers intensify their efforts on progressively smaller areas of floodplain. The farmers fall further and further into debt to their landlords, until a period of less than normal summer rains, or a disastrous flood, brings famine. Famine leads to civil disorder, banditry, and conflict among the overlords and their private armies. Government corruption paralyzes the central authority. The rise in the death rate due to famine results in an actual decrease in population, until a new, powerful ruler appears to recapture authority and to found a new dynasty.

Are these cycles related to changes in the habitat, or are they produced by processes of social change within the culture? This is a fascinating field of study. There are some scholars who think the whole sweep of Chinese history is closely tied to cycles of wet and dry periods which are world-wide, cycles which can be seen in the growth rings of very old trees and in the changes in the shore line of the Caspian Sea.[3] There were times when the pastoral nomads of inner Asia burst into China, into South and Southwest Asia, and into Europe, starting waves of invasion and conquest, notably in the thirteenth century. Were these conquests triggered by a dessication of the steppes on which the pastoral nomads

[3] Ellsworth Huntington, *The Mainsprings of Civilization,* John Wiley and Sons, 1945.

grazed their animals? There can be no doubt that climatic cycles do exist, and that they have given rise to changes in the relations of people to their habitats; but there also seem to be other important social processes involved, which have yet to be examined carefully from a geographic point of view.

China and the Europeans. Chinese culture had been developing for thousands of years. There were times, for instance during the Tang Dynasty (618-906), when China was the strongest country in the world; and there were times when the Chinese people enjoyed the highest standard of living of any people in the world. When Marco Polo came to China from Venice in 1275 he found a civilized people who had skills quite unknown at that time in Europe (such as the use of coal for fuel, the manufacture of paper and gunpowder, and the advanced art of public administration). Traders from the outside world established contacts with China over the ancient overland caravan route through the interior of Asia, and also by sea. The port of Canton was the most accessible sea port because of its geographic position, and became the major center of China's foreign trade. Arabs, Indians, and Malays came regularly to Canton. The first Europeans to reach this part of the world were the Portuguese, and in 1557 they were granted possession of Macao as a trading port downstream from Canton (Map 76). The Chinese were culturally superior to all these aliens who came to trade.

On the other hand the Chinese were quite unprepared to meet the revolutionary new ideas spreading from Europe in the nineteenth century. Science and engineering, the bases of the Industrial Revolution, require abstract thinking—and Chinese scholars had no experience with this approach, for their way of describing nature was immediate and personal rather than abstract. The demand that the individual should have a position of dignity, which is the very basis of the Democratic Revolution, requires a change from the "law of status" to the "law of contract"; but nothing in the Chinese tradition led the individual even to ask for equality before the law. The Europeans who laid claim to Chinese territory in the nineteenth century were able to establish control over the Chinese because they possessed superior weapons and superior facilities for transportation. They profited from the purchase of tea, silk, lacquer, porcelain, wood and ivory carving, and from the sale to China of furs, cotton textiles, ginseng, and opium. As a result of the "Opium War" of 1840 they forced the Chinese to accept large imports of this demoralizing drug.

In 1841 the British occupied the thinly populated island of Hong Kong downstream from Canton; and British possession of this foothold was confirmed by treaty in 1842. In 1860 the colony was enlarged, and in 1898 an additional area on the mainland was leased to the British until 1997 (Map 76). Hong Kong became a major trading port. In addition the Europeans established themselves in other Chinese cities, for instance Shanghai, where they enjoyed the rights of protection by their own police, and of trial in their own courts. The territory of China was divided up into sections: the French claimed the right to control the trade of southwestern China, which they approached through French Indochina; the British controlled the rich Yangtze Valley from Shanghai; the Germans established a base of operations on the Shantung Peninsula; the Japanese claimed Korea and trading rights in southern Manchuria; and the Russians took the rest of Manchuria. However the Russo-Japanese War (1904-1905) excluded the Russians from the ports of southern Manchuria.

The ancient Chinese culture pattern has been subjected to revolutionary change in the modern period. In 1911 a nationalist revolution led by Sun Yat-sen resulted in the overthrow of the Manchu emperor. The Chinese liberals demanded a return of national sovereignty, and an end to a century of humiliation suffered at the hands of the Europeans and the Japanese. But Japan had by now adopted an aggressive policy of conquest and expansion. In 1931 they gained control of Manchuria, and in 1937 started an invasion of the rest of China. After heavy fighting they were able to conquer most of the coastal area, the chief cities, and the areas of greatest population density. The Chinese government was removed to Chungking, beyond the mountains, where it was supplied with munitions over the famous Burma Road.

After the defeat and withdrawal of the Japanese after World War II, the main part of China was in turmoil. The peasants had been torn loose from their ancestral lands; the traditional way of life had been broken; civil war among various minor leaders made the re-establishment of order difficult. It was at this point that the communists first established their regime in Manchuria. In 1949 they extended it to the whole of mainland China. The nationalist government fled to Formosa, just as the remnants of the Ming Dynasty had fled before the conquering Manchus many centuries earlier.

THE PEOPLE'S REPUBLIC OF CHINA

Modern China is still in the process of violent change. The ancient patterns of population and of economic production are no longer the same, and the age-old relations of man to his distinctive habitat are dissolving. In what new form China will finally emerge no one knows.

Population. No census has ever made a reliable count of the population of China, and most of the figures quoted by the authorities on this subject are based on estimates. This was true even in the year A.D. 2, during the Han Dynasty, when the world's first attempt at a census reported a population of 59,600,000. In 1578, during the Ming Dynasty, the population was still only about 60,700,000. But by 1812 it was estimated that the population had reached 362,000,-000. The census carried out by the communist government in 1953 reported 582,603,-417. At that same date it was estimated that there were 8,438,000 people on Formosa, and another 11,743,320 Chinese overseas. The estimated population of mainland China in 1962 was 716,500,000.

The rate of population increase is even more uncertain than the total numbers. If the birth rate is more than 30 per thousand and the death rate under 20 per thousand, this should result in an annual increase of more than 2 per cent, or a figure of some twelve million each year. In any case the total number of people in China will pass the billion mark before very long.

This vast population is concentrated in certain areas—and the striking contrast between areas that are almost empty and areas that are densely crowded is a distinctive feature of the Chinese landscape. The map on pages 4-5 (Map 1) shows that most of the Chinese national territory is empty or very thinly populated, and that enormous concentrations of people occupy the areas where conditions are most favorable to Chinese agricultural techniques. There are six major concentrations: The Yangtze delta, the middle Yangtze Valley, the Yellow Plain, southern Manchuria, the Szechwan Basin, and the Si Valley. Lesser concentrations occupy the coastal fringe of South China, the Wei Valley, and the loess hills. But even within these areas of great density, there are empty strips where the soils are sandy or gravelly, or where there are marshes. More than 1,000 people per square mile are found in all the areas of great concentration. In China as a whole, 90 per cent of the population is grouped together on only 27 per cent of the national territory.

About 14 per cent of the people of mainland China live in cities, and yet there are nine great cities of more than a million people each. The largest is Shanghai with an estimated 7,000,000, followed by Peking and Tientsin with over 3,000,000 each. Other urban centers of more than a million are Mukden (Shenyang) and Harbin (Haerhpin) in Manchuria; the Wuhan conurbation (including Hankou, Hanyang, and Wuchang), and Nanking in the Yangtze Valley; Chungking in the Szechwan Basin; and Canton in the Si Valley.

Agriculture. (Map 77) Farming is the way of life for nearly 70 per cent of the people of China. Before the communists undertook a transformation of the economy, as many as 80 per cent were employed in agriculture. Yet, in 1945, more than half of all the farmers were tenants working on land they did not own, paying what they considered to be high rents to landlords in the cities. Over half of all the farmland was owned by only 5 per cent of the people of China.

Chinese farming is notably labor-intensive. The average size of a farm in 1945 was three and a half acres, although in the crowded areas of the lower Yangtze Valley most farms were less than one acre. The average amount of farmland per capita was 0.43 acres. Traditionally most of the farm work has been done by the farmer, his sons, and perhaps a hired worker. Since the hard work of preparing the soil, planting, cultivating, and harvesting the grain has been done by human and animal muscle-power, the number of acres one man can cultivate during the growing season has been narrowly limited. He has just a few weeks at the beginning of the rainy season in which to plant his crop. Similarly other farm activities require intensive work during brief periods of a few weeks. The farmer cannot afford to cultivate land that does not give high yields per acre. But on the good land he increases yields by the most careful attention to each plant. And he maintains the productivity of the soil by using organic fertilizer. The natural waste, of both human and animal origin, is carefully collected in pits. Mixed with urine and water it is applied by hand around the roots of the plants. Nothing is wasted, and no land that will give sufficient returns under such a system is left uncultivated. But this system cannot be applied to less productive lands. The continued increase in population, therefore, has resulted in a more and more intensive use of the land that is suitable.

Agricultural Regions. Chinese agriculture is organized around two food grains—rice and wheat. Wheat is the chief food grain north of the Tsin Ling Mountains and on the Yellow Plain. Rice is the chief food grain in South China. The Yangtze Valley is midway between the rice and the wheat regions, and produces both of these crops: rice in summer, and wheat in winter on the same fields.

The various crop combinations of China are shown on Map 77. In North China wheat is combined with other hardy grains, such as kaoliang and millet. In the Hwang Ho Valley, the loess hills, and the Yellow Plain the wheat is planted in the fall and harvested in spring; but on the borders of the Gobi and in Manchuria, where winters are severe and the growing season short, the wheat is planted in the spring when the ground thaws out, and harvested in late summer. In Manchuria this spring wheat is mixed with soybeans and kaoliang.

In South China, where rice is the dominant grain, the crop combinations are quite different. The river floodplains are used intensively for paddy rice, which is grown during the summer rainy season. Crops grown in combination with rice in this region are winter wheat and barley, cotton, and mulberry trees (grown on the dikes between the paddies, and used to feed silk worms). In the Szechwan Basin, where the bordering mountains give protection from frosts, the agriculture is exceptionally productive, and the crops include rice, wheat, rapeseed, field peas, beans, sugar cane, tobacco, tung oil, and citrus fruits. On the hilly surface of this basin there are many square miles of rice terraces. Farther south, in the hilly upland south of the Yangtze Valley, rice is found in the narrow valley bottoms and the delta plains along the coast, and is grown in combination with maize and sweet potatoes. On the hilly land there are plantations of tea and tung. In the southernmost part of China, including Hainan and Formosa, the lowlands produce two crops of rice each year. Associated with the rice are maize, sugar cane, and sweet potatoes. On the lower hill slopes the farmers grow tea, tropical fruits, citrus fruits, tobacco, and other crops that require a tropical climate. In the highlands of southwestern China relatively small areas are used to grow rice, wheat, maize, barley, and millet, and on the lower levels fruits and vegetables.

Domestic animals are not so numerous in China as they are in India. Cattle, horses, sheep, and camels are pastured on some of the dry-land margins of inner Asia. In South China the water buffalo is used to plow the rice paddies, and in this part of China the farmers usually raise some hogs and poul-

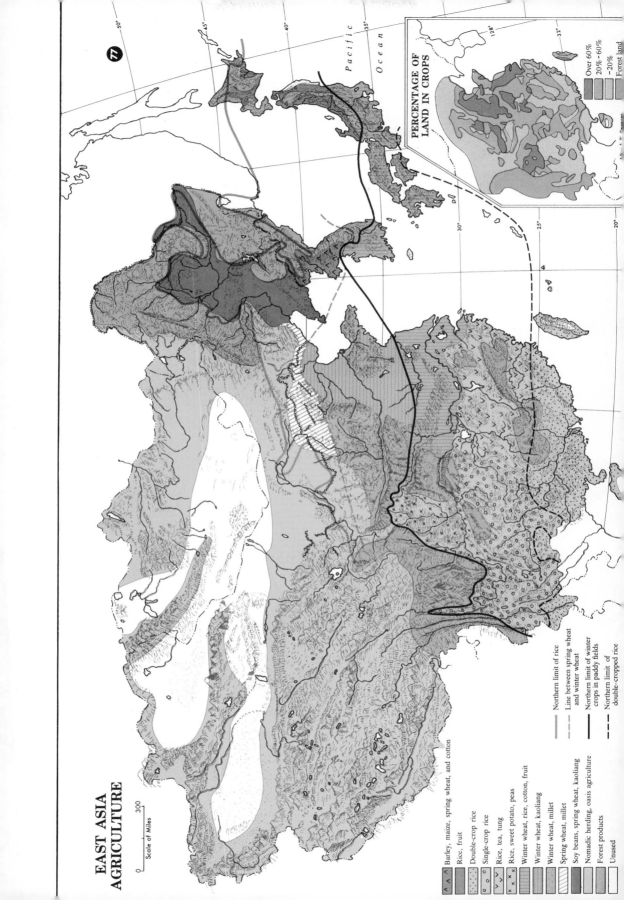

EAST ASIA
AGRICULTURE

Scale of Miles

0   300

PERCENTAGE OF LAND IN CROPS

Over 60%
20% – 60%
– 20%
Forest land

Barley, maize, spring wheat, and cotton
Rice, fruit
Double-crop rice
Single-crop rice
Rice, tea, tung
Rice, sweet potato, peas
Winter wheat, rice, cotton, fruit
Winter wheat, kaoliang
Winter wheat, millet
Spring wheat, millet
Soy beans, spring wheat, kaoliang
Nomadic herding, oasis agriculture
Forest products
Unused

Northern limit of rice
Line between spring wheat
and winter wheat
Northern limit of winter
crops in paddy fields
Northern limit of
double-cropped rice

Pacific

Ocean

try, and sometimes cattle. But where people are so directly dependent on the land for their own food they cannot spare good land for feed crops or pasture.

Fish provide an important additional source of food. On most farms there are fish ponds, carefully stocked and maintained. The chief area for sea fishing is along the coast from Hainan to the mouth of the Yangtze. Farther north fishing conditions are not so good because of the vast quantity of silt poured into the ocean by the Hwang Ho. More than 100,000 junks, equipped with sails, are used to catch fish in the coastal waters; and it is estimated that there are about 1,000,000 people engaged in this form of economic activity.

Changes Introduced by the Communists. In spite of a very large total of human effort expended on agriculture, the Chinese population continued to increase faster than did the production of food. A very large proportion of the people were chronically hungry, and when unfavorable weather reduced crop yields millions were brought face to face with starvation. After World War II, when it seemed that their hunger was not being relieved fast enough by the nationalist government, the peasants gave their support to the Communist Party, which assumed control of mainland China in 1949.

The Communist Party in China undertook to transform the traditional agricultural system in two stages. The first stage was the liquidation of the landlord class, and the redistribution of the expropriated land among the peasants. At this stage the government had the enthusiastic support of the land-hungry farmers. The second stage was the elimination of private ownership or control of property, and the creation of a communist society. At first the peasants with neighboring farms were grouped together in "mutual aid teams" to work their lands together. But in 1957 almost all of the rural people were organized in communes, each under the direction of an appointed manager with control over the total economic, social, and political activities of about five thousand families. Within the communes the people were organized in "work brigades" to perform the necessary agricultural tasks, and also to carry out a vast program of flood control, irrigation, reforestation, and other engineering improvements.

The agricultural program involved a complete break with the past. The family was no longer the basic unit of social organization, and men and women were deprived of their traditional attachment to particular plots of land. The women were freed to work with the men through the establishment of communal nurseries that cared for their children, and communal food services that provided meals. The farm landscape was profoundly altered: fertilizer was spread over large areas by digging out the compost pits, even taking fireplaces to pieces for the wood ashes. The numerous cemeteries which once dotted the rural scene were demolished to make room for more crops. In 1958 the Chinese government announced a 90 per cent increase in agricultural production: 350,000,000 tons of grain and root crops compared with a total of 185,000,000 in 1957.

Among the spectacular construction projects now being undertaken in China is a dam on the Hwang Ho at Sanmen Gorge, located about sixty miles downstream from the junction with the Wei (Map 78). This dam, 394 feet high and three-fifths of a mile long, is designed to control the floods, to increase the area under irrigation, and to generate electric power. The dam and the power plant are scheduled to be completed in 1967.

But the communist program for agricultural improvement has been far from suc-

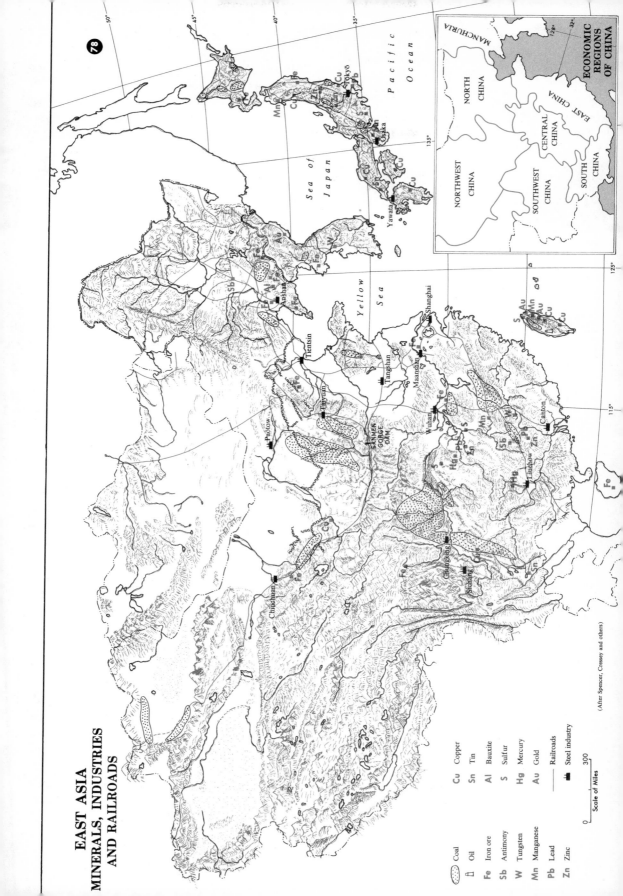

**EAST ASIA
MINERALS, INDUSTRIES
AND RAILROADS**

78

Coal
Oil
Fe Iron ore
Sb Antimony
W Tungsten
Mn Manganese
Pb Lead
Zn Zinc

Cu Copper
Sn Tin
Al Bauxite
S Sulfur
Hg Mercury
Au Gold
— Railroads
Steel industry

Scale of Miles
0   300

(After Spencer, Cressey and others)

Pacific Ocean

Sea of Japan

Tokyo
Osaka
Yawata

Yellow Sea

Tientsin
Taiyuan
Paotow
Anshan
Sb
Tangshan
Maanshan
Shanghai
Wuhan
Canton
Kweiyang
Chungking
Kunming
Chiuchuan

ECONOMIC REGIONS OF CHINA

MANCHURIA
NORTH CHINA
NORTHWEST CHINA
EAST CHINA
CENTRAL CHINA
SOUTHWEST CHINA
SOUTH CHINA

SANMEN GORGE DAM

The new dam on the Hwang Ho at Sanmen Gorge, which is designed to control floods, provide for the irrigation of millions of acres, and generate electricity.

cessful. After 1958 crop yields took a disastrous fall. This has been due partly to inefficient, and even dishonest, administration; partly to the loss of peasant support for the communes; and partly to a succession of natural disasters. By 1961 the work brigades, rather than the communes, were the chief units of authority, and the brigades had been broken down further into small teams of about twenty-five people each. Furthermore, the teams came to be assigned to particular plots of land which they were to cultivate on a long-term basis. Famine became widespread as a result of the decline in food production.

Resources, Transportation, and Industry. (Map 78) The communists plan to transform China from a nation of poor farmers into a modern industrial state. The modernization of agriculture, as we have seen in the chapter on Anglo-America, requires a reduction in the proportion of workers employed in farming, and this, in turn, requires the development of other kinds of employment. In the communist system there are not nearly as many kinds of jobs in service occupations as there are in capitalist countries. However, the communist system calls for a tremendous increase in manufacturing industry, and since 1949 there has been an important increase in this kind of employment,

because about 75 per cent of the investment in new capital formation has gone into industrial plants. Furthermore, much additional effort has been applied to the search for new sources of minerals.

Mineral Resources. China stands third among the nations of the world in terms of its total reserves of coal. Map 78 shows that coal is widely scattered throughout the national territory. The total amount, including all grades of coal, adds up to about 1.2 trillion tons, of which 15 per cent is anthracite, but less than 10 per cent is good coking coal. About 25 per cent of all China's coal is located in the semiarid country on the borders of the Ordos Desert—along the big bend of the Hwang Ho—and another 32 per cent lies just to the east on the edge of the loess hills. These enormous coal reserves were only slightly developed before 1949, and transportation is still not adequate to move the coal to the established industrial centers. The Manchurian coal reserves, making up only 6 per cent of China's total, are the most accessible and have been China's chief source in the past. At Fushun, a little north of Mukden, is the world's thickest coal seam—417 feet thick. Taken together, more than 63 per cent of China's coal is located in North China and Manchuria; the remainder is scattered in small deposits in almost every part of the country.

Before 1949 it was reported that China was not well supplied with iron ore, and that only in Manchuria did iron ore occur in close proximity to coal. But by 1962 new iron ore deposits had been discovered, giving China an estimated reserve of 15 billion tons. Important new iron ore deposits were discovered in the Yangtze Valley and the Szechwan Basin, and at many places throughout the hilly upland of South China. New ore bodies were also found in North China, and a major source has been reported from mountainous southwest China. In many places, therefore, it has now been found that coal and iron ore do, in fact, exist close enough together to support an iron and steel industry.

China is also well endowed with a variety of other minerals. Before World War II China was supplying 75 per cent of the world's antimony, and more than 50 per cent of the world's tungsten. There are adequate supplies of manganese, and some lead, zinc, copper, tin, bauxite, sulfur, mercury, and gold. There are also small supplies of oil. Probably continued geologic exploration of the vast national territory will reveal additional sources of raw materials.

Transportation. China has never been equipped with an adequate system of internal transportation, even for the shipment of food to famine areas. During the nineteenth century the Europeans were concerned about building port facilities, but inland transportation was neglected. There were few railroads, and the canals connecting the Hwang Ho and the Yangtze had been built by the Chinese emperors. Away from the rivers and the railroads most transportation was by pack animal and human porterage, which was both expensive and inefficient. Norton Ginsburg points out that

if 100 units represent the cost of transportation by river steamer in 1937, transportation by railroad cost 112, by river junk 175, by pack animal 425, by handcart 450, and by human porters 890.[4]

Since 1949 the government has greatly expanded the transportation system of China, but much remains to be done. Many thousands of miles of new railroads have been built, and many of the older lines have been double-tracked. The railroads in operation in 1963 are shown on Map 78.

Industries and Economic Regions. When the communist system is applied to a country, however, the volume of transportation is not always so great as in a country developed under the capitalist system. The communists attempt to minimize the need for shipping bulky goods by developing each part of the country on the basis of its own resources. The plan is to divide a large national territory into economic regions, each of which is made as nearly self-sufficient in terms of food and manufactured goods as possible. In each region there is a tightly integrated industrial economy, built around a steel-manufacturing center. This decentralization of industry is costly, because the advantages of large-scale industrial operations are lost; but the country is more uniformly developed, and is less vulnerable to attack.

The communist government is taking steps to develop seven economic regions in mainland China. These regions, the major steel centers in each, and the population of each in 1959, are listed below, and are shown in the inset on Map 78. Each of these regions is to have its own more or less independent industrial structure. In 1962 about half of China's industrial production came from Anshan, Shanghai, and the newly con-

---

[4] Norton Ginsburg (ed.), 1958; p. 242.

ECONOMIC REGIONS OF CHINA 1960[5]

Region	Major Industrial Centers	Population in Millions (1959)
Manchuria	Anshan	50
North China	Paotow	71
East China	Maanshan-Nanking, Shanghai	190
Central China	Wuhan	112
Southwest China	Hsichang, Chungking	82
South China	Liuchow, Canton	57
Northwest China	Chiuchuan	39

structed steel plant at Paotow on the Hwang Ho. However, new steel plants were being erected at Maanshan and Wuhan, and it was planned to expand the steel facilities at Chungking and Canton. New plants were also planned for Hsichang in the mountains west of the Szechwan Basin, Liuchow in the interior of South China, and Chiuchuan on the old caravan route in inner Asia.

Inner Asia. In contrast to the crowded eastern part of China, large areas of western China remain outside the effective national territory. Sinkiang is made up of very thinly populated deserts and mountains; and settled agriculture is possible only where irrigation can be provided along the mountain piedmonts. Many of the people are pastoral nomads. Of the total population of about four million, 80 per cent are Turkic, 8 per

[5] From S. A. Nikolayev and L. I. Molodtsova, "The Present State of the Chinese Iron and Steel Industry," *Geografiya i Khozyaystvo,* 1960, No. 6; pp. 34-44. Translated in *Soviet Geography,* Vol. 1, 1960; pp. 55-71.

The largest iron and steel industry in China, located at Anshan in southern Manchuria.

cent are Kazakh, and only 8 per cent are Chinese.

Tibet is also non-Chinese in culture. Because of the difficulty of reaching the inner part of this high country, the Tibetans were able, for a long time, to keep outsiders from reaching their capital at Lhasa. Traditionally the ruler of Tibet has been the Dalai Lama, believed to be the incarnation of Buddha. In 1912 the Tibetans asserted their independence from China, but in 1951 they accepted the status of an autonomous province within China. In 1959 a revolt in Tibet was put down by Chinese military forces, and the Dalai Lama fled to India. Some of the people are farmers who grow barley and other hardy crops; others are pastoral nomads whose distinctive animal is the yak, used as a draft animal, and to provide meat, wool, hair, and milk.

The Viability of China. Can the communists achieve their goal and transform China into a modern industrial state? Perhaps they have tried to move too fast toward the rebuilding of an ancient culture in a new mold. Perhaps it is not possible to remake the traditional attitudes of the Chinese people. Over the thousands of years of Chinese history, conquerors have again and again attempted to change China, and they have always been assimilated by the culture they attempted to change. It is clear that China has the resources to support a modern industrial state, and the people, when properly taught, can learn the necessary skills. The basic question is whether economic development can be made to move faster than the increase in population. Up to 1962 industrial production had increased between 6 and 7 per cent per year, and the population had grown at a rate of perhaps 2 per cent per year. Even prodigious and well-directed effort, together with massive investments in new capital, may not be enough to create new jobs as fast as people are born to fill them. It may be that China is one of those unhappy countries doomed to choke on its own vast numbers. If China is thrown into convulsions by the ultimate despair of millions of individuals, and if these individuals become aware of the geographic setting of their misery, what is likely to be their avenue of escape? Northward, through Manchuria, into thinly-populated eastern Siberia? Southward, through southeast Asia, perhaps even into thinly-populated Australia? Westward, through Inner Asia, along the ancient routes of invasion, and even into Europe? Or will they be contained in the traditional Chinese homeland by some system of economic development?

THE REPUBLIC OF CHINA[6]

When the communists established control over mainland China in 1949, the nationalist government under Chiang Kai-shek was able to escape to the islands offshore. The nationalist government now maintains control over Formosa (Taiwan), with its capital at Taipei, together with some smaller islands near the coast.

Formosa is a mountainous island located about a hundred miles from the Chinese mainland. The eastern slope is very steep, for the mountains reach elevations of more than 12,000 feet within forty miles of the shore; the western slope is more gentle, and on the western side of the island there is a coastal plain. About 80 per cent of the island's more than 11,000,000 people are concentrated on this plain. On the whole island the density of population is 756 people per square mile.

[6] The People's Republic of China (communist China) and the Republic of China (nationalist China) both claim all of China. Neither one accepts this division of China as permanent.

Farmers on Formosa being shown small farm machinery that can help them to increase production on their limited land holdings.

Formosa has been invaded and conquered again and again. In prehistoric times people from Southeast Asia migrated through Formosa on the way to Japan; and the Chinese came to the island from the mainland during the early periods of expansion from the original culture hearth. In 1590 the Portuguese were the first Europeans to reach the island, and they gave it the name Formosa (meaning "beautiful"). The Dutch and the Spaniards later fought over possession of Formosa; but in 1662 the defeated remnants of the Ming Dynasty, fleeing before the Manchus, invaded and took the island as a place of refuge. They in turn were conquered by the Manchus in 1683. The population was overwhelmingly Chinese when, after the war between China and Japan, the island was surrendered to

the Japanese in 1895. It was returned to China at the conclusion of World War II, and the defeated nationalist armies found refuge there in 1949. Before World War II, under Japanese control, the island produced high-grade oolong tea, and a major share of the world's natural camphor, taken from camphor trees in the mountains.

Formosa faces the usual problems of economic development in the presence of a dense and rapidly increasing population, and chiefly the one of whether the number of jobs can be increased at a rate faster than the numbers of people seeking them. However, the program of economic development does seem to be more successful than the one applied to the People's Republic of China on the mainland.

The first step has been land reform and agricultural improvement. The rents charged by landlords have been reduced to a standard 37.5 per cent from a level of more than 50 per cent of the value of the crop. All paddy-rice lands in excess of 7.2 acres, which were not being worked by the landowner and his family, have been expropriated and resold to the tenants. In addition a large acreage of government land has been made available for sale. The western coastal plain and the lower mountain slopes were already intensively utilized for rice, sugar cane, sweet potatoes, and tea plantations; and a regular flow of forest products came from the mountains (Map 77). But yields per acre of all crops have been increased by technical improvements, and ways have been sought to cut down on losses in the second rice harvest (in September) which is often reduced by typhoons. Sugar and rice, as well as tea, are regular exports.

The second step in economic development has been an increase in mineral and industrial production. Formosa has sources of oil and coal, as well as ores of copper, manganese, mercury, and sulfur (Map 78). New manufacturing industries have been built, with financial assistance from the United States. Manufactured products now include refined sugar, cement, pig iron, machinery, cotton thread, and paper. Between 1958 and 1959 industrial production increased by 14 per cent. And it is hoped that by 1964 Formosa will no longer be dependent on financial aid from outside. The gross national product per capita is already almost double that of the People's Republic of China.

THE MONGOLIAN PEOPLE'S REPUBLIC

Mongolia is the general name given to the Gobi and its grassy margins, an area which is the easternmost part of the dry lands of Inner Asia. The region is traditionally divided into Inner Mongolia and Outer Mongolia, the former being the steppe on the eastern and southern side of the Gobi bordering on densely settled North China, and the latter being the steppe on the northern side of the Gobi bordering on the Soviet Union. The Mongolian People's Republic extends from the Gobi in the south to the mountains on the Soviet border in the north, and includes the steppes of Outer Mongolia (Maps 8 and 74).

This area is included in the East Asian Culture Region because of the historical ties with China. The Mongolian culture is neither Chinese nor Russian: Mongolia is one of those transitional areas that might be included within either of the neighboring major culture regions.

The Mongolian steppes are the ancestral homeland, the culture hearth, of the steppe nomads, whose mobility permitted them to range widely all the way from the borders of China to the eastern part of Europe. In the thirteenth century the Mongols ruled not only China (see table on page 332) and Korea, but also the whole of inner Asia and the grasslands of Europe. The Mongols had much to do with the formation of the Russian culture, as we have seen (page 118). But the semiarid habitat of inner Asia failed to provide the economic strength needed to support a politically-unified empire. After the overthrow of the Mongol Dynasty in China in 1368, the Mongols remained loosely attached to the rulers in Peking. In 1911, when the nationalist revolution swept over China, the Mongols in Outer Mongolia were far enough from the center of power to declare their independence under the rule of the "Living Buddha" of Urga. Both Russia and China attempted to recapture the new country, and in 1921 the Communist Party gained control with the help of Soviet troops. With the death of the Living Buddha in 1924, the Mongolian People's Republic came into existence, and the capital, Urga, was renamed Ulan Bator.

Mongolia is still a pastoral country. It has more livestock per capita than any other country in the world. The animals include sheep (57 per cent), goats (20 per cent), cattle (10 per cent), horses (9 per cent), and camels (4 per cent). These animals graze throughout the year on the grassy steppes which cover more than half of the national territory. There are some coal mines near Ulan Bator, and other smaller mining activities, but most of the industries are involved in the processing of animal products. In Ulan Bator there are modern factories making shoes and other leather goods, sheep skins, and meat products. Ulan Bator is now reached by rail from Peking, and from Ulan-Ude on the Trans-Siberian Railroad.

JAPAN

Japan is the only country of the Oriental world that has gone through all the stages of the Industrial Revolution to achieve a mature economy. It passed through the initial phase a little later than the European countries, between 1880 and 1900, and it reached maturity about 1940. However, the technological transformation was not accompanied by the changes associated with the Democratic Revolution. Democratic ideals were quite alien to the traditional Japanese way of life, which had been derived from the Chinese. Between 1868 and World War II, the Japanese directed a major effort toward rapid industrialization, and toward colonial expansion. This imperialism was undertaken with the purpose of gaining unchallenged access to raw materials and markets. The result was disaster.

The Habitat. Japan has been described, uncritically, as the "Great Britain of Asia." Both countries occupy islands off continental coasts; both countries have led the way to industrialization within their culture regions; and both countries have used the islands as bases for imperial expansion. The similarity of geographic position has been used by the Japanese to justify their policies. But in fact the contrasts between Great Britain and Japan are far more significant than any superficial similarities of position.

The four main Japanese islands form an arc about 1,000 miles long that is a part of the volcanic fringe of the Pacific Ocean basin. The maximum width of the islands is about two hundred miles. Map 74 shows that most of the surface is hilly or mountainous, and that there are only small areas of alluvial plain. The highest mountains are in central Honshū (culminating in Mount Fuji, 12,388 ft.), and here also is the largest area of alluvial lowland—the Kanto Plain.

On all the islands except Shikoku there are symmetrical cone-shaped volcanoes, and earthquakes are common occurrences. Steep slopes and narrow valleys make up most of the surface, and the streams that descend to the coast are short and turbulent.

The Japanese islands extend from roughly 31°N to 45°N—latitudes equivalent to those between South Carolina and Maine in eastern North America. On Hokkaidō the climate is one of severe winters and cool summers. On Kyūshū, Shikoku, and southwestern Honshū the climate is almost tropical, with mild winters and hot summers. Central and northern Honshū are intermediate. In winter the cold air masses from Siberia cross the Sea of Japan and flow against the western sides of the Japanese islands. At this season the western sides have heavy falls of wet snow, while the eastern sides remain mostly cloudless and dry. In summer the prevailing wind direction is from the southeast, and the eastern sides of the islands receive heavy rains. In late summer and early fall typhoons ravage the islands, just as hurricanes pass over parts of eastern North America at the same season.

The Development of Japanese Culture. To this island habitat came people from the mainland of Asia. At a very early period the islands were occupied by Ainus, a Caucasoid people of uncertain origin. Mongoloids came to Japan along the Peninsula of Korea and across the Korean Strait; Malays came from the south by way of Formosa and the Ryūkyū Islands. It was the latter two streams of settlers who began the development of a distinctive Japanese culture, incorporating many traits from Southeast Asia and from the Chinese culture hearth. From the Chinese culture hearth came the form of writing, the Buddhist religion, the emphasis on the family as a unit of social organization, the system of agriculture built around irrigated rice, and many other traits. But in the Japanese culture hearth these traits became transformed.

The Japanese culture was developed in the Yamato Basin at the eastern end of the Inland Sea (Map 75). From this center the Japanese extended their political control northward, forcing the Ainus into northern Honshū and Hokkaidō. They also crossed to Korea and attempted to bring the Korean communities under their control. In A.D. 794 the capital city of Kyōto was established, based on a Chinese city plan; and it remained the capital of the Japanese Empire until 1869. The unity of Japan as a nation was insured in 1281 when the Mongols, who had conquered Korea, attempted to invade the islands. The various more or less separate communities, each with its own military leader, had to join together to resist the invaders. And when this resistance was successful the feeling of coherence, which is an important part of any state-idea, was greatly strengthened.

The earliest European contacts with Japan were made by the Portuguese, followed by the Spaniards and the Dutch. The Portuguese came to trade early in the sixteenth century, and while they traded they attempted to introduce Christianity. The Spaniards challenged the Portuguese monopoly in trade with Japan, and in the resulting struggle, both groups, and the missionaries who represented them, were expelled by the Japanese. At this point, in 1600, a Dutch ship reached Japan. When the Dutch made it clear that trade was their only concern, the Japanese permitted them to establish a permanent post on an island in the harbor of Nagasaki (Map 75). But otherwise the islands were sealed off from outside contacts: no Europeans, other than the Dutch, were permitted to come to Japan, and no Japanese were allowed to visit foreign countries. Even the size of the fishing boats was restricted so that they could not be sailed beyond the coastal waters. Japan became isolated from the rest of the world.

For about two and a half centuries this isolation was maintained, and during that time the Japanese culture was consolidated. Under a feudal system, a small number of leading families owned the land and governed the country. The great mass of the people worked as tenant farmers, growing rice as their basic crop. The aristocracy perfected the Japanese culture, building beauty into the carefully cultivated Japanese landscape, advancing the art of flower arrangement, and creating in this protected paradise a genial and unchanging pattern of living. When Commodore Matthew Perry of the United States Navy entered Yokohama harbor in 1853, he found a thoroughly unified people whose ancestors had not been challenged by foreign ideas for centuries.

The modernization of Japan began with the Meiji Restoration in 1868. The word "Meiji" means "enlightened government." The Japanese had been embarrassed and humiliated by the first contacts with foreigners, and they quickly determined to lead Japan along the path already blazed with such apparent success by the European countries. Plans were drawn up to build factories, to find markets for their exports, and to make up with imports the lack of basic resources. In 1872 the first railroad was built between Tōkyō and Yokohama, and the first docks for oceangoing ships.

Japan began its advance into the initial phase of the Industrial Revolution on the basis of a textile industry. Silk was a native product with obvious possibilities as an export product. The Japanese built factories for the spinning of silk thread, and in a few decades had captured a large part of the world market for silk. So valuable were the cargoes of silk, and so high the insurance rates for every day in transit, that special facilities were developed to rush the product to its markets. In the United States at that time the silk textile industry was concentrated at Paterson, New Jersey. Fast steamers carried the Japanese silk to Seattle, and from Seattle a special silk train was rushed eastward across the continent to New Jersey. Even the best passenger trains stood aside to let the silk train through. The Japanese made large profits from these arrangements.

The Japanese also developed several other industries during the initial phase of industrialization—which took place largely between 1880 and 1900. Cotton textiles were manufactured, largely with cotton imported from the United States; and the cotton fabrics were sold in China, India, and Southeast Asia in competition with British textiles. Japanese industrialists imported coal and iron to feed a new steel industry, and with the steel they began building railroads and oceangoing ships. A chemical industry made its appearance in the early decades of the twentieth century; and chemical fertilizers, applied to the carefully cultivated farms, increased the yields per acre. Japanese fishing fleets began to sail to distant waters, and Japanese canned fish entered the markets all over the world.

But Japanese industrial development took place in a unique social environment. Each industry was directed by a single family. There were five families who controlled all the manufacturing, mining, and trading companies: the Mitsui, Mitsubishi, Sumitomo, Yasuda, and Fuji. In addition, the Satsuma family undertook to provide Japan with a modern navy, and the Choshu family directed the training and equipment of an army. Japanese culture became a strange blend of ancient and modern, of traditional Japanese practices, and of attitudes common in Europe before the Industrial Revolution. The belief that the strength of a nation depended on its self-sufficiency caused serious trouble in Europe, as we have seen, long after it had been made obsolete by the new technology: the belief that an industrial nation must control its markets politically, or at least attempt to do so, dated back to the imperialistic ages of Babylon and Rome.

Imperial Expansion. The stages of Japan's imperial expansion are shown on Map 79. In 1875 the Kuril Islands connecting Hokkaidō with the Peninsula of Kamchatka were acquired by treaty with Russia. In the same year the Bonin Islands in the Pacific Ocean, about five hundred miles south of Tōkyō, were claimed. In 1879 the Japanese gained control of the Ryūkyū Islands. In 1894-1895 they waged war on China, and as one result of the war acquired ownership of Formosa, which they renamed Taiwan. In 1904-1905 Japan fought a war with Russia over Manchuria. The Russians had built a railroad across this Chinese territory to Vladivostok, and had assumed complete control of a zone along the railroad. A branch had been extended south to Port Arthur (now Lüshun), where the Russians were building a naval base that was free from ice. The Japanese were victorious and the Russians were forced out of Port Arthur. As an additional result of the war Japan invaded and later claimed possession of Korea (which was renamed Chosen). The other powers recognized Manchuria as a "sphere of interest" within which Japan might have a free hand to develop resources, build industries, and control trade. Both Korea and Manchuria had just the resources of agricultural land, coal, and iron that were so much needed by Japan.

During World War I, Japan sided with the Allies against Germany. As a result Japan was given the German possessions in East Asia and the islands of the Pacific Ocean, which included the Caroline, Marshall, and Mariana Islands.

In the years leading up to World War II, however, Japan sided with Italy and Germany. In 1931 it gained control of Manchuria, set up a puppet government and named the new state Manchukuo. The sources of good coking coal and iron ore in southern Manchuria were used to support a huge, Japanese-built steel industry, and to manufacture armaments. In 1937, using Manchukuo and its industries as a base, the Japanese invaded China, and eventually gained control over most of eastern China.

By 1941 Japan had experienced sixty years of unchecked imperial expansion. The Japanese found themselves treated as equals among the world's great powers, and their military conquests had proved enormously profitable. They began to look beyond their new borders, to the whole of eastern and southeastern Asia with its vast stores of resources and products. As a first step in the invasion of Southeast Asia, the Japanese attacked Pearl Harbor and crippled the United States Navy which was based there. Facing only minor opposition they swept into Singapore, and on into the Netherlands East Indies. They took over southern Burma, and reached the borders of India. They occupied the northern part of New Guinea, and most of the islands of Oceania. It took four years of hard fighting to defeat the Japanese military forces, and to strip away all the territories and possessions they had gained during this period of imperial expansion.

Now Japan has adopted a new model for its development. Between 1952 and 1962 Japan had the fastest rate of economic growth ever achieved by any nation. The

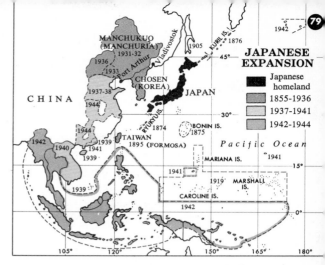

79

JAPANESE EXPANSION

- Japanese homeland
- 1855-1936
- 1937-1941
- 1942-1944

gross national product has increased about 9 per cent per year, and the value of manufactured goods has increased an incredible 20 per cent per year.

This enormous rate of growth has been the result of five programs. First is the program of new capital formation. The Japanese have used 25 per cent per year of their gross national product for new capital formation. Second is the program for the development of a large domestic market for manufactured products. Japan stands second only to the United States in the volume of purchases of such things as household appliances, refrigerators, and TV sets. Third is the transformation of the agriculture, which has changed Japan from an importer of foods to a country that can feed its own population. Fourth is the effort to make education more widespread. In 1963 Japan came third in the world in the proportion of its young people in college. And fifth is the attack on the population problem. Although the death rate has been lowered and life expectancy has been increased from 50 years, before World War II, to 70 years, the birth rate has also been lowered. No longer is Japan threatened by a population explosion.

Modern Japan: Population. Since World War II the United States has worked to put Japan back on its feet, and to reorient Japanese attitudes and objectives. The process has not been simple. Unlike the communist reconstruction of China, which was carried out by force, the reconstruction of Japan has been done largely through education and persuasion. Moreover, the United States bases and armed forces which have remained in Japan have provided the country with a part of the dollars needed to pay for imports.

Japan, shorn of its mainland resources and markets, faced a serious population problem. During the period when Japan was isolated from the rest of the world, the population reached a stable figure of a little less than 30,000,000. After 1868, however, the rate of increase rose sharply as a result of a decrease in the death rate together with a continued high birth rate. During the period of Japanese imperialist expansion large families were encouraged. To be sure there was a slight decline in the birth rate among people living in the cities, but because of the large proportion of young people in the population no large drop in the birth rate was anticipated. The census of 1960 counted a population of 93,400,000. Students of Japanese problems were pessimistic about the possibility that Japan's economy could be built fast enough to stay even with the population growth, let alone gain on it. But since 1960 the Japanese seem to have accomplished something like a miracle. There has been a notable decrease in the birth rate. It is now estimated that the population will not reach 100,000,000 until after 1970.

Japan's population is mostly urban (about 66 per cent). This proportion of urban people is higher than in any other Oriental country. In the 1950's there were four metropolitan areas of more than a million people each: Tōkyō-Yokohama (the world's second largest metropolitan area, with more than 11,000,000, compared with 14,000,000 in Greater New York), Ōsaka, Kyōto, and Nagoya. There were sixty-four cities with populations of over 100,000.

The rural population is clustered with great density in the small areas suitable for agriculture, and is spread thinly over much of the hilly and mountainous surfaces (Map 1, pp. 4-5). Hokkaidō remains the Japanese frontier, and it is on Hokkaidō that the largest rates of population increase are taking place.

Agriculture. The Japanese are able to supply their food requirements from their own farms and fisheries. Although only about 16 per cent of the total national territory is permanently under cultivation, this small area has been made highly productive. About 53 per cent of the cultivated land is used for paddy rice, and only 10 per cent is used for non-food crops such as mulberry trees and cotton. So great is the pressure on the land that very little can be spared to grow feed crops for animals. In southern Shikoku there are two crops of rice each year, and as far north as the line shown on Map 77 the rice paddies are used for a second winter crop such as wheat, barley, millet, soy beans, potatoes, or vegetables. Only in the far north of Hokkaidō is it impossible to grow rice. In the southern half of the country the steep margins of the alluvial lowlands are used for citrus fruits and mulberry trees; and near the coast west of Tōkyō there is a major area of tea cultivation. Tea is also grown on the western part of Kyūshū.

The Japanese increased their production of rice by about 30 per cent in the years between 1955 and 1960, and this they achieved without any significant increase in acreage. This revolution in agriculture was the result of the application of modern technology, together with a fundamental change in the farm system. The large land properties were

A tea plantation in Japan. The crop is grown very successfully in some western parts of the country.

redistributed as private holdings among the former tenants. Farmers the world over are willing to work more efficiently on land that they own—and the Japanese are no exception. The farmers were supplied with improved seeds, with insecticides, and with an increased volume of inorganic fertilizer from Japanese factories. Large applications of lime (from easily available limestone) counteracted the prevailing acidity of Japanese soils. And manual labor was, to a certain extent, replaced by machinery. In 1955 about 47 per cent of the Japanese workers were employed in agriculture, but by 1960 this proportion had been reduced to about 33 per cent. A revolution in agriculture requires a reduction in the proportion of workers employed in farming, and this is being accomplished in Japan. As a result the Japanese lead the world in the yields of crops per acre. *non seq. ?*

One of the exciting changes in the technology of agriculture in Japan is the new use of small, power-driven machines. It has long been said that the Japanese farms have been too small to permit the use of machinery. Certainly, the big tractors and harvesters used in the United States could not be introduced in Japan. But there has been a major break-through in the invention and manufacture of small, power-driven farm machines. There is a two-wheel tractor, moved by a gasoline motor, guided by a farmer who walks behind it. The tractor can draw a small plow, a harrow, or a harvesting machine designed to operate in small fields. The possibilities of using the Japanese technological advances throughout the southern and eastern Asian countries are enormous.

Forests and Fisheries. Forests and forest products play an important part in the Japanese economy. No other densely populated country in the world has such a high proportion of its total area under forest. More than half of the land area of Japan is forested; and from these forests, mostly in the mountains, the Japanese produce more wood than any other country of comparable size. Wood is used for charcoal, and also as the basis for a variety of products, including rayon and paper. The forests are as carefully managed as crops, so that the annual growth does not drop behind the annual cut.

The Japanese catch more fish, eat more fish per person, and export more fish products than do the people of any other country. Fish and other sea food, including seaweed, have long made up an important part of the Japanese diet. Small coastal-fishing boats supply a major part of the fish catch for domestic use, but larger oceangoing ships operate as far south as Singapore, and as far north as the Bering Sea. These large ships are also floating canneries in which the fish are processed immediately. Japanese herring are sold in large quantities in Great Britain, and Japanese tuna is used widely in the United States. Fishing gives employment to more than 1,000,000 people.

Manufacturing Industries. Japan is not well supplied with industrial raw materials other than wood (Map 78). The production of synthetic fibers for the manufacture of modern textiles has brought about a very large reduction in the market for silk. Japan's most important industrial resource is coal, but Japanese coal is not suitable for making steel. There are some small oil fields, but

The Yawata iron and steel industry of northern Kyūshū, Japan.

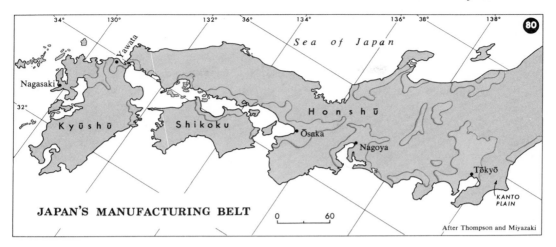

34° 130°   132°   36°   134°   136° 38°   138°   80

Sea   of   Japan

Yawata

Nagasaki

H o n s h ū

32°

Ōsaka

K y ū s h ū   Shikoku

Nagoya

Tōkyō

KANTO
PLAIN

JAPAN'S MANUFACTURING BELT   0 ____ 60

After Thompson and Miyazaki

the reserves are not large. There is a serious lack of iron ore, or of the hardeners of steel, which are now supplied from Brazil. The only mineral resource that provides Japan with a surplus over its own needs is sulfur. On the other hand, Japan is provided with an abundance of small water-power sites. A large supply of electric power comes from numerous small hydroelectric stations, supplemented during the winter dry season by steam-electric stations.

Japan's manufacturing industries are concentrated in a belt running from Tōkyō in the northeast to Nagasaki in the southwest. The belt is about eight hundred miles long. The major concentrations of manufacturing industry are in the Tōkyō-Yokohama metropolitan area, around Nagoya, Ōsaka, and Yawata (Map 80). Along the shores of Japan's Inland Sea (between Shikoku and Honshū) there are numerous small manufacturing towns.

Japan's economy reached maturity about 1940. It has rebuilt its industries since World War II, providing a great variety of manufactured products. The textile industry, which in 1923 accounted for nearly 45 per cent of all Japan's industrial production, by 1950 accounted for less than 20 per cent.

Cotton textiles are still important, but the once-important silk industry is today almost gone. The decline of textiles has been matched by the rise of metals, machinery, and chemicals, by optical goods, precision instruments, and other products requiring an abundance of inexpensive, skilled workers. The steel centers, Tōkyō, Ōsaka, and Yawata, provide support for a variety of metal industries, including shipbuilding, in which field Japan now ranks among the world leaders. There has been an enormous increase in chemical industries—manufacturing fertilizers and synthetic fibers.

The Viability of Japan. Japan's problem has not changed. The islands are occupied by such a large population that they cannot survive with a purely agricultural economy. Lacking the raw materials for industry, Japan has to secure them elsewhere, add value to them through the manufacturing process, and sell the finished products abroad. But in a world in conflict, and with many markets closed to Japanese goods, the future is anything but secure. Could Japan survive the withdrawal of the United States armed forces? Has a decade or so of indoctrination placed the Japanese securely on the road to democracy? Here is an Oriental country that has been deeply shaken by the impact of the great revolutions, and that is now struggling to integrate its economy with that of the free world. Survival is dependent on the success of this effort.

KOREA

The Korean Peninsula serves as a land bridge between China and Japan. People have been coming and going over this bridge for thousands of years. Those who stayed and settled became Koreans. Racially and culturally the Koreans are a mixture, in which Chinese and Japanese traits are the most common. In the north the Chinese element in the mixture is the stronger; in the south the Japanese element is predominant. Yet the Koreans have been able to develop a coherent and distinctive culture, and to maintain their individuality in spite of repeated invasions, conquests, and years of economic exploitation by both China and Japan. However, the increasing strength of the Soviet Union, just to the north, has added a third great power to the two already poised over Korea on its strategically situated bit of land.

The Habitat. The rugged nature of the Korean Peninsula is shown on Map 74. Although the mountains that form the backbone of the peninsula are only six or seven thousand feet in altitude, the slopes are very steep. Rugged mountains form the border between Manchuria and Korea, and these mountains continue southward, rising steeply from the east coast, more gently from the west coast. Rib-like ridges descend from the main range to the western coast, with alluvial lowlands in between. There is not much flat land, and all of it is in the west.

Korea is at about the same latitude as Chesapeake Bay in North America. For the reasons previously explained the winters are colder, latitude for latitude, in eastern Asia than in eastern North America. The summers, especially in the southern part of Korea, are hot and wet.

Korea and Japan. Korea has for many centuries been more or less closely tied to China. It was conquered first by the Mongols. Later it was forced to pay tribute to the Manchus when they came to power in China, but was otherwise left to govern itself.

But Korea gradually came more and more under the influence of Japan. When the Russo-Japanese War began the Japanese guaranteed Korean independence in return for permission to establish bases on Korean soil. In 1910, all pretense cast aside, Japan annexed Korea, renaming it Chosen. Japan made use of Korea as a source of coking coal, and as a route of passage to the richer resources of Manchuria. Although the Koreans were too numerous to raise surplus rice for export, they were forced to send rice to Japan. As a result living standards were painfully reduced. Today the Koreans view any suggestions for closer trade relations with Japan with distaste.

The Partition of Korea. Toward the end of World War II, the Soviet Union declared war on Japan. As a result, when Korea was granted its independence in 1945, the southern half of its territory was occupied by troops from the United States, and the northern half by troops from the Soviet Union. The dividing line was the parallel of 38°N. This has become a permanent dividing line between the communist Democratic People's Republic of Korea, and the Republic of Korea (Map 74). However, in 1950, the North Koreans attempted to invade the southern section of the country. United Nations forces came to the defense of South Korea in its critical position, but it was not until 1953 that the war was brought to an end.

Post-War Korea. In 1962 the population of South Korea was estimated at 26,100,000, while that of North Korea was a little over 8,000,000. South Korea is the part of the peninsula where most of the agriculture is concentrated (Map 77). On the alluvial plains in the southwest the land is used for paddy rice, with barley grown on the paddies as a winter crop. Toward the north, where the growing season is too short for rice, the chief grains are barley, wheat, millet, and maize. The dense population of South Korea is mostly engaged in farming.

North Korea, on the other hand, has the industries, the iron ore mines, the coal, and the hydroelectric power stations (Map 78).

Korea is crippled, and the problem of rebuilding the economy of the country, even with aid from outside, cannot easily be solved. The major difficulty is that South Korea and North Korea form one economic unit with complementary parts. Separated, neither part can develop a strong economy. Moreover, the separation which was imposed by force is no more acceptable to the Korean people than was control by Japan.

SUMMARY

The East Asian Culture Region is one of the world's major theaters of conflict, where the communist and capitalist systems face each other across sharply drawn borders. This is a region dominated by the ancient culture of China. From China came attitudes, objectives, and skills that were highly perfected, and that had been the traditional way of life for countless generations. The Japanese, on their islands, were able to develop a separate and uniquely distinctive variation on the Chinese themes—a coherent and viable culture in an isolated habitat. These two peoples—the Chinese and the Japanese—became as antagonistic in their culture region as did the French and the Germans in the European region.

Now, in the aftermath of World War II, the intensity of conflict in East Asia has reached new heights. And the conflicts are incredibly complex. It is not just a conflict between communism as applied in China and modified capitalism as applied in Japan; it is not just a conflict between those who have property and those who do not; it is not just a conflict between autocracy in the traditional East Asian sense and democracy in the European and American sense: it includes all these conflicts and many more. China now stands in major opposition, within the communist world, to the Soviet Union—and challenges Soviet domination of that world. And the new China has the resources, the manpower, and the skills to become a major military power if power is to be applied. The whole world stands aghast at the impending explosion in the East Asian Culture Region that the great European and American revolutions, and the communist reaction, may have ignited.

But now the militant communists of China face the challenge of the new Japan. Here is another demonstration, for all to see, that economic development can be pushed forward rapidly, and the inequities of landlord-tenant relationships can be eliminated by an orderly process of change in a free society. It may well be that many of the most troublesome problems of the economic development of densely populated countries, such as India or Indonesia, can be attacked successfully with technical assistance from Japan. It may well be that Japan will prove to be one of the most important strongholds in the war with the communist reaction.

10

THE
AFRICAN
CULTURE REGION

Country	Political Status	Latest Estimate Population	Capital City
Angola	Port. Overseas Province	4,900,000 ('62)	Luanda
Basutoland	British Colony	685,000 ('60)	Maseru
Bechuanaland	British Protectorate	340,000 ('60)	
Burundi	Kingdom	2,234,000 ('60)	Usumbura
Cameroun	Republic	4,200,000 ('62)	Douala
Cape Verde Is.	Port. Overseas Province	201,549 ('60)	
Central African Republic	Republic	1,300,000 ('62)	Bangui
Chad	Republic	2,700,000 ('62)	Fort-Lamy
Comoro Is.	French Overseas Territory	183,000 ('60)	
Congo Republic	Republic	900,000 ('62)	Brazzaville
Congo, Rep. of the	Republic	14,800,000 ('62)	Léopoldville
Dahomey	Republic	2,100,000 ('62)	Porto-Novo
Ethiopia Incl. Eritrea	Monarchy	20,000,000 ('62)	Addis Ababa
French Somaliland	French Overseas Territory	67,000 ('60)	Djibouti
Gabon	Republic	500,000 ('62)	Libreville
Gambia	British Colony & Protect.	284,000 ('60)	Bathurst
Ghana	Republic	7,200,000 ('62)	Accra
Guinea	Republic	3,200,000 ('62)	Conakry
Ivory Coast	Republic	3,400,000 ('62)	Abidjan
Kenya	Republic	7,500,000 ('62)	Nairobi
Liberia	Republic	1,300,000 ('60)	Monrovia
Malagasy	Republic	5,700,000 ('62)	Tananarive
Mali	Republic	4,300,000 ('62)	Bamako
Mauritania	Republic	727,000 ('59)	Nouakchott
Mauritius & Depen.	British Colony	700,000 ('62)	
Mozambique	Port. Overseas Province	6,700,000 ('62)	Lourenço Marques
Niger	Republic	3,100,000 ('62)	Niamey
Nigeria	Federal Republic	36,400,000 ('62)	Lagos
Northern Rhodesia	Republic	2,515,000 ('62)	Lusaka
Nyasaland	Republic	2,921,000 ('62)	Zomba
Portuguese Guinea	Port. Overseas Province	571,000 ('60)	Bissau
Reunion Island	French Overseas Dept.	336,000 ('60)	
Rwanda	Republic	2,695,000 ('60)	Kigali
St. Helena group	British Colony		
Incl. St. Helena	British Colony	5,000 ('60)	
Ascension	Dependency	457 ('60)	
Tristan da Cunha	Dependency	292 ('59)	
São Tomé & Principe	Port. Overseas Terr.	67,000 ('60)	
Senegal	Republic	3,000,000 ('62)	Dakar
Seychelles	British Colony	41,425 ('60)	
Sierra Leone	Republic	2,600,000 ('62)	Freetown
Somali Republic	Republic	2,000,000 ('62)	Mogadiscio
South Africa, Rep. of	Republic	16,500,000 ('62)	Pretoria
Southern Rhodesia	Republic	3,848,000 ('62)	Salisbury
Southwest Africa	U.N. Mandate to S. Africa	525,064 ('60)	Windhoek
Spanish Guinea	Spanish Colonies	245,989 ('60)	
Incl. Annobon Corisco, Elobey Fernando Póo		47,000 ('60)	
Rio Muni		169,000 ('60)	
Swaziland	British Protectorate	259,000 ('60)	Mbabane
Tanganyika	Republic	9,600,000 ('62)	Dar es Salaam
Togo	Republic	1,500,000 ('62)	Lomé
Uganda	Republic	7,000,000 ('62)	Entebbe
Upper Volta	Republic	4,400,000 ('62)	Ouagadougou
Zanzibar	Sultanate	307,000 ('60)	Zanzibar

◄ *Kariba Dam, Zambeze River.*

The African Culture Region—Africa south of the Sahara—is the ancestral home of the Negroid peoples. The great interior of Africa has been known to Europeans for scarcely a century, and its potential wealth of resources is only beginning to be appreciated. Throughout most of Europe's history, Africa, beyond the great desert, was known only as a source of Negro slaves and gold, and of such exotic things as ivory and ostrich plumes. Only in the nineteenth and twentieth centuries have people from outside Africa actually settled in parts of the interior, bringing to the long-isolated African communities the revolutionary concepts which were then spreading across the world. Today, in our divided world, the difficult and emotion-laden problems of race relations come to a sharp focus in Africa.

For a long time the continental interior was described as "Darkest Africa." The Greeks and Romans knew only the northern fringe of the desert, and the Nile Valley as far as the first cataract at Syene (now Aswân). The country south of Ethiopia, from which the main stream of the Nile flowed, remained totally unknown. Aristotle, and the Greek and Roman geographers who followed him, had been certain that if temperatures were so high in the northern part of the great desert they must be still higher near the equator. The equatorial part of the Torrid Zone, they taught, was uninhabitable. Muslim traders and missionaries who traveled widely over the world did, however, penetrate Africa south of the Sahara, taking with them the religion of Islam and carrying on a profitable trade in slaves and exotic products. In the fourteenth century Ibn Batuta journeyed southward along the African east coast as far as 10°S, but his main interest was in trade. Starting with the voyage of Gil Eanes in 1433, the Portuguese little by little extended their explorations southward along the west coast, until, in 1473, they crossed the equator and found that temperatures there were not so high as in the northern Sahara. In 1487 Bartholomeu Dias rounded Cape Agulhas at the southern end of Africa, and in 1497-1498 Vasco da Gama sailed all the way to India.

From the sixteenth century on, the coasts of Africa were frequently visited by Europeans—who established the first ports. Ships sailing the Indian Ocean stopped at Cape Town to take on supplies while on their way to and from Europe; and here the Dutch East India Company established a colony in 1652. Slave ships made frequent voyages to such ports as Bathurst, Bissau, Conakry, and Lagos to buy slaves; and so many Negroes were carried away that Africa actually declined in population between the seventeenth and nineteenth centuries. *really?*

But the interior of Africa remained the largest blank area on the maps of the world, apart from the polar regions. In the north, the Sahara effectively blocked the way south into Central Africa for the Europeans. However, in 1796 Mungo Park followed the old route over which slave dealers had brought slaves to Bathurst, and was the first European to reach the Niger River. And meanwhile, in 1772, James Bruce had climbed into Ethiopia and found the source of the Blue Nile. The first European expedition to cross the Sahara reached Lake Chad in 1823. Farther south the way inland was blocked, not only by steep escarpments covered with dense rain forest and by spectacular falls and rapids, but also by the hostility of the African traders, who did not want Europeans to compete in the profitable business of capturing and selling slaves. It was 1856 before John Speke discovered the source of the White Nile, and 1860 before he proved that the Nile actually flowed out of Lake Victoria. The crossing of the Kala-

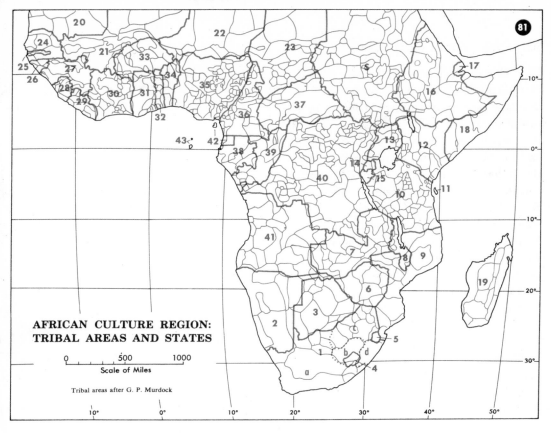

**AFRICAN CULTURE REGION:
TRIBAL AREAS AND STATES**

0   500   1000
Scale of Miles

Tribal areas after G. P. Murdock

KEY TO POLITICAL DIVISIONS IN 1963

Southern Africa

1. Republic of South Africa
   a Cape of Good Hope
   b Orange Free State
   c Transvaal
   d Natal
2. Southwest Africa
3. Bechuanaland
4. Basutoland
5. Swaziland

South-Central and East Africa

6. Southern Rhodesia (Zimbabye)
7. Northern Rhodesia (Zambia)
8. Nyasaland (Malawi)
9. Mozambique
10. Tanganyika
11. Zanzibar
12. Kenya
13. Uganda
14. Rwanda
15. Burundi
16. Ethiopia
17. French Somaliland
18. Somali Republic
19. Malagasy Republic

Western and Central Africa

20. Islamic Republic of Mauritania
21. Republic of Mali
22. Republic of Niger
23. Republic of Chad
24. Republic of Senegal
25. Gambia
26. Portuguese Guinea
27. Republic of Guinea
28. Sierra Leone
29. Liberia
30. Republic of the Ivory Coast
31. Ghana
32. Republic of Togo
33. Republic of Upper Volta
34. Republic of Dahomey
35. Nigeria
36. Republic of Cameroon
37. Central African Republic
38. Gabon Republic
39. Congo Republic
40. Republic of the Congo
41. Angola
42. Spanish Guinea
43. São Tomé, Principe

S. Sudan (Included in the North African-Southwest Asian Culture Region)

hari Desert in southern Africa, and the identification of the main outlines of the drainage pattern of eastern Africa were accomplished by David Livingstone, a Scottish missionary, between 1840 and 1874; and in 1877 Henry M. Stanley crossed from the Indian Ocean to the Atlantic, exploring for the first time the basin of the Congo River. These explorers found most of Africa thinly populated by pastoralists, and by hunters and shifting cultivators in the forest regions. There were only a few areas of relatively dense population: around Lake Victoria; along the lower Congo; in the Sudan west of Lake Chad; and in the forests of southwestern Nigeria and central Ghana.

The partitioning of Africa among the European colonial powers took place rapidly after the Berlin Conference of 1884. Even in 1885 the European territorial claims were mostly restricted to the coasts; but almost at once thereafter the whole interior had been divided up among the Europeans. The insets on Map 82 show the territorial claims of 1885 and of 1910. The German colonies and protectorates included Southwest Africa, Tanganyika, Togo, and Kamerun, all of which were placed under League of Nations mandates after World War I. The European countries that still held colonies in Africa south of the Sahara in 1940 included Great Britain, France, Belgium, Spain, and Portugal.

Then in the 1950's the whole colonial structure abruptly fell to pieces. It has been British and French policy to prepare the colonies to administer their own affairs, and to give support to the training of African political leaders. Belgium, Spain, and Portugal, on the other hand, have not only resisted the rising demand for independence, but have also taken pains to see that ambi-

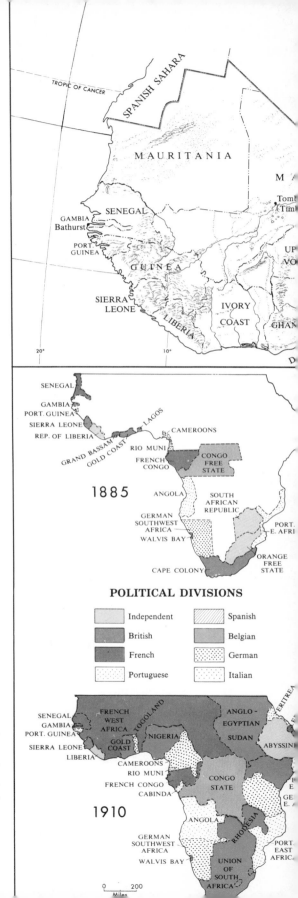

POLITICAL DIVISIONS

	Independent		Spanish
	British		Belgian
	French		German
	Portuguese		Italian

AFRICAN CULTURE REGION
SURFACE FEATURES AND POLITICAL DIVISIONS

82

GERIA

LIBYA

EGYPT

S A H A R A

NIGER

CHAD

SUDAN

Lake Chad

Chari R.

FRENCH
SOMALILAND

ETHIOPIA

Nile R.

Atbara R.

Blue Nile R.

White Nile R.

GERIA

Benue R.

REPUBLIC OF
CAMEROUN

CENTRAL AFRICAN
REPUBLIC

SOMALI REPUBLIC

o Póo

SP GUINEA

GABON

CONGO REPUBLIC

Congo R.

Stanleyville

UGANDA

Lake
Rudolph

Lake
Albert

Mt. Elgon

Mt. Kenya

KENYA

EQUATOR

0°

REPUBLIC

OF THE

CONGO

Lake
Edward

RWANDA

Lake
Victoria

Kilimanjaro

Indian

Brazzaville
Léopoldville

BURUNDI

Ocean

CABINDA

Matadi

Lake
Tanganyika

TANGANYIKA

ANGOLA

Elizabethville

Lake Nyasa

antic

ean

NORTHERN RHODESIA

MOZAMBIQUE

Mozambique Channel

MALAGASY REPUBLIC

Zambezi

Livingstone

Victoria
Falls

SOUTHERN

RHODESIA

Salisbury

Beira

Bulawayo

SOUTHWEST

AFRICA

BECHUANALAND

WALVIS BAY

Limpopo R.

TROPIC OF CAPRICORN

20°

Pretoria

Johannesburg

SWAZILAND

Kimberley

Orange R.

Bloemfontein

BASUTOLAND

SOUTH

AFRICA

30°

Cape Town

Cape Agulhas

0   300   600
Scale of Miles

EUROPE

U.S.S.R.

Atlantic Ocean

SOUTH
AMERICA

Indian Ocean

10°

tious African leaders have been thwarted. Furthermore, the boundaries of the European colonies were originally drawn with scant reference to the realities of African geography, either the realities of physical geography or the geography of tribal groups. Often the boundaries were straight lines drawn on almost blank maps, where the chief features were incorrectly-plotted rivers.

A large part of Africa's current difficulties stems from this discordant relationship of the new states with the underlying tribal areas (Map 81). It is important to understand that tribal loyalties are still strong. In the cities there are European-educated men and women who speak French or English, and who are quite conscious of the problems of building a viable state. But 95 per cent of the Africans still live under primitive conditions, thinking of themselves not as Nigerians, Tanganyikans, or Kenyans, but rather as Yoruba, Chaga, or Masai. There are something like six hundred different tribal groups in this culture region, many of which speak languages that cannot be understood by the people of other tribes, and which have quite different ways of raising food, training children, settling disputes, and even of keeping on good relations with the supernatural. The tribe offers the individual his only security and dignity: for the leaders of a tribe are bound to provide shelter and food for fellow tribesmen in need; and the prestige enjoyed by an individual is determined by tribal custom. But the tribal areas are cut by the state borders, and all but two states include many tribes. The tribes are miniature nationalities, politically self-conscious and occupying more or less clearly defined extents of territory. If they are to be grouped together in viable states it is necessary to formulate state-ideas that

can become stronger than the tribal loyalties. Clearly the present states are not permanent: there are numerous federal groupings that may form eventually, and some of the present states may break into separate parts.

Within the African Culture Region in 1963 there were forty-three separate political entities, including the Spanish and Portuguese possessions on the islands in the Gulf of Guinea (Maps 81 and 82). The population of the whole region (Map 3, p. 7) was estimated to be about 200,000,000: about 6 per cent of the world's population on 16 per cent of the inhabited land area of the world.

THE HABITAT

(Maps 5, 6, 7, 8, and 82) South of the Sahara, Africa, with the exception of West Africa, extends like a massive tableland with steeply scarped edges southward across the equator almost as far as 35°S. There are large areas of level land, which are grass-covered, or covered with a mixture of grass and deciduous woodland; but there are also towering mountain peaks, permanently snow-covered. The unbearable torrid heat that the Greek geographers expected to find does not exist, but there are places where 80° temperatures are combined with high humidity to create a hot-house climate and scenery which is described by the journalists as "steaming jungles." The greater part of Africa, however, is by no means a steaming jungle: much of it is high enough to be continuously cool, and much of it suffers more from a deficiency of moisture than from an excess of it.

Surface Features. The African tableland stands high in southern Africa, and the escarpments that form the margins are especially steep. From a narrow patch of coastal lowland in South Africa the land rises in a series of steps, each with scarped sides. First comes the Southern Karroo, then the Great Karroo, then the Northern Karroo—the latter standing some 4,000 feet above sea level, rising to 6,000 feet in the High Veldt of Transvaal, and to more than 10,000 feet in Basutoland. The high eastern rim of the tableland is known as the Drakensburg: from the crest the escarpment drops 5,000 feet down into Natal. The Orange River, with its large tributary the Vaal, rises at the very crest of the Drakensburg and drains westward, finally dropping over several falls to the Atlantic which it only reaches during the rainy season. To the north of the Orange drainage basin, the Limpopo River gathers water from a wide area of the tableland, draining eastward through a narrow canyon to the lowland along the coast of the Indian Ocean in Mozambique. Still farther north is the Zambezi River which also drains eastward, dropping between two hundred and three hundred feet over the Victoria Falls into a narrow canyon on the border between Southern Rhodesia and Northern Rhodesia.

Some of the earth's most spectacular surface features are to be found in East Africa. This is a region of great rift valleys, where long, narrow blocks of the earth's crust have dropped down between steeply scarped sides. The rifts start in Mozambique, where Lake Nyasa is formed. North of Nyasa one curving system of rifts bends around to the west of Lake Victoria, occupied by lakes Tanganyika, Kivu, Edward, and Albert. Another system of rifts runs due north from Lake Nyasa, east of Lake Victoria. In this rift lies Lake Rudolf. Still farther north the rift cuts through the midst of the Highlands of Ethiopia, and continues northward to form the Red Sea depression, the Gulf of Aqaba, the Dead Sea depression, and the central rift valley of Syria (Map 61, p. 246).

Through these cracks in the earth's crust, molten lava was once squeezed up to the surface. The Highlands of Ethiopia were built up by successive flows of lava, reaching a general elevation of 9,000 feet above sea level, with isolated peaks up to 15,000 feet. Smaller lava accumulations were also located along the margins of the rifts farther south. In Kenya and Tanganyika there are several high, cone-shaped volcanoes, including Mount Kilimanjaro (19,565 ft.), Mount Kenya, and Mount Elgon.

To the west of the rift valleys and the lava plateaus is the vast basin drained by the Congo River and its numerous tributaries. The river rises near the border of Northern Rhodesia and flows northward parallel to the rift valleys, frequently interrupted by falls and rapids as it descends toward the Congo Basin. From Stanleyville to Léopoldville the river flows 1,090 miles across a plain, easily navigable by river boats. The Congo Basin lies about 1,000 feet above sea level; and below Léopoldville the river drops over the Livingstone Falls, descending 852 feet in 220 miles. The lower course of the river is navigable by ocean vessels for about one hundred miles, as far inland as Matadi.

All the rivers that flow northward to the Sahara have one common characteristic. As they approach the region of aridity they rapidly lose volume through evaporation, and they drop much of the load of alluvium that they are carrying. The channels tend to split into separate, or braided channels, and the water spreads out in shallow lakes with marshy shores. The Nile, which drains Lake Victoria, and pours over the edge of the rift valley, over the Murchison Falls, to Lake Albert, then flows northward into the Sudd, a sheet of water about 250 miles long by 200 miles wide, the surface of which is covered by floating papyrus and aquatic grasses. Half of the water is lost by evaporation, and only a shrunken remnant of the Nile continues northward through the Sudan toward Khartoum. The river could scarcely persist in its flow across Egypt to the Mediterranean were it not for two tributaries that join it from the rainy Ethiopian Highlands—the Blue Nile and the Atbara River.

The Niger and the Chari behave in a similar manner as they approach the desert margin. The Niger, which rises in the hilly upland near the border of Sierra Leone, flows northeastward into a three-hundred-mile-long dry lake bed upstream from Tombouctou, from which it once drained northeastward into the Sahara. But the lower Niger, fed by the heavy rains of what is now southern Nigeria, cut its valley headward until it captured the upper Niger and drained it off to the Gulf of Guinea. A tributary of the lower Niger, the Benue, is in the process of cutting its valley headward to capture the western branch of the Chari River. The Chari drains from Central Africa northward to the edge of the desert, where it spreads out into the shallow Lake Chad. Similar behavior can be observed in the southern hemisphere where the rivers reach the edge of the Kalahari Desert, and where the Zambezi River has captured some of the interior drainage.

Climate and Vegetation. The pattern of climate and vegetation in Africa is relatively simple. In the north, forming the northern boundary of the African Culture Region, is the Sahara, the southern limit of which runs more or less east and west from Mauritania to Sudan, passing a little to the north of Tombouctou, Lake Chad, and Khartoum. The dry belt extends southward along the east coast of Africa almost as far as Zanzi-

bar; although this coast of the Indian Ocean is within the area of alternating monsoon winds, these winds are parallel to the land at all seasons along the Somali coast and fail to bring much moisture.

In the southern hemisphere there is another dry-land region at about the same latitudes as the Sahara. This is the Kalahari. Moisture deficiency extends along the Atlantic coast from northern Angola southward to about 32°S. The very dry section of the coast in Southwest Africa, where the land is bathed by the cold Benguela Current, is known as the Namib. The border of the dry region extends inland into Bechuanaland and South Africa as far as the highlands of Basutoland. At the southern end of the continent, around Cape Town, there is a Mediterranean climate with winter rains (May to September) and summer droughts.

The wettest parts of Africa are along the south-facing Guinea Coast and in the northern part of the Congo Basin. In winter, in the northern hemisphere, the north winds from the Sahara reach all the way southward to the Guinea Coast; but in summer the north wind is replaced by a westerly wind that brings heavy rain to Sierra Leone and Liberia, and to the west-facing mountain slopes farther east. The relatively dry belt in eastern Ghana and in Togo is a rain shadow. The current of moist air from the west moves into the northern Congo bringing heavy rains as far as Lake Victoria and the western slopes of the Ethiopian Highlands. In this Congo region there are two rainy seasons (maxima in April and October) separated by two dry seasons.

Temperatures in this culture region are usually not extreme. Map 7 (p. 14) shows that the belt of excessively high temperatures associated with the Sahara reaches southward into the Sudan and the Chari Valley south of Lake Chad, and along the Somali Coast south of the Red Sea. The southern end of the Red Sea, which receives little actual rainfall, is the world's most uncomfortable climate in terms of high temperature and high humidity. Temperatures in the equatorial regions of West Africa and Central Africa are moderately high (average of 83° at Lagos in March), but never so high as farther north (average of 94° at Tombouctou in May). At the higher altitudes of East Africa, even on the equator, temperatures are moderate (average of 71° on the shores of Lake Victoria in March). At elevations over 5,000 feet temperatures are generally below 65°, and these places are relatively free from such insect pests as the tsetse fly.

The vegetation reflects these climatic conditions. Well-defined zones of vegetation mark the decreasing rainfall as one moves northward from the Guinea Coast or the Congo toward the edge of the Sahara. The very rainy areas support rain forests. On the edge of this forest there is a woodland savanna (parkland), which may reflect an extension of the grasslands at the expense of the forests as a result of human action. This is described by Shantz as "high-grass low-tree savanna."[1] Farther north there is a savanna with scattered trees ("acacia tall-grass savanna"), and on the edge of the dry lands there is a belt of xerophytic brush ("acacia desert-grass savanna"). There is a similar sequence of vegetation zones around the Kalahari. The Mediterranean climate of South Africa is reflected in the presence of an evergreen scrub woodland. There is a large area of grassland in South Africa and Southern Rhodesia, including the Veldt; but the higher elevations of Northern Rhodesia, Angola, and Katanga are covered with a seasonal forest (semideciduous). Most of these broad categories of vegetation have been severely modified by human action, which has the effect of extending the dry-land types of vegetation and reducing the area of forest.

SOUTHERN AFRICA[2]

The Republic of South Africa is the only state in the African Culture Region that has started the process of economic development associated with the Industrial Revolution. Yet South Africa has also gained world attention because of the racial conflict within its borders. Five contrasting groups of people occupy this country, each with traditions, customs, and values that do not blend easily with those of the others. Yet none of these groups can claim South Africa as the ancestral homeland. Two centuries ago the whole southern part of Africa was very thinly inhabited by Bushmen (a non-Negro pygmy race) and Hottentots (a nomadic people related to the Bushmen). The invasion of Bantu-speaking Negro tribes from the north forced the earlier inhabitants to flee to the driest and least accessible parts of the Kalahari, where some Hottentots still survive. The people who came into empty southern Africa were the Dutch, the British, the Indians, and the Bantu who were used as slaves. These groups, and the racially mixed *Coloureds*, make up the population of South Africa today.

The Course of Settlement. The first European settlers in Southern Africa were the Portuguese, who established a base at what is now Port Elizabeth late in the fifteenth century. In 1652 the Dutch occupied the

[1] H. L. Shantz and C. F. Marbut, 1923.

[2] Southern Africa includes the Republic of South Africa, which, until 1961, was a member of the British Commonwealth; Southwest Africa, a former German colony, now a United Nations Trust Territory administered by South Africa; and three British Protectorates—Bechuanaland, Basutoland, and Swaziland (Map 82).

harbor at the foot of Table Mountain where Cape Town is now situated. The fact that steep scarps inland from Cape Town impeded access to the interior was unimportant, for the Dutch were only concerned with establishing a base on their sailing route to southern Asia. At the beginning of the eighteenth century the European population of the colony numbered less than two thousand, of whom about half were Dutch, and the remainder Germans and French Huguenots. However, there were also about two thousand Negro slaves who had been brought from the north, and a number of Malays brought by trading ships from Southeast Asia. The descendents of the early Dutch settlers today form one of the five distinct groups in South Africa—the people known as *Afrikaners*, whose language, Afrikaans, is derived from the Dutch.

From the beginning the Afrikaners resented outside authority. Some of them started to migrate, or trek, across the Karroo so that they would be beyond the administrative reach of even the Dutch East India Company. The British gained control of Cape Town as a result of a European war (1795-1803), and British colonists began to move into Cape Town after 1820. As a result the Dutch farmers, known as *Boers*, started the "Great Trek" out of the Karroo and into the more remote interior of the Northern Karroo. The trek, begun in 1836, resulted in the agricultural settlement of the High Veldt, and the establishment of the Transvaal and the Orange Free State. Here the Boers fought with the various tribes of Bantus, especially the Zulus, to establish control of the Veldt. Cape Colony was confirmed as a British possession in 1852, at which time the British recognized the independence of the Transvaal and the Orange Free State. In 1856 Natal, along the coast

to the northeast of Cape Colony, was established as a British Crown Colony, with its administrative center at Durban.

This separation of British and Afrikaners was abruptly ended by the discovery of diamonds along the Orange and Vaal rivers in 1867, and of gold at Johannesburg in 1886. British miners flocked northward, invading the country in which the Afrikaners had laid out their farms. The Afrikaners asked only to be left alone, but the facts of geography were against them. The success of the gold and diamond mines was followed inevitably by a desire on the part of the British for political control of the area. When the Afrikaners resisted, war broke out. As a result of the Boer War (1899-1902), the British gained control of the Transvaal and the Orange Free State. However, they succeeded in regaining the cooperation of the Boers, and in 1910 the Union of South Africa was formed, including as provinces the Cape of Good Hope (Cape Province), Natal, the Transvaal, and the Orange Free State. As a reflection of the composite nature of the Union, the administrative capital was placed at Pretoria, the legislative at Cape Town, and the judicial branch at Bloemfontein.

Population. The population of South Africa was estimated in 1962 at about 16,500,000. Cape Province and the Transvaal have the largest populations. About 43 per cent of the people of South Africa live in cities, of which Johannesburg (with a little over 1,000,000 inhabitants) is the largest (Map 3, p. 7).

The five contrasted groups of people who make up the South African population are not evenly distributed throughout the national territory. The three non-European groups make up 79 per cent of the total. Native Africans of the Bantu group (including Kaffirs, Zulus, Basutos, and Matabeles) make up 67 per cent of the total, and more than 50 per cent of the population of each of the provinces. About 9 per cent of the total are Coloureds, a people of mixed ancestry, partly Bantu and Hottentot, partly Malay, and partly European. Since they are neither wholly Negroid nor wholly Caucasoid, they are caught between the two groups and are the ones who suffer the most from racial conflict. The Coloureds are most numerous in Cape Province. Among the non-Europeans there are also people of Indian ancestry who make up 3 per cent of the total population of South Africa. They are most numerous in Natal, where they were brought about a century ago to work on the sugar cane plantations. The Europeans, who make up 21 per cent of the total population, are divided into two sharply contrasted groups: the Afrikaners who comprise about two thirds of the European group, and the British who make up the other third.

The Africans are an essential part of the labor force throughout the Republic, and in every field of economic activity. About 2,000,000 Africans work as farm hands or as tenants on farms owned by Europeans. There are more than 2,000,000 Africans living in the cities, where they are employed in the manufacturing industries, in transportation, and as servants. About 3,000,000 Africans live in areas that have been reserved for their exclusive use, and within which they administer their own affairs. But the farms within these African areas are not sufficiently productive to support so large a population; about 70 per cent of the able-bodied men take jobs in the mines, leaving their families on the farms. Mine workers are also recruited in the neighboring British protectorates—Bechuanaland, Swaziland, and Basutoland. The mine workers are housed in "compounds" where they live and work behind carefully guarded fences. Although the mine workers are well paid, it is always difficult to find enough workers because of the conditions under which they are made to live. They are separated from their families, and can leave the fenced compounds only with special permission from the police, or when their contracts with the mining companies run out. Since contracts usually run for as much as a year or eighteen months, this long separation from wives and children is a great hardship.

Agriculture. The area reserved for the Africans is intended to provide them with enough land to raise their own subsistence crops. Traditionally the Bantu counts his wealth in terms of the number of cattle he owns. He does not easily accept the idea of private property in land, for in his native culture land is held in common by the tribe, and the chief of the tribe assigns plots of land to the heads of families in accordance with their needs. But animals are private property, and the more animals a man owns the better is his economic position and the higher is his prestige. Usually the farm work is done by the women and children and the older men, while the able-bodied men in their most productive years seek necessary additional income by working in the mines or on the farms of the Europeans. The overworked land is already seriously damaged by soil erosion, and the pastures have been so heavily overgrazed that there has been an invasion of dry-land vegetation from the Kalahari into areas that once supported a good grass cover. This invasion is not due to a change of the climate, as some insist, but rather to a lowering of the groundwater table due to bad farm practices.

Agriculture is no longer the basic element in the South African economy. Although 33 per cent of the workers are still employed in agriculture, this group contributes only 14 per cent of the gross national product. Nearly 75 per cent of the cropland of the Republic is located in the triangular area on the High Veldt of the Orange Free State and the southern Transvaal (Map 83). Here the farms produce maize, wheat, dairy cattle, sheep, and poultry, with peanuts and tobacco on the poorer marginal lands. Maize is the staple food of the Africans, and most of it is eaten directly as human food. Animals are fattened on alfalfa, if they are fattened at all. There are areas of mixed agriculture in the Transvaal and in Cape Province, areas of tropical crops in Natal, and areas of Mediterranean crops near Cape Town. But a large part of the national territory is too dry for crops and is used for range feeding sheep. South Africa stands second only to Australia as a source of wool from Merino sheep, most of which is exported to Great Britain.

Mining. Gold and diamonds are the products for which South Africa is famous, and which provided the support for economic development. Diamonds were discovered in 1867 in the alluvial gravels of the Orange and Vaal rivers, and in 1870 the great diamond source at Kimberley was opened up. In 1886 the gold in the Witwatersrand (the ridge of white waters), or simply the "Rand", was discovered, and gave rise to a gold rush. In 1870 there were only 69 miles of railroad in the whole of South Africa, but by 1886 there were 1,800 miles. By 1895 Johannesburg was connected by rail with Cape Town, Port Elizabeth, East London, Durban, and Lourenço Marques. At the present time South Africa produces nearly half of all the gold produced in the world each year, and a large share of the gem diamonds.

Diamond mining is concentrated near Kimberley and Pretoria, and along the

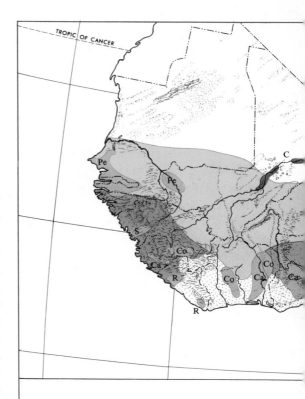

AFRICAN CULTURE REGION

AGRICULTURE

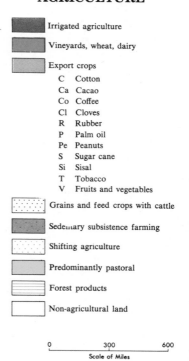

Irrigated agriculture

Vineyards, wheat, dairy

Export crops
  C   Cotton
  Ca   Cacao
  Co   Coffee
  Cl   Cloves
  R   Rubber
  P   Palm oil
  Pe   Peanuts
  S   Sugar cane
  Si   Sisal
  T   Tobacco
  V   Fruits and vegetables

Grains and feed crops with cattle

Sedentary subsistence farming

Shifting agriculture

Predominantly pastoral

Forest products

Non-agricultural land

0   300   600
Scale of Miles

After Hance, Kotschar, and Peterec

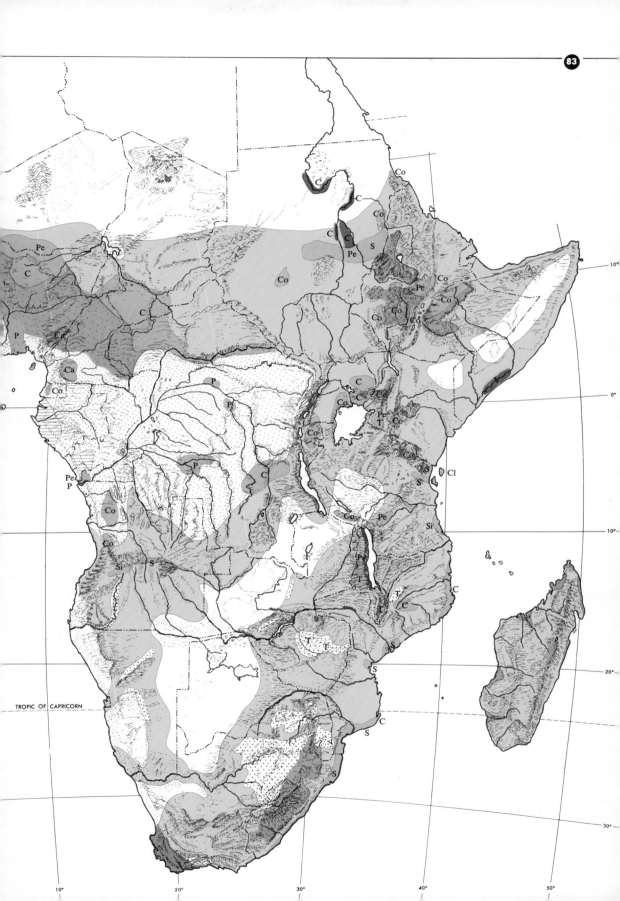

83

Pe

C

P

Co

Ca

Co

Pe
P

Co

Co

Si

Co

S

S

P

P

P

P

Co

Co

Co

Co

C

Co

C

Pe

C

C

C

Co

Co

Co

Co

Co

Co

Co

Pe

S

Co

Pe

Pe
T

S

Co

Pe

Co

Si

S

Cl

Pe

T

T

T

C

S

S

T

T

T

C

C

S

C

S

TROPIC OF CAPRICORN

10°

0°

10°

20°

30°

10°

20°

30°

40°

50°

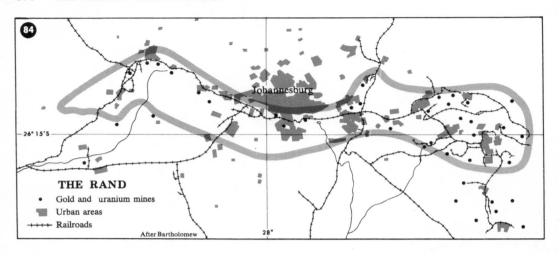

THE RAND
- • Gold and uranium mines
- ▥ Urban areas
- ┼┼┼┼ Railroads

After Bartholomew

lower Orange River (Map 85). The Orange River operations are on the surface since here the diamonds are found in the alluvial gravels. At Kimberley and Pretoria the diamonds are found embedded in a blue clay around the zone of contact between old volcanic vents and the bedrock. In the early decades these vents were opened up as enormous surface pits; and it was from the pit near Pretoria that the famous Cullinan diamond—the largest ever found—was taken in 1905. At present most of the mining is done underground. The diamond mines are controlled by a few large firms.

Gold mining actually produces a larger share of the gross national product. Between 1887 and 1949 South Africa produced a total of 469,000,000 ounces of gold. The central Rand alone produced nearly half of South Africa's gold, while the Rand as a whole accounted for 97 per cent. Since 1946 the discovery of new gold-bearing rocks in the Rand area, and in the Orange Free State farther south, has guaranteed that South Africa will continue for some time as the world's chief source of gold. The Rand mines have already been dug to a depth of about 9,000 feet below the surface, and about 3,000 feet below sea level. The rock temperature at this depth is 109°, and ex-

pensive air-cooling machinery has to be used. It is estimated that even if the gold in the quartz veins continues at its present degree of concentration, mining below 12,-000 feet will be impossible because of the high costs involved.

Gold and diamonds are not the only minerals in South Africa. It has now been discovered that the slag piles at the mine openings contain uranium, and large plants are being built to work over these old mine dumps. A large part of the known coal reserves of Africa are in the southern part of the Transvaal and neighboring parts of the Orange Free State and Natal. Nearby there are large supplies of high-grade iron ore. In the same general area there are also ores of copper, manganese, chromium, and a number of other industrial metals.

Manufacturing Industries. South Africa completed the initial phase of the Industrial Revolution in about 1950. Large-scale steel industries have been built around Pretoria and Johannesburg, and in other cities of the southern Transvaal and Natal. Around the steel plants there are now many manufacturing industries that make use of steel in the production of consumer goods. By mid-century South Africa was producing more than 60 per cent of its steel needs.

Since 1950 many new kinds of industries have been built, including, at the time of its building, the largest refinery in the world for making gasoline from coal—a process invented by the Germans. A woolen textile industry, using domestic wool supplies, has been developed at Cape Town, Port Elizabeth, and Durban. At these coastal cities there are now also food and tobacco-processing plants, clothing and leather factories, and factories making a variety of machines.

The Viability of South Africa. The Republic of South Africa faces serious problems of policy. Each of the five groups that make up the population has felt the impact of economic development in a somewhat different way, and each has its own approach to the formulation of a workable state-idea.

The major problem involves the treatment of the Africans, and on this question there are sharp differences of opinion. Cape Province, long dominated by the British, has a tradition of "equal rights for all educated men" regardless of color. Many of the Coloureds have been able to secure a good education and have entered business occupations and the professions. A smaller number of Africans have been able to get training as lawyers and doctors. In the rest of South Africa, on the other hand, the Afrikaner majority insists on the strict separation of the races. The native Africans are tolerated only because their labor is essential. In South Africa as a whole, the Afrikaners outnumber the people of British origin two to one. And to the Afrikaners any relaxation of the policy of apartheid is unthinkable.

The native Africans have generally not been rebellious. The African is quite familiar with autocratic authority within his own tribe, and he would scarcely object to the regulations that restrict his activities if it were not for the enforced separation from his family. The need for African workers in the mines and industries is so great that the managers have had to undertake recruitment programs even outside South Africa; and yet when the Africans come to live and work in the cities they are housed in barracks and carefully guarded.

The policy of apartheid has fallen with special severity on the Cape Coloureds. With no language and no cultural tradition of their own, the Coloureds have been treated as "an appendage of the white race." Many of them are not distinguishable from Caucasoids. The restrictions adopted by the majority of the voters are now applied to them as fully as they are to the people of Negroid race. Yet the Africans do not accept the Coloureds, and many Coloureds are as bitterly antagonistic toward the Negroes as are the Afrikaners.

The Indian problem is of concern chiefly in Natal. The Indians of this province have lived in Natal for many generations and regard it as their homeland. They are small-traders, laborers, and farm owners, and a few have become wealthy. But the one attitude shared by Europeans and Africans in Natal is dislike of the Indians. The Europeans dislike the Indians because of their willingness to accept a low standard of living, and in some cases because of their financial success. The Africans dislike the Indians because of the widespread feeling that the Indian traders exploit their African customers. The Indians are said to be "more concerned with political rights and to possess fewer of them than any other group in South Africa."

The problem of formulating an acceptable state-idea that will bring all the South African groups together in support of one state is not easy to solve.

Dependent Territories. Southern Africa also includes four dependent territories (Map 82). The former German colony of

An air view of Johannesburg, South Africa, showing the mine dumps of the Rand.

Southwest Africa, since World War I administered by South Africa, includes the driest part of the Kalahari and the Namib. The entire population is only about 500,000, of which about 25 per cent is European or Coloured and the remainder African and Hottentot. There are some minerals: diamonds are found in the stream gravels of the Namib, and in the north vanadium, copper, manganese, lead, and zinc are mined. But most of the area that is used at all is used for sheep grazing.

Bechuanaland, which borders Southwest Africa on the east, also includes a large area of the Kalahari. Most of the northern and western part of the area is a dry brushland where the only human inhabitants are primitive nomads. The extensive marshes, where the rivers from the north spread out on reaching the dry-land margin, are in-

fested with the tsetse fly—the carrier of sleeping sickness—and are at the present time essentially uninhabitable. The 340,000 people, of whom 2,000 are Europeans, occupy the higher area in the southeast where some water is available. Bechuanaland is a British protectorate.

The other two British protectorates are Swaziland and Basutoland. Swaziland was created by the British early in the nineteenth century to provide farmland for the Swazi tribes that were being pushed northward by the Afrikaners and southward by the Zulus. Basutoland is the most densely populated of the four dependent territories. This is the rugged country at the eastern rim of the Northern Karroo. Early in the nineteenth century four Bantu tribes (Zulus, Matabeles, Basutos, and Koranas) moved into the mountain valleys to escape the pressure of other Bantus moving in from the north. In the shelter of the rugged terrain a powerful chief was able to accomplish a rare thing: he brought the four tribes together under one political authority, which was strong enough to withstand the invasion of the Afrikaners. In 1869 the native king made a treaty with the British which established his country as a protectorate. Basutoland is now an important source of laborers for South Africa. The steeply-sloping land is badly eroded due to poor agricultural techniques and to overgrazing.

SOUTH-CENTRAL AND EAST AFRICA [3]

South-Central and East Africa includes the colonies and former colonies of the high country of tropical Africa and of the coastal margins. In this part of the African Culture Region Africans and Europeans live together in the same political units, and are attempting to face together the problems of race relations in states newly emerging from colonial status. The concepts of the great contemporary revolutions of Europe have been brought to this part of Africa by British settlers and administrators. As a result of an attack on illiteracy and ill-health, more and more Africans are learning about the possibilities of economic development; but there are still not nearly enough Africans trained as engineers or technically skilled workers, or even trained to accept the world of science and logical thought in exchange for the world of witch doctors. Even now the more prosperous Africans are hardly ready to give up cattle as a measure of wealth. But even if the desire to invest in new capital formation were more widespread, the very low incomes per capita of these countries would scarcely allow for the postponement of consumption necessary to start the initial phase of the Industrial Revolution. A vast amount of foreign capital will be needed.

[3] South-Central and East Africa includes Southern and Northern Rhodesia (Zimbabye and Zambia), Nyasaland (Malawi), Mozambique, Tanganyika, Zanzibar, Rwanda, Burundi, Kenya, Uganda, Ethiopia, the Somali Republic, and the Malagasy Republic (Map 82).

SOUTHERN RHODESIA, NORTHERN RHODESIA, AND NYASALAND

The Rhodesias and Nyasaland are located on the high country of South-Central Africa, just to the south of the Congo drainage basin. This is beyond the area originally settled by the Afrikaners. The Europeans who moved into the thinly-populated strip along the stream-divides north of the Limpopo River were mostly British pioneer farmers. They pushed the frontier of European settlement northward with the extension of the railroads. A railroad reached Bulawayo from Johannesburg in 1897; and in 1899 a line was completed, through Salisbury, down to the port of Beira in Portuguese Mozambique (Map 85). In 1904 a bridge was built across the gorge of the Zambezi River, just downstream from the Victoria Falls; and the railroad was promptly extended northward through the forests of Northern Rhodesia, reaching Elisabethville, in the Katanga Province of what was then the Belgian Congo, in 1910. From Elisabethville the railroad was eventually built northward to reach navigable water in the Congo system. And in 1931 a long rail line was built across Portuguese Angola to the Atlantic port of Lobito, thus providing a much shorter export route to Europe and America. This was the period of rapid mining development in Northern Rhodesia and Katanga, and it was in the mining towns, and especially in Elisabethville, that the pioneer farmers found markets for their food products.

In 1923 the British settlers in Rhodesia were offered a chance to join the Union of South Africa. They rejected the offer, preferring to set up Southern Rhodesia as a self-governing colony, while Northern Rhodesia and Nyasaland remained British protectorates. In 1953 Southern Rhodesia, Northern Rhodesia, and Nyasaland were joined together in the Federation of Rhodesia and Nyasaland; but the forces of disintegration remained stronger than those of integration, and in 1963 it was finally decided to abandon this scheme. Instead each country was to achieve independence separately during 1964.

In 1962 it was estimated that the Federation had a population of about 8,800,000. Southern Rhodesia had about 3,800,000, with a core of Europeans numbering about 223,000. Northern Rhodesia had about 2,500,000, and only 76,000 Europeans. Nyasaland, with about the same total population as Northern Rhodesia, had only about 9,300 Europeans.

Southern Rhodesia is better off than the rest of the former Federation in terms of its economic development. Although most of the Europeans live in the cities, some are farmers, and the farms they operate are much more productive than those operated by the native Africans. This difference is due in part to the fact that the Europeans hold the better lands, but it is also due to the better farm techniques used by the Europeans, and to the severe soil erosion on the African farms. The Europeans raise tobacco, maize, peanuts, and other food crops.

The economy of Southern Rhodesia is given additional support by mining and manufacturing. The largest supply of bituminous coal in tropical Africa is in this area (May 85). At Que Que, on the railroad

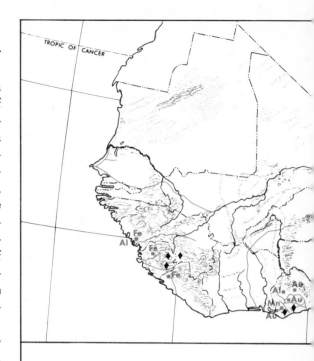

AFRICAN CULTURE REGION

MINERALS, INDUSTRIES AND RAILROADS

——	Railroads
⊙	Industrial centers
⛏	Steel industry
⬭	Coal fields
Fe	Iron
Al	Bauxite
Cu	Copper
Au	Gold
Zn	Zinc
Pb	Lead
Mn	Manganese
W	Tungsten
U	Uranium
Co	Cobalt
Cr	Chromium
V	Vanadium
Sn	Tin
◆	Diamonds
Gr	Graphite
Mo	Monazite

0   300   600
Scale of Miles

After Hance, Kotschar, and Peterec

Sn

Au
Au

EQUATOR   0°

Cu
Sn
Sn   Cu   Sn
W   Cu   W

Indian

Ocean

W   Pb

Au   10°

Mn

Mn Cu   Zn Cu   Mn
Mn   Cu
Au   Cu
Elisabethville
Co   Cu

Fe

Zn   Atlantic
Pb   Cu Fe   Ocean
Cu   Au
Fe   Au

KARIBA DAM   Fe

Zn V   W   Cu
Zn Pb   W   Cr   Cu   Au
Pb Cu   V   Au   Pb   Pb   Sn
Cu   Mn   Fe   Au   Fe
Que Que   Cr
Bulawayo   Pb   Cr

Cu   U   20°
Cu
TROPIC OF CAPRICORN
Cr   Fe
Cu
Mn   Pretoria   Mo
Au U
Pb   Au   Johannesburg
Fe   Fe
Kimberley   Fe
Mn
Bloemfontein
Cu
Durban   30°

Cape Town

Port Elizabeth

10°   20°   30°   40°   50°

between Bulawayo and Salisbury, there is a body of high-grade iron ore; and nearby a large iron and steel industry has been built. There are also mines producing cobalt, manganese, chromium, tungsten, and asbestos.

In 1960 the electric generators started to operate at the great Kariba Dam, built in the gorge of the Zambezi River downstream from Victoria Falls, northwest of Salisbury. The lake behind the dam is 175 miles long and a maximum of 20 miles wide, with a maximum depth of 390 feet. This enormous volume of water operates giant generators in one of the world's largest hydroelectric plants, and will be able to provide power for new manufacturing industries. Nevertheless, the net rate of population increase is faster than the possible rate of increase in the numbers of new jobs. Southern Rhodesia still faces a serious problem in its need to speed up its economic growth.

In Northern Rhodesia the problems involved in economic development are even more difficult than in Southern Rhodesia. The great majority of the people are African farmers and herders who make a poor living from the land. A small group of British farmers raise export crops such as tobacco and peanuts, and produce milk and butter for sale in Elisabethville and Salisbury. The farms operated by the Europeans are mostly strung along the railroad.

Northern Rhodesia is also well supplied with minerals, and produces copper, lead, zinc, iron, cobalt, manganese, and other industrial metals, most of which are exported to Europe and America. From the Kariba Dam the copper smelters are now receiving a much needed increase in electric power. Northern Rhodesia would be better off economically if it were attached to its natural market in Southern Rhodesia. But the native leaders prefer independence to economic growth.

Nyasaland has shared little of the economic development of the Rhodesias. Most of the native African farmers grow subsistence crops or pasture cattle; the chief commercial products—tobacco, cotton, peanuts, pyrethrum, and tea—are raised by the Europeans.

MOZAMBIQUE

Mozambique, or Portuguese East Africa, is of importance chiefly because the railroads, that give access to the Transvaal and to Southern Rhodesia, pass through its territory. Two rail lines extend inland, one of which starts at the port of Beira and runs into Southern Rhodesia. About 80 per cent of Beira's trade is traffic to and from Rhodesia or the Republic of the Congo to the north. The other rail line extends from Lourenço Marques to Pretoria and Johannesburg. The rail lines and ports were built with British money, primarily to serve the hinterland (Map 85).

The population of about 6,700,000 is made up chiefly of subsistence farmers. There are only a few areas devoted to commercial plantation crops. Around Lourenço Marques there is an area where sugar cane is grown, from which Portugal gets most of its supply of sugar. New plantations of cotton and of various tropical fruits have also been developed in this area. The chief crop of the native Africans is maize.

TANGANYIKA

To the north of the Rhodesias and Nyasaland, on the highland of East Africa, is the former Germany colony of Tanganyika. After World War I it was placed under British administration. A small part of the former German colony north of Lake Tanganyika, Ruanda-Urundi, was placed under Belgian administration. In 1961 Tanganyika became an independent state, and Ruanda-Urundi was scheduled for independence, or

A rhinoceros in the woodland savanna that is to be found extensively in southern and eastern parts of Africa.

for incorporation with neighboring states, as soon as the political problems could be worked out. This occurred in 1962, when Rwanda and Burundi emerged as two separate independent states.

Tanganyika has about 9,600,000 inhabitants, very unevenly distributed over its territory (Map 3, p. 7). The density of population around the shores of Lake Victoria is nearly five hundred per square mile. There is a moderate density along the border of Kenya, and a string of settlements along the railroad from Dar es Salaam to Lake Tanganyika. But there are large areas that are almost unoccupied because they are infested with the tsetse fly. There is no large-scale economic production. Since World War II the crops of chief value have been sisal, cotton, and coffee. Sugar cane plantations have been started southwest of Dar es Salaam.

Tanganyika is famous for its ill-fated experiments with the large-scale production of peanuts. After World War II the British government decided to make use of heavy machinery to clear the land and to plant and harvest peanuts as a source of vegetable oil. The work was started in 1947, but was finally abandoned in 1951, after providing the world with a clear demonstration of how economic development should not be undertaken. In the first place, the promoters of the plan were too impatient to wait for a careful and methodical survey of the land itself. Not until the machines had been imported and the work started was it realized that the machines could not clear the cover of scrubby but deep-rooted trees. Furthermore, as the heavy machines passed over the soil they packed it down so firmly that it was not fit for planting. No one believed that tropical soils could be anything but highly productive. Only when the peanut plants failed to appear did the essential infertility of tropical savanna soils become apparent.

Tanganyika is not lacking in minerals, but the mines have yet to be fully developed. There is some lignite, there are some ores of tin and uranium; and the diamond deposits are said to be the largest in the world, larger even than those of Kimberley. An increase in production will require large amounts of capital.

ZANZIBAR

Off the coast of Tanganyika are two islands still ruled over by the Sultan of Zanzibar. Muslim traders who extended their activities far to the south of the world that the Greeks had known, founded a trading

A village of the Kikuyu tribe in Kenya.

post on Zanzibar. Through this port many slaves were exported to Arabia. When the Europeans colonized Africa the Germans laid claim to the islands off Tanganyika. But in 1890 Great Britain exchanged Helgoland, an island in the North Sea, for Zanzibar, and established a protectorate over the islands. In 1961 the inhabitants voted by a narrow margin to seek independence, gained in 1963, rather than to join Tanganyika.

Zanzibar is of economic interest as the world's leading producer of cloves. About 80 per cent of the world supply comes from clove plantations on the islands, and cloves and clove-oil make up 60 per cent of the value of all exports.

KENYA

Kenya lies astride the equator and east of Lake Victoria. Here outpourings of lava once filled the rift depression and formed a highland with excellent volcanic soils. The area above 5,000 feet has temperatures that average below 60° for several months each year. This has always been too cool for the native Africans who have concentrated, as a result, on the lower and warmer lands near Lake Victoria. Here the soils, like those of Tanganyika, are not very productive.

The British assumed control of Kenya in 1888; but it was not until after 1920 that the higher and cooler parts of the east African plateau, between Mount Kenya and Mount Elgon, were opened up to British pioneer settlers. The whole country was divided into areas reserved for British farmers, areas reserved for native Africans, areas reserved for the protection of the forest cover, and crown lands which were not occupied by any group (Map 86). The parts of Kenya reserved for the Africans were used for agriculture. But the Africans were accustomed to farm a piece of land for a few years and then to move on to a new location, permitting the old farm to lie idle for a long time and slowly regain its productivity. This kind of farming was concentrated along the eastern shore of Lake Victoria. The whole eastern part of the country bordering Somalia is too dry for agriculture without irrigation, and the native Africans had no knowledge of the techniques of irrigation.

In 1962 Kenya had a population of 7,500,-000. The great majority were Africans belonging to six different tribes. There were also about 170,000 Indians, about 25,000 Arabs, and almost 70,000 British colonists. The British were mostly settled in and around Nairobi, although about a third of them were farmers living away from the city.

The conflict between European colonists and native Africans came about as a result of an unforeseen chain of events. British administration brought about a rapid increase in the native population. Medical services reduced the number of deaths from disease. Intertribal warfare was stopped. The railroad from Mombasa made possible the importation of foodstuffs, so that each year fewer people died from famine. As a result, the population on the land reserved for Africans doubled between 1920 and 1932. In some of the already densely settled areas, the density increased to more than a thousand people per square mile. Within a few years the native farmers were forced to give up their traditional practice of shifting agriculture, and to cultivate each piece of land year after year without a break. But the soil cannot maintain this permanent kind of farming without the use of fertilizer, and without the use of better farming methods than those familiar to the Africans. As a result, the land reserved for the native Africans has not been sufficient to continue supporting them. The Africans, faced again

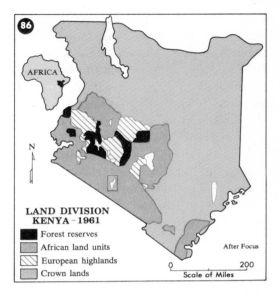

LAND DIVISION KENYA - 1961

- ■ Forest reserves
- ▦ African land units
- ▨ European highlands
- ▥ Crown lands

After Focus

0   200
Scale of Miles

with starvation, have attempted to push out the European settlers. Meanwhile the British farmers, who in good faith purchased their lands in areas reserved for white settlement, have not been at all inclined to retreat.

The only solution to the problem would seem to be an increased use of modern farming methods. It is clear that even if all the European settlers were to leave the country, the land thus made available to the Africans would not provide support for the whole population. But it is not easy to teach new farming methods to an unwilling people in an atmosphere of violence.

Most of the present exports of Kenya come from the European farms. These exports are coffee, sisal, tea and pyrethrum. The farmers also raise maize, wheat, barley, oats, and other foodstuffs for personal consumption.

UGANDA

The situation in Uganda is quite different from that in Kenya. Long before the arrival of the Europeans, the native population along the northern side of Lake Victoria was so dense that the practice of shifting cultivation had to be abandoned. Fortunately this part of the Victoria region has better soils than those found to the east or south of the lake. As a result, although the same fields are cultivated year after year, the farmers are able to grow enough food to support the dense population.

Uganda became a protectorate of Great Britain in 1890. A census taken in 1959 counted over 6,000,000 Africans. In the area just north of Lake Victoria the density of population was over two hundred people per square mile. The 1959 census also counted almost 11,000 Europeans, 72,000 Indians, and about 2,000 Arabs. The British attempted to hasten the independence of Uganda, but the usual difficulties appeared when the separate tribes were asked to accept an over-all government. In 1961 Buganda, a tribe occupying the southern part of Uganda on the western side of Lake Victoria, attempted to establish a separate state. However, when Uganda was granted independence in 1962 Buganda was included, but was given local autonomy.

Most of the people of Uganda are farmers. In the areas of dense settlement, the land is marked off into permanent and intensively cultivated fields. Part of each farm is used to grow bananas, and there are also small patches of sweet potatoes, manioc, maize, and beans. Most farmers raise some tobacco and some cotton which they sell to the Indian traders. At the higher altitudes there are coffee plantations.

RWANDA AND BURUNDI

To the south of Uganda are two small states which also became independent in 1962. These are Rwanda and Burundi (the former Belgian Trust Territory of Ruanda-Urundi). The total population of these two states is about five million. The population density of about 200 people per square mile is the greatest rural density in Central Africa.

Rwanda and Burundi are unique in the African Culture Region because each is made up of a single tribe (Map 81). Actually matters are not so simple as the map suggests. Both the Rwanda and the Burundi tribes are composed of three chief groups of people who form sharply-defined social and economic classes within the tribe. The majority of the people (84 per cent) are of Bantu stock, and do most of the farming. Under them are remnants of the Pygmies who once inhabited this area (1 per cent of the population). But ruling over the Bantus and the Pygmies are the Watusi, who make up a minority of the population (14 per cent). The other 1 per cent are Indians and Europeans. The Watusi are a very tall, slender people who migrated into this part of Africa from Egypt and Ethiopia along the rift valleys. With them they brought cattle and the technique of milking them. The Watusi became the hereditary rulers of the local tribes which they either conquered or joined.

The political situation in Rwanda and Burundi differs. In Burundi, the southern country, the Watusi king still holds power and maintains order and loyalty among the Bantus. But in Rwanda the Bantus were successful in deposing their king. An election in 1961, supervised by the United Nations, ended the Watusi claim to political control. Something like 60,000 Watusi fled from Rwanda, and many were killed. Rwanda was established as an independent republic. Efforts to make the two tribes agree to form one country failed, for obvious reasons.

The economy of both countries is based on agriculture. To be sure, the Watusi count their wealth in terms of cattle, but the cattle contribute only in a minor way to the economy. The majority of the people are subsistence farmers, growing manioc, bananas, and sweet potatoes. In 1962 the food production was sufficient to supply the needs of the inhabitants of the two countries, but the rapid net rate of population increase due to a decrease in the death rate will soon create problems. At the higher elevations there are coffee plantations, and coffee is the chief commercial crop.

ETHIOPIA[4]

Ethiopia has been an independent state for a long time. The Ethiopian kings, as previously noted, at certain periods even extended their rule over Egypt. Moreover, except for the brief period between 1935 and 1941, they were never invaded successfully by an outside power. In the fourth century A.D. the people of Ethiopia adopted Coptic Christianity, which makes their's one of the oldest Christian countries. The steep mountain slopes, surrounded on all sides by hot and arid lowlands, made defense possible against invaders even for people with relatively primitive weapons. An invading Italian army was defeated at the Battle of Aduwa in 1896. It was the Italians, however, who in 1935 finally succeeded in conquering the highlands. They maintained control of Ethiopia until the country was liberated by British and Indian troops in 1941.

Ethiopia has a long history of isolation and self-sufficiency. The inner part of the highlands remained almost unknown, even while events of history were taking place in the North African-Southwest Asian Culture Region nearby. Finally in 1918 a railroad, that had been started in 1894, was completed from Djibouti in French Somaliland

[4] Often popularly known as Abyssinia, a Portuguese mispronunciation of the Arabic name El Habesha.

to the Ethiopian capital, Addis Ababa. The impact of the modern world was not felt until the reign of Haile Selassie (who became prince regent in 1916, and emperor in 1930). The first steps have now been taken to transform Ethiopia from a primitive, feudal, self-sufficient country, into a modern state with products for export.

The Ethiopians think of their country as divided into three zones. From sea level to about 5,500 feet is the *Kolla*, a hot zone which is deficient in moisture and thinly populated. Above that, to about 8,000 feet, is the most densely populated zone, the *Woina Dega*, where temperatures are moderate, and where there is usually abundant rainfall in summer. Here most of Ethiopia's crops are grown, including millet, wheat, barley, maize, tobacco, cotton, and coffee. The country's chief exports, coffee and beeswax, are produced in this zone. Above 8,000 feet is the *Dega*, a zone in which the air is always cool and the moisture abundant. Some grains are raised in this zone below 11,000 feet, but most of the land is used to pasture animals.

Ethiopia is made up of a variety of peoples. Although no census has ever been taken, it was estimated in 1962 that the population was close to 20,000,000. About 2,000,000 people form the ruling group that controls the government, owns the land, and carries on the business affairs. These people are Christian, and speak a language different from that used by other Ethiopians. The remainder of the population is made up of a remarkable mixture of religious, racial, and language groups, who are, nevertheless, strongly conscious of being Ethiopian. Traditionally the people are self-sufficient herders and farmers, but in modern times an effort is being made to increase the production of crops for export, especially of coffee which grows very well in the Woina Dega. The national territory has yet to be explored for mineral ores.

Eritrea, which is the coastal strip between the Highlands of Ethiopia and the Red Sea, was seized by Italy in 1889 and was administered by that country until World War II. In 1952 Ethiopia and Eritrea were joined in a federation. But Ethiopia's chief port is still Djibouti in French Somaliland.

THE SOMALI REPUBLIC

The Somali Republic, made up of territory formerly included in Italian Somaliland and British Somaliland, gained its independence in 1960. The population, estimated at 2,000,000 in 1962, included, in addition to Negroes, 31,000 Arabs, 2,000 Indians, and 3,000 Europeans, of whom most were Italians. The people are mostly nomadic herders who form permanent settlements only where water is available in the dry stream beds. The country seems to lack most of the elements necessary for the formation of a viable state.

THE MALAGASY REPUBLIC

The Malagasy Republic occupies the island of Madagascar. This island, located about 250 miles off the African east coast, is about 975 miles long and 300 miles wide. It is mostly mountainous, with elevations reaching 9,450 feet above sea level. The land slopes steeply to the east coast which is swampy, with many lagoons, and more gently to the west, where there is a wide belt of hilly upland. The eastern side of the island is very rainy, but the southwestern side receives less than twenty inches. In the highlands there is a rainy season from November through March, and the rest of the year is very dry.

Madagascar was settled by Malays and Indians, who maintained regular connections between Asia and the island, using the alternation of the monsoons to make the long sea voyage back and forth across the Indian Ocean. Negroes make up an important part of the population only along the western side of the island where Africans were brought many generations ago as slaves. In 1962 the population was estimated at about 5,700,000, including some 80,000 Europeans. There are also Chinese and Arab minorities. The Malgache people (the people of the Malagasy Republic) belong to eleven different tribes (Map 81, p. 359), but thanks to the efforts of a native king of the early nineteenth century, they all speak the same language. This is a new state—and a member of the French Community—in which there is a strong state-idea, fostered, to be sure, by the isolation of the island from the outside world. The people insist that they are not African and not Asian—they are something unique.

The Malgache population lives chiefly from agriculture and the pasturing of cattle. Scarcely 3 per cent of the land is under cultivation, and most of this in small concentrations in the mountain valleys and along the coasts. The chief crop, which occupies about 6 per cent of the cultivated land, is paddy rice; but associated with the rice are maize, peanuts, manioc, sorghum, vegetables, and bananas. The most important export crop is coffee, grown on about 12 per cent of the cultivated area. There are also a wide variety of other export crops. These include—in addition to coffee and rice—cloves, tobacco, vanilla, raffia, peanuts, sugar cane, tapioca, essential oils, sisal, pears, and pepper. But the greater part of the area of Madagascar is used to pasture zebu cattle, originally introduced from India.

There is almost no industrial development and very little mining. Nevertheless, Madagascar has the resources for considerable mining development. Its resources include some low-grade coal, graphite, mica, quartz crystals (for use in electronic equipment), uranium, monazite, and semiprecious stones.

The Malagasy Republic is viable as a state partly because of the advantages of an isolated position to a people in the early stage of economic development. However, the Malgache economy needs repair. To be sure, there is a long list of exports, but none are large in world terms. A considerable ex-pansion of agriculture is possible, because only a small part of the potentially arable land is used. A basic problem to be over-come is the tradition of owning cattle as a symbol of wealth. The cattle are neither milked nor eaten, and they are not even sa-cred as in Hindu India. They are a net loss to the economy.

WEST AFRICA AND CENTRAL AFRICA[5]

West Africa and Central Africa are not clearly defined areas. In general, West Africa lies south of the Sahara and north of the Gulf of Guinea. The south-facing coast of this area is called the Guinea Coast. Central Africa lies between West Africa and East Africa.

This is a part of the African Culture Region in which the withdrawal of the Euro-pean colonial administrations has resulted in the emergence of a large number of separate states. Few of these states can be considered definitely viable, and many changes and many new combinations may yet be expected. None of the new states has a gross national product which is ade-quate to start economic development with-out a large amount of foreign financial and technical aid. And all of the new states face the problems of integrating numerous sepa-rate tribes, and of commanding the support of people who speak different languages and in some cases practice different reli-gions. Map 81 shows the relations between the new states and the underlying pattern of tribes.

SIERRA LEONE

Sierra Leone is a former British colony that started as a settlement of liberated slaves. In 1787 a group of abolitionists in Britain founded a colony at Freetown on the Guinea Coast, where the heavy summer rains (May to October) support a dense rain forest. Later the British government took over administration of the settlement as a Crown Colony, and in 1961 Sierra Leone was granted independence and membership in the Commonwealth.

Sierra Leone's economy is based on the commercial production of a few plantation crops, and on the export of minerals. There are plantations around Freetown producing palm oil (for use in soap and oleomarga-rine), piassava fiber, kola nuts, ginger, and cacao. But most of the inhabitants are sub-sistence farmers raising rice, manioc, sweet potatoes, and peanuts. The rice is mostly upland rice, and only about 10 per cent of the land suitable for paddy rice is used for this crop. Of major importance to Sierra Leone are the iron mines, the chromium and platinum mines, and the alluvial dia-monds.

LIBERIA

Liberia was also first established as a colony for liberated slaves. From 1822 to 1847 the colony was administered by the American Colonization Society, but in the latter year the 3,000 American Negroes who had set-tled in Liberia adopted a constitution pat-terned on that of the United States, and became independent. Liberia even adopted a flag consisting of horizontal red and white stripes, with one white star on a blue field.

[5] The political divisions of West Africa and Cen-tral Africa are shown on Map 82, page 361.

As late as 1925, about a century after the first settlement of American Negroes, Liberia remained economically underdeveloped. Furthermore, the only support that the Liberian government was able to command was that of the people who lived within a zone some twenty miles wide along the coast. The African natives of the interior not only resented their masters, but also remained essentially independent of them. Even today the Liberian of American descent considers himself superior to the native African, and takes care not to mix with him socially.

Since 1925 Liberia has made important economic progress. The Firestone Company was granted land in the interior on which to develop rubber plantations. There are now plantations of oil palms, coffee, cacao, and piassava. And American, Swedish, and West German companies are also developing several important iron ore bodies, for which special transportation facilities have been provided. A contribution of no small importance to the Liberian economy is made by the large number of ships registered under the Liberian flag.

GHANA AND TOGO

Ghana, the former British colony and protectorate, is the world's leading producer of cacao (32 per cent of the world's production in 1960-1961). The export of cacao has given Ghana a gross national product that is second only to that of South Africa in the African Culture Region, and the cacao farmers enjoy a standard of living considerably higher than that of most other Africans. Ghana became an independent state, and member of the Commonwealth, in 1956.

Before World War I the British colony of the Gold Coast (as Ghana was then called) was bordered on the east by the German colony of Togoland. After World War I, Togoland was divided into three parts: the western part was included in the Gold Coast; the eastern part was included in French West Africa (now Dahomey); and the central part became the République de Togo. In 1960 the République de Togo became independent.

The western part of Ghana is the area from which most of the cacao now comes (Map 83). Cacao trees (indigenous to Central America) were imported into the Gold Coast in 1879 from Spanish Guinea. They were planted by the African farmers on small farms averaging only about three acres in size. The cacao tree grows well in a very wet climate, where there are no high winds and no cool seasons, and produces best when grown in the shade of taller trees. The plantations have been located in the midst of the uncleared forest. British traders buy Ghana's cacao and ship it to distant markets, but the income from cacao production is widely shared among the small farmers of the country.

Ghana may not continue for long to be the world's largest producer of cacao. Before World War II this little country was shipping out about two thirds of the world's cacao supply. But this crop, like so many tropical crops, has been attacked by plant diseases, and this has resulted in a reduction in the yield per tree. In spite of every effort, no way has been found to eliminate the diseases. Although the country is still the world's leading cacao producer, it has accounted for only one third of world production in the years since World War II. The farmers are now being urged to diversify their crops, and especially to devote a considerable part of their farmland to rice and oil palms.

Ghana bases a part of its prosperity on mining; and the country is on the thresh-

The inauguration of Kwame Nkrumah as the first President of the new Ghana Republic in 1960.

hold of an important development of manufacturing industry. From the mines comes about 4 per cent of the world supply of manganese, as well as small quantities of gold and diamonds. The country also contains an important supply of bauxite. Plans have been drawn up for the construction of a hydroelectric station on the Volta River, which enters the sea a little to the east of Accra. An aluminum manufacturing plant will use electricity from this source to refine the bauxite, and thus provide a major new source of economic support for the country.

NIGERIA

Nigeria has the largest population of any country in West Africa. In 1960, when the country became independent, and a member of the Commonwealth, the population was estimated at 34,000,000. The British had been leading Nigeria forward to independence as fast as possible, and had not only built railroads and power plants, developed mines and plantations, and established schools, but had also given the Nigerians training in the procedures of public administration. However, in Nigeria there are many different tribes, and hundreds of different languages and contrasted ways of making a living, so that the task of uniting them all in support of one state is a difficult one.

Nigeria is located on the easternmost part of the Guinea Coast, and extends northward across the several zones of climate and vegetation previously discussed. There is a very great contrast in habitat between the rainy, densely forested southern area, and the semiarid savannas west of Lake Chad in the northern part of the national territory. The country is drained by the Niger River and its large tributary, the Benue.

Nigeria is made up of three quite different parts in terms of population and economy. The economic core of the country is in the southwest, behind Lagos. This area, occupied by the Yoruba tribe (16 per cent of the total population of Nigeria), was claimed as a British colony in 1861. The Yoruba were at one time shifting cultivators who planted their subsistence crops in temporary clearings in the tropical forest. But the British administration ended the destructive system of shifting cultivation. The death rate was reduced so that today there is a population density of over five hundred people per square mile. The economy is now based on plantation crops— chiefly oil palms and cacao. The Yoruba are Muslim.

The second of the three major parts of Nigeria is in the southeast, east of the Niger River and south of the Benue River. This is the homeland of the Ibo tribe, which also forms 16 per cent of the total population of Nigeria. Like the Yoruba, these people used to be shifting cultivators raising subsistence crops. During the period when slaves were captured and shipped out, the Ibo were the people from among whom large numbers were taken. The Ibo are partly Christian, partly Pagan. Under British protection the population has been increasing rapidly in the twentieth century, and the population density is about the same as in southwestern Nigeria—more than five hundred per square mile. There are few plantations in this region. The people are still subsistence farmers raising yams, manioc, maize, rice, beans, bananas, and plantains. The pressure of population is so great, however, that the practice of shifting cultivation is no longer possible, and the hard-worked land is showing declining crop yields. This is one of Nigeria's chief problem areas.

The third concentration of people is in the north around Kano, the homeland of the Fulani and Hausa tribes. The Fulani make up about 10 per cent of the population of Nigeria, and the Hausa about 18 per

Bags of peanuts awaiting shipment from Kano in northern Nigeria.

cent. Both are Muslim. Most of the Fulani are nomadic herdsmen who pasture cattle, sheep, goats, and other animals, and whose major concern is the eradication of the tsetse fly through the clearing of the natural brush in which the fly breeds. The Hausa are sedentary farmers whose crops include millet and peanuts. Instead of conflicting with the herders who occupy the same general region, the Hausa actually pay the Fulani to pasture animals on their farms in order to enrich the soil with manure. This part of Nigeria also has a population density of more than five hundred per square mile. It generates a considerable amount of trade through Kano, a city of more than 100,000. One of its unique products is the high-quality leather made from glazed goatskins, known as Morocco leather. A major problem has been created in the north through increases in the size of the herds and the serious overgrazing of the pastures. On pastures that are occupied by too many animals the useful feed plants are destroyed, and the weeds and brush come back in again. And with the brush comes the tsetse fly which spreads disease among the herds.

In between these densely populated parts of Nigeria there are zones of relatively thin population. In the woodland savanna north of the forests the population density is less than ten per square mile, except for small concentrations along the railroad between Lagos and Kano, and around the mines of tin and columbium (important in the manufacture of jet engines).

Since 1960 Nigeria has been successful not only in establishing a democratic and stable government among the tribal diversities, but also has produced a burst of economic development. Lagos has been modernized with new air-conditioned office buildings, and sky-scrapers—one of them 25 stories high. There are supermarkets and a TV station. Many of the more successful Nigerians can afford to buy a family automobile. At Ibadan, inland from Lagos, there is a new university, and throughout the country there are well-attended primary and secondary schools. In the eastern part of southern Nigeria, east of the Niger River, coal, iron ore, and limestone have been discovered, and it is planned to build a steel plant here—in an area that formerly was a poverty-spot. Plans have also been made to build a huge dam on the Niger River in the northern region to provide water for irrigation and electric power for the new factories of Kano.

CAMEROON, GUINEA, AND MALI

Cameroon, Guinea, and Mali—at one time parts of the French colonial system—decided to sever all ties with France when they became independent. Cameroon had a population estimated at a little over 3,000,000 when it became independent in 1960. Guinea had a population of less than 3,000,000, and Mali nearly 4,000,000. The great majority of the people in all three countries are Africans coming from many different tribes.

The countries are poorly developed economically. Cameroon is the most productive part of the former French Equatorial Africa, since it does have some minerals, including some undeveloped sources of bauxite and manganese. Guinea also has bauxite, iron ore, chromium, diamonds, and gold. Agriculture is the primary occupation but provides only a meager living. Export crops include cacao, coffee, palm oil, and peanuts.

THE FRENCH COMMUNITY AND THE COUNCIL OF THE ENTENTE

Five independent countries carved out of the former French colonies have decided to remain within the French Community. The members of the Community enjoy complete freedom to draw up their own constitutions, to select their own forms of government, and to select their own political leaders. They agree, however, that certain matters are to be administered by a committee, on which all the member states, and France, are represented. These matters include foreign policy, national defense, economic and financial policy, policies regarding the use of natural resources, and higher education.

The French Community in Africa includes six states: the republics of Senegal, Chad, Gabon, the Central African Republic, the Congo Republic (the latter not to be confused with the Republic of the Congo, the former Belgian Congo), and the Malagasy Republic. Some other former colonies have agreements with France outside the Community and are members of the Council of the Entente. This latter includes the republics of Dahomey, Ivory Coast, Niger, and Upper Volta.

The population of the members of the French Community and of the Council of the Entente is mostly African, largely illiterate, and very poor. The great majority of the people are engaged in agriculture and cattle raising. In a few places commercial agriculture has been developed. Where irrigation can be provided along the desert margin cotton constitutes an important commercial crop. Farther south, where rainfall is more plentiful, the chief commercial crops include cacao, coffee, peanuts, and palm oil. Gabon, with a small area and only about 500,000 inhabitants, is one of the most productive countries of the French Community. It has a large timber industry, and important resources of iron ore and manganese. Even here, however, jobs are scarce and the standard of living remains low for the rapidly increasing population.

THE REPUBLIC OF THE CONGO

The Republic of the Congo is the former Belgian colony which gained its independence in 1960. It was first established by the King of Belgium in 1885 as the Congo Free State. In 1907 possession passed from the King to the government of Belgium, and the colony was administered by the Belgians. The colonial administration provided schools, medical services, and transportation. But the Belgians, unlike the British, did not attempt to prepare the native political leaders to assume control. In fact, they did not even allow the natives to obtain an education abroad, since they felt that the students might bring back disturbing ideas. But when the wave of independence began to sweep over tropical Africa, the Belgians agreed to grant self-government to the Congo in 1963. The Congolese leaders, however, insisted on immediate independence, and it became effective in 1960.

In late 1958 the Belgians made an estimate of the population. It was calculated at that time that the total population was made up of about 13,500,000 Africans, 113,000 Europeans (including 89,000 Belgians), and 1,600 Indians. The capital city, Léopoldville, had a little less than 400,000 inhabitants. But all these people were spread over an area almost eighty times larger than Belgium—and three and a half times the size of Texas. A large part of the Congo is very thinly populated.

The map of tribal areas (Map 81) shows the complexity of the Congo problem. None of the native leaders can be certain of the loyalty of the people over whom he claims to rule. There are great differences among these tribes. Most of them make use of variations of the basic Bantu language, and most are shifting cultivators who raise subsistence crops in temporary clearings in the forest. There are also Pygmy tribes, peoples who, in the past, used to depend entirely on the hunting of wild animals in the forest. Traditionally, they located their temporary settlements close to the Bantu villages, and exchanged meat for the vegetables and grains produced by the Bantus. In modern times, the Pygmies have copied the farming methods of their neighbors, and now raise most of their own food. Tribes in the more remote parts of the forest still make a living by collecting rubber, and ivory from elephant tusks. Along the forest foot-trails they bring these items to the European trading posts. The contrast between life among these primitive tribes, and life in such modern cities as Léopoldville is enormous.

From an economic point of view the Congo is more important for its minerals than for its agriculture. In the years from 1890 to 1892 a Belgian geologist, exploring the Congo Basin, discovered and mapped rich ores of copper in the southernmost part of the area, called Katanga (Map 85). The Kantanga District, lying partly in the Congo and partly across the border in Northern Rhodesia, is now recognized as the world's richest source of copper ore. The Belgians developed the mining industries, and built copper smelters at Elisabethville. At one time Katanga produced about 20 per cent of the world's copper. In addition to copper this same district is also important for its cobalt, uranium, tin, and industrial diamonds.

The large-scale production of minerals in Katanga began about 1911. It was made possible by the construction of railroads through Rhodesia and Mozambique to the Portuguese port of Beira, and through Angola to the Portuguese port of Lobito (Map 85). A railroad was also built from Elisa-

bethville northwestward to reach navigable water on one of the Congo tributaries. Products carried on this route, however, have to be transferred from railroad to river steamer, and then back again to railroad. They pass the Livingstone Falls by rail and are loaded eventually onto ocean steamers, which can only sail up the Congo as far as Matadi.

The future of the newly independent Congo is by no means clear. Its native leaders are having to struggle among themselves before the one person can emerge who has the power to command the obedience of the others. So far none of them can be sure of the support of the illiterate tribes among whom the territory is divided. Meanwhile, production at the mines and smelters has dropped. And in the entire country in 1960 there was not a single Congolese doctor, lawyer, dentist, or engineer. The one feeling everyone shares is dislike of the foreigners, and the one thing everyone desires is freedom from outside interference. With all the pressures and conflicts of the modern world, how can such a country survive?

ANGOLA

Southwest of the Republic of the Congo is the Portuguese colony of Angola. This is mostly a semiarid plateau covered with woodland savanna which is thinly populated. It has about 4,900,000 inhabitants, most of them shifting cultivators and herders. Where irrigation is possible along the dry coast there are spots of green. The exports include maize, coffee, beans, sisal, palm oil, and cottonseed. Some diamonds are taken from the stream gravels in the northern interior, near the border of the Congo.

Angola came to the notice of the public outside Africa when, in 1931, the long rail line from Rhodesia and Elisabethville was completed all the way across Angola to Lobito. This provided a more direct route for export to Europe and America than did the route through Beira, and it now carries a considerable part of the traffic that once went through Mozambique.

The native leaders of Angola, as unprepared for leadership as those of the Congo, are nevertheless demanding independence, and the Portuguese are resisting the demands. The future of Angola remains uncertain.

OTHER EUROPEAN COLONIES

There are several small bits of territory in tropical Africa that remain as European possessions. These are remnants of the world-wide empires, once controlled by Great Britain, Portugal, and Spain.

One small remnant is the British possession of Gambia in West Africa (Map 82). This is a narrow strip of territory along the Gambia River inland from Bathurst. It is entirely surrounded on the land side by Senegal, and negotiations are now in progress to combine the two.

South of Gambia there are some Portuguese and Spanish colonies. One is Portuguese Guinea, inland from the port of Bissau. Portugal also owns the Cape Verde Islands, and the two little islands in the Gulf of Guinea—São Tomé and Principe. The Spanish possessions include Rio Muni on the mainland, and the island Fernando Póo, which together make up the colony of Spanish Guinea.

SUMMARY

The African Culture Region has only recently felt the impact of the great world revolutions. It is important to keep in mind that even as late as the 1870's explorers were still engaged in tracing the courses of African rivers, and that not until the 1890's were European traders, miners, and missionaries making extensive contacts with the primitive Negro tribes of the African interior. Yet the Africans are now taking the long stride forward to hasten political independence and economic development in the most modern ways. If conflict and confusion arise this is very understandable.

With financial and technical assistance from outside the economic development of Africa need not be too long postponed. The continent contains a vast wealth of raw materials which are needed by the insatiable industries of the countries with mature economies. The old nineteenth-century colonial relationship of an industrial country with its suppliers of raw material is no longer acceptable. The people of this culture region, as elsewhere in the world, are demanding a larger share of the rewards of economic production. A major question to be faced is whether the African people will be ready to postpone consumption in order to save and invest in new capital—as is required by the process of economic development in a capitalist system—or whether this saving will have to be enforced by a central dictatorship, either fascist or communist. In few places are the pre-conditions for economic development in existence: in places where cattle constitute a measure of wealth there is a reluctance to shift from cattle to capital; and in most places there is resistance to the pressure to abandon magic in favor of science and engineering. But there are a number of outstanding African leaders who know what the problems are, and who are trying to face them.

Can the aspirations of the people of this culture region be satisfied within the framework of a democratic society? Here, as elsewhere, there are many who are impatient with the delays and compromises that seem to stand in the way of change. Yet the demand for equality of status among races cannot be denied. The traditional position of the African as inferior to all outsiders, of whatever origin, can neither be preserved by force, nor be defended on grounds of morality. The country, or group of countries, that can first realize and accept this completely will be able to exert a tremendous influence on Africa in the changing conditions of the world.

11

THE AUSTRALIA-NEW ZEALAND CULTURE REGION

Country	Political Status	Latest Estimate Population	Capital City
Australia	Federal State	10,700,000 ('62)	Canberra
Excl.			
Christmas Isl.	Dependency	3,000 ('60)	
Cocos Is.	Dependency	1,000 ('60)	
Macquarie Is.	Dependency		
Norfolk Isl.	Dependency	1,000 ('60)	
New Zealand	Parliamentary State	2,500,000 ('62)	Wellington
Incl.			
Antipodes Is.			
Auckland Is.			
Bounty Is.	External Territories		
Chatham Is.			
Kermadec Is.			

The Australia-New Zealand Culture Region is characterized by remoteness and isolation. These geographic qualities, however, need to be interpreted differently at different periods. For a long time remoteness and isolation were natural conditions of being at the end of the string of peninsulas and islands reaching southeastward from the Asian continent. Along this corridor plants and animals had spread away from the source region in southern Asia where they later became eliminated by the more recently developed species. When the land connection was broken, these forms of life were caught in a kind of sanctuary where they could survive and develop unchallenged by the evolving flora and fauna of the Asian continent. As a result there are many kinds of plants and animals in Australia that originally were found nowhere else in the world: for instance the genus eucalyptus, of which Australia has some six hundred species; and the distinctive family of marsupials known as the kangaroo, of which there are several genera and many species.

Australia was also the end of the line for migrating man. Paleolithic people who lived by collecting, hunting, and fishing, and who knew nothing of cultivated crops or of domestic animals other than the dog, were forced out of southern Asia after the first of the great revolutions of human history. The Neolithic people, who could form more effective connections with earth resources, forced their less skilled brothers into the more remote parts of the earth—to southern Africa, to southern South America, and to Australia. When the Europeans first came to Australia they found the Tasmanians living as Stone Age people had lived. The Tasmanians in many ways resembled the Fuegians in southern South America. On the mainland of Australia there were aborigines who were culturally related to the Bushmen of southern Africa. Until the arrival of the Europeans these people with their simple way of life had their own exclusive refuge from the pressures of more complex cultures.

The remoteness and isolation of Australia and New Zealand must be given a new interpretation with each change in the technology of transport. For the Europeans who first came to these places the break in the land bridge, which had provided protection for the aborigines, was no longer significant. For the Europeans with their sailing ships remoteness now had to be measured in terms of ocean distances, wind directions, and currents. The attack on remoteness led to the construction of two great canals, far from Australia, but of vital concern to the people of this region. And now the world has again been transformed by the new technology of air transport. Australia and New Zealand remain remote and isolated, but these conditions are now measured by still another geographic fact: that this culture region lies wholly outside the Land Hemisphere (Map inside the front cover, and Map 13, p. 36). The Australia-New Zealand Culture Region dominates the Water Hemisphere, yet it forms only 6 per cent of the inhabited area of the earth, and is occupied by only 1 per cent of the world population.

AUSTRALIA

Australia stands sixth among the countries of the world in terms of total area. Among the larger countries it has the largest proportion of land that is unproductive because of aridity. The population of Australia, which is smaller than that of metropolitan New York, is concentrated in certain parts of the country, leaving a vast extent of territory either quite empty or very thinly occupied (Map 4, p. 8). As in the case of Canada, the over-all ratio of population to area is a meaningless figure: to say that Australia has only about three persons per square mile really tells very little about the population distribution. A very large part of the country lies outside the effective national territory. A ratio of population to area that could be compared with the ratios of other countries, would have to be based on the density in the part of the total national territory which is effectively used.

The presence of so large an unoccupied area relatively close to the crowded lands of eastern and southern Asia raises several important questions. First, whether more people could support themselves in Australia if different techniques of making a living were used, or if different economic and political institutions were introduced. Second, whether the existence of so much thinly populated territory would be likely to tempt any of the densely populated Asian countries to occupy Australia by force.

The Australians have followed a policy that excludes from permanent settlement all peoples who are not of the Caucasoid race —a decision which is known as the "white Australia policy." But, if some other state really tried to take this empty territory by force, would the Australians be able to defend themselves?

Australia, for a variety of reasons, is listed among the world's most progressive and prosperous countries. It stands fifth among the countries of the world in terms of gross national product per capita (Map 11, p. 30). Supported by income from gold mining, and by food-processing and consumer-goods industries, Australia passed through the initial phase of the Industrial Revolution between 1930 and 1945, and is now well on the road to maturity. Furthermore, the ideals of democratic society have been implanted by the British, and flourish unchallenged.

The Habitat. (Maps 5, 6, 7, 8, and 87) Perhaps in none of the other large countries of the world is the population so concerned with moisture deficiency, and so preoccupied with variations in the rainfall. Nearly 40 per cent of the total area receives less than an average of ten inches of rain a year; and under 9 per cent receives more than forty inches. Furthermore, the parts of the country which receive enough rain to be classed as humid are generally mountainous. The whole central part of Australia is arid; but around the margins of the dry heart there are zones of increasing humidity which pro-

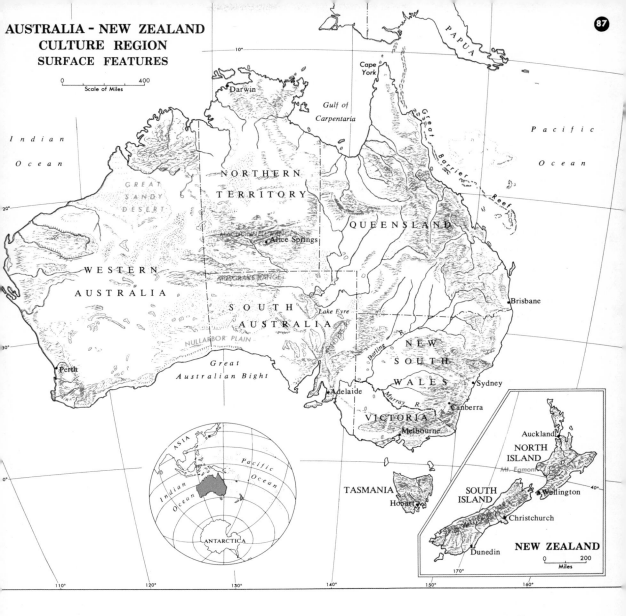

duce a concentric arrangement of the habitats. The only river system of importance is the Murray-Darling in the southeast.

Surface Features. The greater part of Australia is a shield of ancient, massive, crystalline rock. The edges of the shield are relatively steep, in places forming escarpments; but the central part of it is monotonously level, standing 1,000–2,000 feet above sea level. Owing to the arid climate this part of Australia is a vast hamada, covered in places by fixed dunes, and surmounted near the center by two ancient and much eroded ranges—the Macdonnell Range and the Musgrave Range—both less than 5,000 feet in elevation. These ranges are not high enough to bring much rainfall, and as a result there are no radiating systems of wadis to interrupt the expanse of the hamada, as there are in the western Sahara. Furthermore, this is the only great dry-land area in the world which is not crossed by an exotic river. Around the margins of the shield there are a few block ranges of moderate elevation, such as the Flinders Range north of Adelaide.

Where the crystalline shield is bordered by geologically younger, sedimentary strata, there are basins and lowland plains. Such basins occur near the coast in the northwest, and on either side of Perth in the southwest. In the south, at the head of the Great Australian Bight, is the Nullarbor Basin, where limestones have been formed into sinks and underground caverns. The only large area of plain borders the crystalline shield on the east, extending from the Gulf of Carpentaria to the southern coast east of Adelaide. The northern part drains intermittently into the Lake Eyre depression; the southern part drains into Australia's one major river system—the Murray-Darling.

Only the eastern margin of Australia is hilly or mountainous. Rugged country extends about 2,400 miles from Cape York to the southern tip of Tasmania. The Great Dividing Range, as this feature of the Australian mainland is called, slopes sharply to the east, leaving only disconnected patches of coastal lowland along the sea. For much of its length it is no more than a hilly upland, but it is much dissected by streams, and there are few easy pass routes across. The range culminates in the Australian Alps, southwest of Canberra (Mount Kosciusko, 7,305 feet).

Climate and Vegetation. The Australian climate gives the land a distinctive pattern. The driest part of the country is around the Lake Eyre depression, but there is a vast area which receives less than ten inches of rainfall a year, so that moisture deficiency is a major handicap to settlement in all but the continental margins. Furthermore, there is a great variability of rainfall from year to year. Along the northern coast, where there is a monsoonal alternation of wind directions, most of the rain falls during the summer months—November through April. There are

two areas of winter rain and summer drought, one around Perth in the southwest, the other around Adelaide (at Adelaide most of the rain comes between April and October). Along the eastern rim, south of Brisbane, the rainfall is quite evenly distributed throughout the year. Tasmania and the south-facing coast around Melbourne have cool summers and mild winters, but the rest of Australia has hot summers—in the dry areas the temperatures frequently climb above 110°.

The vegetation cover found by the European explorers and settlers reflected the arrangement of climatic features. The greater part of the area was covered by a sparse xerophytic shrub. Around the margin of the dry lands there was a belt of brush and woodland, made up largely of eucalyptus. In the wetter part of the Lake Eyre depression there was a short-grass steppe, perhaps the result of aboriginal burning. Where conditions were somewhat more moist there was a light forest, and in the small spots of heavy rainfall there were patches of rain forest.

Settlement. The people who first came to Australia had migrated from Southeast Asia along the island bridge, which at that time was perhaps continuous, or almost continuous land. The people who came first had a very simple culture, and were pushed to the less habitable areas by those with somewhat more elaborate cultures who came later. Australia offered a poor living for these people: the northern shore was not one to tempt hunters or collectors, and there were no great rivers to offer routes of travel inland. The Tasmanians, by following the belt of heavier rainfall to the east, finally reached "the end of the earth." The aborigines who occupied the Australian mainland were estimated at the time of the first European colonization to number less than 300,000. Today about 75,000 descendants of these aborigines survive on reservations, mostly in the tropical north. The last of the Tasmanians died in 1876.

The only Europeans who ever settled in Australia were the British. Their first settlement, made in 1788, was a penal colony located just south of Sydney to which debtors and assorted criminals were deported from England. The colony was soon moved to Sydney itself, where one of the world's finest harbors attracted people whose chief connections were overseas. In 1803 another penal colony was founded at Hobart on Tasmania. Ten years later—in 1813—only this southeastern section of Australia was even explored. The British settlements formed a strip about 150 miles long on either side of Sydney, and not more than 50 miles wide. But soon after that exploring parties began to cross the Great Dividing Range into the Murray-Darling Basin. In 1824 another penal colony was settled at Brisbane, and in 1826 still another at Perth in Western Australia. Moreover, colonies of free pioneers settled near Melbourne in 1834, and near Adelaide in 1836. Still, it was not until 1862 that an expedition crossed the desert from south to north, and not until 1874 that a party made the journey overland all the way across the country from Adelaide to Western Australia.

The continent was eventually divided into five separate colonies. At first there were just New South Wales and Tasmania (so named in 1853). In 1831 Western Australia was established as a separate colony, and in 1836 South Australia was established with its center at Adelaide. Victoria, focusing on Melbourne, became a separate colony in 1851, and Queensland in 1859. Thereafter, until 1901 when Australia was first formed into a political unit, each of the colonies was administered separately, and each had closer connections with London than with the other parts of Australia.

Population. The population of Australia during this whole period of settlement grew slowly and irregularly. Up to World War II it was formed exclusively of English, Scottish, Irish, and Welsh immigrants; but since World War II the government has tried to increase the number of immigrants, and now there are some Germans, Scandinavians, Italians, Greeks, and Poles included in the population. By 1962 the total number of Australians reached about 10,700,000. Of these 60 per cent lived in cities—57 per cent in cities of over 20,000. There were two leading cities of almost equal size—Sydney and Melbourne.

Apart from the cities most of the national territory is very thinly inhabited (Map 4, p. 8). The only exceptions are the rural area around Melbourne where there is a density of more than 125 people per square mile, and the patches of dense rural population around the other cities. The greater part of Australia has less than two people per square mile, and there are vast areas that remain outside the effective national territory.

Ranching. The Australian economy was built on sheep ranching. Early in the nineteenth century, when the British pioneers had opened a way across the hilly upland west of Sydney, they found that the Murray-Darling plains offered ideal conditions for the grazing of sheep. The clearing of the woodlands permitted the development of pastures: the climate was suitable for the growth of grasses, and the native animals did not include the kind of predators that make sheep raising in many other countries hazardous. At just about this time the steam

88

AUSTRALIA - NEW ZEALAND
AGRICULTURE

Scale of Miles
0   400

Indian Ocean

Pacific Ocean

Darwin

Gulf of Carpentaria

PAPUA

NORTHERN TERRITORY

Alice Springs

QUEENSLAND

WESTERN AUSTRALIA

SOUTH AUSTRALIA

Lake Eyre

Perth

Adelaide

NEW SOUTH WALES

Brisbane

Sydney

Canberra

VICTORIA

Melbourne

TASMANIA

Hobart

Dairy
Sugar cane, dairy
Wheat and sheep
Sheep range
Cattle range
Forest products
Non-agricultural land

Auckland

NORTH ISLAND

SOUTH ISLAND

Wellington

Christchurch

Dunedin

NEW ZEALAND

0   200
Miles

engine was introduced in the woolen textile factories of England (p. 56), and the demand for raw wool was increased beyond the capacity of the local wool producers of the Pennine Hills. As a result the British colonists in remote Australia were able to get a sufficiently high price for their wool to pay for the long voyage back to England. By 1850 Australia had become the world's leading producer of wool, and it has kept this position ever since. In 1960 it produced 20 per cent of the total world supply of wool, and 77 per cent of the Merino wool.

Since 1850 sheep ranching has spread over most of the lowland area west of the Great Dividing Range, and over a large area of the southwest (Map 88). In the tropical north cattle do better than sheep, and this has become the leading area for the grazing of beef cattle. Where conditions are good for wool sheep they occupy the land to the exclusion of other animals, the greatest concentrations being in the Murray-Darling Basin and in the southwest. The sheep that are raised on the mountain pastures of the east, and in rainy Tasmania, are mutton rather than wool sheep.

The development of the Australian ranching economy has raised a series of problems. The first of these is the water supply. As long as the sheep were allowed to move freely from place to place they could travel to water. But when grazing expanded to the drier north, and when fencing was introduced in order to control the breeding of the animals, it became necessary to drill wells. The drilling of deep wells in the plains of southwestern Queensland has revealed the existence of a major natural resource, hitherto unknown. This is the Great Artesian Basin. Layers of porous, sedimentary rock dip gently westward from the Great Dividing Range where the edges of the strata are exposed. Water seeps into these rock layers, soaked up as if by blotting paper. Many miles to the west, and at elevations much lower than those of the mountains where the strata reach the surface, drilled wells can tap this underground water source. The water, which is under pressure, rises in the wells and flows out at the surface without the use of pumps. These are artesian wells. Some water can be provided in this way, even far out to the west of the uplands; but if water is taken out faster than it is absorbed at the intake the resource will eventually be exhausted.

Another problem that the ranchers have had to face relates to the amazing spread of rabbits over Australia. In 1863 a rabbit breeder near Melbourne permitted some rabbits to escape. Finding themselves in a habitat which was largely free from natural enemies, the rabbits increased rapidly and began to spread (Map 89). It is estimated

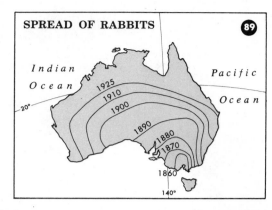

SPREAD OF RABBITS   89

that there are now something like 500,000,-000 rabbits eating the pasture grasses and drinking the water which would otherwise be available for sheep. Ranchers estimate that they could graze one additional sheep for every six rabbits that are killed. Large sums have been spent in an effort to control the pests, for instance in the construction of thousand-mile-long rabbit fences (which failed to stop the spread of the rabbits), and in the innoculation of the rabbits with a virus disease (which has also failed to reduce their numbers).

Furthermore, the rabbits have provided a new source of food for the wild dogs, or dingoes. The dingoes are the descendants of dogs brought into Australia by the earliest migrants from southern Asia. They never found much to eat until the rabbits appeared. But now they have increased rapidly, and they, too, have become a problem for the sheep herders. Each year the dingoes kill thousands of sheep, especially in the Lake Eyre Basin, in spite of the efforts of the herders.

Similar problems have arisen because of the spread of the prickly pear, a kind of cactus that chokes out the pasture grasses, and the tick, that spreads Texas cattle fever. Here too the problems are due to the peculiar nature of the Australian flora and

Rabbits gathered round a water hole in the Australian "outback" north of Adelaide.

fauna, which allows imported plants and animals to spread rapidly in the absence of natural enemies.

Agriculture. The development of agriculture in Australia was retarded by conflict between the farmers and the ranchers. The ranchers were the first to occupy the plains west of the coastal hilly belt, many of them as "squatters"—that is, they leased Crown lands on which to graze their sheep. Agriculture, in 1860, was largely confined to four areas: first, in the hilly land around Sydney; second, in the hills and valleys west of Melbourne; third, in the hilly belt around Adelaide; and fourth, in northern Tasmania. The sheepmen resisted the spread of the farmers. After 1861 laws were passed in the several colonies to permit settlers to gain titles to land within certain prescribed limits, and these limits were intended to separate the lands suitable for farming from those that were reserved for pasture. Two things followed: first, a new frontier of farm settlement developed, forming a crescent around the margins of the Murray-Darling Basin from Adelaide in the west to the northern border of New South Wales in the east; and second, many sheep ranchers gained titles

to some of the best land within the agricultural zone where rainfall is most dependable. By 1884 the conflict between farmers and ranchers was largely concluded because the two had learned to accept each other within the chief agricultural area, and to make the compromises which permitted both systems to exist side by side. Sheep ranching spread far to the north and west: many isolated "stations" were then more than a day's overland journey from the next settlement—although they are now tied together by radio and airplane. The frontier of farm settlement also spread out beyond the original limits, but with disastrous results during years of drought.

There are three chief agricultural types in Australia (Map 88). These are in addition to the small areas of truck farming close to the cities, and the irrigated areas along the lower Murray River where there are small citrus orchards and vineyards. The three major types include the wheat-sheep regions, the dairy regions, and the sugar cane region.

The wheat-sheep regions are in two chief locations. The major concentration of both wheat and sheep is in the Murray-Darling Basin, and extends around the inner margin of the uplands. But there is also a similar agricultural combination in Western Australia, inland from Perth. This is a distinctively Australian agricultural type. The sheep are grazed on cultivated pastures, which after three or four years are plowed and planted with wheat or barley. This form of rotation, combined with the use of chemical fertilizer, maintains the productivity of the soil, and gives the farmer two sources of income. This type of farming occupies the parts of the Australian plains where the rainfall is most nearly dependable.

The second agricultural type is made up of dairy farming with cultivated pastures. This kind of land use is found in the hilly lands of Tasmania, around Melbourne and Sydney, and southwest of Perth—all areas of relatively heavy rainfall. Sheep in these areas are raised for mutton rather than wool. Hay and other feed crops are harvested. But the most valuable products are milk, cheese, and butter. The dairy farms provide more employment than any other form of rural activity.

The third agricultural type is sugar cane growing, and is located along the rainy east coast north of Brisbane. When the cane plantations were first developed along this low-latitude coast in the middle of the nineteenth century it was assumed that Europeans could not do the necessary field work because of the climate. Laborers were imported from the islands of Melanesia, and the work was supervised by British managers. When the Commonwealth of Australia was formed in 1901, Queensland was required by the other provinces to accept the white Australia policy, and the non-European workers had to be sent back to their homelands. In compensation the cane growers were given a high protective tariff against imported sugar. Since the beginning of the twentieth century the planters have used people of European origin to do the work, and none of the expected health problems have appeared—due in part to the excellent medical services and the careful attention to hygiene.

In addition to these three agricultural types, there are vast areas in northern Australia which are used to graze beef cattle; and there are sheep stations scattered over all but the driest parts of the continent.

Mining. The discovery of gold in Australia took place in 1851, before the period of rapid agricultural development. It was discovered in the stream gravels on the western margin of the highlands west of Sydney. Soon additional gold sources were discovered, the most productive of which were located just west of Melbourne. News of the gold strike resulted in a rush of immigrants, and diverted attention for a while from the possibilities of agricultural development. But placer mining began to decline within a decade, and attention shifted to vein mining. Today, the major source of gold is at Kalgoorlie in Western Australia (Map 90).

The chief mineralized area of Australia is around the margins of the crystalline shield. Broken Hill, near the eastern end of the hilly country north of Adelaide, has proved to be one of the world's most valuable sources of silver, lead, and zinc. And on the edge of the shield, north of Adelaide, there are excellent iron ores. In the crystalline rocks of Tasmania there are ores of silver, copper, zinc, and tin. And at Mount Isa, at the end of the railroad in northern Queensland, there is another source of silver, lead, and zinc.

Until recently Australia had no known sources of oil and gas. The large area of crystalline rocks reduces the extent of territory within which one can expect to find oil. In 1961, however, an oil field was discovered on the inner margin of the hilly belt

AUSTRALIA - NEW ZEALAND
MINERALS, INDUSTRIES
AND RAILROADS

Scale of Miles

Indian

Ocean

DARWIN

Gulf of
Carpentaria

P a c i f i c

O c e a n

NORTHERN

TERRITORY

HIGHWAY
CONNECTION
TO DARWIN

Alice Springs

QUEENSLAND

WESTERN

AUSTRALIA

Au

Au

SOUTH

AUSTRALIA

Lake Eyre

Brisbane

Perth

Darling R.

NEW

SOUTH

WALES

Adelaide

Murray R.

Sydney

Canberra

VICTORIA

Melbourne

■ Steel industry
⊙ Industrial center
Coal
Oil
Fe Iron
Cu Copper
Pb Lead
Zn Zinc
Au Gold
—— Railroads

TASMANIA

Zn

Hobart

Auckland

NORTH
ISLAND

SOUTH
ISLAND

Wellington

Christchurch

NEW ZEALAND

Dunedin

Miles

---

west of Brisbane, and hopes mounted for the discovery of additional oil and gas sources.

Australia is abundantly supplied with good-quality coal. The most productive field is located in New South Wales, inland from Newcastle. But there are other important coal fields along the eastern margin of Australia.

Manufacturing Industry. In spite of the existence of these mineral resources, Australia did not make a start toward industrialization until World War I. Before that the provinces had been treated as colonies, which sent raw materials home to supply the British factories, and provided a market for the manufactured products. But during World War I the usual flow of consumer goods was greatly reduced, and Australia had to go without many things or turn to manufacturing for its own market. The earliest industries were engaged in food processing and the manufacture of a variety of other consumer goods. A steel industry was built at Newcastle, making use of the local supplies of coal. Pig iron was, and still is, manufactured at Whyalla, near the sources of iron ore, and shipped by coastal vessels to Newcastle. Now a variety of new industries, which make use of steel in the manufacture of consumer goods, supply the domestic market.

The Australian industries have been growing steadily. The initial phase of the Industrial Revolution was passed before World War II, and the drive to maturity is well under way. The factories now account for about half of the gross national product. They produce machinery and metal goods, foods, beverages, tobacco, clothing and textiles, chemicals, and paper. New hydroelectric developments in the southeast are providing a new source of inexpensive power.

Transportation. Australia's drive to maturity is dependent on a continued development of the transportation facilities. Traditionally coastal shipping has provided a major part of domestic transportation. Highways are of less importance in Australia than in any other country of comparable economic development. The longest highway was built for military reasons in 1940, and extends from the end of the railroad at Alice Springs northward to Darwin. The small airplane is of greater importance, however, in providing connections with the widely scattered settlements of the "outback."

Land transportation is provided chiefly by the railroads (Map 90). But when the rail systems developed each colony adopted its own plan, and its own gauge. Victoria has the most dense network of rail lines, all built on a gauge of 5 feet 3 inches. New South Wales, with a larger total mileage of railroads, made use of the British standard gauge—4 feet 8½ inches. Queensland, with many long rail tentacles extending into the interior, built the lines with a gauge of 3 feet 6 inches. South Australia built some lines with a gauge of 3 feet 6 inches and some with one of 5 feet 3 inches. Western Australia used the gauge of 3 feet 6 inches. The long transcontinental line connecting Sydney with Perth involves two changes of gauge along the way. The Australian government is trying to convert all the lines to a standard gauge; but this is costly, and is opposed by those who prefer the gauge with which they are familiar.

The Viability of Australia. Until 1901 the various parts of Australia were administered as separate colonies, and the closest connection of each colony was with Great Britain. It is for this reason, perhaps, that Australia has no primate city. Since 1901 it has been necessary to develop a state-idea with an appeal strong enough to overcome the tendency toward provincial separateness. The fact that this has been done is no small accomplishment.

One important element in the state-idea is the capital, Canberra. When Australia was granted independence the selection of a capital city became a serious problem. And as long as the problem remained unsolved it exerted a disintegrating force on the state. But the selection of a site in 1908 provided a compromise that was acceptable both to Sydney and Melbourne. Canberra was founded in 1913, on a broad stretch of level land surrounded by hills. The seat of government was transferred to the newly built city in 1927.

The geographic arrangement of the population and the productive areas in a series of concentric circles, with most of the people and most of the production around the rim of the land in the east, southeast, and southwest, is an adverse factor in the viability of Australia. It is unlikely that any important new wave of settlement will take

Modern equipment being used in a coal mine in New South Wales.

place in the "dead heart" of Australia. Mining communities will continue to develop, but these will remain isolated islands of settlement in the midst of the vast empty areas. The crystalline shield will certainly remain one of the least habitable parts of the earth for a long time because of the absence of wadis and the lack of exotic rivers. Even if fresh water can be made available from sea water there are many places along the coast where the use of such water would be much less costly than in the interior. Furthermore, the application of modern techniques to agriculture and stock raising requires the services of fewer and fewer rural people: the tendency, wherever economic development is taking place, is for the thinly peopled areas to lose

population, and for the densely peopled areas to gain. The population pattern of Australia is not likely to change in any important way, unless some quite unexpected technological development occurs.

Australia is still remote from the center of the Land Hemisphere. From Perth to London by way of Colombo and Suez is 9,537 miles, and the distance by way of South Africa is much greater. From Sydney to Liverpool by way of Panama is 12,222 miles. The route around the southern end of South America is longer still. Australia's interest in the Suez Canal and the Panama Canal is clear, although the country would now be able to supply its own basic needs if these long sea routes were cut. At the same time the increase in trade with Britain, that has resulted from the development of a mature economy, ties the Australian standard of living to the maintenance of these distant connections. Australia still supplies Britain with 74 per cent of the wool used in that country, with 18 per cent of the butter, 13 per cent of the sugar, and from 5 to 7 per cent of the wheat, meat, and cheese. But Australia is now able to purchase a much larger volume and variety of manufactured goods from Britain than was possible when there were only a few factories in Australia and little employment in manufacturing and service occupations.

NEW ZEALAND

The other state included in this culture region is New Zealand, also a member of the Commonwealth of Nations. New Zealand was claimed by Great Britain in 1840, and its 27,000 British settlers were granted local self-government in 1852. The people of this remote island, located in the midst of the Water Hemisphere almost exactly opposite to Great Britain, have nevertheless continued to speak of Britain as "home" and to maintain close contacts with the mother country. New Zealand is still primarily a pastoral country, although only about 18 per cent of its labor force is employed in farming, fishing, forestry, and mining. The country ranks third in the world in terms of gross national product per capita (Map 11, p. 30). Its total area is a little larger than the area of Great Britain, but its population is only about 2,500,000.

The Habitat. The main part of New Zealand is made up of two mountainous islands —North Island and South Island (Map 87). The central part of North Island is a volcanic plateau on which there are hot springs, geysers, and other volcanic features. Standing above the plateau is a cone-shaped volcano, a little over 9,000 feet in elevation. On the southwest coast there is another volcano, Mount Egmont, the strikingly symmetrical cone of which rises 8,260 feet above the sea. Elsewhere North Island is hilly, even the long narrow peninsula on which Auckland is situated that extends about three hundred miles to the north. South Island, separated from North Island by a strait only sixteen miles wide at its narrowest point, is very rugged. Along its western side are the heavily glaciated Southern Alps, the highest peaks of which are more than 12,300 feet above sea level. The west coast is deeply fiorded. Along the eastern side of the island there are hilly uplands, and two small plains—one at the southern end of the island, and one south of Christchurch, known as the Canterbury Plain.

New Zealand is located in the middle latitudes, extending from about 34°S. to beyond 47°S. In many respects its climate resembles that of Great Britain. Its temperatures are never very high, and seldom very low. The prevailing westerly winds bring heavy rainfall to the western mountain slopes: in the Southern Alps there is deep snow in winter, and there are many glaciers. A zone of somewhat less rain is found on the eastern sides of the islands, but no part of New Zealand suffers from lack of moisture.

Settlement and Economy. When the Dutch explorer Abel Janszoon Tasman first reached New Zealand in 1642 he found a Polynesian people inhabiting both islands. They had probably migrated to this remote part of the world during the fourteenth century A.D., and finding it unoccupied had settled first on North Island, and then on the more protected parts of South Island. These were the people known as Maoris.

A flock of sheep on South Island, New Zealand. The New Zealand Alps are in the background.

The British did not establish a colony in New Zealand until 1840, and from that date until 1871 there was almost continuous warfare with the Maoris. As a result the earlier inhabitants were almost wiped out, and only those survived who could adjust to the way of life of the British. Now, the people of Maori ancestry, accepted as members of the New Zealand state, have increased to almost 160,000, or about 7 per cent of the total population.

More than half of the people of New Zealand live in cities of over 20,000 in population. There are four chief cities: Auckland, Wellington, the capital, Christchurch, and Dunedin (Map 87). Auckland is the primate city of New Zealand with almost twice the population of the second city, Wellington.

New Zealand's prosperity is based on a large per capita production, and on the export of butter, wool, frozen meat, cheese, and hides. The farmers of North Island are involved in the production of high-grade dairy cattle and sheep. The greatest concentration of dairying is on the gentle lower slopes of Mount Egmont. As one travels southward through South Island sheep, reared for both wool and mutton, become more important than cattle. There are a few areas where wheat is grown, chiefly on the Canterbury Plain; and on the plains at the southern end of South Island there are mixed crop and livestock farms.

Manufacturing industries provide a large part of all employment. These are located in the cities, and are mostly engaged in the processing, packaging, and shipping of farm products. In addition to foodstuffs the industries make metal goods and machines, textiles and clothing, wood products, cement, and building materials. Hydroelectric plants provide abundant power; and there is some mining of coal near the southern end of South Island.

In many ways New Zealand is a model of economic and social development. As in Australia there has been no hindrance to the growth of democratic institutions, or to the rapid acceptance of the new technology of the Industrial Revolution.

SUMMARY

These two remote, and almost unoccupied, lands came into the possession of Great Britain when the latter country had already started the great changes that we have called the Industrial Revolution and the Democratic Revolution. The British colonists brought the new concepts to these distant places, where they developed free from hindrance or the need to compromise. Both Australia and New Zealand developed their economies on the export of foods—dairy products, meat, and wheat—which were essential to the crowded population of the mother country. Both are major suppliers of wool for the British textile factories. But in the present century both countries have devoted a necessary proportion of their gross national products to new capital formation, and especially to the manufacture of consumer goods. The people enjoy a large purchasing power, which allows them to absorb, not only the products of their domestic industry, but also imports from other industrial countries. Remoteness and isolation have not saved the Australians and New Zealanders from participation in the major wars of this century; but they have saved them from direct experience in the destruction and the generation of fear that these conflicts have created in places closer to the center of the Land Hemisphere.

12

THE
PACIFIC
CULTURE REGION

Country	Political Status	Latest Estimate Population	Capital City
Western Samoa	Constitutional Monarchy	114,427 ('61)	Apia
Australian Pacific Islands			
New Guinea Incl. Bismarck Archipelago	Trust Territory	1,402,000 ('60)	
Papua Incl. New Britain, New Ireland, Admiralty Is.	External Territory	503,000 ('60)	
British Pacific Islands			
British Solomon Is. Incl. Choiseul Guadalcanal Lord Howe Is. Malaita Mitre New Georgia Reef & Daff Groups San Cristobal Santa Cruz Santa Isabel	British Protectorate	124,076 ('59)	
Fiji Islands	British Colony	394,000 ('60)	
Gilbert & Ellice Is.	British Colony	46,000 ('60)	
Pitcairn Is. Incl. Aeno, Henderson, Ducie	British Colony	147 ('60)	
Tonga	Protected Kingdom of U.K.	63,000 ('60)	
French Pacific Islands			
French Polynesia Incl. Society, Tahiti, Marquesas, Tuamotu		76,327 ('56)	
New Caledonia Wallis & Futuna		77,000 ('60)	
New Zealand Pacific Islands			
Cook Islands	Dependency	18,174 ('60)	
Tokelau		1,929 ('60)	
Niue		4,860 ('60)	
United States Pacific Islands			
American Samoa	U.S. Unincorporated Territory	20,051 ('60)	
Guam	Unincorporated Territory	67,044 ('60)	
Bonin, Volcano Is.	Military Administrations	204 ('60)	
Marshall, Caroline, Mariana Islands	U.S. Trusteeship	75,836 ('60)	
Johnston			
Midway		2,356 ('60)	
Wake		1,097 ('60)	
Baker, Howland, Jarvis, Kingman Reef, Palmyra			
Condominiums in the Pacific			
Canton & Enderbury	U.S.—British	320 ('60)	
New Hebrides	French—British	59,000 ('60)	

◄ *Light over the Pacific Ocean.*

The Pacific Culture Region is an island world. It is made up of the tens of thousands of islands, islets, and reefs that dot the surface of the southwestern quarter of the Pacific Ocean (Map inside front cover, and Map 91). Only a small proportion of them are large enough to be habitable, or even to be named on a map. The distances involved are enormous: from northern Australia to the northernmost of the Marianas is 2,400 miles; from eastern Australia to Easter Island, 6,000 miles; from Easter Island to the Hawaiian Islands, 5,000 miles; from the Hawaiian Islands to the Marianas, 3,700 miles. These are the dimensions within which the island world is spread out; and to the north and east, beyond these limits, the other three quarters of the Pacific Ocean is largely empty of islands.

The Pacific Culture Region, like Australia, was peopled by migrants from southern Asia. People moved in successive waves away from the Asian mainland along the land bridge to New Guinea; and from there some went southward into Australia, and some continued eastward as far as they could go. At the end of the last glacial period a rise in the world sea level cut the land connections with Asia, and also separated New Guinea from Australia and from the lands that existed farther to the east. When the land bridge was broken migrants continued to spread into the Pacific Culture Region by sea, reaching as far as the Hawaiian Islands and Easter Island—and perhaps even as far as Peru. When the Europeans discovered this region, and laid claim to it, they found a variety of native cultures ranging from very simple to quite elaborate ones with a high degree of seafaring skill. But none of the cultures could resist the power of the newcomers. Life on the islands changed only little by little, but received a

very sudden transformation with the arrival of military forces during World War II. The war and its aftermath left a mark on this region that will never be erased.

The region is commonly divided into three parts, based on differences of race and culture. *Melanesia* includes New Guinea and the smaller islands that extend eastward to the Fiji Islands. *Micronesia* includes the island clusters lying north of the equator and generally west of longitude 180°, with the exception of the Ellice Islands. *Polynesia* is the easternmost part of the region, extending to the Hawaiian Islands, Easter Island, and New Zealand. The Hawaiian Islands and New Zealand are no longer included in this Pacific Culture Region, although before the arrival of the Europeans and the Americans they were a part of Polynesia. The whole land area forms only 1 per cent of the world's inhabited lands, and is occupied by only a fraction of 1 per cent of the world's population.

THE HABITAT

(Maps 5, 6, 8, 91, and 92) The ocean habitat is by no means uniform in its physical and biotic characteristics. There are geographic regions of the ocean as there are of the lands. Within this culture region there are differences of climate, differences in the character and movement of the ocean water, and in the plants and animals that live in it, differences in the landforms and soils of the islands, and differences in the vegetation.

The Climates. In the low latitudes temperatures over the open ocean are never extreme, and differences between day and night, and between the seasons, are slight. It is a climate that may be called the "temperate climate of the tropics." This is the only part of the world where truly temper-

REGIONAL DIVISIONS

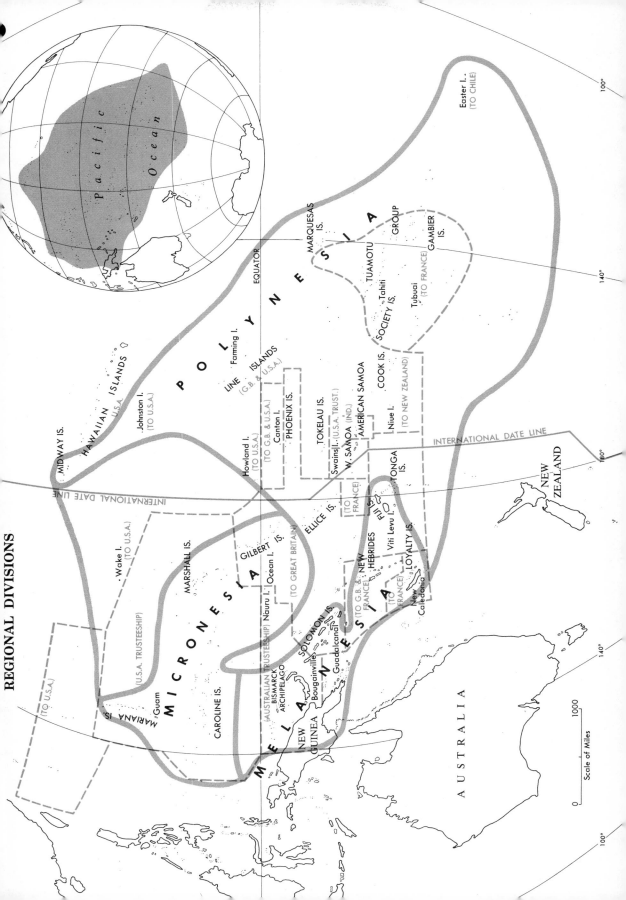

Pacific Ocean

Easter I.
(TO CHILE)

MARQUESAS IS.

P O L Y N E S I A

TUAMOTU GROUP

GAMBIER IS.

Tahiti
SOCIETY IS.

Tubuai
(TO FRANCE)

EQUATOR

Fanning I.
LINE ISLANDS
(G.B. & U.S.A.)

COOK IS.
(TO NEW ZEALAND)

Niue I.

HAWAIIAN ISLANDS
U.S.A.

Johnston I.
(TO U.S.A.)

MIDWAY IS.

Canton I.
(TO G.B. & U.S.A.)
PHOENIX IS.

TOKELAU IS.

Swains I. (U.S.A. TRUST.)
AMERICAN SAMOA
W. SAMOA (IND.)

INTERNATIONAL DATE LINE

Howland I.
(TO U.S.A.)

NEW ZEALAND

INTERNATIONAL DATE LINE

Wake I.
(TO U.S.A.)

(U.S.A. TRUSTEESHIP)

MARSHALL IS.

GILBERT IS.

Ocean I.
(TO GREAT BRITAIN)

ELLICE IS.

(TO FRANCE)

TONGA IS.

FIJI
Viti Levu I.

NEW HEBRIDES
(TO G.B. & FRANCE)

LOYALTY IS.

New Caledonia
(TO FRANCE)

M I C R O N E S I A

(AUSTRALIAN TRUSTEESHIP)

Nauru I.

(TO U.S.A.)

MARIANA IS.

Guam

CAROLINE IS.

BISMARCK ARCHIPELAGO

SOLOMON IS.
Bougainville
Guadalcanal

M E L A N E S I A

NEW GUINEA

A U S T R A L I A

Scale of Miles
0   1000

ate conditions exist. Average annual temperatures vary between 75° and 85°. At Malden Island, only 4° north of the equator, the average is 84.8°, ranging from an average of 85.2° in the warmest month to 84.2° in the coolest month. At Apia, on Samoa, more than 13° south of the equator, the average is 79.7°, ranging from 78° to 80°. In these places temperatures as high as 100° are not experienced, and there are never any cold waves.

The prevailing winds are from the east in both hemispheres. These are the trade winds—strong, steady winds that ruffle the surface of the ocean and cause huge waves to roll unceasingly on the east-facing shores of the islands.

The rainfall is largely dependent on exposure to these winds. The warm air passing over the warm water picks up a large amount of moisture, and wherever the air is forced to rise the rainfall is heavy. Rising air and heavy rain are found where the oceanic whirls of the northern and southern hemispheres converge. An average rainfall of more than two hundred inches may be expected on the windward slopes of mountainous islands: Mount Waialeale on the island of Kauai in the Hawaiian group holds the world record for average annual rainfall (an average of 460 inches per year in the period from 1911 to 1957). But on such islands the lee sides of the mountains, only a short distance from the very rainy parts, are very dry. There are places with more than 100 inches of rain and places with less than 20 inches within less than a mile of each other.

The western part of the Pacific Ocean, like the corresponding part of the Atlantic Ocean, is occasionally visited by violent storms, known in the Pacific as typhoons (hurricanes in the Atlantic). These great whirling storms, measuring perhaps three hundred miles across, move slowly along lines that correspond to the movement of the oceanic whirls. They originate about 10° away from the equator on either side—never on the equator itself: those in the southern hemisphere, an average of three a year, move to the southwest, reaching as far as the east coast of Australia; those in the northern hemisphere, an average of twenty each year, sweep across the islands of Micronesia and do great damage in the Philippines, Japan, and even on the coast of China. Typhoons are always accompanied by torrential rain. The islands of Polynesia are too far east to feel the effects of typhoons very often.

The Ocean Currents. The ocean currents, like the winds, move generally from east to west. But just a little to the north of the equator there is a narrow, and sharply-defined, equatorial counter current, moving back eastward. In the northern part of the region, at about latitude 30°N, there is a line of convergence between the west-moving tropical water and the east-moving mid-latitude water. There is no cold water in the region, but a long tongue of water, somewhat cooler than the water near the equator, extends westward as far as the Philippines. These various currents were well-known to the Polynesians.

The Ocean Basin and the Islands. The southwest Pacific, if drained of its water, would be the most rugged part of the earth's surface. The islands of Melanesia stand on a continental platform which once extended southeastward from Asia as far as the Fiji Islands and New Zealand. This platform is now broken by faults, as well as being submerged by the general rise of the sea level. The island arcs of Micronesia, like those of the Philippines and Japan, are related to

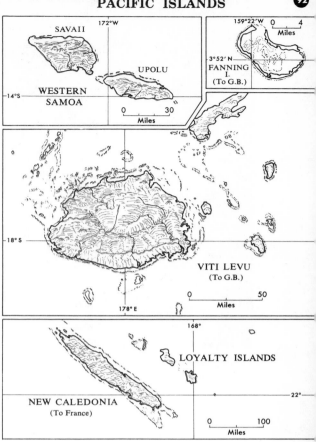

the festoons of mountains along the eastern side of Asia. There is a deep trench in the ocean floor along the eastern side of each of these arcs. The deepest of these—the Mindanao Trench—is now known to reach a depth of 36,804 feet (the deepest point in any ocean). Many of the islands of Polynesia are, in reality, submerged mountains of immense size. The highest mountain on the island of Hawaii, the dormant volcano Mauna Kea (13,825 feet above sea level), rises to the greatest height above its base on the sea floor of any mountain in the world (a total of 32,024 feet from base to summit).

This is a part of the world ocean in which coral reefs form. The coral is a small lime-secreting animal that lives in large colonies in sea water under certain conditions. The water must never get colder than 68°, and it must be clear. The reefs are formed below sea level as deep as bubbles from the surf can reach, and above sea level as high as the spray can reach. They are built from the skeletons of these tiny animals, cemented into solid rock by a variety of lime-secreting algae. Corals form fringing reefs around all the shores of the tropical oceans that are free from the mud brought down by rivers. If the land is rising in relation to the sea limestone collars encircle the central mountains, or the reefs stand as platforms elevated above the sea. If the land is sinking the land area of the island becomes smaller, its valleys are drowned, and the former fringing reef, now some distance off the shore, becomes a barrier reef. If sinking continues the island may completely disappear, leaving only a circular atoll surrounding a lagoon (Map 92).

The Island Habitats. Seven chief kinds of island habitats can be identified in the Pacific Culture Region. These are listed as follows, with examples of each type (Map 91):[1]

1. Treeless atolls (Canton Island, Johnston Island, Howland Island).

2. Atolls with scrub woodland (Marshall Islands, Ellice Islands, some of the Tuamotu Group, and the northern Cook Islands).

3. Atolls with dense rain forest (Gilbert Islands, Tokelau Islands, Swains Island, Fanning Island—Map 92).

4. Raised coral islands (Niue Island, Nauru Island, Ocean Island).

5. New volcanic islands, with little depth of soil (northern Marianas).

6. Old volcanic islands, with deep soil derived from lava or ash (Hawaiian Islands, Society Islands, Samoa—Map 92).

[1] Douglas L. Oliver, 1952; pp. 12-14.

An air view of Swains Island in the Pacific, showing the forested coral atoll encircling a lagoon.

7. Continental islands, with complex rock structures associated with large land masses (New Guinea, Viti Levu—Map 92—New Caledonia, Guadalcanal, and most of the other islands of Melanesia).

MELANESIA

Most of the islands of Melanesia belong to the category of continental islands. They extend from New Guinea to the Fiji Islands (Map 91). The total land area is about 400,-000 square miles, but of this New Guinea comprises 300,000 square miles. These are islands with complex rock structures folded and faulted into mountain ranges, whether above or below sea level. The land surfaces above the sea are deeply dissected. The islands are bordered by fringing reefs and barrier reefs (Map 92). These islands belong to three countries. The western half of New Guinea is now a part of Indonesia and so is included in the Southeast Asian Culture Region. Australia owns the southeastern part of New Guinea (known as Papua), and administers the northeastern part (formerly a German colony). Australia also administers the former German colony in the Bismarck Archipelago, and the island of Bougainville in the Solomon Islands. The remainder of the Solomons are a possession of Great Britain, as are also the Fiji Islands. France owns New Caledonia and the Loyalty Islands, and administers the New Hebrides jointly with Great Britain.

Population and Economic Development. The first people to migrate from the Asian mainland were short, dark-skinned, frizzy-haired Negritos who had no knowledge of agriculture or of domestic animals, and whose culture was well adjusted to the food resources of the rain forests. Some of these people turned southward from New Guinea into Australia; but others continued eastward through what, during the last glacial period, was a much more extensive land area than it is now. They were followed by a racially very different people—also non-agricultural. These later migrants were lighter in skin color, with wavy rather than frizzy hair. The Negritos were similar to the Pygmies of Central Africa; but the lighter-skinned people, who are thought to have been at least partly Caucasoid in origin, were more closely related to the Ainus of Japan. These in turn were followed by still another group—a dark-skinned people with wavy hair who were akin to the earliest inhabitants of South Asia. All these Paleolithic peoples intermingled to produce, eventually, a composite population in which dark color predominated.

After the Neolithic revolution, migrants with crops and animals moved eastward along the land bridge. They were light in color, with straight black hair, and high cheek bones. With their taro roots, bananas, yams, coconuts, breadfruit, pigs, and domestic fowl they could make a much better living than the peoples who had preceded them. The latter were soon driven out of the more accessible coastal areas, and forced to take refuge in the mountainous interior, especially of New Guinea. The Pygmies and the Papuans did, however, adopt crops, and also the domestic pig, from the more advanced peoples, and today both groups still practice a kind of shifting agriculture based on taro, rice, sweet potatoes, chickens and pigs.

When the Europeans came to Melanesia during the first half of the nineteenth century they found the inhabitants warlike and uncooperative. The missionaries first had the task of stopping the practice of cannibalism. This they did, but the newcomers also introduced many diseases to which the Melanesians had no immunity. There were about 3,000,000 Melanesians in the area when the Europeans first arrived, but they have been declining steadily in numbers ever since.

The British, the French, and the Germans introduced commercial plantation crops such as sugar cane and copra—made from coconuts and used in the manufacture of soap. Before World War II Melanesia produced about 12 per cent of the world's supply of copra. Unfortunately the Melanesians have not only been decreasing in numbers, they have also rejected the European ideas about steady work. Over time many Indians have been brought in to develop the plantations. In the Fiji Islands today the population is about 50 per cent Indian, 40 per cent Fiji Islander, and 10 per cent British, Chinese, Polynesian, and Micronesian. With the money earned from work on the plantations the inhabitants purchased imported cotton cloth to make garments (which the missionaries insisted on), and kerosene oil to light their lamps.

World War II created havoc in Melanesia. First came the Japanese invasion, and with it the hasty departure of the European plantation managers. Then the ships that used to call at the many little ports among the islands no longer returned. The islanders were left without wages, and without the supplies on which they had learned to depend. Then came the military forces of the United States and Australia: in some cases they had to fight for possession of the islands; in other cases they were able to occupy them without resistance, and built air bases. Where, before, ships had come to the islands once every two or three weeks, now several ships would arrive within a week. The Melanesians were given employment in the construction of buildings, air strips, docks, and warehouses, and in the loading and unloading of ships. The women made more money than they had ever dreamed of by washing clothes for service personnel, and by selling souvenirs. On many of the islands the land was used to grow fresh vegetables such as cabbages, maize, onions, cucumbers, squash, and watermelons. The Melanesians, supplied with unaccustomed wealth, purchased tobacco, chewing gum, canned beef, canned salmon, and other previously unknown articles. And Melanesians who were given medals for bravery during the war began to wear shirts so as to have something on which to pin them.

Then the war was over, and the military forces withdrew. Suddenly there were no jobs, no good wages, no ships coming with supplies. The plantations of coconuts had been profitable in the past because of the low wages paid, but now the Melanesians would not work for such low wages. The war created wants and aspirations among the Melanesians that the peacetime economy could not satisfy. Among the ruins of the South Sea paradise the natives now dream of the war years.

Mining. The only part of Melanesia where mining is important is on New Caledonia. This island is the administrative center of the French possessions of the South Pacific. In the mountains of New Caledonia there are mines of nickel, chromium, manganese, and iron ore. There are about 70,000 people on the island, of whom only about 20,000 are Europeans—mostly French. The work in the mines and on some of the commercial plantations is done by about 10,000 Javanese and others who come from the former French Indochina. The plantations produce copra, cacao, and coffee.

MICRONESIA

Micronesia contains four chief island clusters (Map 91). The Gilbert Islands are a possession of Great Britain; and since World War II the Marianas, the Carolines, and the Marshalls have been administered by the United States as trust territories. The island of Guam, in the southern part of the Marianas, has been a possession of the United States since 1898.

Except for the northern Marianas, which are new volcanic islands, most of Micronesia is made up of low-lying coral islands. They never did form a connected land bridge, and the Paleolithic peoples, therefore, did not occupy them: they were still empty of human inhabitants when the Neolithic people spread into the region, using outrigger canoes to sail from island to island. The islands offered several useful plants which the newcomers added to the crops they brought with them. This is the native home of the areca palm, the source of the betel nut, a delicacy enjoyed now by the inhabitants of all the islands. The people who occupied these islands also cultivated taros and breadfruit, and even some rice. But the chief commercial crop was the coconut, which does very well on the low coral lands, and is not severely damaged by typhoons.

For the Micronesians the coconut is the basis of life. It provides food, clothing, and shelter. Inside the unripe nut is a milky fluid with a faint coconut taste, a much prized drink in a habitat not abundantly supplied with fresh water. The white meat of the ripe coconut is used for food. The hollowed shell is used as a bowl or spoon. From the fiber around the husk a coarse cloth can be woven. From the trunk of the palm comes timber for houses and boats; and the leaf can be used as thatch. The meat inside the ripe nut can be scraped out and dried to make copra, for which nearby Japan offers a steady market. And the coconut husks have been found to make the most effective charcoal for use in gas masks.

In modern Micronesia there are very few Europeans. Chinese traders came into this part of the Pacific, as they came into Southeast Asia, and they now form the largest minority group, usually controlling the retail businesses, commerce and banking.

The only islands that have ever produced anything but agricultural products are Nauru Island and Ocean Island (Map 91). These are raised coral reefs which for countless years have provided nesting places for sea birds. The bird droppings, reacting chemically with the coral limestone, have created a deep accumulation of phosphate rock, rich in nitrogen, and excellent as a fertilizer. After World War II the islands were placed under an Australian mandate, and since that time they have been so heavily mined that the resource is now virtually exhausted. In 1962 the 2,456 inhabitants of Nauru were offered the choice of moving to Australia or of remaining on Nauru without any means of economic support.

POLYNESIA

The Polynesians are a large-framed, soft-featured, brown-skinned people with black

A native village on the coast of Guadalcanal in the Solomon Islands. These continental islands are part of Melanesia.

wavy hair, and large brown eyes. They are readily distinguished from the brown-skinned Micronesians, and from the small, dark, frizzy-haired Melanesians. All of the islands in this area, including the Hawaiian Islands and New Zealand, were occupied by these seafaring people. Throughout the area the way of life was remarkably uniform, and there was the same basic language. Study of the differences of dialect shows clearly that Polynesia was occupied by people coming from the direction of Asia, not from America. Pigs, poultry, and rats, as well as taros, sugar cane, and breadfruit, came from Southeast Asia. Yet the sweet potato, which the Polynesians cultivated along with the Asian plants, came originally from America. There can be no doubt that in their large outrigger canoes the Polynesians were able to navigate vast distances across the ocean, migrating from island to island when there was too much overcrowding, or when feuds between clans became too fierce to endure.

The Polynesians were overwhelmed by the Europeans. They were first discovered in the late eighteenth century by Captain James Cook, whose explorations between 1767 and 1779 placed the outlines of the Pacific Ocean on the map. Early in the nineteenth century missionaries came to the various islands, and at about the same time traders and whalers. Commercial plantations were laid out in the better-favored places, as they were on the Hawaiian Islands (see p. 188). The Polynesians step by step lost control of their islands, and in many places found themselves all but submerged by the flow of immigrants—Europeans, Americans, Chinese, and many others. However, in the period since World War II the introduction of better medicine and hygiene, and the fact that the surviving Polynesians have now adjusted to the way of life of the Europeans and Americans, is resulting in a rapid increase in population. Already there is not enough room on some of the islands, and regular currents of migration are again appearing, especially into Melanesia and New Zealand. The population of Polynesia as a whole is increasing at a faster rate than are opportunities for employment.

Most of the Polynesian islands are possessions or trust territories of the United States, Great Britain, New Zealand, or France. American Samoa has been a possession of the United States since 1872. Great Britain owns the Ellice Islands and the Tonga Islands. The Marquesas Islands, the Tuamotu Group, and the Society Islands, including Tahiti, belong to France. The Cook Islands and Niue Island are administered by New Zealand; and Easter Island is a possession of Chile.

Western Samoa, formerly administered by New Zealand, became, in 1962, the first Polynesian state to gain independence in the twentieth century (Map 92). With a total area of 1,133 square miles, and a population of 114,427, the new state will continue to depend for economic aid on New Zealand. The chief products are copra, cacao, and bananas. The people have been trained by the New Zealanders to manage their own political affairs. The form of government that they have selected by majority vote is based on the traditional authority of the heads of the families and clans, the *matais*. The political leadership will be held jointly by the heads of the two leading families. Even if the gross national product remains small, and the standard of living seems low by European standards, the people are happy that they are no longer members of someone else's empire.

SUMMARY

In the Pacific Culture Region the original inhabitants have been submerged by the tide of European conquest, from which only Western Samoa has so far escaped. The Hawaiian Islands have been successfully transformed as a part of Anglo-America, and New Zealand has also been successful in the integration of British and Polynesian institutions. The thousands of other islands throughout the region have not escaped from invasion, but they have not been integrated with any modern states.

The airplane and the radio bring even these remote spots of land close to the centers of the world's population. Yet it is true that neither resources nor strategic positioning place any part of this region at the focus of international interest. The great conflicts of our time are mostly being worked out within the Land Hemisphere. These islands are beyond the horizon, on the edge of events. But even these remote places would feel the effects of global warfare, just as they were forced to join in the events of World War II. The paradise that once existed for the original inhabitants can now only be re-created synthetically for the tourists.

13 CONCLUSION:

THE
SEARCH FOR
SIGNIFICANCE

For each of the eleven culture regions which divide our one world into distinctive parts we have considered the areal association and the interactions of four groups of phenomena. These four groups are 1) the physical and biotic features of the habitat; 2) the density, growth, character, and arrangement of the populations; 3) the nature and stage of economic development in relation to the earth resources; and 4) the political organization and attitudes, and the viability of the states.

Let us follow the sequence of ideas carefully:

1. Our one world is differentiated by variations in the physical and biotic character of habitats, and by variations in the resource base of states.

2. It is differentiated, also, by variations in the population, the economy, and the political conditions.

3. For some two centuries two great processes of fundamental and revolutionary change—the Industrial Revolution and the Democratic Revolution—have been going on, and have been spreading unevenly from the culture hearth around the North Sea.

4. As the two revolutions spread they also undergo a continuation of the process of development, so that they do not make the same impact today along their advancing fronts as they did a century ago.

5. Distinctive social, economic, and political reactions have been produced by the impact of these revolutionary changes on pre-existing societies—the pre-industrial and pre-democratic societies.

6. In each distinctive culture area, so defined, the significance to man of the features of the habitat changes with changes in the culture, requiring with each change a new evaluation of the resource base.

7. Such re-evaluation is aided by grouping the resulting cultures into culture regions, in each of which there is a distinctive association of demographic conditions, economic development, and political expression.

8. This distinctive regional character is most clearly observable in the cores of the regions.

9. Eleven such regions can tentatively be defined; this number may be subject to change as a result of more precise study or of the continuation of the revolutionary processes.

10. The geographic arrangement of these distinctive regions on the globe has a meaning not found in the separate consideration of the elements that make them up, and this meaning is relevant to the formulation of economic, political, or military policy.

The Significance of Position on the Earth. We have presented the argument for the pre-eminent importance of the Land Hemisphere (Map 12, p. 36). But can one measure the relative importance of one part of the earth to the other parts?

We may assume that what we are trying to measure is the extent to which the actions and decisions of people in any one area affect or influence the lives and actions of people in other areas. The actions and decisions involved in this problem relate to such matters as population growth, economic development, increased volume of trade, increase in gross national products, and a variety of political decisions and policies. The more accessible one population is to another, the greater will be its influence on the other, the greater will be the number of contacts that are made, or the number of messages exchanged—unless man-made barriers are set up between them.

Accessibility is a condition that can be measured: the influence of one population on another varies directly with the size of the two populations, and inversely with the distance between them.[1] This basic concept

[1] John Q. Stewart, 1947.

◄ President Eisenhower addressing the United Nations General Assembly.

has been used to establish a theoretical model in relation to which actual contacts and exchanges between populations can be measured. But in the modern world this relationship is complicated because the numbers of people must be balanced against the degree to which the people are economically productive. The more productive the population the greater is the influence it exerts, the greater the number of contacts with other populations, and the greater the volume of exchanges. We may rephrase the principle then and say that accessibility can be measured by multiplying the gross national products per capita of two populations and dividing by the distance between them.

But we know that population and economic production are not evenly spread over national territories and culture regions. The population exerts the greatest influence where it is most dense and most productive. In each state there is an economic core, within which 70 per cent or more of the gross national product originates; and usually within the core there is a primate city, or perhaps there are two cities of nearly equal size. The core of the culture region is that part in which the characteristics of the region as a whole are most clearly developed. The cores of states or regions need to be identified for the purpose of measuring distances to other cores.

This suggests a number of calculations that could be made in order to give quantitative expression to the concept of accessibility. These would show that the majority of state and regional cores are more closely accessible to the center of the Land Hemisphere in Western Europe than they are to any other part of the world. The actions and policy decisions of Western Europe affect more people than do actions and policies appearing elsewhere. The closer a state or region is to the center of the Land Hemisphere, the greater is its importance in the modern world.

The Patterns of Population. One group of phenomena with which we have been concerned in characterizing the culture regions relates to the density, growth, character, and arrangement of the population.

People are very unevenly spread over the earth. This is true whether population is considered for the world as a whole, or whether it is considered in topographic detail so that specific features of human occupance of the land can be examined. There are vast areas of the earth where there are no human inhabitants, and from which no economic products are taken. On the other hand, over half of the world's population is crowded onto about one tenth of the earth's land area in southern and eastern Asia. Furthermore, 39 per cent of the world's population lives on the 7 per cent of the world's land area, in the lower middle latitudes, that was originally covered by seasonal forests (Mid-Latitude Mixed Forest). Why is population so unevenly spread, and is the uneven spread likely to change?

A historical study of the changes in the patterns of population suggests that there are no simple explanations for the present arrangement of people on the earth. The people who occupy the seasonal forests of the lower middle latitudes, for example, have concentrated in such habitats at different times and for different reasons. Furthermore, men have not always agreed about the kinds of habitats that could be considered suitable for human settlement and the kinds that could be considered unsuitable. The Greek geographers of antiquity reported that Europe north of the Alps could not be occupied by civilized man because it was necessary to spend so much time huddled in furs around great fires just to keep warm. These geographers also believed that human beings could not survive the intense heat that was thought to exist close to the equator. Modern techniques of house building, and of heating and cooling houses, makes many of these long cherished ideas now seem absurd.

Does nature set limits beyond which man may not go in his settlement of the earth? All living things on the earth are dependent on the existence of water in liquid form—which is one of the peculiar characteristics of our otherwise quite ordinary planet. In the arid regions where water is scarce, and in the polar regions where it is usually frozen, human settlement is not easy. Yet the historical view of man's settlement in such regions suggests that the limits are flexible, and that there is no place on earth where settlement cannot take place if it seems desirable. There are some who think that man will soon be establishing colonies elsewhere in the universe. At any one period of time with a given set of attitudes, objectives, and technical skills, certain nature-given limits have become significant; but with changes in the culture new natural limits have gained significance. The spread of farm settlement toward the dry lands has reached limits beyond which it is not wise to go; but these limits have been made significant by human technology, or by the balance of costs and prices, or by the preconceptions of Soviet planners, or by other factors inherent in the human culture.

Population Growth. Great differences exist in the rate of growth among the world's populations. The demographers have suggested that there are at least five different population types in terms of growth and decline. These are:

1. The essentially stationary population, with a high birth rate and a high death rate —characteristic of a pre-industrial society.

2. The early period of expansion, with a high birth rate and a declining death rate, a large proportion of young people in the population, and a high population growth potential.

3. The late period of expansion, with a declining birth rate and a low death rate, a large proportion of older people in the population, and a low population growth potential.

4. The essentially stationary population, with a low birth rate and a low death rate—characteristic of a mature economy.

5. The declining population, with a birth rate lower than the death rate.

Among the world's culture regions some have gone through the stages of economic development associated with the Industrial Revolution, and are now characterized by the third and fourth population types—for example the European and Anglo-American regions. Other regions are just starting the Industrial Revolution, and are advancing from Type 1 to Type 2—for example Latin America and parts of the North African-Southwest Asian region. Others again are still pre-industrial, but are trying to advance their economic growth as rapidly as possible: they are clearly still in Type 1, but will soon be shifting to Type 2—for example South Asia, part of East Asia, and perhaps Africa.

With very large numbers of people on the verge of shifting from Type 1 to Type 2, the demographers forecast a large increase in population by the year 2000. In 1950 there were about 2,406,000,000 people in the world, and during the decade of the 50's there were something like 170 births and 90 deaths every minute—each minute the world as a whole had 80 new mouths to feed, and 80 new pairs of hands to employ. Estimates of the world population in the year 2000 range from a minimum of three billion to more than five billion.

Shifts of Population. The population patterns involve more than just total numbers and rates of growth. They also involve shifts of population from place to place, currents of migration both external and internal. One principle seems quite clear: the areas that are now densely populated are becoming more densely populated, and those that are thinly populated are declining in population. To be sure, in the Soviet Culture Region, and in communist East Asia, the government planners are trying to avoid excessive concentrations of people, and are making the assumption that the optimum size for a city in the Soviet Union is about 100,000. The Soviet territory is marked off into "economic regions," and development within each region is planned with the aim of spreading people more uniformly over the national territory. Yet the populations of both the Soviet Union and China remain strongly concentrated, leaving vast areas very thinly occupied.

In Anglo-America the development of huge conurbations is continuing rapidly. Megalopolis is the name Jean Gottman applies to the great urban concentration of the eastern United States between Portland, Maine, and Washington, D.C.[2] It is forecast that by the year 2000 metropolitan New York will have increased by nearly 150 per cent to about 25,000,000, while the cities of the next order—such as Chicago and Detroit—will have increased by 100 per cent. Map 46f (p. 166) shows the great urban concentrations of this region.

Similar urban concentrations are appearing, or will appear, in the other culture regions. There may be a certain amount of scattering of urban centers in the Soviet Region through the establishment of satellite cities, but even here the increased concentration of people in cities is taking place. The Soviet ideal is to eliminate the difference between urban and rural by making

[2] Jean Gottman, 1961.

it possible for farm workers, as well as industrial workers, to enjoy the advantages of living together in cities. All over the world one of the essential features of the Industrial Revolution is this increased concentration of population.

Under what circumstances, then, can we declare that an area has too many people. What is "overpopulation?"

Economic Development and Earth Resources. The answer to this question has changed radically as a result of the Industrial Revolution. In a pre-industrial society overpopulation exists when there is not enough food. In 1798, in his *Essay on Population*, Malthus pointed out that populations tended to increase in geometric progression (2-4-8-16 . . .), whereas food supplies could only be increased in arithmetic progression (2-4-6-8 . . .). When the population outgrew the food supply the death rate would rise and the numbers of people would decline. He saw famine, epidemic, and war as the great checks to population growth. In his day the only way to increase the food supply was to open up a new frontier of pioneer farm settlement and so increase the agricultural area. It was the movement of farm settlement onto the mid-latitude grasslands of the world, after the middle of the nineteenth century, that made possible the provision of food to support the spectacular increase in population then occurring in Europe and America.

Conditions have changed radically. We have seen that an increase in the food supply without a rise in food prices now requires a reduction in the numbers of farmers, and a withdrawal of agriculture from areas that are less favorably situated in terms of markets. An increase in the food supply now requires capital investment—pioneer zones where farm settlers move onto new lands are no longer a solution. In the countries that have been transformed by the Industrial Revolution a condition of overpopulation exists when there are not enough jobs to keep the working force fully employed. In the long run an increase in the number of jobs requires new capital formation—in Anglo-America it takes between $10,000 and $20,000 of new capital investment in industry to create one job. The problem of population can be phrased as follows: can the economy be developed fast enough to stay ahead of the increase in numbers?

The Stages of Economic Growth. All over the world people are demanding the higher standards of living that are supposed to result from economic development. Modern media of communication—radio, television, periodicals, newspapers—are making known even to the most isolated people that the technical knowledge now exists to provide more food, better clothing, and more adequate shelter, and to ease the burden of working merely for survival. But not every one understands how this knowledge can be applied.

Before economic development can get started there are certain pre-conditions that must be satisfied. Among the very poor countries of the world—those with gross national products per capita of less than $200 (Map 11, p. 30)—all available income is needed to purchase the basic necessities of life. Such countries need massive financial aid, especially when they are also densely populated. But economic development eventually requires domestic savings: the well-to-do people must somehow be persuaded, or forced, to devote some of their incomes to new capital formation, rather than to luxury-living. In the communist world this class is liquidated and all capital is transferred to the state, which decrees the proportion of income that is to be saved and invested. In the parts of the world where persuasion rather than dictation is the preferred method of establishing policy, an attitude favorable to the investment of savings has to be created; and where such a change of attitude is resisted, economic development may be retarded. No one has really devised a more workable method for increasing domestic investment in new capital than the so-called "profit motive," the desire of the individual to better his own economic status.

Another pre-condition for economic development is the popular acceptance of change as a way of life. Societies that tend to force individuals to conform to traditional attitudes are not easily transformed. In many pre-industrial societies prestige is granted to those who own land, whether or not the land is used productively. The landowner class constitutes the aristocracy, and a landowner who sells his land and invests his money in dometic industry may lose status. This was not the case in eighteenth-century Britain. When Matthew Boulton sold his estate and invested the money in James Watt's steam engine he did not thereby face widespread disapproval. A basic problem in the African Culture Region, as we have pointed out, is how to break down the tradition of cattle ownership as a sign of wealth. Such a change is a pre-condition of economic development.

Still another pre-condition is the disposition to accept the findings of scientists and engineers. The Industrial Revolution, with its new control over a wider and wider range of natural processes, is incompatible with belief in magic. In the European Culture Region men like Roger Bacon, Galileo, and Newton made the basic assault on superstition and ignorance, and laid the foundations on which the Industrial Revolution could be developed.

There must also be certain economic developments that precede the initial phase of the Industrial Revolution. The countries that have already started their transformation have, in every case, derived financial support from the export of some commodity. In the case of Anglo-America it was wheat; in Australia-New Zealand it was wool; in Japan it was silk; in Brazil it was coffee; in South Africa it was gold. It has yet to be proved that economic development can get under way without such a source of income. And economic development also requires the building of certain features of "social overhead" such as roads and railroads, ports, electric power systems, and other facilities that are often made possible either through private foreign investment or through government loans.

In many parts of the world we have observed the process of economic development passing through the stages to maturity. In order to start the initial phase between 5 and 10 per cent of the gross national product has to be invested in new capital formation each year for a period of two or three decades. Thereafter the ratio of investment rises to between 10 and 20 per cent—to 30 per cent in the Soviet Union. The drive to maturity takes about fifty years, during which time all the other changes associated with the Industrial Revolution take place: the increase in the size of cities; the decrease in the proportion of people employed in agriculture; the increase in total population; the tremendous growth of production, requiring a vast increase in the supply of raw materials of all kinds; the shift from a self-sufficient economy to one that is frankly dependent on the economies of other states. These and many other changes have the effect of completely transforming the societies that succeed in making a start. Thereafter economic development is self-sustaining, and the contrast between those countries that have gone through the revolution and those that have not becomes enormous.

The Mature Economy. According to the analysis of W. W. Rostow, countries that achieve maturity have a choice of alternative policies.[3] Some states have followed the time-honored tradition inherited from the Early Civilizations—they have used their power to expand the national territory at the expense of other states. They have attempted to expand their *lebensraum* by conquering their neighbors; they have built empires, and have forcibly annexed the territory of other nations. This, in fact, was the usual policy in the nineteenth century, and one that has been brought into the twentieth century by Germany, Japan, and the Soviet Union. But now there are other alternatives. A country with a mature economy may elect to seek security for its citizens by building a welfare state. Or it may expand the use of consumer goods by developing an economy of high mass consumption.

It is instructive to see what the achievement of a mature economy has meant in the core of the European Culture Region. For many decades the benefits that might have been derived from the achievement of maturity were withheld because of policies of national economic self-sufficiency. The attempt to maintain the partition of Europe into nineteen separate national economies left the Europeans thoroughly frustrated. But finally, under the pressure of circumstances, the European Economic Community was established in 1957, and it was planned to wipe out tariff barriers and other

[3] W. W. Rostow, 1960.

restrictions in a series of steps. The six states that first made up the European Economic Community experienced such an unprecedented burst of economic growth and widespread prosperity that the whole operation was speeded up, and other European states applied for admission. During the period from 1957 to 1962 the member states experienced a rate of sustained economic growth never before achieved on the European continent. The gross national product of the Economic Community as a whole increased 7 per cent between 1959 and 1960, and industrial production increased 12 per cent. Not only are the people of Europe now enjoying luxuries they have never been able to reach before, but the increase in economic production has also created a new major center of power in the world. This new major power, comparable in skills and resources to the United States and the Soviet Union, and located at the center of the Land Hemisphere, is the single most significant development in the period since World War II.

Meanwhile the economy of Anglo-America continues to grow. One of the essential features of a mature economy with high mass consumption is the continuation of technological change. Research and development become a way of life. Previews of what life will be like in the year 2000 seem fantastic: it is forecast that the gross national product of the United States will increase four times, while the average work week will be cut almost in half; large jet planes will carry people from New York to California in a little more than an hour; the commuter problem will be solved through the use of helicopters, interurban trains riding smoothly on rubber tires at 90 miles an hour, fast downtown monorail services, and moving sidewalks; motor trucks will be replaced by pneumatic pipelines for the ship-

ment of goods; cities will be remodeled to correspond more nearly to the vision of what they could be like; satellites in outer space will provide world-wide telephone and television coverage; medicine will have made further strides in the conquest of disease; and discoveries in distant worlds will stimulate the thinking of earth-bound people much as the voyages of discovery from the fifteenth to the eighteenth centuries stimulated Europe at that time.

Even if only a few of these forecasts prove to be correct there are two conclusions of a geographic nature that will necessarily follow. The first is that the present contrast between the developed economies, and those that are not yet developed, is likely to become greater rather than less. Our one world is likely to be more sharply divided in the year 2000 than it is today—unless one devastated world is produced by nuclear warfare. And the other conclusion is that the demand for earth resources will reach astronomic heights. Anglo-America alone will need twelve times as much aluminum as it needed in 1960, three times as much timber, twice as much iron ore, and two and a half times as much fresh water. Can these enormous increases be provided?

Earth Resources. The answer to this question is disputed vigorously, even among specialists. There are some who forecast the collapse of a civilization that is dependent on the large-scale use of non-renewable resources: there are others who believe that advances in technology will permit the indefinite expansion of resource use. The answer probably lies somewhere between the two extremes.

It is important to understand the economic problem involved in the use of non-renewable resources. What is the real cost of changing a given volume of ore into a useful form, and of transporting it to where it is wanted? There are two elements involved in real cost: the number of hours of human work, and the amount of capital needed. During the twentieth century the real cost of resource use in Anglo-America has been declining due to the development of engineering skills; and this decline has contributed to the continued rise of the American standard of living, as a larger and larger proportion of the people are able to purchase and use the products of the factories and farms. The basic problem is whether the future needs of the mature economy can be met without a rise in real costs.

Is there an ample supply of minerals and fuels in the world, or are the world resources about to be exhausted? To answer this question we must return to what was said previously about natural resources (p. 14): resources are produced by natural processes, but they become resources as a result of human technology. We have considered the story of bituminous coal—which only became a major natural resource in the 1850's when the large-scale conversion of this kind of coal into coke, and the use of coke in steel manufacturing, were made possible by new technological developments. Since the second half of the nineteenth century mining has become a large-scale operation, and this has meant that small ore bodies have ceased to be resources, and the work of extracting minerals from the earth has been concentrated in the relatively few localities where the resources are especially rich. More fuels and more mineral raw materials were taken out of the earth between 1940 and 1960 than in all preceding time, and as a result some of the richest ore bodies have already been exhausted—for instance the high-quality iron ore bodies of the Mesabi Range in Minnesota. Mining has to shift to other high-quality ores, but these also will eventually be exhausted. Experts forecast that even by 1980 minerals such as lead, zinc, and tin, will be close to exhaustion.

There is a delicately adjusted relationship between the price of a raw material and the amount of it that is considered to be available. A rise in the price stimulates geologic exploration, which may bring to light previously unknown ore bodies. The rise in price permits the use of ore bodies that were formerly considered to be sub-marginal, and it also stimulates the search for more efficient techniques both for extracting the ore and for using it in industry. For example, in the United States in the 1950's when manganese, an essential hardener of steel, was worth four cents a pound it was in such short supply in the parts of the world accessible to the United States that the government began to create a stockpile. But it was estimated, at the same time, that if the price were raised to one dollar a pound the reserves of manganese available for mining would increase ten times. With the price at one dollar a pound technologists would have worked vigorously to find ways of using the steel hardener more efficiently.

There can be no doubt that the rocks of the earth's crust, and the water in the oceans, contain a vast store of minerals. It is reported, for example, that one hundred tons of an average igneous rock contain 16,000 pounds of aluminum, 10,000 pounds of iron, and smaller amounts of titanium, manganese, chromium, nickel, vanadium, copper, tungsten, and lead. The same rock also contains enough uranium and thorium to provide the energy necessary to extract these minerals, if only techniques for doing so could be worked out.[4] It is well known that the deuterium in ordinary sea water could provide an incredible amount of en-

[4] Harrison Brown, quoting K. Rankama and T. G. Sahama, in W. L. Thomas (ed.), 1956.

ergy if a way could be found to control a nuclear-fusion reaction outside the "H-Bomb."

These technical possibilities are certainly no more incredible than are the rocket systems that will carry man to the moon and beyond. But there are some students of resource problems who believe that it is dangerous to count on continued technological improvement. They say that the slow and almost imperceptible rise in the prices of minerals, as the richer sources are used up, will eventually bring an end to the system of high mass consumption. One writer describes it as "irresponsible folly" to expect the scientists to find adequate substitutes for lead, zinc, and tin, before these minerals become too expensive to use. There is no sure answer to this problem—except that the Industrial Revolution will certainly lead to disaster and collapse unless larger and larger amounts of effort and capital are devoted to science and engineering.

Applying this consideration to an evaluation of potential military power we find another significant principle. Before World War II military potential was closely related to the productive capacity of a nation's industries: but in the second half of the twentieth century industrial potential is less important than are the trained personnel and the facilities devoted to research and development. Industrial equipment is quickly rendered obsolete by the invention of better machines and procedures. It is the continuous flow of new technology from laboratories and drawing boards that produces economic and military strength.

Democracy and Autocracy. The Democratic Revolution is the other fundamental change that is transforming our one world into distinct and sometimes antagonistic parts. Democratic ideas were not new in the second half of the eighteenth century when revolutionary movements in Europe and America first gained momentum. The ideas came from ancient Athens, from the teachings of Jesus, from the experience of the British in formulating basic laws that could be applied equally to every man, from the struggle of the people of the Netherlands to throw off the alien Spanish rule, and from many other sources. But between 1760 and 1800 revolutionary attacks on traditional political and social institutions were successful in France and Anglo-America, in the Netherlands, Switzerland, Italy, Poland, and Ireland. Even the word "democracy" did not enter the popular vocabulary until the 1780's. But around that time democratic constitutions were being written and adopted in many European countries and in the United States.

The five elements of the Democratic Revolution (p. 30) are different aspects of the demand for one basic right: respect for the dignity of the individual. This demand is an assertion that every person is important, too important to be disregarded, or to be placed in a position of subservience to another. This is not to say that all men are equal, or that one should not recognize persons in authority, or that one should not treat with respect those whose accomplishments are superior. But it does mean that no man should command obedience or respect because of inherited status, race, or creed. It means that the "law of status" is replaced by the "law of contract."

The Democratic Revolution has taken different forms in different culture regions. Resistence to these new ideas has been especially strong outside the core of the European Culture Region, and is now reflected in the existence of fascist and communist dictatorships within which all the democratic ideas are specifically banned. It is an interesting fact, not only in Europe but all over the world, that where revolutionary changes inspired by democratic ideas have been strong and successful, communism is weak. The Communist Party has been successful in establishing control only over those countries that have not had successful liberal democratic movements—with the one exception, perhaps, of the Czech part of Czechoslovakia. The Democratic Revolution has proceeded most rapidly in Anglo-America, in Australia-New Zealand, and in parts of Latin America. Latin America today is in the process of rapid change: there is a tidal wave of revolutionary fervor which is demanding an end to special privileges for landowners, army officers, and foreigners. A similar democratic ferment has appeared among the newly-educated urban workers and students of the North African-Southwest Asian Culture Region. In the parts of the world that were formerly British colonies many of the institutions and practices of democracy have already been introduced, and now provide a framework for the nurture of democratic ideas.

In one form or another the Democratic Revolution has been sweeping over the colonial world since World War II. Where the revolutionary groups are resisted, and become impatient, open violence breaks out; and it is at this stage, when traditional institutions are crumbling, and when democratic ideas are not yet established, that the communists are most successful in gaining control and establishing a "dictatorship of the people," a people's democracy. This use of the word "democracy" refers only to economic equality, not to social or political equality—in fact the Communist Party, as we have seen, is established as a new privileged class in the place of the former landowners and owners of capital. For persons frustrated by the compromises and delays inherent in the democratic system the

communist program may have a strong appeal. Therefore, any policy for dealing with the problems of the modern world that does not take into account the reality and the permanence of the revolt against status and privilege, and that fails to recognize the difference between communist revolutionaries and genuine supporters of liberal democracy, will very certainly be doomed to failure.

A Program for Americans. Our "One World Divided" is not likely soon to be unified. The divisions are deep and fundamental, derived from the spread of the most revolutionary new ideas to appear on the earth since the rise of the Early Civilizations around 4000 B.C. The last two centuries represent only a very short period in relation to the sweep of human history, and the revolutionary changes have in no sense reached completion. Thousands of years from now historians could well report that revolutionary changes had only just started, and that in the second half of the twentieth century the shape of the new world had yet to be seen. It is clear that at this stage two great systems of living are locked in a struggle where compromise is impossible. Autocracy and democracy are two incompatible concepts; and so far wherever communism has been established this has been through force, and it has been maintained by autocracy. Eventually one or the other concept must prevail; and if the struggle of ideas is interrupted by armed conflict this will only postpone the eventual solution of the ideological challenge.

What kind of a program does this suggest for Americans? In this struggle of ideas it is not enough just to be against communism—for no battle and no contest was ever won by defense alone. A program for Americans calls for positive and enlightened support for the continued spread of the Democratic

Revolution, of which the peoples of Anglo-America, Australia and New Zealand, as well as of Europe, are the custodians; it calls for continued efforts to enlarge and perfect democratic ideas, and to apply them more fully within the United States; it calls for a study of the concepts written in the Constitution, and the acceptance by every individual of the responsibility for patterning a way of life based on these concepts. It is necessary to realize that in this revolutionary period there can be no policy that leads to real security: there can only be choices among risks.

APPENDIXES

CONVERSION SCALES

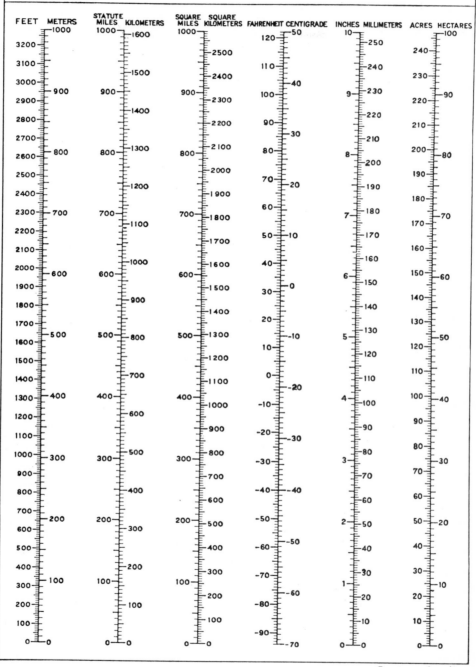

APPENDIX A. CLIMATES OF THE WORLD

Climate is the average state of the atmosphere over a period of years—as opposed to weather which is the state of the atmosphere at any one time. The climate of a place is described in terms of averages of temperature, rainfall, humidity, wind velocity and wind direction, cloudiness, air pressure, and other elements.

The Atmosphere. The atmosphere is a thin film of gases clinging to the earth's surface. It is made up of nitrogen (about 78 per cent), oxygen (about 21 per cent), and small amounts of water vapor, carbon dioxide, and other gases. Most of the weather changes take place within the lower part of the atmosphere, the *troposphere*, which ranges in height from about 20,000 feet in the high latitudes to about 40,000 feet near the equator. Above the troposphere is the *stratosphere*, which thins out gradually with increasing distance from the earth. In comparison with the 7,926 miles which is the equatorial diameter of the earth, the height of the troposphere is so small that it can scarcely be measured on an ordinary globe. Yet it is the changing physical state of this thin film of gases that produces the earth's daily weather, and its average pattern of climates.

The climatic features are regularly arranged over the earth in relation to latitudinal and longitudinal position on the oceans and continents. If the latitude of a place is known, and also its position in relation to land and water (west side of ocean basin, east side of ocean basin, west side of continent, interior of continent, or east side of continent), then it is possible to describe the general character of its climate. The regularity of the climatic pattern is explained by the physical controls of climate.

Latitude. The first of the controls of climate is latitude—that is, distance north or south of the equator. Because the earth's axis is tilted 23½° from the plane of the earth's orbit around the sun, all the latitudes from 23½° N. (the Tropic of Cancer) to 23½° S. (the Tropic of Capricorn) receive the sun's rays vertically twice during the year. As one proceeds northward from the Tropic of Cancer, or southward from the Tropic of Capricorn, the sun's rays reach the surface of the earth at larger and larger angles from the vertical, or zenith. Much more heat is received at the earth's surface when the sun's rays are vertical than when they reach the earth at an angle. Very little heat is received when the sun rises only a little above the horizon even at noon. The low latitudes and the lower middle latitudes of the earth (from the equator to latitude 38° in both hemispheres) absorb more solar radiation than they radiate, while the higher middle latitudes and the high latitudes radiate more than they absorb.

The atmosphere receives most of its heat from the surface of the earth. The sun's radiation passes through the gases of the atmosphere, affecting their temperature only to a small degree. But direct contact with the earth, or radiation from the earth, does affect the air temperature. Therefore, the air has a higher temperature close to the earth, and temperature decreases with increasing altitude in the troposphere. At the earth's surface the lower the latitude the higher, generally, is the average annual temperature. If the surface of the earth were all land, or all water, temperature would correspond quite closely to latitude.

Land and Water. The surface of the earth, however, is anything but uniform.

The simple arrangement of temperature by latitude, therefore, is modified by the effect of land and water; so much so that in some places the direction of greatest temperature contrast is east and west instead of north and south. For a variety of reasons the land heats up by day, and in summer, much more rapidly than the water does; and at night, and in winter, the land cools off much more rapidly than the water. The air over the water, therefore, has a more equable temperature than does the air over the land. At any given latitude the summers are hotter and the winters colder over the land than over the water. Ranges of temperatures between coldest and warmest months increase with increasing latitude and distance from the sea. A distinction is recognized between *marine* climates and *continental* climates.

Land and water also have an important effect on the distribution of rainfall. Rain is produced in nature through the cooling of moist air—that is, air in which there is a relatively large amount of water vapor. Air picks up water vapor by evaporation. Because evaporation is very much more rapid from warm water than from cold water the one major source of atmospheric moisture in the world is warm ocean water. Map 8 shows that each ocean has about the same regular pattern of warm and cold water, as well as of water of intermediate temperature. From a comparison of the map of rainfall (Map 6) with the map of ocean waters (Map 8) it can be seen that rainfall is generally greater over warm water, and over the margins of the continents bathed by warm water. Rainfall is low over cold water, and over the continental margins bordered by cold water. Rainfall is also low in the continental interiors distant from warm ocean water.

The Circulation of the Atmosphere. There is a tendency for air equatorward of 38° to move from places with an excess of energy to places at higher latitudes which have a deficit of energy. Furthermore, there is a tendency for air at the earth's surface to move from cold places (where the air is chilled and becomes relatively heavy) toward warm places, displacing the warm and relatively lighter air as it moves.

All these air movements, however, take place on the surface of a rotating sphere. Except for air which is close to the equator all moving air in the northern hemisphere swings to the right of its course, and all moving air in the southern hemisphere swings to the left of its course. Outside the equatorial regions, therefore, air movements tend to become whirls. Instead of moving from areas of high pressure directly toward areas of low pressure, the air in the northern hemisphere swings to the right, until it reaches a position with high pressure to its right and low pressure to its left. Only where friction with the earth's surface, or other things, interfere, can air actually move into an area of low pressure.

The air that starts moving from lower to higher latitudes in both hemispheres, and is deflected to the right in the northern hemisphere and to the left in the southern hemisphere, feeds into the *jet streams* which, in both hemispheres, move at high velocity from west to east between latitudes 30° and 35°. The jet streams are narrow, sharply defined currents of air, moving at speeds of 200 to 300 miles per hour, and at elevations just below the top of the troposphere (20,000 to 40,000 feet). There are periods when the jet streams move in nearly straight courses, but there are other periods when the courses are very wavy, or when the streams break into detached pieces. The position of the jet streams determines the wind directions and the weather at the earth's surface: it is during wavy periods that there is a large amount of interaction between cold air masses of polar origin and warm air masses of tropical origin, which causes changeable weather in the middle latitudes.

The jet streams pile up zones of high pressure to the right in the northern hemisphere and to the left in the southern hemisphere. But at the earth's surface where there are contrasts between land and water these pressure zones, at about latitude 30° in both hemispheres, tend to break up into cells, and to give rise to great whirls of surface winds. The cells center over the eastern sides of the oceans. In the southern hemisphere, where there are vast expanses of ocean, the high pressure forms a nearly unbroken zone over the water.

As a result of these conditions and movements of the atmosphere a regular pattern of winds at the earth's surface can be recognized. There are three elements in this general pattern (Map 6). First are the *oceanic whirls*. These whirls are centered over the cold ocean water on the eastern sides of the five ocean basins (North Atlantic, South Atlantic, North Pacific, South Pacific, South Indian) at about latitude 30°. The air circulates in a clockwise direction in the northern hemisphere and in a counterclockwise direction in the southern hemisphere. The whirls are so large that they cover most of the ocean basins and the bordering margins of the continents. Air circulating around the North Atlantic whirl, for example, moves through the low latitudes from the northeast and east. Approaching eastern North America it comes from the southeast and south. In the middle latitudes, on the northern side of the whirl, the air crosses the North Atlantic from the southwest, west, and northwest. Over the western side of Europe and North Africa the wind is from the north. Only near the equator can the air move in a straight line. In South

America air from the North Atlantic oceanic whirl passes all the way across Brazil to the eastern side of the Andes. But in the middle latitudes air circulating in these whirls cannot reach the continental interiors, which are consequently dry.

The *polar outbursts* are the second element in the general pattern of winds. Over the permanent icecaps of Greenland and Antarctica, and over the very cold snow-covered surfaces of northern North America and northern Eurasia in winter, the air over the land is greatly chilled. It becomes very cold and heavy. Cold air accumulates until it becomes so heavy in relation to warmer and lighter air that it slides off, moving toward the nearest warm place where air is light and pressure low. These cold air masses move like drops of water on a window-pane—with a steep, rolling front and a streamlined top. Because the air is heavy it stays close to the earth, and the deflective force of the earth's rotation has little effect. The cold air masses burrow into the poleward parts of the oceanic whirls creating rotating eddies known as cyclonic storms. The cold air moves under the relatively warm and light oceanic air and pushes it up. The oceanic air is thereby cooled, and if it contains enough water vapor it drops this moisture in the form of rain or snow. It is the interaction of these polar outbursts with the oceanic whirls that brings the variable weather of the middle latitudes. Especially stormy are the higher middle latitudes of the southern hemisphere around Antarctica. But also very stormy are the North Atlantic and the North Pacific.

The third element in the world's surface winds either reinforces or interrupts the first two elements along certain of the continental coasts. This consists of the *monsoons—* winds which tend to blow in approximately opposite directions at different seasons. On coasts in the low latitudes that face toward the equator the alternation of wind directions seems to be related to shifts in the position of the jet stream. In southern Asia, for example, the jet stream in winter is bifurcated by the Himalayas, and the southern arm passes over northern India. The surface air movement at this time is from the northeast. But in summer the jet stream remains north of the Himalayas, and a stream of air moves from the Indian Ocean from the southwest onto the southern and eastern part of the continent of Asia. Similarly, in the southern hemisphere the surface air in winter moves from Australia toward the tropical islands to the north and northwest; but in summer the flow of air is reversed. There are similar alternations of wind direction along the Guinea Coast of Africa, the southern coast of Central America, and the Gulf Coast of North America. The monsoons of the east-facing coasts in the middle latitudes of the northern hemisphere (eastern North America and eastern Asia) are the result of the alternation between cold air masses from the north and warm air masses from the southeast. The polar outbursts prevail during the winter, and the oceanic whirls during the summer.

Climatic Regions. The patterns of temperature, rainfall, and wind direction, together with other climatic elements, combine to form the climatic regions of the world. It should be noted that the traditional division of the world into temperate, torrid, and frigid zones is unacceptable to geographers; for, in spite of its simplicity, it obscures more important climatic relationships than it reveals. The world's highest and the world's lowest temperatures close to sea level occur in the so-called temperate zone; the only truly temperate climates in the world occur over the tropical oceans in the so-called torrid zone.

The system presented in this book (Map 5, pp. 10-11) is one which was devised by a German geographer, Wladimir Köppen. It is a system based on quantitative definitions, and, as such, can be applied to any part of the earth where climatic data are available.[1] Qualitative definitions for the letter symbols used on Map 5 are given below.

[1] For these quantitative definitions see P. E. James, *A Geography of Man*, Ginn and Company, 2nd ed., 1959; pp. 534-543.

KÖPPEN'S CLASSIFICATION OF CLIMATES

Af-Afi Am-Ami	Tropical rainy climate with no cool season, with little range of temperature, and with no dry season or only a short dry season
Aw-Awi	Tropical climate with no cool season, with little range of temperature, and with a distinct rainy season and a distinct dry season
Bsh	Hot, semiarid climate
Bsk-Bsk'	Cool, semiarid climate
Bwh	Hot, arid climate
Bwk-Bwk'	Cool, arid climate
Cwbi-Cfbi	High altitude, low latitude climate
Cwa-Cwb	Mid-latitude climate with mild, dry winters and rainy summers
Csa	Mid-latitude climate with mild, rainy winters, and hot, dry summers
Csb	Mid-latitude climate with mild, rainy winters, and cool, dry summers
Cfa	Mid-latitude continental and east coast climate with mild winters and hot summers, and with no dry season
Cfb	Mid-latitude marine climate with mild winters and cool summers, and with no dry season

Cfc	Mid-latitude marine climate with mild winters and short, cool summers, and with no dry season
Dfa	Mid-latitude continental climate with severe winters and hot summers, and with no dry season
Dfb	Mid-latitude continental climate with severe winters and cool summers, and with no dry season
Dfc	Mid-latitude continental climate with severe winters and short, cool summers, and with no dry season
Dwa, Dwb Dwc	Same as Dfa, Dfb, and Dfc, but with very dry winters
Dfd, Dwd	Same as above, but with extremely low winter temperatures
E	High latitude or high altitude climate with no summers

APPENDIX B. SURFACE FEATURES

The Face of the Earth. The major lineaments of the face of the earth are the continents and ocean basins. The continents are composed of relatively upstanding masses of the earth's rock crust, which are floating on heavier rock masses. The range in elevation, or relief, above and below sea level averages only about three miles, or less than 1/1300 of the radius of the earth. The maximum difference in elevation is about twelve miles (between Mount Everest, 29,028 feet above sea level, and the Cook Deep in the Mindanao Trench, 36,804 feet below sea level). But even this is only about 1/330 of the earth's radius. Small as are these differences compared with the size of the earth, they nevertheless measure the major relief features of its surface.

Only 29.4 per cent of the surface, however, stands above the sea. Water fills the ocean basins and, overflowing these, inundates also the margins of the continental masses. As a result the continents are for the most part isolated, while the oceans are relatively continuous. There is more than twice as much land north of the equator as south of it. Except for Antarctica all the continents are broadest in the north, even those in the southern hemisphere. There is an almost complete ring of land around the basin of the Arctic Ocean, while, in contrast, the tapering of the continents toward the south leaves an almost uninterrupted sea in the higher middle latitudes of the southern hemisphere.

All these various continental masses are tied together by more or less continuous chains of high mountains. These mountain ranges, passing from continent to continent or festooned around the oceans in strings of islands, form a framework to which are joined the other major lineaments of the earth's face. If one ignores the complexity of detail, the general distribution pattern of high mountains is one of relative simplicity but profound significance. In a sense the central and southeastern part of Asia is the core of the world's lands; and in the present-day world it is composed of a complex knot of towering mountain ranges. From this core mountain axes extend in three directions: one westward through southern Asia, southern Europe, and northern Africa; one southeastward through Indonesia and

New Guinea to New Zealand; and one starts northeastward through Asia, crosses into the Americas while still continuing in a more or less straight line on the globe, and extends on to form the axis of North America, South America, and Antarctica. The land masses of the world, unlike the climates, are not regularly arranged with reference to the poles and the lines of latitude and longitude.

Surface Features of the Dry Lands. Looking at these major lineaments more closely we see that the surfaces of the continents are differentiated by a number of different kinds of features—in addition to the high mountains. But the nature of the surface features depends on the kinds of processes of erosion that have been forming them, and these in turn depend on the climate. In the world's dry lands there are two chief kinds of desert surface: the *basin and range desert,* and the *hamada and erg desert.*

The first desert type, known as the basin and range desert (or mountain and bolson desert), is characterized by scattered ranges of barren hills or low mountains separated by more or less extensive basins or bolsons. In this kind of country most of the rain falls on the highlands. Because of the steep slopes and the violent nature of the showers, a very large part of the rainfall runs off over the surface, rapidly eroding deep V-shaped ravines and gullies. Although the desert rains may be infrequent, and many years may elapse between showers, most of the work of sculpturing the mountain ranges is accomplished by the violent rains and resulting floods. When the flood waters emerge from the mountains and enter the basin, however, their rate of flow is suddenly checked. Much of the load of sand and gravel picked up in the mountains is deposited in the form of alluvial fans, which spread out in front of each valley mouth

along the margins of the basin. During a cloudburst, and for a short time after, water may actually cross the alluvial fans and reach the center of the basin, there forming a temporary shallow lake. But the rapid evaporation speedily removes the water from such a lake, leaving in its bed an accumulation of dazzling white salt. In some of the larger basins enough water may enter to support a shallow salt lake permanently, like Great Salt Lake in Utah; but more commonly the lakes in the basins are temporary, known technically as *playa* lakes, their beds marked most of the time by salt accumulations left over from the repeated evaporation of water.

There are, then, three chief divisions of the surface of basin and range deserts. There are the mountain ranges with their steep, rocky slopes; there are the alluvial fans smoothing the angles between bordering mountains and basin bottoms; and in the lowest part of the basin there is the playa—either a shallow salt lake with fluctuating shores or simply a flat salt plain over which, at rare intervals, the flood waters may form a lake. It is the alluvial fans of such regions which offer the best sites for human settlement; for by irrigating the fans with water from the mountain streams and permitting it to drain off easily to the playa, rich oases may be formed.

The second type of desert is composed of rocky plateaus of relatively slight relief, in some places interspersed with extensive sand-filled basins. The Saharan terms are adopted in Anglicized form to describe these features: for the rocky plateaus, the term *hamada;* for the sandy areas, the term *erg.*

Although the surface of the hamada is covered with a regolith of angular rock fragments, this mantle is not very thick and does not obscure the underlying rock. The character and position of the geologic formations are therefore of primary importance in determining the landforms of the hamada. Especially varied are the forms which appear in areas of stratified rocks where the strata are of varying degrees of resistance to weathering and erosion. The weaker formations are quickly excavated, leaving the stronger rocks standing out in bold relief as *mesas* or *cuestas*.

Many hamadas are shaped as broad, flattish domes. Erosion by streams or wind may strip off the layers of sedimentary strata from the higher parts of the dome, leaving a core of massive crystalline rocks exposed in the center. In desert areas many of the crystalline rocks disintegrate more easily than the sedimentary strata, so that the rocks in the center of the structural dome may be worn away to form a surface basin. A few types of crystalline rocks, however—especially recent igneous rocks—may stand out boldly. Around the crystalline center a series of infacing cuestas correspond to the outcrops of resistant strata. This is a common geologic structure not only in the dry lands but also in many other parts of the world.

There are many other kinds of hamadas, however, besides those formed of simple horizontal layers of stratified rock or those produced by a broad doming. Some hamadas possibly represent the final product in the erosion of mountain ranges, and the neighboring ergs may be bolsons of earlier geologic periods which have become filled. It is not uncommon to find the monotonous surfaces of such hamadas surmounted by a few mountain remnants. Steep-sided pinnacles of crumbling rock rise so abruptly from the rocky platforms on which they stand that, viewed from a distance, they resemble islands rising from a sea. Because of this the Germans have given them the descriptive name *inselberge,* or "island mountains." All stages of transition, from

the well-defined mountain and bolson desert to the subdued surfaces of the hamada and erg type, may be observed in the various parts of the world's dry lands.

The dry desert valley cut, perhaps deeply, into the surface of the hamada, is a characteristic and striking element of the desert landscape. Excavated by the recurring floods over long periods of time, these steep-sided ravines remain quite dry most of the time. When rain does fall, torrents fill the ravines from wall to wall; but as the waters subside the load of alluvium, which is being swept along by the floods, is deposited in the channels. The ravine bottoms, therefore, are flat and are composed of a fill of coarse sand or gravel. To designate these dry desert valleys the Arabic term *wadi* has been adopted (they are known as *arroyos* in the western United States).

Of all the desert surfaces, however, the one which is most familiar to people who have never visited the dry lands is the erg, or sandy desert. The ergs are extensive basins, or depressions, filled with sand which the wind forms into great dune ridges. Here we find the standard desert scene of the "movies," although actually this kind of surface is less extensive than any of the other types. Unlike the bolsons, the ergs do not usually have playa lakes, for the water which drains into them through the wadis of the neighboring hamadas is rapidly absorbed by the porous sands.

Surface Features of the Humid Lands. The surface features of the humid lands of the world are quite different from those of the dry lands. There are, to be sure, the same kinds of geologic structures and rocks in both; but the manner in which the rock structures have been sculptured by the processes of erosion in the rainy lands is very different from that in the dry lands. Under rainy tropical conditions, where there is a dense cover of forest vegetation, the rock surfaces are usually decomposed to great depths by chemical action. The mantle of loose earth which covers the solid rock is molded into rounded forms quite different from the angular forms of the deserts. Rivers find their way to the ocean and carry with them large quantities of alluvium. Where structural basins occur, which in the dry lands might form bolsons, they are filled with water. The rift depressions of East Africa, which are filled with fresh-water lakes, are very similar in geologic structure to such dry-land rifts as Death Valley in California or the Dead Sea depression of Palestine.

The larger surface features that stand out when we examine continental maps—and which are comparable to such dry-land features as basin and range, or hamada and erg, are five in number: plains, plateaus, hilly uplands, low mountains, and high mountains. The words used to describe these five major surface features are all common in non-technical language. The words used by geographers to describe the surface features of the dry lands are strange to most people who speak English, but every such person thinks he knows what is meant by the words plain, plateau, hill, or mountain. Yet the actual use of these words in naming the features of the land suggests that in the popular vocabulary there is no very careful definition of them. The Turtle Mountains of North Dakota, for example, are only a few hundred feet high above the plain upon which they stand; they are really a part of the plain, but the local people call them mountains. If they are to be called mountains, then the Berkshire Hills of Massachusetts should certainly be renamed. To use these words in a more exact sense in geography we must define them more carefully than the dictionary does; but in so doing we must be prepared to find that features which are popularly called mountains are really

plains, that features called plateaus are really hills, or that features called hills are really plateaus. We must be ready to distinguish between proper names and the more or less technical geographic terms which describe them.

These four categories of surface features may be given somewhat more accurate definition as follows. A *plain* is an area of low relief,[1] generally less than five hundred feet. It is low-lying with reference to bordering areas, and is usually, but not in every case, low in altitude. A *plateau* stands distinctly above bordering areas, at least on one side; and it has a large part of its total surface at or near the summit level. Its local relief may be very great in cases where it is cut by canyons; or it may have as small a local relief as a plain, from which it differs in such a case only because of its position with reference to bordering areas. A *hilly upland* has more than five hundred feet of local relief, and has a relatively small proportion of its surface at or near the summit level. *Low mountains* have more than a thousand feet of local relief, and, like hilly lands, have a relatively small proportion of the surface near the summit level. *High mountains* have more than three thousand feet of local relief, and also have a relatively small proportion of the surface near the summit level.

---

[1] The relief of an area is the difference in elevation between the highest and lowest points. Relief is different from altitude, which is usually measured from mean sea level. There may be surfaces of very slight local relief standing at very high altitudes—for example, the Plateau of Tibet; or there may be very steep slopes and great differences of local relief within an area which lies below sea level—as on the slopes of Death Valley. Local relief may be defined as difference in elevation within any selected area of restricted size. See V. C. Finch, G. T. Trewartha, A. H. Robinson, and E. H. Hammond, *Elements of Geography, Physical and Cultural*, McGraw-Hill Book Company, Inc., 1957; pp. 213-216, and 265-355.

APPENDIX C. WORLD VEGETATION[1]

The map of world vegetation (Map 8, pp. 16-17) divides the plant cover into seven broad categories based on the dominant layer of growth. The use of only seven basic types of vegetation allows the map to be relatively free from possibly confusing detail, while each category differs in some significant way from all the others in its vegetative characteristics. The actual mapping of world vegetation is limited by the lack of adequate data for some parts of the world. Furthermore, because vegetation boundaries are usually far from sharp, their location on maps is often somewhat subjective. The major world patterns of vegetation are, however, quite clear, and a comparison between them and the related patterns of climate and soil should be very instructive. The seven categories include five which represent largely undisturbed formations, while the other two (grassland and parkland) owe their characters in large measure to the results of disturbance.

Rain Forest is distinguished by a luxuriant evergreen canopy and the relative absence of mechanisms for dormancy. There is little or no vegetation in the world that is not prepared in some degree to withstand unfavorable conditions for growth, but a rain forest is not normally subject to severe or regularly unfavorable periods. Included within rain forest are luxuriant and evergreen but xerophytic types with small, tough or needle-like leaves. The year around sameness of these xerophytic formations that grow in tropical highland and middle latitude marine areas suggests the absence of severe unfavorable seasons, but the thick

leaves imply chronically poor growing weather. The luxuriance is achieved by prolonged, even though slow, growth during each year. The rain forest is distinctly denser in growth than the following vegetation types, although in some areas rain forest blends through a gradual transition into seasonal forest.

Seasonal Forest has a tree canopy that displays well developed mechanisms for regular dormancy. It lacks the luxuriance of the rain forest where frequently, when the two come together, there is a distinct change from a complex growth, for the most part of sensitive trees, to a uniform stand of a few hardy tree species. Seasonal forest regularly becomes dormant during a part of the year as a result of seasonally unfavorable conditions for growth—either excessive cold or drought. Trees withstand either type of prolonged stress in one of two ways: sensitive leaves are discarded and the tree stands bare (deciduous); or the leaves themselves are adapted to endure by means of a thick cuticle, surface hairs, resin, reduced surface, etc. (xerophytic). Normally a seasonal forest is made up of trees of which some use one method of defense and some the other—for this condition the terms mixed or semideciduous are used. Because seasonal forests are dominated at most by a few kinds of trees, and not uncommonly by just one (e.g., oak, eucalyptus), it is no surprise that forests which are all deciduous, or all evergreen-xerophytic, are widespread.

Woodland is characterized by a cover of trees whose crowns do not mesh, with the result that branches extend to the ground. Woodland normally grows in the semiarid zones of the world, although essentially the same kind of formation is also found on the

[1] This appendix and the map of vegetation (Map 8) were prepared by Professor David J. deLaubenfels.

cold margins of the seasonal forests. Continuous brush is included in the areas mapped as woodland. Brush intermingles with woodland in complex mosaics as a rule, apparently because of variable amounts of disturbance or because of edaphic differences.

Desert vegetation has a discontinuous cover of plants. While bushes and herbaceous plants such as grass grow among and between the trees of a woodland, bare ground becomes dominant in desert vegetation. Deserts are characterized by a great variety of plant forms: trees in the less arid parts, bushes, herbaceous plants, and many bizarre growths that have in one way or another become adapted to survive under virtually continuous stress. It should be noted that desert grasslands cover extensive areas; the fact that herbaceous plants are the rule does not make such an area any less of a desert.

Tundra is the name applied to all areas which are too cold to allow trees to grow. There are actually three major kinds of tundra. The most typical is a prostrate cover of plants crowded together on the surface, which in a less extreme form becomes simply brush. Alternatively there may be grass and other herbaceous plants—essentially a grassland. Finally, in the most difficult areas climatically there may be what amounts to desert vegetation. None of these sub-formations is unique in the larger sense, and tundra can well be thought of as simply a cold desert. Where other deserts tend to meet the tundra, as in inner Asia, there may be difficulty in distinguishing tundra from other vegetation formations.

Parkland refers to areas where clumps of trees alternate with grassland, but where neither becomes an extensive, uninterrupted stand. Parkland normally results from the disturbance of forest or woodland. Not only may the forest be opened up in this way, but the trees may also be stunted to a smaller size than they achieve through uninterrupted growth. There are limited areas where rain forest alternates with parkland, but in general it appears to alternate with seasonal forest, and frequently borders on grassland.

Grassland is a cover of herbaceous plants where grass and grass-like plants are most prominent. Individual stands may be dominated by clump types, prostrate types, or upright but sod-forming types three feet and more high; but all types coalesce into a continuous cover, as they must in order to form a true grassland. It is generally thought that the world's great grasslands are the result of fires because they alternate with seasonal forest and woodland, and often lie between the two. Sharp boundaries are likely to be edaphically controlled; otherwise a zone of parkland, in most cases, intervenes between grassland and the woody formations. When fires are controlled in grassland areas the growth reverts to bushes or trees as the seeds become available. A grass desert must not be thought of as a grassland; each is caused by different conditions.

APPENDIX D. REFERENCE TABLES
EUROPEAN CULTURE REGION

Country	Political Status	Population & Date of Latest Census	Population & Date of Latest Estimate
Andorra	Republic	5,664 ('54)	8,000 ('60)
Austria	Federal Republic	7,067,432 ('61)	7,100,000 ('62)
Belgium	Constitutional Monarchy	8,512,195 ('47)	9,300,000 ('62)
Cyprus	Republic	571,225 ('60)	600,000 ('62)
Denmark	Constitutional Monarchy	4,448,401 ('55)	4,600,000 ('62)
Faeroe Is.	Autonomous part of Denmark	32,456 ('55)	34,000 ('60)
Greenland	Integral part of Denmark	26,933 ('55)	31,000 ('60)
Finland	Republic	4,449,000 ('60)	4,500,000 ('62)
France	Republic	42,843,520 ('54)	46,400,000 ('62)
Incl. Corsica			
Germany, West	Federal Republic	53,187,277 ('56)	56,900,000 ('62)
Incl. W. Berlin			
Greece	Constitutional Monarchy	8,385,000 ('61)	8,500,000 ('62)
Iceland	Republic	143,973 ('50)	200,000 ('62)
Ireland, Rep. of	Republic	2,960,593 ('51)	2,800,000 ('62)
		2,815,000 ('61)	
Italy	Republic	50,463,762 ('61)	50,463,762 ('61)
Liechtenstein	Constitutional Monarchy	16,628 ('60)	16,628 ('60)
Luxembourg	Constitutional Monarchy	314,889 ('60)	314,889 ('60)
Malta	Constitutional Monarchy	319,620 ('57)	328,461 ('60)
Monaco	Monarchy	22,297 ('61)	22,297 ('61)
Netherlands	Constitutional Monarchy	11,468,045 ('60)	11,800,000 ('62)
Norway	Constitutional Monarchy	3,278,546 ('50)	3,600,000 ('62)
Excl. Svalbard Arch.			
& Jan Mayen		3,769 ('50)	4,276 ('57)
Portugal	Republic	8,920,787 ('60)	9,300,000 ('62)
Incl.			
Azores		317,409 ('50)	318,558 ('56)
Madeira		266,990 ('50)	280,000 ('56)
San Marino	Republic	9,796 ('06)	17,000 ('60)
Spain	Monarchy	27,976,755 ('50)	30,600,000 ('62)
Incl.			
Balearic Is.		419,628 ('50)	441,842 ('59)
Canary Is.		807,773 ('50)	908,718 ('59)
Sweden	Constitutional Monarchy	7,495,129 ('60)	7,600,000 ('62)
Switzerland	Federal Republic	5,429,061 ('60)	5,600,000 ('62)
United Kingdom of Great Britain & Northern Ireland	Constitutional Monarchy	52,675,556 ('61)	53,200,000 ('62)
Incl. England Wales		46,071,604 ('61)	46,071,604 ('61)
Scotland		5,178,490 ('61)	5,178,490 ('61)
Northern Ireland		1,425,462 ('61)	1,425,462 ('61)
Excl. Gibraltar	British Colony	23,232 ('51)	26,000 ('60)
Isle of Man		48,150 ('61)	48,150 ('61)
Channel Is.		108,471 ('61)	108,471 ('61)
Vatican City State	Ecclesiastical State	1,000—Normal population	

Area Sq. Miles	Capital City	Largest City	Percent of Pop. Urban	Percent of Workers in Agric. & Fish.	Gross Nat'l Product Per Capita ($)
175	Andorra	Andorra			
32,374	Vienna	Vienna	49.2	32	703
11,779	Brussels	Brussels	62.7	12	1,239
3,572	Nicosia	Nicosia	27.0	37	374
16,619	Copenhagen	Copenhagen	69.0	23	1,074
540				42	
840,000				46	
130,119	Helsinki	Helsinki	37.0	39	843
212,821	Paris	Paris	55.9	26	1,067
95,920	Bonn	W. Berlin	71.1	13	1,035
51,182	Athens	Athens	36.8	53	342
39,768	Reykjavík	Reykjavík	72.8	40	1,237
27,136	Dublin	Dublin	41.5	40	571
116,294	Rome	Rome	44.6	28	548
60	Vaduz	Vaduz		18	
999	Luxembourg	Luxembourg	58.3	26	
121	Valleta	Valleta	51.5	12	
0.57			100.0		
12,616	Amsterdam	Amsterdam	54.6	19	857
125,064	Oslo	Oslo	32.8	26	1,104
23,957					
35,527	Lisbon	Lisbon	31.2	48	230
24	San Marino				
194,988	Madrid	Madrid	39.8	49	295
1,936					
2,808					
173,624	Stockholm	Stockholm	47.5	13	1,433
15,941	Bern	Zurich	36.5	12	1,464
93,895	London	London	66.9	5	1,224
58,345	London	London	80.8	5	
	Cardiff	Cardiff			
29,795	Edinburgh	Edinburgh	82.9	16	
5,459	Belfast	Belfast	53.1	7	
2					
221			53.1	11	
75					
0.2					

SOVIET CULTURE REGION

Country	Political Status	Population & Date of Latest Census	Population & Date of Latest Estimate
Union of Soviet Socialist Republics	Federal Soviet Republic	170,467,186 ('39) 208,826,650 ('59)	221,000,000 ('62)
Incl. SSRs:			
Armenia		1,768,000 ('59)	
Azerbaydzhan		3,700,000 ('59)	
Byelorussia		8,055,000 ('59)	8,226,000 ('60)
Estonia		1,196,000 ('59)	
Georgia		4,049,000 ('59)	
Kazakh		9,301,000 ('59)	
Kirghiz		2,063,000 ('59)	
Latvia		2,094,000 ('59)	
Lithuania		2,713,000 ('59)	
Moldavia		2,880,000 ('59)	
Russian SFSR		117,494,000 ('59)	
Tadzhik		1,982,000 ('59)	
Turkmen		1,520,000 ('59)	
Ukraine		41,869,046 ('59)	43,091,000 ('60)
Uzbek		8,113,000 ('59)	
Albania	People's Republic	1,625,378 ('60)	1,700,000 ('62)
Bulgaria	People's Republic	7,613,709 ('56)	8,000,000 ('62)
Czechoslovakia	People's Republic	13,741,529 ('61)	13,900,000 ('62)
Germany, East	Democratic Republic	18,388,172 ('50)	17,200,000 ('62)
Hungary	People's Republic	9,976,530 ('60)	10,100,000 ('62)
Poland	People's Republic	29,731,009 ('60)	30,400,000 ('62)
Romania	People's Republic	17,489,450 ('56)	18,800,000 ('62)
Yugoslavia	Federal People's Republic	18,538,000 ('61)	18,800,000 ('62)

ANGLO-AMERICAN CULTURE REGION

Country	Political Status	Population & Date of Latest Census	Population & Date of Latest Estimate
Canada	Federal State	18,238,247 ('61)	18,600,000 ('62)
United States	Federal Republic	179,323,175 ('60)	185,822,000 ('62)
St. Pierre & Miquelon	French Overseas Territories	4,822 ('57)	5,000 ('60)

Area Sq. Miles	Capital City	Largest City	Percent of Pop. Urban	Percent of Workers in Agric. & Fish.	Gross Nat'l Product Per Capita ($)
*8,650,069	Moscow	Moscow	47.9	35	682
11,506	Yerevan				
33,436	Baku				
80,154	Minsk		30.8		
17,413	Tallinn				
26,911	Tbilisi				
1,064,092	Alma-Ata				
76,641	Frunze				
24,595	Riga				
25,174	Vilnius				
13,012	Kishinev				
6,593,391	Moscow				
55,019	Dyushambe				
188,417	Ashkhabad				
232,046	Kiev		45.7		
158,069	Tashkent				
11,099	Tiranë	Tiranë	28.5	70	
42,818	Sofia	Sofia	33.6	64	285
49,336	Prague	Prague	51.2	38	543
41,635	E. Berlin	E. Berlin	71.7	23	
35,919	Budapest	Budapest	39.7	38	387
120,347	Warsaw	Warsaw	47.5	57	468
91,699	Bucharest	Bucharest	31.7	70	320
98,766	Belgrade	Belgrade	18.5	66	203

* Includes the area of the White Sea (34,749) and the Sea of Azov (15,444).

Area Sq. Miles	Capital City	Largest City	Percent of Pop. Urban	Percent of Workers in Agric. & Fish.	Gross Nat'l Product per Capita ($)
3,851,809	Ottawa	Montreal	66.6	11	1,903
3,615,208	Washington, D.C.	New York City	64.0	12	2,538

93

LATIN AMERICA CULTURE REGION

Country	Political Status	Population & Date of Latest Census	Population & Date of Latest Estimate
Argentina	Federal Republic	20,008,945 ('60)	21,300,000 ('62)
Bahama Islands	British Colony	84,841 ('53)	105,000 ('60)
Bermuda	British Colony	42,640 ('60)	42,640 ('60)
Bolivia	Republic	3,019,031 ('50)	3,600,000 ('62)
Brazil	Federal Republic	52,021,786 ('50)	70,528,625 ('61)
British Guiana	British Colony	375,701 ('46)	600,000 ('62)
		560,620 ('60)	
British Honduras	British Colony	59,220 ('46)	90,381 ('60)
		90,381 ('60)	
Chile	Republic	7,339,546 ('60)	7,900,000 ('62)
Colombia	Republic	11,548,172 ('51)	14,800,000 ('62)
Costa Rica	Republic	800,875 ('50)	1,300,000 ('62)
Cuba	Socialist Republic	5,829,029 ('53)	6,800,000 ('62)
Dominican Republic	Republic	2,135,872 ('50)	3,200,000 ('62)
		3,013,525 ('60)	
Ecuador	Republic	3,202,757 ('50)	4,600,000 ('62)
Incl. Galápagos Is.	Dependency		
El Salvador	Republic	1,855,917 ('50)	2,800,000 ('62)
Falkland Islands	British Colony	2,230 ('53)	2,191 ('59)
French Guiana	Fr. Overseas Department	27,863 ('54)	31,000 ('60)
Guadeloupe	Fr. Overseas Department	229,120 ('54)	270,000 ('60)
Guatemala	Republic	2,790,868 ('50)	4,000,000 ('62)
Haiti	Republic	3,097,304 ('50)	4,300,000 ('62)
Honduras	Republic	1,883,173 ('61)	2,000,000 ('62)
Jamaica	Republic	1,613,880 ('60)	1,647,000 ('62)
Martinique	Fr. Overseas Department	239,130 ('54)	277,000 ('60)
Mexico	Federal Republic	25,791,017 ('50)	37,200,000 ('62)
		34,923,129 ('60)	
Netherlands	Integral part of the		
Antilles	Netherlands Realm	76,304 ('30)	190,000 ('60)
Incl.			
Curaçao		50,165 ('30)	124,000 ('60)
Aruba		15,659 ('30)	56,000 ('60)
Bonaire		5,733 ('30)	6,000 ('60)
Saba			1,016 ('60)
St. Eustatius		5,084 ('30)	1,094 ('60)
St. Martin			1,537 ('60)
Nicaragua	Republic	1,057,023 ('50)	1,600,000 ('62)
Panamá	Republic	1,075,541 ('60)	1,100,000 ('62)
Panama Canal Zone	U.S. Military Reservation	42,122 ('60)	42,122 ('60)
Paraguay	Republic	1,408,400 ('50)	1,900,000 ('62)
Peru	Republic	10,364,620 ('61)	10,600,000 ('62)
Puerto Rico	Self-govn'g Commonwealth of the U.S.	2,349,544 ('60)	2,500,000 ('62)
Surinam	Integral part of Neth. Realm	209,681 ('50)	308,000 ('60)
Swan Islands	U.S. Possession	28 ('60)	28 ('60)
Trinidad & Tobago	Republic	827,957 ('60)	900,000 ('62)
Turks & Caicos	British Colony	5,716 ('60)	5,716 ('60)
Uruguay	Republic	1,042,686 ('08)	3,000,000 ('62)

Area Sq. Miles	Capital City	Largest City	Percent of Pop. Urban	Percent of Workers in Agric. & Fish.	Gross Nat'l Product per Capita ($)
1,072,746	Buenos Aires	Buenos Aires	62.5	25	185
4,404		Nassau		40	200
20			11.6	6	
424,162	Sucre	La Paz	33.9	63	60
3,287,195	Brasília	São Paulo	36.2	58	202
83,000		Georgetown	27.6	46	311
8,867		Belize	53.7	40	
286,396	Santiago	Santiago	60.2	30	386
439,512	Bogotá	Bogotá	45.8	54	185
19,695	San José	San José	33.5	55	412
44,218	Habana	Habana	57.0	41	397
18,703	Santo Domingo	Santo Domingo	30.5	56	232
105,684	Quito	Guayaquil	28.5	49	198
8,260	San Salvador	San Salvador	36.7	63	214
4,618		Port Stanley			
35,135		Cayenne			
687		Pointe-à-Pitre	43.9		
42,042	Guatemala	Guatemala	25.0	68	189
10,714	Port-au-Prince	Port-au-Prince	12.2	83	78
43,277	Tegucigalpa	Tegucigalpa	31.0	66	206
4,411	Kingston	Kingston	29.0	45	265
431		Fort-de-France	50.5		
760,335	Mexico City	Mexico City	44.1	58	282
394		Willemstad			
178			44.4		
71					
112					
5					
12					
16					
57,143	Managua	Managua	39.9	68	218
28,753	Panamá	Panamá	36.0	50	327
362				2	
157,047	Asunción	Asunción	34.6	54	133
496,222	Lima	Lima	44.3	62	126
3,435	San Juan	San Juan	40.5	37	511
55,143		Paramaribo	40.5	65	356
2 mi. long					
1,980	Port-of-Spain	Port-of-Spain	75.1	25	185
169					
72,152	Montevideo	Montevideo		37	559

Country	Political Status	Population & Date of Latest Census	Population & Date of Latest Estimate
Venezuela	Federal Republic	7,555,799 ('61)	7,800,000 ('62)
Virgin Islands	British Colony	7,338 ('60)	7,338 ('60)
Virgin Islands Incl.	U.S. Unincorporated Territory	32,099 ('60)	32,099 ('60)
St. Croix		14,973 ('60)	14,973 ('60)
St. Thomas		16,201 ('60)	16,201 ('60)
St. John		925 ('60)	925 ('60)
West Indies Incl.	British Colony		
Antigua		54,354 ('60)	54,354 ('60)
Barbados		232,085 ('60)	232,085 ('60)
Cayman Islands		7,616 ('60)	7,616 ('60)
Dominica		59,916 ('60)	59,916 ('60)
Grenada		88,677 ('60)	88,677 ('60)
Montserrat		12,157 ('60)	12,157 ('60)
St. Kitts-Nevis & Anguilla		56,658 ('60)	56,658 ('60)
St. Lucia		86,108 ('60)	86,108 ('60)
St. Vincent		79,948 ('60)	79,948 ('60)

NORTH AFRICAN-SOUTHWEST ASIAN CULTURE REGION

Country	Political Status	Population & Date of Latest Census	Population & Date of Latest Estimate
Afghanistan	Constitutional Monarchy		13,800,000 ('60)
Algeria	Republic	9,144,971 ('54)	11,700,000 ('62)
Bahrain Islands	Sheikhdom; Brit. Protect.	143,135 ('59)	147,000 ('60)
Ifni	Spanish Colony	38,295 ('50)	54,000 ('60)
Iran	Monarchy	18,954,704 ('56)	21,200,000 ('62)
Iraq	Constitutional Monarchy	6,538,109 ('57)	7,500,000 ('62)
Israel	Republic	2,170,082 ('61)	2,300,000 ('62)
Jordan	Constitutional Monarchy	1,329,174 ('52)	1,800,000 ('62)
Kuwait	Sheikhdom; Brit. Protect.	206,473 ('57)	300,000 ('62)
Lebanon	Republic		1,700,000 ('62)
Libya	Monarchy	1,088,889 ('54)	1,200,000 ('62)
Morocco	Independent Kingdom	9,325,000 ('52) 11,626,470 ('60)	12,300,000 ('62)

Area Sq. Miles	Capital City	Largest City	Percent of Pop. Urban	Percent of Workers in Agric. & Fish.	Gross Nat'l Product per Capita ($)
352,142	Caracas	Caracas	53.8	41	1,019
59					
133		Charlotte Amalie	55.9	11	
171			39.8		
166		Bridgetown	52.6	27	80
100					
305			25.7		
133			14.4		
32					
153			27.8		
238			18.3		
150			13.7		

Area Sq. Miles	Capital City	Largest City	Percent of Pop. Urban	Percent of Workers in Agric. & Fish.	Gross Nat'l Product per Capita ($)
250,000	Kābul	Kābul	7.5	85	48
113,912	Algiers	Algiers	22.9	75	217
231		Manama	65.7		
579					
636,293	Tehrān	Tehrān	30.1	55	145
171,599	Baghdad	Baghdad	37.3	81	160
7,993	Jerusalem	Tel Aviv	75.9	17	982
37,313	'Ammān	'Ammān	37.7	54	111
6,000	Kuwait	Kuwait	47.0		
4,015	Beirut	Beirut	23.0		358
679,536	Al Bayḍā'	Tripoli	18.4		107
174,471	Rabat	Casablanca	29.3	71	169

Country	Political Status	Population & Date of Latest Census		Population & Date of Latest Estimate	
Muscat & Oman	Sultanate (In close treaty relationship with Britain) Incl. enclave in Trucial territory			544,000	('60)
Qatar	Sheikhdom; Brit. Protect.			45,000	('60)
Saudi Arabia	Monarchy			6,000,000	('62)
South Arabia, Federation of					
Incl. Aden	British Colony & Protectorate	138,441	('55)	155,000	('60)
Spanish Sahara	Spanish Territory	7,749	('50)	25,000	('60)
Incl.					
Río de Oro		1,304	('50)		
Saguia el Hamra		6,445	('50)		
Sudan	Republic	10,262,536	('56)	12,400,000	('62)
Syrian Arab Republic	Republic	4,555,267	('60)	5,100,000	('62)
Trucial Coast	Seven Sheikhdoms; British Protected			86,000	('60)
Tunisia	Republic	3,943,273	('56)	4,300,000	('62)
Turkey	Republic	27,829,198	('60)	29,200,000	('62)
United Arab Republic	Republic	26,059,000	('60)	27,200,000	('62)
Yemen	Monarchy			5,000,000	('62)

SOUTH ASIAN CULTURE REGION

Country	Political Status	Population & Date of Latest Census		Population & Date of Latest Estimate	
Bhutan	Formal Protectorate of India			700,000	('62)
Ceylon	Republic	8,154,580	('53)	10,500,000	('62)
India	Republic	434,807,245	('61)	434,807,245	('61)
Incl.					
Andaman & Nicobar Is.	Owned by India				
Laccadive, Minicoy, & Amindivi Is.	Dependencies				
Excl.					
Kashmir-Jammu		3,583,585	('61)	3,583,585	('61)
Maldive Is.	Sultanate; Brit. Protect.	81,950	('56)	89,000	('60)
Nepal	Constitutional Monarchy	9,407,127	('61)	9,500,000	('62)
Pakistan	Republic	93,812,000	('61)	96,600,000	('62)
Incl.					
W. Pakistan		33,779,555	('51)	37,396,000	('58)
E. Pakistan		42,062,610	('51)	46,500,000	('56)
Sikkim	Formal Protectorate of India	161,080	('61)	161,080	('61)

Area Sq. Miles	Capital City	Largest City	Percent of Pop. Urban	Percent of Workers in Agric. & Fish.	Gross Nat'l Product per Capita ($)
82,000	Muscat	Muscat			
8,500		Doha			
872,722	Riyadh	Mecca	9.5		169
		Aden	93.3	0	
102,703					
967,491	Khartoum	Khartoum	8.3		70
71,227	Damascus	Damascus	38.8	70	142
32,278		Sharja			
48,332	Tunis	Tunis	35.6	68	190
301,380	Ankara	Istanbul	28.8	77	151
386,100	Cairo	Cairo	36.9	64	136
75,290	San'a	San'a	0.6		75

Area Sq. Miles	Capital City	Largest City	Percent of Pop. Urban	Percent of Workers in Agric. & Fish.	Gross Nat'l Product per Capita ($)
19,305	Thimbu Tashi Chho Dzong	Thimbu			
25,332	Colombo	Colombo	17.6	53	130
1,234,012	New Delhi	Calcutta	17.3	71	76
115			10.3		
54,362	Katmandu	Katmandu	2.8	93	40
364,737	Rawalpindi (Islamabad)	Karachi	10.4	65	66
310,236					
54,501					
2,774	Gangtok	Gangtok	2.0		

SOUTHEAST ASIAN CULTURE REGION

Country	Political Status	Population & Date of Latest Census	Population & Date of Latest Estimate
Brunei	British Colony	83,877 ('60)	83,877 ('60)
Burma	Federal Republic	16,823,798 ('41)	21,700,000 ('62)
Cambodia	Constitutional Monarchy	4,845,000 ('59)	5,200,000 ('62)
Indonesia	Republic	95,189,000 ('61)	96,600,000 ('62)
Laos	Constitutional Monarchy		2,000,000 ('62)
Malaysia, Federation of			
Malaya		6,278,763 ('57)	7,400,000 ('62)
Sabah		454,421 ('60)	500,000 ('62)
Sarawak		744,529 ('60)	800,000 ('62)
Philippines	Republic	27,455,799 ('60)	29,600,000 ('62)
Portuguese Timor	Port. Overseas Province	442,378 ('50)	502,000 ('60)
Singapore		1,445,928 ('57)	1,700,000 ('62)
Thailand	Constitutional Monarchy	25,519,965 ('60)	28,000,000 ('62)
Vietnam:			
Republic of			
Vietnam (So.)	Republic		15,300,000 ('62)
Democratic Rep.			
of Vietnam	People's Republic	15,916,955 ('60)	16,600,000 ('62)

EAST ASIAN CULTURE REGION

Country	Political Status	Population & Date of Latest Census	Population & Date of Latest Estimate
China:			
People's Republic			
of China	People's Republic	582,603,417 ('53)	716,500,000 ('62)
Republic of			
China	Republic	9,367,661 ('56)	11,400,000 ('62)
Hong Kong	Colony & Lease of U.K.	3,128,044 ('61)	3,300,000 ('62)
Japan	Constitutional Monarchy	93,418,501 ('60)	94,900,000 ('62)
Korea:			
North Korea	People's Republic		8,300,000 ('62)
South Korea	Republic	24,994,117 ('60)	26,100,000 ('62)
Macao	Port. Overseas Province	187,772 ('50)	220,000 ('60)
Mongolian People's			
Republic	People's Republic	1,019,000 ('63)	—
Ryūkyū Islands	U.S. Military Possession	883,052 ('60)	883,052 ('60)

Area Sq. Miles	Capital City	Largest City	Percent of Pop. Urban	Percent of Workers in Agric. & Fish.	Gross Nat'l Product Per Capita ($)
2,226	Brunei	Brunei		55	
261,789	Rangoon	Rangoon	8.2	85	53
66,606	Phnom Penh	Phnom Penh	16.0	80	94
575,893	Djakarta	Djakarta	9.1	66	59
85,907	Vientiane	Luang Prabang	4.0	90	50
50,700	Kuala Lumpur	Kuala Lumpur	42.7	57	250
29,388	Jesselton	Sandakan	13.4	85	298
47,500	Kuching	Kuching	10.8	58	
115,707	Quezon City	Manila	35.3	59	218
7,332	Dili	Dili			
224	Singapore	Singapore	62.6	8	
198,263	Krung-Thep	Krung-Thep	11.8	82	102
65,958	Saigon	Saigon			133
60,156	Hanoi	Hanoi			

Area Sq. Miles	Capital City	Largest City	Percent of Pop. Urban	Percent of Workers in Agric. & Fish.	Gross Nat'l Product per Capita ($)
3,691,502	Peking	Shanghai	14.2	69	56
13,885	Taipei	Taipei	56.0	50	104
398		Victoria	94.0	7	292
142,767	Tōkyō	Tōkyō	65.7	33	302
47,862	Pyŏngyang	Pyŏngyang			
37,424	Seoul	Seoul	32.3	80	99
6	Macao	Macao			
591,119	Ulan Bator	Ulan Bator	40.8	71	
1,447			36.2	44	

AFRICAN CULTURE REGION

Country	Political Status	Population & Date of Latest Census	Population & Date of Latest Estimate
Angola	Port. Overseas Province	4,145,266 ('50)	4,900,000 ('62)
Basutoland	British Colony	641,674 ('56)	685,000 ('60)
Bechuanaland	British Protectorate	327,305 ('56)	340,000 ('60)
Burundi	Kingdom		2,234,000 ('60)
Cameroun	Republic		4,200,000 ('62)
Cape Verde Is.	Port. Overseas Province	201,549 ('60)	201,549 ('60)
Central African Republic	Republic		1,300,000 ('62)
Chad	Republic		2,700,000 ('62)
Comoro Is.	French Overseas Territory	183,133 ('58)	183,000 ('60)
Congo Republic	Republic		900,000 ('62)
Congo, Rep. of the	Republic		14,800,000 ('62)
Dahomey	Republic	1,934,447 ('60)	2,100,000 ('62)
Ethiopia Incl. Eritrea	Monarchy		20,000,000 ('62)
French Somaliland	French Overseas Territory		67,000 ('60)
Gabon	Republic		500,000 ('62)
Gambia	British Colony & Protect.		284,000 ('60)
Ghana	Republic	4,118,450 ('48) 6,690,730 ('60)	7,200,000 ('62)
Guinea	Republic	2,570,219 ('55)	3,200,000 ('62)
Ivory Coast	Republic		3,400,000 ('62)
Kenya	Republic	5,405,966 ('48)	7,500,000 ('62)
Liberia	Republic		1,300,000 ('60)
Malagasy	Republic		5,700,000 ('62)
Mali	Republic		4,300,000 ('62)
Mauritania	Republic		727,000 ('59)
Mauritius & Depen.	British Colony	516,556 ('52)	700,000 ('62)
Mozambique	Port. Overseas Province	5,738,911 ('50)	6,700,000 ('62)
Niger	Republic	2,822,732 ('60)	3,100,000 ('62)
Nigeria	Federal Republic	30,418,025 ('53)	36,400,000 ('62)
Northern Rhodesia	Republic		2,515,000 ('62)
Nyasaland	Republic		2,921,000 ('62)
Portuguese Guinea	Port. Overseas Province	510,777 ('50)	571,000 ('60)
Reunion Island	French Overseas Dept.	274,370 ('54)	336,000 ('60)
Rwanda	Republic		2,695,000 ('60)
St. Helena group Incl. St. Helena	British Colony British Colony	4,642 ('56)	5,000 ('60)
Ascension	Dependency	390 ('56)	457 ('60)
Tristan da Cunha	Dependency	186 ('38)	292 ('59)
São Tomé & Principe	Port Overseas Territory	60,159 ('50)	67,000 ('60)

Area Sq. Miles	Capital City	Largest City	Percent of Pop. Urban	Percent of Workers in Agric. & Fish.	Gross Nat'l Product per Capita ($)
481,351	Luanda	Luanda	4.7		70
11,716	Maseru	Maseru			
275,000					
10,747	Usumbura	Usumbura			
183,376	Douala	Yaoundé	4.1		150
1,557					
241,699	Bangui	Bangui			
495,752	Fort-Lamy	Fort-Lamy			
832					
134,749	Brazzaville	Brazzaville	15.4		
905,063	Léopoldville	Léopoldville	15.8	85	85
44,696	Porto-Novo	Cotonou	5.5		
457,142	Addis Ababa	Addis Ababa	1.7		46
8,996	Djibouti	Djibouti	32.4		
102,317	Libreville	Libreville			
4,010	Bathurst	Bathurst	7.7		
92,100	Accra	Accra	6.4	70	210
94,925	Conakry	Conakry			
124,503	Abidjan	Abidjan	6.8		58
224,960	Nairobi	Nairobi	5.0		85
43,000	Monrovia	Monrovia			112
230,035	Tananarive	Tananarive	8.0	7	119
464,873	Bamako	Bamako			
451,351	Nouakchott	Nouakchott			
804			34.9	45	
303,073	Lourenço Marques	Lourenço Marques	1.6	75	
489,206	Niamey	Niamey			
356,669	Lagos	Lagos	10.5	59	81
290,724	Lusaka	Kitwe	11	67	
45,747	Zomba	Blantyre-Limbe		90	
13,948	Bissau	Bissau		44	50
969			45.0		
10,169	Kigali	Kigali			
47					
34					
40					
372					

Country	Political Status	Population & Date of Latest Census	Population & Date of Latest Estimate
Senegal	Republic	2,973,285 ('60)	3,000,000 ('62)
Seychelles	British Colony	41,425 ('60)	41,425 ('60)
Sierra Leone	Republic		2,600,000 ('62)
Somali Republic	Republic		2,000,000 ('62)
South Africa, Republic of	Republic	15,841,128 ('60)	16,500,000 ('62)
Southern Rhodesia	Republic		3,848,000 ('62)
Southwest Africa	U.N. Mandate to South Africa	525,064 ('60)	525,064 ('60)
Spanish Guinea	Spanish Colonies	245,989 ('60)	245,989 ('60)
Incl. Annoboń		1,403 ('50)	
Corisco		513 ('50)	
Elobey		96 ('50)	
Fernando Póo		40,475 ('50)	47,000 ('60)
Rio Muni		156,176 ('50)	169,000 ('60)
Swaziland	British Protectorate	256,000 ('56)	259,000 ('60)
Tanganyika	Republic	8,788,466 ('57)	9,600,000 ('62)
Togo	Republic	1,439,772 ('60)	1,500,000 ('62)
Uganda	Republic	6,538,031 ('59)	7,000,000 ('62)
Upper Volta	Republic		4,400,000 ('62)
Zanzibar	Sultanate	299,111 ('58)	307,000 ('60)

AUSTRALIA-NEW ZEALAND CULTURE REGION

Country	Political Status	Population & Date of Latest Census	Population & Date of Latest Estimate
Australia	Federal State	10,547,510 ('61)	10,700,000 ('62)
Excl.			
Christmas Isl.	Dependency	2,619 ('57)	3,000 ('60)
Cocos Is.	Dependency	1,814 ('47)	1,000 ('60)
Macquarie Is.	Dependency		
Norfolk Isl.	Dependency	942 ('54)	1,000 ('60)
New Zealand°	Parliamentary State	2,414,064 ('61)	2,500,000 ('62)

° The New Zealand data includes the following external island territories: Antipodes, Aukland, Bounty, Chatham, and Kermadec.

Area Sq. Miles	Capital City	Largest City	Percent of Pop. Urban	Percent of Workers in Agric. & Fish.	Gross Nat'l Product per Capita ($)
76,124	Dakar	Dakar			
156			25.4		
27,925	Freetown	Freetown	3.1	90	70
246,201	Mogadiscio	Mogadiscio	18.1		39
472,733	Pretoria	Johannesburg	42.6	33	398
150,333	Salisbury	Salisbury	5.0		
317,725	Windhoek	Windhoek	16.0	80	
			6.0		
6					
5					
0.7					
786					
10,045					
6,704	Mbabane	Mbabane	2.6		
362,688	Dar es Salaam	Dar es Salaam	4.1		48
21,853	Lomé	Lomé	2.8		
93,981	Entebbe	Entebbe	0.9		58
105,839	Ouagadougou	Ouagadougou	5.3		
1,020	Zanzibar	Zanzibar	26.5	64	

Area Sq. Miles	Capital City	Largest City	Percent of Pop. Urban	Percent of Workers in Agric. & Fish.	Gross Nat'l Product Per Capita ($)
2,971,081	Canberra	Sydney	82	13	1,351
62					
5					
1					
13					
103,736	Wellington	Christchurch	60	16	1,395

PACIFIC CULTURE REGION

Country	Political Status	Population & Date of Latest Census	Population & Date of Latest Estimate
Western Samoa	Constitutional Monarchy	114,427 ('61)	114,427 ('61)
Australian Pacific Islands			
New Guinea Incl. Bismarck Archipelago	Trust Territory		1,402,000 ('60)
Papua Incl. New Britain New Ireland Admiralty Is.	External Territory		503,000 ('60)
British Pacific Islands			
British Solomon Is. Incl. Choiseul Guadalcanal Lord Howe Is. Malaita Mitre New Georgia Reef & Daff Groups San Cristobal Santa Cruz Santa Isabel	British Protectorate	124,076 ('59)	124,076 ('59)
Fiji Islands	British Colony	345,737 ('56)	394,000 ('60)
Gilbert & Ellice Is.	British Colony	35,919 ('47)	46,000 ('60)
Pitcairn Is. Incl. Aeno Henderson Ducie	British Colony	124 ('47)	147 ('60)
Tonga	Protected Kingdom of U.K.	56,838 ('56)	63,000 ('60)
French Pacific Islands			
French Polynesia Incl. Society Tahiti Marquesas Tuamotu		76,327 ('56)	76,327 ('56)
New Caledonia Wallis & Futuna		68,480 ('56)	77,000 ('60)
New Zealand Pacific Islands			
Cook Islands	Dependency	16,680 ('56)	18,174 ('60)
Tokelau		1,619 ('56)	1,929 ('60)
Niue		4,707 ('56)	4,860 ('60)

Area Sq. Miles	Capital City	Largest City	Percent of Pop. Urban	Percent of Workers in Agric. & Fish.	Gross Nat'l Product per Capita ($)
1,090	Apia	Apia	18.7		
93,000					
90,540					
11,500					
7,055			18.3	57	
360					
19					
270					
1,544				54	
8,487				54	
61					
194					

Country	Political Status	Population & Date of Latest Census	Population & Date of Latest Estimate
United States Pacific Islands			
American Samoa	U.S. Unincorporated Territory	18,937 ('50) 20,051 ('60)	20,051 ('60)
Guam	Unincorporated Territory	59,498 ('50) 67,044 ('60)	67,044 ('60)
Bonin, Volcano Islands	Military Administrations	148 ('50) 204 ('60)	204 ('60)
Marshall, Caroline, Mariana Islands	U.S. Trusteeship	54,843 ('50) 75,836 ('60)	75,836 ('60)
Johnston		46 ('50)	
Midway		2,356 ('60)	2,356 ('60)
Wake		1,097 ('60)	1,097 ('60)
Baker, Howland, Jarvis, Kingman Reef, Palmyra			
Condominiums in the Pacific			
Canton & Enderbury	U.S.—British	320 ('60)	320 ('60)
New Hebrides	French—British		59,000 ('60)

The following are the main sources for the data in the tables:
United Nations, *Demographic Yearbook* (1960)
Statistical Yearbook (1961)
International Labour Office, *Yearbook of Labour Statistics* (1962)
N. Ginsburg, *Atlas of Economic Development* (1961)
Life Pictorial Atlas of the World (1961)

Area Sq. Miles	Capital City	Largest City	Percent of Pop. Urban	Percent of Workers in Agric. & Fish.	Gross Nat'l Product per Capita ($)
76				53	
209					
41					
687					
20					
9					
5,700					

REFERENCES
AND
INDEX

REFERENCES

The following list of references is intended to offer the student a selection of additional readings to supplement and enlarge upon the topics covered in this book. The references are both to geographical sources and to sources in related fields that contribute to an understanding of the division of the world into various culture regions.

There are several bibliographic sources where additional geographic materials can be found. The most important of these is the *Bibliographie géographique internationale*, published annually since 1891 by Armand Colin in Paris. In the United States the American Geographical Society (Broadway at 156th Street, New York, has published, since 1938, its *Current Geographical Publications: Additions to the Research Catalogue of the American Geographical Society* (it is published every month, except for July and August). These, and many other bibliographies throughout the world, are listed and described in J. K. Wright and E. T. Platt, *Aids to Geographic Research*, American Geographical Society (Research Series No. 22), second edition, New York, 1947.

For material published in pamphlet form covering many of the world's countries, and many topics of general interest, the student is referred to *Focus*, published monthly by the American Geographical Society. Also for a wealth of information about the world's habitats, and man's use of them, reference should be made to Paul Vidal de la Blache and Lucien Gallois, *Géographie universelle* (15 volumes by various authors), Armand Colin, Paris (starting in 1927). For additional material on the major groups of natural regions and man's use of them, and on the principles of climatology, geomorphology, hydrography, and cartography, see Preston E. James, *A Geography of Man*, Ginn and Company, second edition, 1959.

GENERAL AND TOPICAL

CARLETON S. COON, *The Story of Man*, 2nd ed., Alfred A. Knopf, Inc., New York, 1962.

CLAIR WILCOX, WILLIS D. WEATHERFORD, JR., AND HOLLAND HUNTER, *Economies of the World Today: Their Organization, Development, and Performance*, Harcourt, Brace and World, Inc., New York, 1962.

JACK P. GIBBS, "Growth of Individual Metropolitan Areas: A Global View," *Annals of the Association of American Geographers*, Vol. 51, 1961, pp. 380–391.

NORTON GINSBURG, *Atlas of Economic Development*, The University of Chicago Press, Chicago, 1961.

LEWIS MUMFORD, *The City in History: Its Origins, Its Transformations and Its Prospects*, Harcourt, Brace and World, Inc., New York, 1961.

R. M. ADAMS, "The Origin of Cities," *Scientific American*, Vol. 203, 1960, pp. 153–168.

ROBERT J. BRAIDWOOD, "The Agricultural Revolution," *Scientific American*, Vol. 203, 1960, pp. 130–148.

NORTON GINSBURG (ed.), *Essays on Geography and Economic Development*, University of Chicago, Department of Geography, Research Paper No. 62, Chicago, 1960.

WILLIAM H. HOWELLS, "The Distribution of Man," *Scientific American*, Vol. 203, 1960, pp. 113–127.

W. W. ROSTOW, *The Stages of Economic Development, A Non-Communist Manifesto*, Cambridge University Press, Cambridge, England, 1960.

ROBERT R. PALMER, *The Age of the Democratic Revolution*, Princeton University Press, Princeton, New Jersey, 1959.

NORTON GINSBURG (ed.), *The Pattern of Asia*, Prentice-Hall, Inc., Englewood Cliffs, New Jersey, 1958.

HANS W. WEIGERT, *et al.*, *Principles of Political Geography*, Appleton-Century-Crofts, Inc., New York, 1957.

W. GORDON EAST AND A. E. MOODIE (eds.), *The Changing World, Studies in Political Geography*, George G. Harrap & Company, Ltd., London, and Harcourt, Brace and World, Inc., New York, 1956.

WILLIAM L. THOMAS, JR. (ed.), *Man's Role in Changing the Face of the Earth* (Published for the Wenner-Gren Foundation for Anthropological Research and for the National Science Foundation), The University of Chicago Press, Chicago, 1956.

JOSEPH E. SPENCER, *Asia East by South, A Cultural Geography*, John Wiley & Sons, Inc., New York, 1954.

JOHN Q. STEWART, "Empirical Mathematical Rules Concerning the Distribution and Equilibrium of Population," *Geographical Review*, Vol. 37, 1947, pp. 461–485.

GEORGE B. CRESSEY, *Asia's Lands and Peoples*, McGraw-Hill Book Company, Inc., New York, 1944; 3rd ed., 1963.

A. M. CARR-SAUNDERS, *World Population: Past Growth and Present Trends*, Oxford University Press, London, 1935.

EUROPEAN CULTURE REGION

CHARLES A. FISHER, "The Changing Significance of the Commonwealth in the Political Geography of Great Britain," *Geography*, Vol. 48, 1963, pp. 113–129.

M. J. WISE, "The Common Market and the Changing Geography of Europe," *Geography*, Vol. 48, 1963, pp. 129–138.

MICHAEL SHANKS AND JOHN LAMBERT, *The Common Market Today—and Tomorrow*, Frederick A. Praeger, Inc., New York, 1962.

J. FREDERIC DEWHURST, JOHN O. CAPPOCK, P. LAMARTINE YATES, *et al.*, *Europe's Needs and Resources*, The Twentieth Century Fund, New York, 1961.

ARTHUR P. WHITAKER, *Spain and the Defense of the West: Ally and Liability*, Harper & Row, Publishers, New York, 1961.

ALEX SOMME (ed.), *A Geography of Norden*, John Wiley & Sons, Inc., New York, 1960.

F. J. MONKHOUSE, *A Regional Geography of Western Europe*, Longmans, Green & Co., Ltd., London, and John Wiley & Sons, Inc., New York, 1959.

DAN STANISLAWSKI, *The Individuality of Portugal. A Study in Historical-Political Geography*, University of Texas Press, Austin, Texas, 1959.

DENIS HAY, *Europe: The Emergence of an Idea*, Edinburgh University Press, Edinburgh, 1957.

ALAN G. OGILVIE, *Europe and its Borderlands*, Thomas Nelson & Sons, Ltd., Edinburgh, 1957.

GEORGE W. HOFFMAN (ed.), *A Geography of Europe*, The Ronald Press Company, New York, 1953; revised ed., 1961.

HAJO HOLBORN, *The Political Collapse of Europe*, Alfred A. Knopf, Inc., New York, 1951.

GORDON EAST, *An Historical Geography of Europe*, Methuen & Co., Ltd., London, and E. P. Dutton & Co., Inc., New York, 1935; revised ed., 1950.

E. C. SEMPLE, *The Geography of the Mediterranean Region: Its Relation to Ancient History*, Henry Holt and Company, Inc., New York, 1931.

ALAN G. OGILVIE (ed.), *Great Britain: Essays in Regional Geography*, Cambridge University Press, Cambridge, England, 1928.

T. S. ASHTON, *Iron and Steel in the Industrial Revolution*, Manchester University Press, Manchester, England, and Barnes & Noble, Inc., New York, 1924; 2nd ed., 1951.

HALFORD J. MACKINDER, *Democratic Ideals and Reality*, Henry Holt and Company, Inc., New York, 1919; W. W. Norton &

Company, Inc. (paperback), New York, 1962.

Leon Dominian, *The Frontiers of Language and Nationality in Europe*, Henry Holt and Company, Inc., New York, 1917.

Lucien Gallois, *Régions naturelles et noms de pays, étude sur la région parisienne*, A. Colin, Paris, 1908.

Halford J. Mackinder, "The Geographical Pivot of History," *Geographical Journal*, Vol. 23, 1904, pp. 421–437.

SOVIET CULTURE REGION

Paul E. Lydolph, *Geography of the U.S.S.R.*, John Wiley & Sons, 1964.

George B. Cressey, *Soviet Potentials: A Geographic Appraisal*, Syracuse University Press, Syracuse, New York, 1962.

J. Edgar Hoover, *A Study of Communism*, Holt, Rinehart and Winston, Inc., New York, 1962.

Maurice Hindus, *House Without a Roof*, Doubleday & Company, Inc., New York, 1961.

W. A. Douglas Jackson, *The Russo-Chinese Borderlands*, D. Van Nostrand Company, Inc., Princeton, New Jersey (Searchlight Book No. 2), 1961.

Georges Jorré, *The Soviet Union: The Land and its People*, Trans. by E. D. Laborde, 2nd ed., Longmans, Green & Co., Ltd., London, and John Wiley & Sons, Inc., New York, 1961.

Alec Nove, *The Soviet Economy: An Introduction*, Frederick A. Praeger, Inc., New York, 1961.

S. P. Suslov, *Physical Geography of Asiatic Russia* (Editor of American edition, Joseph E. Williams), W. H. Freeman & Co., San Francisco, California, 1961.

David J. M. Hooson, "The Middle Volga—An Emerging Focal Region of the Soviet Union," *The Geographical Journal*, Vol. 126, 1960, pp. 180–190.

Richard E. Lonsdale and John H. Thompson, "A Map of the U.S.S.R.'s Manufacturing," *Economic Geography*, Vol. 36, 1960, pp. 36–52.

Norman J. G. Pounds, "The Industrial Geography of Modern Poland," *Economic Geography*, Vol. 36, 1960, pp. 231–253.

Michael K. Roof and Frederick A. Leedy, "Population Redistribution in the Soviet Union, 1939–1956," *Geographical Review*, Vol. 49, 1959, pp. 208–221.

M. Gardner Clark, *The Economics of Soviet Steel*, Harvard University Press, Cambridge, Massachusetts, 1956.

George W. Hoffman, "Yugoslavia in Transition: Industrial Expansion and Resource Bases," *Economic Geography*, Vol. 32, 1956, pp. 295–315.

Dmitri B. Shimkin, "Economic Regionalization in the Soviet Union," *Geographical Review*, Vol. 42, 1952, pp. 591–614.

William Mandel, *The Soviet Far East and Central Asia*, The Dial Press, New York, 1944.

ANGLO-AMERICAN CULTURE REGION

Hans H. Landsberg, Leonard L. Fischman, and Joseph L. Fisher, *Resources in America's Future: Patterns of Requirements and Availabilities, 1960–2000* (Published for Resources for the Future), The Johns Hopkins Press, Baltimore, Maryland, 1963.

Harvey S. Perloff and Vera W. Dodds, *How a Region Grows: Area Development in the U. S. Economy*, Committee for Economic Development, Supplementary Paper No. 17, March, 1963.

Jean Gottmann, *Megalopolis—The Urbanized Northeastern Seaboard of the United States*, The Twentieth Century Fund, New York, 1961.

Simon Kuznets and others, *Population Re-*

distribution and Economic Growth: United States 1870–1950, American Philosophical Society, Philadelphia, 1960.

HARVEY S. PERLOFF, EDGAR S. DUNN, JR., ERIC E. LAMPARD, AND RICHARD F. MUTH, *Regions, Resources, and Economic Growth* (Published for Resources for the Future), The Johns Hopkins Press, Baltimore, Maryland, 1960.

EDWARD HIGBEE, *American Agriculture,* John Wiley & Sons, Inc., New York, 1958.

HOWELL WILLIAMS (ed.), *Landscapes of Alaska; Their Geologic Evolution,* University of California Press, Berkeley, California, 1958.

D. F. PUTNAM AND D. P. KERR, *A Regional Geography of Canada,* J. M. Dent & Sons, Ltd., Toronto, 1956.

MERRILL JENSEN (ed.), *Regionalism in America,* The University of Wisconsin Press, Madison, Wisconsin, 1951.

VAL HART, *The Story of American Roads,* William Sloane Associates, Inc., New York, 1950.

HANS KURATH, *A Word Geography of the Eastern United States,* The University of Michigan Press, Ann Arbor, 1949.

EDWARD L. ULLMAN, "The Railroad Pattern of the United States," *Geographical Review,* Vol. 39, 1949, pp. 242–256.

WALTER ISARD, "Some Locational Factors in the Iron and Steel Industry since the Early 19th Century," *Journal of Political Economy,* Vol. 56, 1948, pp. 203–217.

J. C. MALIN, *The Grassland of North America: Prolegomena to its History,* J. W. Edwards, Publishers, Inc., Ann Arbor, Mich., 1947.

R. H. BROWN, *Mirror for Americans: Likeness of the Eastern Seaboard, 1810,* American Geographical Society, New York, 1943.

MERLE CURTI, *The Growth of American Thought,* Harper & Row, Publishers, New York, 1943; 2nd ed., 1951.

H. R. FRIIS, "A Series of Population Maps of the Colonies and the United States," *Geographical Review,* Vol. 30, 1940, pp. 463–470.

U. B. PHILLIPS, *Life and Labor in the Old South,* Little, Brown & Company, Boston, 1929.

LATIN-AMERICAN CULTURE REGION

GERALD CLARK, *The Coming Explosion in Latin America,* David McKay Company, New York, 1962.

CHARLES O. PORTER AND ROBERT J. ALEXANDER, *The Struggle for Democracy in Latin America,* The Macmillan Company, New York, 1961.

PRESTON E. JAMES, *Latin America,* 3rd ed., The Odyssey Press, New York, 1959.

WILLIAM S. STOKES, *Latin American Politics,* Thomas Y. Crowell Company, New York, 1959.

PEDRO C. M. TEICHERT, "Analysis of Real Growth and Wealth in the Latin American Republics," *Journal of Inter-American Studies,* Vol. 1, 1959, pp. 173–202.

KINGSLEY DAVIS (ed.), "A Crowding Hemisphere: Population Change in the Americas," *The Annals of the American Academy of Political and Social Science,* Vol. 316, 1958, pp. 1–136.

JOHN J. JOHNSON, *Political Change in Latin America: The Emergence of the Middle Sectors,* Stanford University Press, Stanford, California, 1958.

CLARENCE SENIOR, *Land Reform and Democracy,* The University of Florida Press, Gainesville, 1958.

THOMAS W. PALMER, JR., *Search for a Latin American Policy,* The University of Florida Press, Gainesville, 1957.

T. LYNN SMITH, *Brazil: People and Institutions,* Louisiana State University Press, Baton Rouge, 1954.

ARTHUR P. WHITAKER, *The Western Hemisphere Idea: Its Rise and Decline,* Cornell University Press, Ithaca, New York, 1954.

SIMON G. HANSON, *Economic Development in Latin America*, Inter-American Affairs Press, Washington, D. C., 1951.

NATHAN L. WHETTEN, *Rural Mexico*, The University of Chicago Press, Chicago, 1948.

EYLER N. SIMPSON, *The Ejido: Mexico's Way Out*, The University of North Carolina Press, Chapel Hill, 1937.

NORTH AFRICAN-SOUTHWEST ASIAN CULTURE REGION

JOHN I. CLARKE, "Oil in Libya: Some Implications," *Economic Geography*, Vol. 39, 1963, pp. 40–59.

GEORGE B. CRESSEY, *Crossroads: Land and Life in Southwest Asia*, J. B. Lippincott Company, Philadelphia, 1960.

GAMAL ABDEL NASSER, *The Philosophy of the Revolution*, Smith, Keynes & Marshall, Buffalo, New York, 1959.

R. R. PLATT AND M. B. HEFNY, *Egypt: A Compendium*, American Geographical Society, New York, 1958.

J. H. G. LEBON, "Population Distribution and the Agricultural Regions of Iraq," *Geographical Review*, Vol. 43, 1953, pp. 223–228.

ALEXANDER MELAMID, "Political Geography of Trucial, Oman and Qatar," *Geographical Review*, Vol. 43, 1953, pp. 194–206.

WILLIAM BAYNE FISHER, *The Middle East: A Physical, Social, and Regional Geography*, E. P. Dutton & Co., Inc., New York, 1950.

DOREEN WARRINER, *Land and Poverty in the Middle East*, Royal Institute of International Affairs, London, 1948.

WILLIAM BAYNE FISHER, "Unity and Diversity in the Middle East," *Geographical Review*, Vol. 37, 1947, pp. 414–435.

R. H. FORBES, "The Transsaharan Conquest," *Geographical Review*, Vol. 33, 1943, pp. 197–213.

JEAN GOTTMANN, "Economic Problems of French North Africa," *Geographical Review*, Vol. 33, 1943, pp. 175–196.

E. F. GAUTIER, "The Ahaggar, Heart of the Sahara," *Geographical Review*, Vol. 16, 1926, pp. 378–394.

SOUTH ASIAN CULTURE REGION

WILFRED MALENBAUM, *The Prospects for Indian Development*, Center for International Studies, Massachusetts Institute of Technology, Cambridge, Massachusetts, 1962.

PRADYUMNA P. KARAN, "Sikkim and Bhutan: A Geographical Appraisal," *Journal of Geography*, Vol. 60, 1961, pp. 58–66.

BARBARA WARD, *India and the West*, W. W. Norton & Company, Inc., New York, 1961.

PRADYUMNA P. KARAN, *Nepal: A Cultural and Physical Geography*, The University of Kentucky Press, Lexington, 1960.

PRADYUMNA P. KARAN AND WILLIAM M. JENKINS, JR., "Geography of Manufacturing in India," *Economic Geography*, Vol. 35, 1959, pp. 269–278.

V. P. MENON, *The Story of the Integration of the Indian States*, The Macmillan Company, New York, 1956.

ROBERT C. MAYFIELD, "A Geographic Study of the Kashmir Issue," *Geographical Review*, Vol. 45, 1955, pp. 181–196.

O. H. K. SPATE, *India and Pakistan*, Methuen & Co., Ltd., London, and E. P. Dutton & Co., Inc., New York, 1954.

F. J. FOWLER, "Some Problems of Water Distribution Between East and West Punjab," *Geographical Review*, Vol. 40, 1950, pp. 583–599.

JOHN E. BRUSH, "The Distribution of Religious Communities in India," *Annals* of the Association of American Geographers, Vol. 39, 1949, pp. 81–98.

SOUTHEAST ASIAN CULTURE REGION

CHARLES A. FISHER, "The Malaysian Federation, Indonesia, and the Philippines: A Study in Political Geography," *Geographical Journal*, Vol. 129, 1963, pp. 311–328.

ROBERT L. PENDLETON, *Thailand: Aspects of Landscape and Life* (An American Geographical Society Handbook), Duell, Sloan and Pearce, New York, 1962.

ALDEN CUTSHALL, "The Philippine Sugar Industry: Status and Problems," *Journal of Geography*, Vol. 60, 1961, pp. 5–9.

EDWARD L. ULLMAN, "Trade Centers and Tributary Areas of the Philippines," *Geographical Review*, Vol. 50, 1960, pp. 203–218.

B. W. HODDER, *Man in Malaya*, University of London Press, Ltd., London, 1959.

NORTON GINSBURG AND CHESTER F. ROBERTS, JR., *Malaya*, University of Washington Press, Seattle, 1958.

J. E. SPENCER, *Land and People in the Philippines*, University of California Press, Berkeley, 1954.

D. W. FRYER, "The 'Million City' in Southeast Asia," *Geographical Review*, Vol. 43, 1953, pp. 474–494.

CARL O. SAUER, *Agricultural Origins and Dispersals*, American Geographical Society, New York, 1952.

KARL J. PELZER, *Pioneer Settlement in the Asiatic Tropics*, American Geographical Society, New York, 1945.

J. O. M. BROEK, "Diversity and Unity in Southeast Asia," *Geographical Review*, Vol. 34, 1944, pp. 175–195.

E. H. G. DOBBY, "Settlement Patterns in Malaya," *Geographical Review*, Vol. 32, 1942, pp. 211–232.

EAST ASIAN CULTURE REGION

CHIAO-MIN HSIEH, *Taiwan—Ilha Formosa*, Butterworths & Co., Ltd. (Publishers), London, 1963.

JOHN K. FAIRBANK, *Communist China and Taiwan in United States Foreign Policy*, Brien McMahon Lectures, University of Connecticut, November 21, 1960.

C. T. HU, *China: Its People, Its Society, Its Culture*, Taplinger Publishing Company, Inc., New York, 1960.

IRENE B. TAEUBER, "Japan's Demographic Transition Re-examined," *Population Studies*, Vol. 14, 1960, pp. 28–39.

A. DOAK BARNETT, *Communist Economic Strategy: The Rise of Mainland China*, National Planning Association, Washington, D. C., 1959.

THEODORE HERMAN, "Group Values toward the National Space: The Case of China," *Geographical Review*, Vol. 49, 1959, pp. 164–182.

JOHN H. THOMPSON AND MICHIHIRO MIYAZAKI, "A Map of Japan's Manufacturing," *Geographical Review*, Vol. 49, 1959, pp. 1–17.

SHANNON McCUNE, *Korea's Heritage, A Regional and Social Geography*, Charles E. Tuttle Co., Tokyo, 1956.

RHOADS MURPHEY, "China's Transport Problem and Communist Planning," *Economic Geography*, Vol. 32, 1956, pp. 17–28.

GEORGE B. CRESSEY, *Land of the 500 Million: A Geography of China*, McGraw-Hill Book Company, Inc., New York, 1955.

GLENN T. TREWARTHA, "Chinese Cities: Origins and Functions," *Annals of the Association of American Geographers*, Vol. 42, 1952, pp. 69–93.

GLENN T. TREWARTHA, *Japan: A Physical, Cultural, and Regional Geography*, The University of Wisconsin Press, Madison, Wisconsin, 1945.

J. RUSSELL SMITH, "Grassland and Farmland as Factors in the Cyclical Development of Eurasian History," *Annals of the Association of American Geographers*, Vol. 33, 1943, pp. 135–161.

OWEN LATTIMORE, *Inner Asian Frontiers of China*, American Geographical Society, New York, 1940.

WALTER H. MALLORY, *China: Land of Famine*, American Geographical Society, New York, 1926.

AFRICAN CULTURE REGION

WALTER DESHLER, "Cattle in Africa: Distribution, Types, and Problems," *Geographical Review*, Vol. 53, 1963, pp. 52–58.

PETER R. GOULD (ed.), *Africa, Continent of Change*, Wadsworth Publishing Co., Inc., Belmont, California, 1961.

R. J. HARRISON CHURCH, *West Africa: A Study of the Environment and of Man's Use of it*, Longmans, Green & Co., Ltd., London, 1960.

GEORGE H. T. KIMBLE, *Tropical Africa* (2 vols.), The Twentieth Century Fund, New York, 1960.

GEORGE P. MURDOCK, "Staple Subsistence Crops of Africa," *Geographical Review*, Vol. 50, 1960, pp. 523–540.

VIRGINIA THOMPSON AND RICHARD ADLOFF, *The Emerging States of French Equatorial Africa*, Stanford University Press, Stanford, California, 1960.

GEORGE P. MURDOCK, *Africa: Its Peoples and their Culture History*, McGraw-Hill Book Company, Inc., New York, 1959.

H. L. SHANTZ AND B. L. TURNER, *Photographic Documentation of Vegetational Changes in Africa over a Third of a Century*, University of Arizona, College of Agriculture, Report No. 169, 1958.

WILLIAM A. HANCE AND IRENE S. VAN DONGEN, "The Port of Lobito and the Benguela Railroad," *Geographical Review*, Vol. 46, 1956, pp. 460–487.

KEITH BUCHANAN, "The Northern Region of Nigeria: The Geographical Background

of its Political Duality," *Geographical Review*, Vol. 43, 1953, pp. 451–473.

L. DUDLEY STAMP, *Africa, A Study in Tropical Development*, John Wiley & Sons, Inc., New York, 1953.

J. K. MATHESON AND E. W. BOVILL (eds.), *East African Agriculture: A Short Survey of the Agriculture of Kenya, Uganda, Tanganyika, and Zanzibar*, Oxford University Press, London, 1950.

RODERICK PEATTIE, *Struggle on the Veld*, Vanguard Press, Inc., New York, 1947.

CLEMENT GILLMAN, "A Population Map of Tanganyika Territory," *Geographical Review*, Vol. 26, 1936, pp. 353–375.

H. L. SHANTZ AND C. F. MARBUT, *The Vegetation and Soils of Africa*, American Geographical Society (Research Series No. 13), New York, 1923.

AUSTRALIA-NEW ZEALAND CULTURE REGION

DONALD W. MEINIG, *On the Margins of the Good Earth: The South Australian Wheat Frontier, 1868–1884*, Rand McNally & Company, Chicago, 1962.

G. J. R. LINGE, "The Concentration and Dispersion of Manufacturing in New Zealand," *Economic Geography*, Vol. 36, 1960, pp. 326–343.

ANDREW H. CLARK, *The Invasion of New Zealand by People, Plants and Animals: The South Island*, Rutgers University Press, New Brunswick, New Jersey, 1949.

KENNETH CUMBERLAND, "A Century's Change: Natural to Cultural Vegetation in New Zealand," *Geographical Review*, Vol. 31, 1941, pp. 529–554.

STEPHEN H. ROBERTS, "History of the Pioneer Fringes in Australia," in W. L. G. Joerg (ed.), *Pioneer Settlement*, American Geographical Society (Special Publication No. 14), New York, 1932, pp. 392–404.

GRIFFITH TAYLOR, "The Pioneer Belts of Australia," in W. L. G. Joerg (ed.), *Pioneer Settlement*, American Geographical Society (Special Publication No. 14), New York, 1932, pp. 360–391.

PACIFIC CULTURE REGION

HAROLD J. WIENS, *Pacific Island Bastions of the United States*, D. Van Nostrand Company, Inc. (Searchlight Book No. 4), Princeton, New Jersey, 1962.

DOUGLAS L. OLIVER, *The Pacific Islands*, Harvard University Press, Cambridge, Massachusetts, 1952.

ROBERT G. BOWMAN, "Army Farms and Agricultural Development in the Southwest Pacific," *Geographical Review*, Vol. 36, 1946, pp. 420–446.

JOHN WESLEY COULTER, "Impact of the War on South Sea Islands," *Geographical Review*, Vol. 36, 1946, pp. 409–419.

INDEX

Note: References to maps, drawings, and diagrams are in boldface type.

MANUFACTURED IN THE UNITED STATES OF AMERICA

CDEFGHIJK 069876